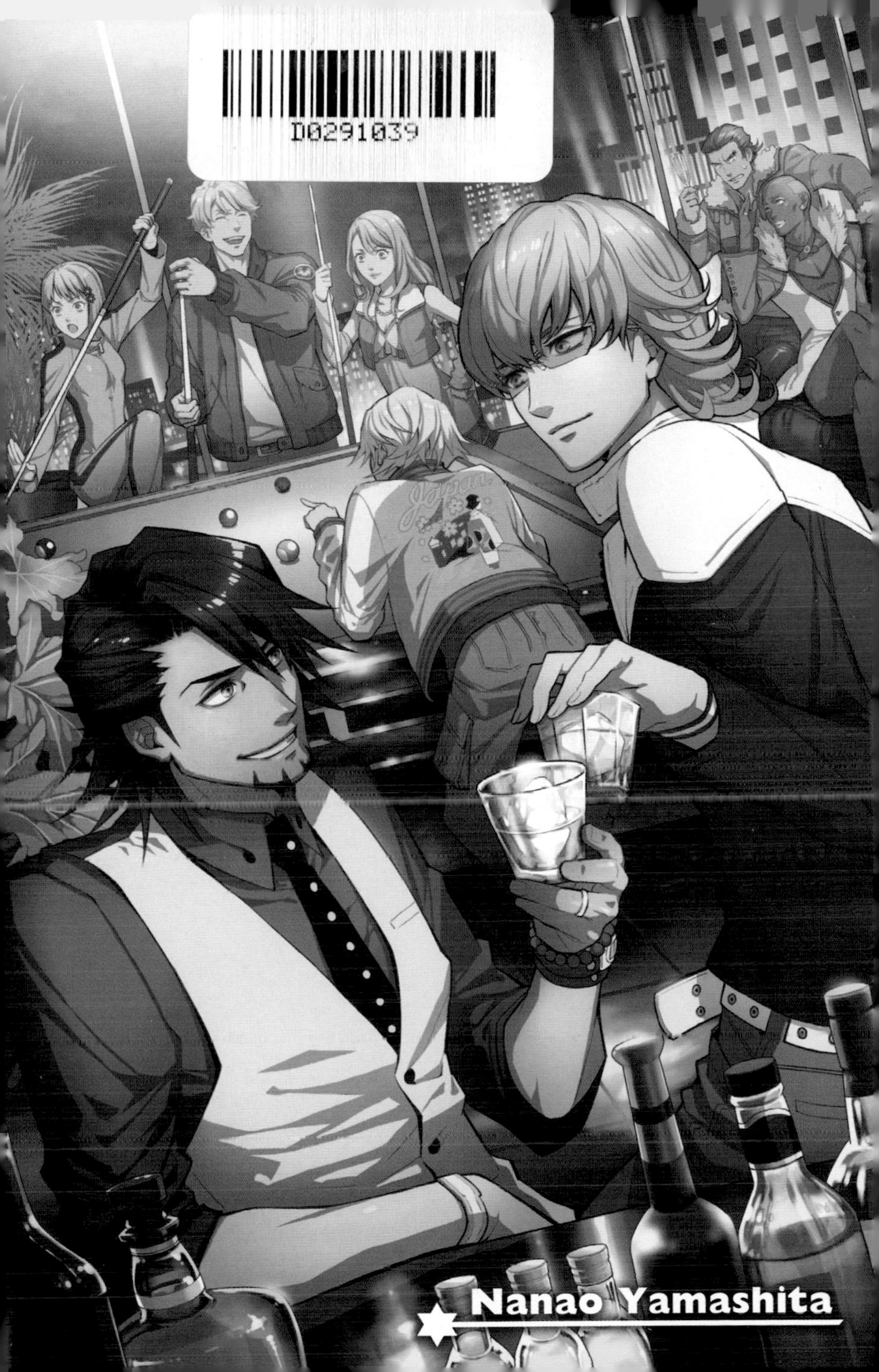
Nanao Yamashita

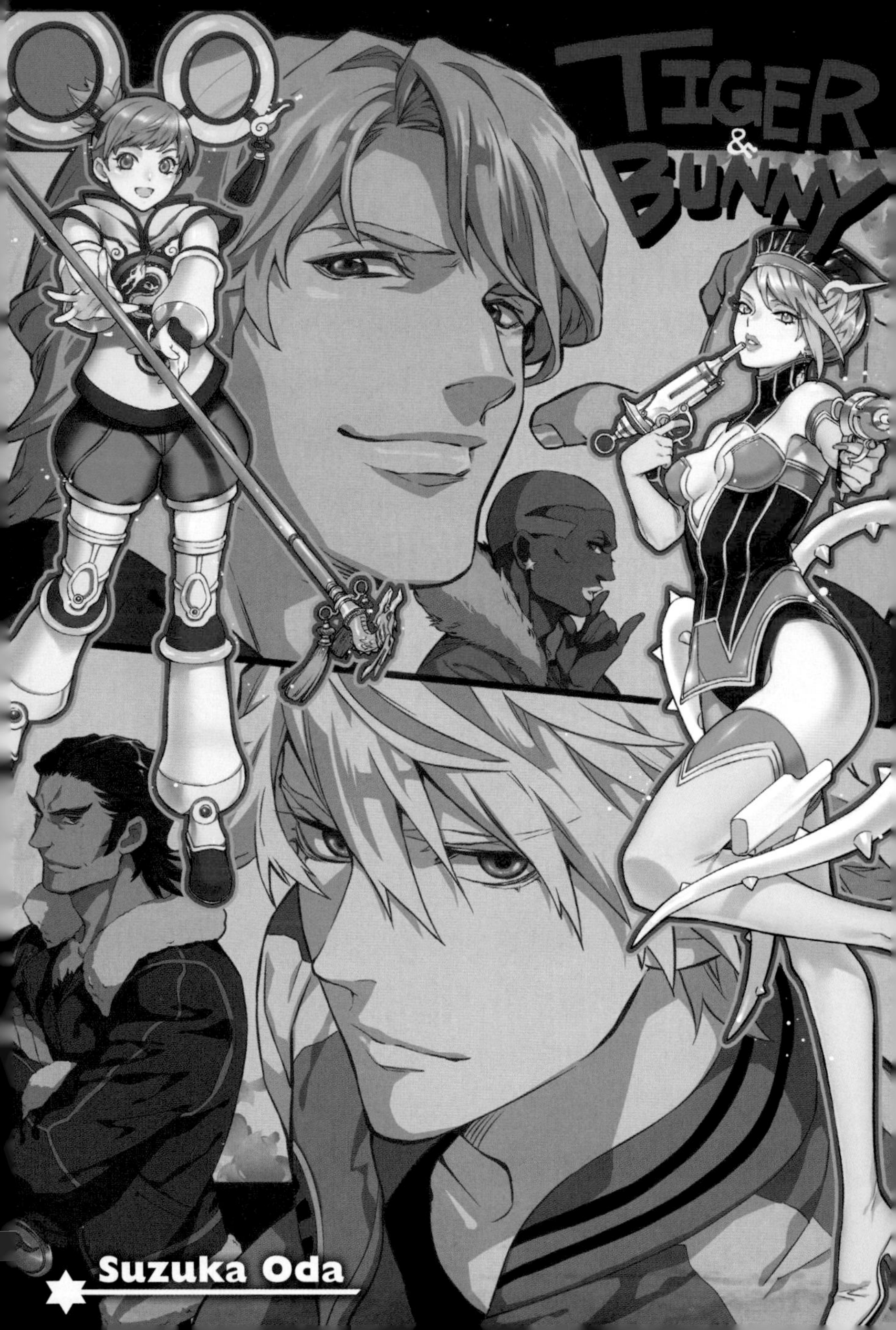
TIGER & BUNNY
Suzuka Oda

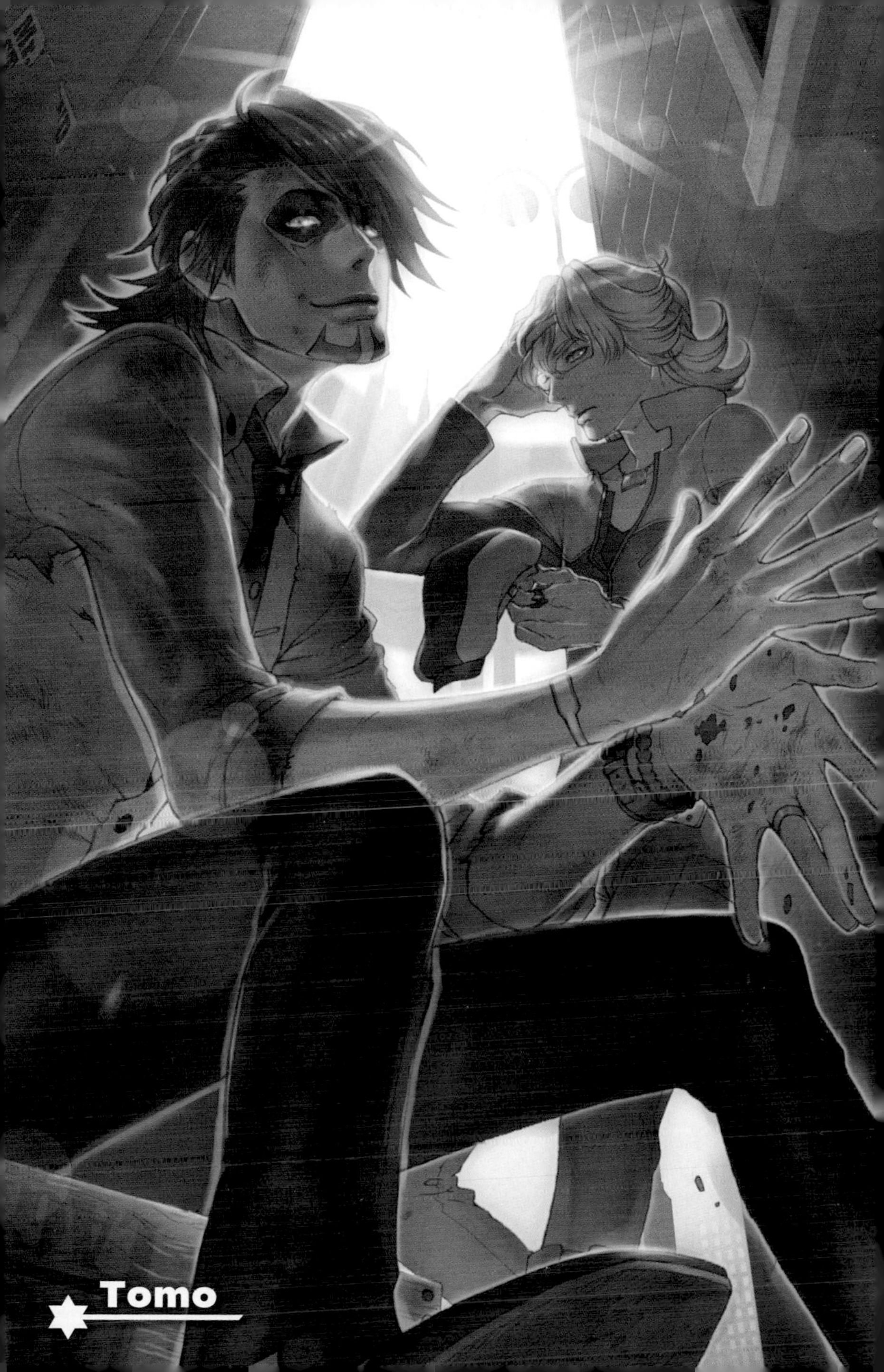
Tomo

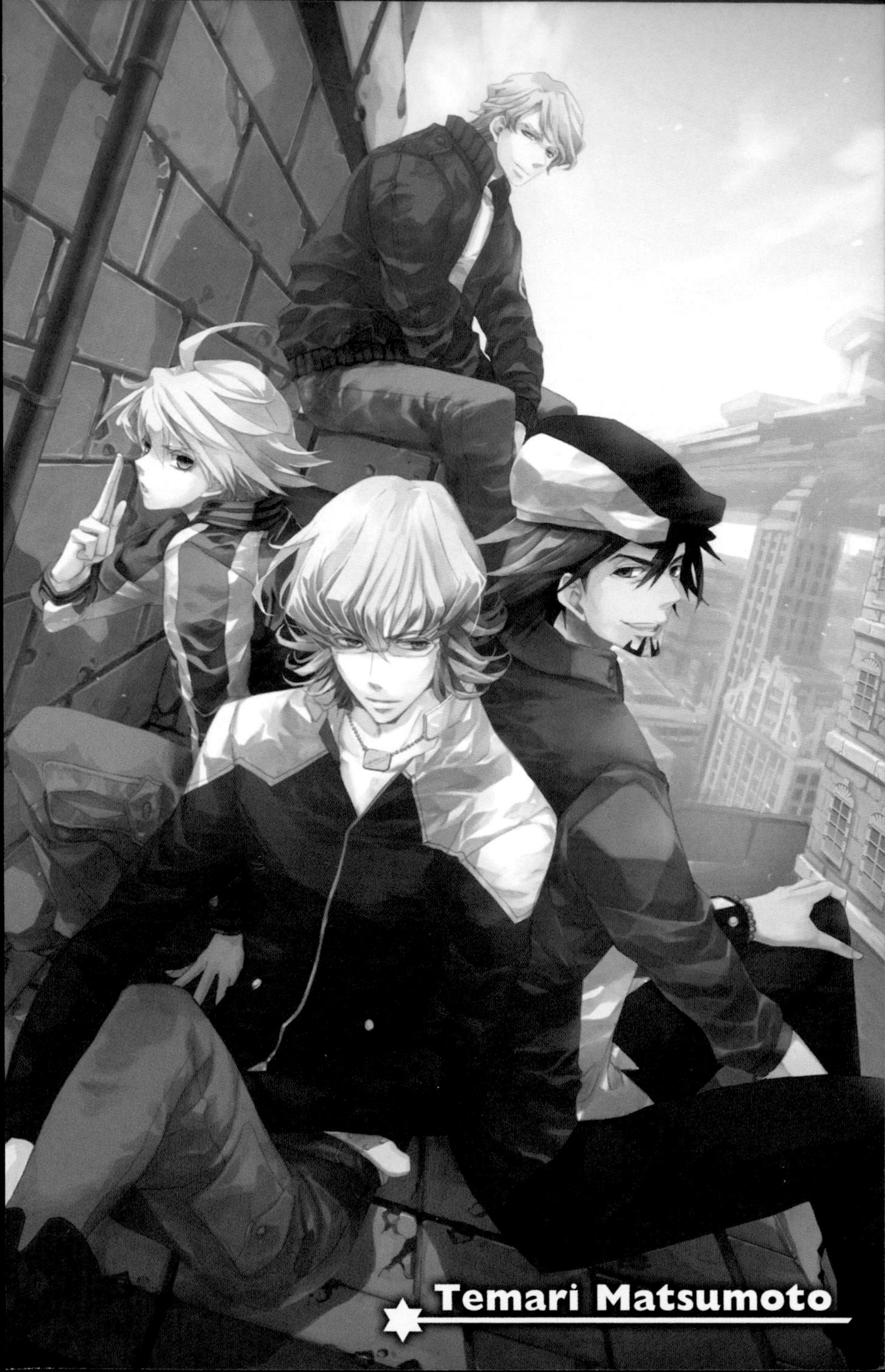
Temari Matsumoto

TIGER & BUNNY

COMIC ANTHOLOGY

1

It Takes Two to Make a Quarrel

EDITED BY: **Asuka Henshubu** | PRODUCTION: **SUNRISE**

TIGER & BUNNY COMIC ANTHOLOGY 1

It Takes Two to Make a Quarrel

CONTENTS

WE RESPECT TIGER & BUNNY

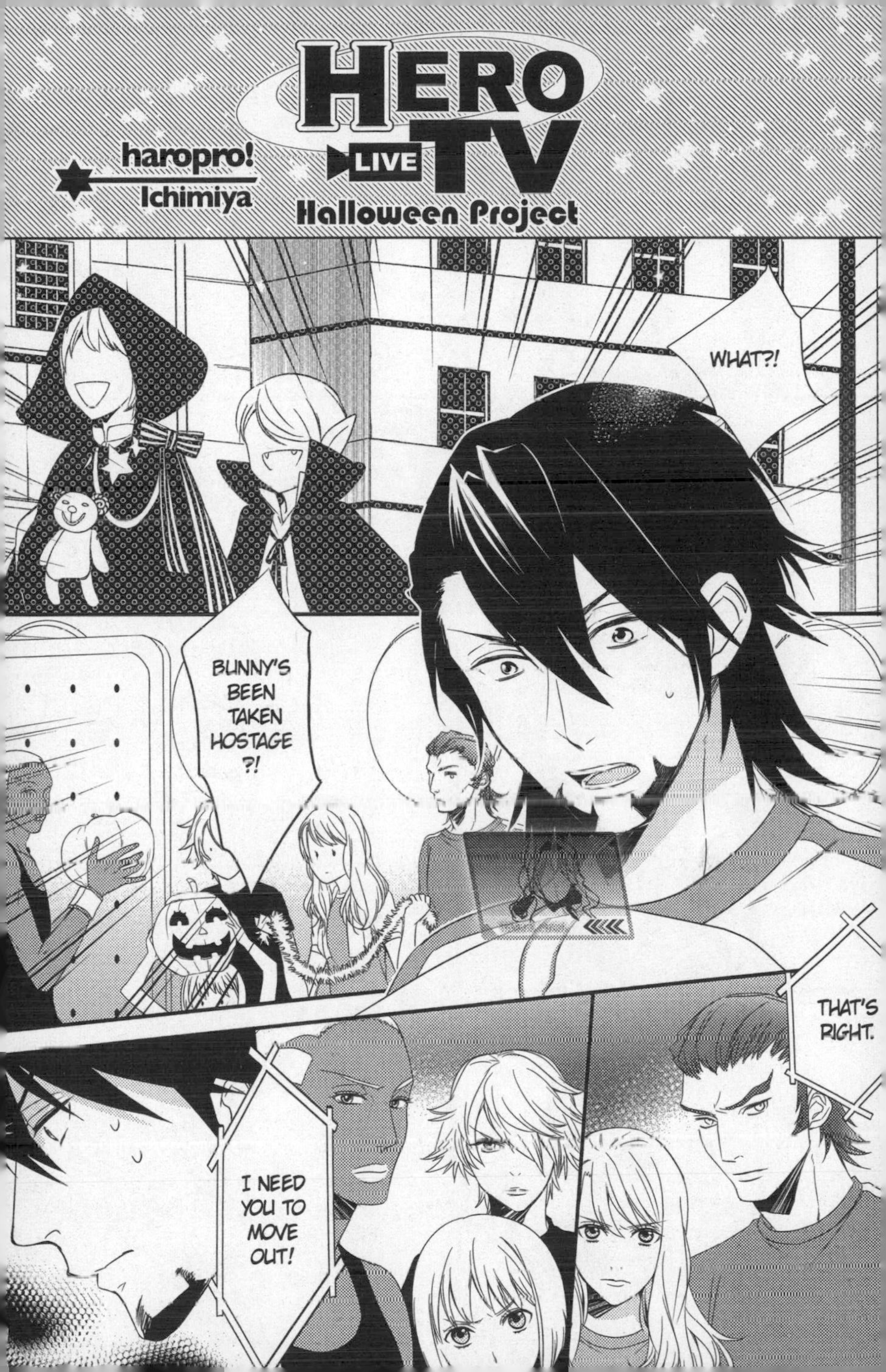
HERO TV
LIVE
Halloween Project
haropro!
Ichimiya
WHAT?!
BUNNY'S BEEN TAKEN HOSTAGE ?!
THAT'S RIGHT.
I NEED YOU TO MOVE OUT!

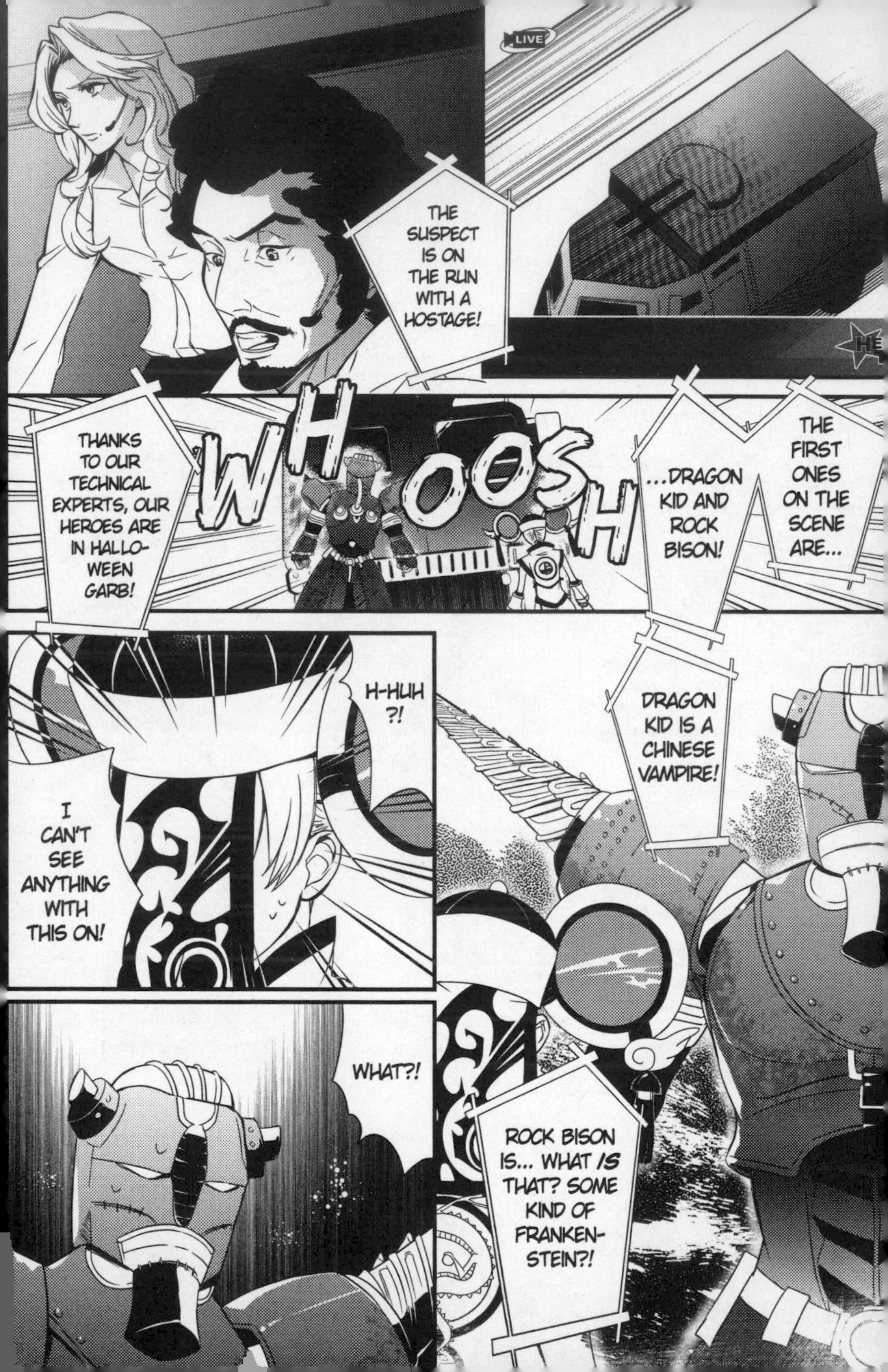
LIVE
THE SUSPECT IS ON THE RUN WITH A HOSTAGE!
THE FIRST ONES ON THE SCENE ARE...
...DRAGON KID AND ROCK BISON!
WHOOSH
THANKS TO OUR TECHNICAL EXPERTS, OUR HEROES ARE IN HALLO-WEEN GARB!
DRAGON KID IS A CHINESE VAMPIRE!
ROCK BISON IS... WHAT *IS* THAT? SOME KIND OF FRANKEN-STEIN?!
H-HUH?!
I CAN'T SEE ANYTHING WITH THIS ON!
WHAT?!

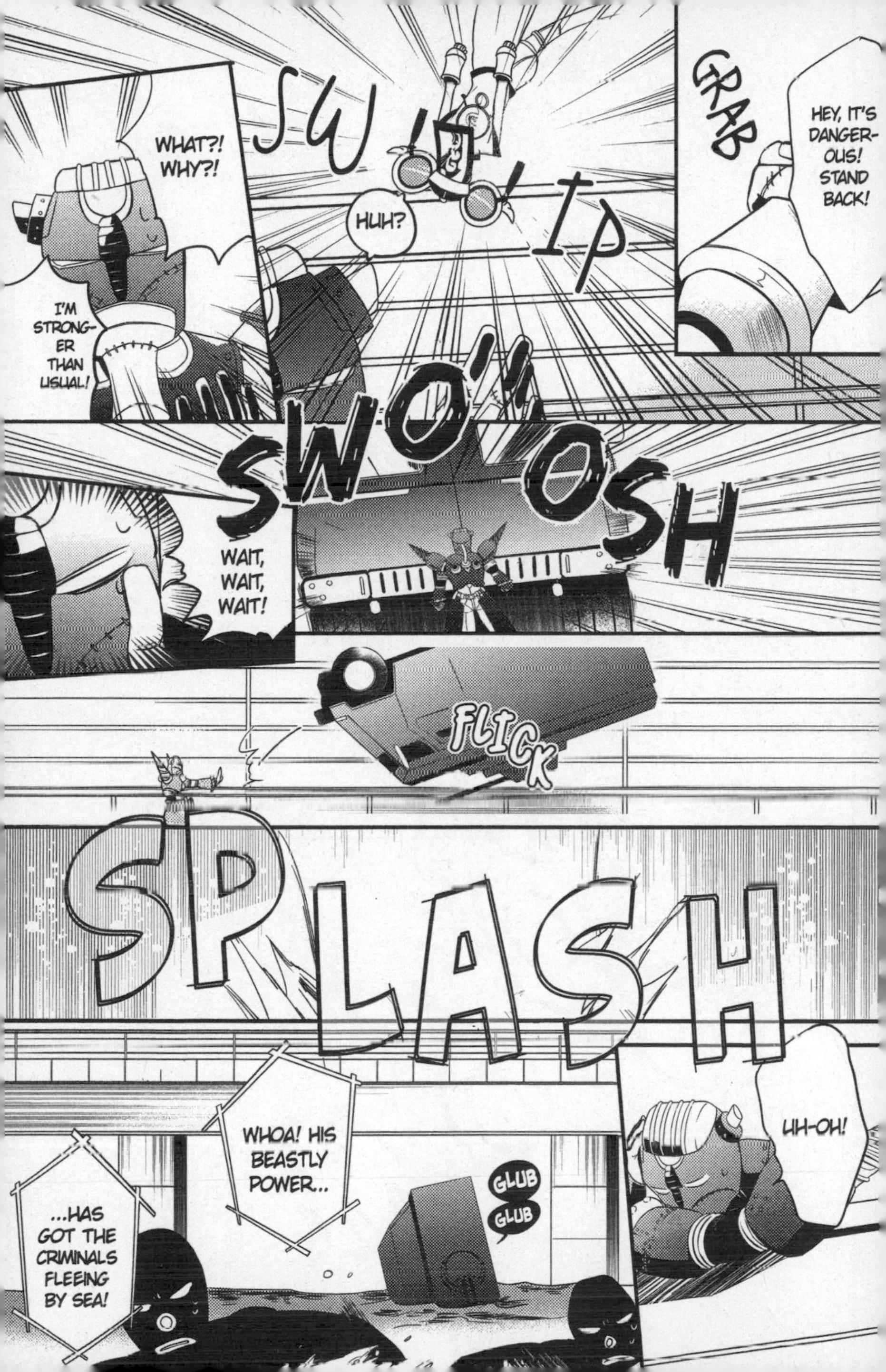

GRAB
HEY, IT'S DANGER-OUS! STAND BACK!
SWIP
HUH?
WHAT?! WHY?!
I'M STRONG-ER THAN USUAL!
SWOOSH
WAIT, WAIT, WAIT!
FLICK
SPLASH
UH-OH!
GLUB GLUB
WHOA! HIS BEASTLY POWER...
...HAS GOT THE CRIMINALS FLEEING BY SEA!

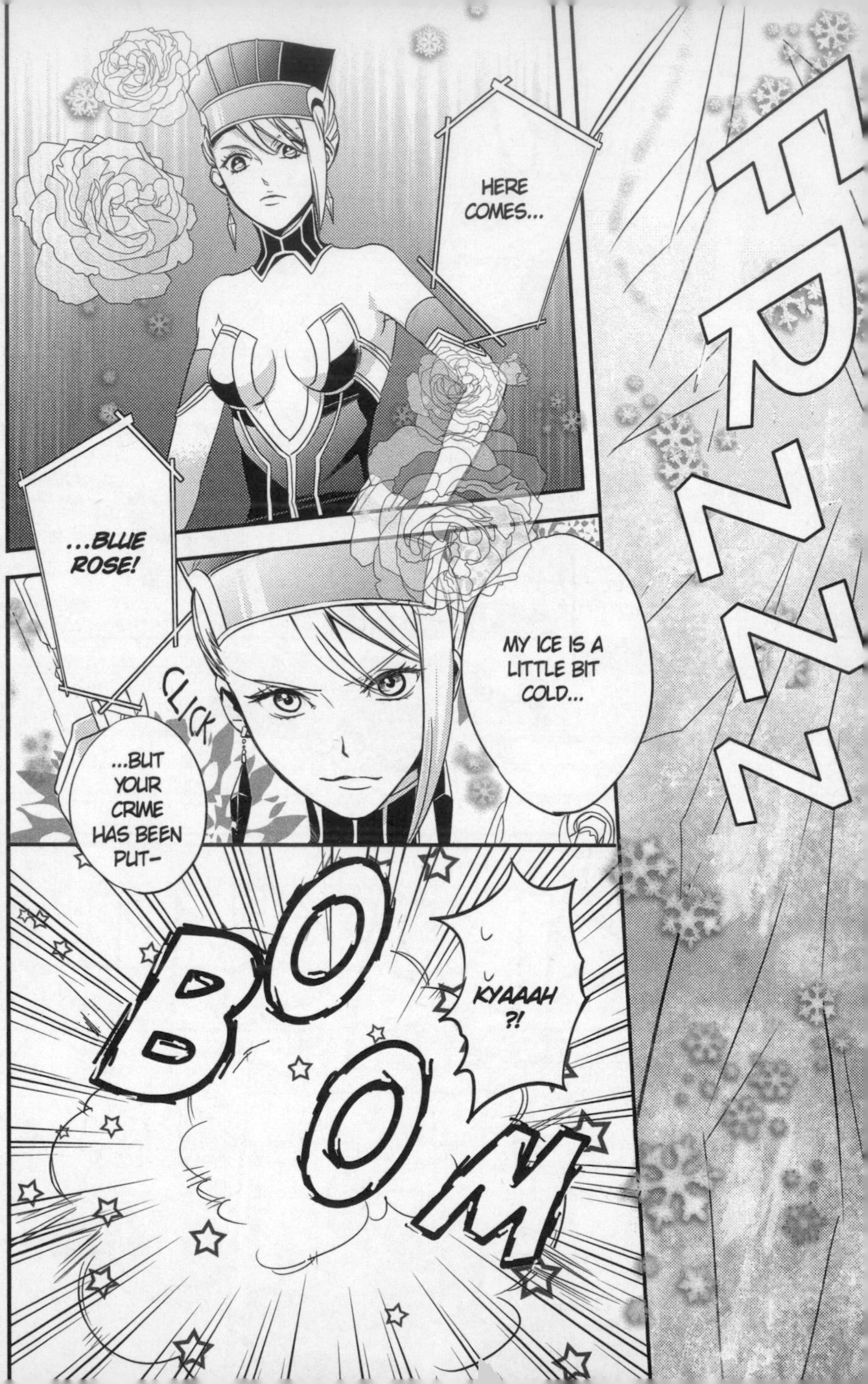
FRZZZ
HERE COMES...
...BLUE ROSE!
MY ICE IS A LITTLE BIT COLD...
CLICK
...BUT YOUR CRIME HAS BEEN PUT-
KYAAAH ?!
BOOM

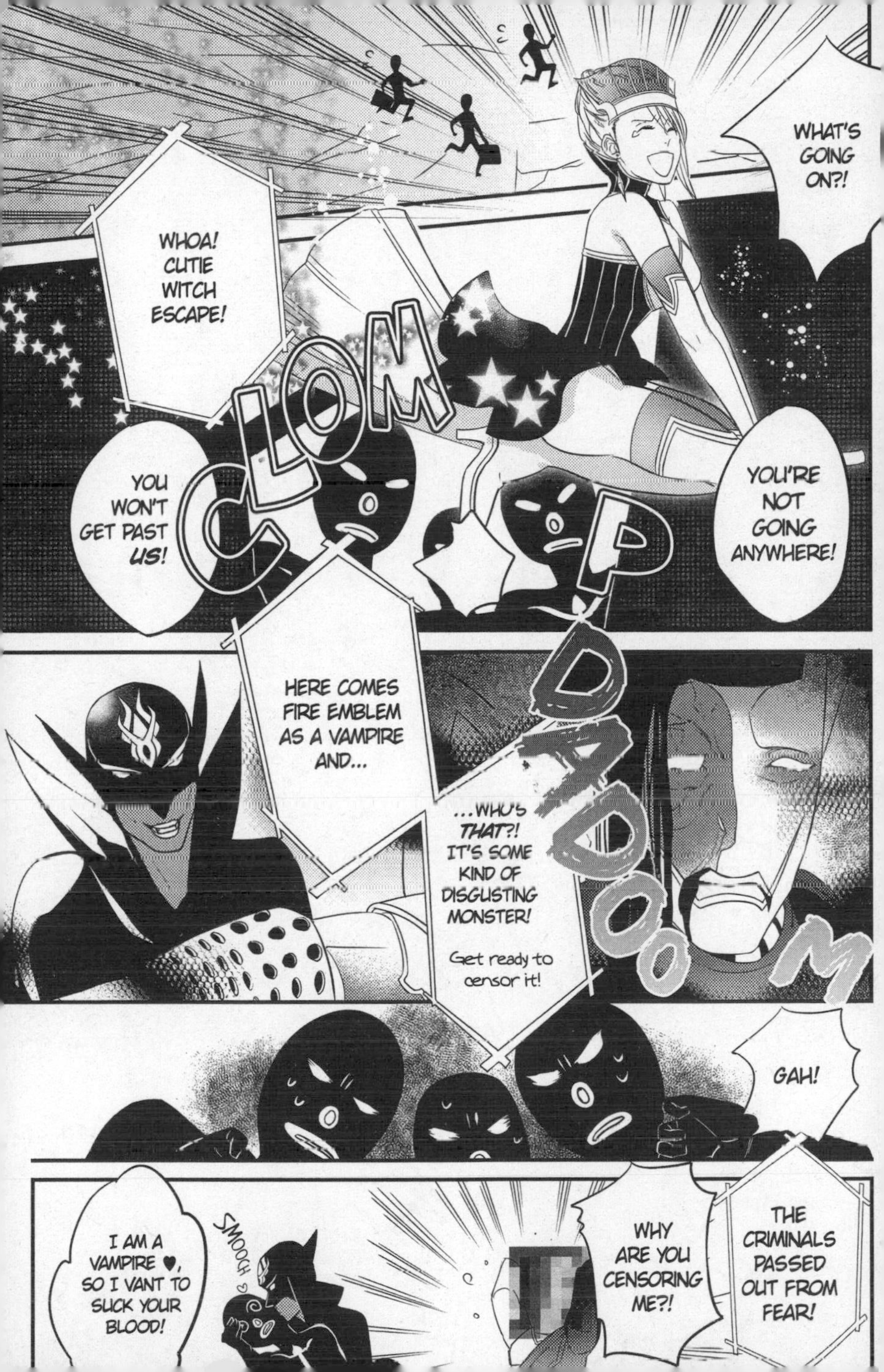
WHAT'S GOING ON?!
WHOA! CUTIE WITCH ESCAPE!
YOU'RE NOT GOING ANYWHERE!
CLOMP
YOU WON'T GET PAST *US*!
HERE COMES FIRE EMBLEM AS A VAMPIRE AND...
DADOOM
...WHO'S *THAT*?! IT'S SOME KIND OF DISGUSTING MONSTER!
Get ready to censor it!
GAH!
THE CRIMINALS PASSED OUT FROM FEAR!
WHY ARE YOU CENSORING ME?!
SMOOCH
I AM A VAMPIRE ♥, SO I VANT TO SUCK YOUR BLOOD!

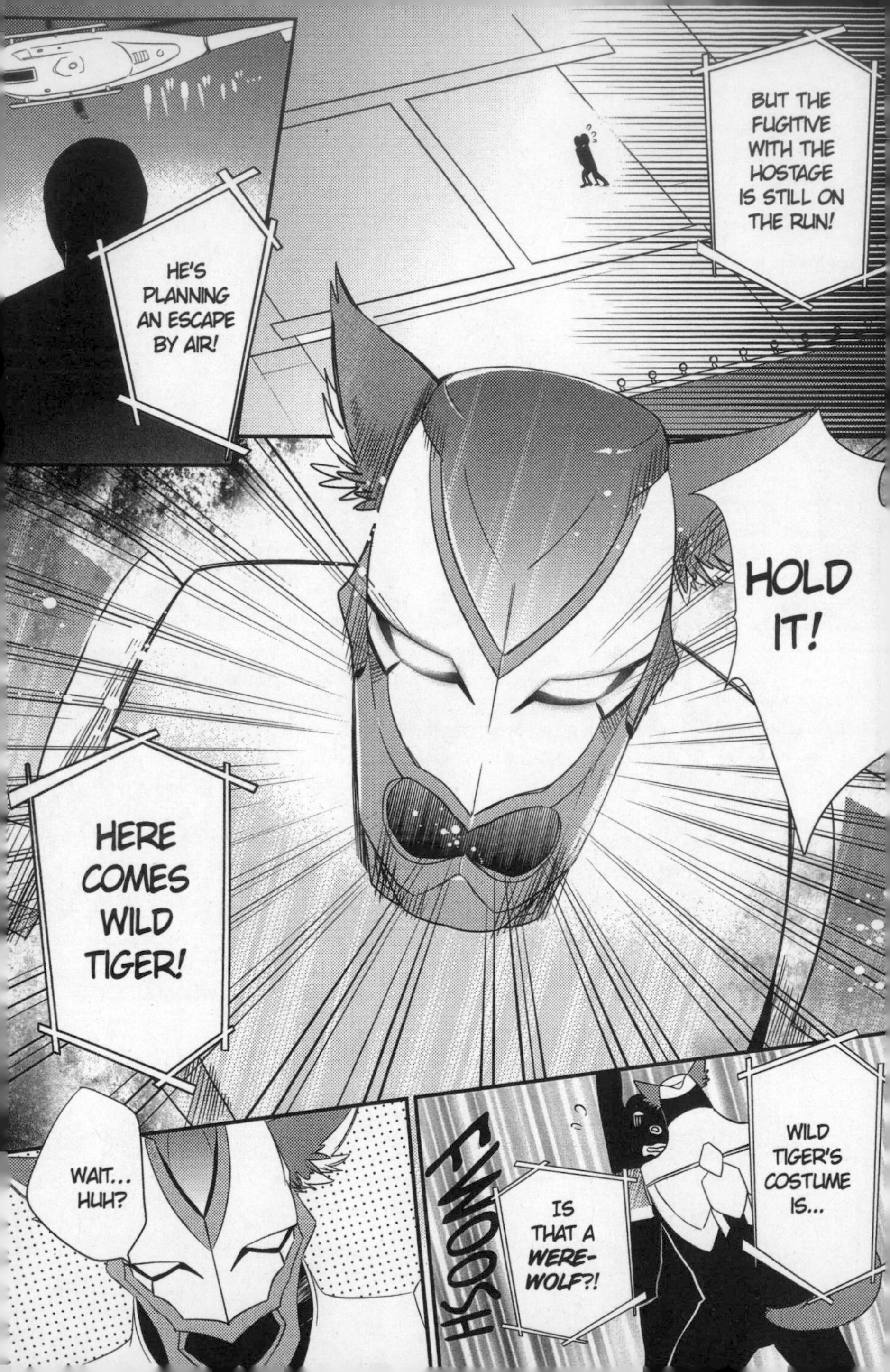
BUT THE FUGITIVE WITH THE HOSTAGE IS STILL ON THE RUN!
HE'S PLANNING AN ESCAPE BY AIR!
HOLD IT!
HERE COMES WILD TIGER!
WILD TIGER'S COSTUME IS...
IS THAT A WERE-WOLF?!
FWOOSH
WAIT... HUH?

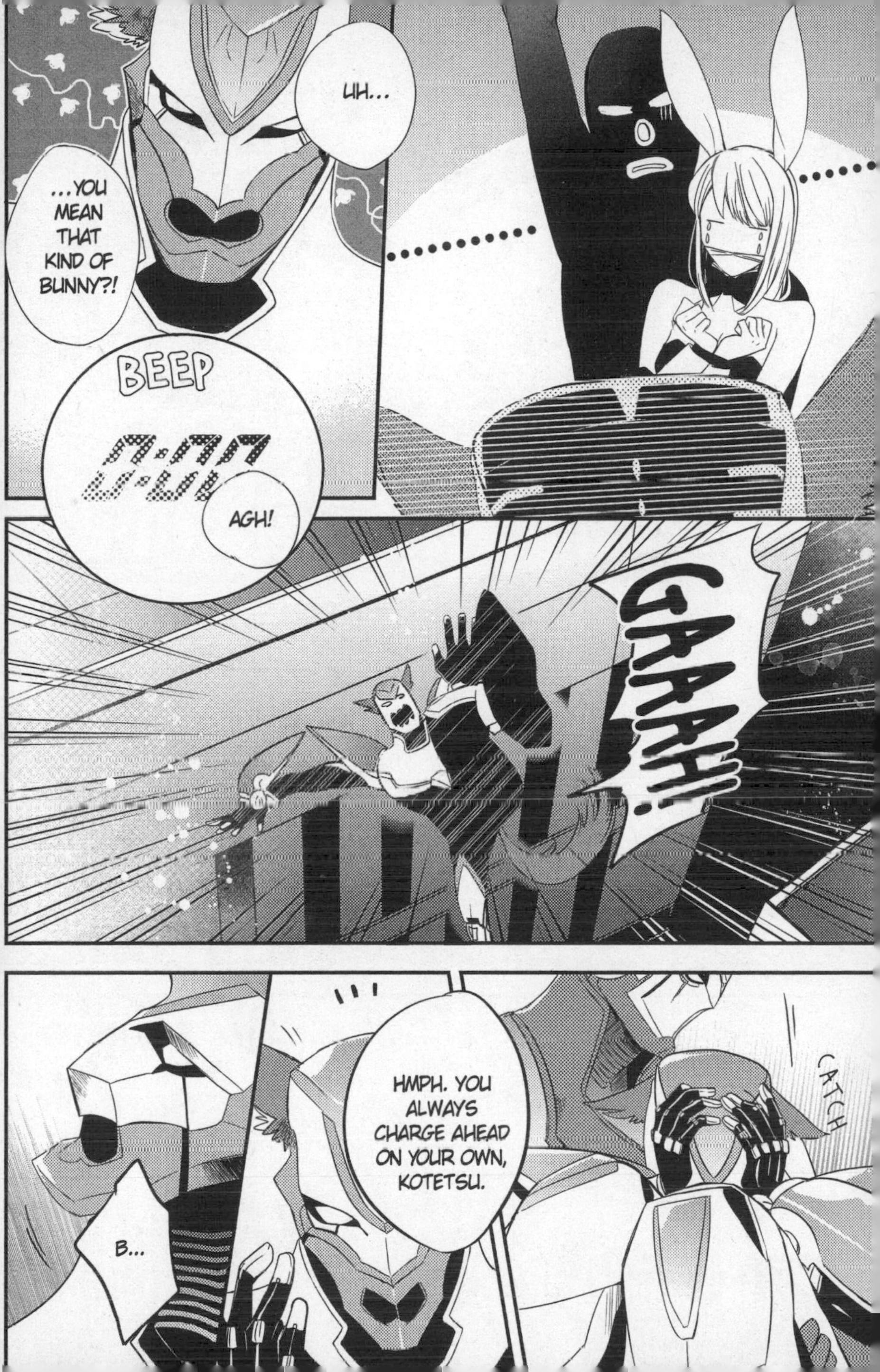
UH...
...YOU MEAN THAT KIND OF BUNNY?!
BEEP
0:00
AGH!
GAAAH!!
CATCH
HMPH. YOU ALWAYS CHARGE AHEAD ON YOUR OWN, KOTETSU.
B...

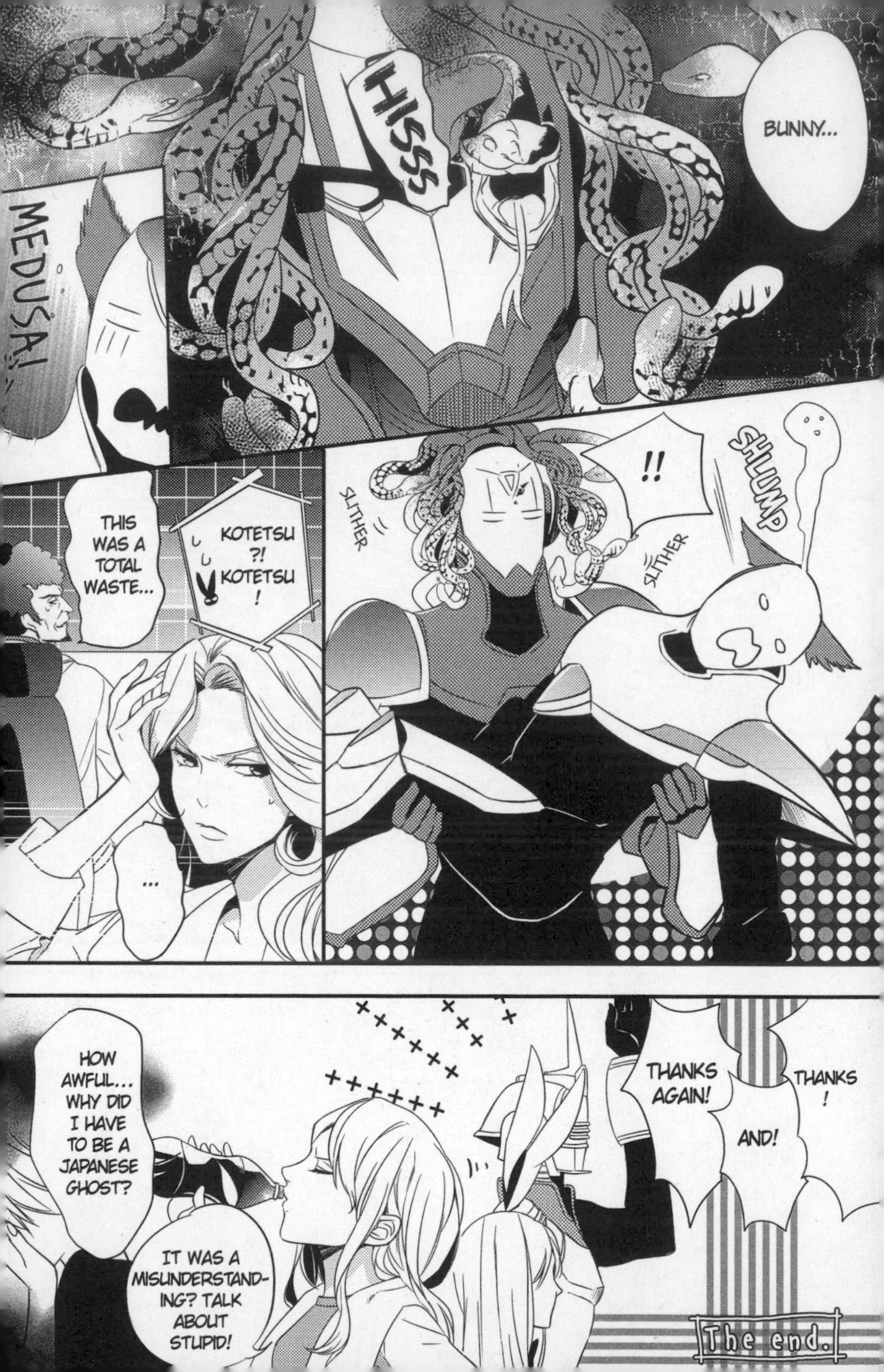

BUNNY...
HISSS
MEDUSA!
!!
SHLUMP
SLITHER
SLITHER
KOTETSU ?! KOTETSU !
THIS WAS A TOTAL WASTE...
...
THANKS !
THANKS AGAIN!
AND!
HOW AWFUL... WHY DID I HAVE TO BE A JAPANESE GHOST?
IT WAS A MISUNDERSTANDING? TALK ABOUT STUPID!
The end.

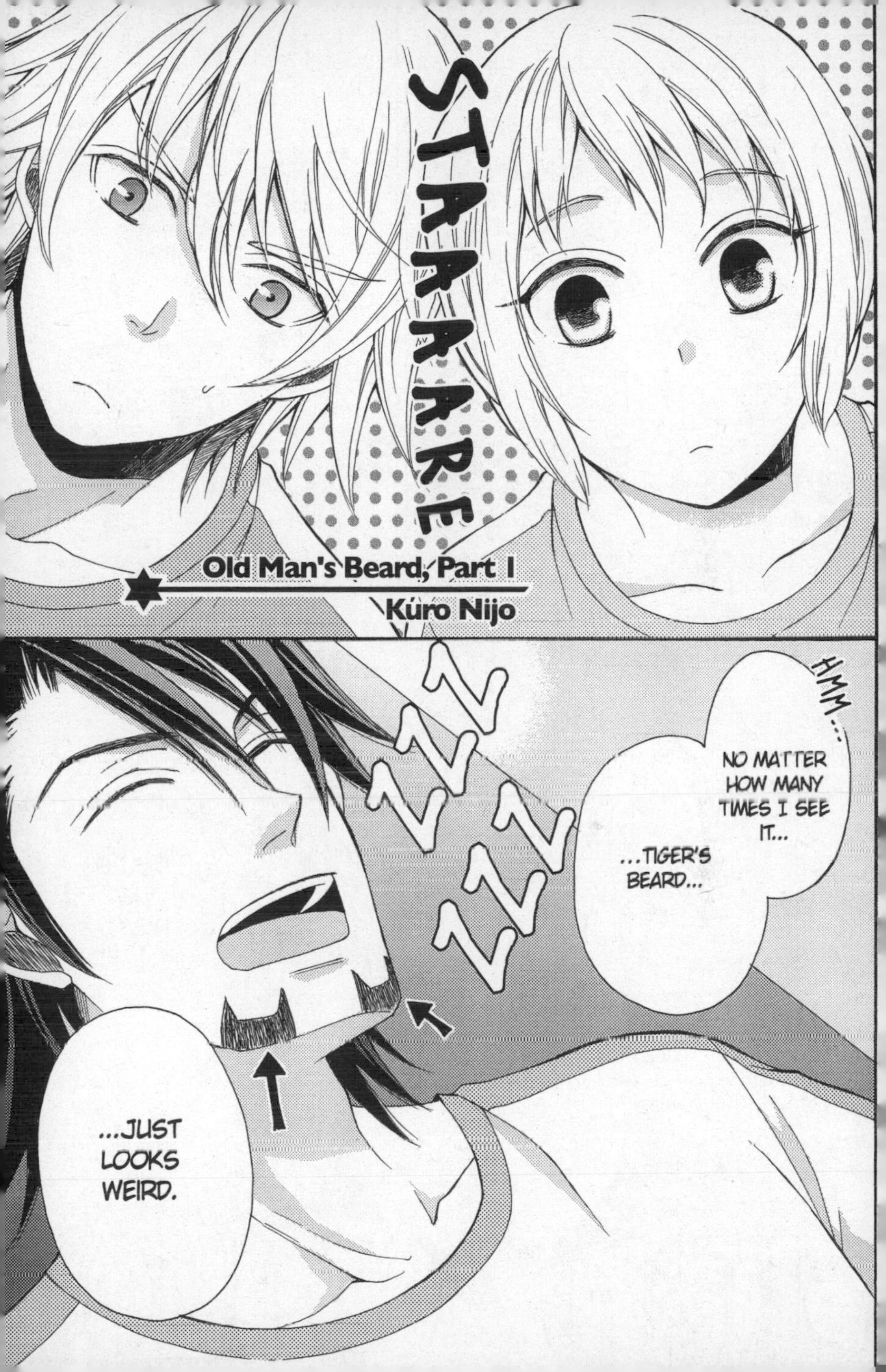
STAAARE
Old Man's Beard, Part 1
Kuro Nijo
HMM...
NO MATTER HOW MANY TIMES I SEE IT...
...TIGER'S BEARD...
ZZZ ZZZ
...JUST LOOKS WEIRD.

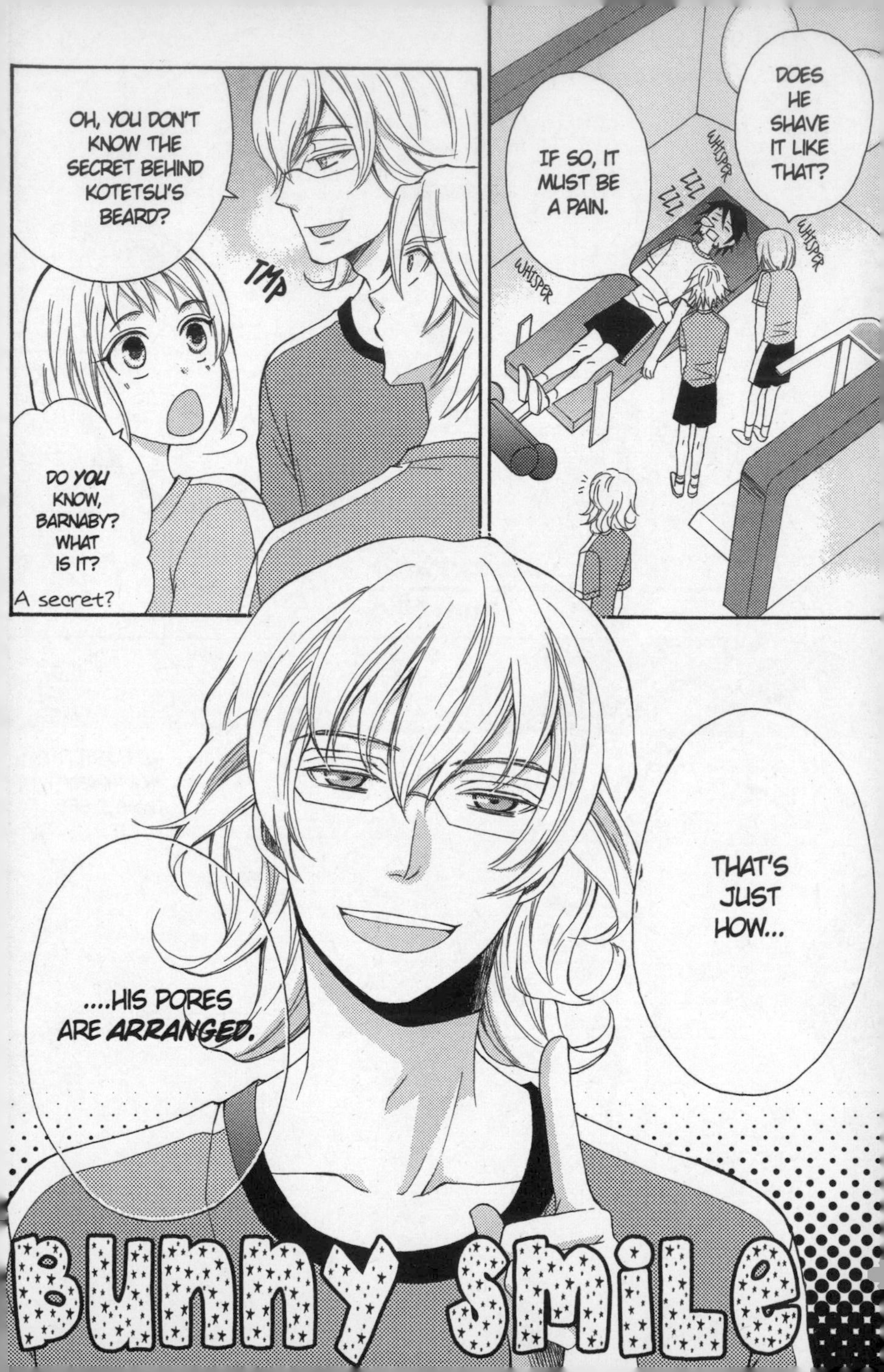
DOES HE SHAVE IT LIKE THAT?
WHISPER
IF SO, IT MUST BE A PAIN.
WHISPER
ZZZ ZZZ
WHISPER
OH, YOU DON'T KNOW THE SECRET BEHIND KOTETSU'S BEARD?
TMP
DO *YOU* KNOW, BARNABY? WHAT IS IT?
A secret?
THAT'S JUST HOW...
....HIS PORES ARE *ARRANGED*.
BUNNY SMILE

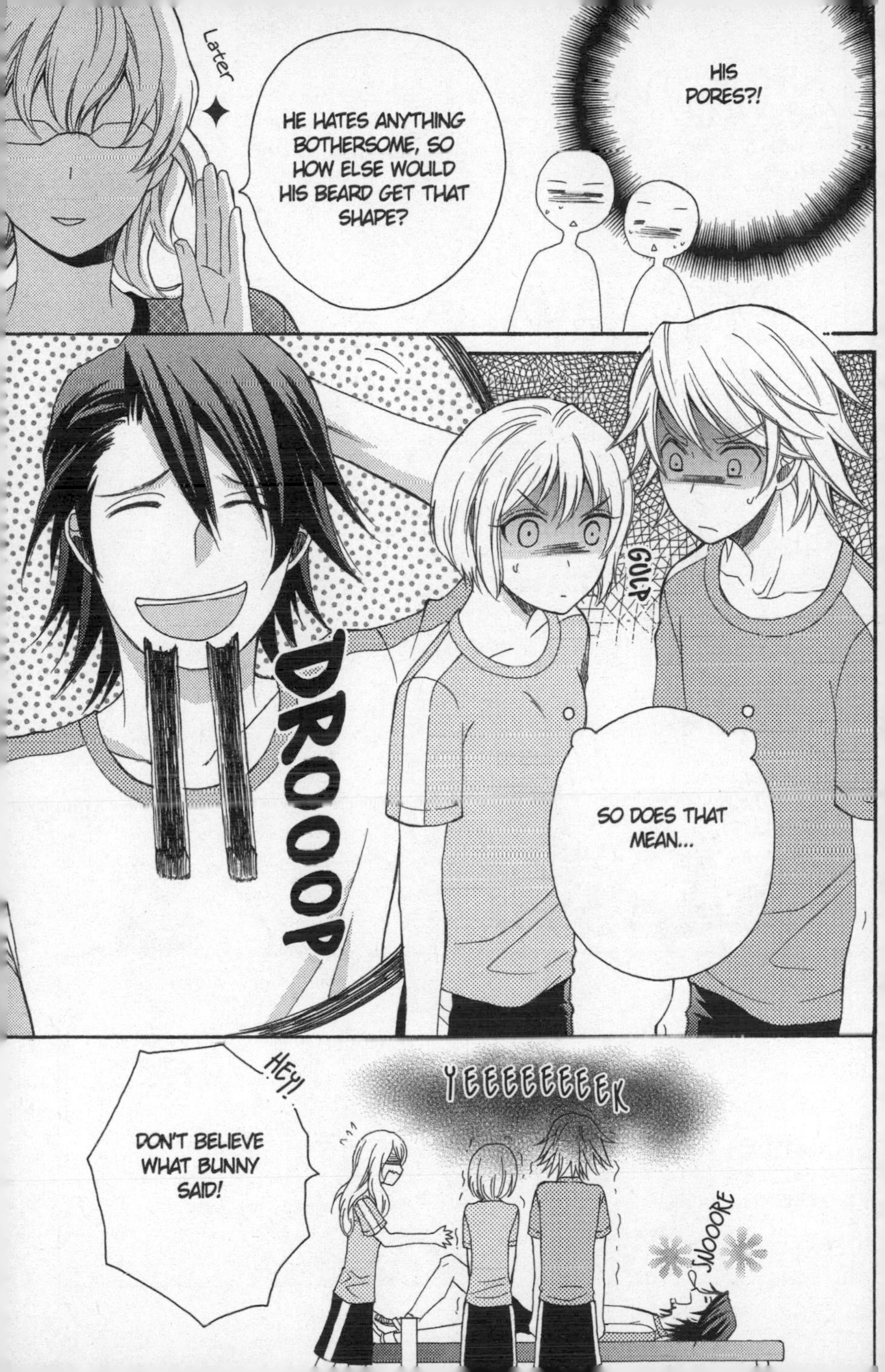

HIS PORES?!
Later
HE HATES ANYTHING BOTHERSOME, SO HOW ELSE WOULD HIS BEARD GET THAT SHAPE?
GULP
SO DOES THAT MEAN...
DROOOOP
YEEEEEEEEK
SNOOORE
HEY!
DON'T BELIEVE WHAT BUNNY SAID!

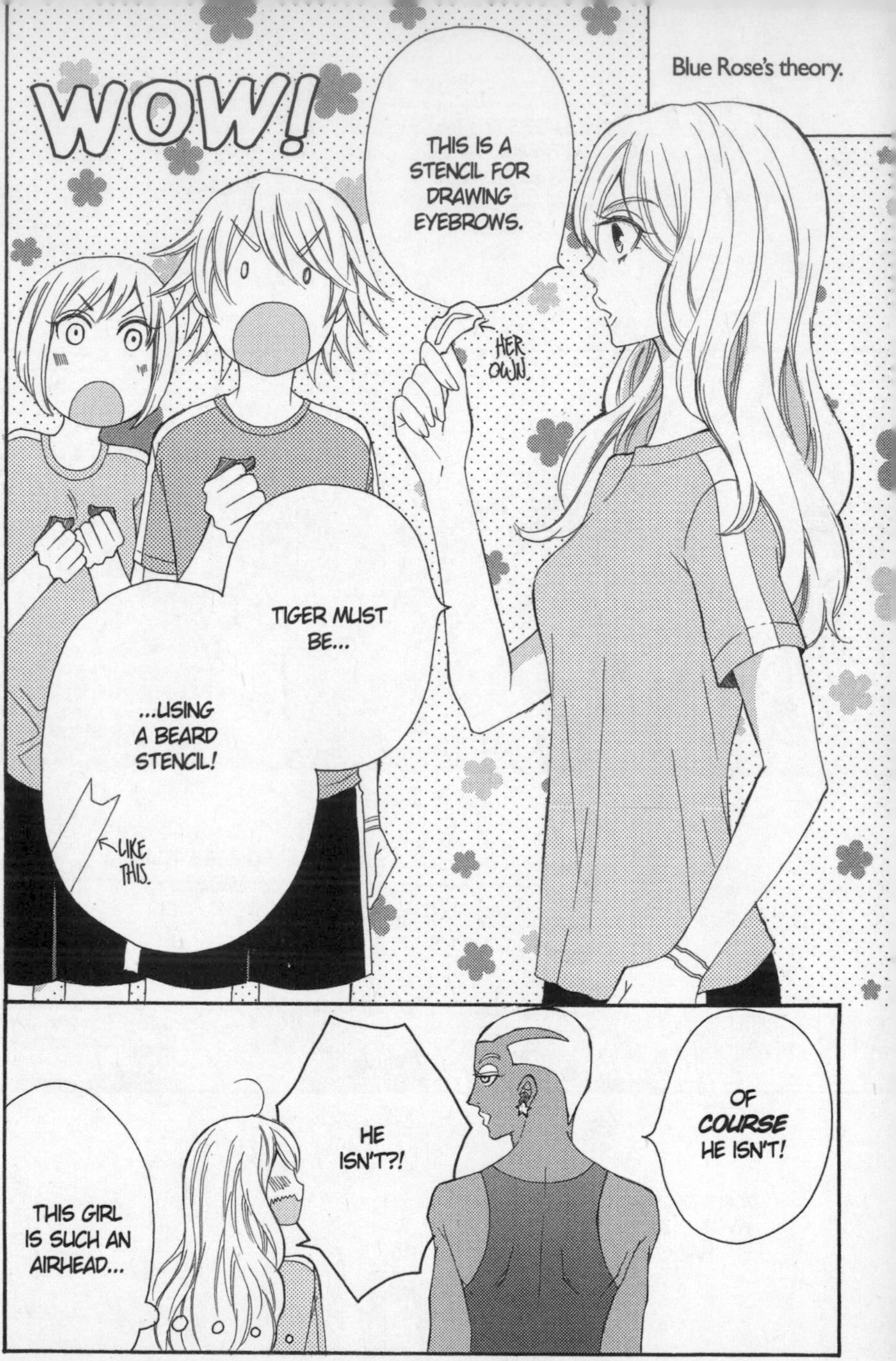
Blue Rose's theory.
THIS IS A STENCIL FOR DRAWING EYEBROWS.
HER OWN.
WOW!
TIGER MUST BE...
...USING A BEARD STENCIL!
LIKE THIS.
OF *COURSE* HE ISN'T!
HE ISN'T?!
THIS GIRL IS SUCH AN AIRHEAD...

Old Man's Beard, Part 2

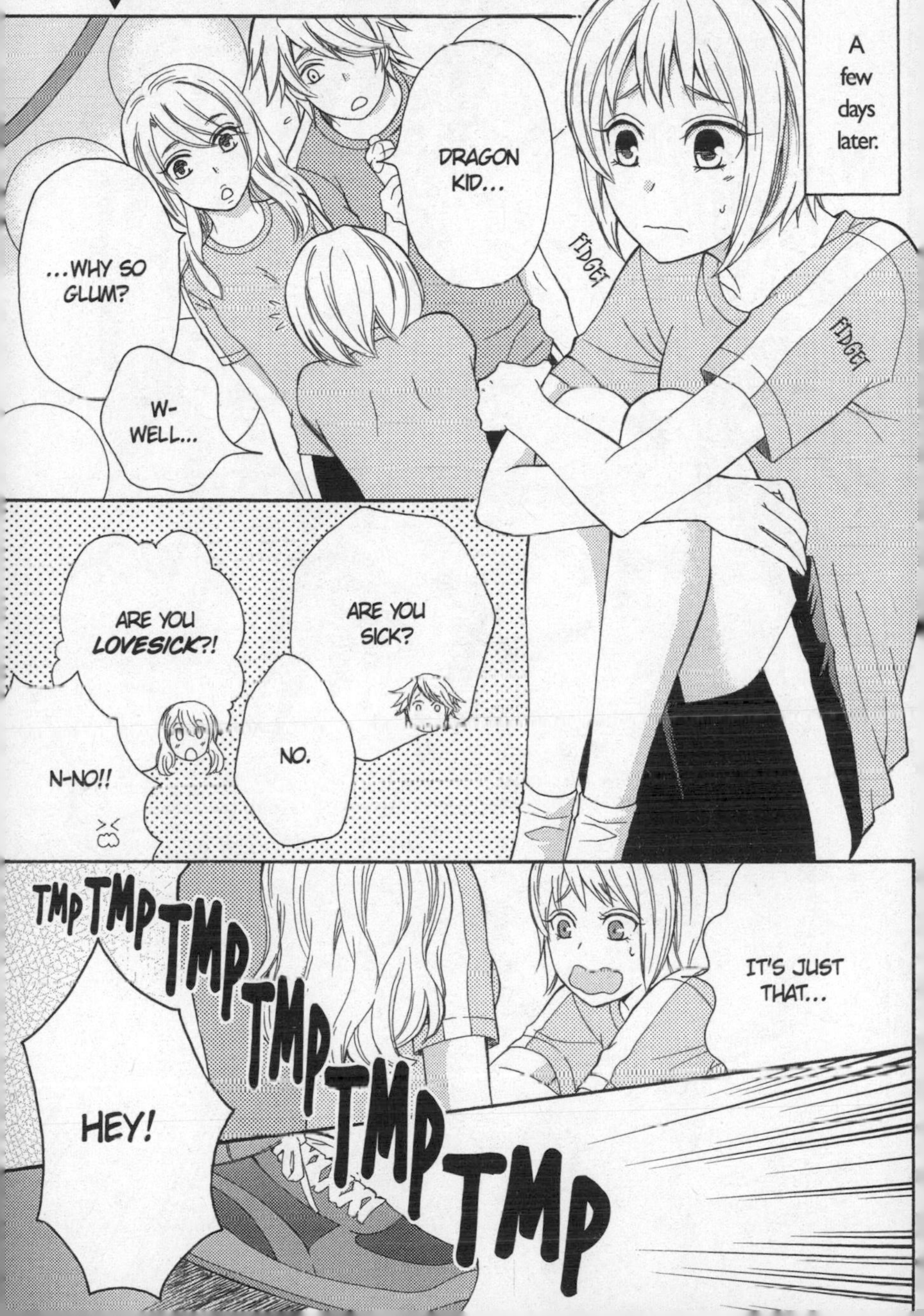
A few days later.
FIDGET
FIDGET
DRAGON KID...
...WHY SO GLUM?
W-WELL...
ARE YOU SICK?
NO.
ARE YOU LOVESICK?!
N-NO!!
IT'S JUST THAT...
TMP TMP TMP TMP TMP TMP TMP TMP
HEY!

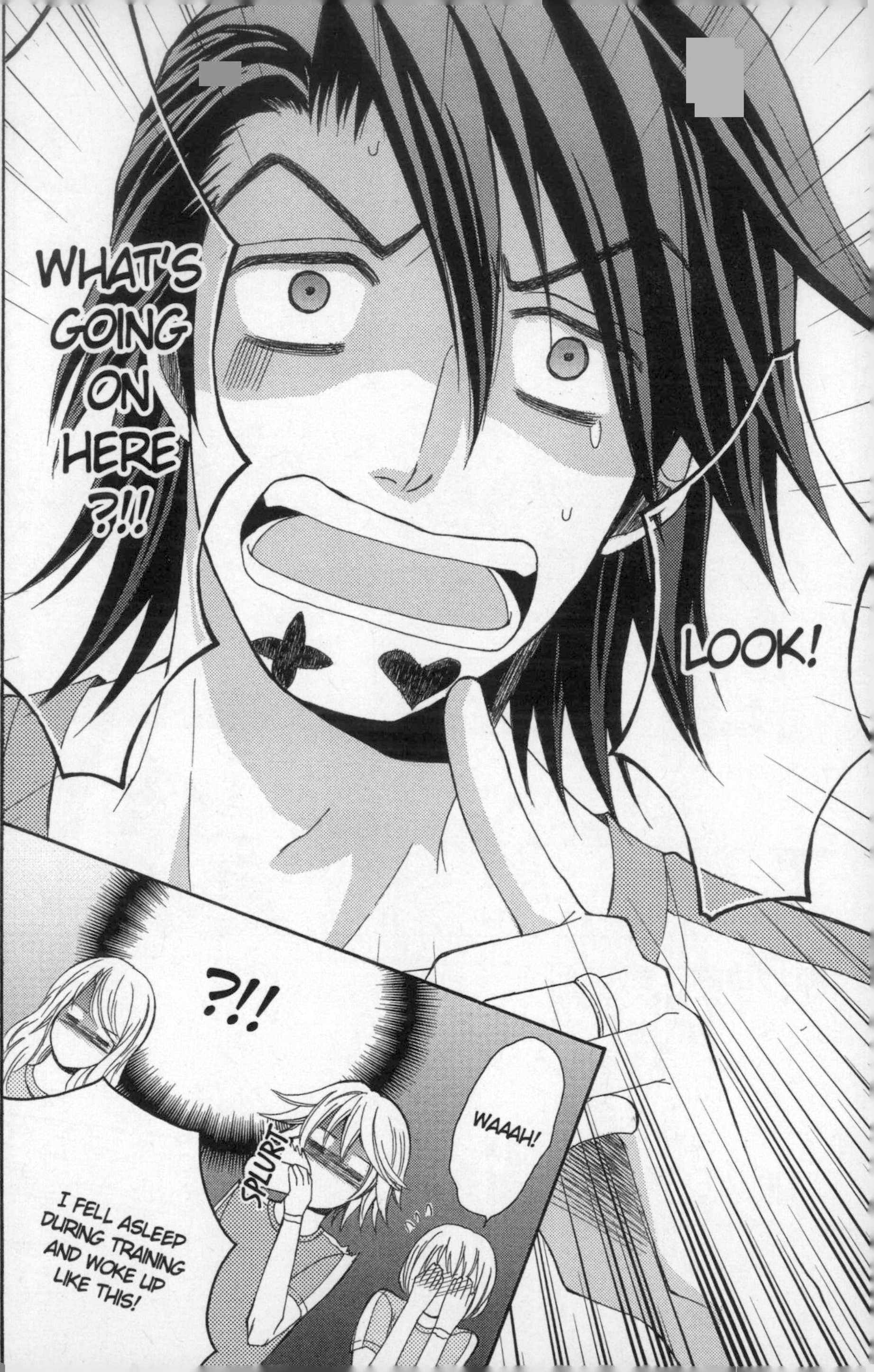
WHAT'S GOING ON HERE ?!!
LOOK!
?!!
WAAAH!
SPLURT
I FELL ASLEEP DURING TRAINING AND WOKE UP LIKE THIS!

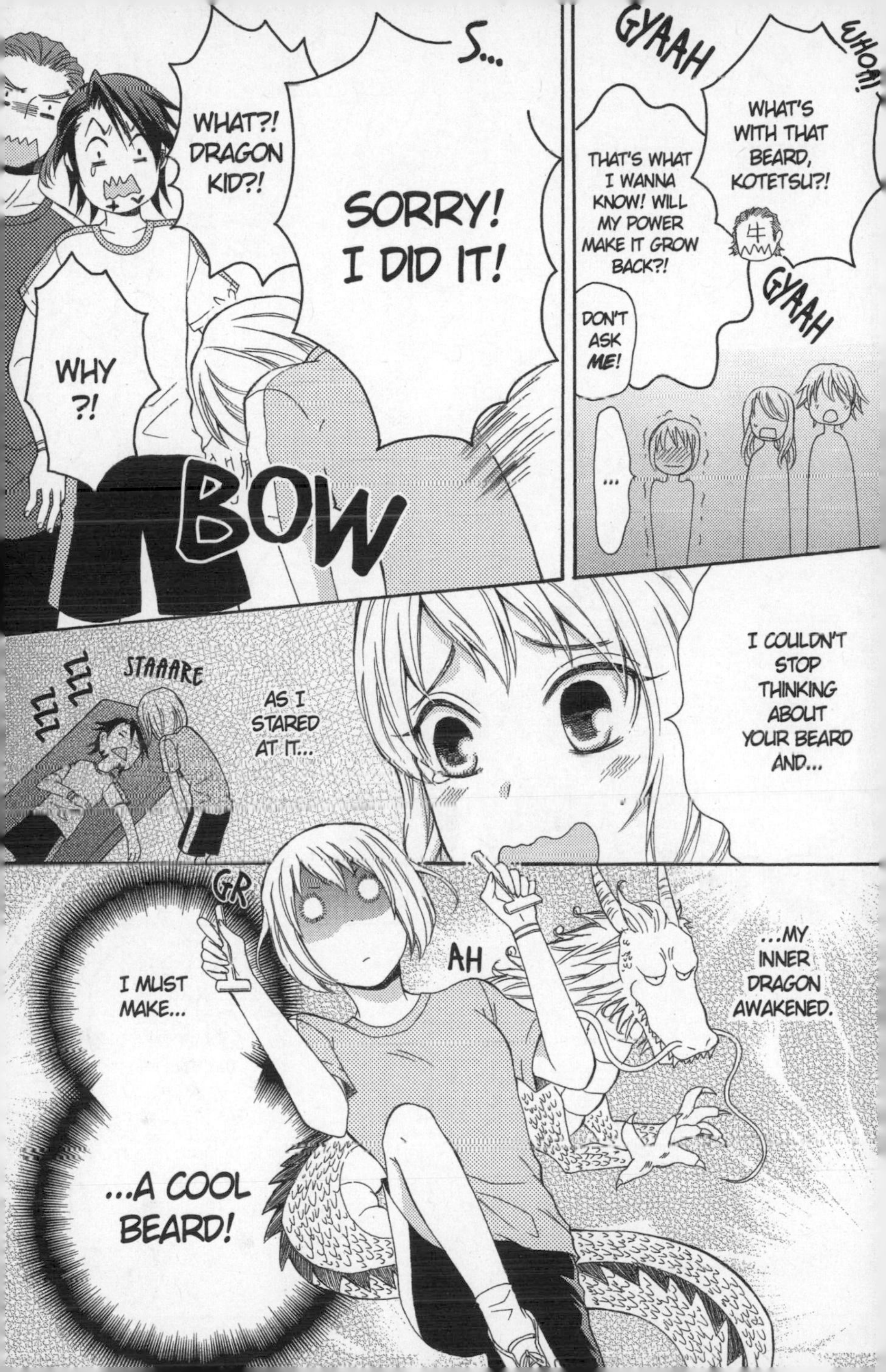
WHOA?!
WHAT'S WITH THAT BEARD, KOTETSU?!
GYAAH
GYAAH
THAT'S WHAT I WANNA KNOW! WILL MY POWER MAKE IT GROW BACK?!
DON'T ASK ME!
...
S...
SORRY! I DID IT!
WHAT?! DRAGON KID?!
WHY ?!
BOW
I COULDN'T STOP THINKING ABOUT YOUR BEARD AND...
AS I STARED AT IT...
STAAARE
ZZZ
ZZZ
...MY INNER DRAGON AWAKENED.
AH
GR
I MUST MAKE...
...A COOL BEARD!

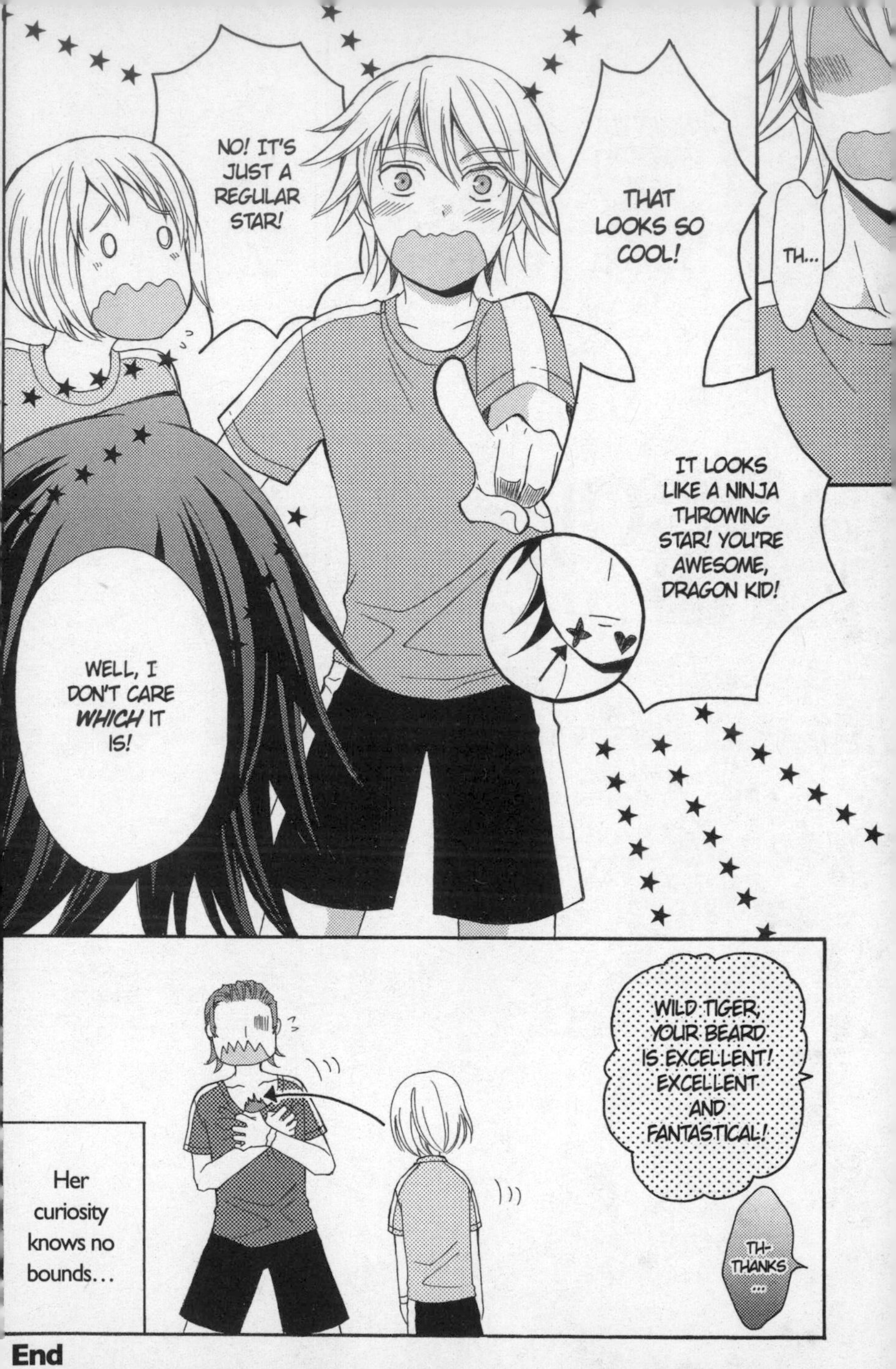
TH...
THAT LOOKS SO COOL!
IT LOOKS LIKE A NINJA THROWING STAR! YOU'RE AWESOME, DRAGON KID!
NO! IT'S JUST A REGULAR STAR!
WELL, I DON'T CARE *WHICH* IT IS!
WILD TIGER, YOUR BEARD IS EXCELLENT! EXCELLENT AND FANTASTICAL!
TH-THANKS...
Her curiosity knows no bounds…

End

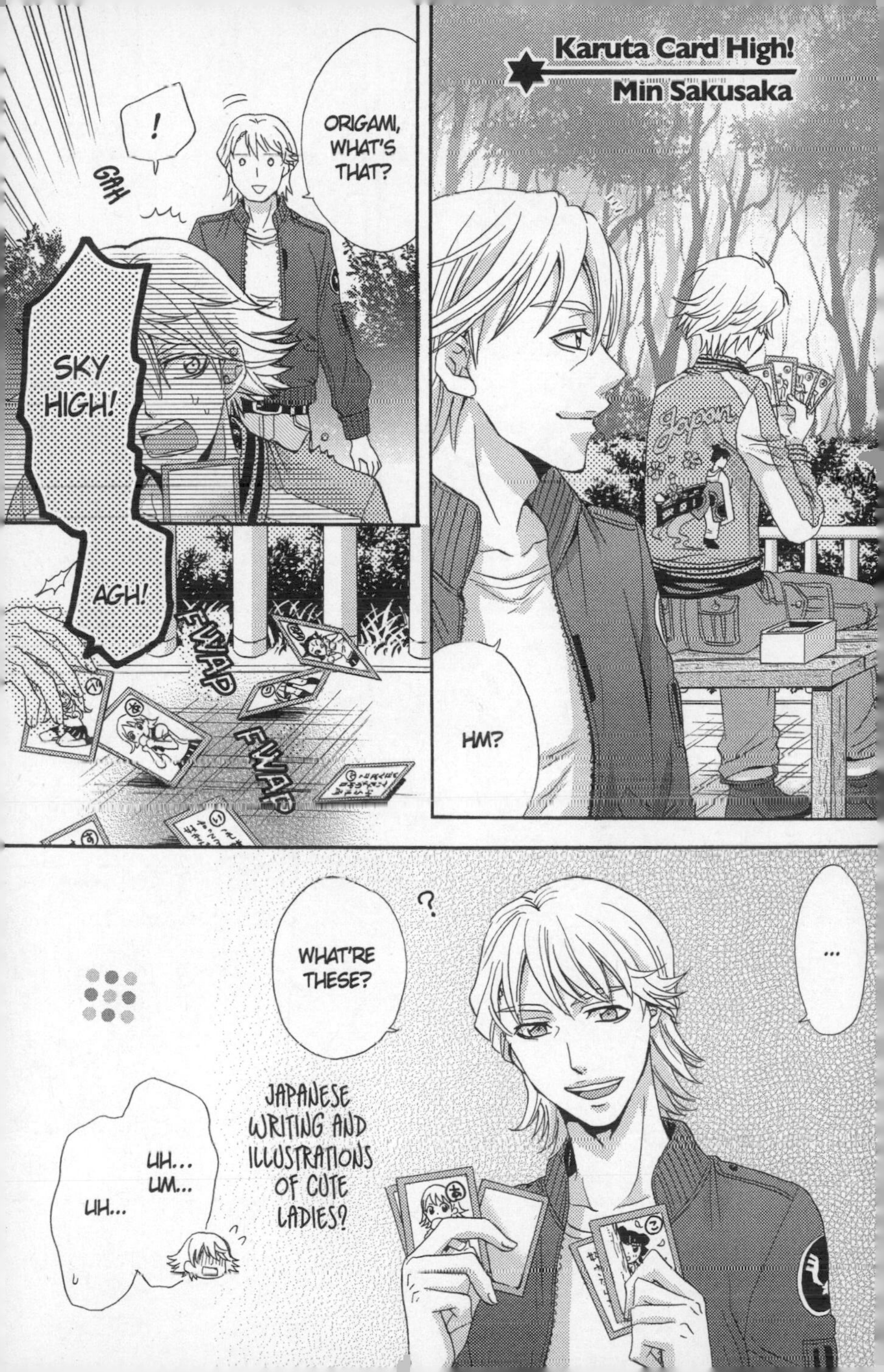

Karuta Card High!
Min Sakusaka
HM?
ORIGAMI, WHAT'S THAT?
!
GAH
SKY HIGH!
AGH!
FWAP
FWAP
...
?
WHAT'RE THESE?
JAPANESE WRITING AND ILLUSTRATIONS OF CUTE LADIES?
UH... UM...
UH...

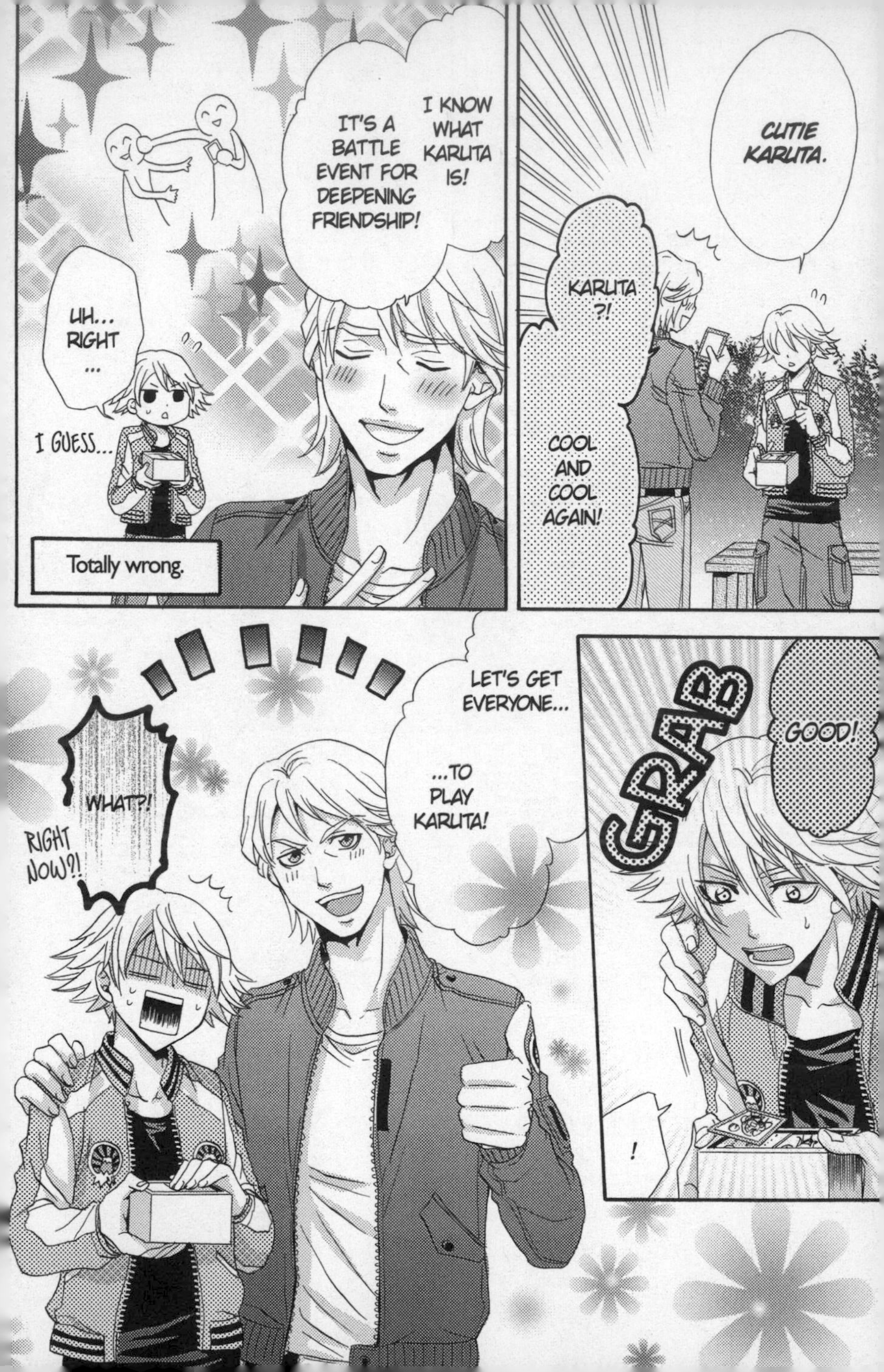
CUTIE KARUTA.
KARUTA ?!
COOL AND COOL AGAIN!
I KNOW WHAT KARUTA IS!
IT'S A BATTLE EVENT FOR DEEPENING FRIENDSHIP!
UH... RIGHT ...
I GUESS...
Totally wrong.
GOOD!
GRAB
!
LET'S GET EVERYONE...
...TO PLAY KARUTA!
WHAT?!
RIGHT NOW?!

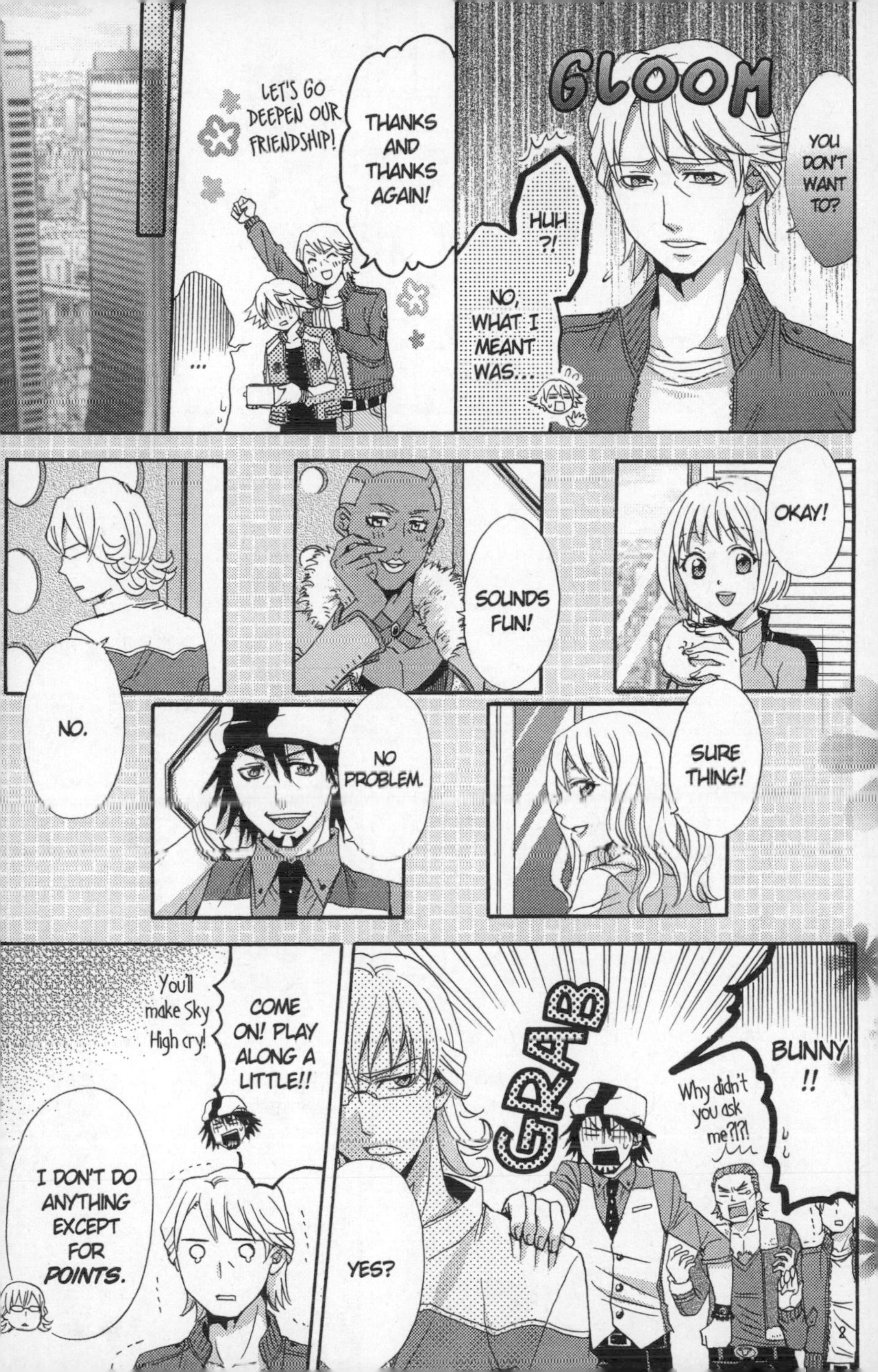
GLOOM
YOU DON'T WANT TO?
HUH ?!
NO, WHAT I MEANT WAS...
THANKS AND THANKS AGAIN!
LET'S GO DEEPEN OUR FRIENDSHIP!
...
OKAY!
SOUNDS FUN!
NO.
SURE THING!
NO PROBLEM.
BUNNY !!
Why didn't you ask me?!?!
GRAB
YES?
COME ON! PLAY ALONG A LITTLE!!
You'll make Sky High cry!
I DON'T DO ANYTHING EXCEPT FOR *POINTS*.

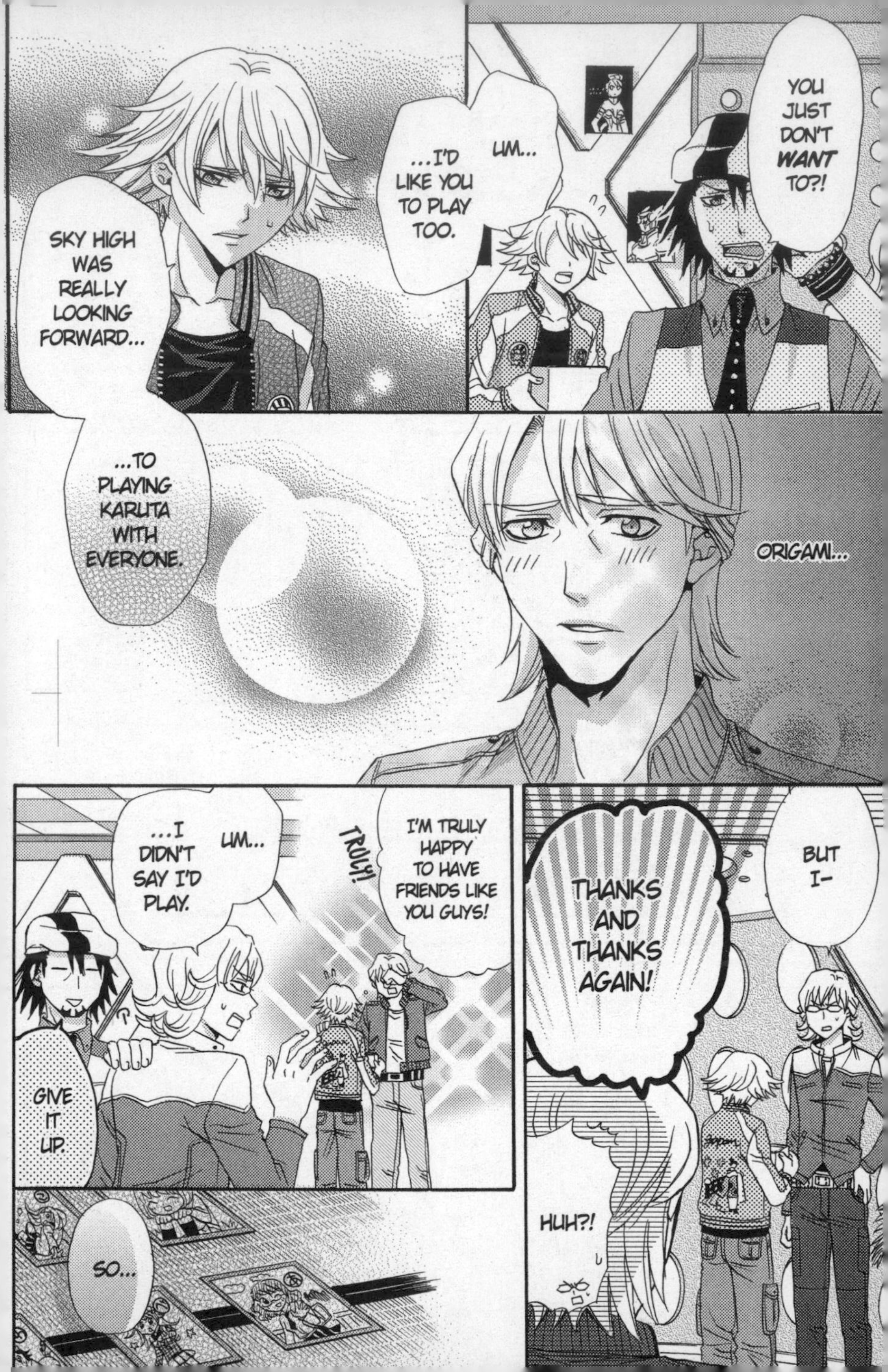
YOU JUST DON'T WANT TO?!
UM...
...I'D LIKE YOU TO PLAY TOO.
SKY HIGH WAS REALLY LOOKING FORWARD...
...TO PLAYING KARUTA WITH EVERYONE.
ORIGAMI...
BUT I-
THANKS AND THANKS AGAIN!
HUH?!
I'M TRULY HAPPY TO HAVE FRIENDS LIKE YOU GUYS!
TRULY!
UM...
...I DIDN'T SAY I'D PLAY.
GIVE IT UP.
SO...

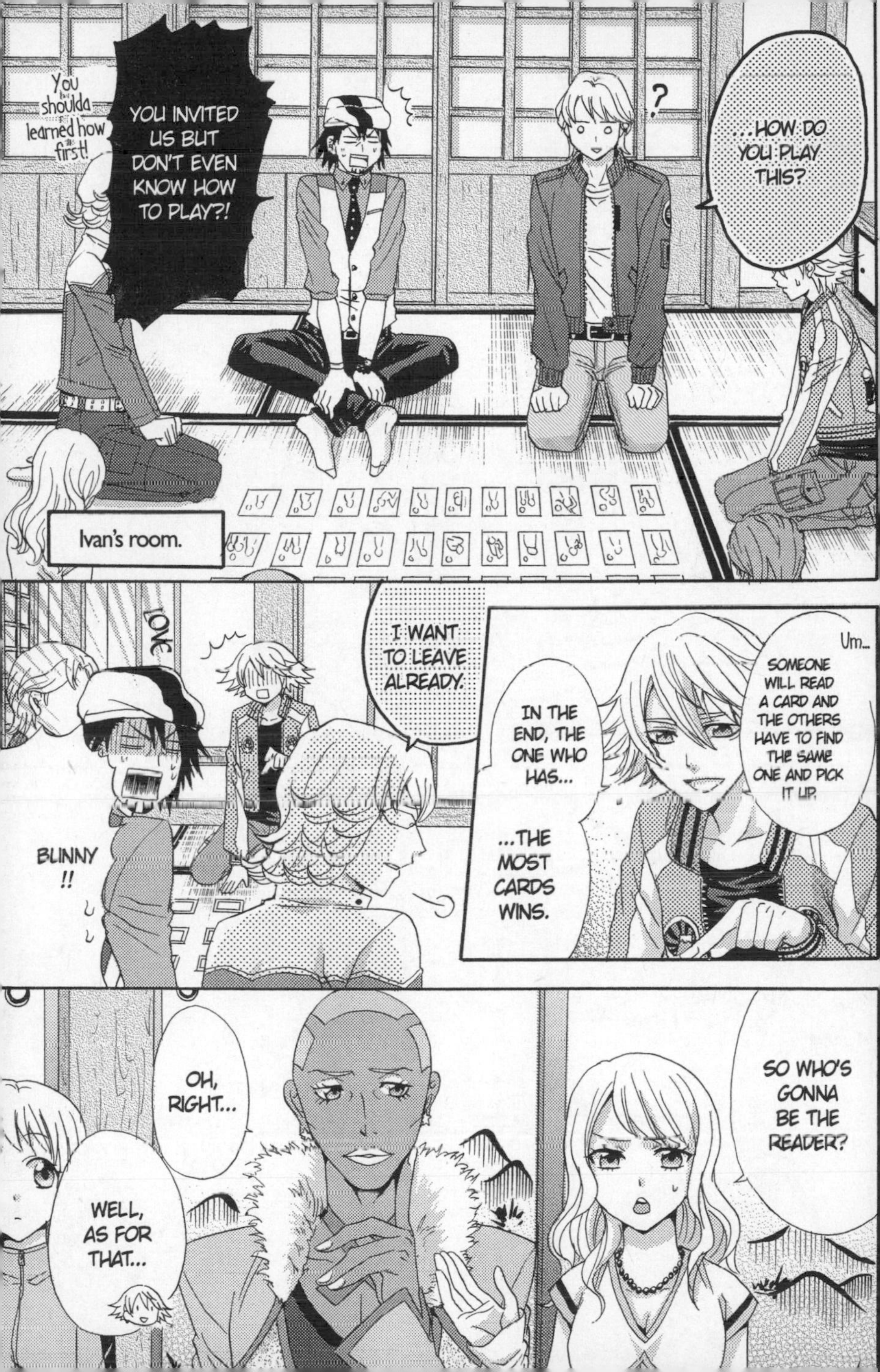
?
...HOW DO YOU PLAY THIS?
YOU INVITED US BUT DON'T EVEN KNOW HOW TO PLAY?!
You shoulda learned how first!
Ivan's room.
Um...
SOMEONE WILL READ A CARD AND THE OTHERS HAVE TO FIND THE SAME ONE AND PICK IT UP.
IN THE END, THE ONE WHO HAS...
...THE MOST CARDS WINS.
I WANT TO LEAVE ALREADY.
LOVE
BUNNY !!
SO WHO'S GONNA BE THE READER?
OH, RIGHT...
WELL, AS FOR THAT...

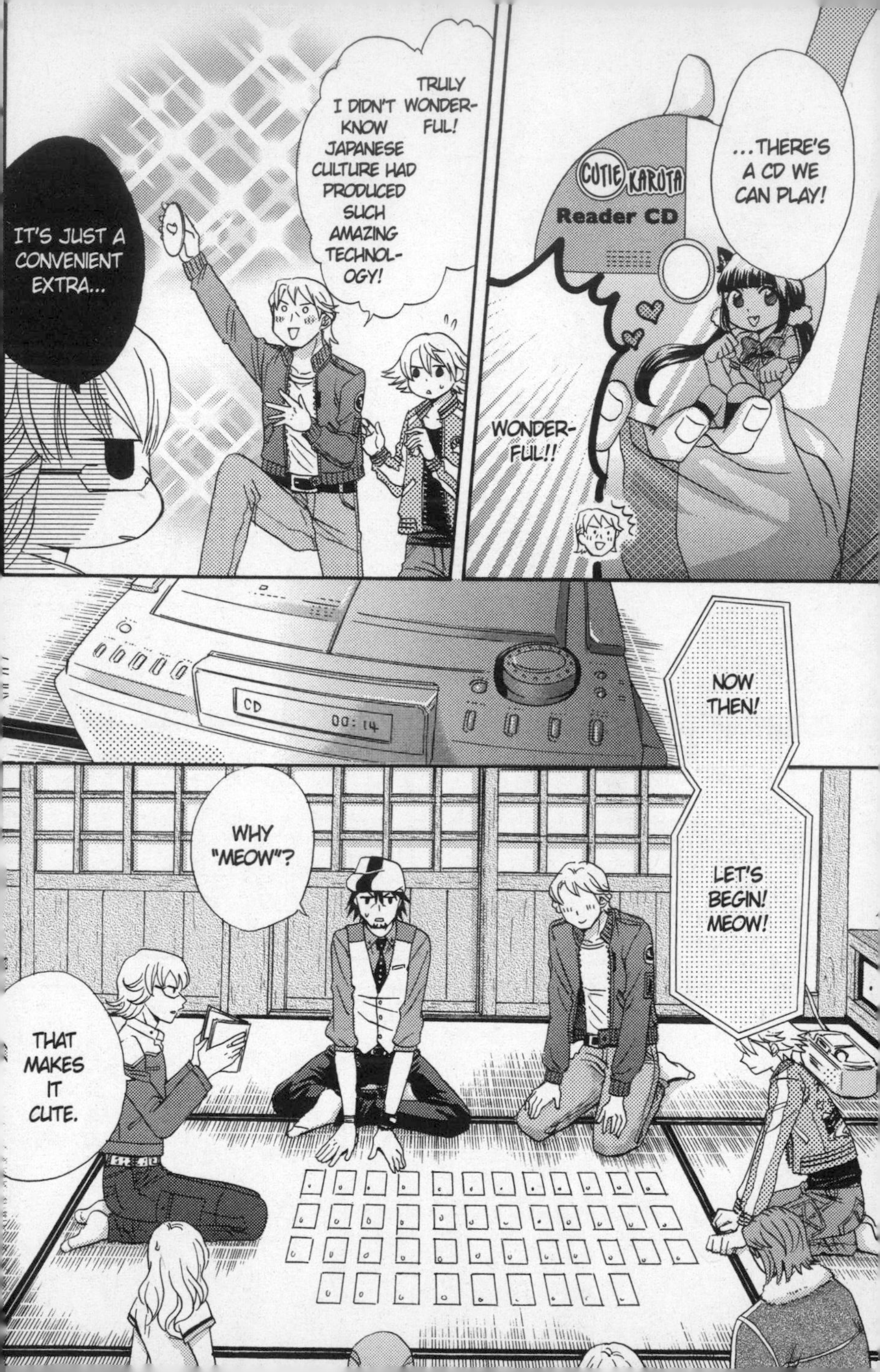
...THERE'S A CD WE CAN PLAY!
CUTIE KARUTA
Reader CD
WONDERFUL!!
I DIDN'T KNOW JAPANESE CULTURE HAD PRODUCED SUCH AMAZING TECHNOL-OGY! TRULY WONDER-FUL!
IT'S JUST A CONVENIENT EXTRA...
NOW THEN!
CD 00:14
LET'S BEGIN! MEOW!
WHY "MEOW"?
THAT MAKES IT CUTE.

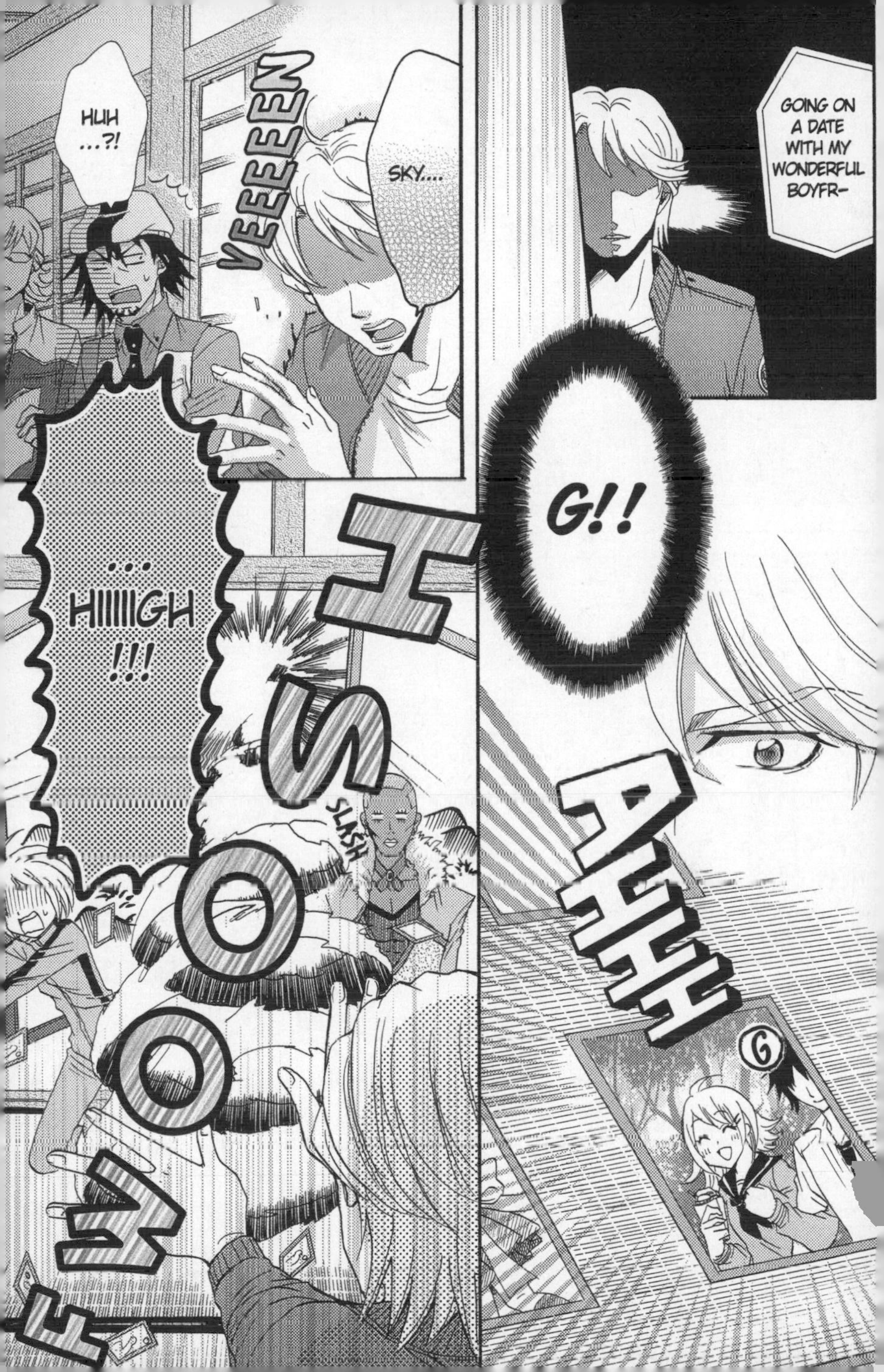
GOING ON A DATE WITH MY WONDERFUL BOYFR-
SKY....
VEEEEEN
HUH ...?!
G!!
AHHH
WHOOSH
SLASH
... HIIIIGH !!!

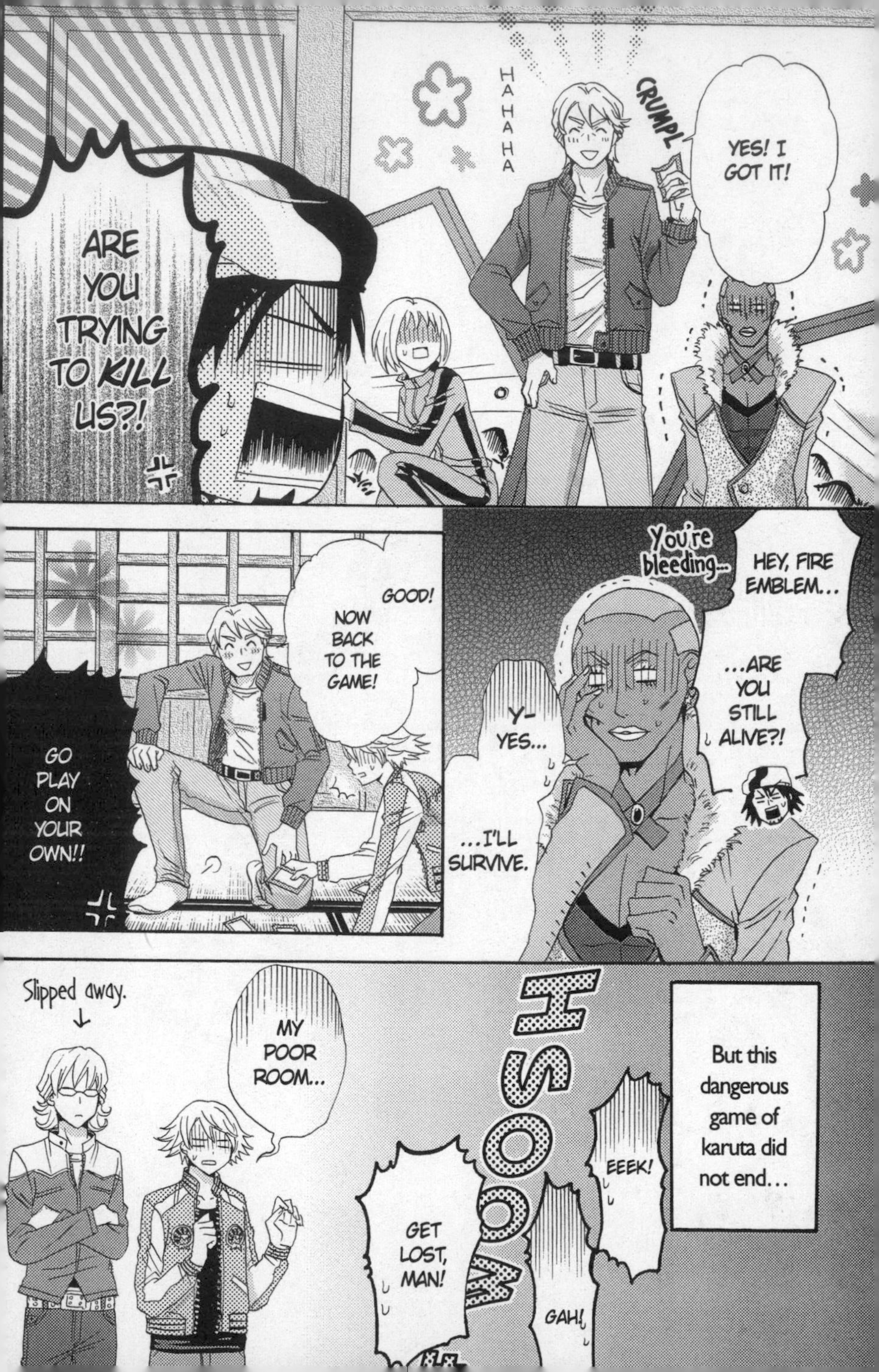
YES! I GOT IT!
CRUMPL
HAHAHA
ARE YOU TRYING TO KILL US?!
HEY, FIRE EMBLEM...
You're bleeding...
...ARE YOU STILL ALIVE?!
Y- YES...
...I'LL SURVIVE.
GOOD! NOW BACK TO THE GAME!
GO PLAY ON YOUR OWN!!
But this dangerous game of karuta did not end...
WHOOSH
EEEK!
GET LOST, MAN!
GAH!
MY POOR ROOM...
Slipped away.

Blue Rose's Mission: Dieting!

Ayumi Karino

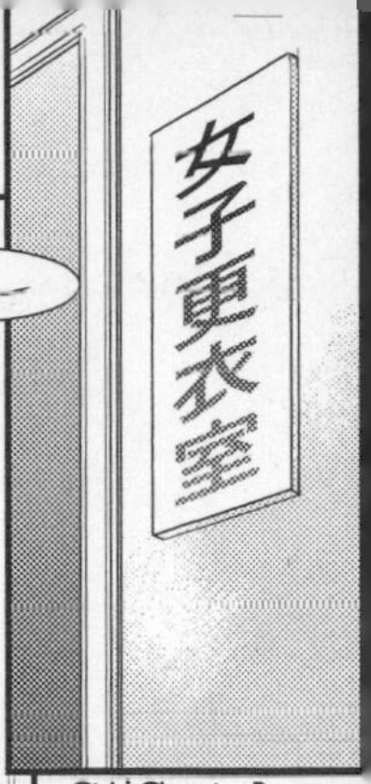
女子更衣室
Girls' Changing Room

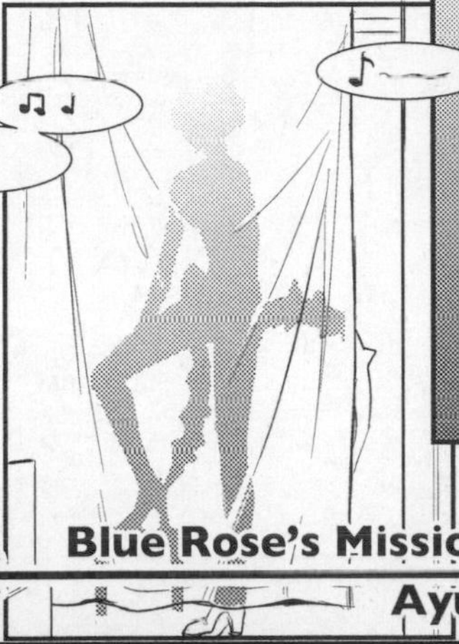
♪〜〜
♫♩
♪

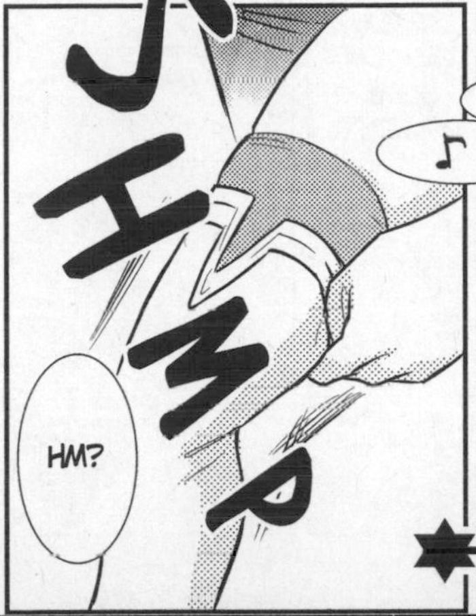
HM?

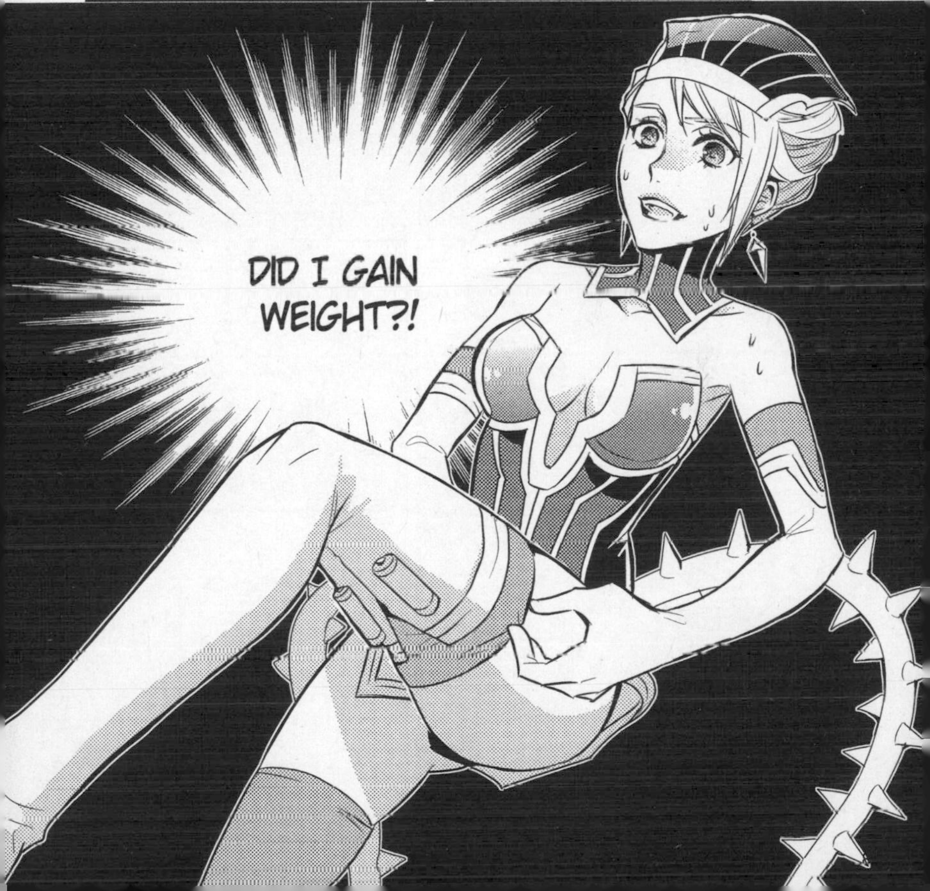
DID I GAIN WEIGHT?!

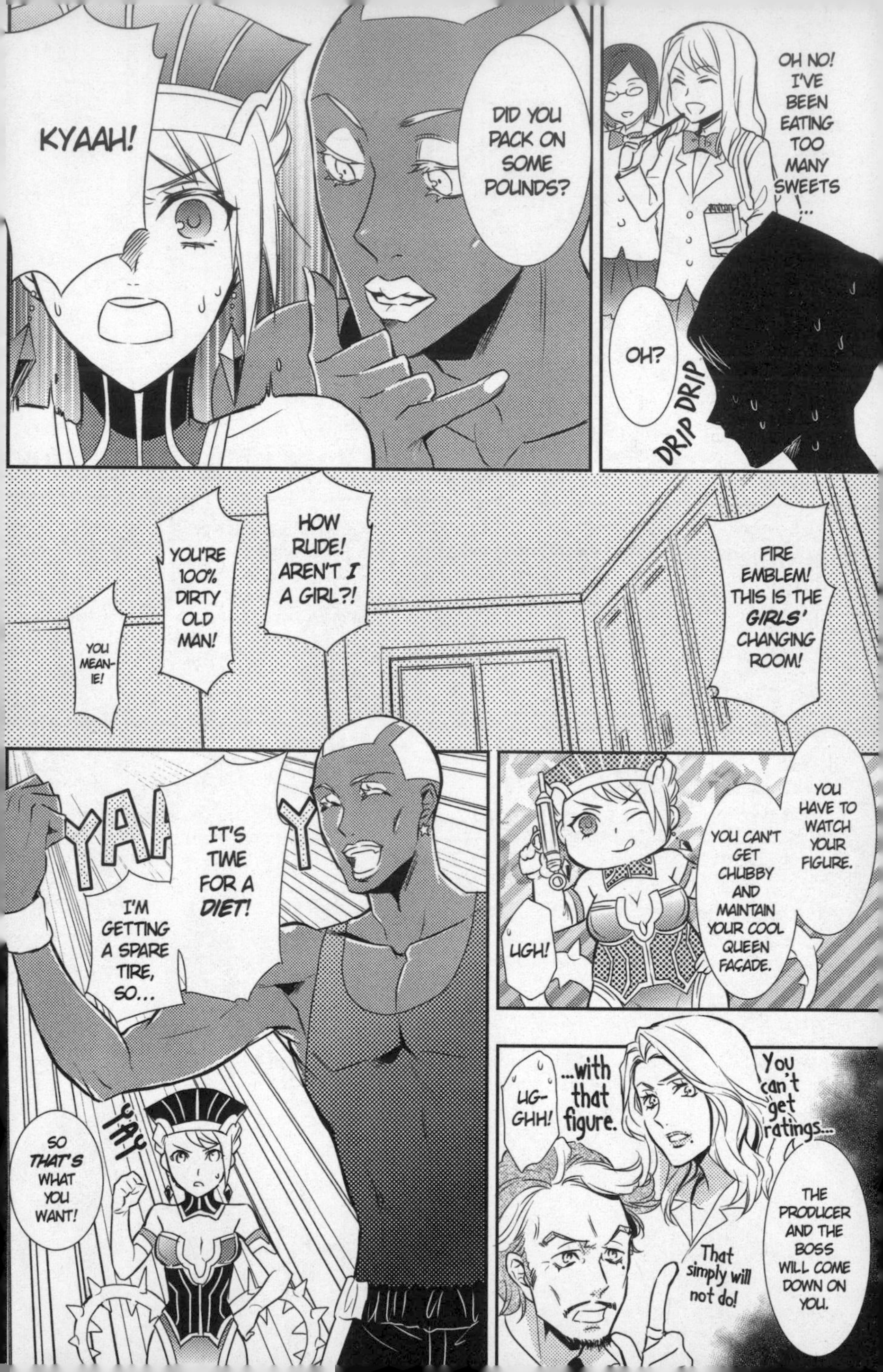
OH NO! I'VE BEEN EATING TOO MANY SWEETS...
OH?
DRIP DRIP
DID YOU PACK ON SOME POUNDS?
KYAAH!
FIRE EMBLEM! THIS IS THE GIRLS' CHANGING ROOM!
HOW RUDE! AREN'T I A GIRL?!
YOU'RE 100% DIRTY OLD MAN!
YOU MEANIE!
YOU HAVE TO WATCH YOUR FIGURE.
YOU CAN'T GET CHUBBY AND MAINTAIN YOUR COOL QUEEN FAÇADE.
UGH!
You can't get ratings...
...with that figure.
UG-GHH!
THE PRODUCER AND THE BOSS WILL COME DOWN ON YOU.
That simply will not do!
IT'S TIME FOR A DIET!
I'M GETTING A SPARE TIRE, SO...
YAY
SO THAT'S WHAT YOU WANT!

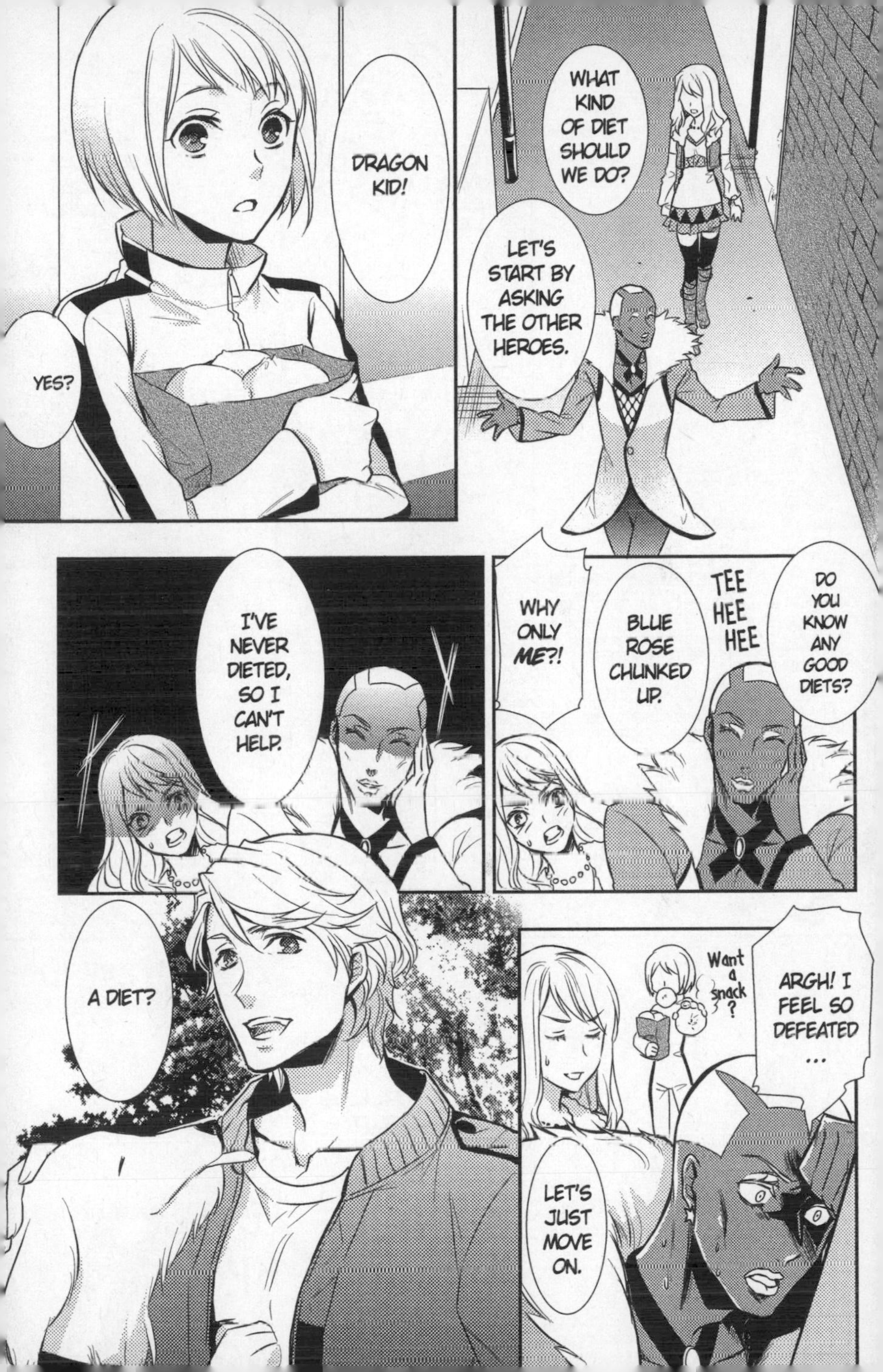
WHAT KIND OF DIET SHOULD WE DO?
LET'S START BY ASKING THE OTHER HEROES.
DRAGON KID!
YES?
DO YOU KNOW ANY GOOD DIETS?
TEE HEE HEE
BLUE ROSE CHUNKED UP.
WHY ONLY *ME*?!
I'VE NEVER DIETED, SO I CAN'T HELP.
ARGH! I FEEL SO DEFEATED ...
Want a snack?
LET'S JUST MOVE ON.
A DIET?

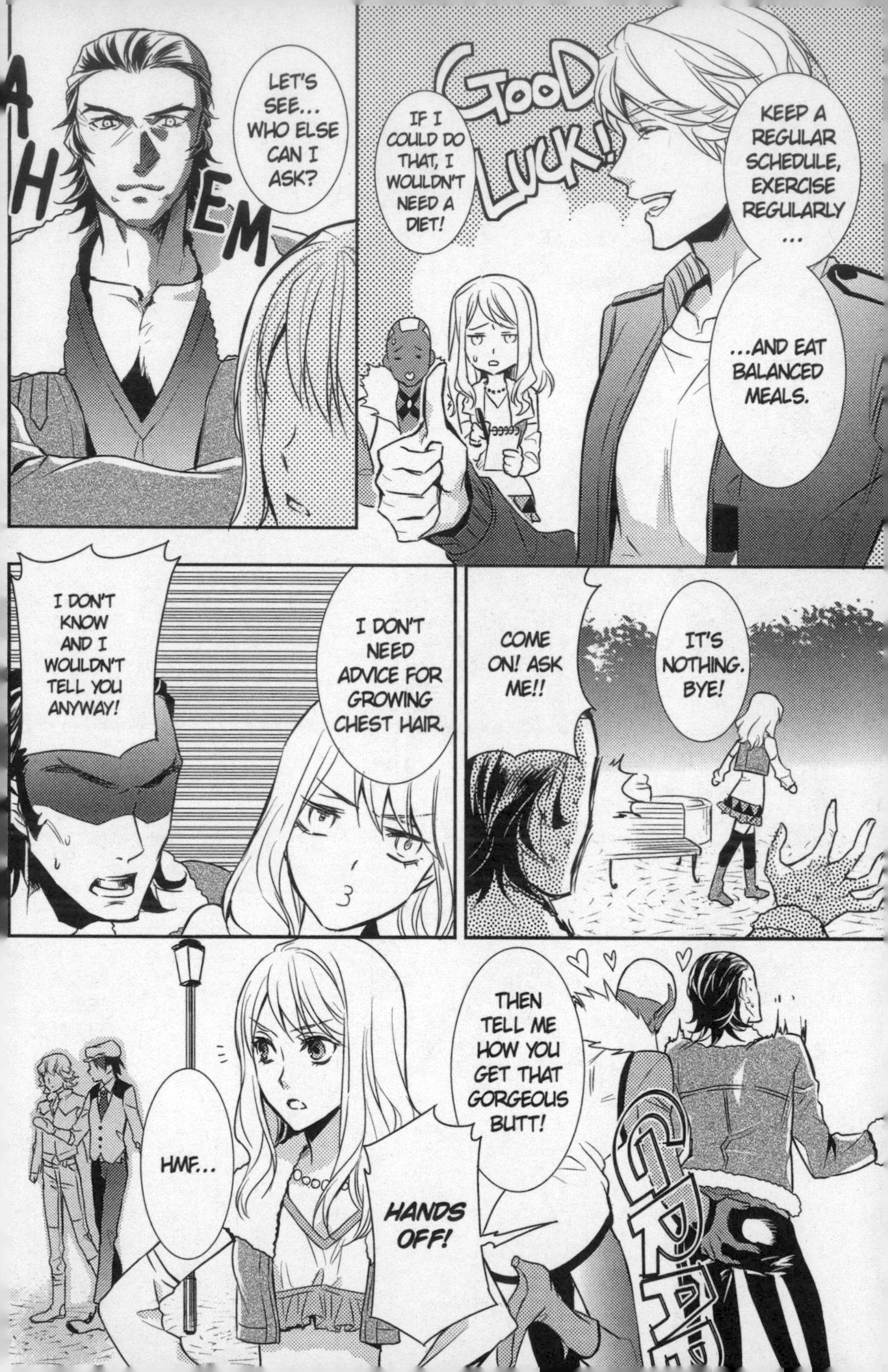
KEEP A REGULAR SCHEDULE, EXERCISE REGULARLY ...
...AND EAT BALANCED MEALS.
GOOD LUCK!
IF I COULD DO THAT, I WOULDN'T NEED A DIET!
AHEM
LET'S SEE... WHO ELSE CAN I ASK?
IT'S NOTHING. BYE!
COME ON! ASK ME!!
I DON'T NEED ADVICE FOR GROWING CHEST HAIR.
I DON'T KNOW AND I WOULDN'T TELL YOU ANYWAY!
THEN TELL ME HOW YOU GET THAT GORGEOUS BUTT!
GRAB
HANDS OFF!
HMF...

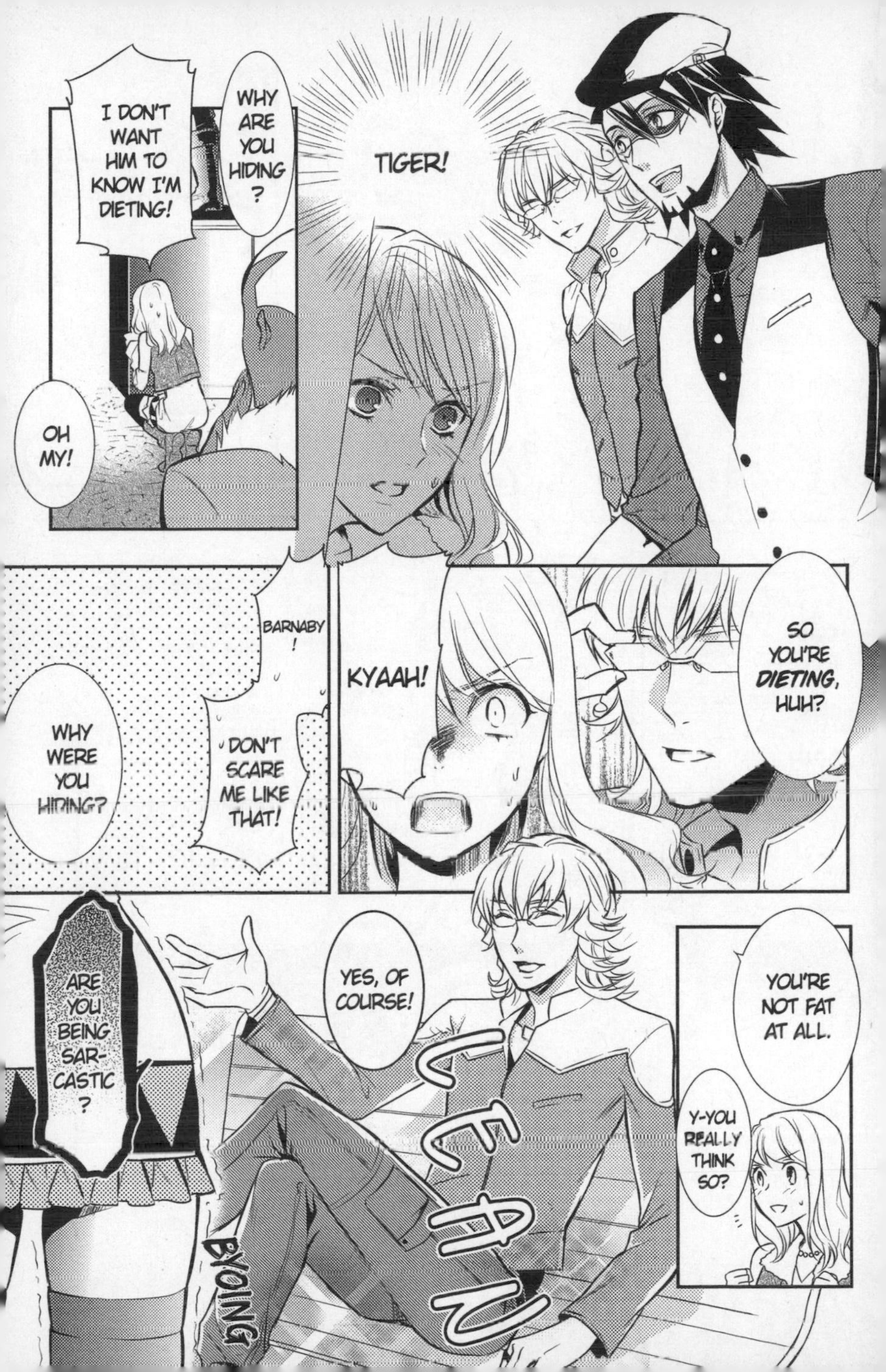
TIGER!
WHY ARE YOU HIDING?
I DON'T WANT HIM TO KNOW I'M DIETING!
OH MY!
SO YOU'RE DIETING, HUH?
KYAAH!
BARNABY!
DON'T SCARE ME LIKE THAT!
WHY WERE YOU HIDING?
YOU'RE NOT FAT AT ALL.
Y-YOU REALLY THINK SO?
YES, OF COURSE!
ARE YOU BEING SAR-CASTIC?
BYOING

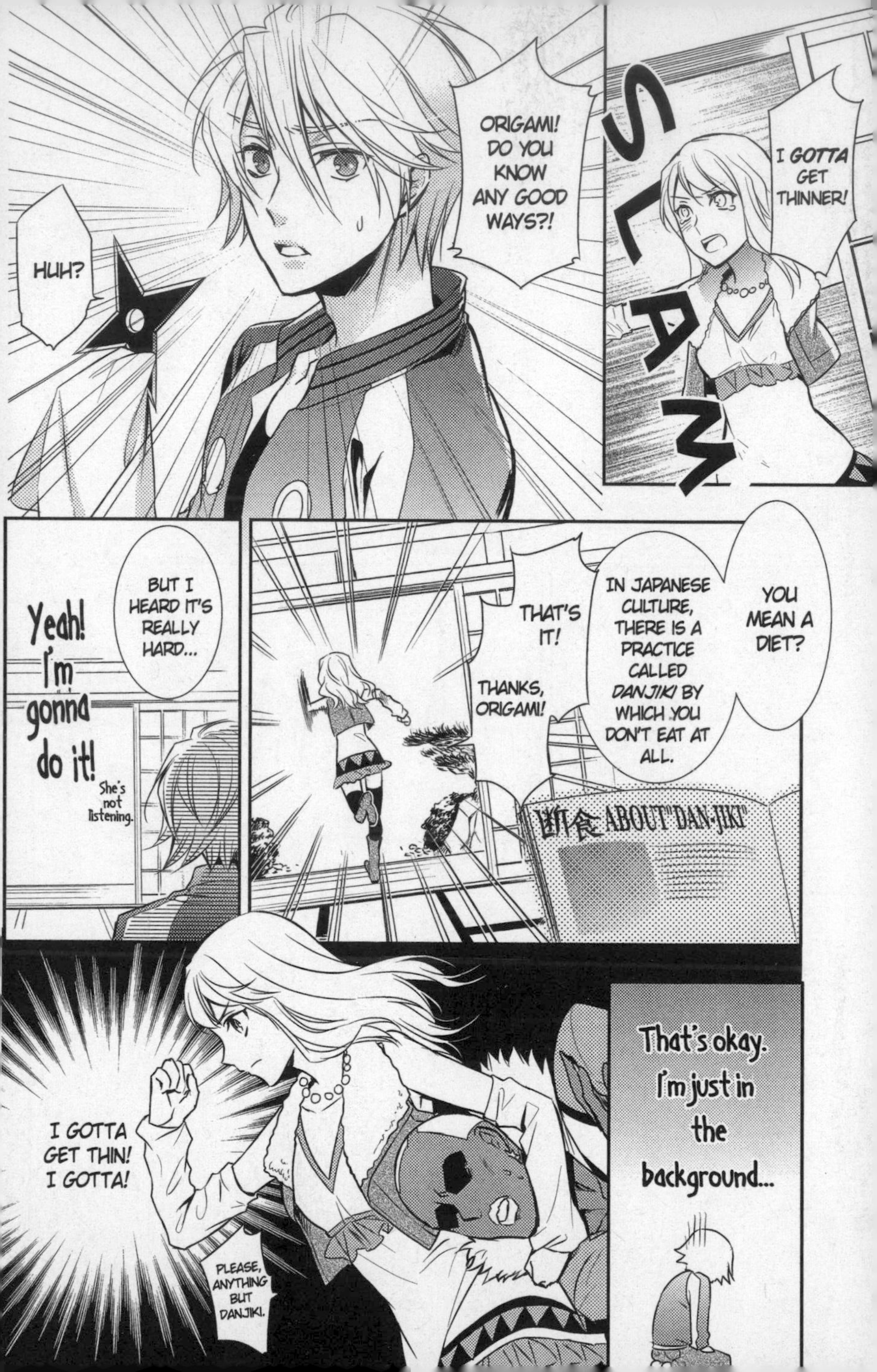
SLAM
I GOTTA GET THINNER!
ORIGAMI! DO YOU KNOW ANY GOOD WAYS?!
HUH?
YOU MEAN A DIET?
IN JAPANESE CULTURE, THERE IS A PRACTICE CALLED DANJIKI BY WHICH YOU DON'T EAT AT ALL.
THAT'S IT!
THANKS, ORIGAMI!
断食 ABOUT "DAN-JIKI"
BUT I HEARD IT'S REALLY HARD...
Yeah! I'm gonna do it!
She's not listening.
That's okay. I'm just in the background...
I GOTTA GET THIN! I GOTTA!
PLEASE, ANYTHING BUT DANJIKI.

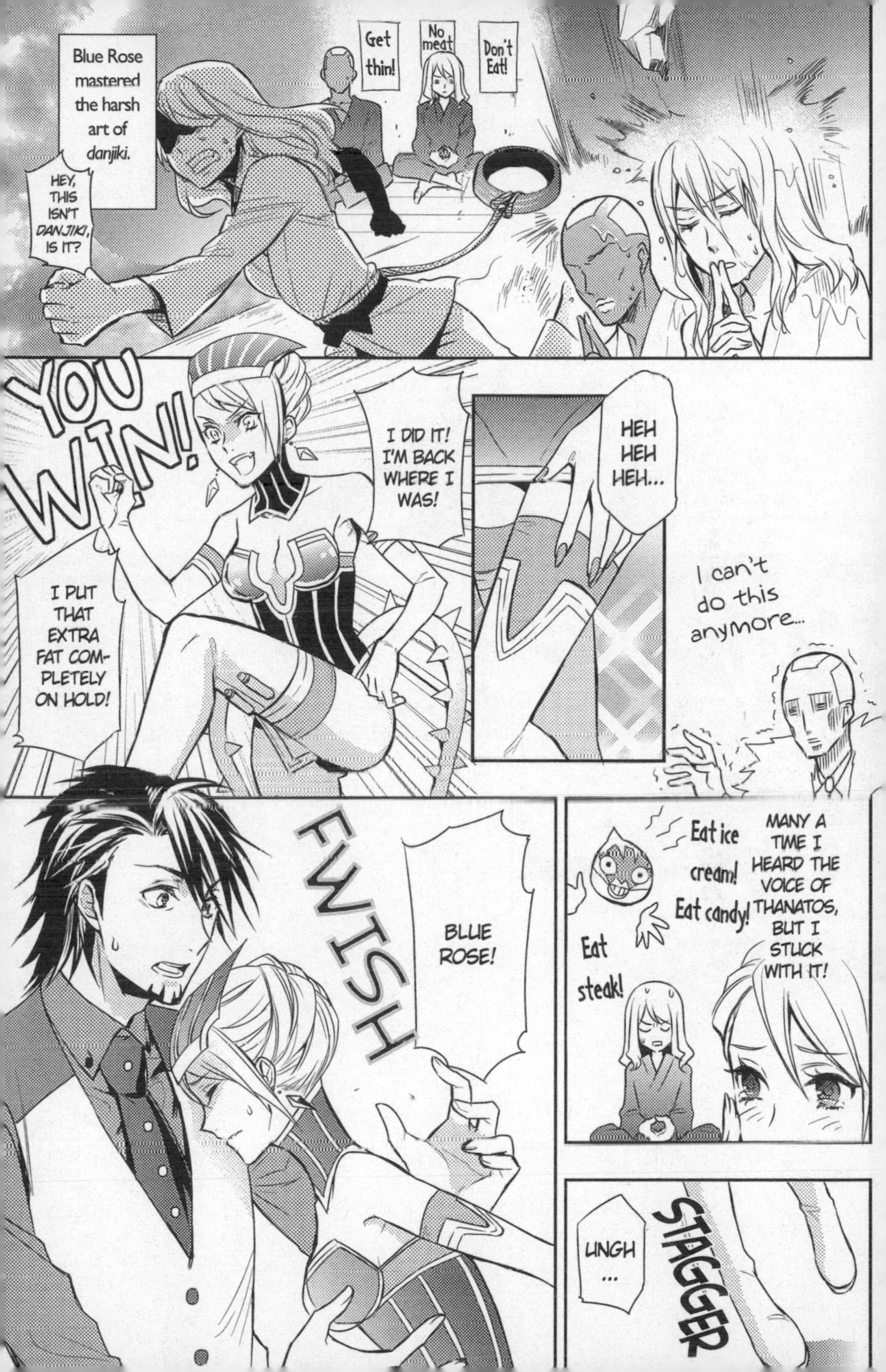
Don't Eat!
No meat
Get thin!
Blue Rose mastered the harsh art of *danjiki*.
HEY, THIS ISN'T *DANJIKI*, IS IT?
HEH HEH HEH...
I can't do this anymore...
I DID IT! I'M BACK WHERE I WAS!
YOU WIN!
I PUT THAT EXTRA FAT COMPLETELY ON HOLD!
MANY A TIME I HEARD THE VOICE OF THANATOS, BUT I STUCK WITH IT!
Eat ice cream!
Eat candy!
Eat steak!
STAGGER
UNGH ...
BLUE ROSE!
FWISH

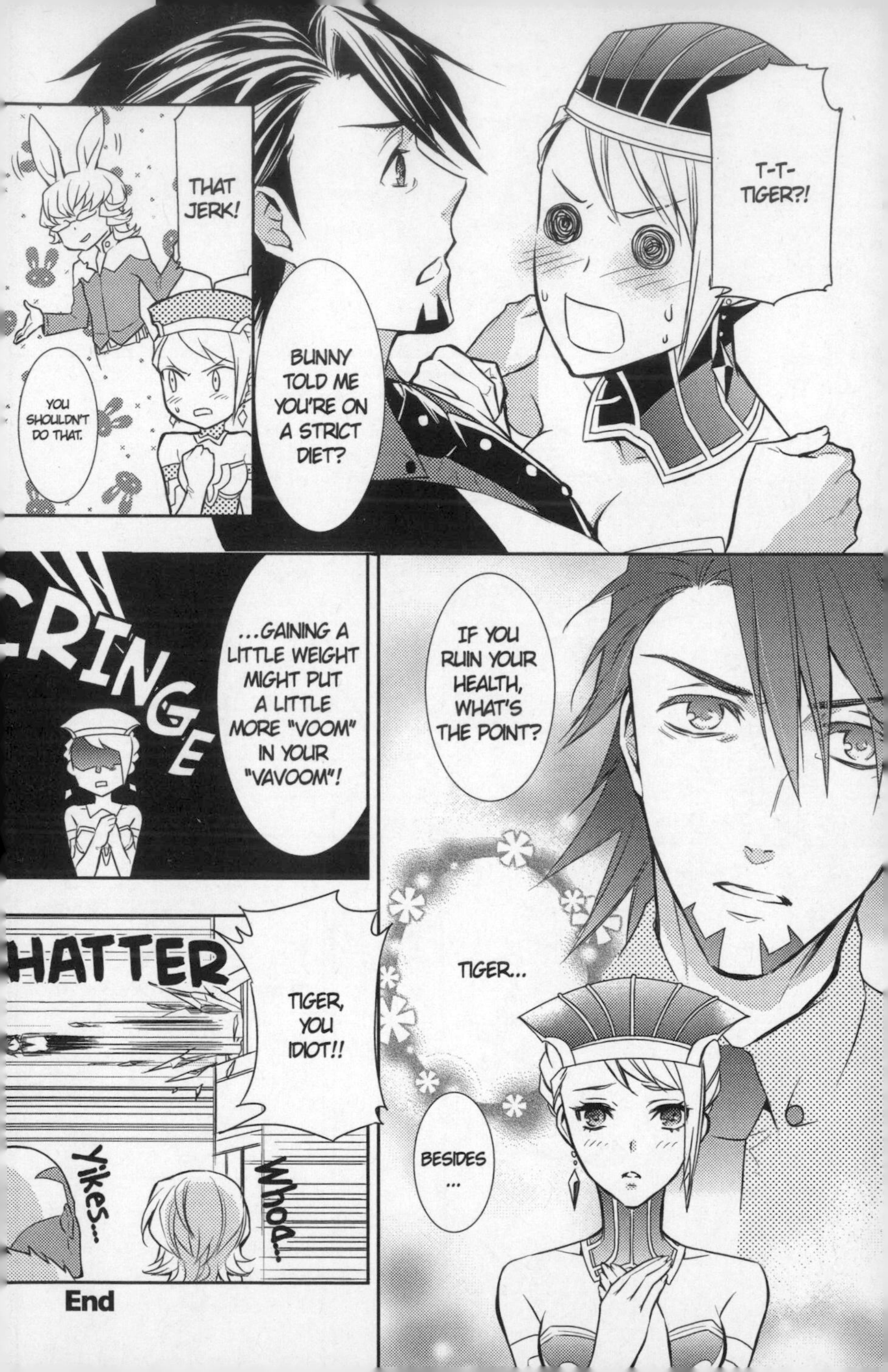
T-T-TIGER?!
BUNNY TOLD ME YOU'RE ON A STRICT DIET?
THAT JERK!
YOU SHOULDN'T DO THAT.
IF YOU RUIN YOUR HEALTH, WHAT'S THE POINT?
TIGER...
BESIDES ...
...GAINING A LITTLE WEIGHT MIGHT PUT A LITTLE MORE "VOOM" IN YOUR "VAVOOM"!
CRINGE
TIGER, YOU IDIOT!!
HATTER
Whoa...
Yikes...
End

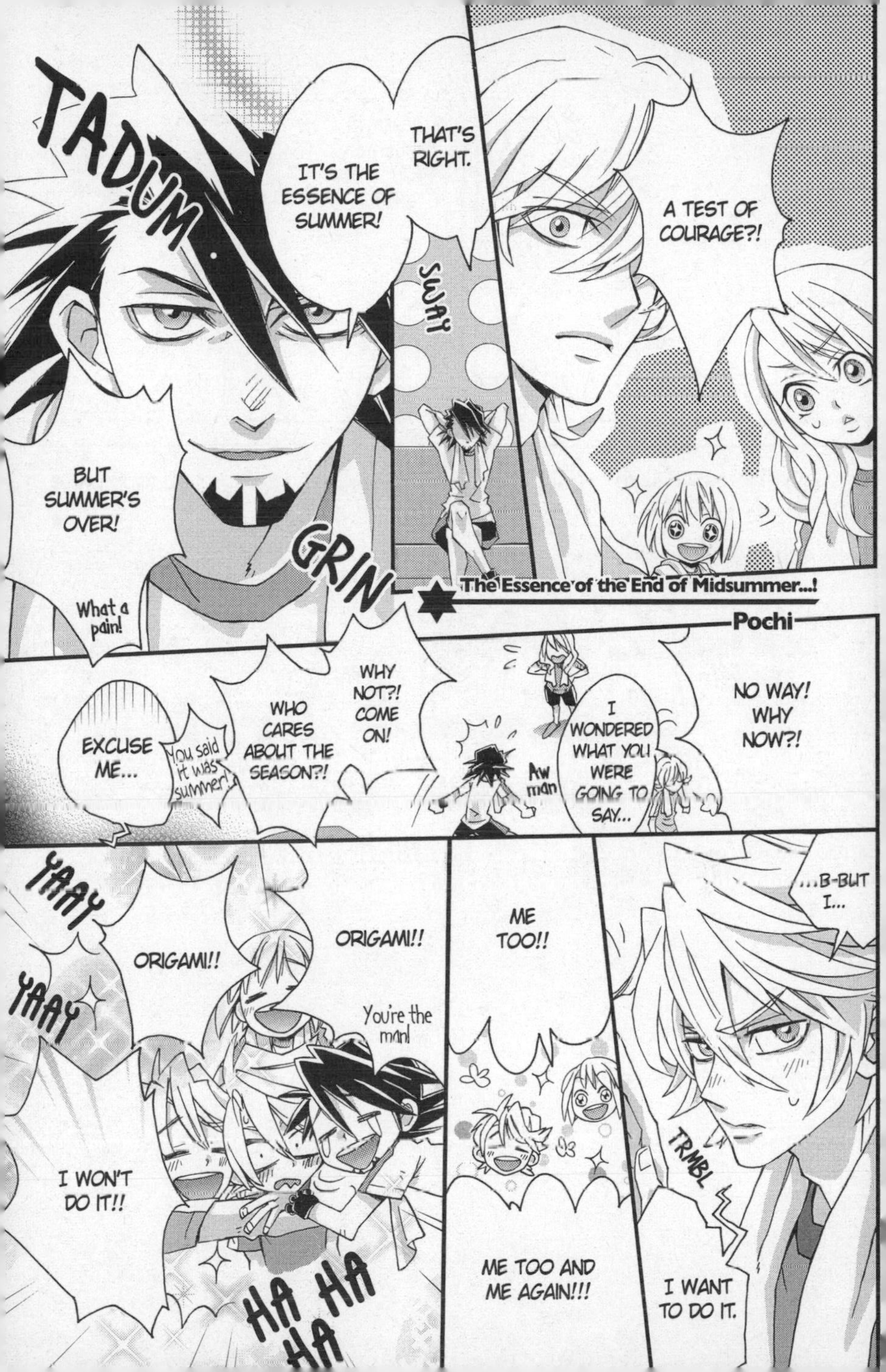
A TEST OF COURAGE?!
THAT'S RIGHT.
IT'S THE ESSENCE OF SUMMER!
SWAY
TADUM
BUT SUMMER'S OVER!
GRIN
What a pain!
The Essence of the End of Midsummer...!
Pochi
NO WAY! WHY NOW?!
I WONDERED WHAT YOU WERE GOING TO SAY...
Aw man
WHY NOT?! COME ON!
WHO CARES ABOUT THE SEASON?!
You said it was summer!
EXCUSE ME...
...B-BUT I...
TRMBL
I WANT TO DO IT.
ME TOO!!
ME TOO AND ME AGAIN!!!
ORIGAMI!!
ORIGAMI!!
You're the man!
YAAY
YAAY
I WON'T DO IT!!
HA HA HA

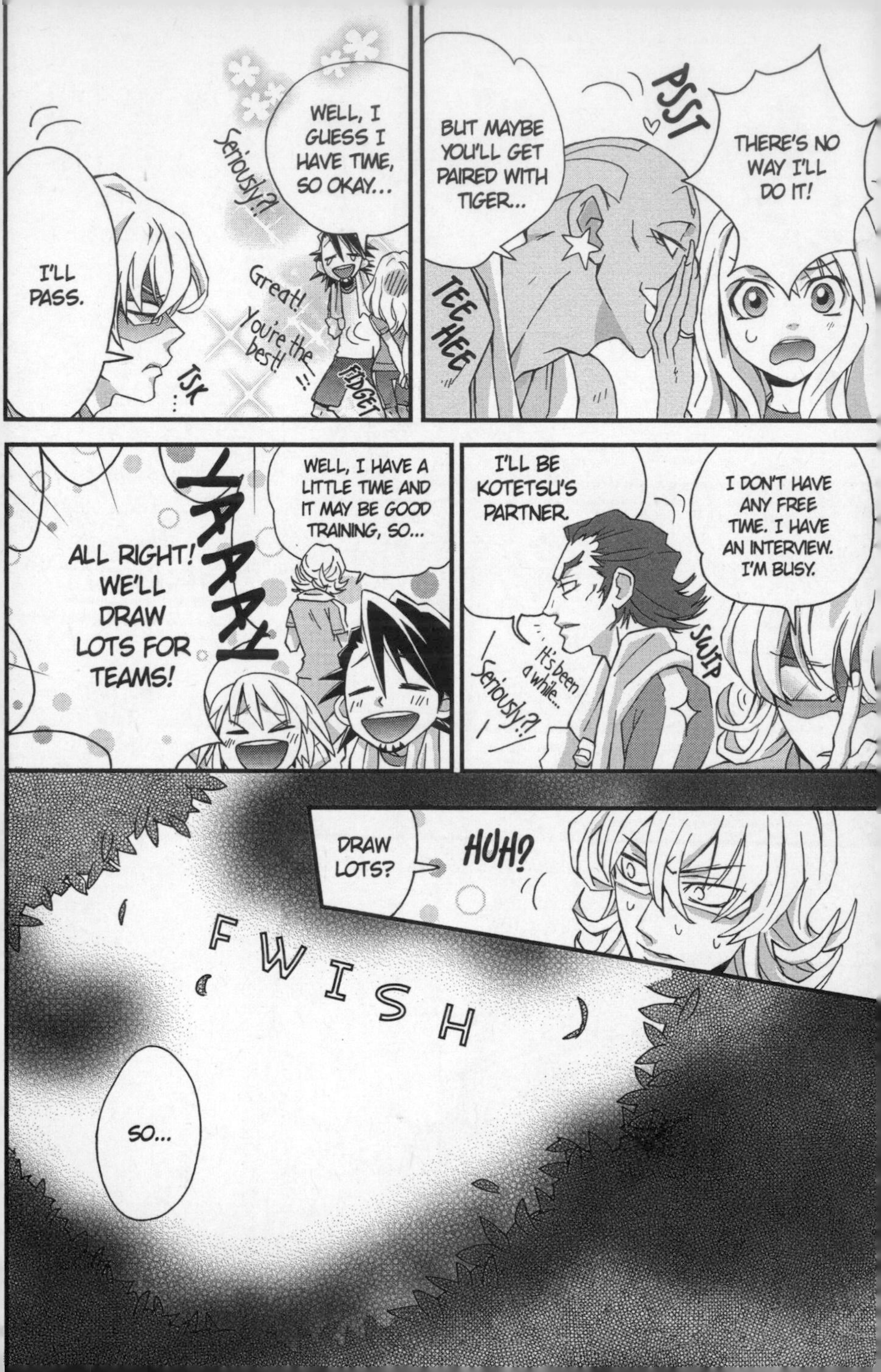
THERE'S NO WAY I'LL DO IT!
PSST
BUT MAYBE YOU'LL GET PAIRED WITH TIGER...
TEE HEE
WELL, I GUESS I HAVE TIME, SO OKAY...
Seriously?!
I'LL PASS.
Great! You're the best!!
FIDGET
TSK...
I DON'T HAVE ANY FREE TIME. I HAVE AN INTERVIEW. I'M BUSY.
I'LL BE KOTETSU'S PARTNER.
SWIP
It's been a while...
Seriously?!
WELL, I HAVE A LITTLE TIME AND IT MAY BE GOOD TRAINING, SO...
YAAAY
ALL RIGHT! WE'LL DRAW LOTS FOR TEAMS!
HUH?
DRAW LOTS?
FWISH
SO...

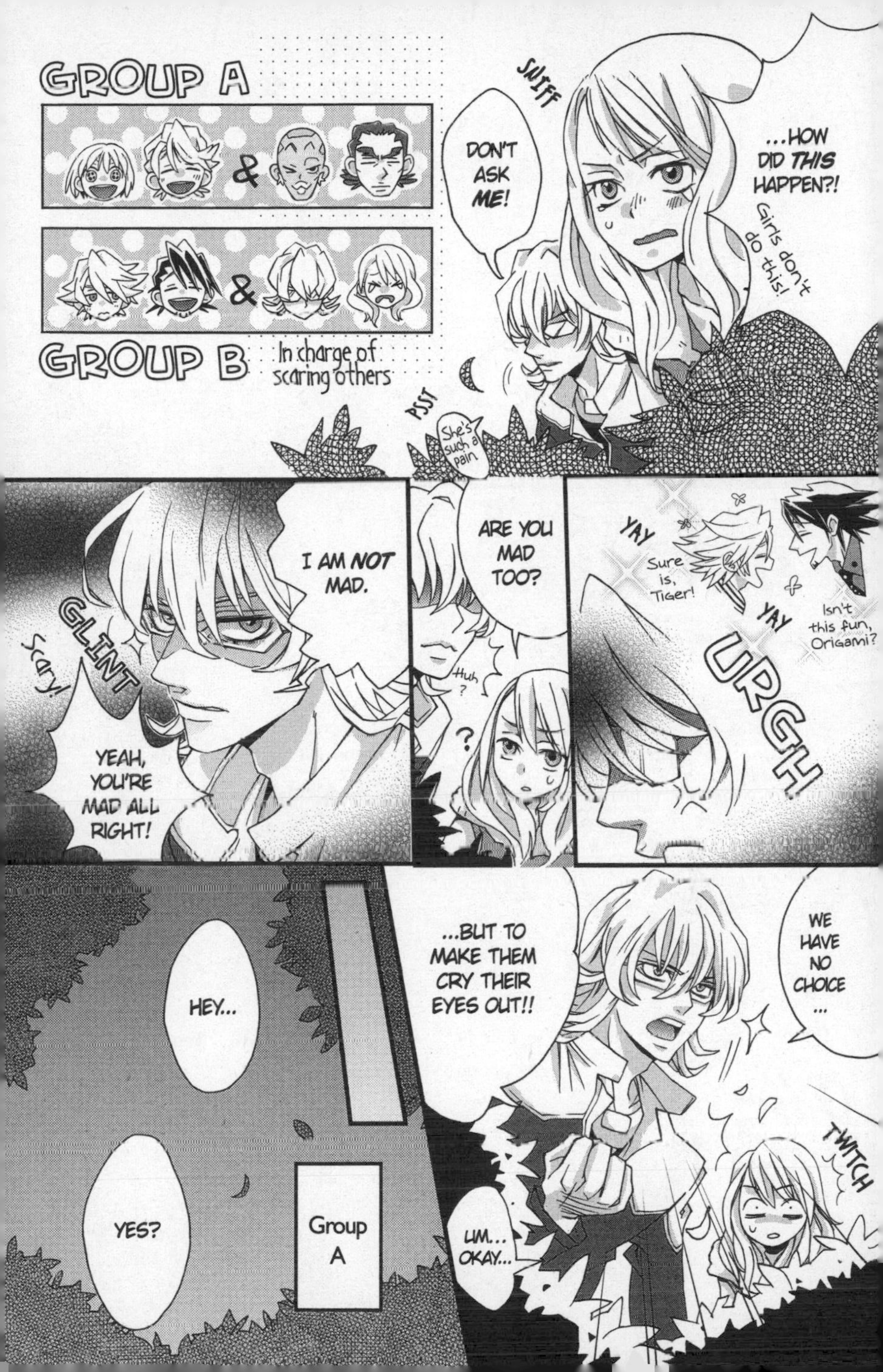
...HOW DID THIS HAPPEN?!
Girls don't do this!
SNIFF
DON'T ASK ME!
PSST
She's such a pain.
GROUP A
GROUP B
In charge of scaring others
Isn't this fun, Origami?
YAY
Sure is, Tiger!
YAY
URGH
ARE YOU MAD TOO?
Huh?
?
I AM NOT MAD.
GLINT
Scary!
YEAH, YOU'RE MAD ALL RIGHT!
WE HAVE NO CHOICE...
...BUT TO MAKE THEM CRY THEIR EYES OUT!!
TWITCH
UM... OKAY...
HEY...
YES?
Group A

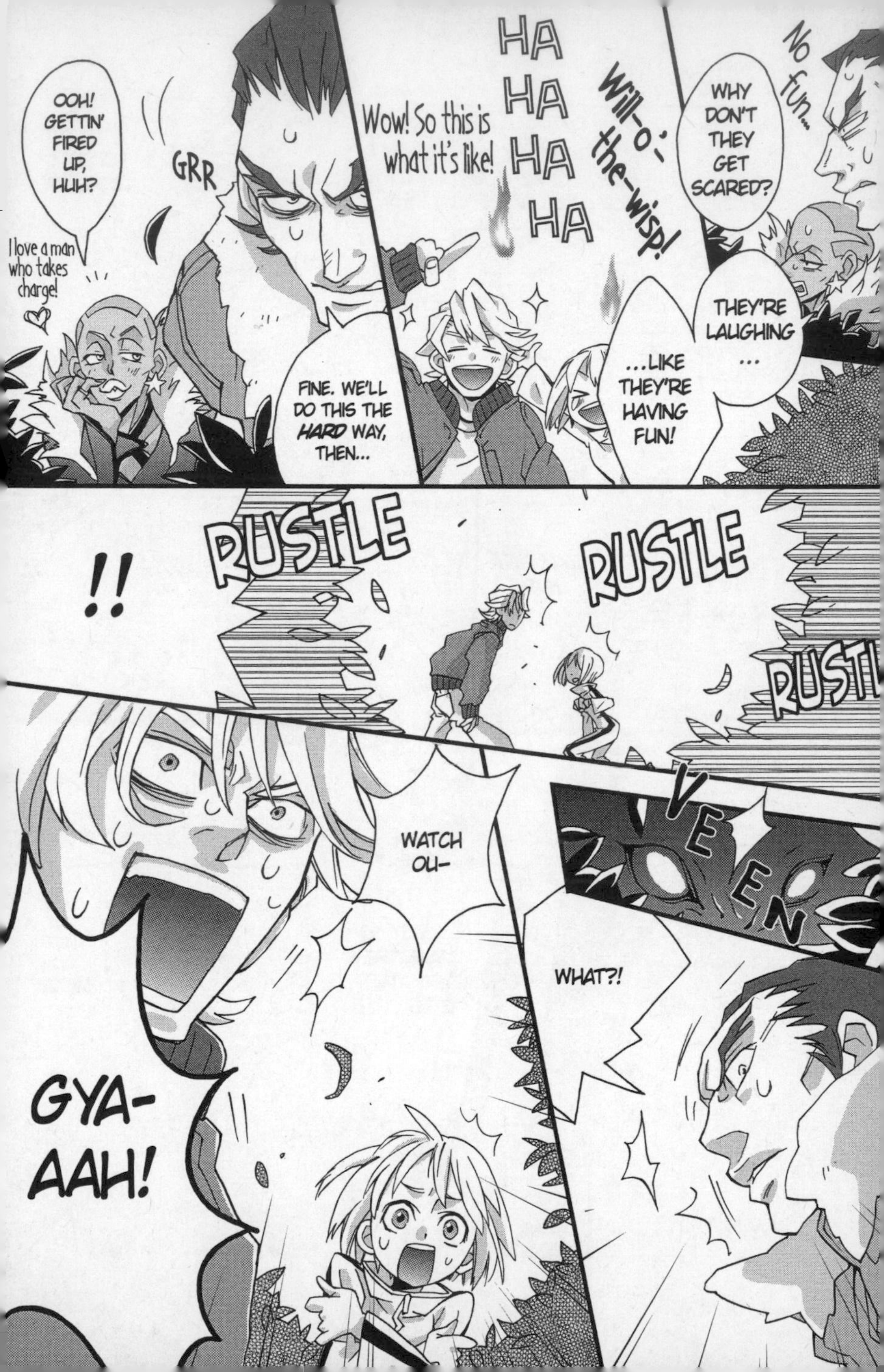
No fun...
WHY DON'T THEY GET SCARED?
THEY'RE LAUGHING ...
...LIKE THEY'RE HAVING FUN!
Will-o'-the-wisp!
HA HA HA HA
Wow! So this is what it's like!
GRR
OOH! GETTIN' FIRED UP, HUH?
I love a man who takes charge!
FINE. WE'LL DO THIS THE *HARD* WAY, THEN...
RUSTI
RUSTLE
RUSTLE
!!
VEEEN
WHAT?!
WATCH OU-
GYA-AAH!

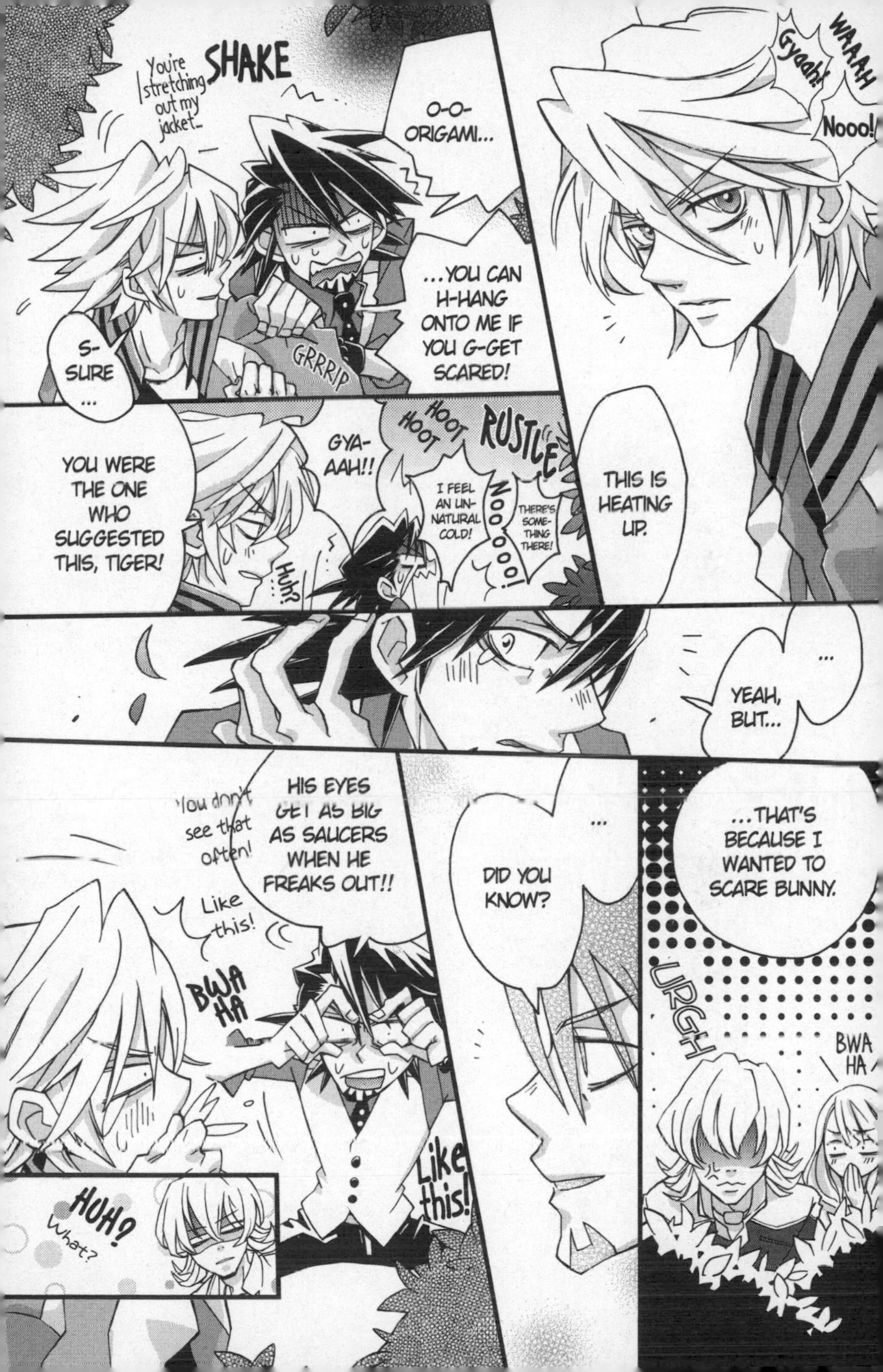
WAAAH
Gyaah!
Nooo!
THIS IS HEATING UP.
O-O-ORIGAMI...
SHAKE
You're stretching out my jacket...
...YOU CAN H-HANG ONTO ME IF YOU G-GET SCARED!
GRRRIP
S-SURE...
HOOT HOOT
RUSTLE
GYA-AAH!!
NOOOOOO!
THERE'S SOME-THING THERE!
I FEEL AN UN-NATURAL COLD!
YOU WERE THE ONE WHO SUGGESTED THIS, TIGER!
Huh?
...
YEAH, BUT...
...THAT'S BECAUSE I WANTED TO SCARE BUNNY.
URGH
BWA HA
...
DID YOU KNOW?
HIS EYES GET AS BIG AS SAUCERS WHEN HE FREAKS OUT!!
You don't see that often!
Like this!
BWA HA
Like this!
HUH?
What?

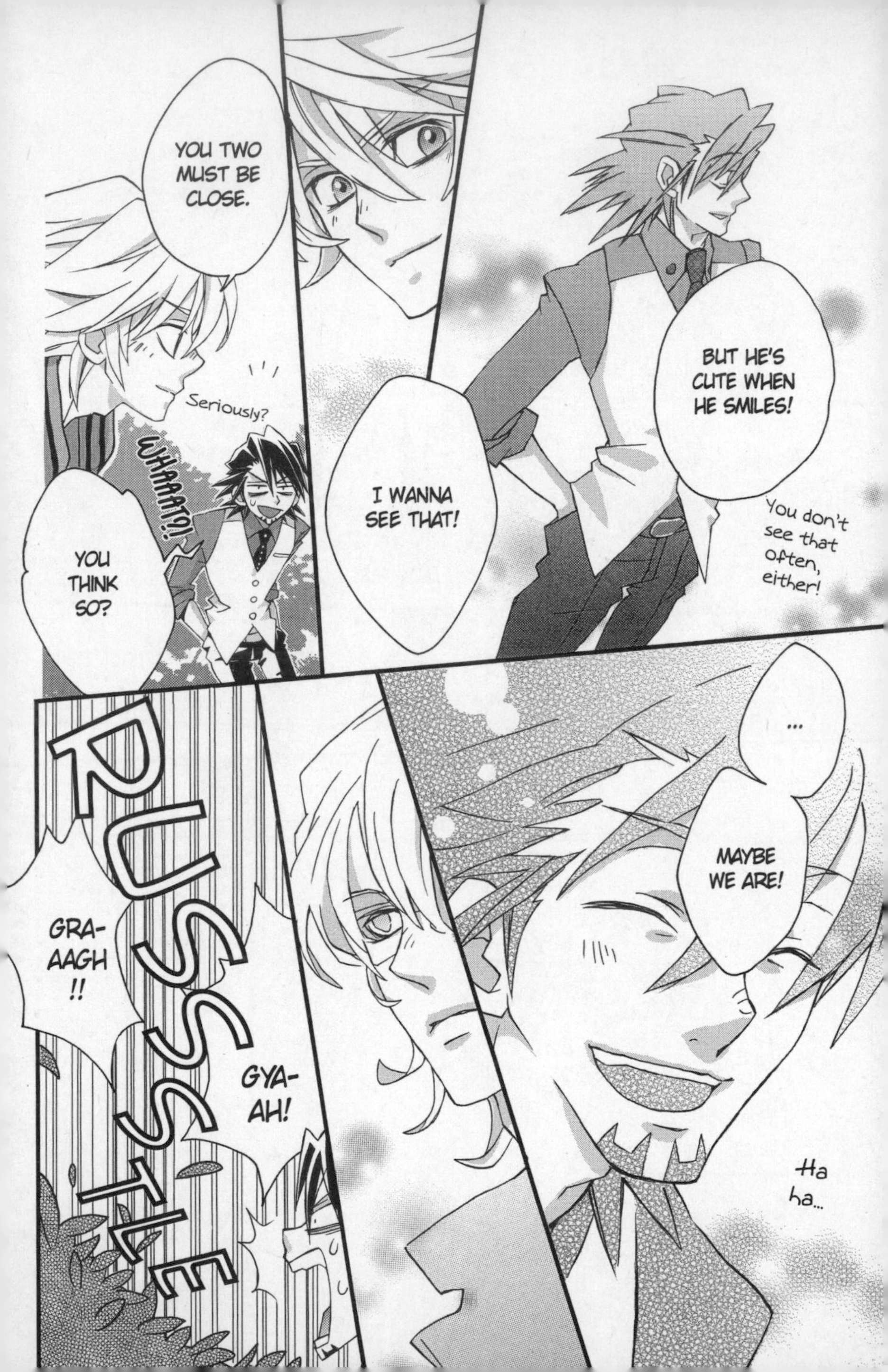
BUT HE'S CUTE WHEN HE SMILES!
You don't see that often, either!
I WANNA SEE THAT!
YOU TWO MUST BE CLOSE.
Seriously?
WHAAAT?!
YOU THINK SO?
...
MAYBE WE ARE!
Ha ha...
RUSSSTLE
GRA-AAGH!!
GYA-AH!

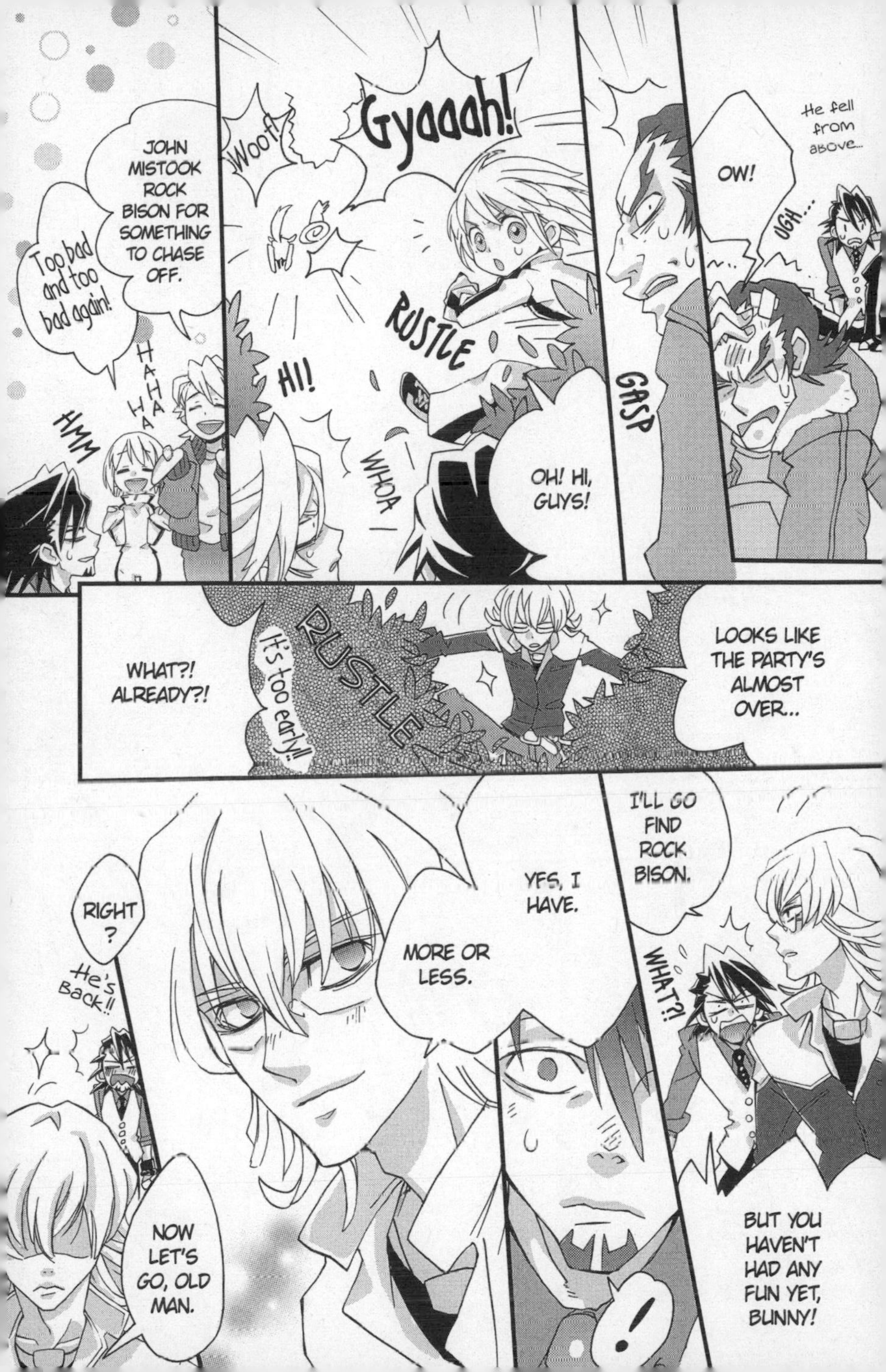
He fell from above...
OW!
UGH...
GASP
Gyaaah!
Woof!
RUSTLE
HI!
WHOA
OH! HI, GUYS!
JOHN MISTOOK ROCK BISON FOR SOMETHING TO CHASE OFF.
Too bad and too bad again!
HAHAHA
HMM
LOOKS LIKE THE PARTY'S ALMOST OVER...
RUSTLE
It's too early!!
WHAT?! ALREADY?!
I'LL GO FIND ROCK BISON.
WHAT?!
BUT YOU HAVEN'T HAD ANY FUN YET, BUNNY!
YES, I HAVE.
MORE OR LESS.
!
RIGHT?
He's Back!!
NOW LET'S GO, OLD MAN.

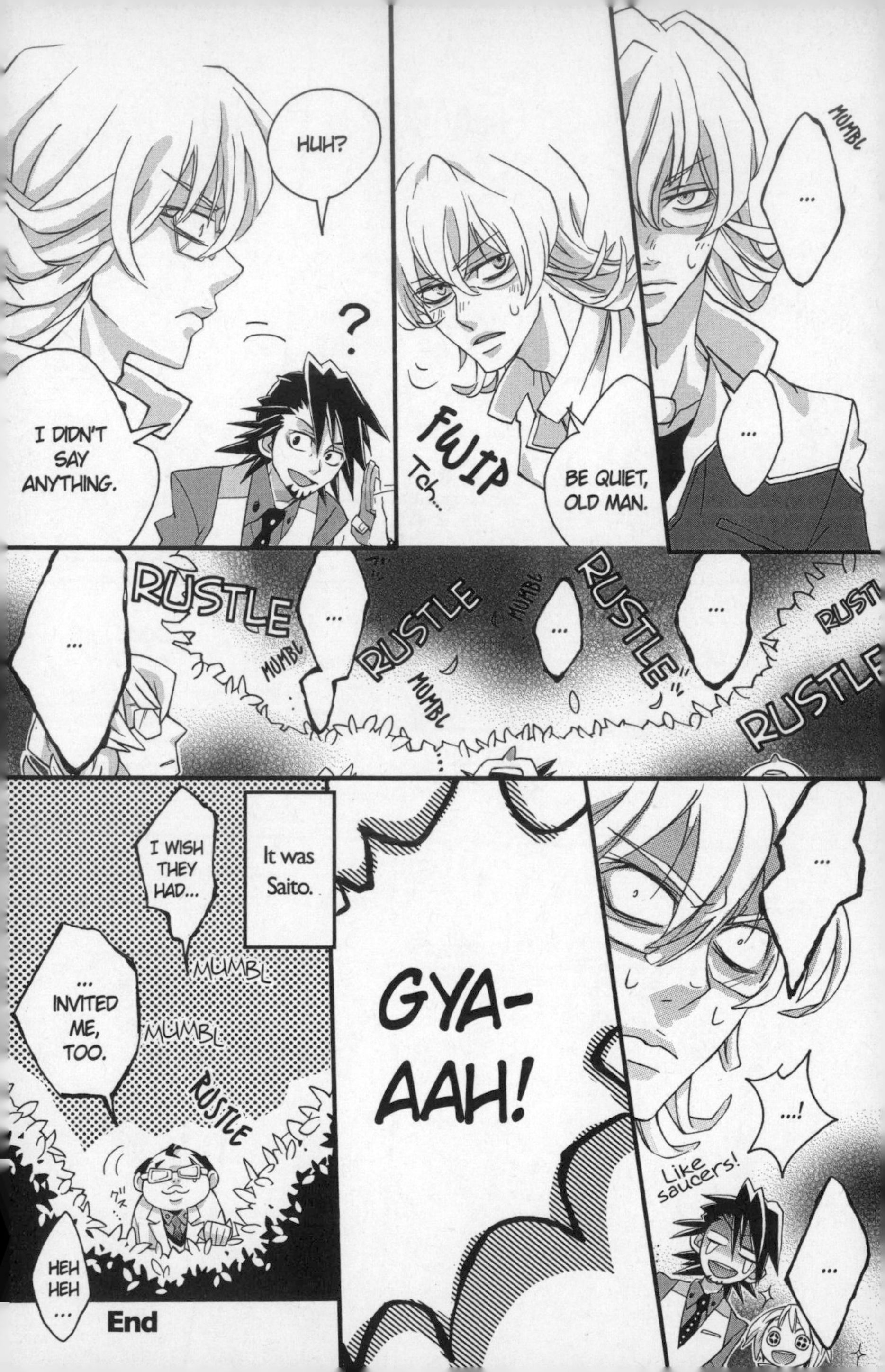
MUMBL
...
...
BE QUIET, OLD MAN.
FWIP
Tch...
HUH?
?
I DIDN'T SAY ANYTHING.
RUSTLE
RUSTLE
...
RUSTLE
MUMBL
...
MUMBL
RUSTLE
MUMBL
...
RUSTLE
...
...
...!
Like saucers!
...
GYA-AAH!
It was Saito.
I WISH THEY HAD...
MUMBL
... INVITED ME, TOO.
MUMBL
RUSTLE
HEH HEH ...
End

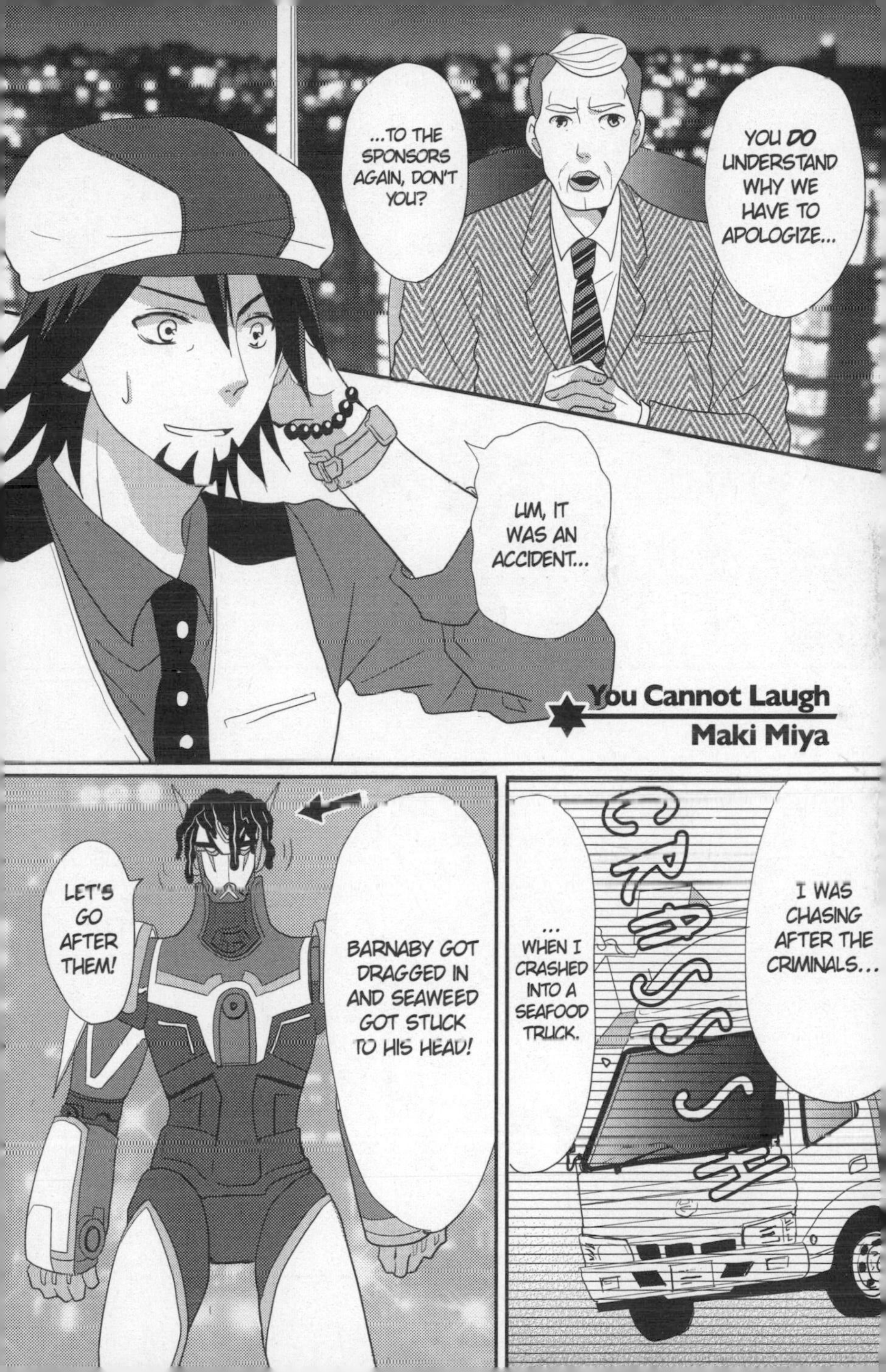
YOU *DO* UNDERSTAND WHY WE HAVE TO APOLOGIZE...
...TO THE SPONSORS AGAIN, DON'T YOU?
UM, IT WAS AN ACCIDENT...
You Cannot Laugh
Maki Miya
I WAS CHASING AFTER THE CRIMINALS...
...WHEN I CRASHED INTO A SEAFOOD TRUCK.
BARNABY GOT DRAGGED IN AND SEAWEED GOT STUCK TO HIS HEAD!
LET'S GO AFTER THEM!

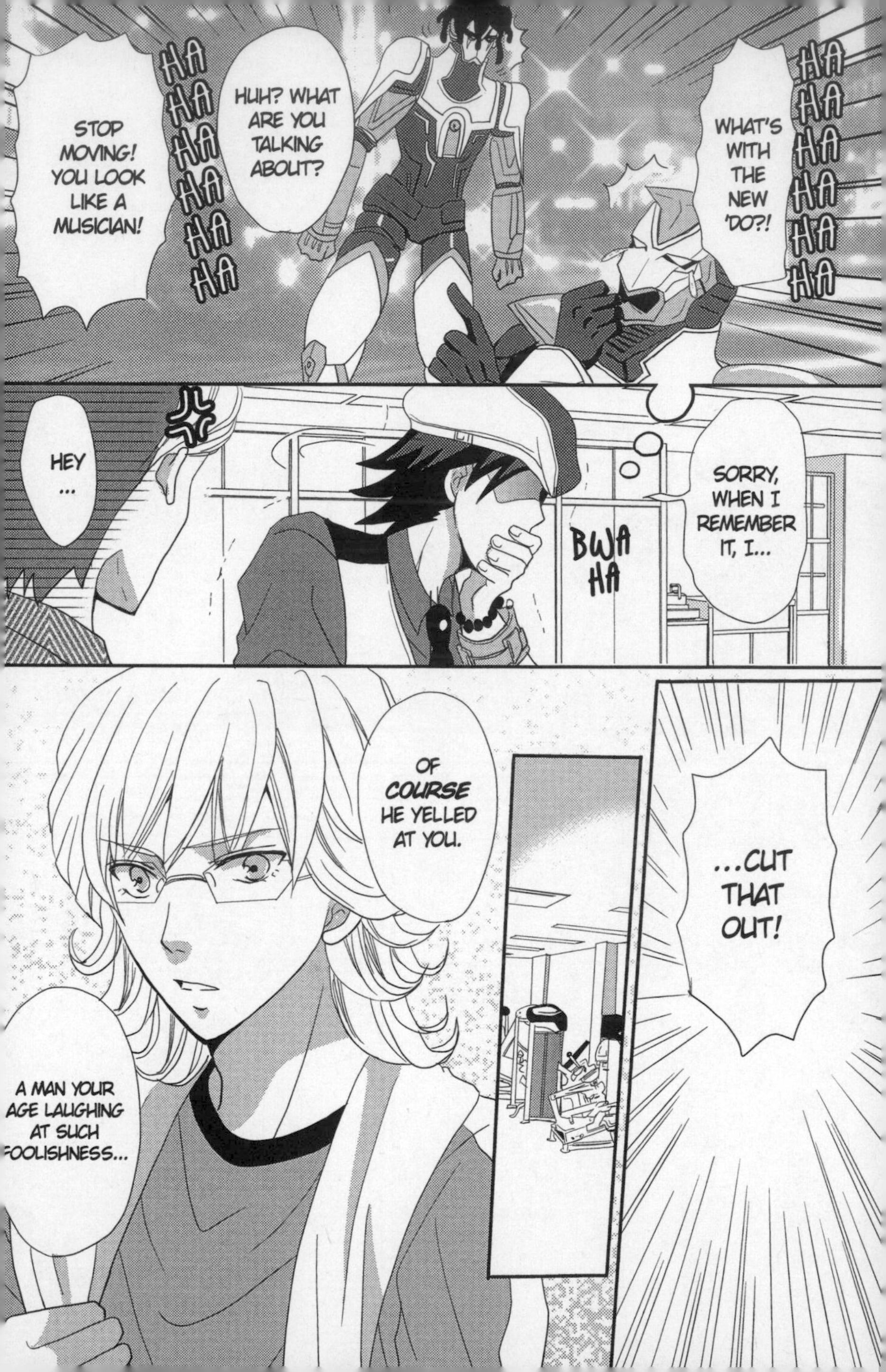
WHAT'S WITH THE NEW 'DO?!
HA HA HA HA HA HA HA
HUH? WHAT ARE YOU TALKING ABOUT?
HA HA HA HA HA HA HA
STOP MOVING! YOU LOOK LIKE A MUSICIAN!
SORRY, WHEN I REMEMBER IT, I...
BWA HA
HEY ...
...CUT THAT OUT!
OF COURSE HE YELLED AT YOU.
A MAN YOUR AGE LAUGHING AT SUCH FOOLISHNESS...

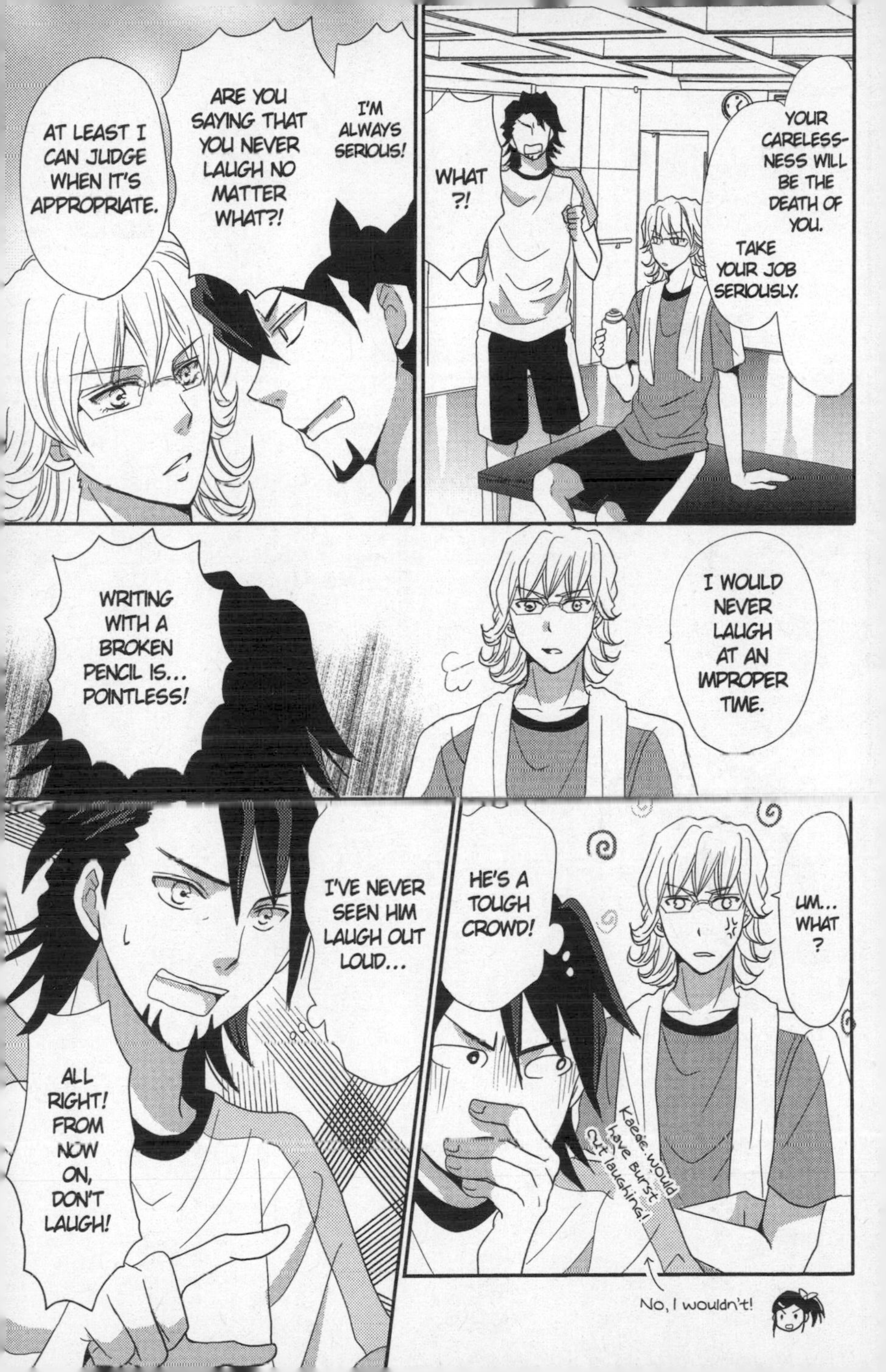
YOUR CARELESSNESS WILL BE THE DEATH OF YOU.
TAKE YOUR JOB SERIOUSLY.
WHAT?!
I'M ALWAYS SERIOUS!
ARE YOU SAYING THAT YOU NEVER LAUGH NO MATTER WHAT?!
AT LEAST I CAN JUDGE WHEN IT'S APPROPRIATE.
I WOULD NEVER LAUGH AT AN IMPROPER TIME.
WRITING WITH A BROKEN PENCIL IS... POINTLESS!
UM... WHAT?
HE'S A TOUGH CROWD!
Kaede would have burst out laughing!
I'VE NEVER SEEN HIM LAUGH OUT LOUD...
ALL RIGHT! FROM NOW ON, DON'T LAUGH!
No, I wouldn't!

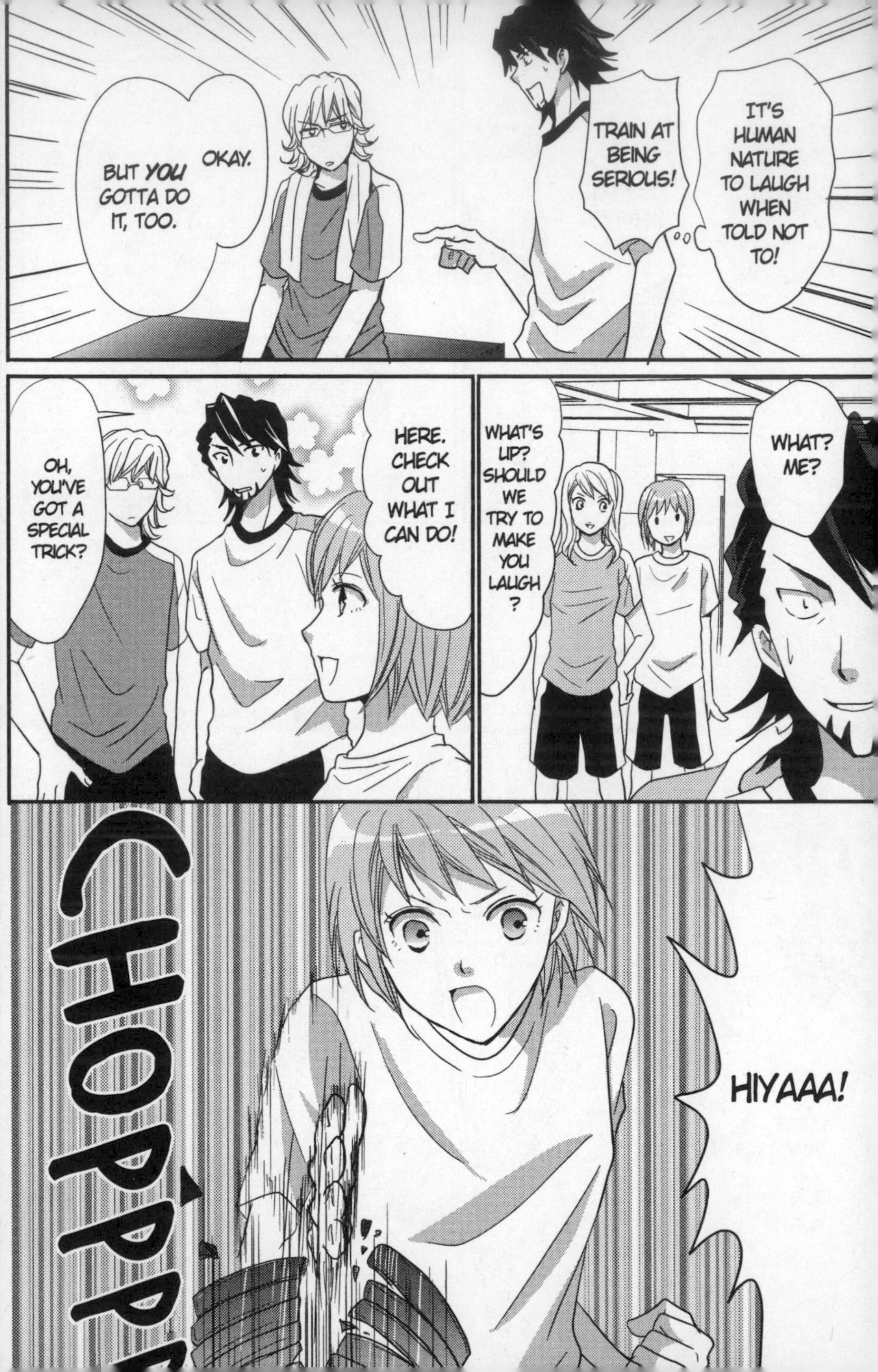
IT'S HUMAN NATURE TO LAUGH WHEN TOLD NOT TO!
TRAIN AT BEING SERIOUS!
OKAY.
BUT *YOU* GOTTA DO IT, TOO.
WHAT? ME?
WHAT'S UP? SHOULD WE TRY TO MAKE YOU LAUGH?
HERE. CHECK OUT WHAT I CAN DO!
OH, YOU'VE GOT A SPECIAL TRICK?
HIYAAA!
CHOPP

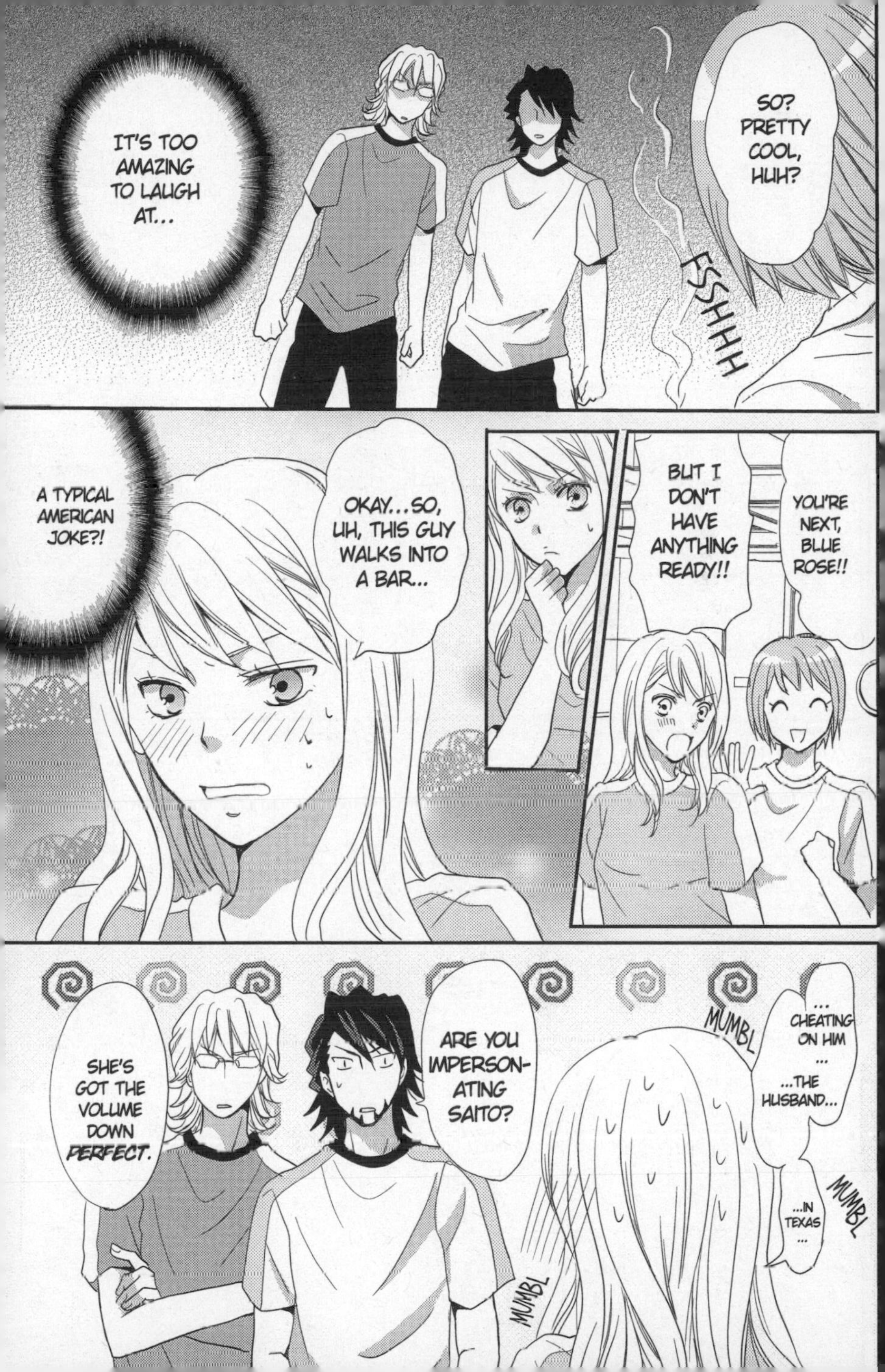
SO? PRETTY COOL, HUH?
FSSHHH
IT'S TOO AMAZING TO LAUGH AT...
YOU'RE NEXT, BLUE ROSE!!
BUT I DON'T HAVE ANYTHING READY!!
OKAY...SO, UH, THIS GUY WALKS INTO A BAR...
A TYPICAL AMERICAN JOKE?!
MUMBL
... CHEATING ON HIM ... ...THE HUSBAND...
MUMBL
...IN TEXAS ...
MUMBL
ARE YOU IMPERSON-ATING SAITO?
SHE'S GOT THE VOLUME DOWN ***PERFECT***.

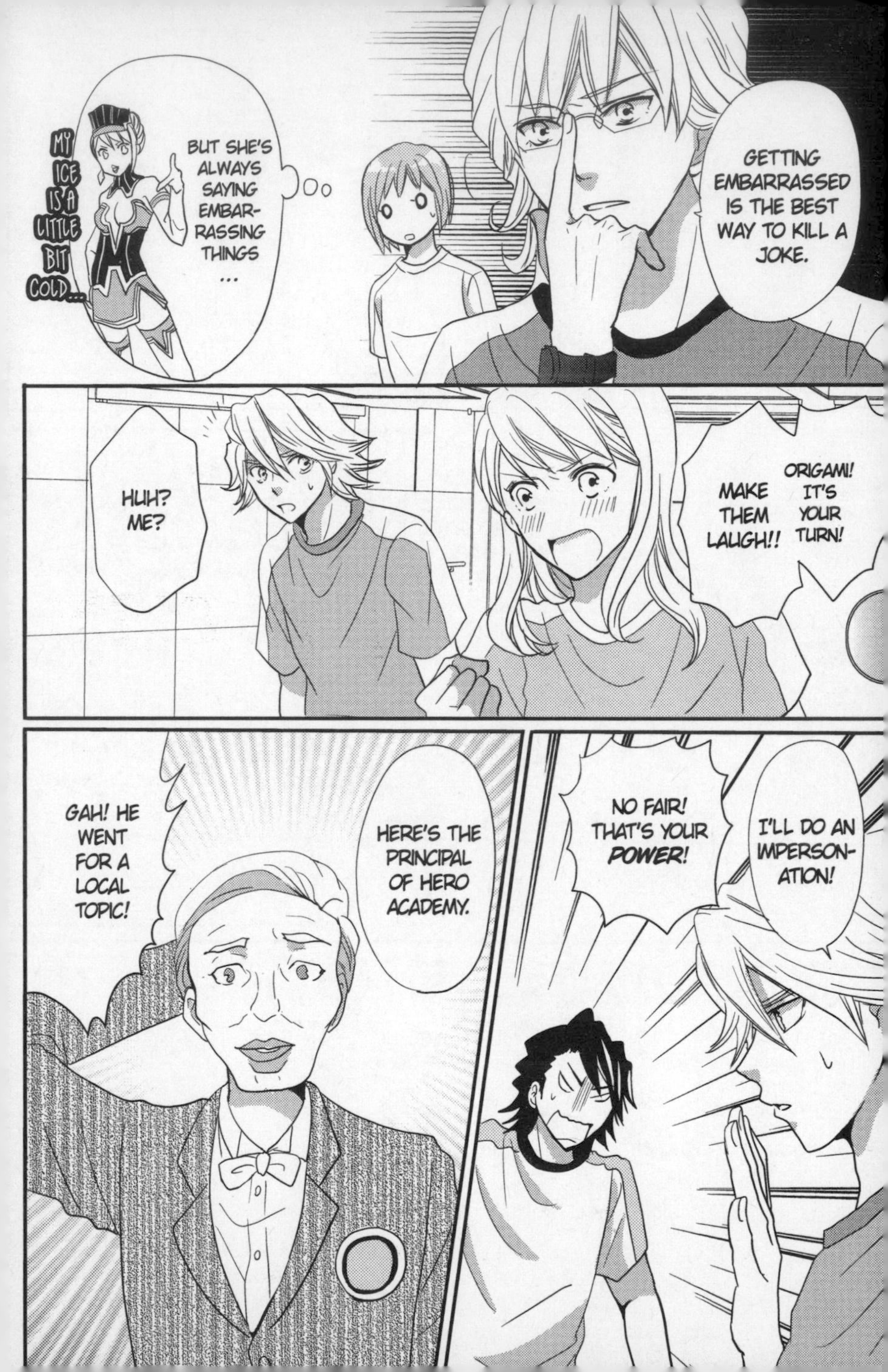
GETTING EMBARRASSED IS THE BEST WAY TO KILL A JOKE.
BUT SHE'S ALWAYS SAYING EMBAR-RASSING THINGS ...
MY ICE IS A LITTLE BIT COLD...
ORIGAMI! IT'S YOUR TURN!
MAKE THEM LAUGH!!
HUH? ME?
I'LL DO AN IMPERSON-ATION!
NO FAIR! THAT'S YOUR *POWER*!
HERE'S THE PRINCIPAL OF HERO ACADEMY.
GAH! HE WENT FOR A LOCAL TOPIC!

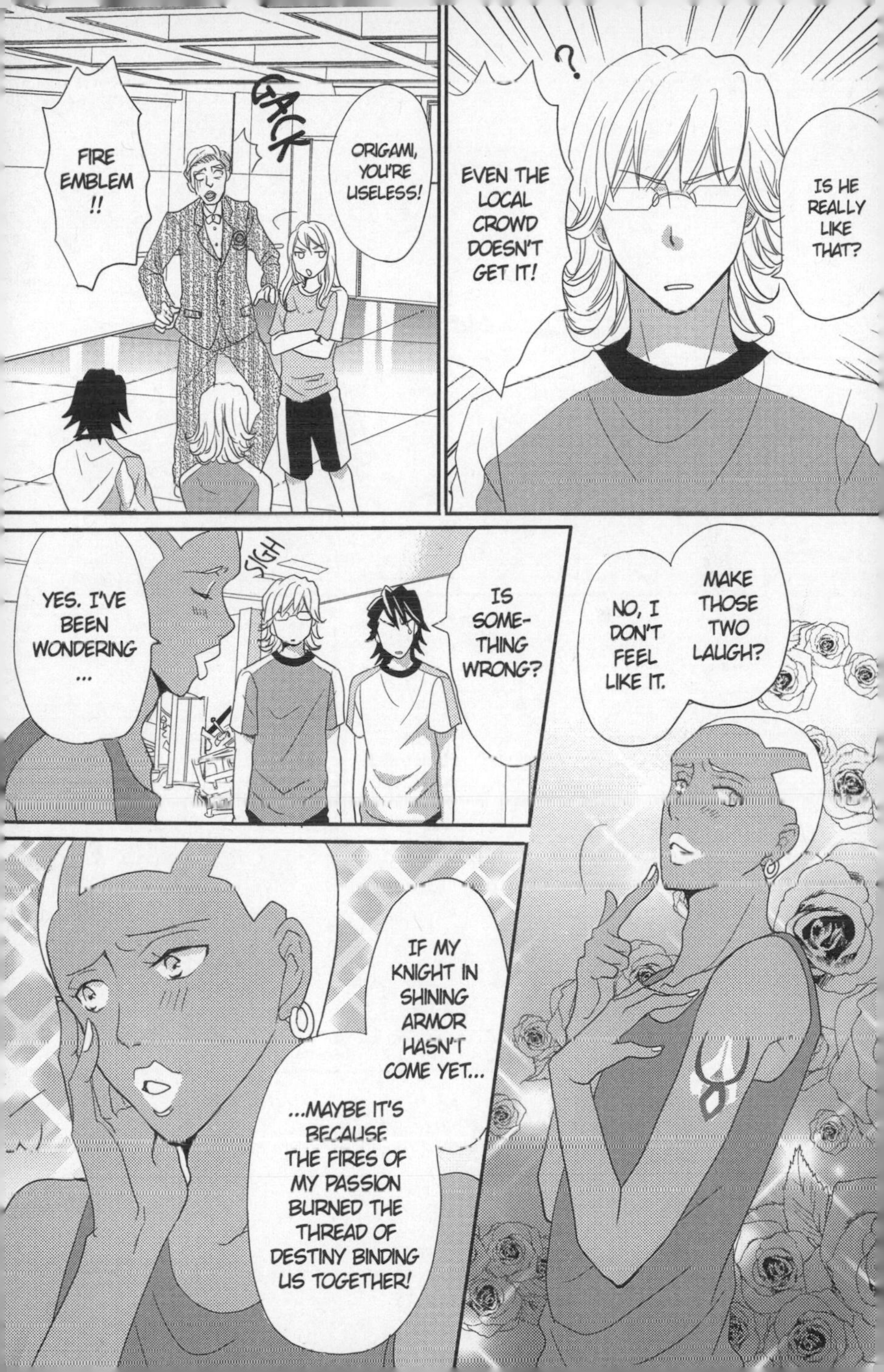
?
IS HE REALLY LIKE THAT?
EVEN THE LOCAL CROWD DOESN'T GET IT!
ORIGAMI, YOU'RE USELESS!
GACK
FIRE EMBLEM !!
MAKE THOSE TWO LAUGH?
NO, I DON'T FEEL LIKE IT.
IS SOME-THING WRONG?
SIGH
YES. I'VE BEEN WONDERING ...
IF MY KNIGHT IN SHINING ARMOR HASN'T COME YET...
...MAYBE IT'S BECAUSE THE FIRES OF MY PASSION BURNED THE THREAD OF DESTINY BINDING US TOGETHER!

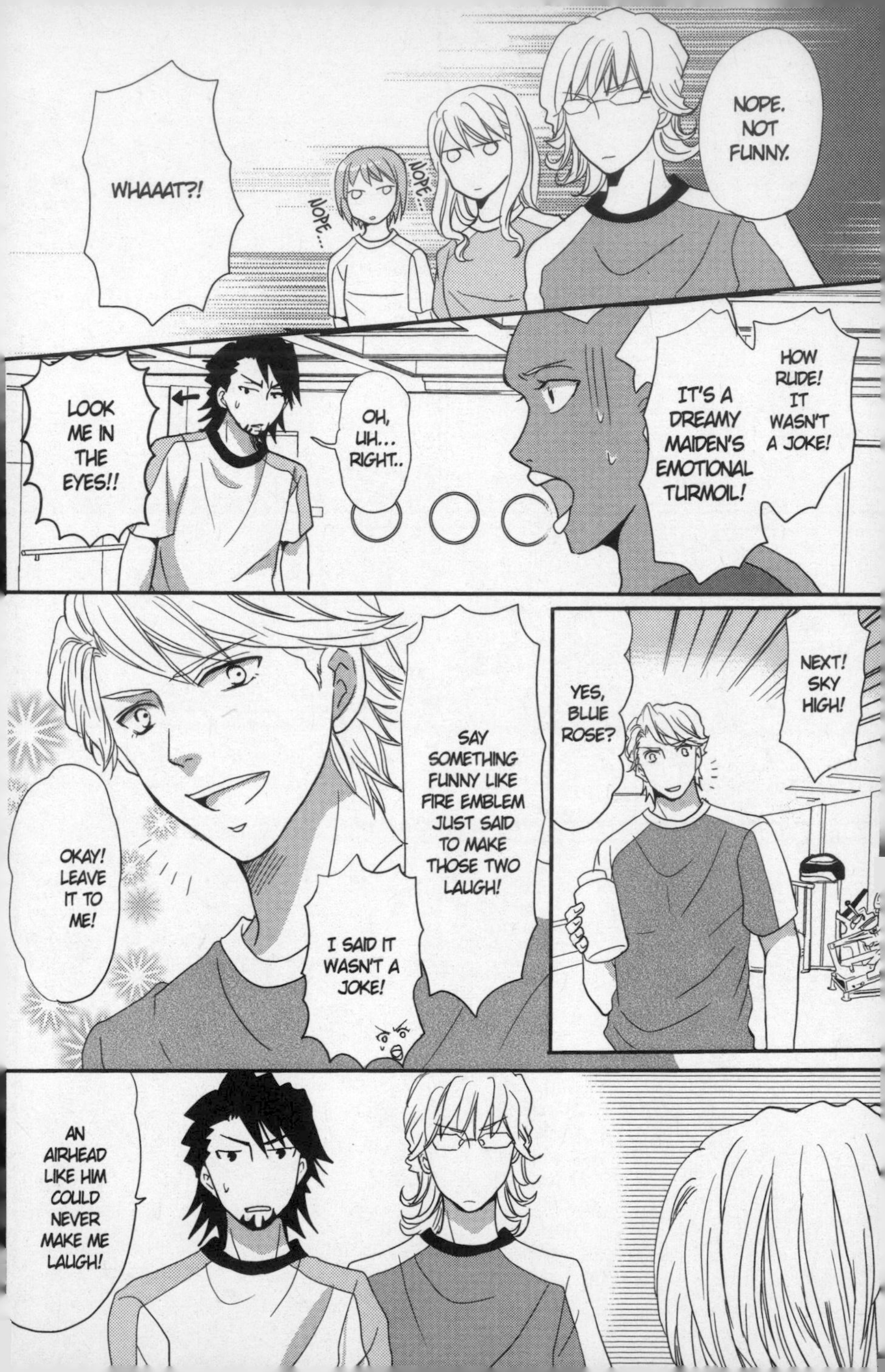
NOPE. NOT FUNNY.
NOPE...
NOPE...
WHAAAT?!
HOW RUDE! IT WASN'T A JOKE!
IT'S A DREAMY MAIDEN'S EMOTIONAL TURMOIL!
OH, UH... RIGHT..
LOOK ME IN THE EYES!!
NEXT! SKY HIGH!
YES, BLUE ROSE?
SAY SOMETHING FUNNY LIKE FIRE EMBLEM JUST SAID TO MAKE THOSE TWO LAUGH!
I SAID IT WASN'T A JOKE!
OKAY! LEAVE IT TO ME!
AN AIRHEAD LIKE HIM COULD NEVER MAKE ME LAUGH!

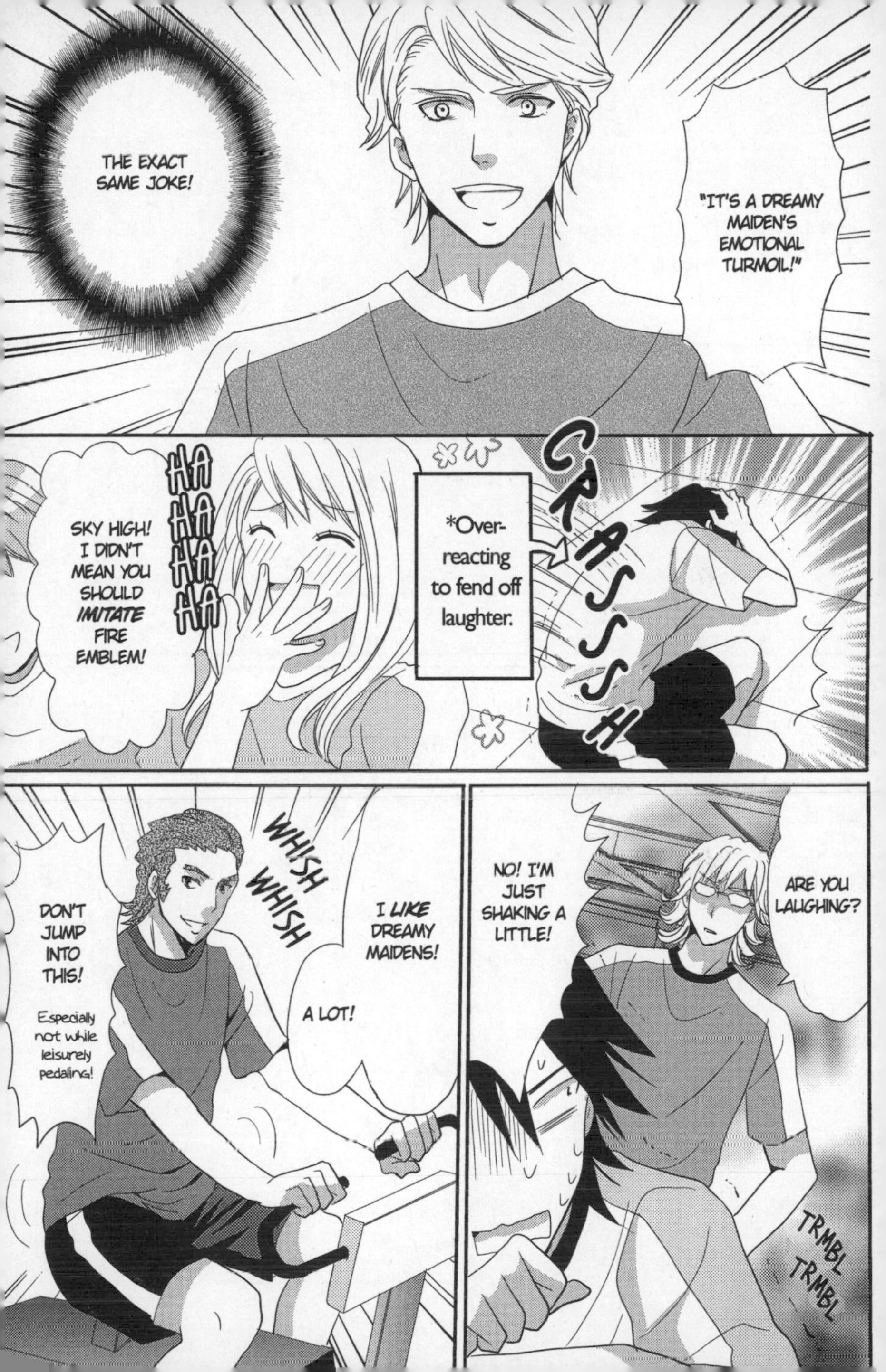
"IT'S A DREAMY MAIDEN'S EMOTIONAL TURMOIL!"
THE EXACT SAME JOKE!
CRASSSH
*Over-reacting to fend off laughter.
HA HA HA HA
SKY HIGH! I DIDN'T MEAN YOU SHOULD *IMITATE* FIRE EMBLEM!
ARE YOU LAUGHING?
NO! I'M JUST SHAKING A LITTLE!
TRMBL TRMBL
I *LIKE* DREAMY MAIDENS!
A LOT!
WHISH WHISH
DON'T JUMP INTO THIS!
Especially not while leisurely pedaling!

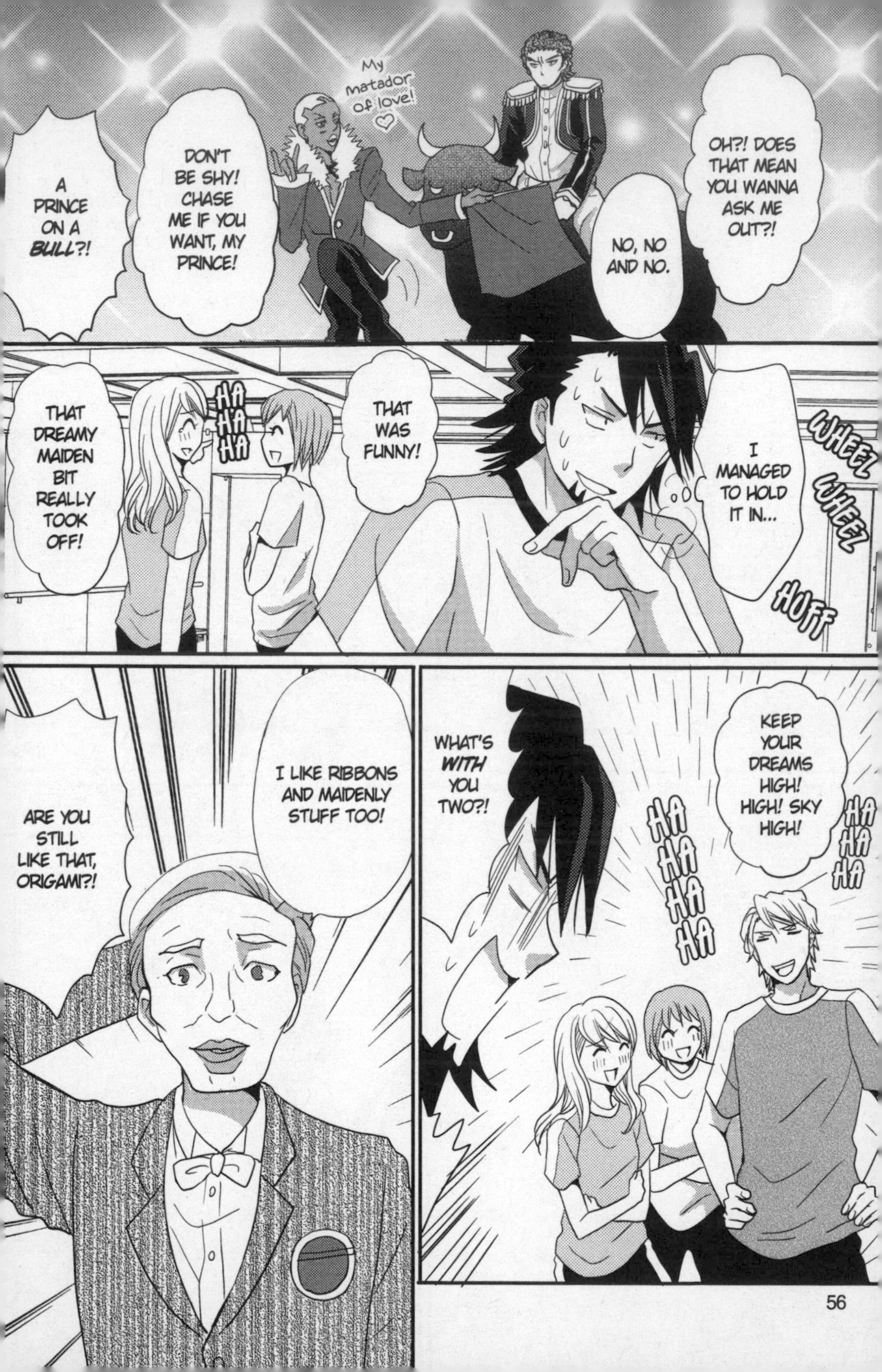
OH?! DOES THAT MEAN YOU WANNA ASK ME OUT?!
NO, NO AND NO.
My Matador of love! ♡
DON'T BE SHY! CHASE ME IF YOU WANT, MY PRINCE!
A PRINCE ON A *BULL*?!
WHEEL WHEEL
HUFF
I MANAGED TO HOLD IT IN...
THAT WAS FUNNY!
HA HA HA
THAT DREAMY MAIDEN BIT REALLY TOOK OFF!
KEEP YOUR DREAMS HIGH! HIGH! SKY HIGH!
HA HA HA
HA HA HA HA HA
WHAT'S *WITH* YOU TWO?!
I LIKE RIBBONS AND MAIDENLY STUFF TOO!
ARE YOU STILL LIKE THAT, ORIGAMI?!

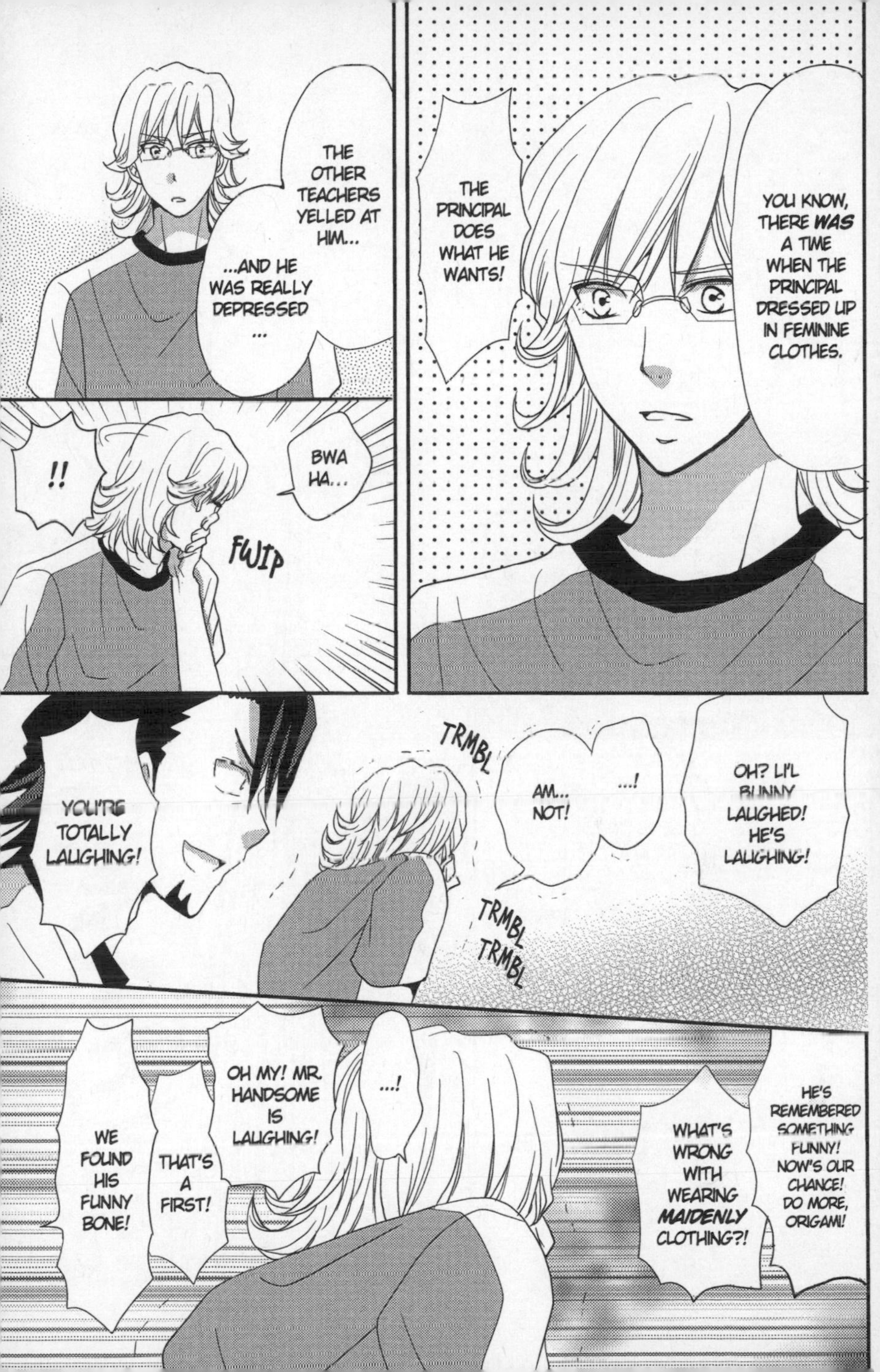
YOU KNOW, THERE WAS A TIME WHEN THE PRINCIPAL DRESSED UP IN FEMININE CLOTHES.
THE PRINCIPAL DOES WHAT HE WANTS!
THE OTHER TEACHERS YELLED AT HIM...
...AND HE WAS REALLY DEPRESSED ...
BWA HA...
!!
FWIP
OH? LI'L BUNNY LAUGHED! HE'S LAUGHING!
...!
AM... NOT!
TRMBL
TRMBL TRMBL
YOU'RE TOTALLY LAUGHING!
HE'S REMEMBERED SOMETHING FUNNY! NOW'S OUR CHANCE! DO MORE, ORIGAMI!
WHAT'S WRONG WITH WEARING MAIDENLY CLOTHING?!
...!
OH MY! MR. HANDSOME IS LAUGHING!
THAT'S A FIRST!
WE FOUND HIS FUNNY BONE!

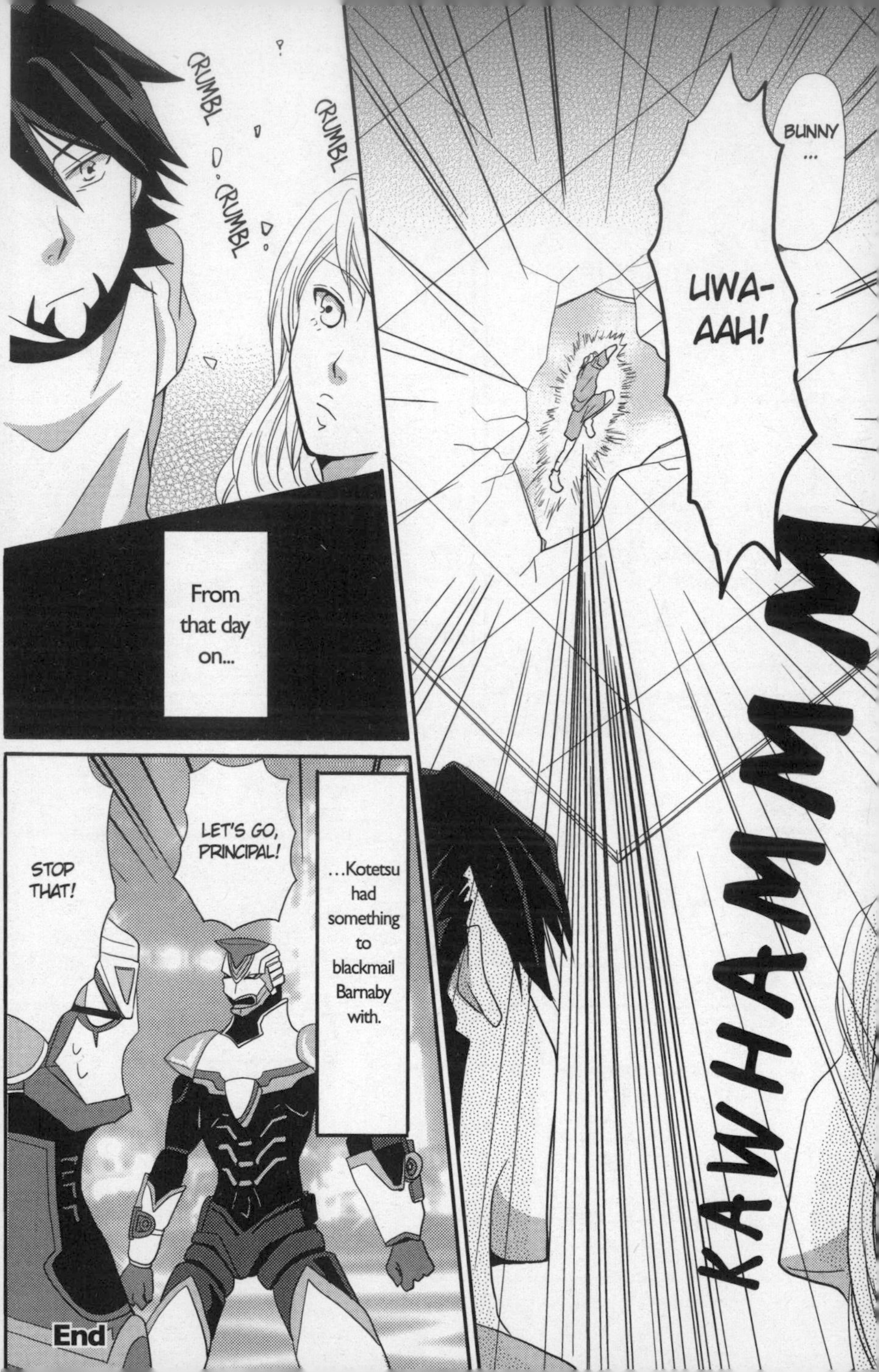
BUNNY ...
UWA-AAH!
KAWHAMMMM
CRUMBL
CRUMBL
CRUMBL
CRUMBL
From that day on...
...Kotetsu had something to blackmail Barnaby with.
LET'S GO, PRINCIPAL!
STOP THAT!
End

Barnaby in Season 1

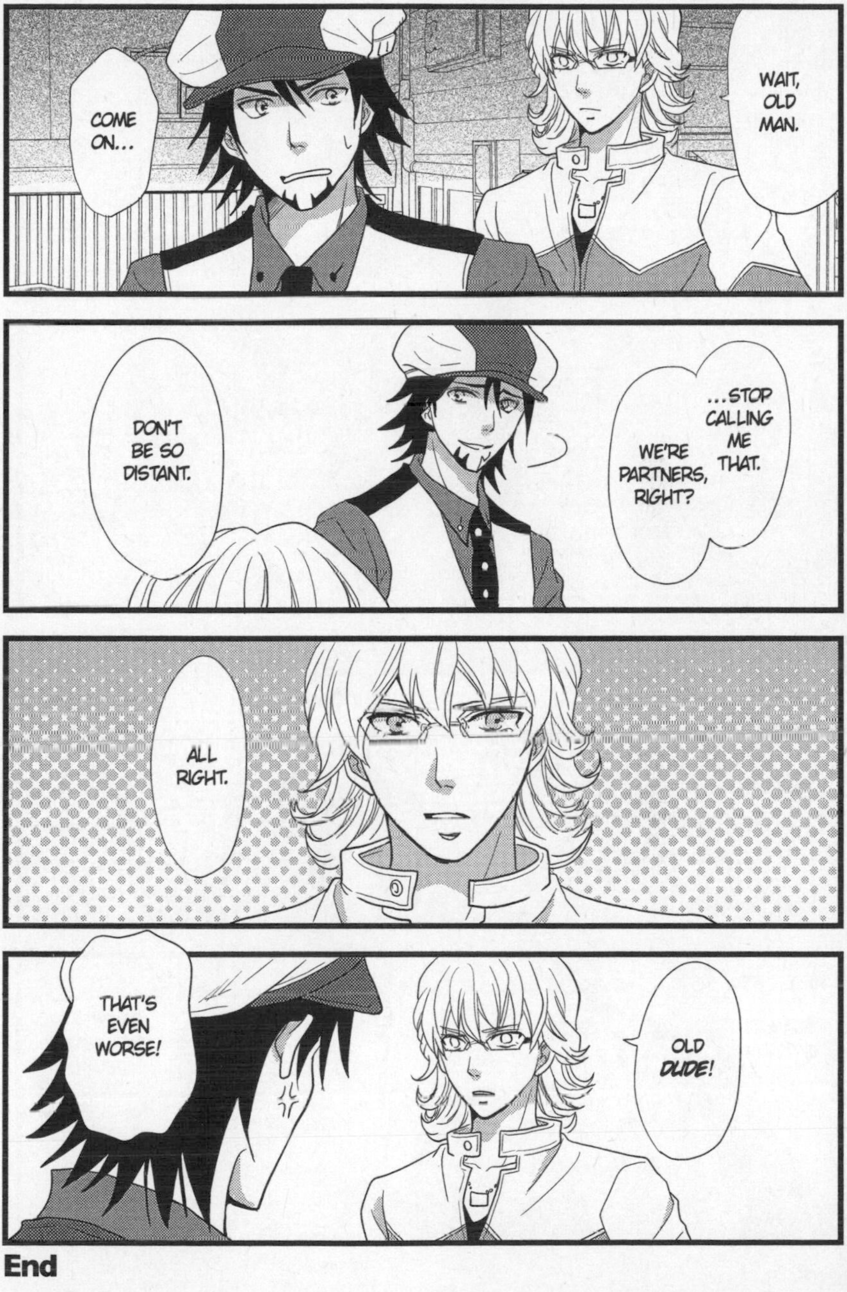
WAIT, OLD MAN.
COME ON...
...STOP CALLING ME THAT.
WE'RE PARTNERS, RIGHT?
DON'T BE SO DISTANT.
ALL RIGHT.
OLD DUDE!
THAT'S EVEN WORSE!

End

Can't Read

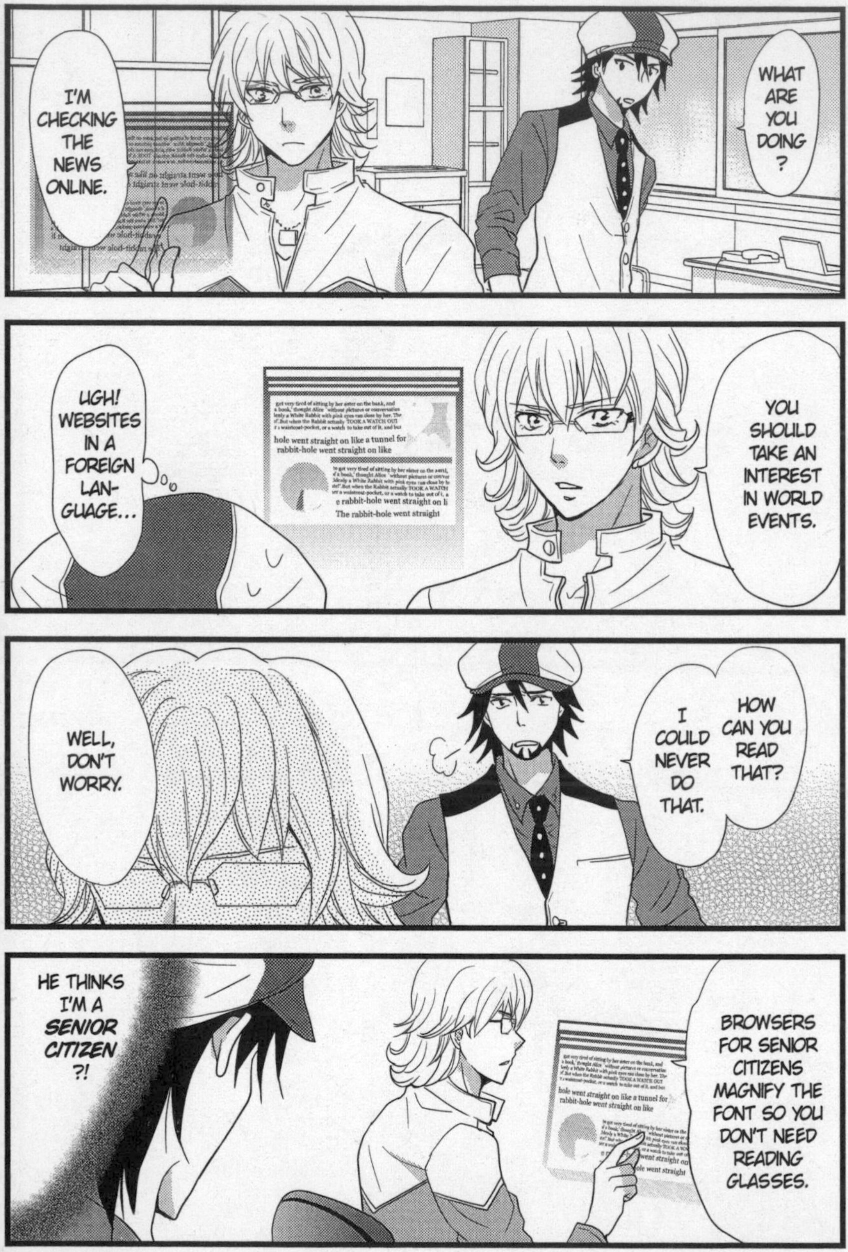
WHAT ARE YOU DOING?
I'M CHECKING THE NEWS ONLINE.
YOU SHOULD TAKE AN INTEREST IN WORLD EVENTS.
UGH! WEBSITES IN A FOREIGN LAN-GUAGE...
HOW CAN YOU READ THAT?
I COULD NEVER DO THAT.
WELL, DON'T WORRY.
BROWSERS FOR SENIOR CITIZENS MAGNIFY THE FONT SO YOU DON'T NEED READING GLASSES.
HE THINKS I'M A *SENIOR CITIZEN*?!

End

Business Smile

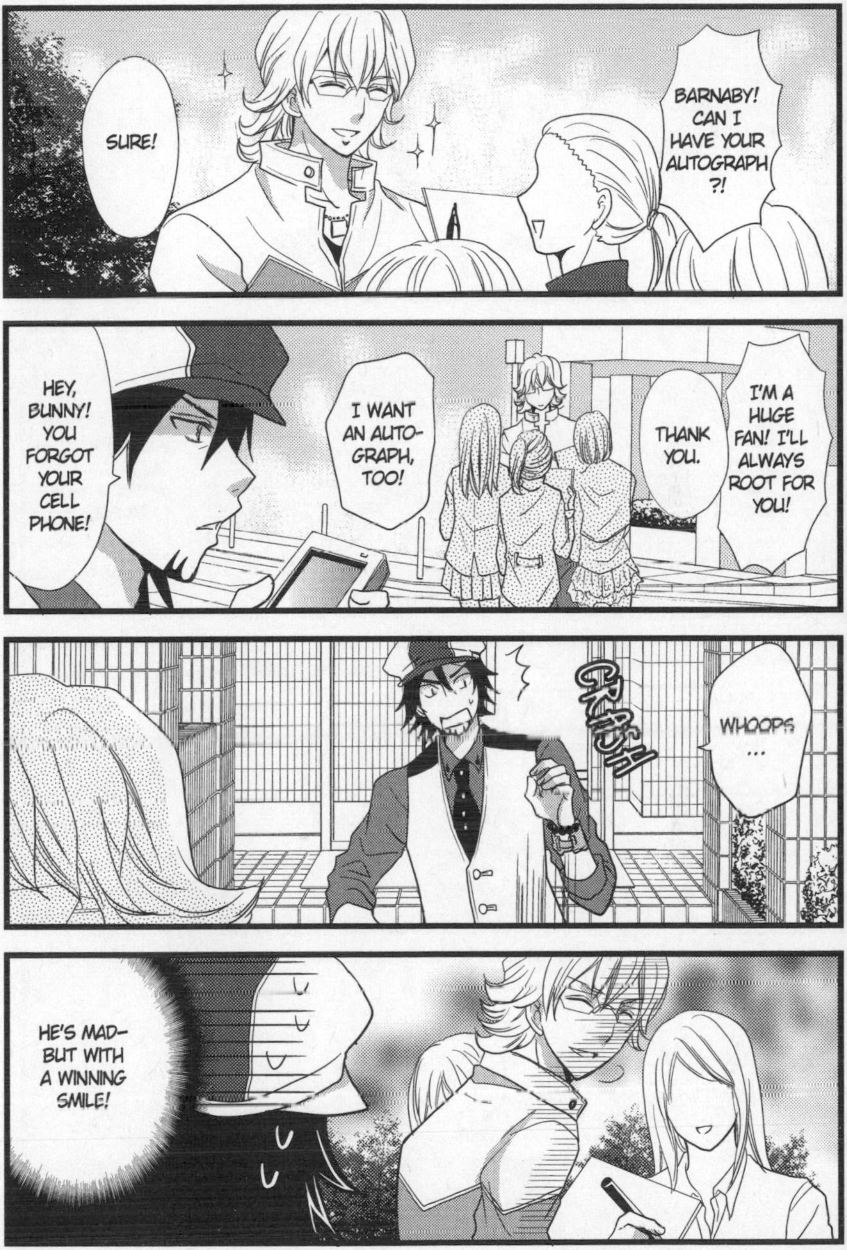
BARNABY! CAN I HAVE YOUR AUTOGRAPH?!
SURE!
I'M A HUGE FAN! I'LL ALWAYS ROOT FOR YOU!
THANK YOU.
I WANT AN AUTO-GRAPH, TOO!
HEY, BUNNY! YOU FORGOT YOUR CELL PHONE!
WHOOPS...
CRASH
HE'S MAD-BUT WITH A WINNING SMILE!

End

Maiden's Heart

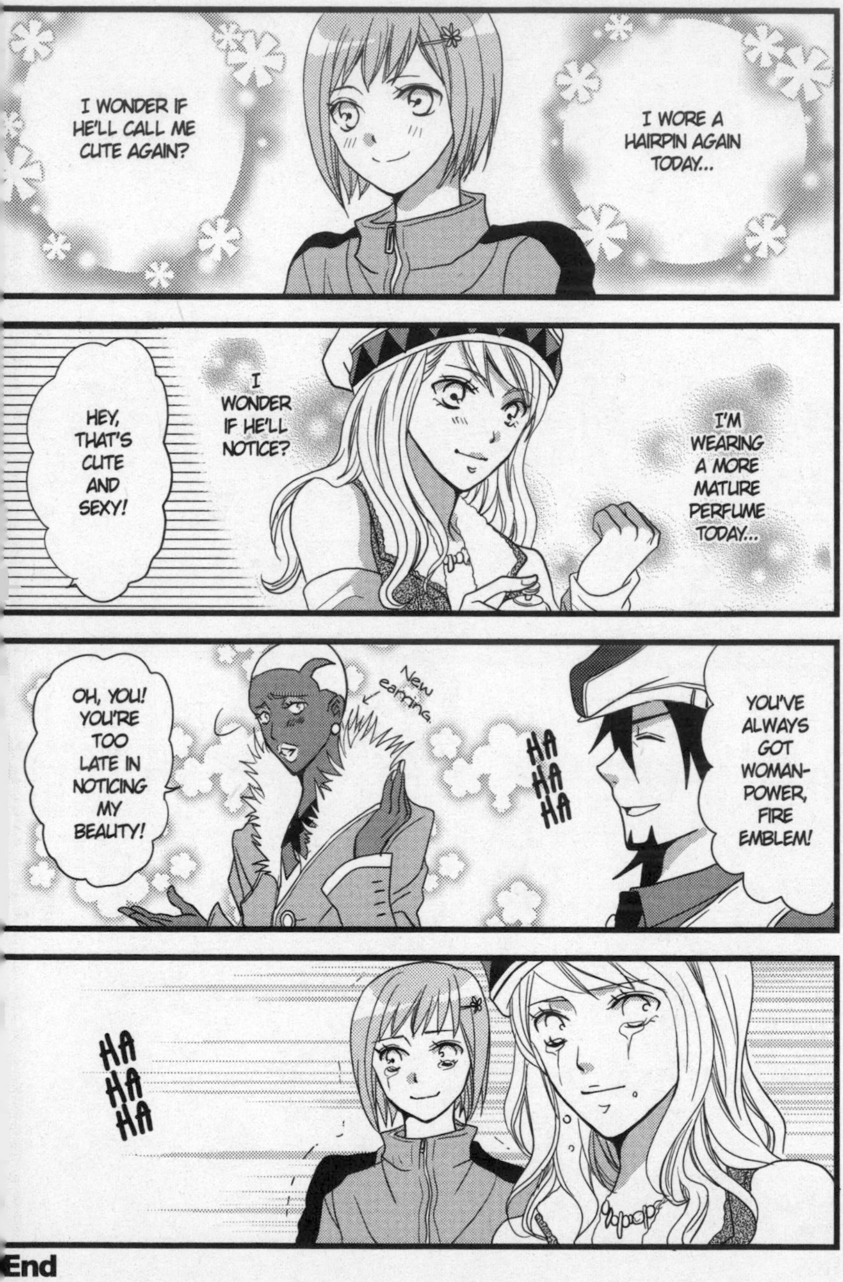
I WORE A HAIRPIN AGAIN TODAY...
I WONDER IF HE'LL CALL ME CUTE AGAIN?
I'M WEARING A MORE MATURE PERFUME TODAY...
I WONDER IF HE'LL NOTICE?
HEY, THAT'S CUTE AND SEXY!
YOU'VE ALWAYS GOT WOMAN-POWER, FIRE EMBLEM!
HA HA HA
New earring.
OH, YOU! YOU'RE TOO LATE IN NOTICING MY BEAUTY!
HA HA HA

End

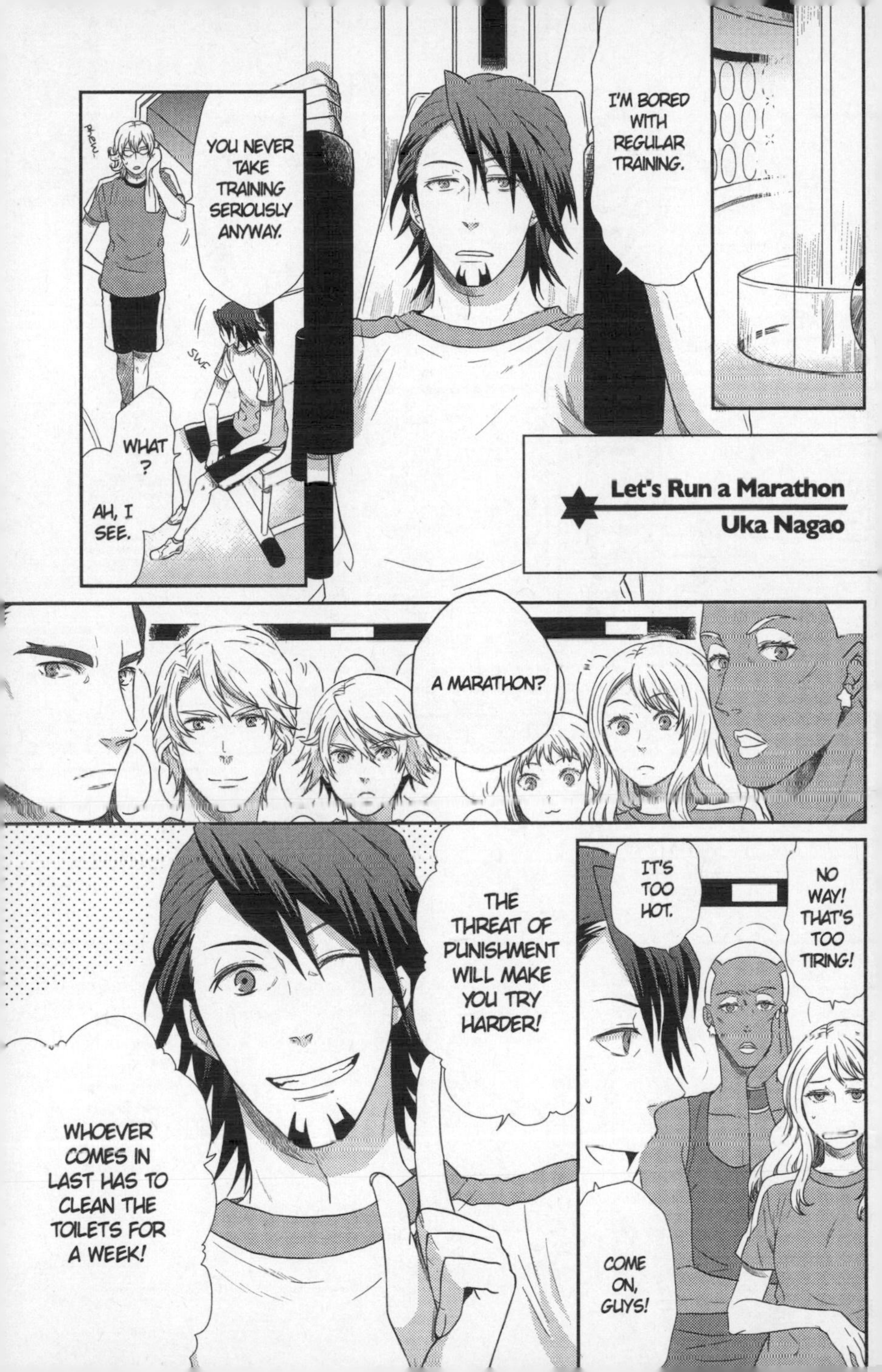
I'M BORED WITH REGULAR TRAINING.
Let's Run a Marathon
Uka Nagao
phew
YOU NEVER TAKE TRAINING SERIOUSLY ANYWAY.
SWF
WHAT?
AH, I SEE.
A MARATHON?
NO WAY! THAT'S TOO TIRING!
IT'S TOO HOT.
COME ON, GUYS!
THE THREAT OF PUNISHMENT WILL MAKE YOU TRY HARDER!
WHOEVER COMES IN LAST HAS TO CLEAN THE TOILETS FOR A WEEK!

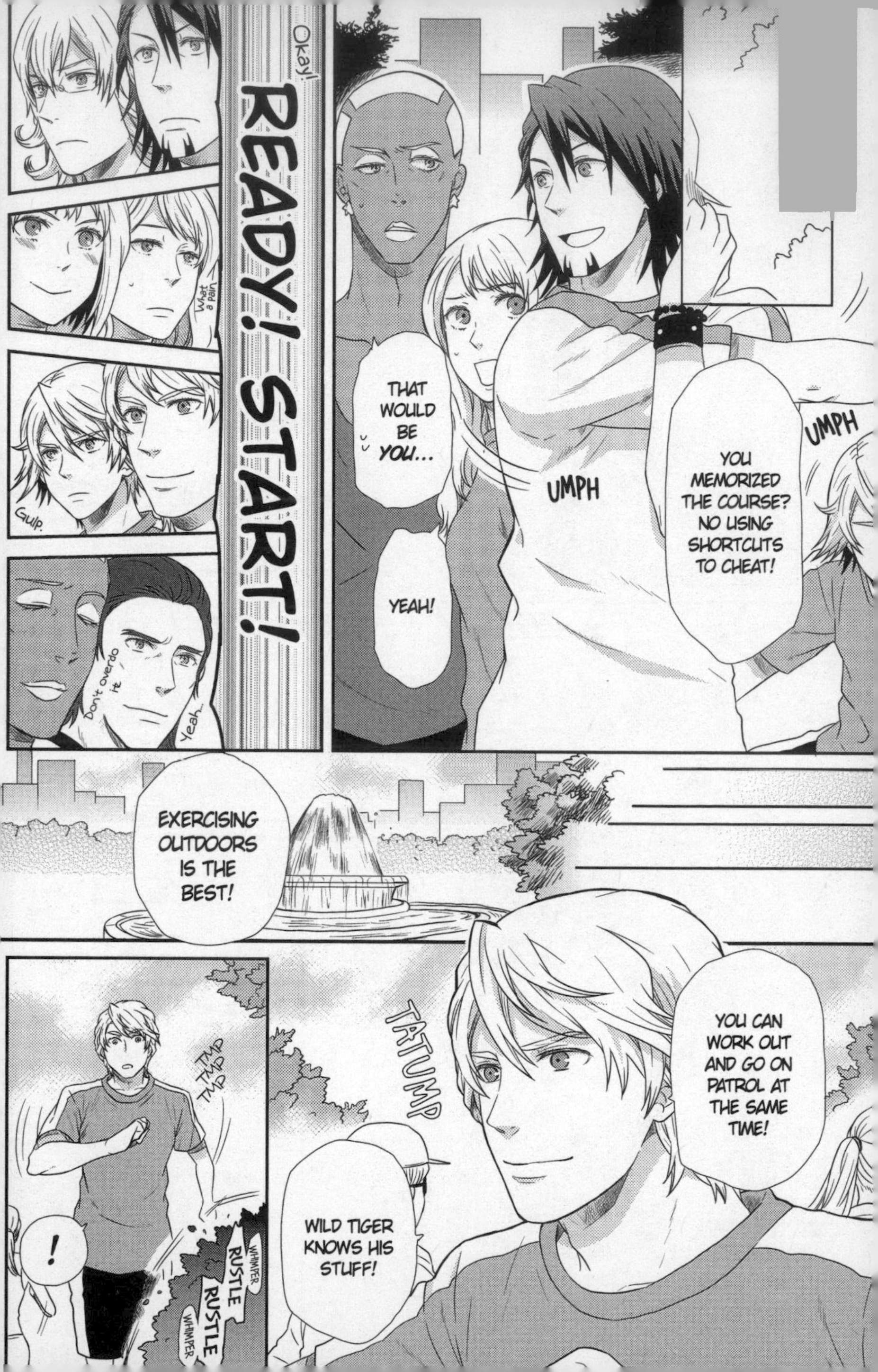
UMPH
YOU MEMORIZED THE COURSE? NO USING SHORTCUTS TO CHEAT!
UMPH
THAT WOULD BE *YOU*...
YEAH!
Okay!
READY! START!
What a pain
Gulp.
Don't overdo it
Yeah...
EXERCISING OUTDOORS IS THE BEST!
YOU CAN WORK OUT AND GO ON PATROL AT THE SAME TIME!
TATUMP
WILD TIGER KNOWS HIS STUFF!
TMP TMP TMP
WHIMPER
RUSTLE RUSTLE
WHIMPER
!

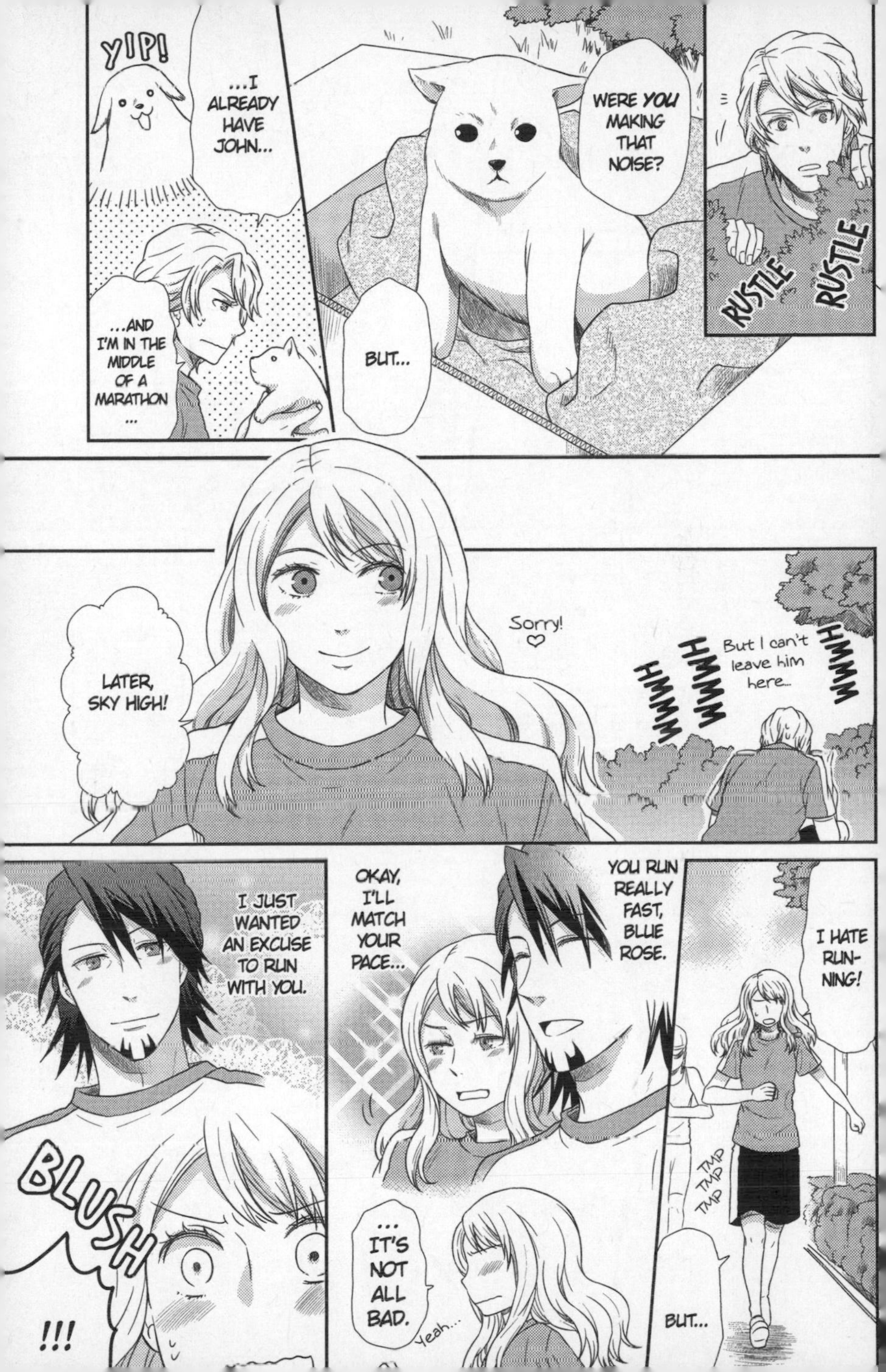
RUSTLE
RUSTLE
WERE YOU MAKING THAT NOISE?
BUT...
YIP!
...I ALREADY HAVE JOHN...
...AND I'M IN THE MIDDLE OF A MARATHON...
HMMMM
But I can't leave him here...
HMMMM
HMMMM
Sorry! ♡
LATER, SKY HIGH!
I HATE RUN-NING!
TMP TMP TMP
BUT...
YOU RUN REALLY FAST, BLUE ROSE.
OKAY, I'LL MATCH YOUR PACE...
...IT'S NOT ALL BAD.
Yeah...
I JUST WANTED AN EXCUSE TO RUN WITH YOU.
BLUSH
!!!

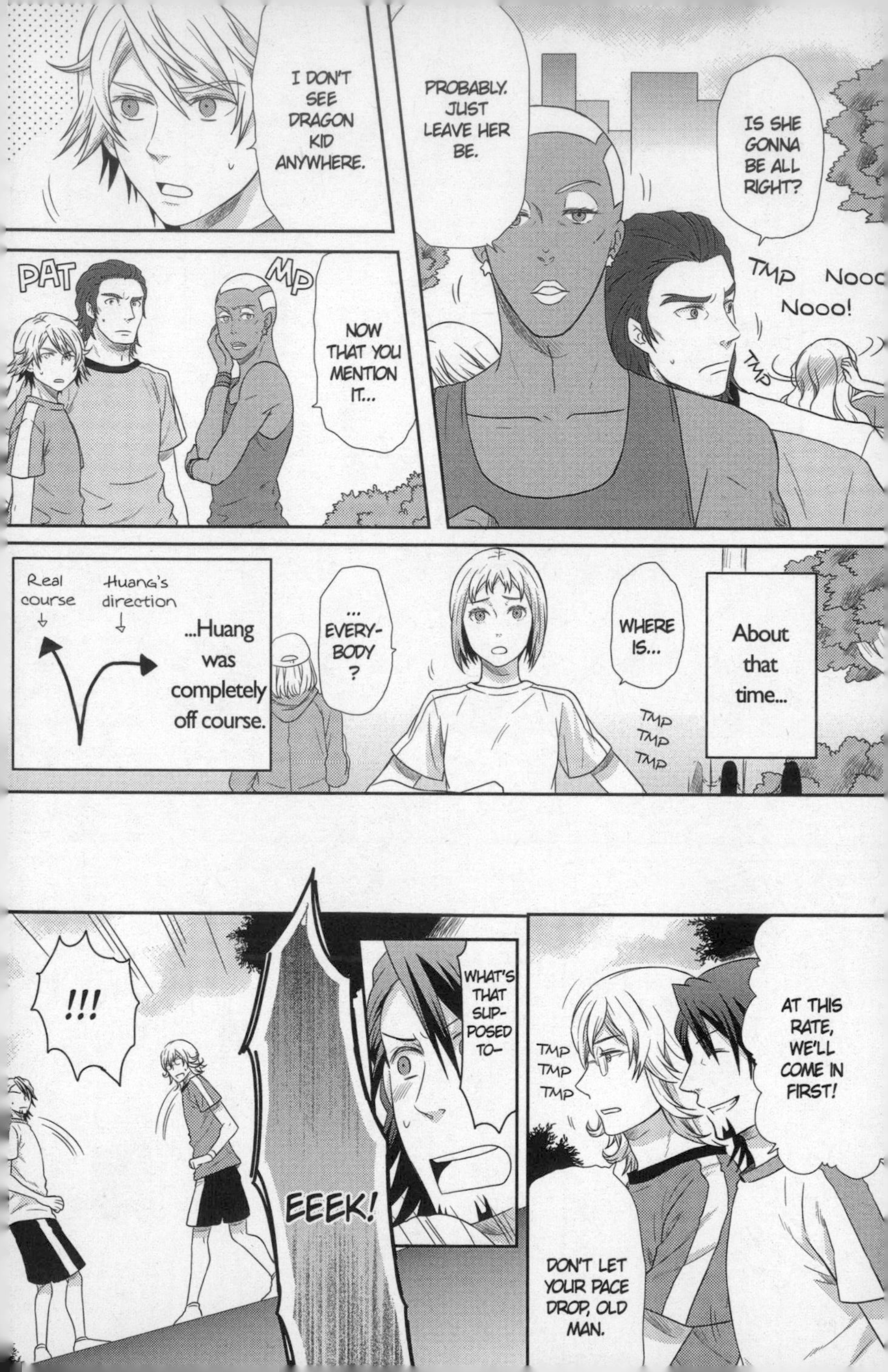
IS SHE GONNA BE ALL RIGHT?
PROBABLY. JUST LEAVE HER BE.
TMP
Nooo Nooo!
TMP
I DON'T SEE DRAGON KID ANYWHERE.
MP
PAT
NOW THAT YOU MENTION IT...
About that time...
WHERE IS...
...EVERYBODY?
TMP TMP TMP
Real course
Huang's direction
...Huang was completely off course.
AT THIS RATE, WE'LL COME IN FIRST!
TMP TMP TMP
DON'T LET YOUR PACE DROP, OLD MAN.
WHAT'S THAT SUP-POSED TO-
EEEK!
!!!

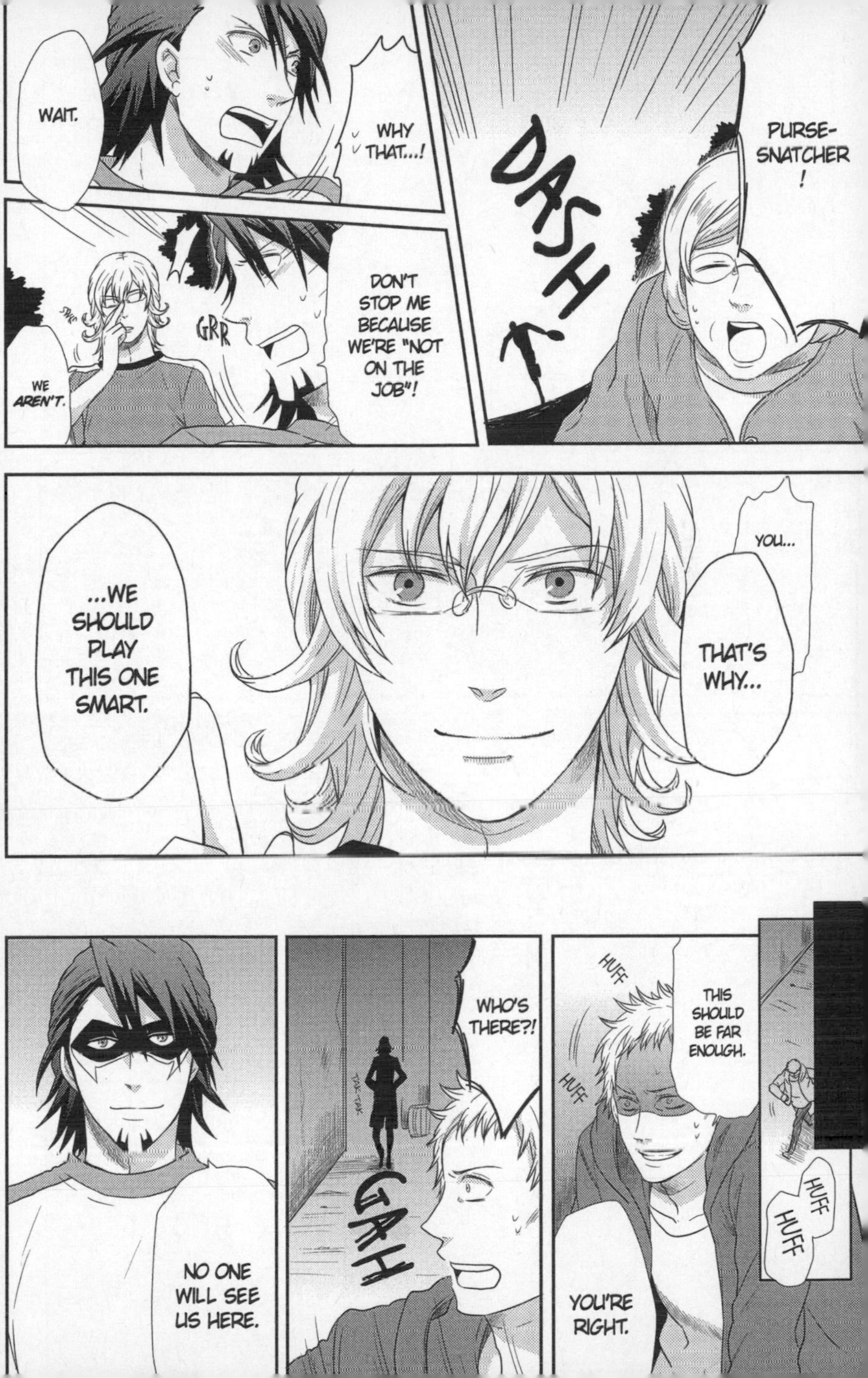
PURSE-SNATCHER!
DASH
WHY THAT...!
WAIT.
DON'T STOP ME BECAUSE WE'RE "NOT ON THE JOB"!
GRR
WE AREN'T.
YOU...
THAT'S WHY...
...WE SHOULD PLAY THIS ONE SMART.
HUFF HUFF
THIS SHOULD BE FAR ENOUGH.
HUFF
HUFF
YOU'RE RIGHT.
WHO'S THERE?!
GAH
NO ONE WILL SEE US HERE.

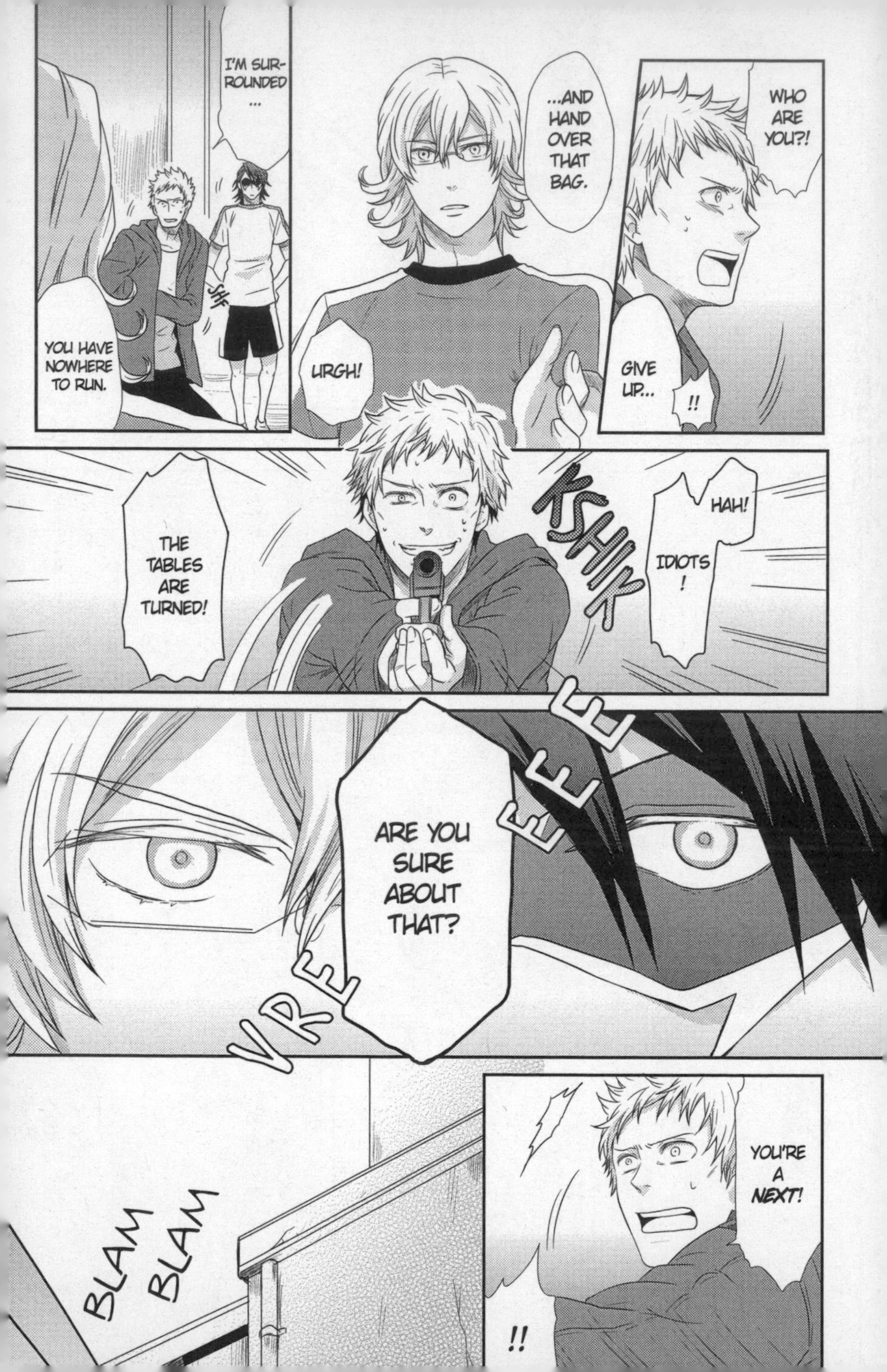
WHO ARE YOU?!
GIVE UP...
!!
...AND HAND OVER THAT BAG.
URGH!
I'M SURROUNDED...
SHF
YOU HAVE NOWHERE TO RUN.
HAH! IDIOTS!
KSHIK
THE TABLES ARE TURNED!
VREEEEE
ARE YOU SURE ABOUT THAT?
YOU'RE A NEXT!
!!
BLAM BLAM

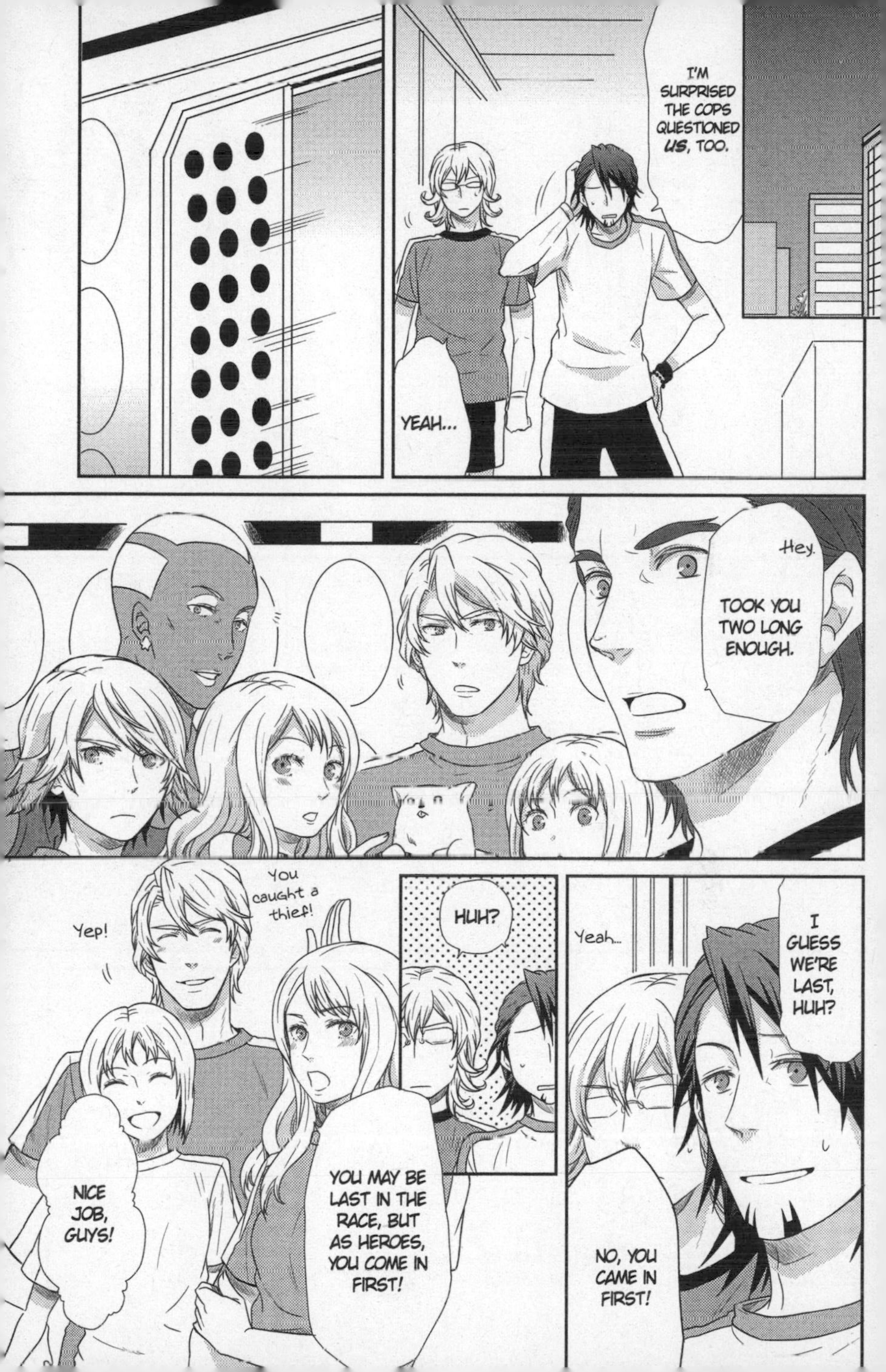
I'M SURPRISED THE COPS QUESTIONED *US*, TOO.
YEAH...
Hey.
TOOK YOU TWO LONG ENOUGH.
I GUESS WE'RE LAST, HUH?
Yeah...
NO, YOU CAME IN FIRST!
HUH?
You caught a thief!
Yep!
YOU MAY BE LAST IN THE RACE, BUT AS HEROES, YOU COME IN FIRST!
NICE JOB, GUYS!

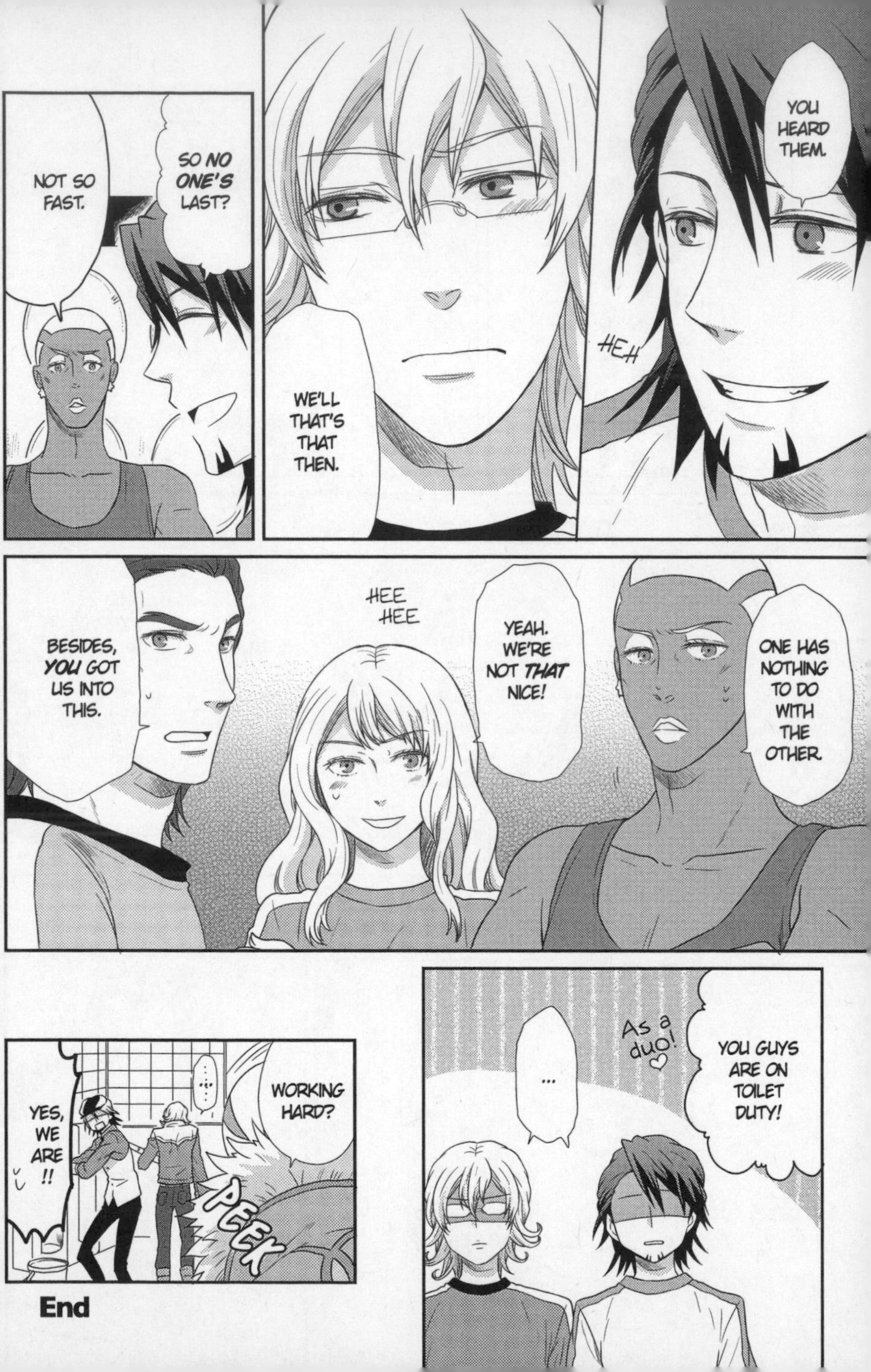
YOU HEARD THEM.
HEH
WE'LL THAT'S THAT THEN.
SO *NO ONE'S* LAST?
NOT SO FAST.
ONE HAS NOTHING TO DO WITH THE OTHER.
YEAH. WE'RE NOT *THAT* NICE!
HEE HEE
BESIDES, *YOU* GOT US INTO THIS.
YOU GUYS ARE ON TOILET DUTY!
As a duo! ♡
...
WORKING HARD?
PEEK
...
YES, WE ARE!!

End

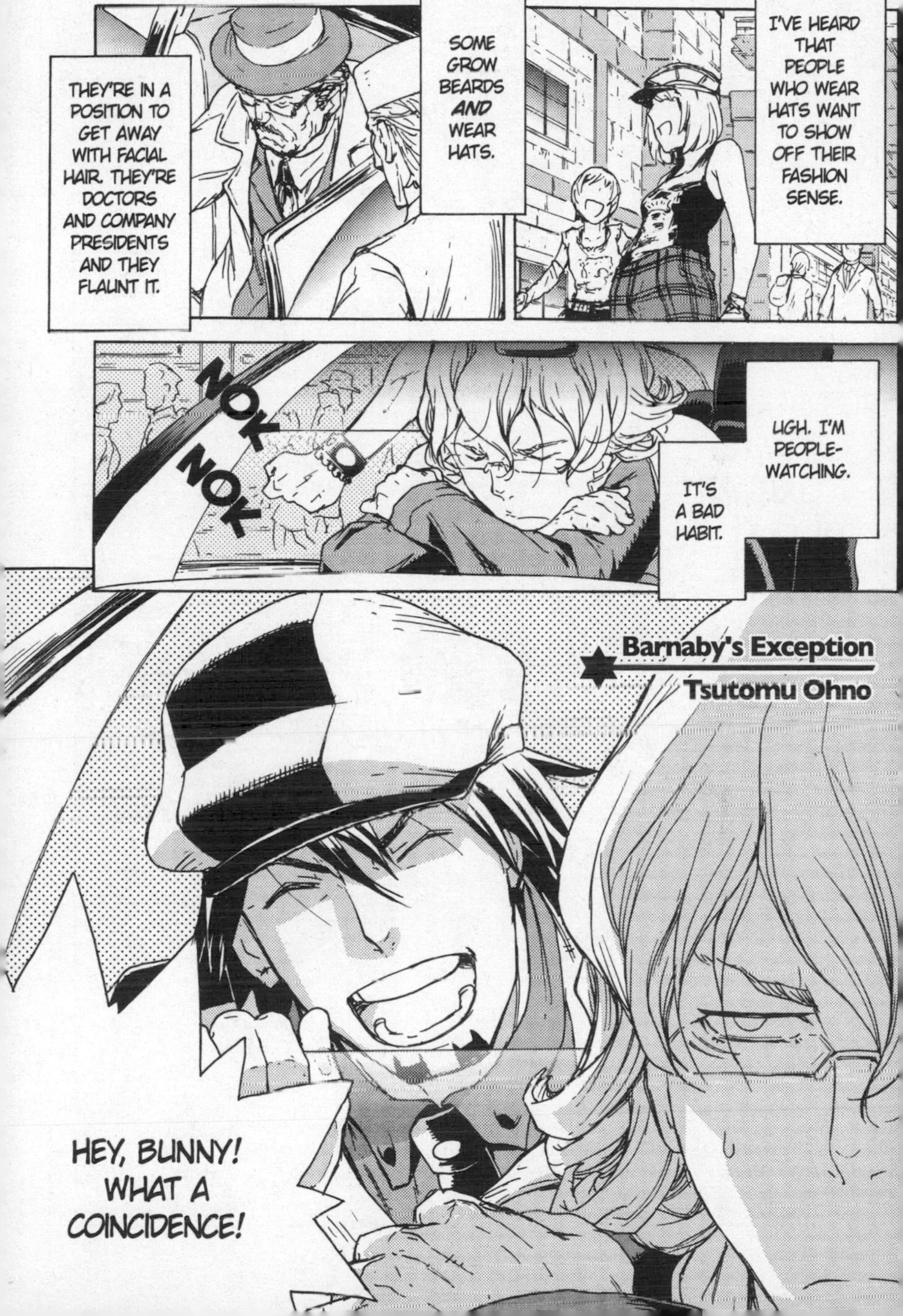
I'VE HEARD THAT PEOPLE WHO WEAR HATS WANT TO SHOW OFF THEIR FASHION SENSE.
SOME GROW BEARDS AND WEAR HATS.
THEY'RE IN A POSITION TO GET AWAY WITH FACIAL HAIR. THEY'RE DOCTORS AND COMPANY PRESIDENTS AND THEY FLAUNT IT.
UGH. I'M PEOPLE-WATCHING.
IT'S A BAD HABIT.
NOK NOK
Barnaby's Exception
Tsutomu Ohno
HEY, BUNNY! WHAT A COINCIDENCE!

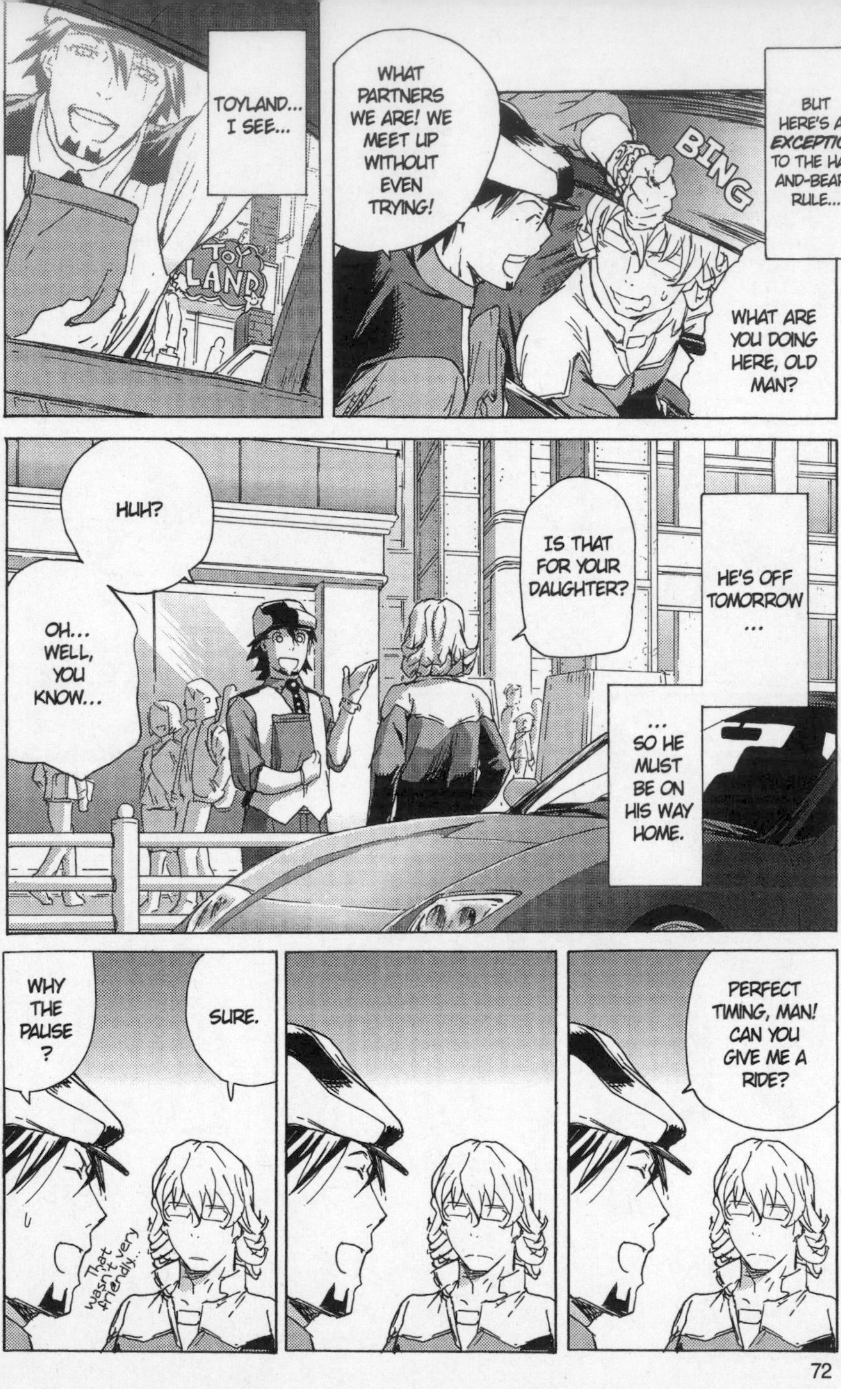
BUT HERE'S AN EXCEPTION TO THE HAT-AND-BEARD RULE...
BING
WHAT PARTNERS WE ARE! WE MEET UP WITHOUT EVEN TRYING!
WHAT ARE YOU DOING HERE, OLD MAN?
TOYLAND... I SEE...
TOY LAND
HE'S OFF TOMORROW ...
... SO HE MUST BE ON HIS WAY HOME.
IS THAT FOR YOUR DAUGHTER?
HUH?
OH... WELL, YOU KNOW...
PERFECT TIMING, MAN! CAN YOU GIVE ME A RIDE?
SURE.
WHY THE PAUSE ?
That wasn't very friendly...

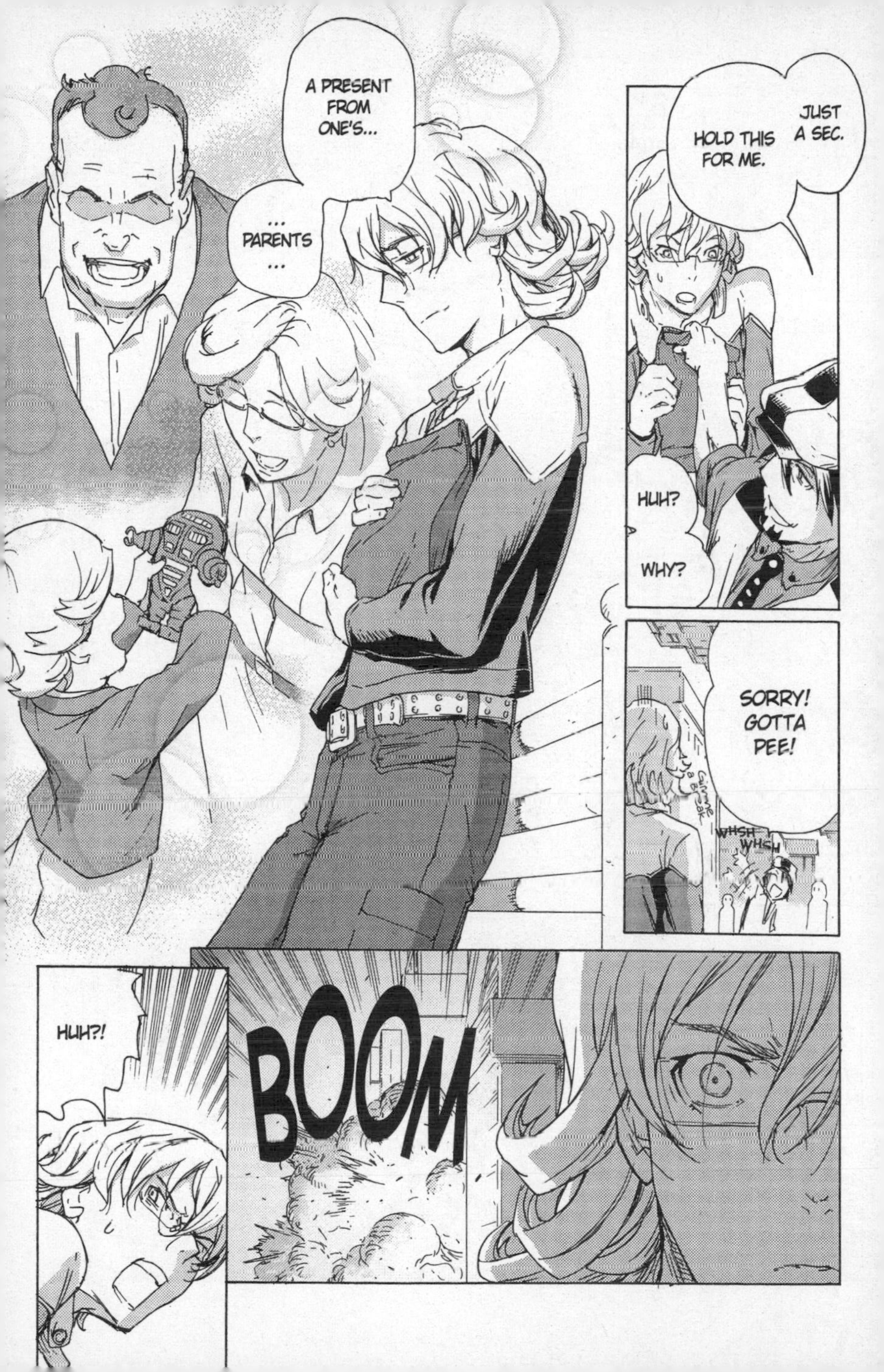
JUST A SEC.
HOLD THIS FOR ME.
HUH?
WHY?
SORRY! GOTTA PEE!
Gimme a break
WHSH WHSH
A PRESENT FROM ONE'S...
... PARENTS ...
BOOM
HUH?!

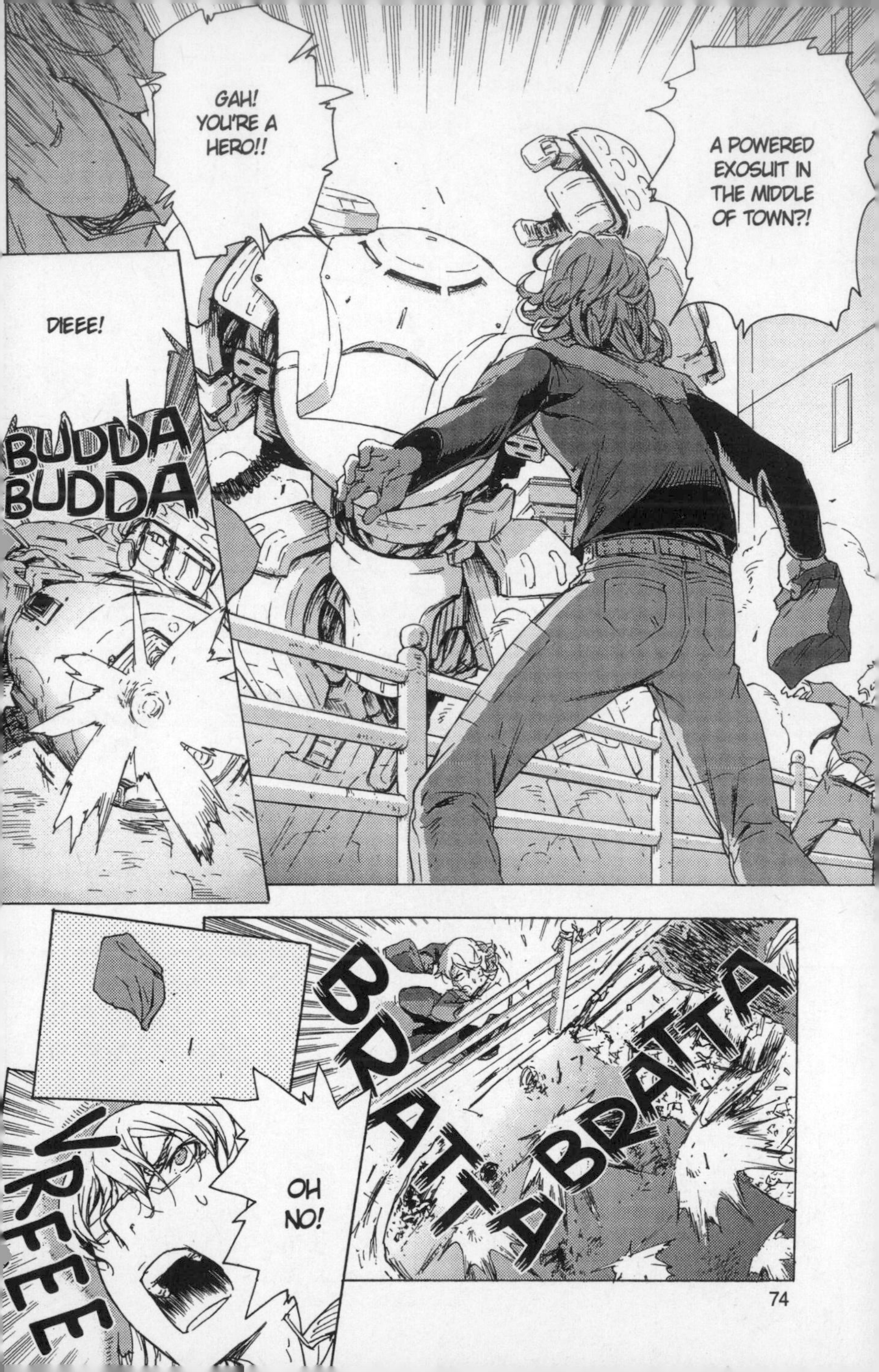
A POWERED EXOSUIT IN THE MIDDLE OF TOWN?!
GAH! YOU'RE A HERO!!
DIEEE!
BUDDA BUDDA
BRATA
BRATTA
OH NO!
VREEE

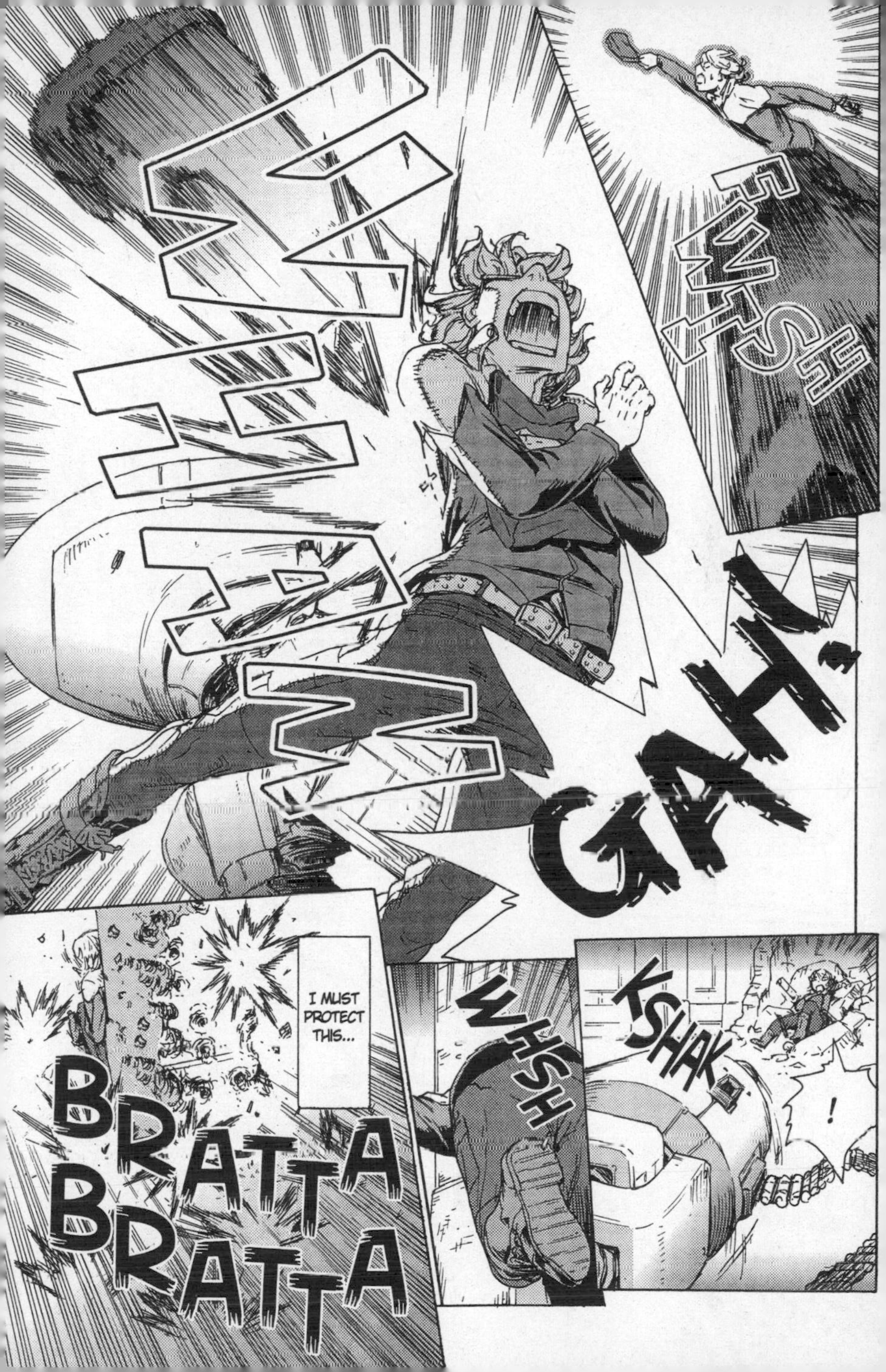
FWISH
WHAM
GAH!
KSHAK
!
WHSH
I MUST PROTECT THIS...
BRATTA BRATTA

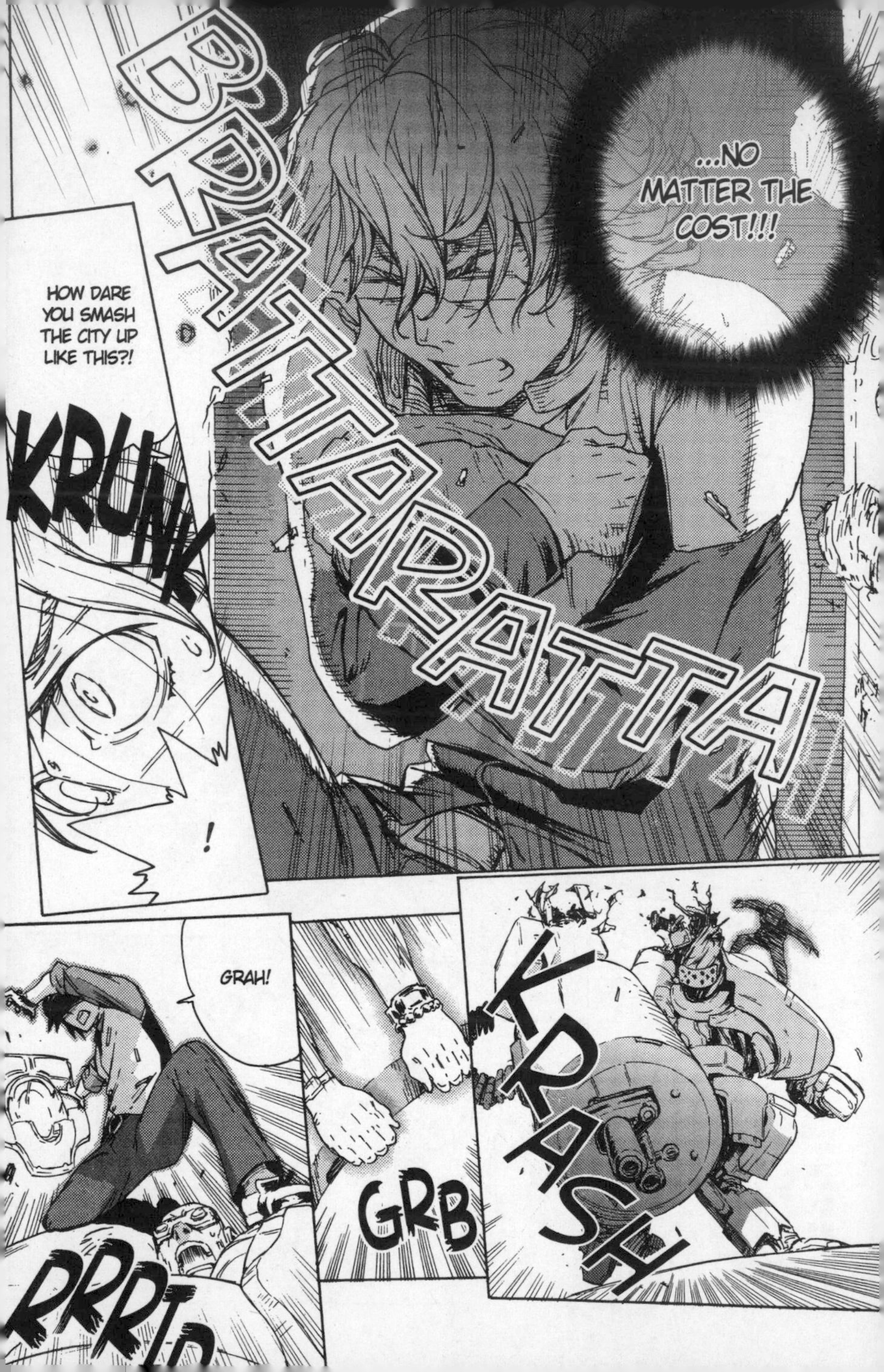
...NO MATTER THE COST!!!
BRATTARATTA
HOW DARE YOU SMASH THE CITY UP LIKE THIS?!
KRUNK
!
KRASH
GRB
GRAH!

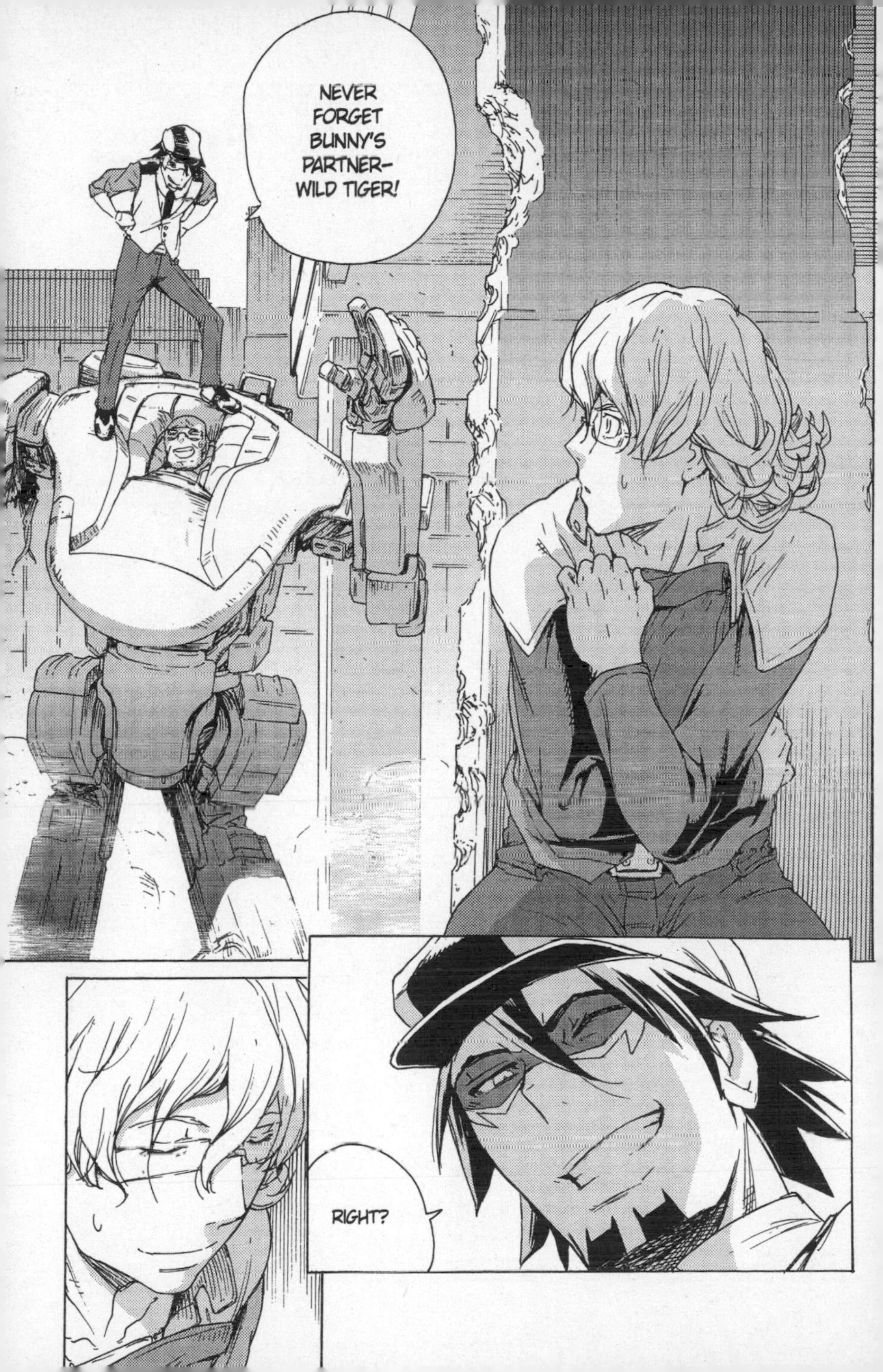
NEVER FORGET BUNNY'S PARTNER–WILD TIGER!
RIGHT?

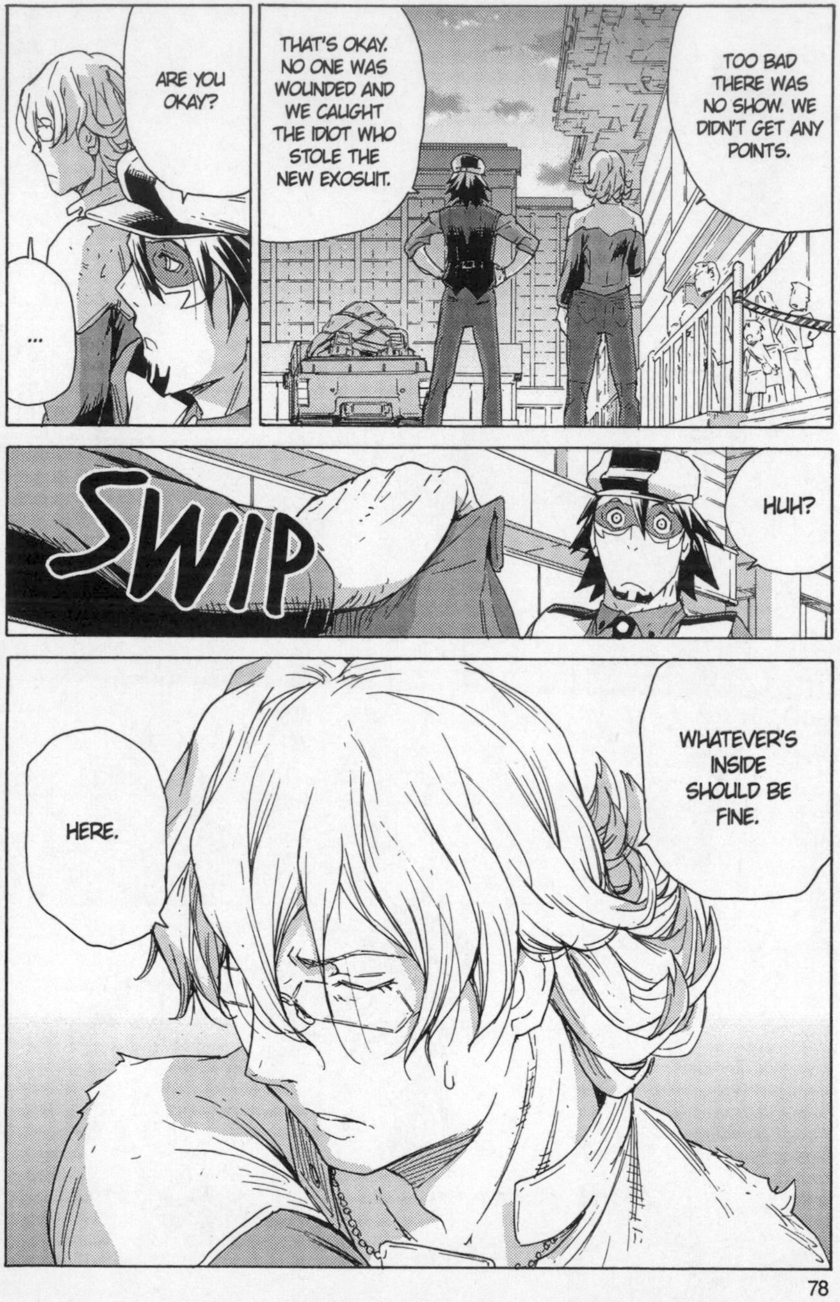
TOO BAD THERE WAS NO SHOW. WE DIDN'T GET ANY POINTS.
THAT'S OKAY. NO ONE WAS WOUNDED AND WE CAUGHT THE IDIOT WHO STOLE THE NEW EXOSUIT.
ARE YOU OKAY?
...
HUH?
SWIP
WHATEVER'S INSIDE SHOULD BE FINE.
HERE.

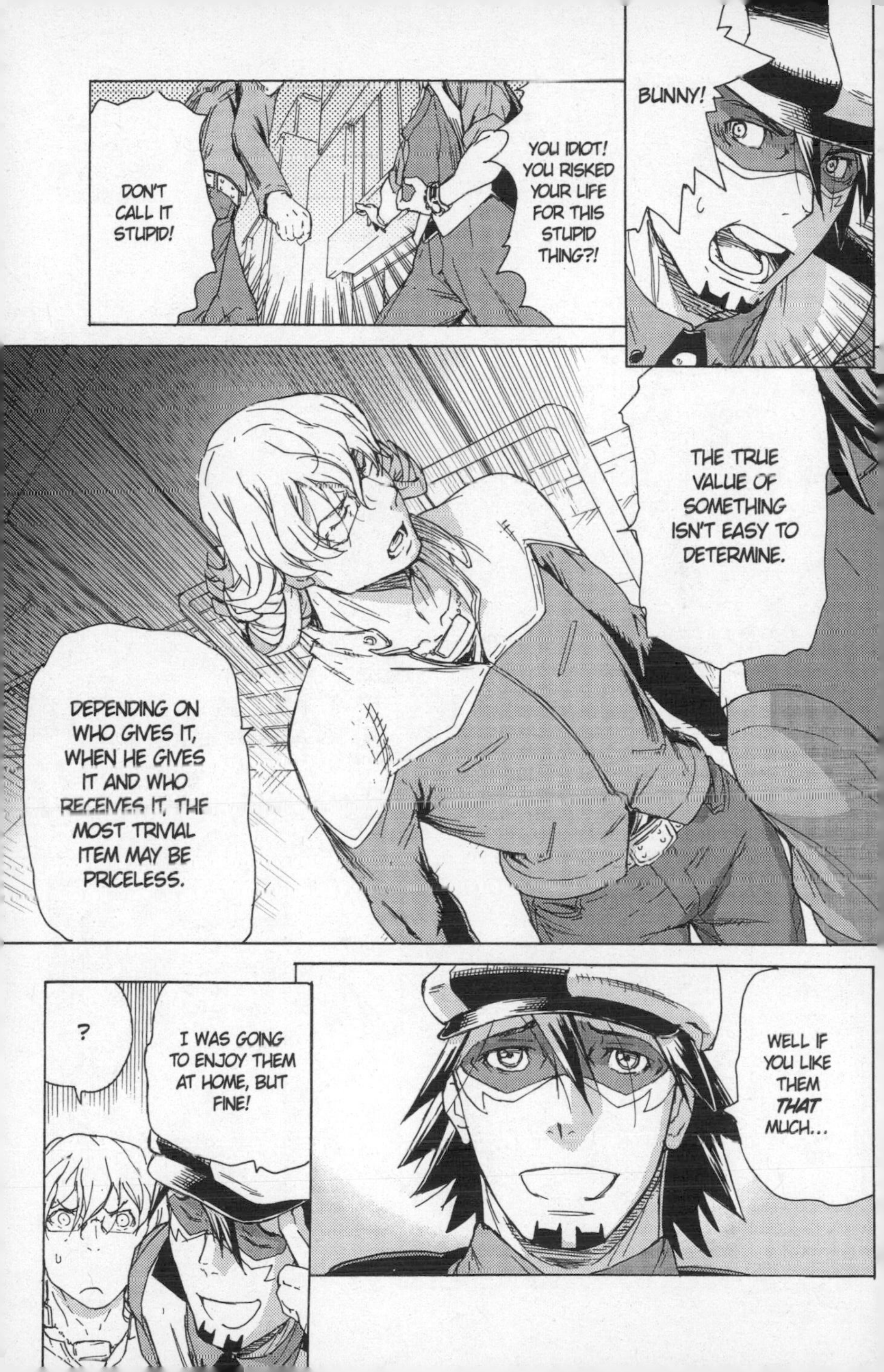
BUNNY!
YOU IDIOT! YOU RISKED YOUR LIFE FOR THIS STUPID THING?!
DON'T CALL IT STUPID!
THE TRUE VALUE OF SOMETHING ISN'T EASY TO DETERMINE.
DEPENDING ON WHO GIVES IT, WHEN HE GIVES IT AND WHO RECEIVES IT, THE MOST TRIVIAL ITEM MAY BE PRICELESS.
WELL IF YOU LIKE THEM *THAT* MUCH...
I WAS GOING TO ENJOY THEM AT HOME, BUT FINE!
?

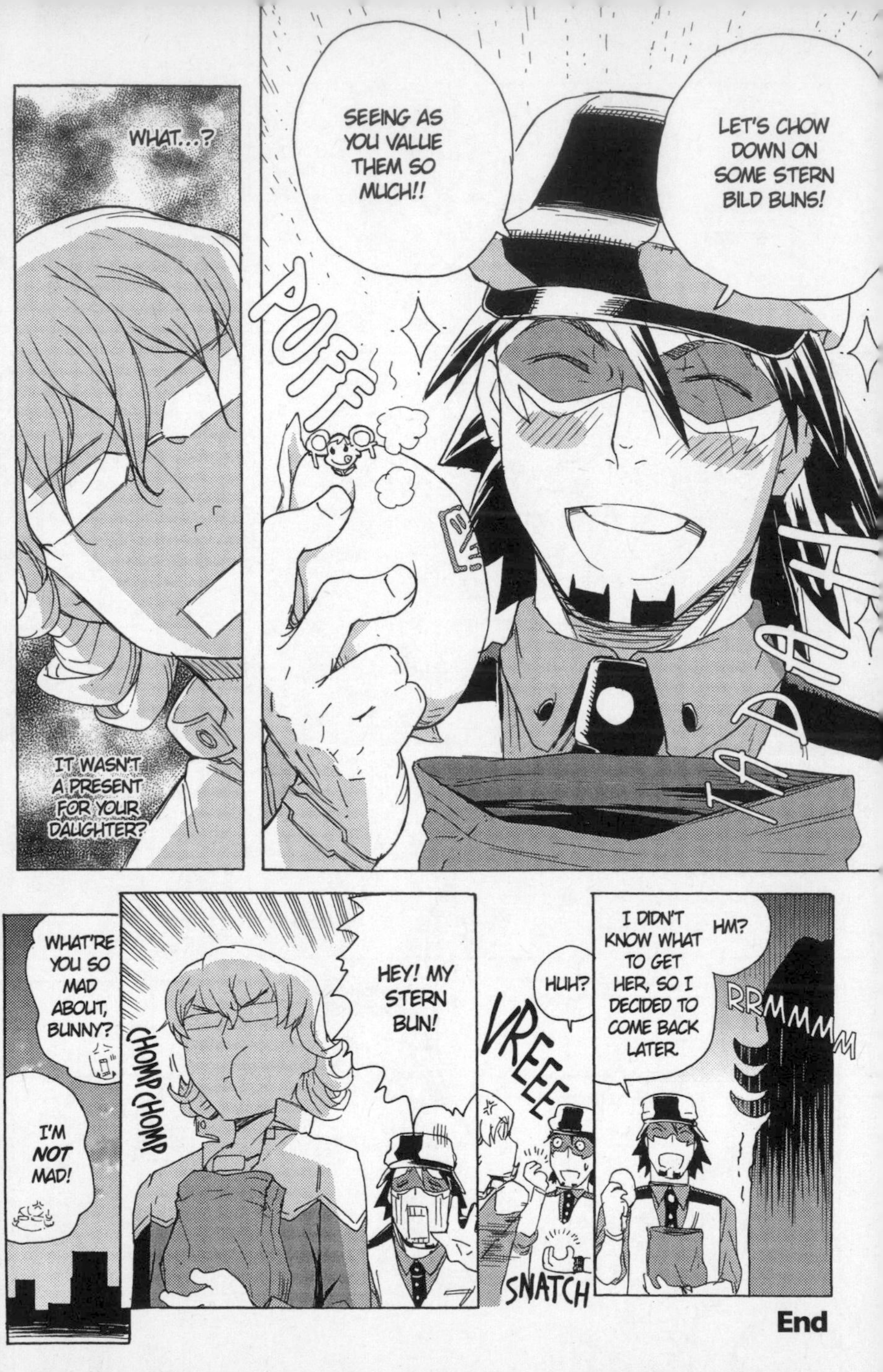
LET'S CHOW DOWN ON SOME STERN BILD BUNS!
SEEING AS YOU VALUE THEM SO MUCH!!
HA HA HA HA
PUFF
WHAT...?
IT WASN'T A PRESENT FOR YOUR DAUGHTER?
HM?
I DIDN'T KNOW WHAT TO GET HER, SO I DECIDED TO COME BACK LATER.
RRMMMMM
HUH?
VREEE
SNATCH
HEY! MY STERN BUN!
CHOMP CHOMP
WHAT'RE YOU SO MAD ABOUT, BUNNY?
I'M *NOT* MAD!

End

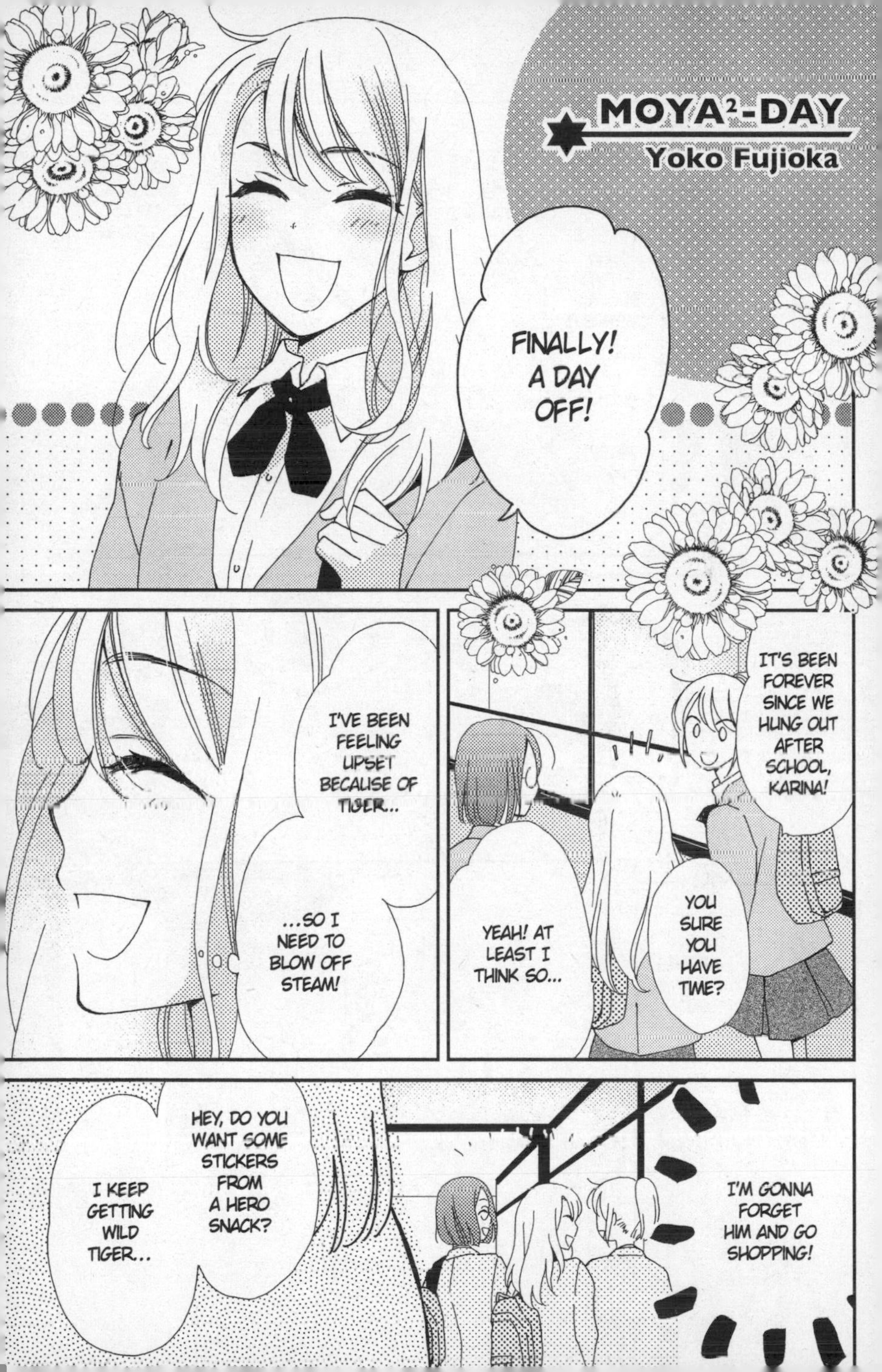
MOYA²-DAY
Yoko Fujioka
FINALLY! A DAY OFF!
IT'S BEEN FOREVER SINCE WE HUNG OUT AFTER SCHOOL, KARINA!
YOU SURE YOU HAVE TIME?
YEAH! AT LEAST I THINK SO...
I'VE BEEN FEELING UPSET BECAUSE OF TIGER...
...SO I NEED TO BLOW OFF STEAM!
I'M GONNA FORGET HIM AND GO SHOPPING!
HEY, DO YOU WANT SOME STICKERS FROM A HERO SNACK?
I KEEP GETTING WILD TIGER...

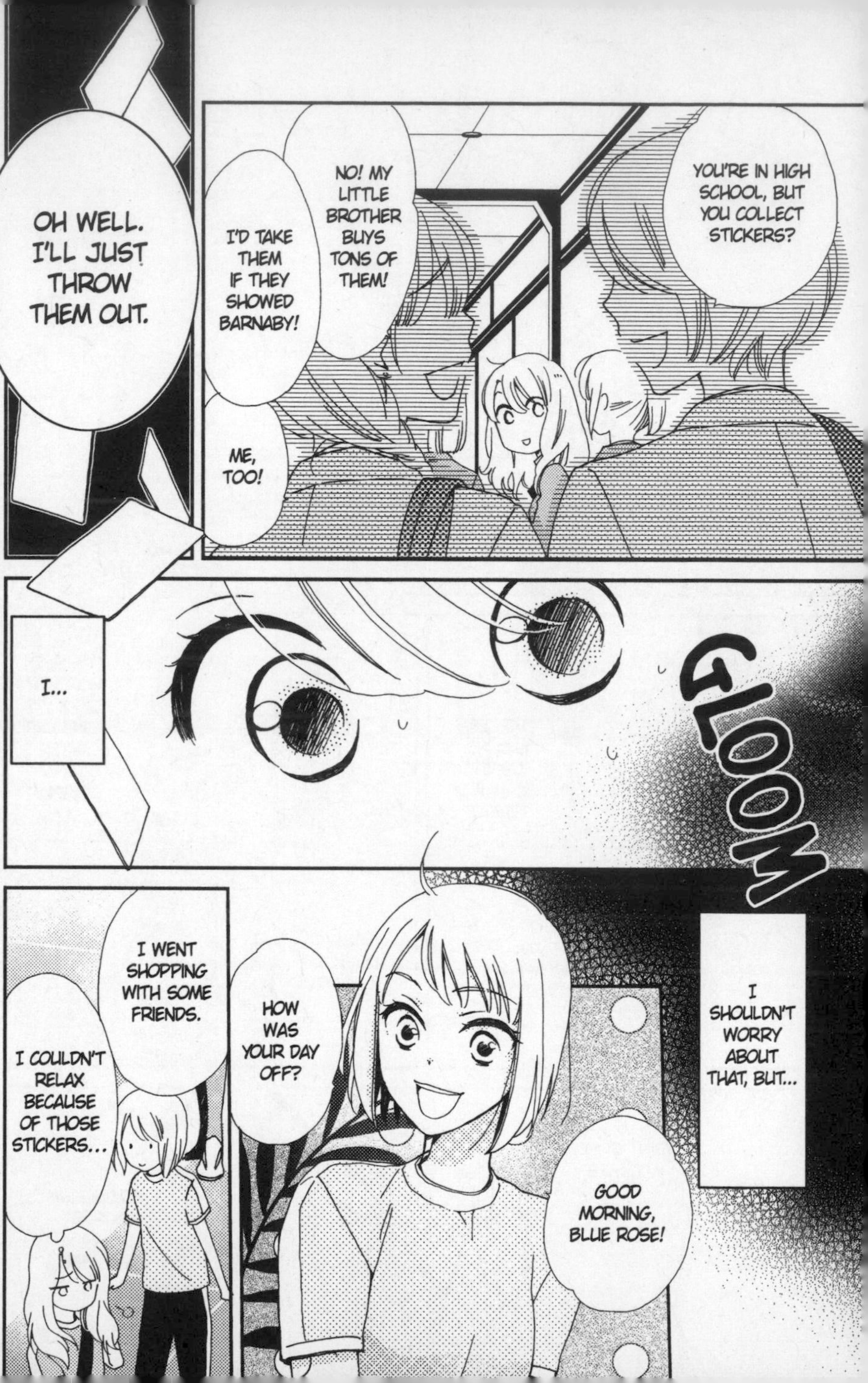
YOU'RE IN HIGH SCHOOL, BUT YOU COLLECT STICKERS?
NO! MY LITTLE BROTHER BUYS TONS OF THEM!
I'D TAKE THEM IF THEY SHOWED BARNABY!
ME, TOO!
OH WELL. I'LL JUST THROW THEM OUT.
GLOOM
I...
I SHOULDN'T WORRY ABOUT THAT, BUT...
GOOD MORNING, BLUE ROSE!
HOW WAS YOUR DAY OFF?
I WENT SHOPPING WITH SOME FRIENDS.
I COULDN'T RELAX BECAUSE OF THOSE STICKERS...

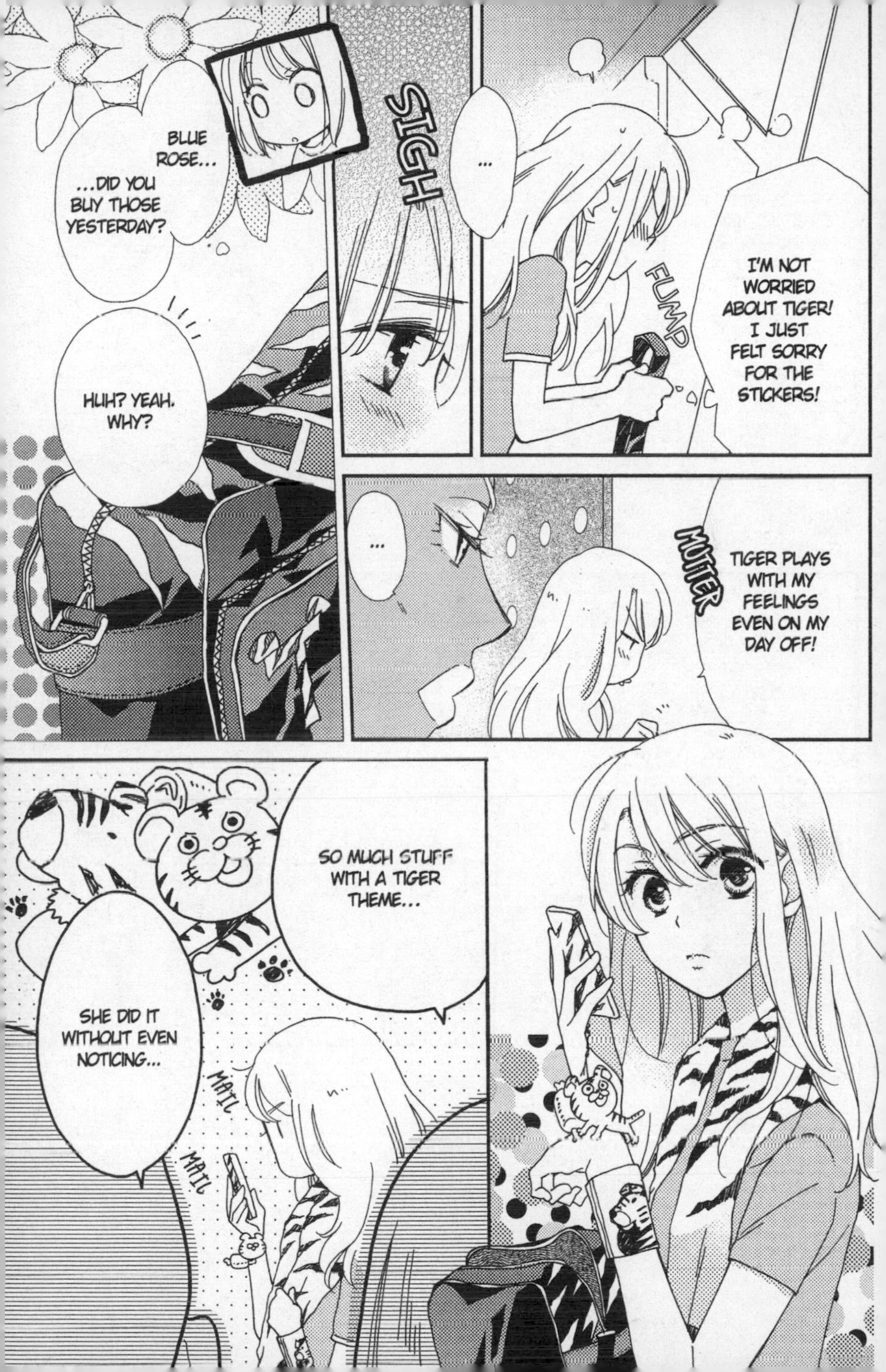
I'M NOT WORRIED ABOUT TIGER! I JUST FELT SORRY FOR THE STICKERS!
FUMP
...
SIGH
MUTTER
TIGER PLAYS WITH MY FEELINGS EVEN ON MY DAY OFF!
...
BLUE ROSE...
...DID YOU BUY THOSE YESTERDAY?
HUH? YEAH. WHY?
SO MUCH STUFF WITH A TIGER THEME...
SHE DID IT WITHOUT EVEN NOTICING...
MAIL
MAIL

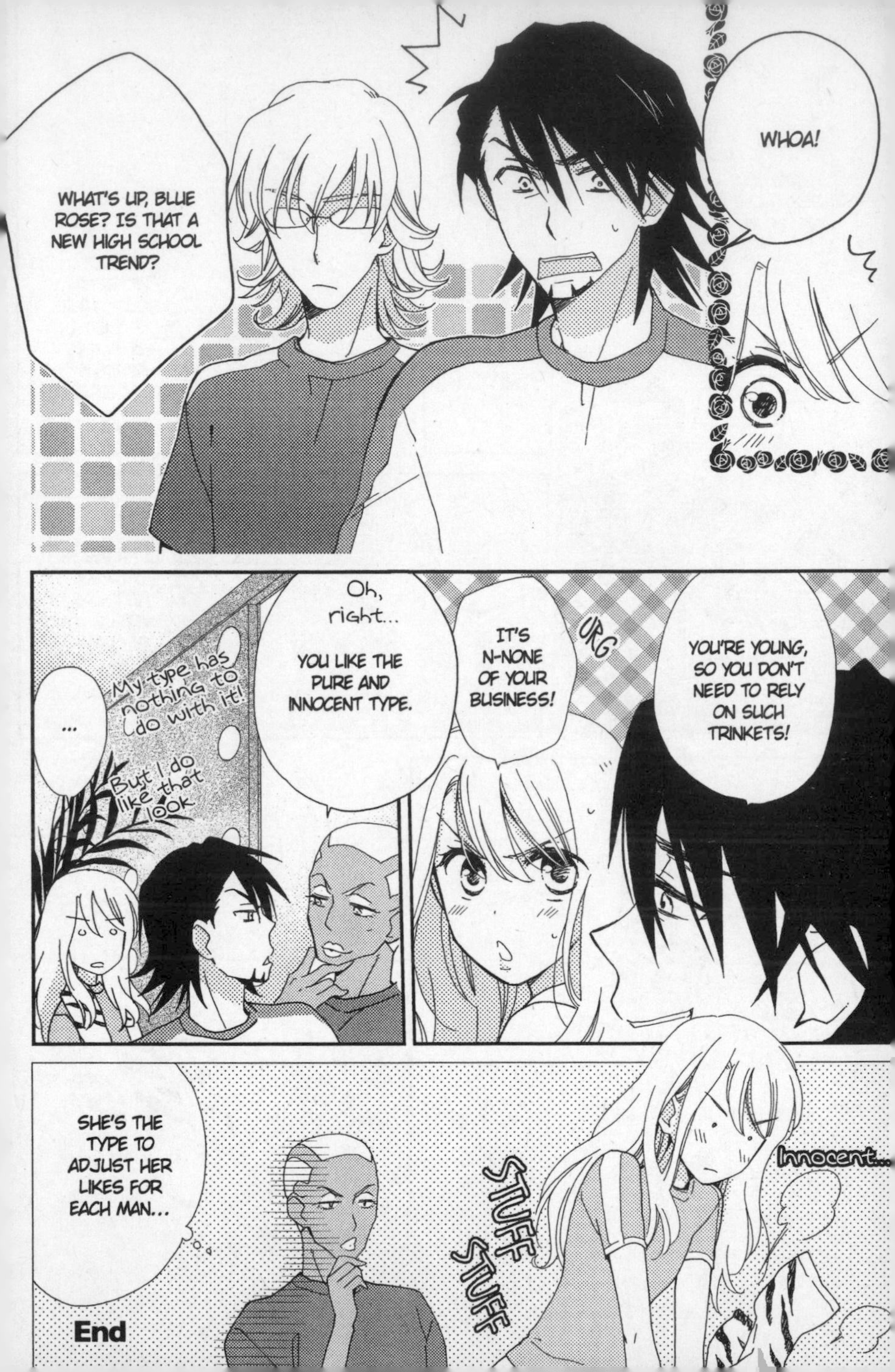
WHOA!
WHAT'S UP, BLUE ROSE? IS THAT A NEW HIGH SCHOOL TREND?
YOU'RE YOUNG, SO YOU DON'T NEED TO RELY ON SUCH TRINKETS!
URG
IT'S N-NONE OF YOUR BUSINESS!
Oh, right...
YOU LIKE THE PURE AND INNOCENT TYPE.
My type has nothing to do with it!
But I do like that look
...
Innocent...
STUFF STUFF
SHE'S THE TYPE TO ADJUST HER LIKES FOR EACH MAN...
End

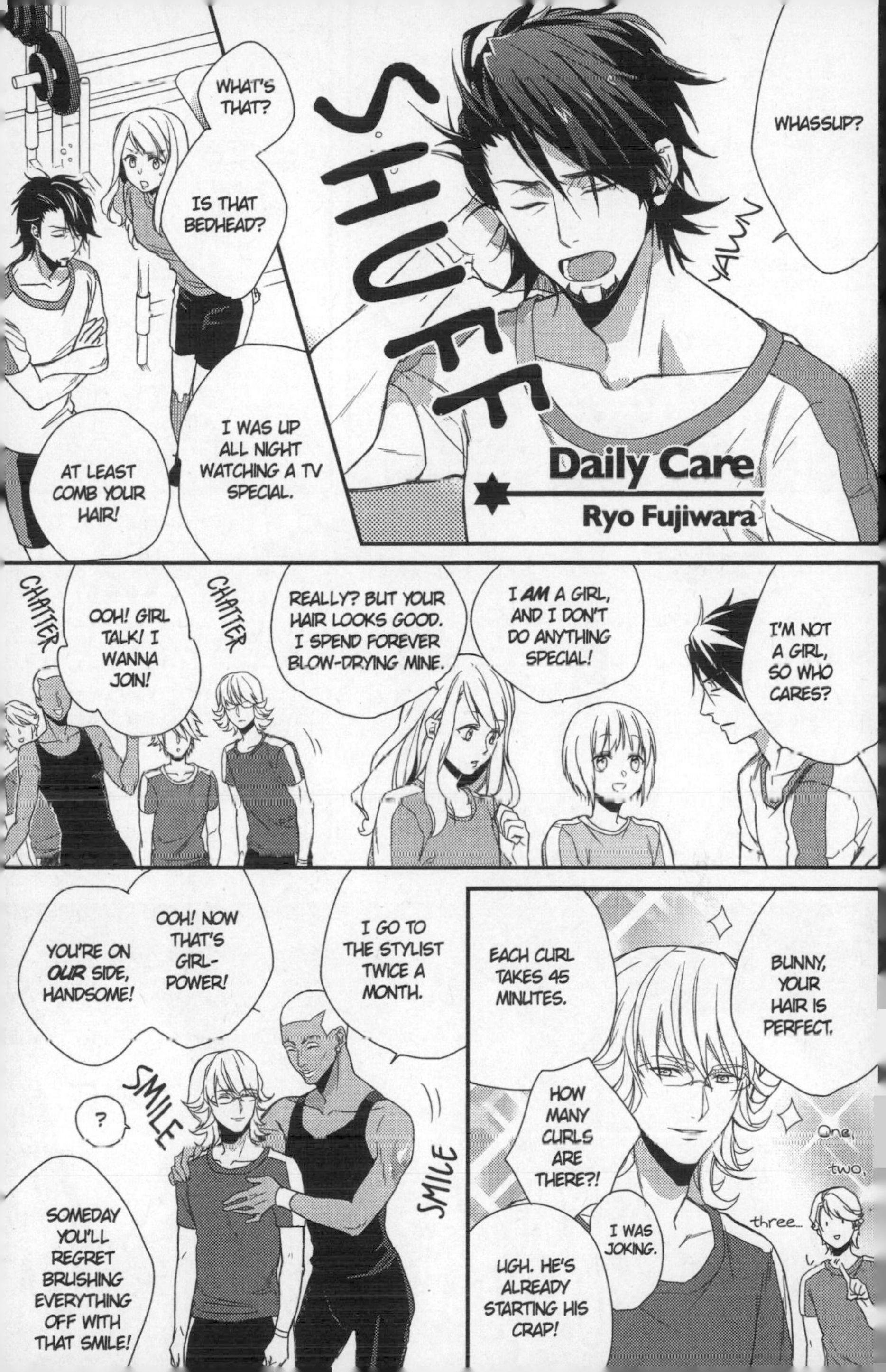

WHASSUP?
YAWN
SHUFF
Daily Care
Ryo Fujiwara
WHAT'S THAT?
IS THAT BEDHEAD?
I WAS UP ALL NIGHT WATCHING A TV SPECIAL.
AT LEAST COMB YOUR HAIR!
I'M NOT A GIRL, SO WHO CARES?
I *AM* A GIRL, AND I DON'T DO ANYTHING SPECIAL!
REALLY? BUT YOUR HAIR LOOKS GOOD. I SPEND FOREVER BLOW-DRYING MINE.
CHATTER
OOH! GIRL TALK! I WANNA JOIN!
CHATTER
BUNNY, YOUR HAIR IS PERFECT.
EACH CURL TAKES 45 MINUTES.
One, two, three...
HOW MANY CURLS ARE THERE?!
I WAS JOKING.
UGH. HE'S ALREADY STARTING HIS CRAP!
I GO TO THE STYLIST TWICE A MONTH.
OOH! NOW THAT'S GIRL-POWER!
YOU'RE ON *OUR* SIDE, HANDSOME!
SMILE
SMILE
?
SOMEDAY YOU'LL REGRET BRUSHING EVERYTHING OFF WITH THAT SMILE!

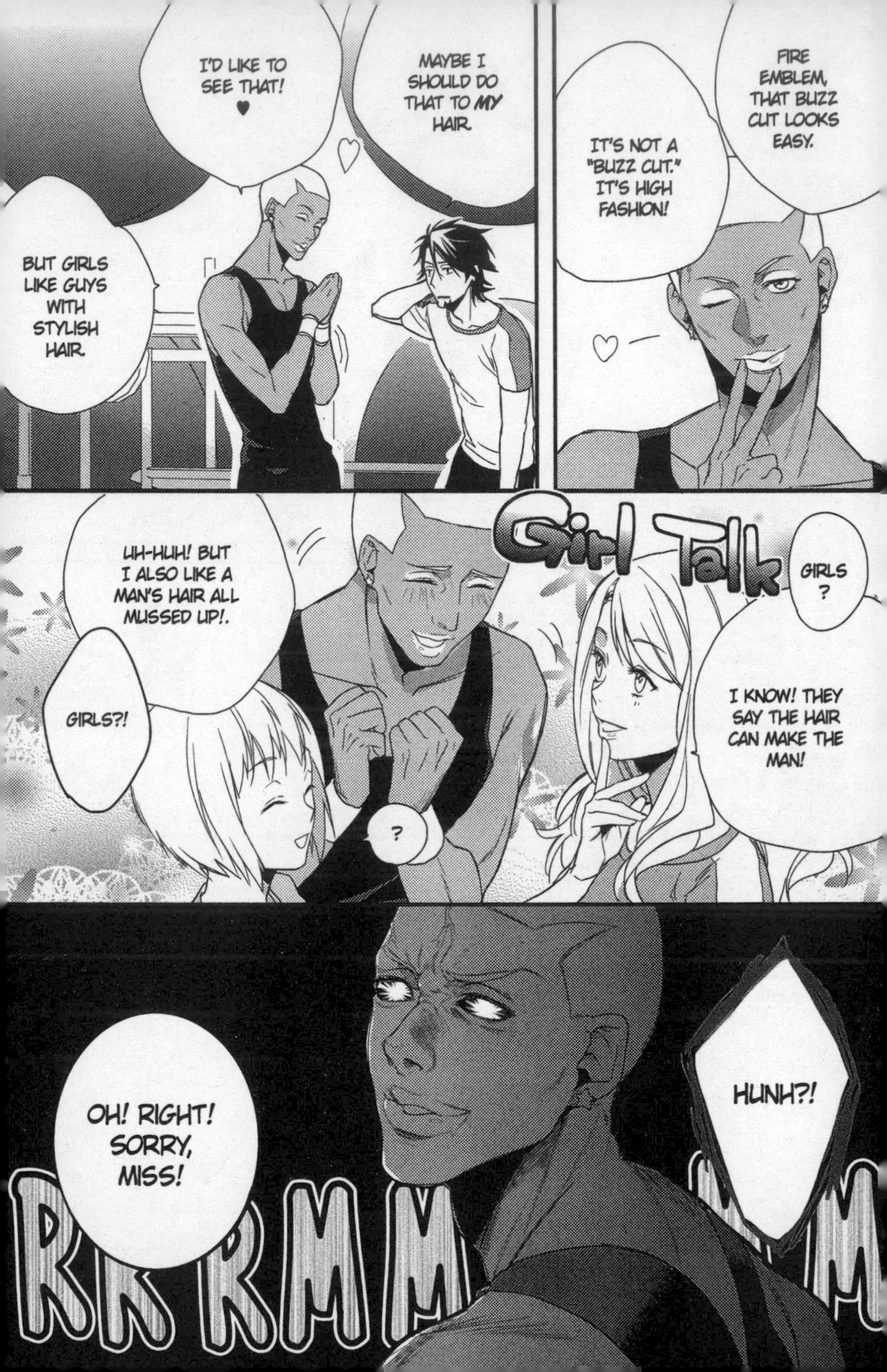
FIRE EMBLEM, THAT BUZZ CUT LOOKS EASY.
IT'S NOT A "BUZZ CUT." IT'S HIGH FASHION!
MAYBE I SHOULD DO THAT TO *MY* HAIR.
I'D LIKE TO SEE THAT! ♥
BUT GIRLS LIKE GUYS WITH STYLISH HAIR.
Girl Talk
GIRLS ?
I KNOW! THEY SAY THE HAIR CAN MAKE THE MAN!
UH-HUH! BUT I ALSO LIKE A MAN'S HAIR ALL MUSSED UP!.
GIRLS?!
?
HUNH?!
OH! RIGHT! SORRY, MISS!
RRRMM

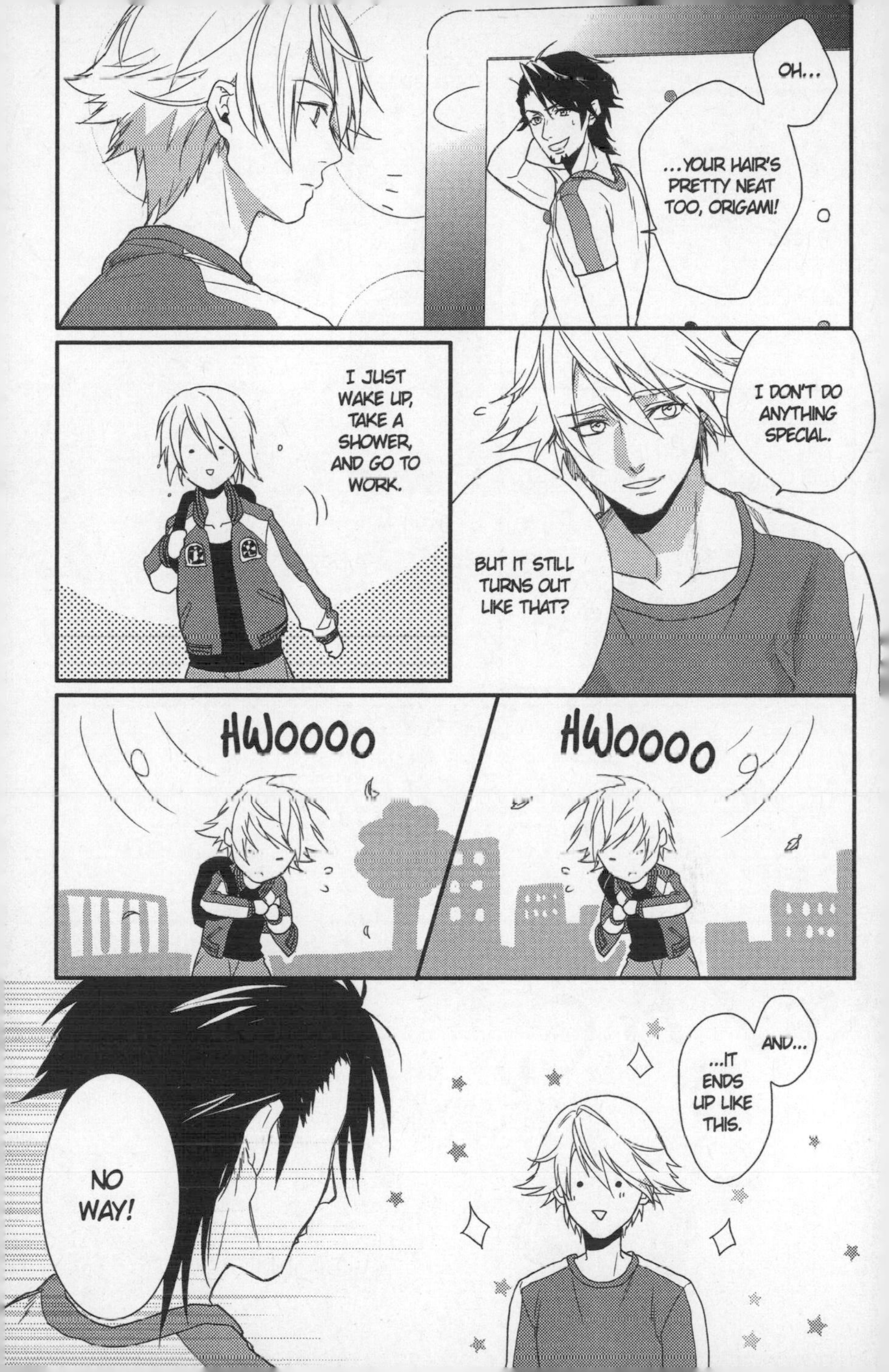
OH...
...YOUR HAIR'S PRETTY NEAT TOO, ORIGAMI!
I DON'T DO ANYTHING SPECIAL.
BUT IT STILL TURNS OUT LIKE THAT?
I JUST WAKE UP, TAKE A SHOWER, AND GO TO WORK.
HWOOOO
HWOOOO
AND...
...IT ENDS UP LIKE THIS.
NO WAY!

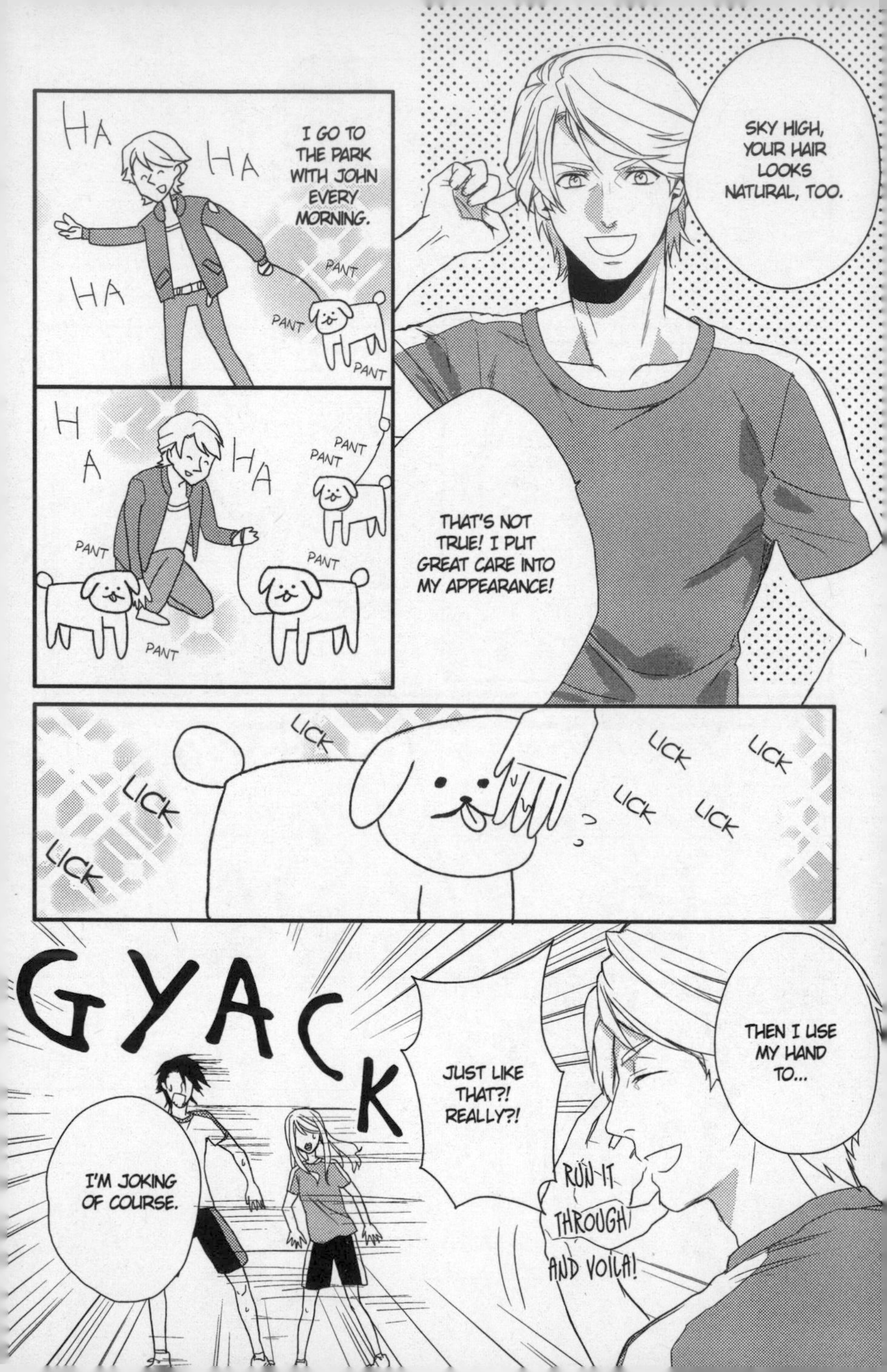

SKY HIGH, YOUR HAIR LOOKS NATURAL, TOO.
THAT'S NOT TRUE! I PUT GREAT CARE INTO MY APPEARANCE!
I GO TO THE PARK WITH JOHN EVERY MORNING.
HA HA HA
PANT
PANT
PANT
HA HA HA
PANT
PANT
PANT
PANT
PANT
LICK
LICK
LICK
LICK
LICK
LICK
LICK
THEN I USE MY HAND TO...
RUN IT THROUGH
AND VOILA!
JUST LIKE THAT?! REALLY?!
GYACK
I'M JOKING OF COURSE.

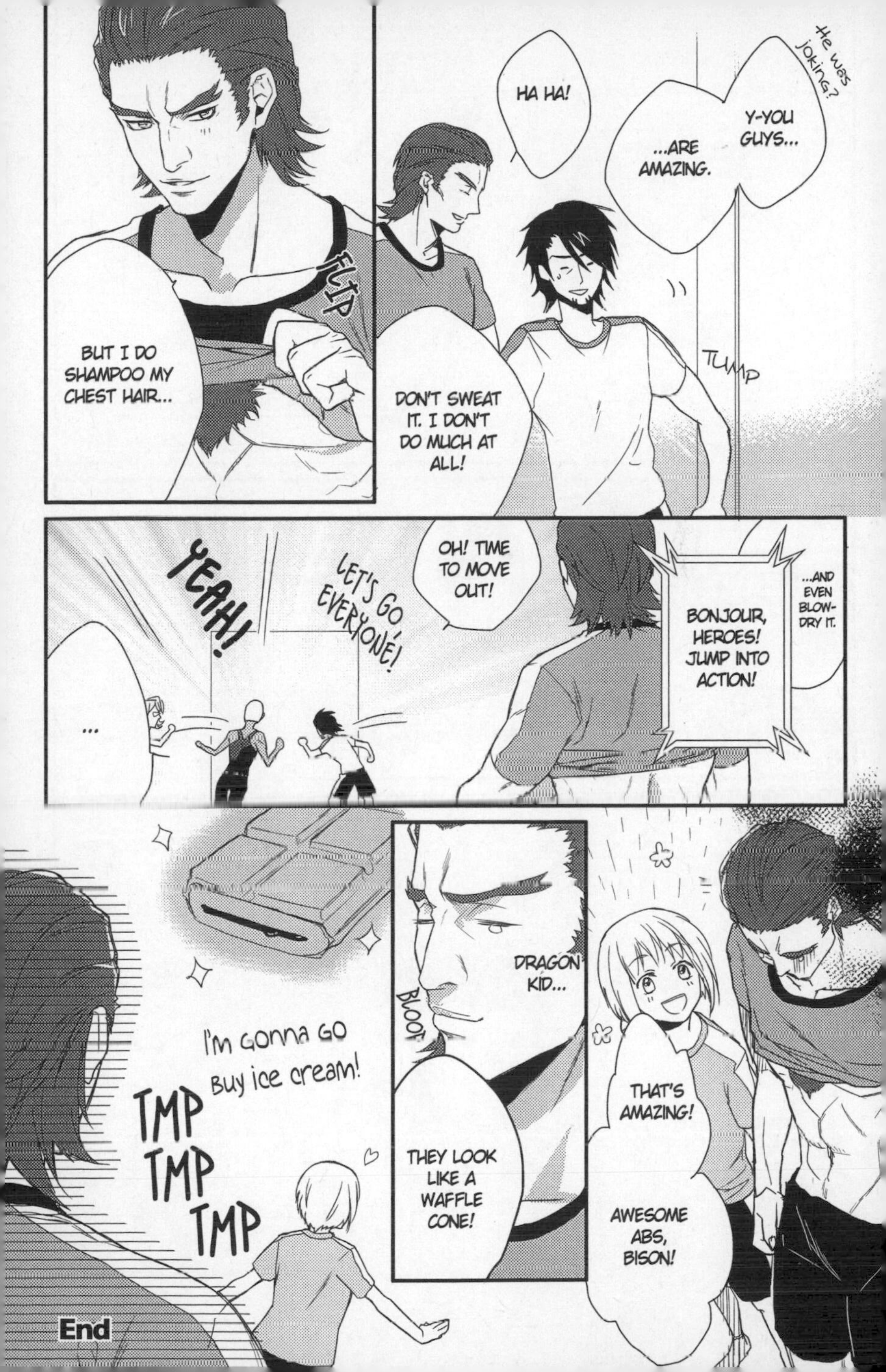
He was joking?
Y-YOU GUYS...
...ARE AMAZING.
HA HA!
TUMP
DON'T SWEAT IT. I DON'T DO MUCH AT ALL!
FLIP
BUT I DO SHAMPOO MY CHEST HAIR...
...AND EVEN BLOW-DRY IT.
BONJOUR, HEROES! JUMP INTO ACTION!
OH! TIME TO MOVE OUT!
LET'S GO EVERYONE!
YEAH!
...
THAT'S AMAZING!
AWESOME ABS, BISON!
DRAGON KID...
BLOOT
THEY LOOK LIKE A WAFFLE CONE!
I'm gonna go buy ice cream!
TMP
TMP
TMP
End

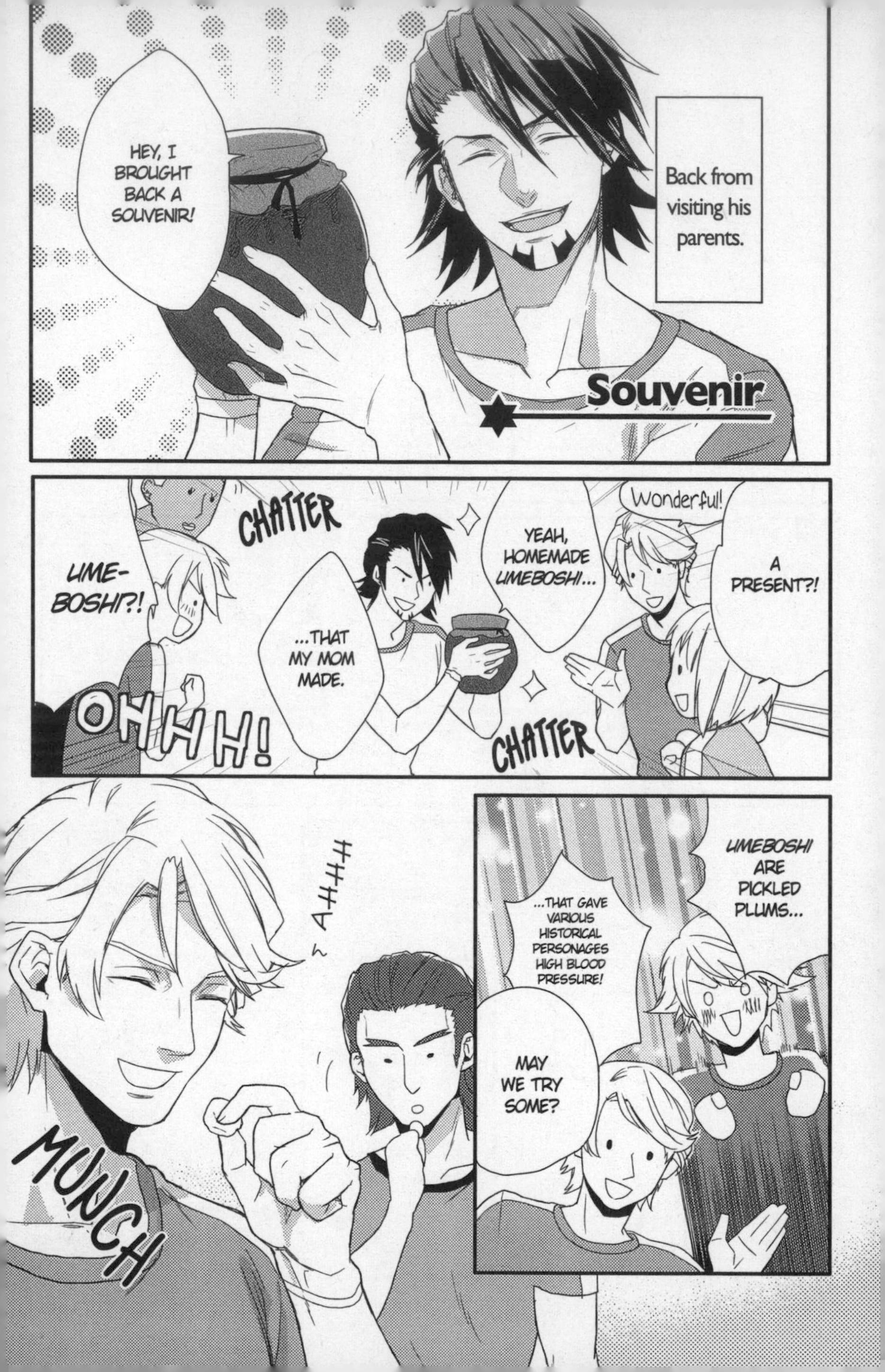
Souvenir
Back from visiting his parents.
HEY, I BROUGHT BACK A SOUVENIR!
A PRESENT?!
Wonderful!
YEAH, HOMEMADE UMEBOSHI...
...THAT MY MOM MADE.
CHATTER
UME-BOSHI?!
CHATTER
OHHHH!
UMEBOSHI ARE PICKLED PLUMS...
...THAT GAVE VARIOUS HISTORICAL PERSONAGES HIGH BLOOD PRESSURE!
MAY WE TRY SOME?
AHHHH
MUNCH

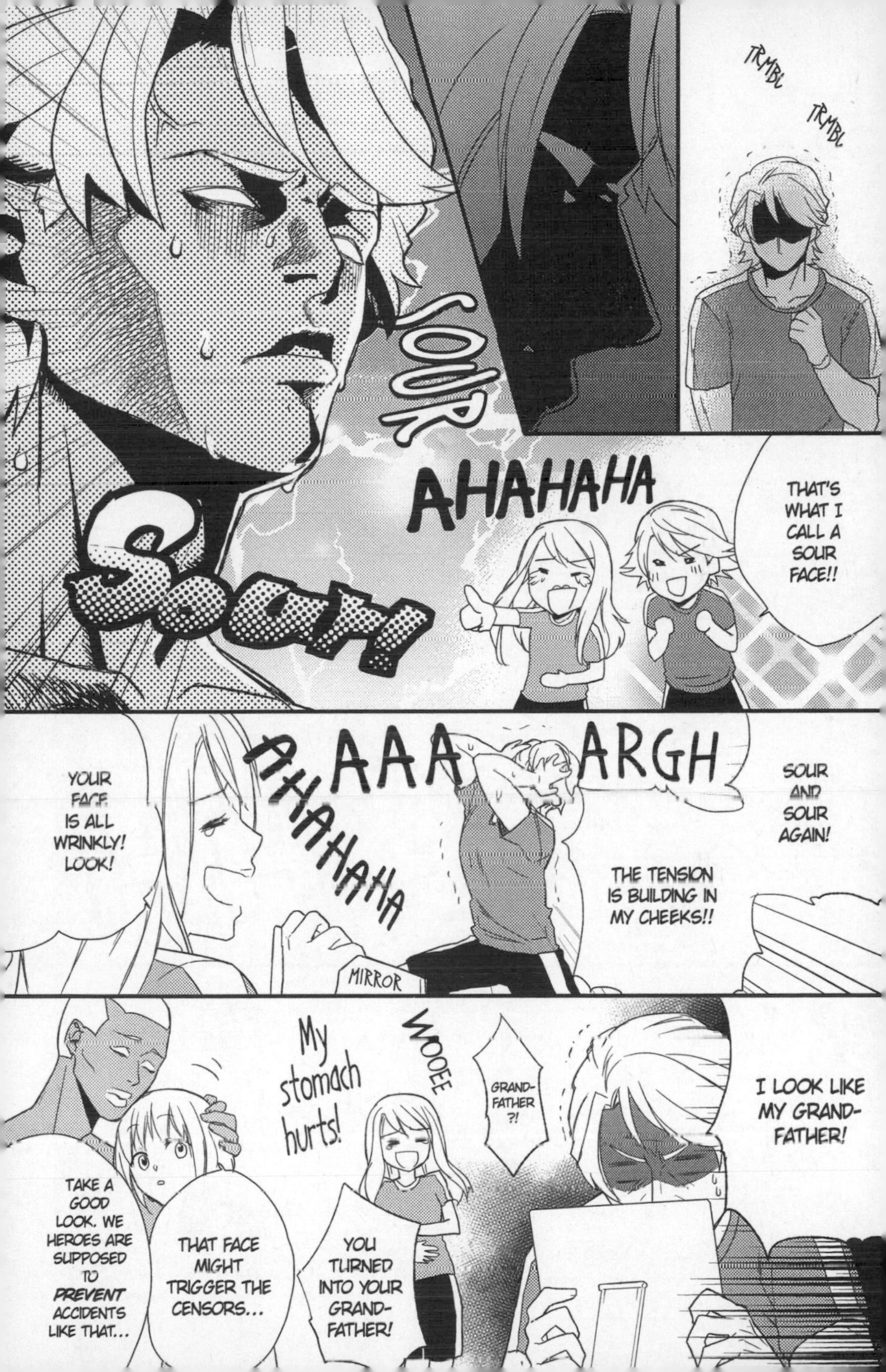
TRMBL
TRMBL
SOUR
SOUR!
AHAHAHA
THAT'S WHAT I CALL A SOUR FACE!!
SOUR AND SOUR AGAIN!
AAA ARGH
THE TENSION IS BUILDING IN MY CHEEKS!!
AHAHAHAHA
YOUR FACE IS ALL WRINKLY! LOOK!
MIRROR
I LOOK LIKE MY GRAND-FATHER!
GRAND-FATHER ?!
WOOEE
My stomach hurts!
YOU TURNED INTO YOUR GRAND-FATHER!
THAT FACE MIGHT TRIGGER THE CENSORS...
TAKE A GOOD LOOK. WE HEROES ARE SUPPOSED TO *PREVENT* ACCIDENTS LIKE THAT...

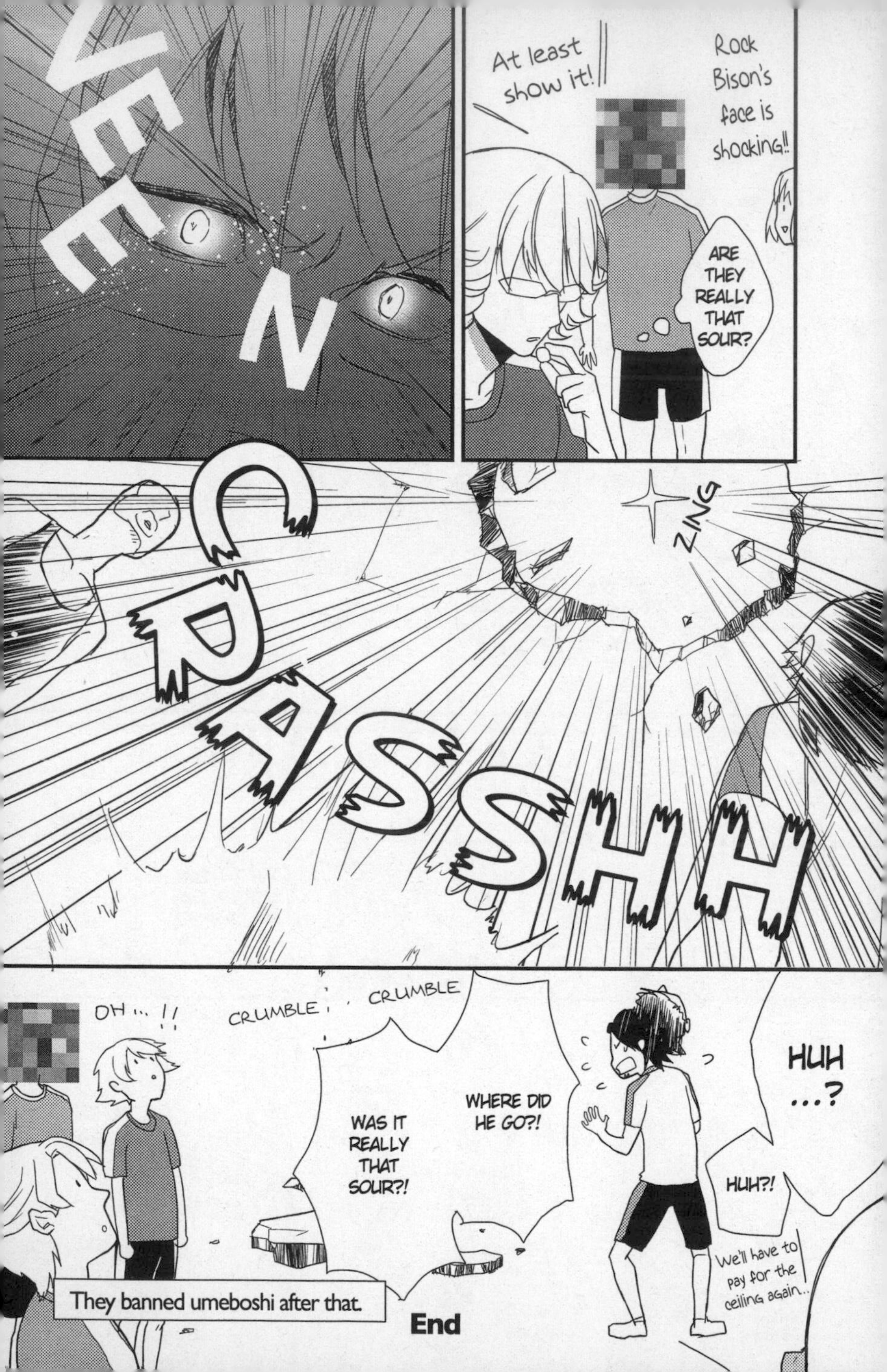
Rock Bison's face is shocking!!
At least show it!
ARE THEY REALLY THAT SOUR?
VEEN
ZING
CRASSHH
HUH ...?
HUH?!
We'll have to pay for the ceiling again...
WHERE DID HE GO?!
WAS IT REALLY THAT SOUR?!
CRUMBLE CRUMBLE
CRUMBLE
OH... !!
They banned umeboshi after that.
End

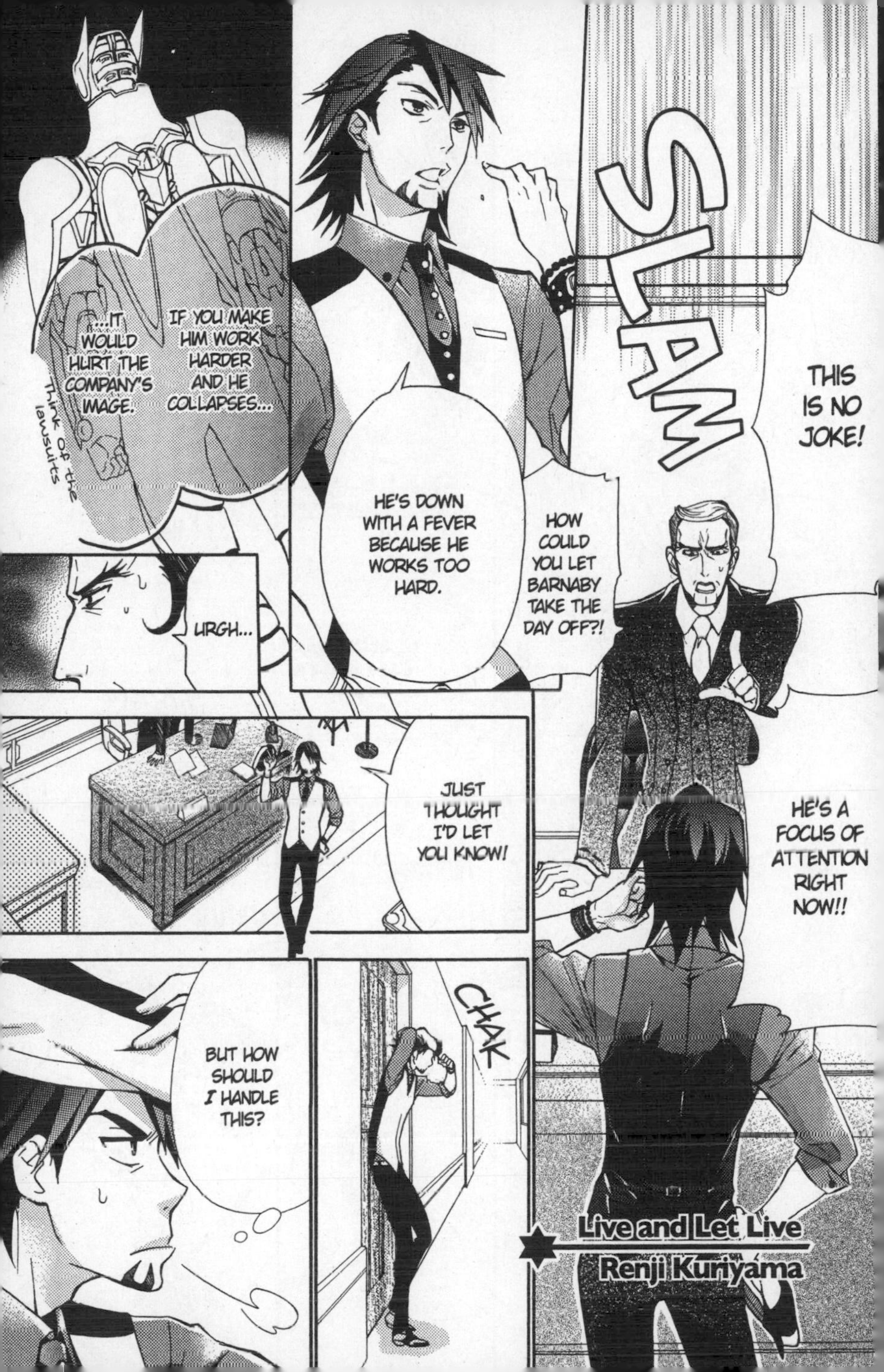
SLAM
THIS IS NO JOKE!
HOW COULD YOU LET BARNABY TAKE THE DAY OFF?!
HE'S A FOCUS OF ATTENTION RIGHT NOW!!
HE'S DOWN WITH A FEVER BECAUSE HE WORKS TOO HARD.
IF YOU MAKE HIM WORK HARDER AND HE COLLAPSES...
...IT WOULD HURT THE COMPANY'S IMAGE.
Think of the lawsuits
URGH...
JUST THOUGHT I'D LET YOU KNOW!
CHAK
BUT HOW SHOULD I HANDLE THIS?
Live and Let Live
Renji Kuriyama

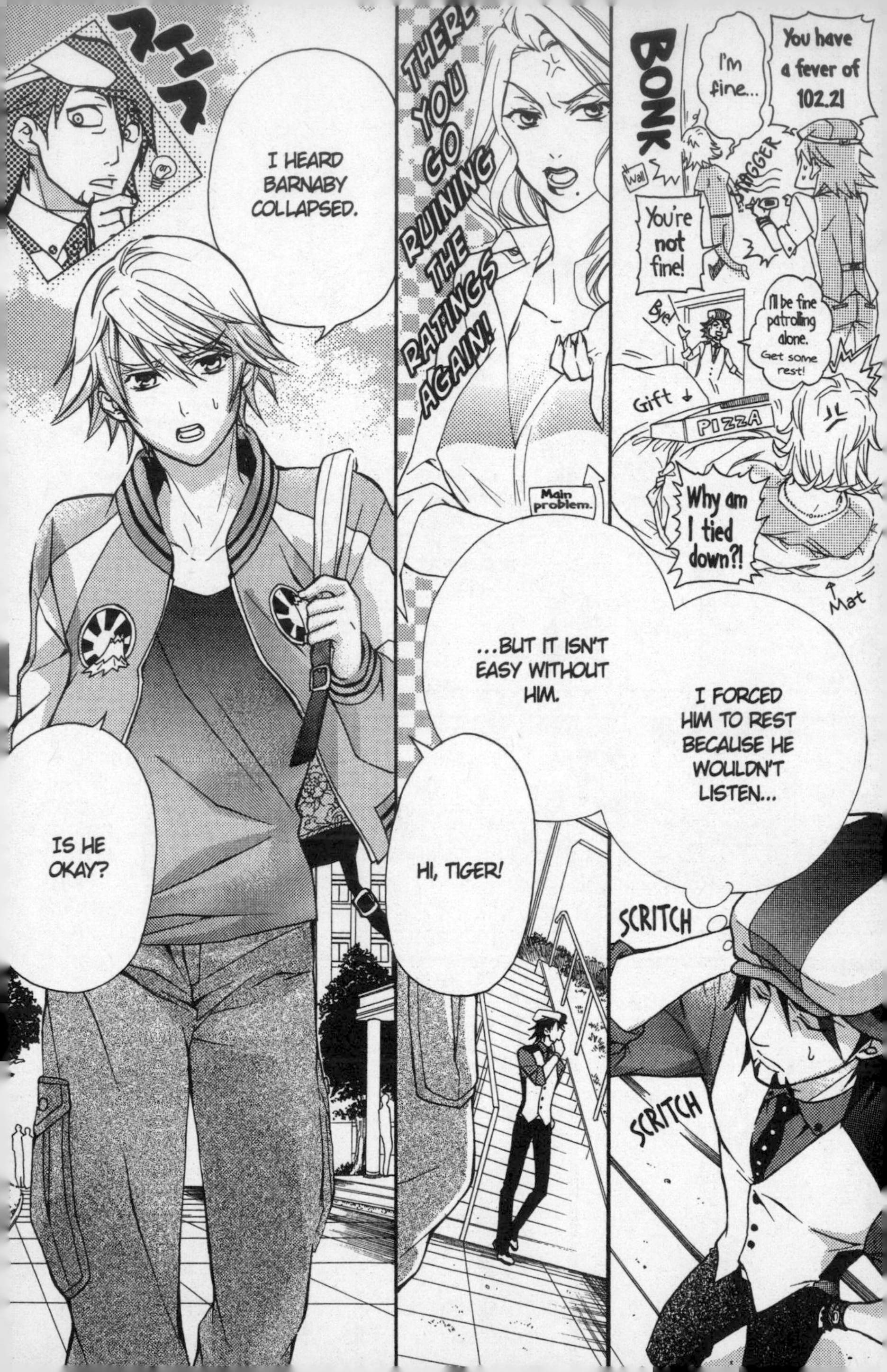
You have a fever of 102.2!
I'm fine...
BONK
Wall
STAGGER
You're not fine!
Bye!
I'll be fine patrolling alone. Get some rest!
Gift ↓
PIZZA
Why am I tied down?!
↑ Mat
I FORCED HIM TO REST BECAUSE HE WOULDN'T LISTEN...
SCRITCH
SCRITCH
THERE YOU GO RUINING THE RATINGS AGAIN!
Main problem.
...BUT IT ISN'T EASY WITHOUT HIM.
HI, TIGER!
I HEARD BARNABY COLLAPSED.
IS HE OKAY?

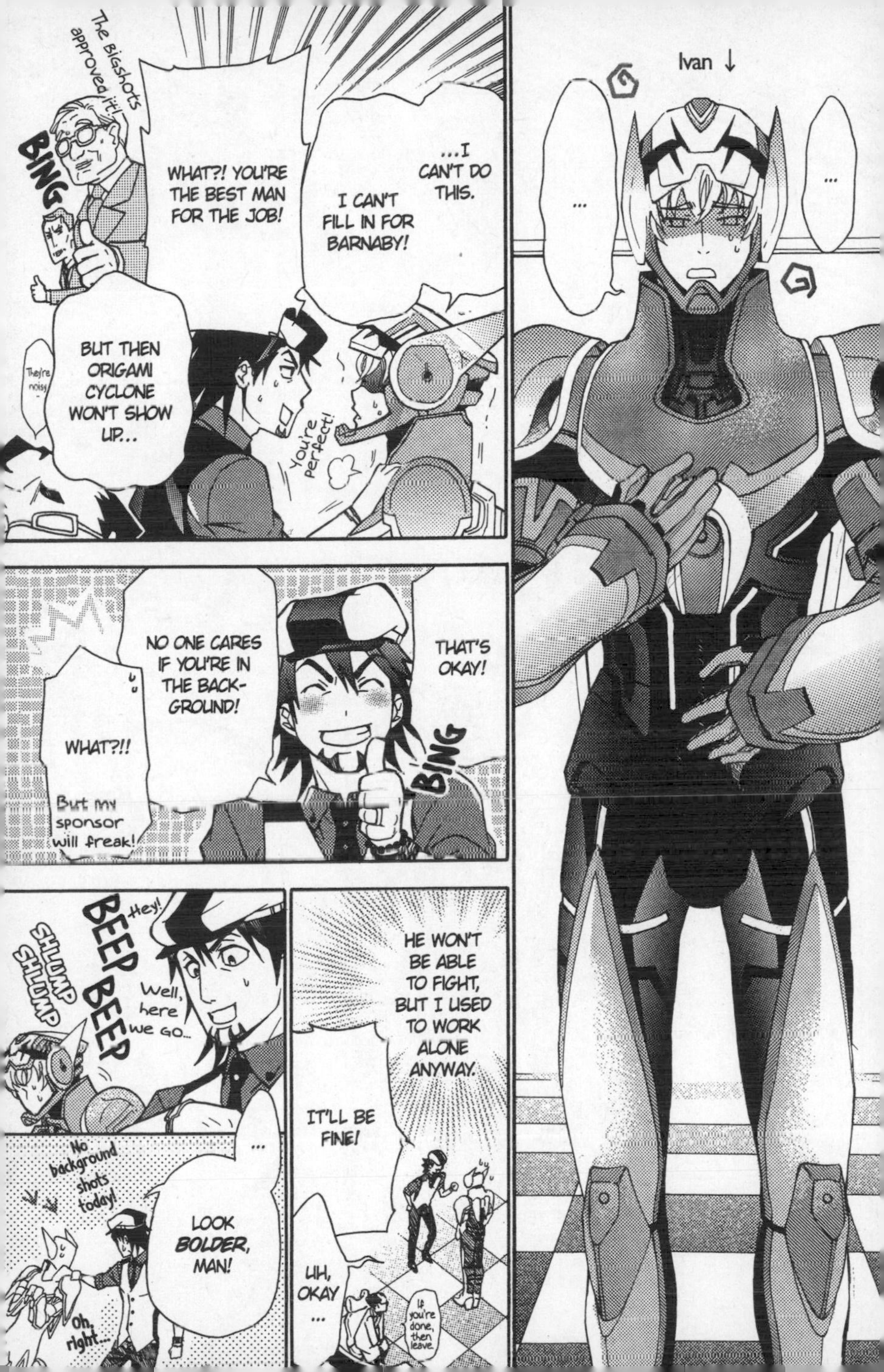
Ivan ↓
...
...
...I CAN'T DO THIS.
I CAN'T FILL IN FOR BARNABY!
WHAT?! YOU'RE THE BEST MAN FOR THE JOB!
The Bigshots approved it!
BING
You're perfect!
BUT THEN ORIGAMI CYCLONE WON'T SHOW UP...
They're noisy.
THAT'S OKAY!
NO ONE CARES IF YOU'RE IN THE BACK-GROUND!
BING
WHAT?!!
But my sponsor will freak!
HE WON'T BE ABLE TO FIGHT, BUT I USED TO WORK ALONE ANYWAY.
IT'LL BE FINE!
If you're done, then leave.
UH, OKAY ...
Hey!
BEEP BEEP
Well, here we go...
SHLUMP SHLUMP
...
No background shots today!
LOOK BOLDER, MAN!
Oh, right...

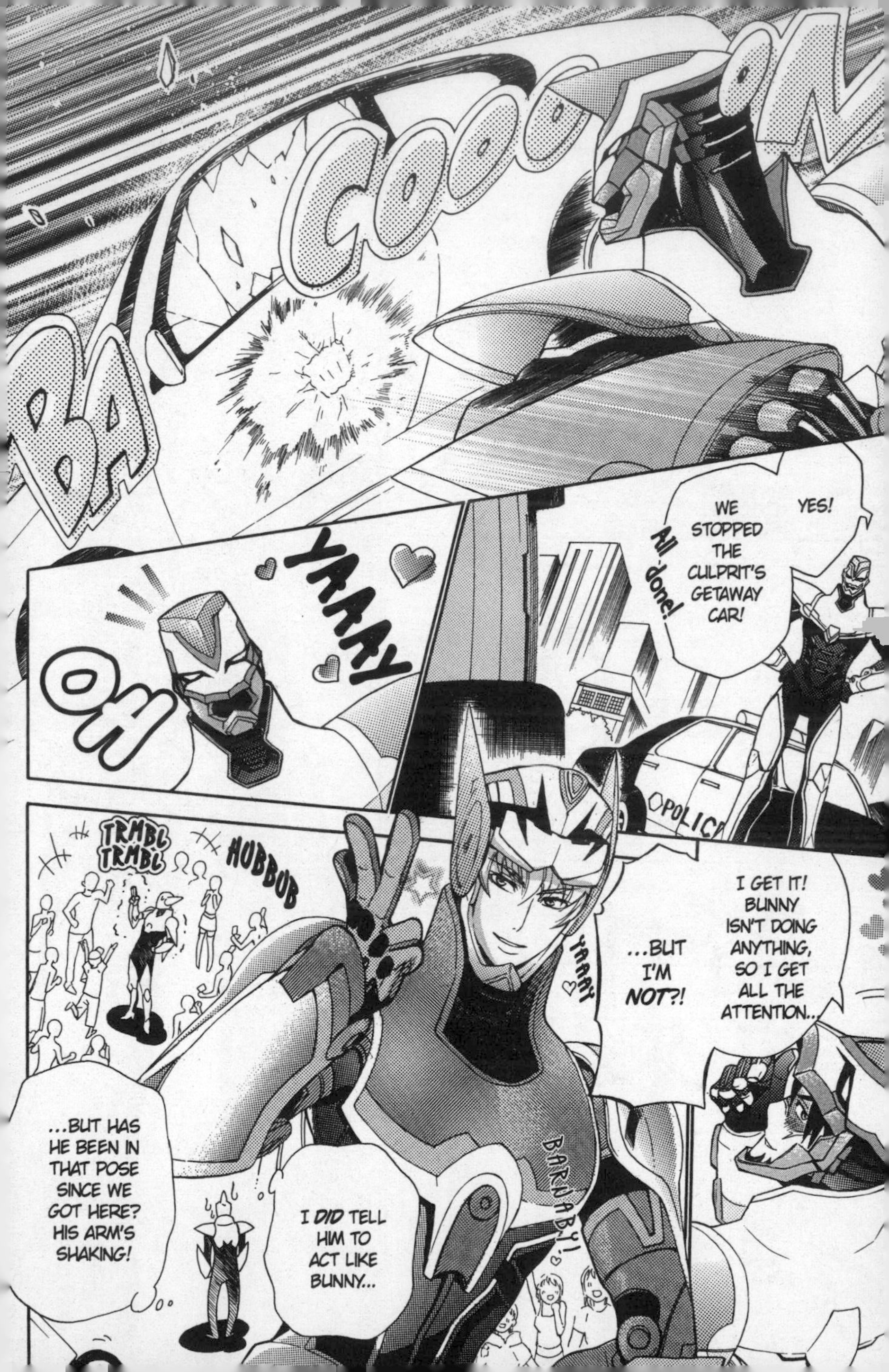
BACOOOON
YES!
WE STOPPED THE CULPRIT'S GETAWAY CAR!
All done!
YAAAY
OH
I GET IT! BUNNY ISN'T DOING ANYTHING, SO I GET ALL THE ATTENTION...
...BUT I'M *NOT*?!
YAAAY
BARNABY!
HUBBUB
TRMBL TRMBL
I *DID* TELL HIM TO ACT LIKE BUNNY...
...BUT HAS HE BEEN IN THAT POSE SINCE WE GOT HERE? HIS ARM'S SHAKING!

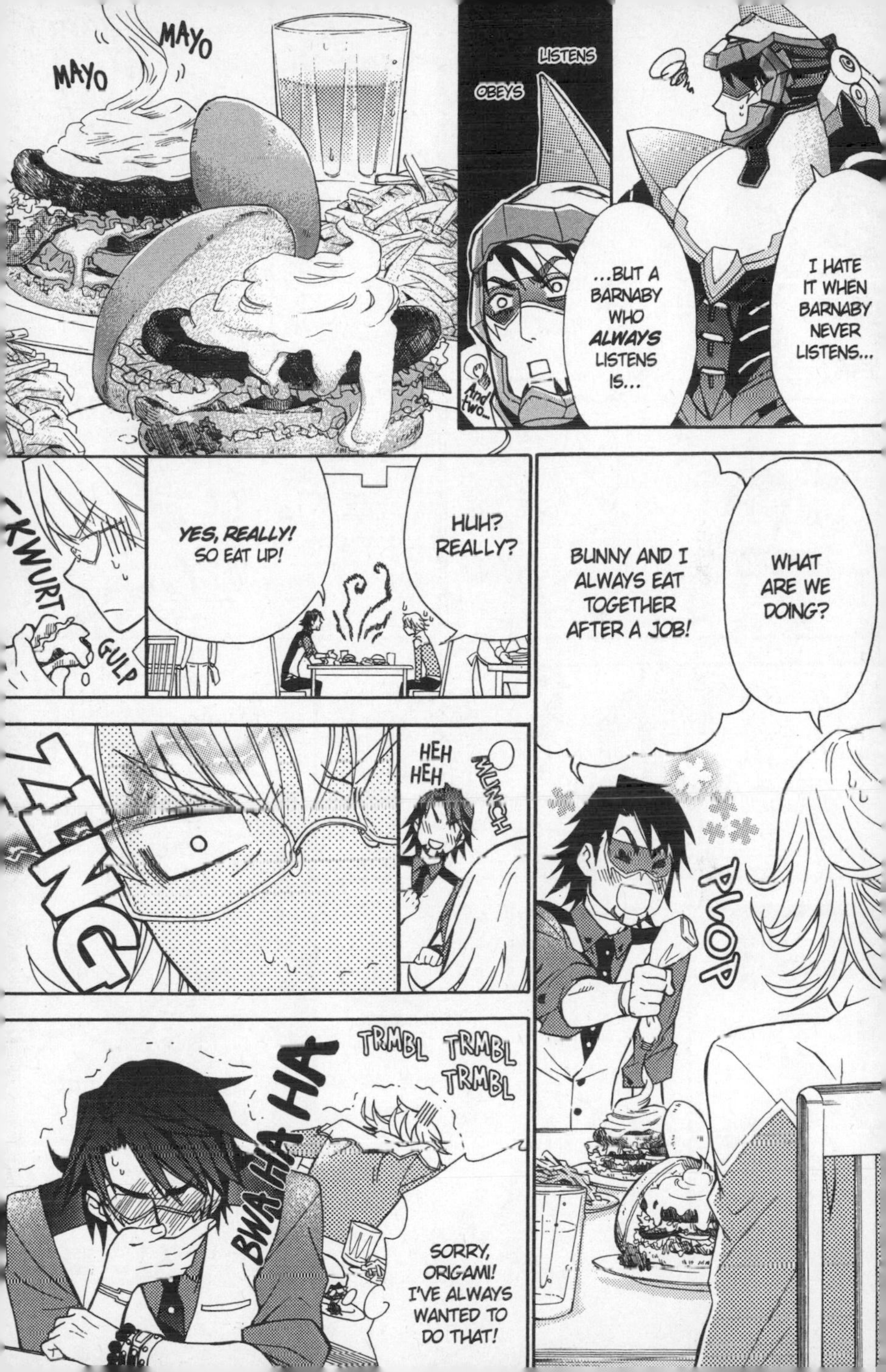
LISTENS
OBEYS
I HATE IT WHEN BARNABY NEVER LISTENS...
...BUT A BARNABY WHO *ALWAYS* LISTENS IS...
And two...
MAYO
MAYO
WHAT ARE WE DOING?
BUNNY AND I ALWAYS EAT TOGETHER AFTER A JOB!
PLOP
HUH? REALLY?
YES, REALLY! SO EAT UP!
-KWURT
GULP
MUNCH
HEH HEH
ZING
TRMBL TRMBL TRMBL
BWA HA HA
SORRY, ORIGAMI! I'VE ALWAYS WANTED TO DO THAT!

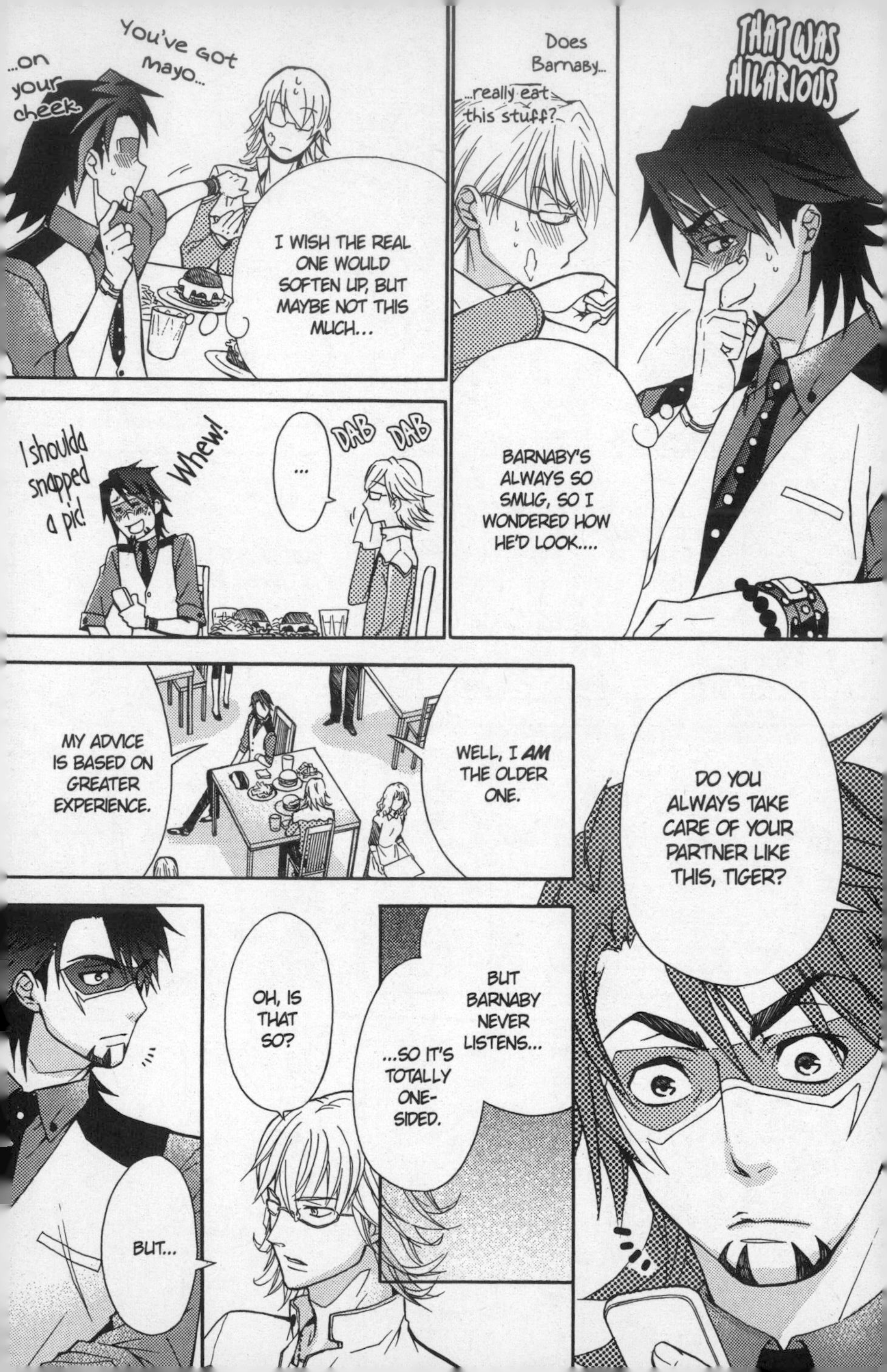
THAT WAS HILARIOUS
BARNABY'S ALWAYS SO SMUG, SO I WONDERED HOW HE'D LOOK....
Does Barnaby...
...really eat this stuff?
You've got mayo...
...on your cheek
I WISH THE REAL ONE WOULD SOFTEN UP, BUT MAYBE NOT THIS MUCH...
DAB DAB
...
Whew!
I shoulda snapped a pic!
DO YOU ALWAYS TAKE CARE OF YOUR PARTNER LIKE THIS, TIGER?
WELL, I *AM* THE OLDER ONE.
MY ADVICE IS BASED ON GREATER EXPERIENCE.
BUT BARNABY NEVER LISTENS...
...SO IT'S TOTALLY ONE-SIDED.
OH, IS THAT SO?
BUT...

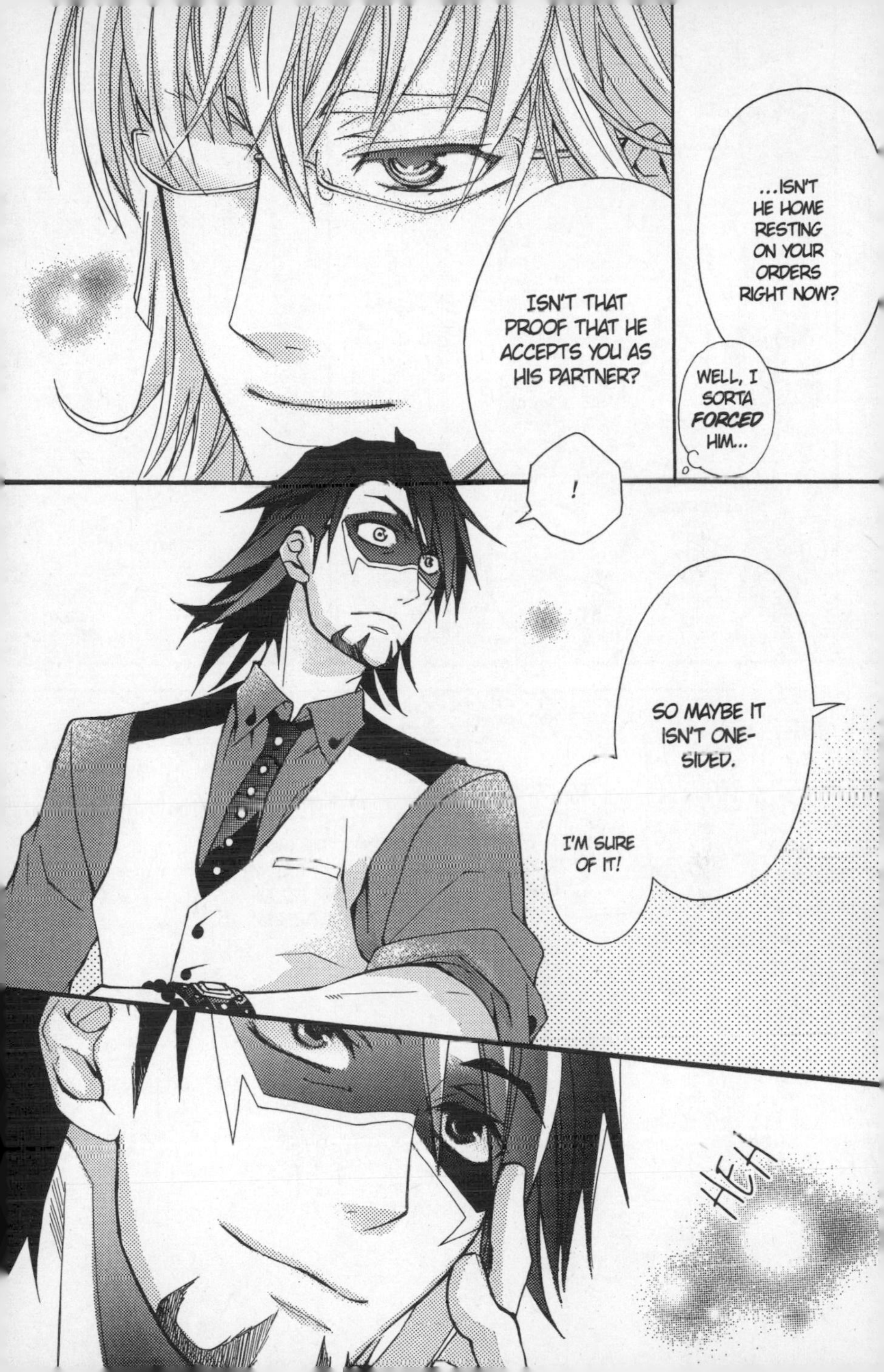
...ISN'T HE HOME RESTING ON YOUR ORDERS RIGHT NOW?
WELL, I SORTA *FORCED* HIM...
ISN'T THAT PROOF THAT HE ACCEPTS YOU AS HIS PARTNER?
!
SO MAYBE IT ISN'T ONE-SIDED.
I'M SURE OF IT!
HEH

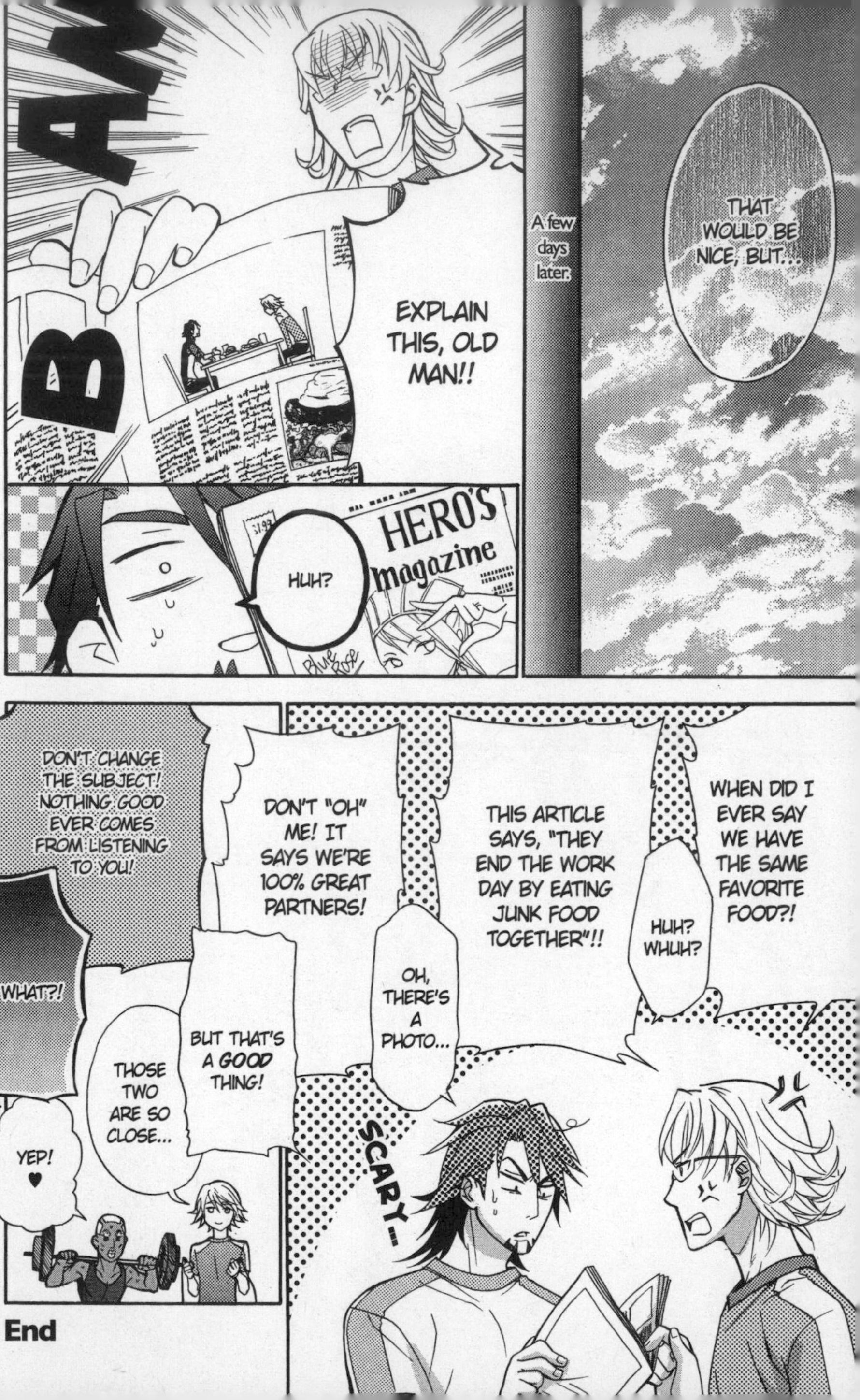
THAT WOULD BE NICE, BUT...
A few days later.
BAM
EXPLAIN THIS, OLD MAN!!
HERO'S magazine
HUH?
WHEN DID I EVER SAY WE HAVE THE SAME FAVORITE FOOD?!
HUH? WHUH?
THIS ARTICLE SAYS, "THEY END THE WORK DAY BY EATING JUNK FOOD TOGETHER"!!
OH, THERE'S A PHOTO...
DON'T "OH" ME! IT SAYS WE'RE 100% GREAT PARTNERS!
BUT THAT'S A *GOOD* THING!
SCARY...
DON'T CHANGE THE SUBJECT! NOTHING GOOD EVER COMES FROM LISTENING TO YOU!
WHAT?!
THOSE TWO ARE SO CLOSE...
YEP! ♥
End

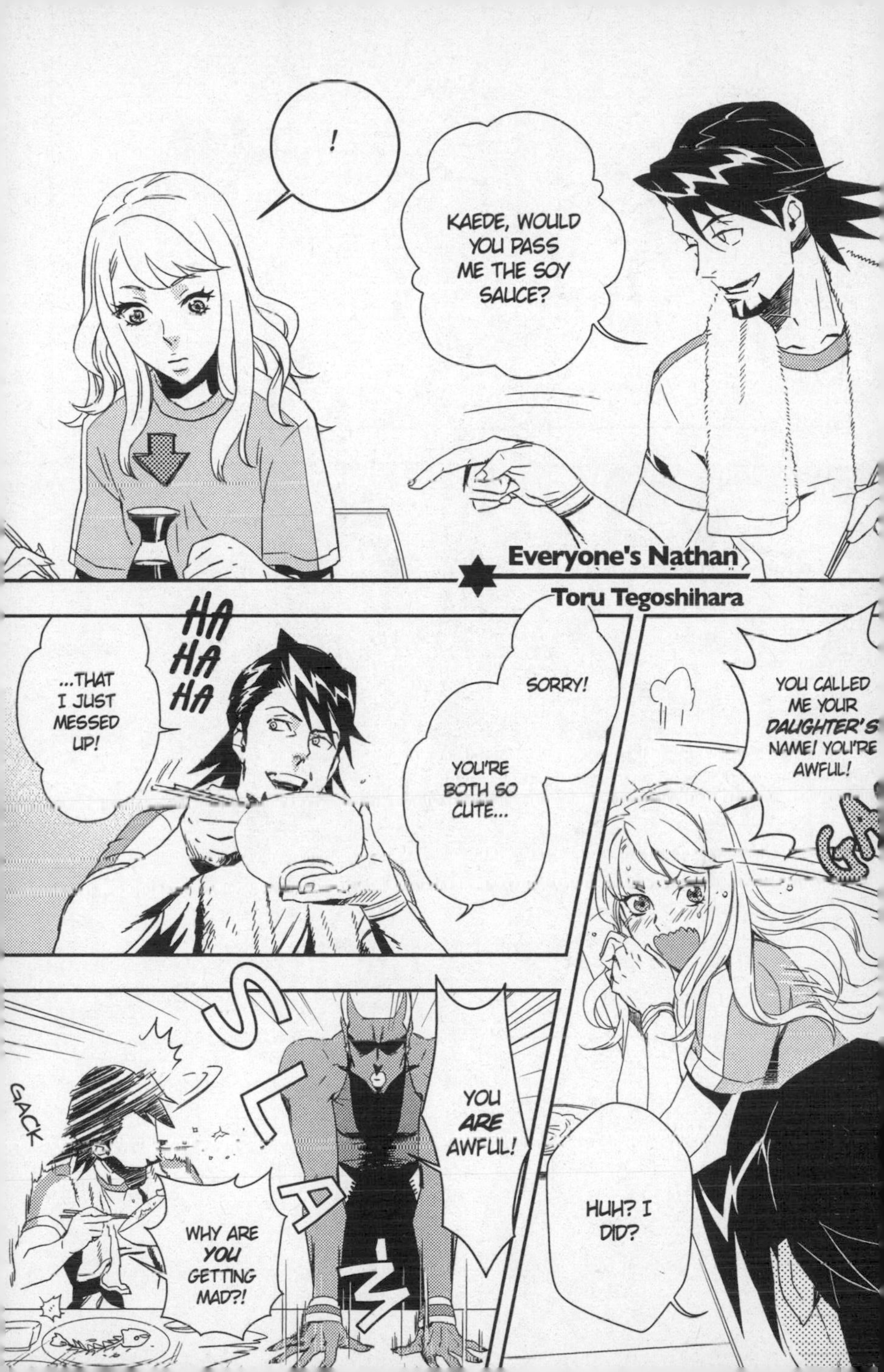
KAEDE, WOULD YOU PASS ME THE SOY SAUCE?
!
Everyone's Nathan
Toru Tegoshihara
YOU CALLED ME YOUR DAUGHTER'S NAME! YOU'RE AWFUL!
HUH? I DID?
SORRY!
YOU'RE BOTH SO CUTE...
HA HA HA
...THAT I JUST MESSED UP!
YOU ARE AWFUL!
SLAM
WHY ARE YOU GETTING MAD?!
GACK

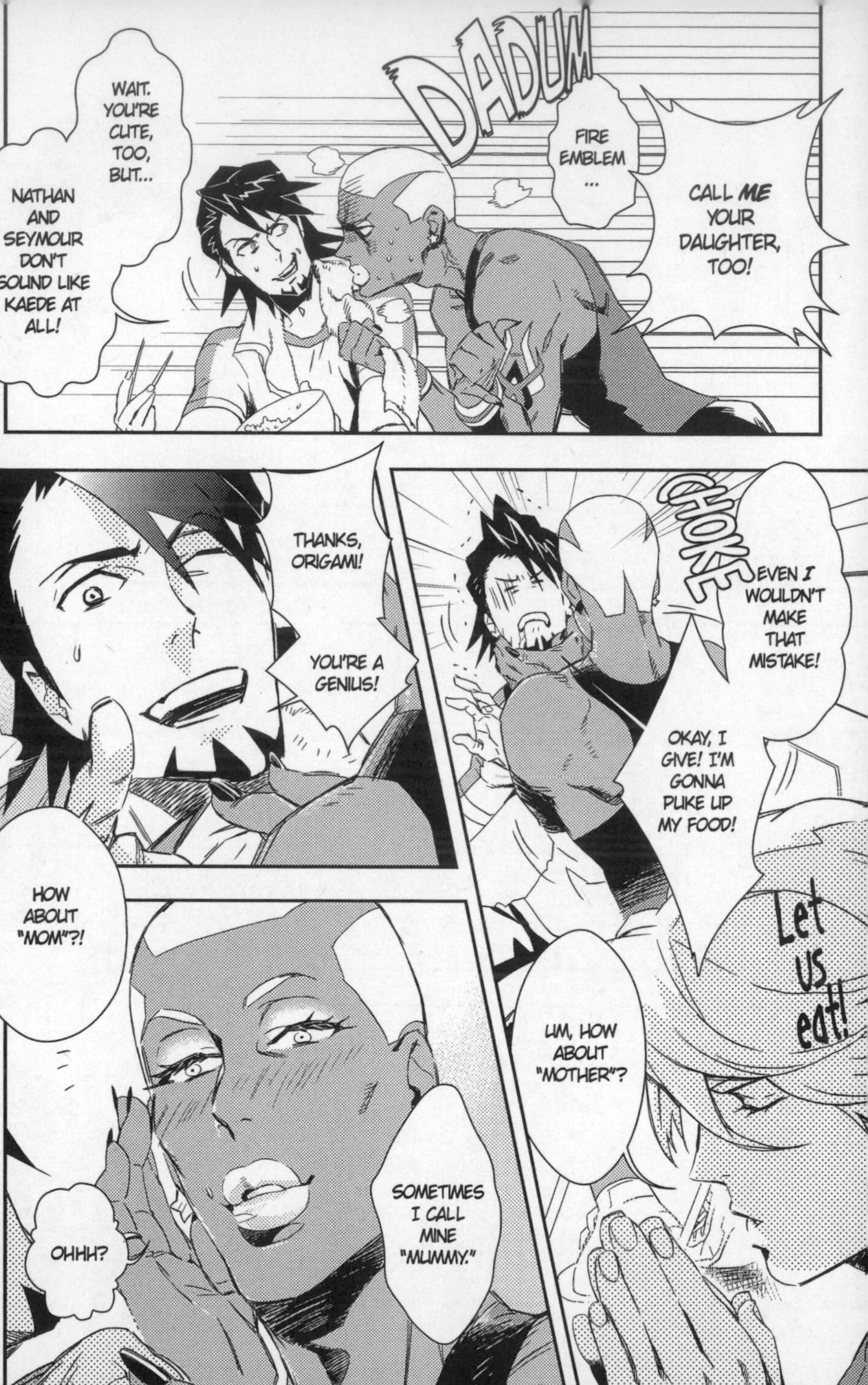
DADUM
CALL ME YOUR DAUGHTER, TOO!
FIRE EMBLEM ...
WAIT. YOU'RE CUTE, TOO, BUT...
NATHAN AND SEYMOUR DON'T SOUND LIKE KAEDE AT ALL!
CHOKE
EVEN I WOULDN'T MAKE THAT MISTAKE!
OKAY, I GIVE! I'M GONNA PUKE UP MY FOOD!
Let us eat!
UM, HOW ABOUT "MOTHER"?
THANKS, ORIGAMI!
YOU'RE A GENIUS!
HOW ABOUT "MOM"?!
OHHH?
SOMETIMES I CALL MINE "MUMMY."

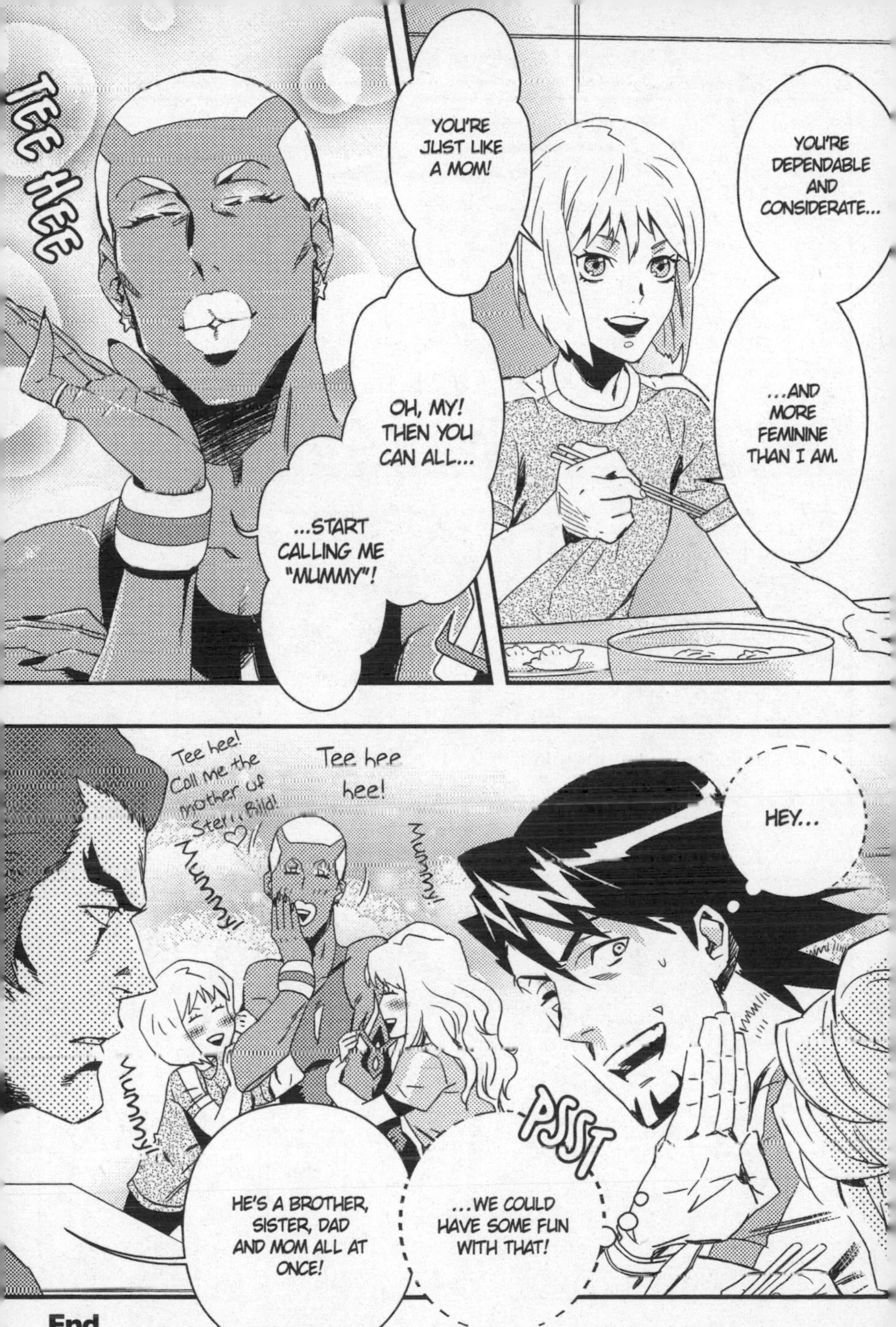
YOU'RE DEPENDABLE AND CONSIDERATE...
...AND MORE FEMININE THAN I AM.
YOU'RE JUST LIKE A MOM!
OH, MY! THEN YOU CAN ALL...
...START CALLING ME "MUMMY"!
TEE HEE
HEY...
PSSST
...WE COULD HAVE SOME FUN WITH THAT!
HE'S A BROTHER, SISTER, DAD AND MOM ALL AT ONCE!
Mummy!
Tee hee hee!
Mummy!
Tee hee! Call me the mother of Stern Bild!
Mummy!

End

A Hero's Worry - Sky High Chapter -

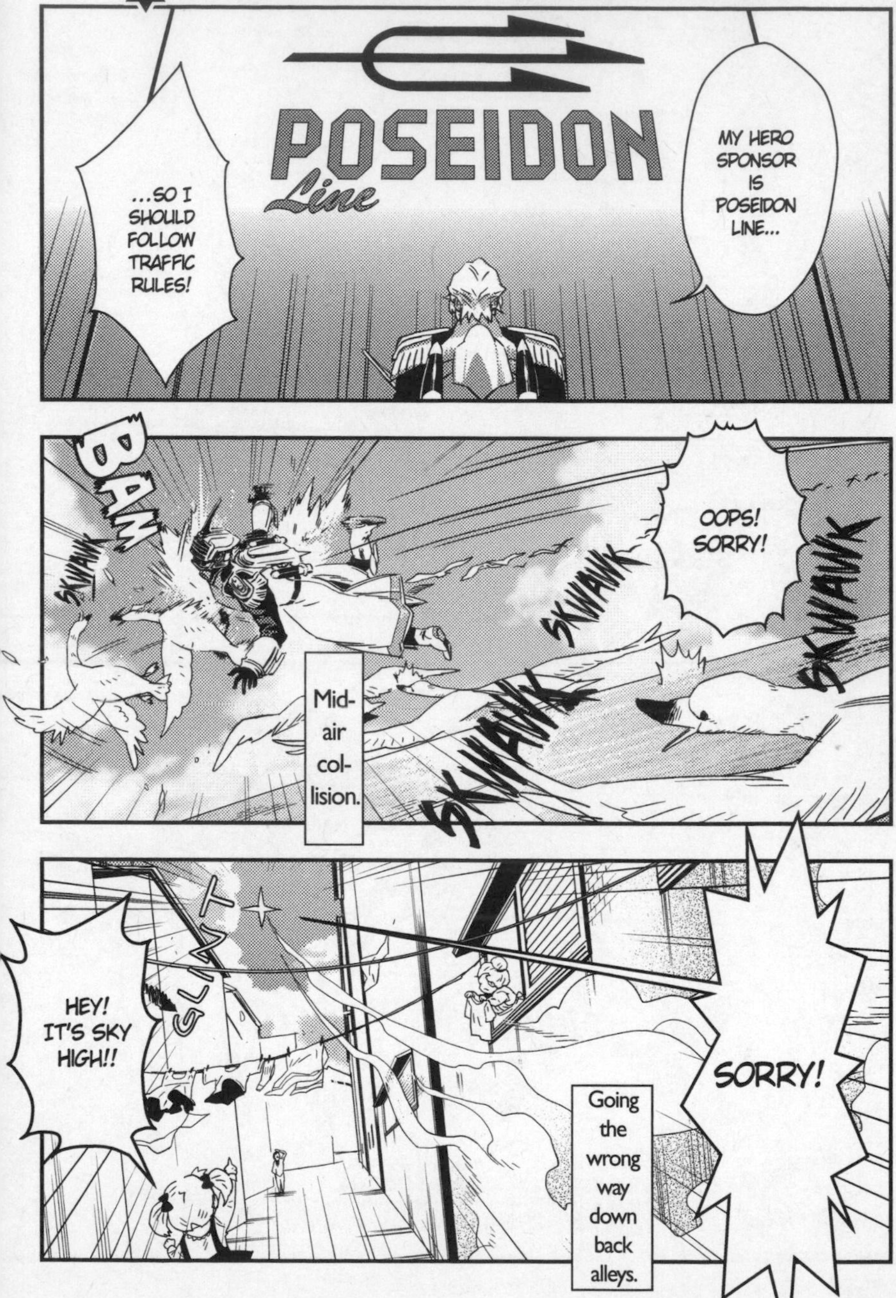
MY HERO SPONSOR IS POSEIDON LINE...
POSEIDON Line
...SO I SHOULD FOLLOW TRAFFIC RULES!
OOPS! SORRY!
SKWAWK
SKWAWK
BAM
SKWAWK
SKWAWK
SKWAWK
Mid-air col-lision.
SORRY!
Going the wrong way down back alleys.
HEY! IT'S SKY HIGH!!

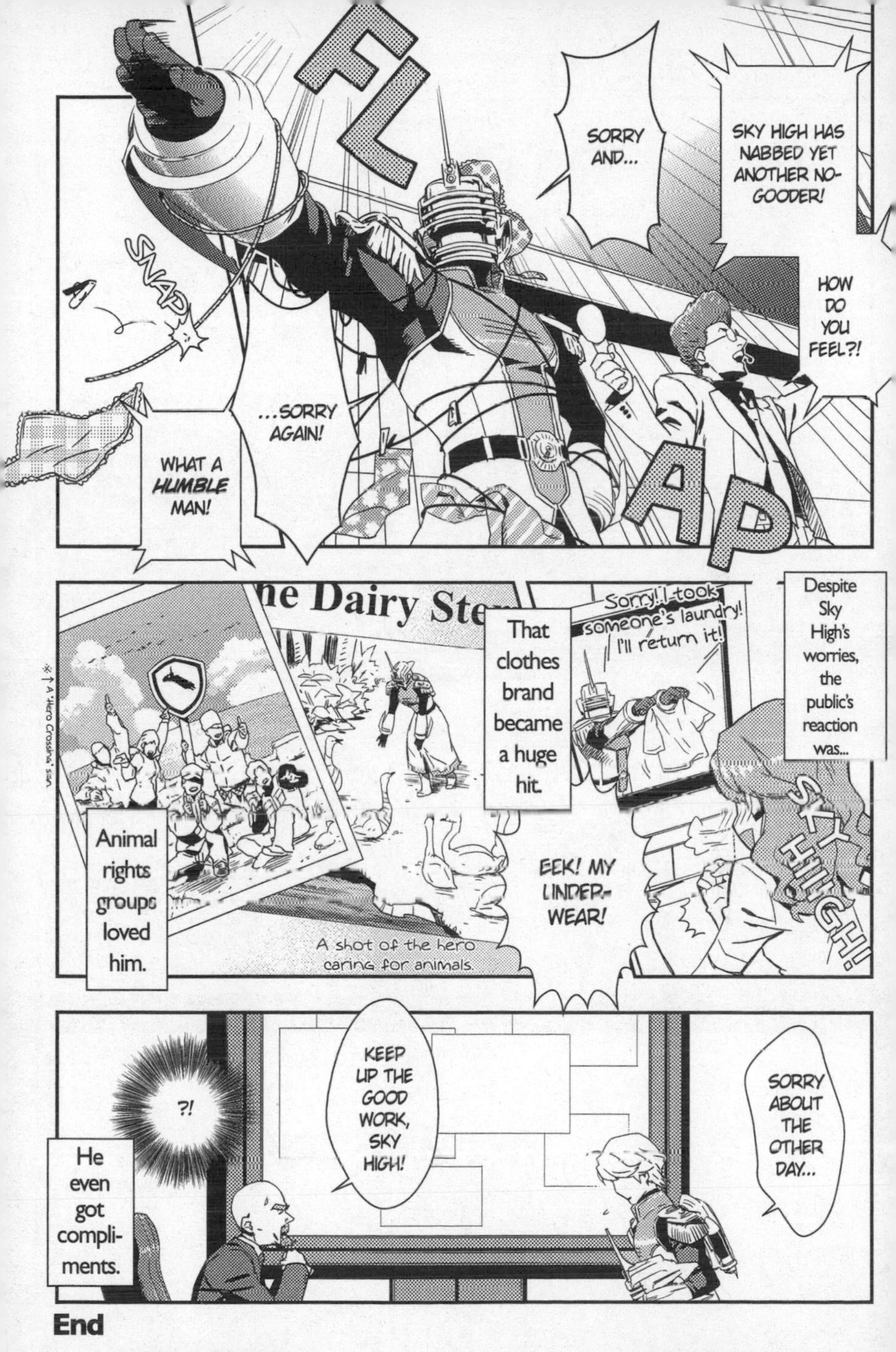
FL
SKY HIGH HAS NABBED YET ANOTHER NO-GOODER!
SORRY AND...
HOW DO YOU FEEL?!
AP
SNAP
...SORRY AGAIN!
WHAT A *HUMBLE* MAN!
Despite Sky High's worries, the public's reaction was...
SKY HIGH!
EEK! MY UNDERWEAR!
Sorry! I took someone's laundry! I'll return it!
That clothes brand became a huge hit.
he Dairy Ste
A shot of the hero caring for animals.
※↑ A "Hero Crossing" sign
Animal rights groups loved him.
SORRY ABOUT THE OTHER DAY...
KEEP UP THE GOOD WORK, SKY HIGH!
?!
He even got compli-ments.

End

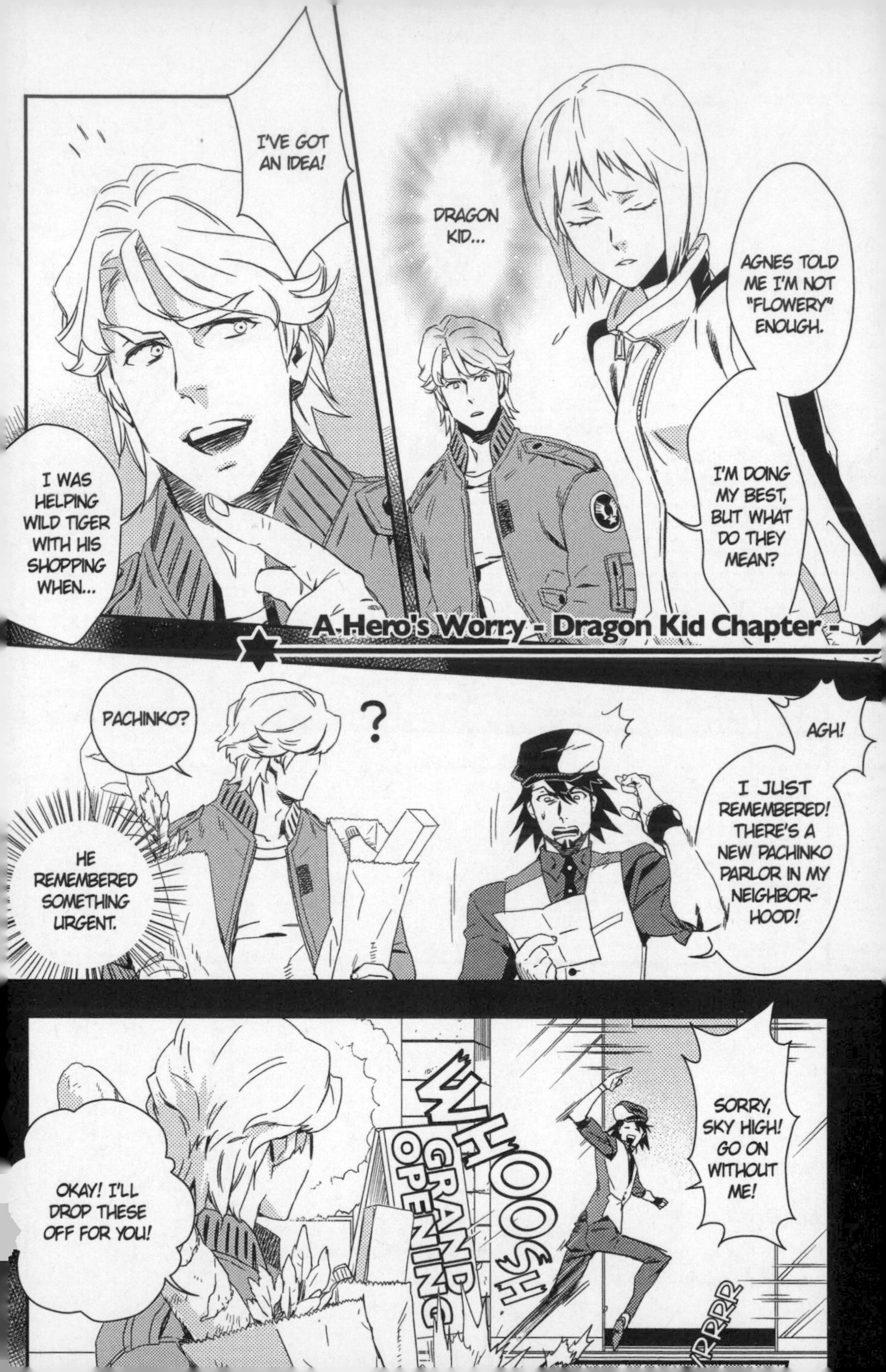
AGNES TOLD ME I'M NOT "FLOWERY" ENOUGH.
I'M DOING MY BEST, BUT WHAT DO THEY MEAN?
DRAGON KID...
I'VE GOT AN IDEA!
I WAS HELPING WILD TIGER WITH HIS SHOPPING WHEN...
A Hero's Worry - Dragon Kid Chapter -
AGH!
I JUST REMEMBERED! THERE'S A NEW PACHINKO PARLOR IN MY NEIGHBOR-HOOD!
PACHINKO?
?
HE REMEMBERED SOMETHING URGENT.
SORRY, SKY HIGH! GO ON WITHOUT ME!
WHOOOSH
GRAND OPENING
OKAY! I'LL DROP THESE OFF FOR YOU!

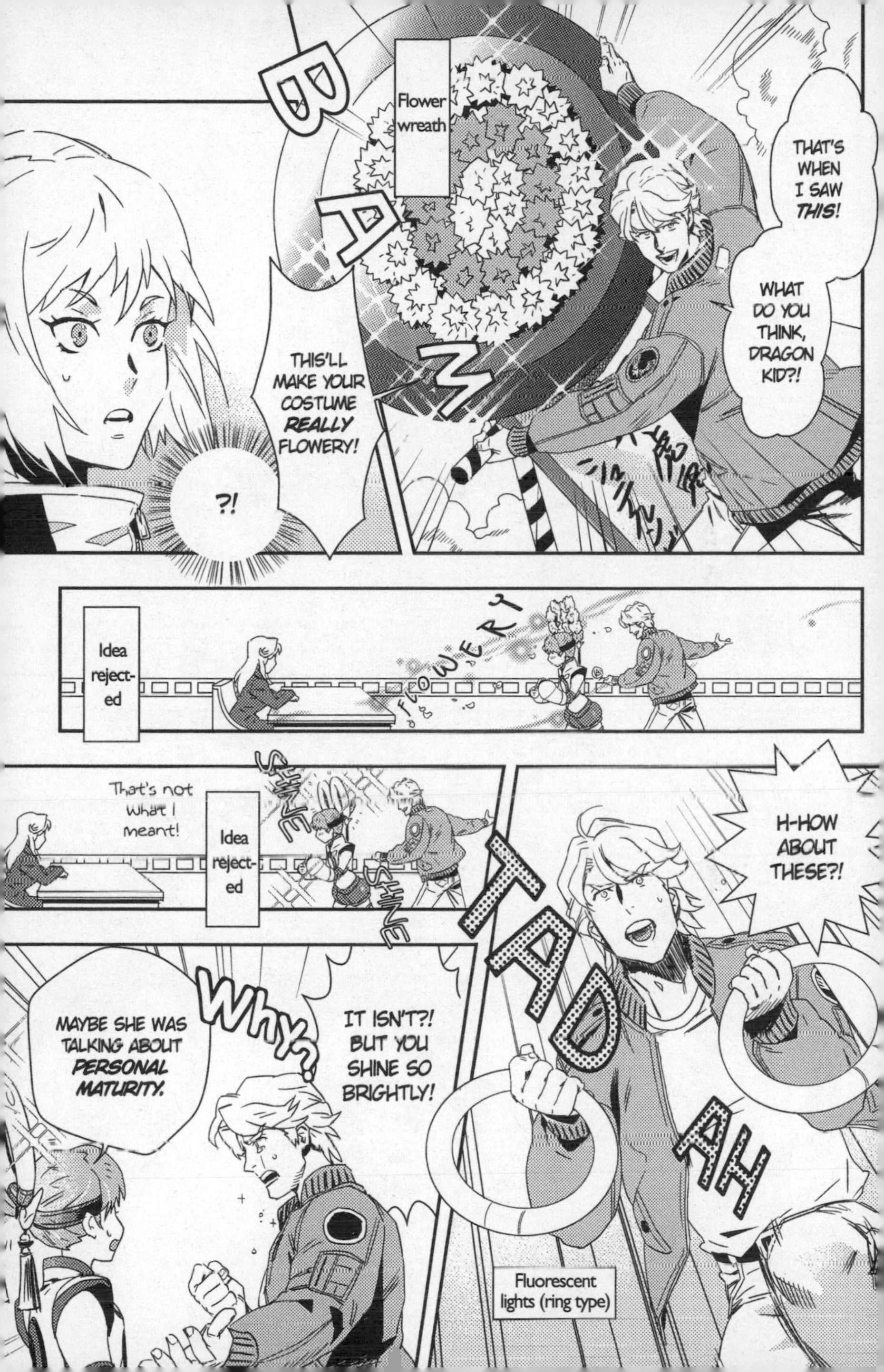
BAM
Flower wreath
THAT'S WHEN I SAW THIS!
WHAT DO YOU THINK, DRAGON KID?!
THIS'LL MAKE YOUR COSTUME REALLY FLOWERY!
?!
FLOWERY
Idea rejected
H-HOW ABOUT THESE?!
TADAH
Fluorescent lights (ring type)
SHINE
SHINE
Idea rejected
That's not what I meant!
IT ISN'T?! BUT YOU SHINE SO BRIGHTLY!
Why?
MAYBE SHE WAS TALKING ABOUT PERSONAL MATURITY.

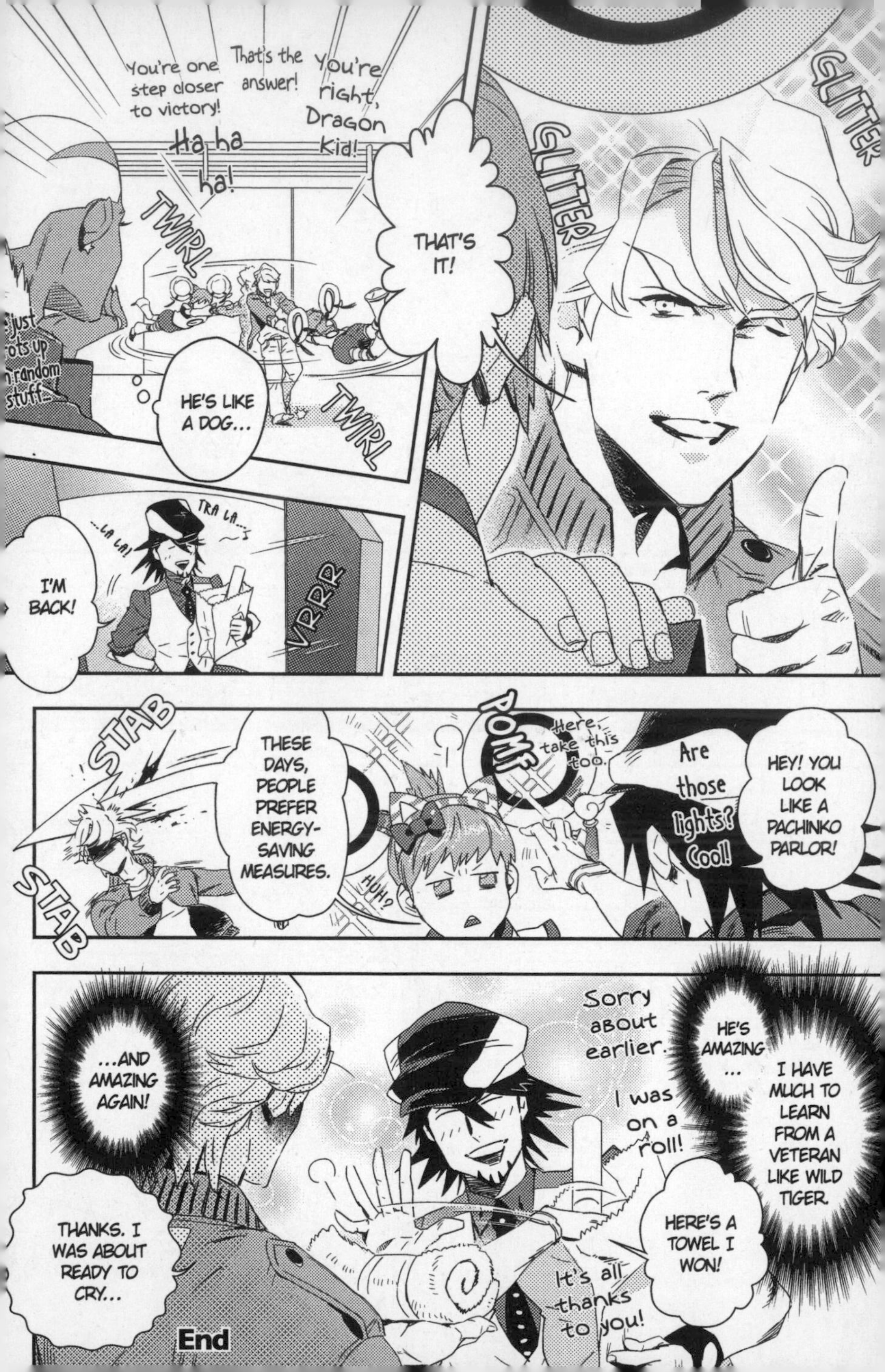
GLITTER
GLITTER
THAT'S IT!
You're right, Dragon kid!
That's the answer!
You're one step closer to victory!
Ha ha ha!
TWIRL
e just ots up n random stuff...
HE'S LIKE A DOG...
TWIRL
VRRR
TRA LA...
...LA LA!
I'M BACK!
HEY! YOU LOOK LIKE A PACHINKO PARLOR!
Are those lights? Cool!
Here, take this too.
POMF
HUH!?
THESE DAYS, PEOPLE PREFER ENERGY-SAVING MEASURES.
STAB
STAB
HE'S AMAZING...
I HAVE MUCH TO LEARN FROM A VETERAN LIKE WILD TIGER.
Sorry about earlier.
I was on a roll!
HERE'S A TOWEL I WON!
It's all thanks to you!
...AND AMAZING AGAIN!
THANKS. I WAS ABOUT READY TO CRY...
End

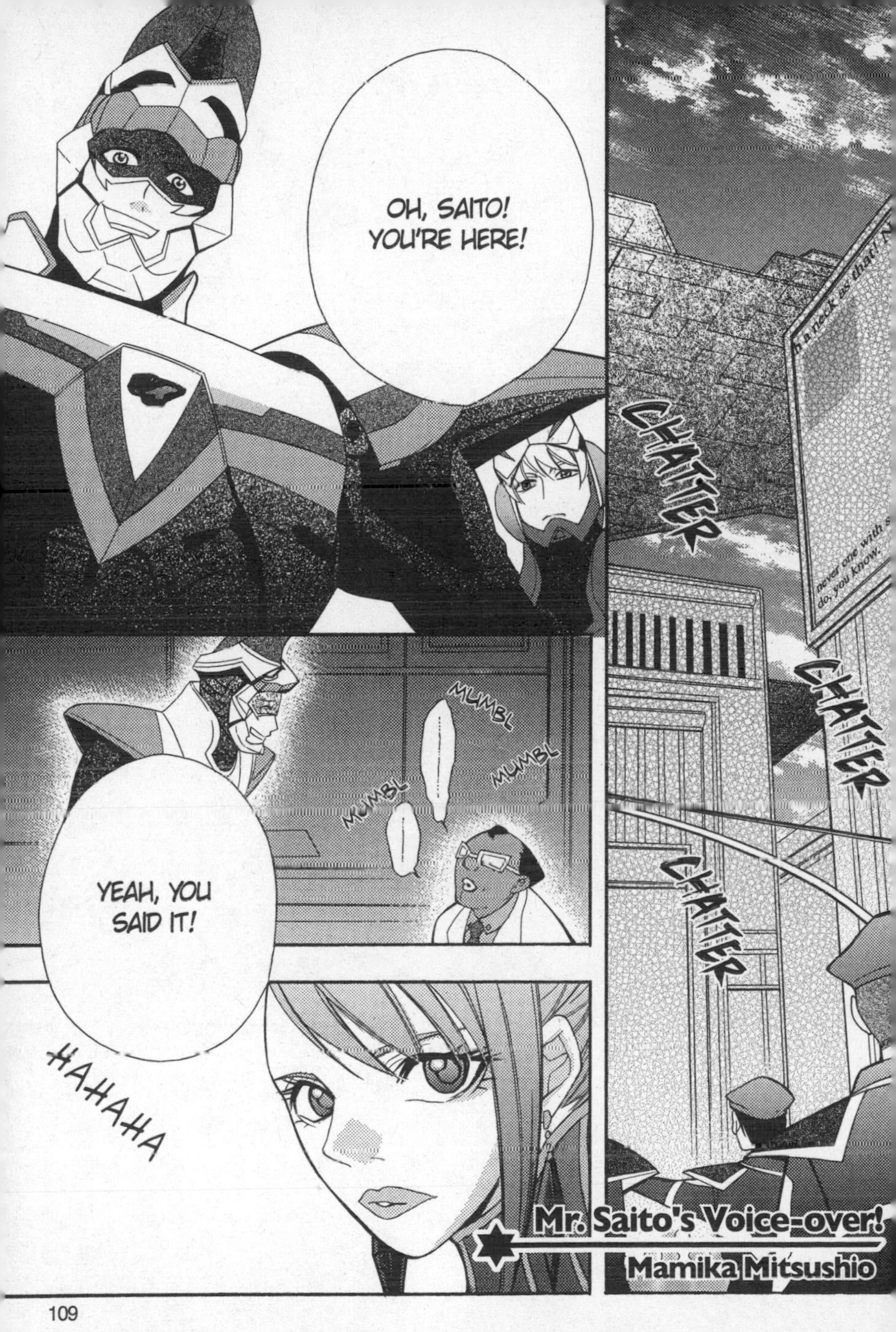
CHATTER
CHATTER
CHATTER
Mr. Saito's Voice-over!
Mamika Mitsushio
OH, SAITO! YOU'RE HERE!
MUMBL
MUMBL
MUMBL
YEAH, YOU SAID IT!
HAHAHA

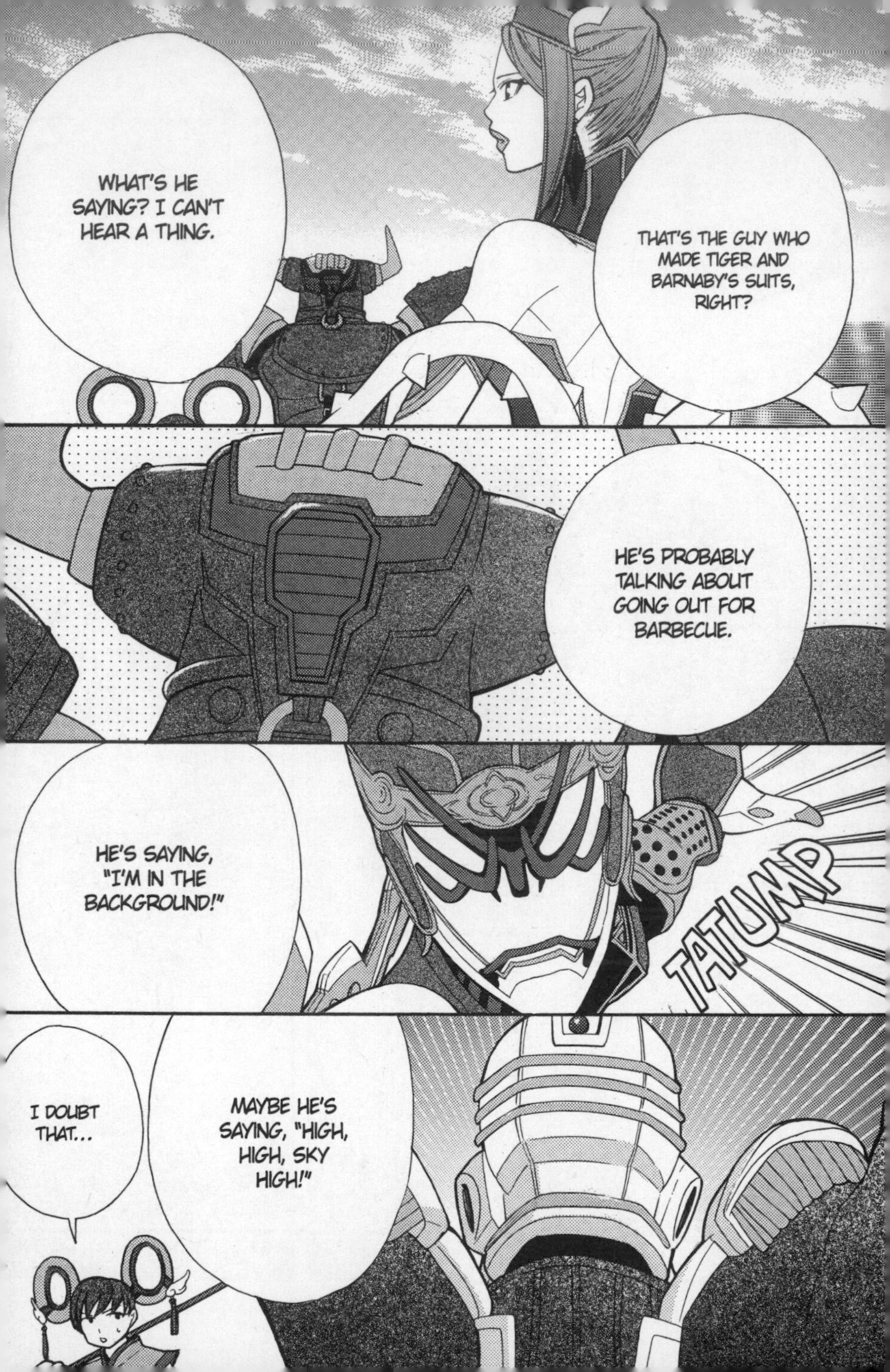

THAT'S THE GUY WHO MADE TIGER AND BARNABY'S SUITS, RIGHT?
WHAT'S HE SAYING? I CAN'T HEAR A THING.
HE'S PROBABLY TALKING ABOUT GOING OUT FOR BARBECUE.
TATUMP
HE'S SAYING, "I'M IN THE BACKGROUND!"
MAYBE HE'S SAYING, "HIGH, HIGH, SKY HIGH!"
I DOUBT THAT...

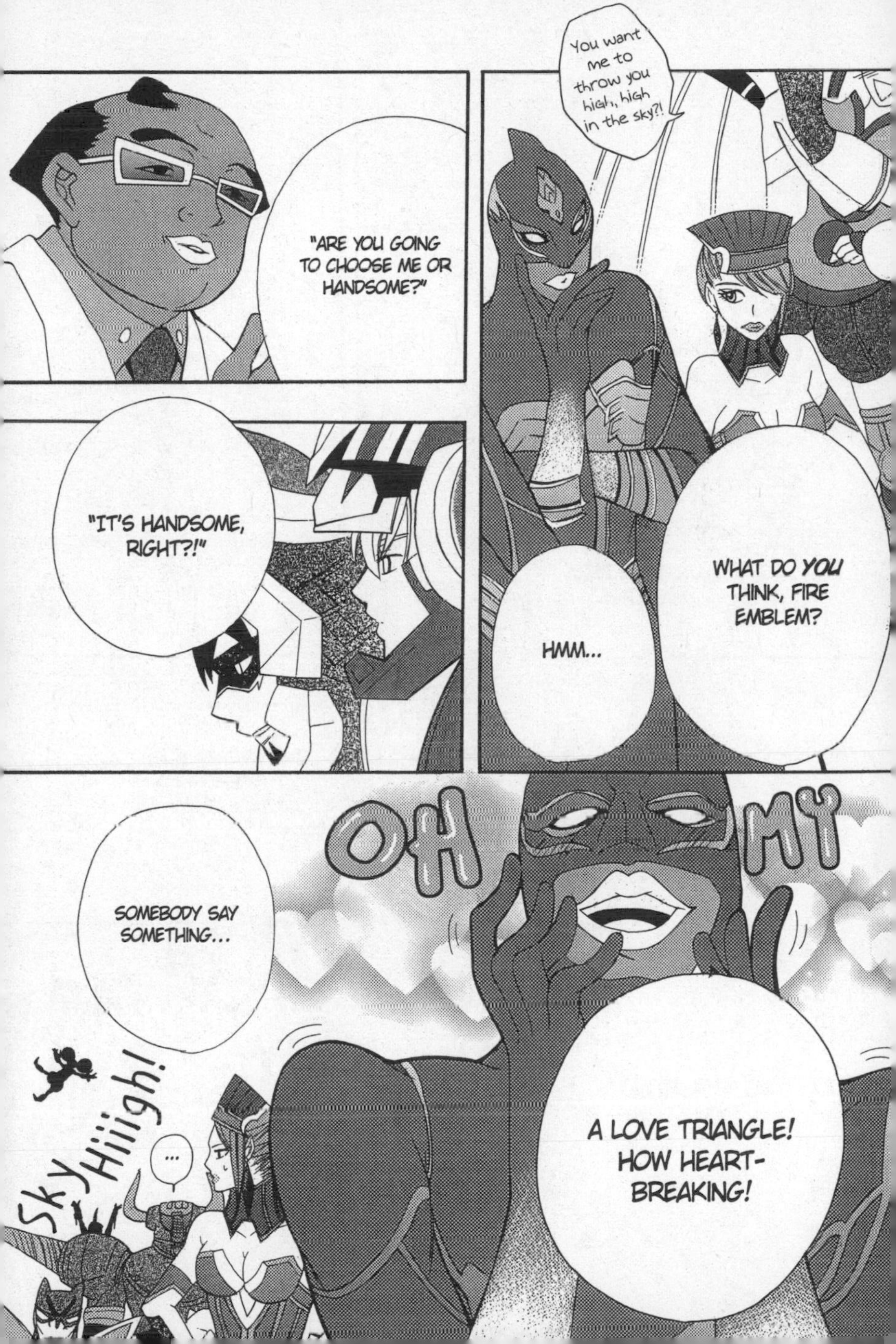
You want me to throw you high, high in the sky?!
WHAT DO *YOU* THINK, FIRE EMBLEM?
HMM...
"ARE YOU GOING TO CHOOSE ME OR HANDSOME?"
"IT'S HANDSOME, RIGHT?!"
OH MY
A LOVE TRIANGLE! HOW HEART-BREAKING!
SOMEBODY SAY SOMETHING...
...
Sky Hiiiigh!

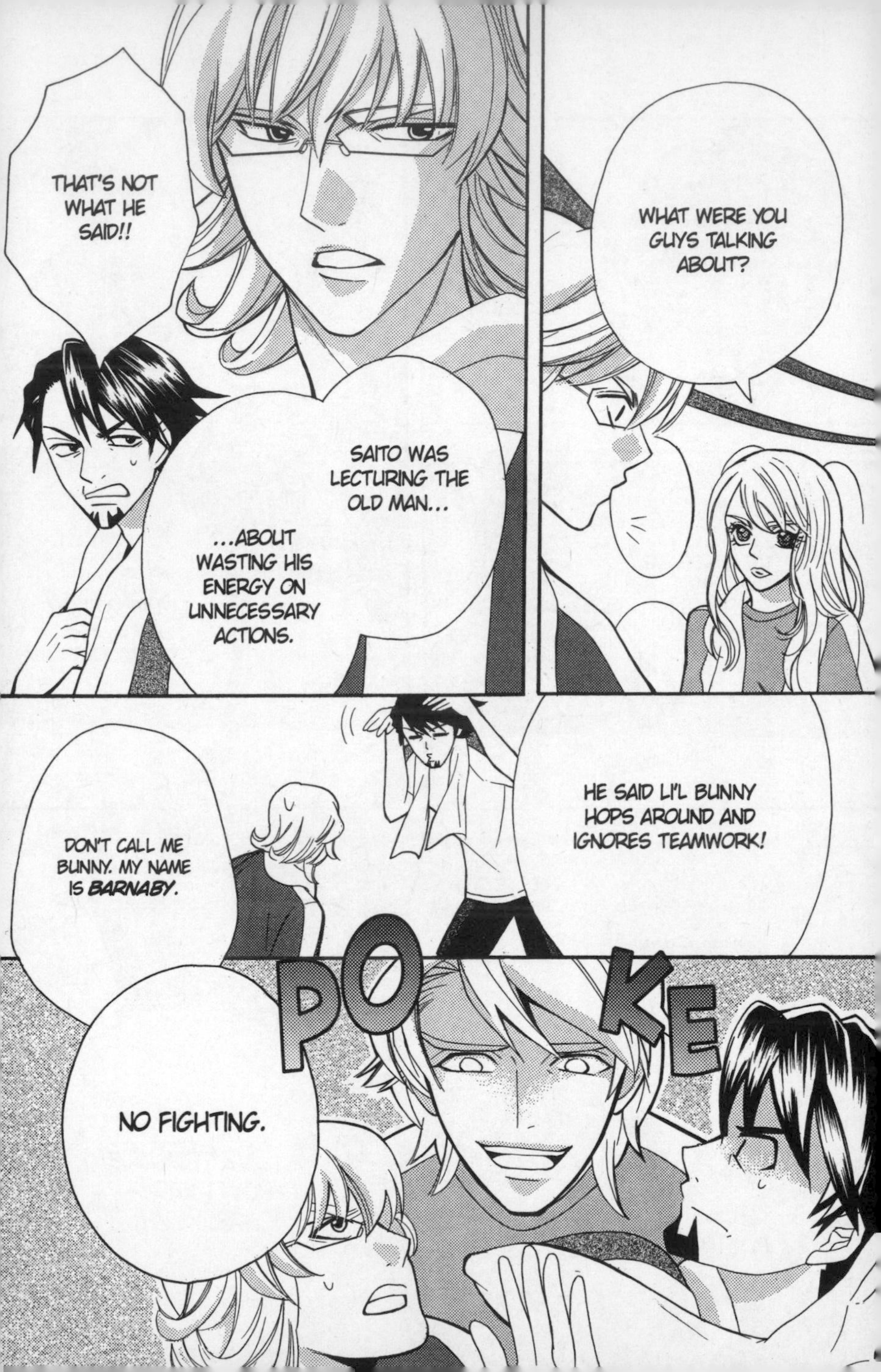
WHAT WERE YOU GUYS TALKING ABOUT?
SAITO WAS LECTURING THE OLD MAN...
...ABOUT WASTING HIS ENERGY ON UNNECESSARY ACTIONS.
THAT'S NOT WHAT HE SAID!!
HE SAID LI'L BUNNY HOPS AROUND AND IGNORES TEAMWORK!
DON'T CALL ME BUNNY. MY NAME IS *BARNABY*.
POKE
NO FIGHTING.

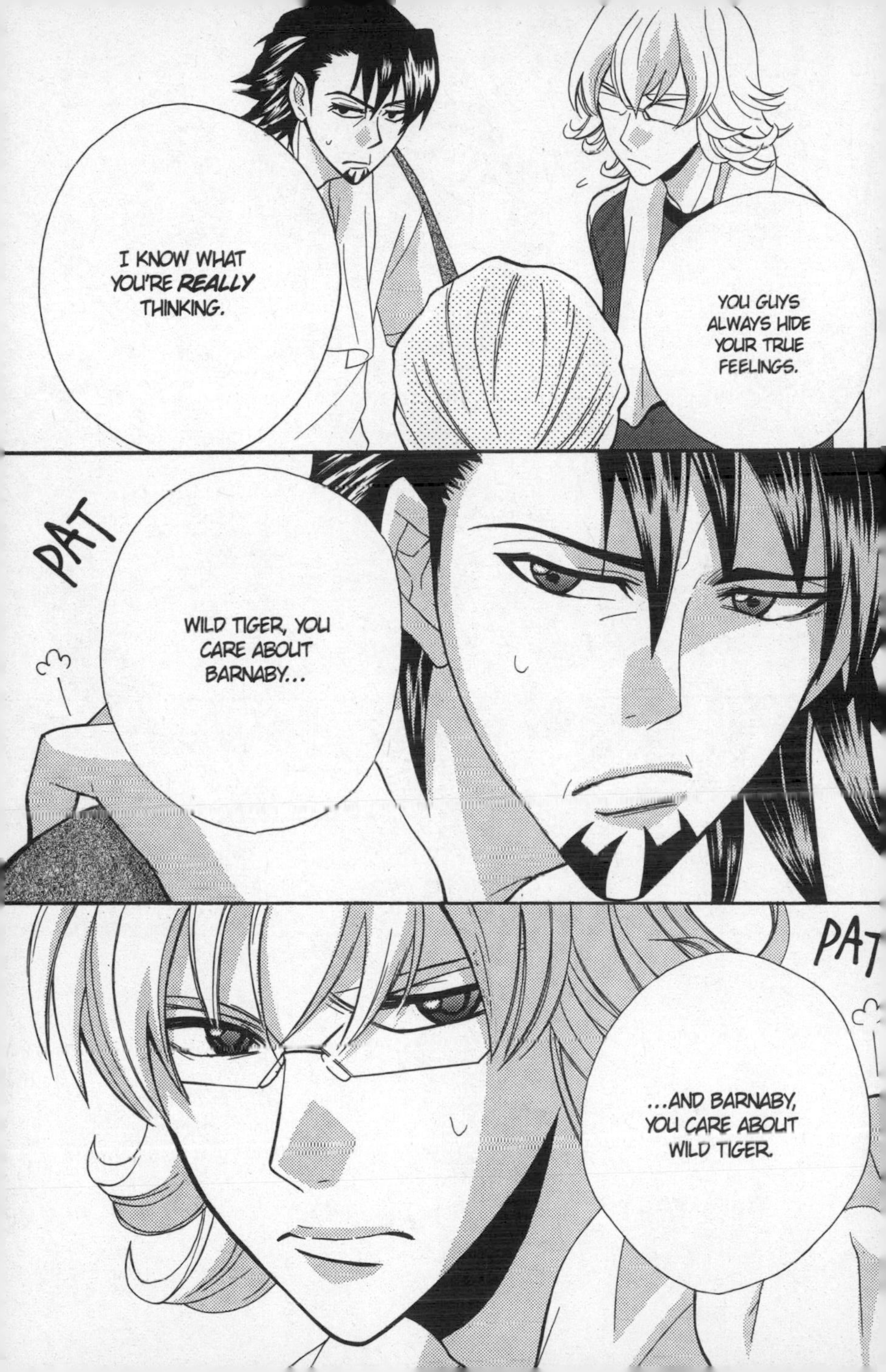
YOU GUYS ALWAYS HIDE YOUR TRUE FEELINGS.
I KNOW WHAT YOU'RE *REALLY* THINKING.
PAT
WILD TIGER, YOU CARE ABOUT BARNABY...
PAT
...AND BARNABY, YOU CARE ABOUT WILD TIGER.

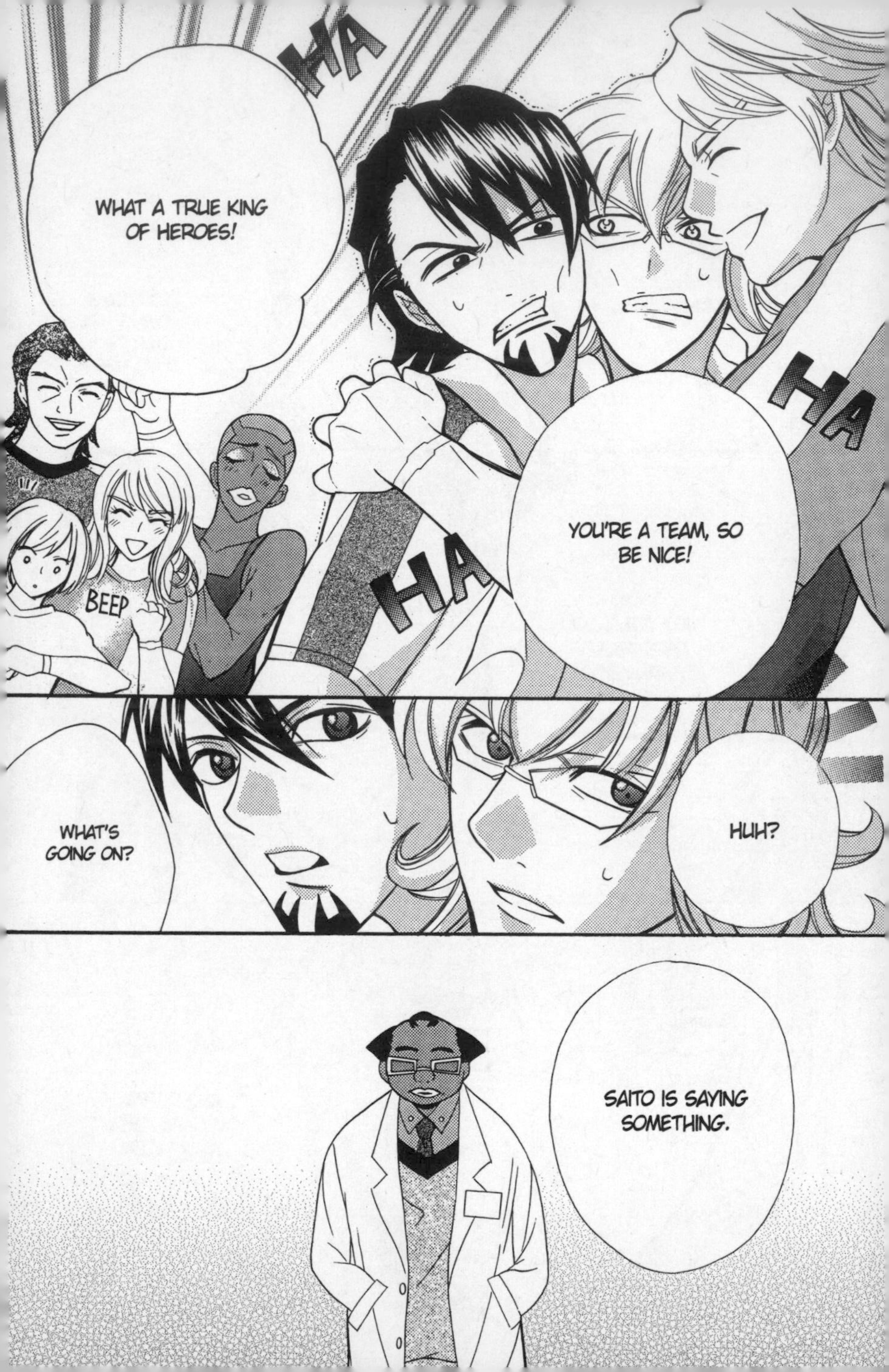
HA
YOU'RE A TEAM, SO BE NICE!
HA
WHAT A TRUE KING OF HEROES!
HA
BEEP
HUH?
WHAT'S GOING ON?
SAITO IS SAYING SOMETHING.

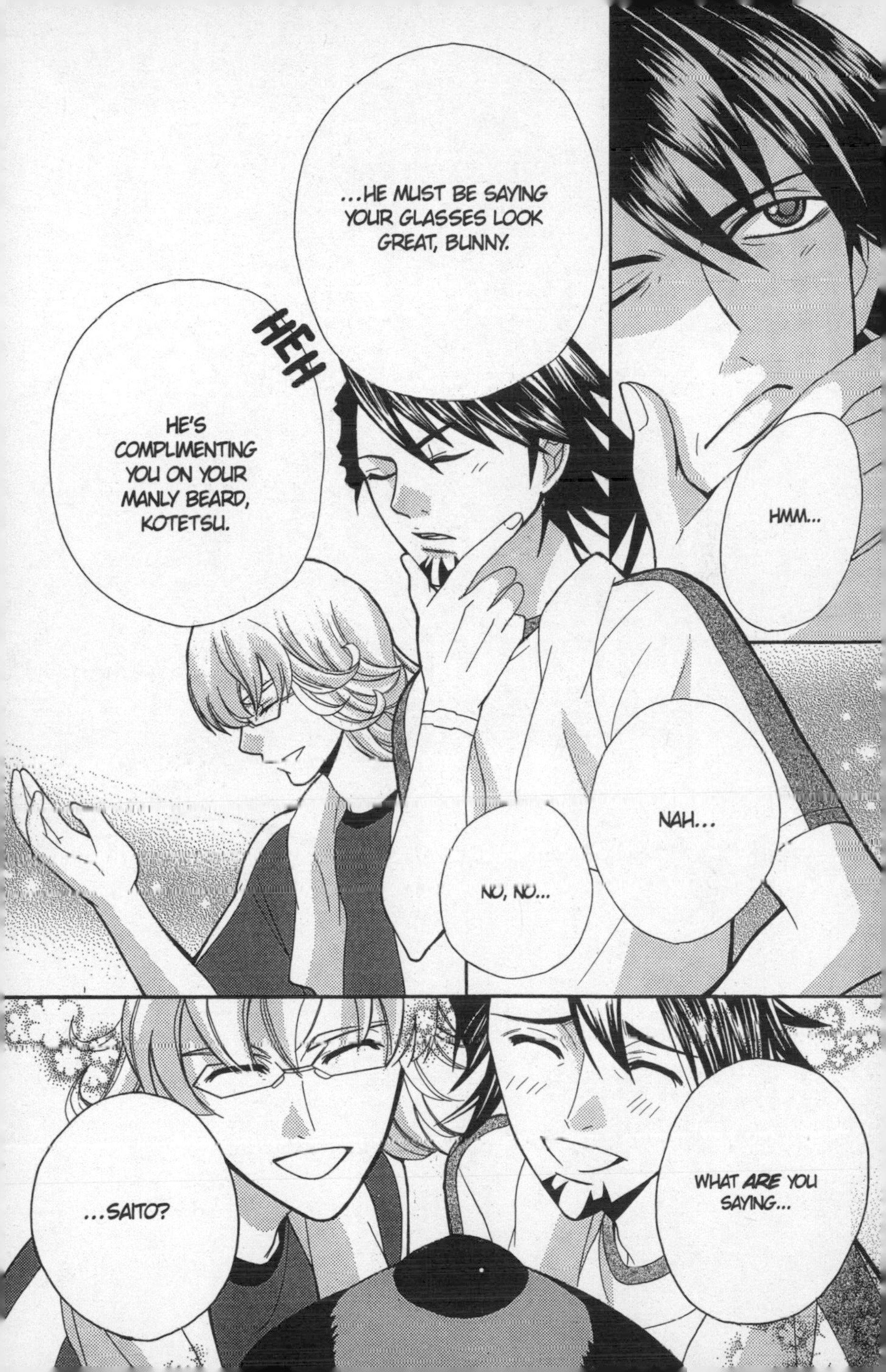
HMM...
...HE MUST BE SAYING YOUR GLASSES LOOK GREAT, BUNNY.
HEH
HE'S COMPLIMENTING YOU ON YOUR MANLY BEARD, KOTETSU.
NAH...
NO, NO...
WHAT *ARE* YOU SAYING...
...SAITO?

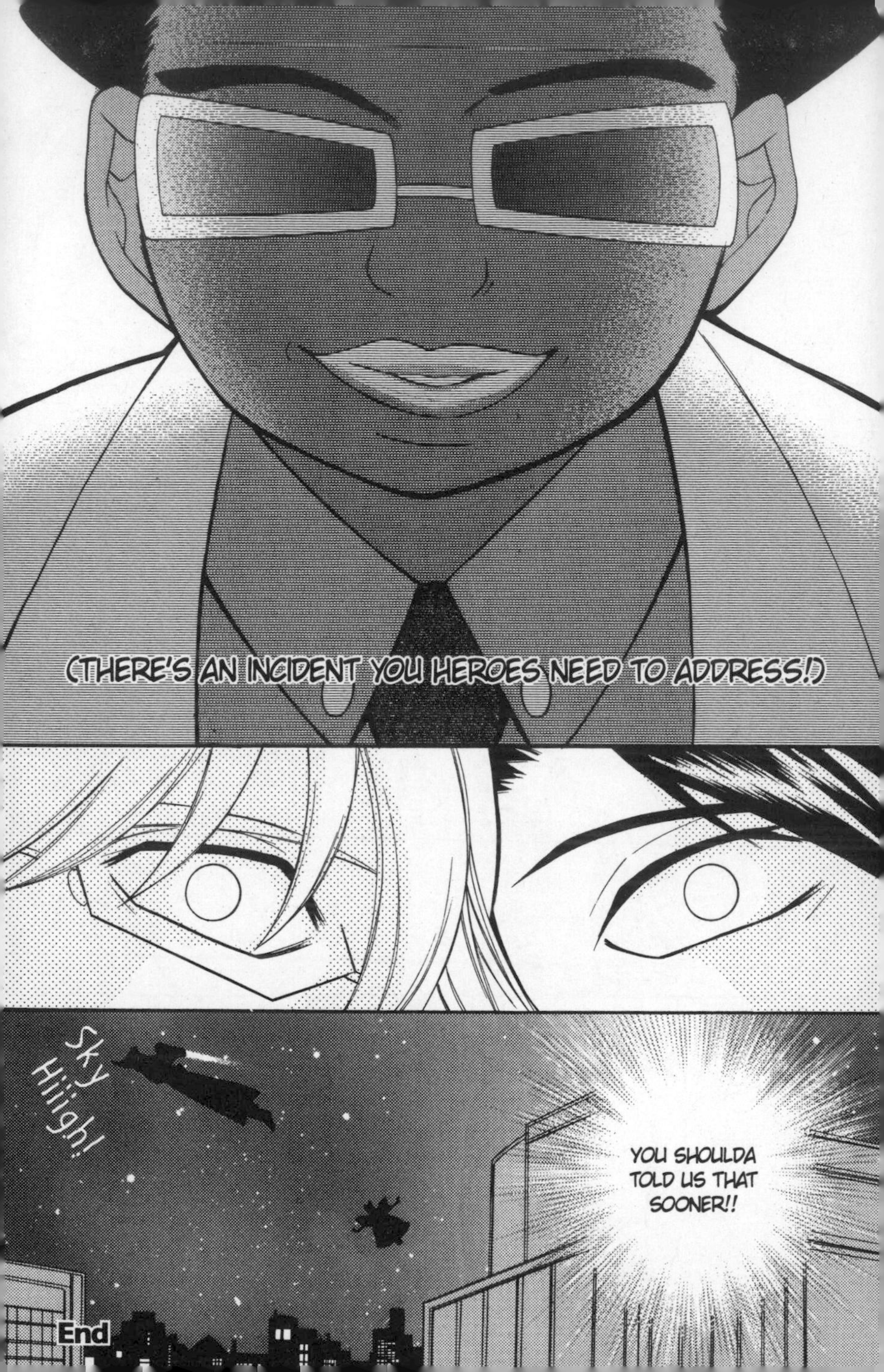
(THERE'S AN INCIDENT YOU HEROES NEED TO ADDRESS!)
YOU SHOULDA TOLD US THAT SOONER!!
Sky Hiiigh!
End

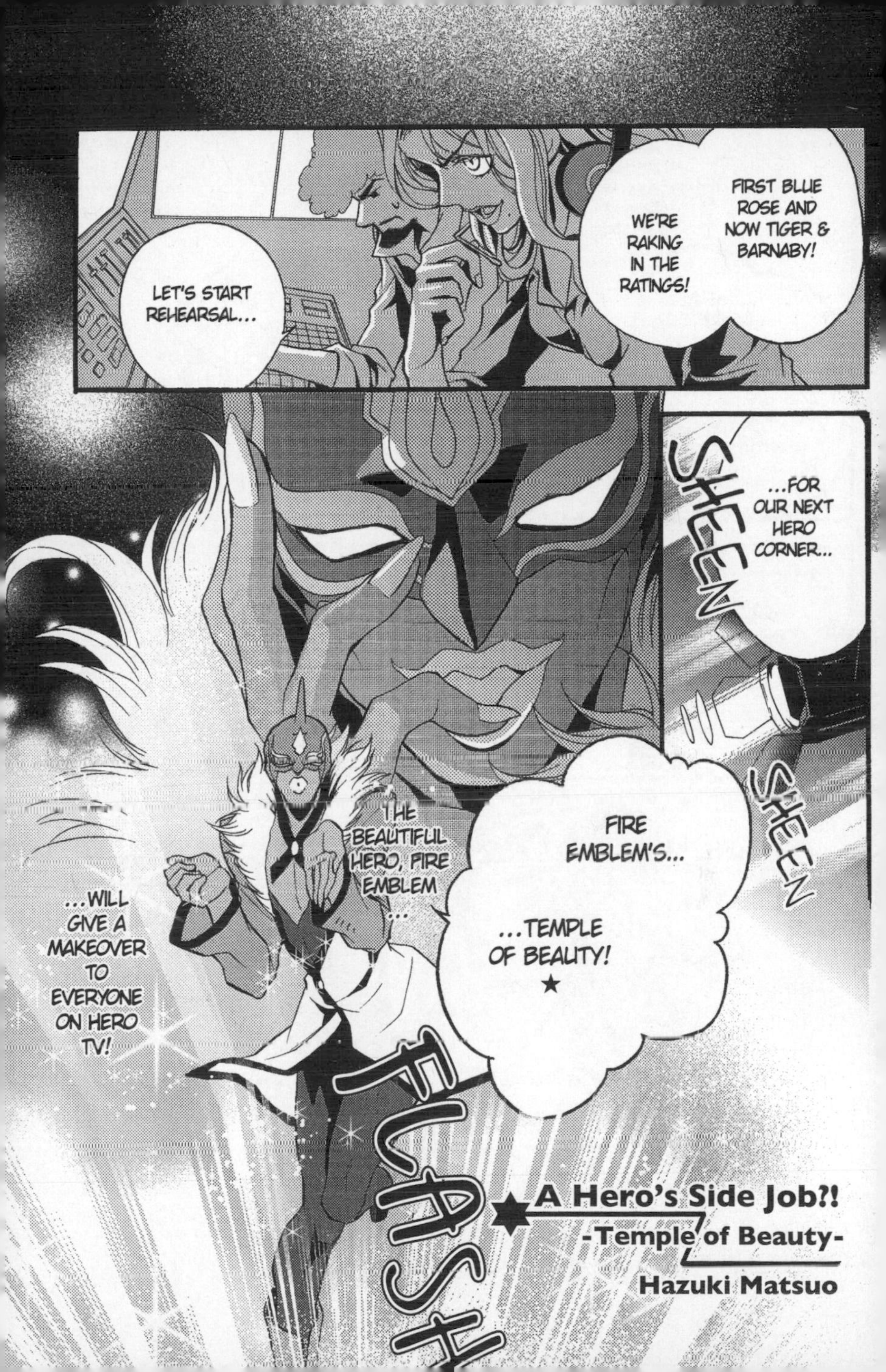
FIRST BLUE ROSE AND NOW TIGER & BARNABY!
WE'RE RAKING IN THE RATINGS!
LET'S START REHEARSAL...
...FOR OUR NEXT HERO CORNER...
SHEEN
SHEEN
FIRE EMBLEM'S... ...TEMPLE OF BEAUTY! ★
THE BEAUTIFUL HERO, FIRE EMBLEM...
...WILL GIVE A MAKEOVER TO EVERYONE ON HERO TV!
FLASH
A Hero's Side Job?!
-Temple of Beauty-
Hazuki Matsuo

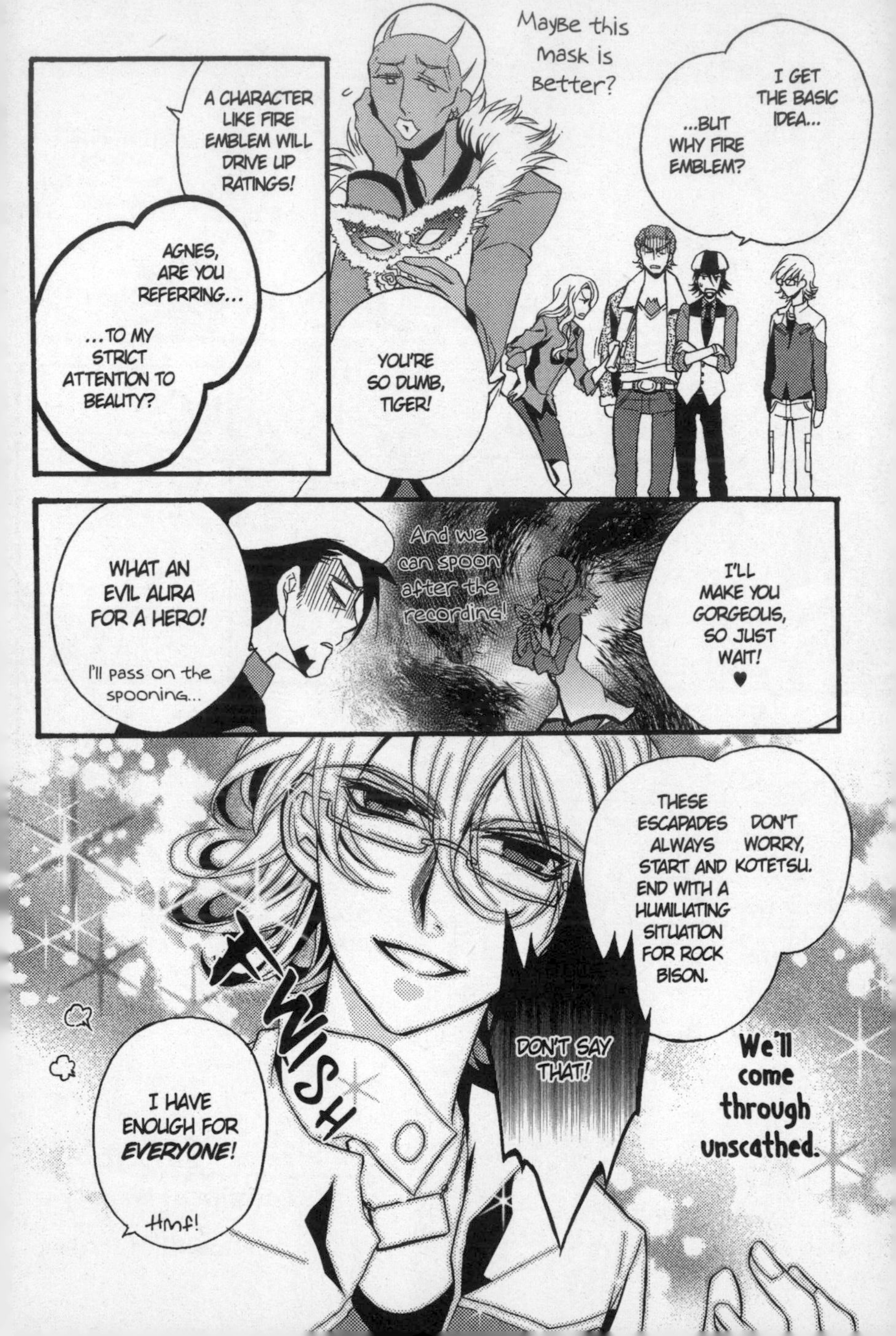
I GET THE BASIC IDEA...
...BUT WHY FIRE EMBLEM?
Maybe this Mask is Better?
A CHARACTER LIKE FIRE EMBLEM WILL DRIVE UP RATINGS!
YOU'RE SO DUMB, TIGER!
AGNES, ARE YOU REFERRING...
...TO MY STRICT ATTENTION TO BEAUTY?
I'LL MAKE YOU GORGEOUS, SO JUST WAIT! ♥
And we can spoon after the recording!
WHAT AN EVIL AURA FOR A HERO!
I'll pass on the spooning...
We'll come through unscathed.
DON'T WORRY, KOTETSU.
THESE ESCAPADES ALWAYS START AND END WITH A HUMILIATING SITUATION FOR ROCK BISON.
DON'T SAY THAT!
TWISH
I HAVE ENOUGH FOR *EVERYONE*!
Hmf!

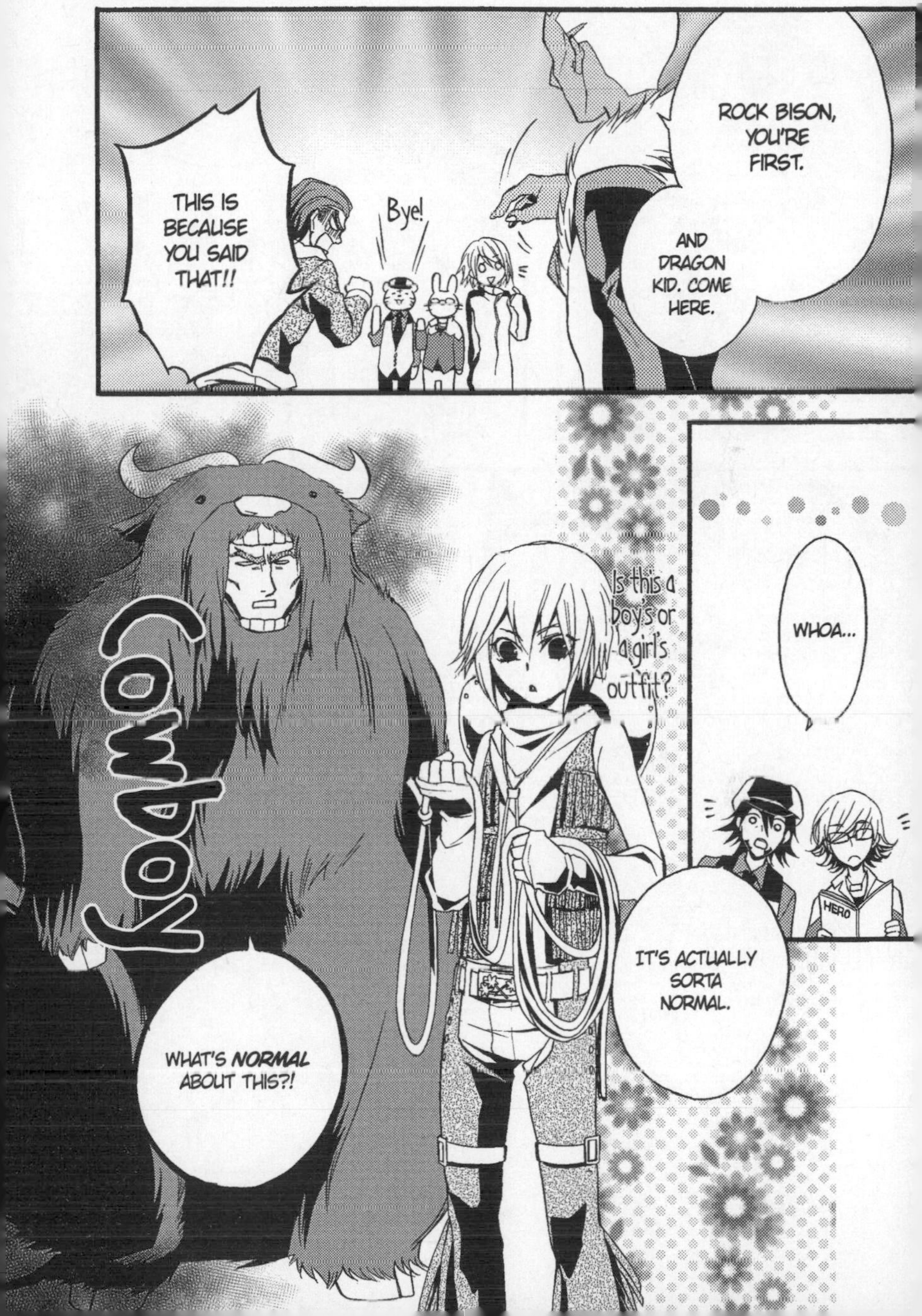
ROCK BISON, YOU'RE FIRST.
AND DRAGON KID. COME HERE.
Bye!
THIS IS BECAUSE YOU SAID THAT!!
WHOA...
IT'S ACTUALLY SORTA NORMAL.
Is this a boy's or a girl's outfit?
Cowboy
WHAT'S **NORMAL** ABOUT THIS?!

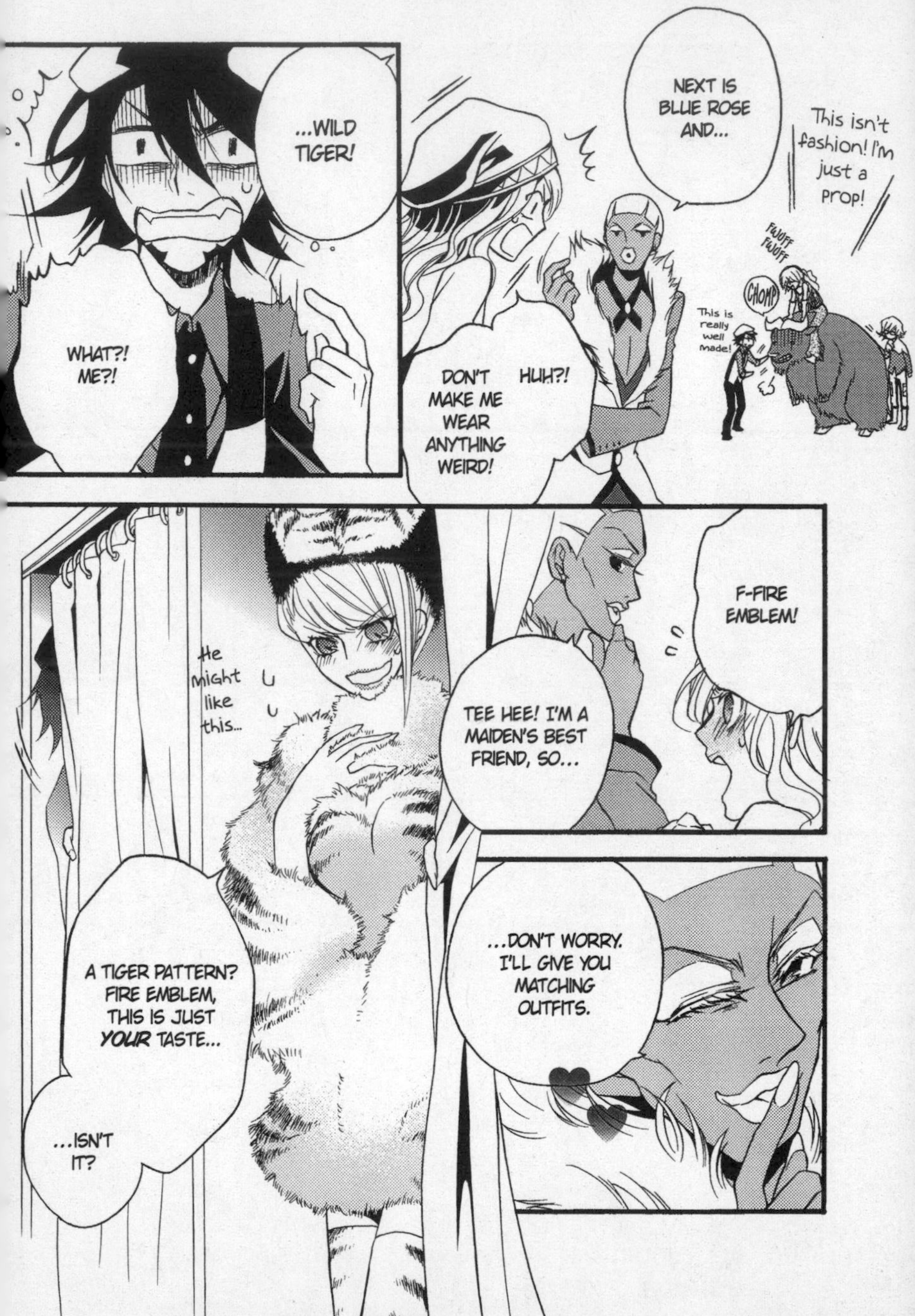
NEXT IS BLUE ROSE AND...
This isn't fashion! I'm just a prop!
FWUFF FWUFF
CHOMP
This is really well made!
HUH?!
DON'T MAKE ME WEAR ANYTHING WEIRD!
...WILD TIGER!
WHAT?! ME?!
F-FIRE EMBLEM!
TEE HEE! I'M A MAIDEN'S BEST FRIEND, SO...
...DON'T WORRY. I'LL GIVE YOU MATCHING OUTFITS.
He might like this...
A TIGER PATTERN? FIRE EMBLEM, THIS IS JUST *YOUR* TASTE...
...ISN'T IT?

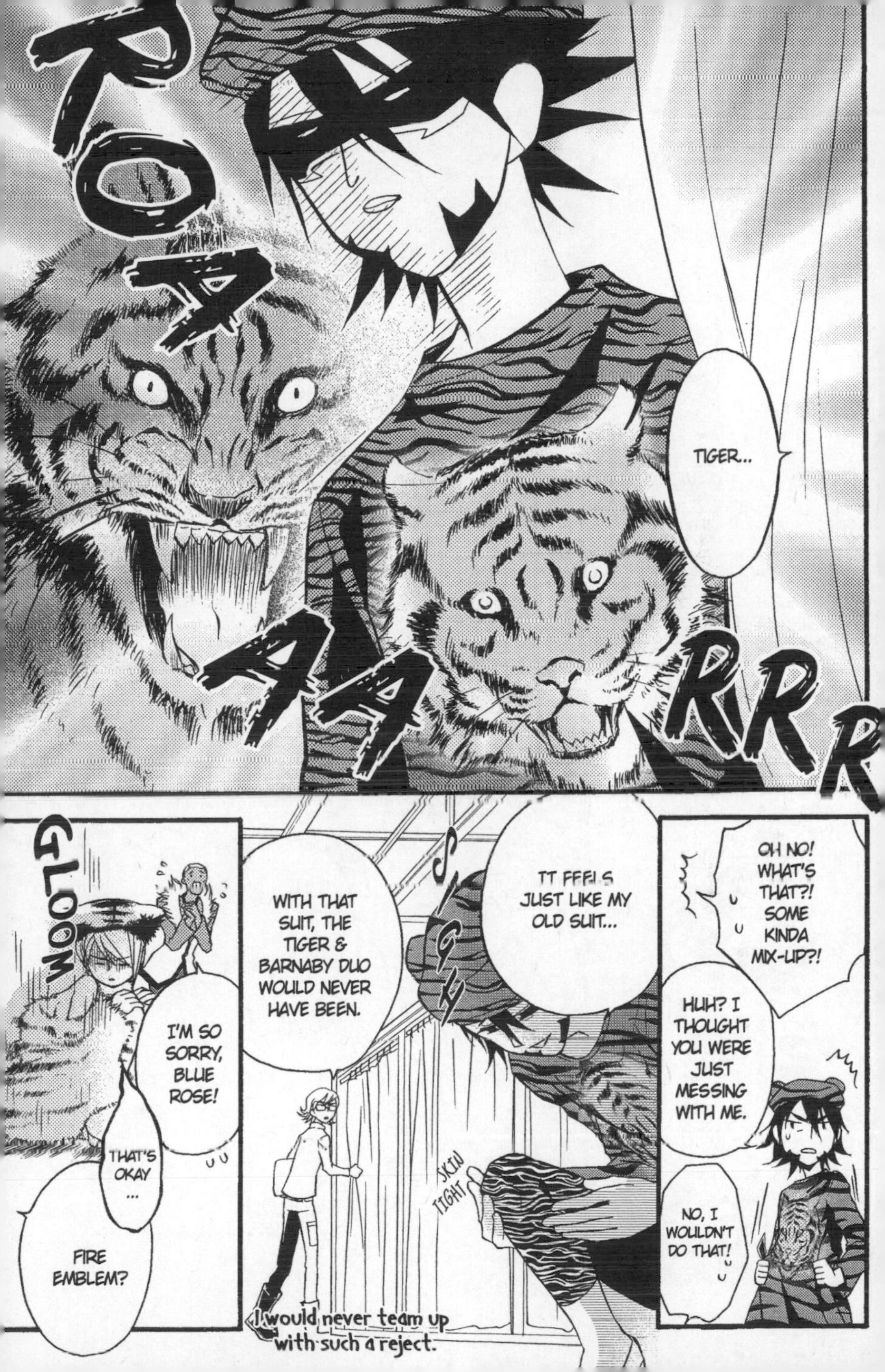
ROAAARRR
TIGER...
OH NO! WHAT'S THAT?! SOME KINDA MIX-UP?!
HUH? I THOUGHT YOU WERE JUST MESSING WITH ME.
NO, I WOULDN'T DO THAT!
SIGH
IT FEELS JUST LIKE MY OLD SUIT...
WITH THAT SUIT, THE TIGER & BARNABY DUO WOULD NEVER HAVE BEEN.
SKIN TIGHT
I would never team up with such a reject.
GLOOM
I'M SO SORRY, BLUE ROSE!
THAT'S OKAY ...
FIRE EMBLEM?

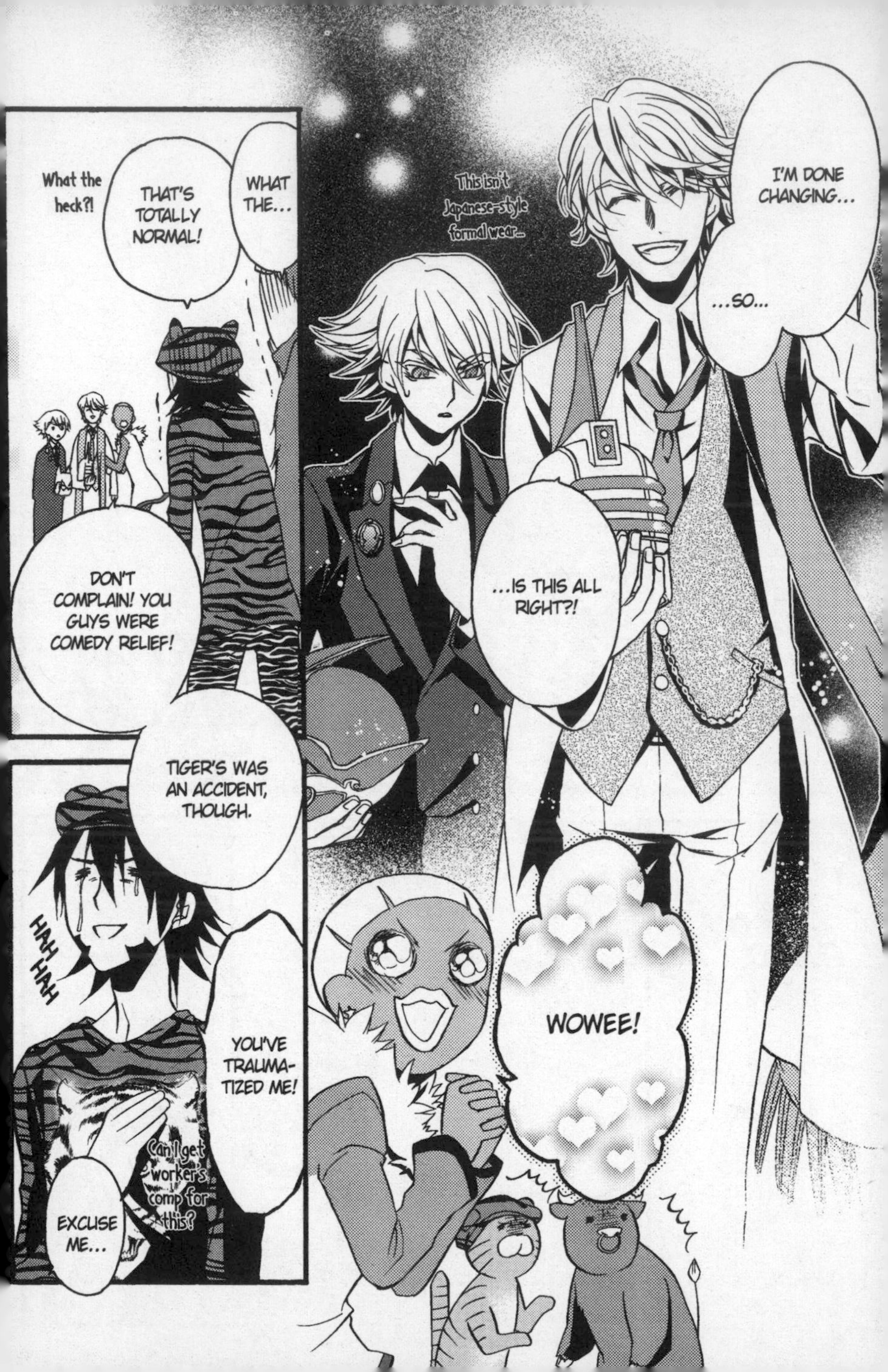
I'M DONE CHANGING…
…SO…
This isn't Japanese-style formal wear…
…IS THIS ALL RIGHT?!
WOWEE!
WHAT THE…
THAT'S TOTALLY NORMAL!
What the heck?!
DON'T COMPLAIN! YOU GUYS WERE COMEDY RELIEF!
TIGER'S WAS AN ACCIDENT, THOUGH.
HAH HAH
YOU'VE TRAUMATIZED ME!
Can I get worker's comp for this?
EXCUSE ME…

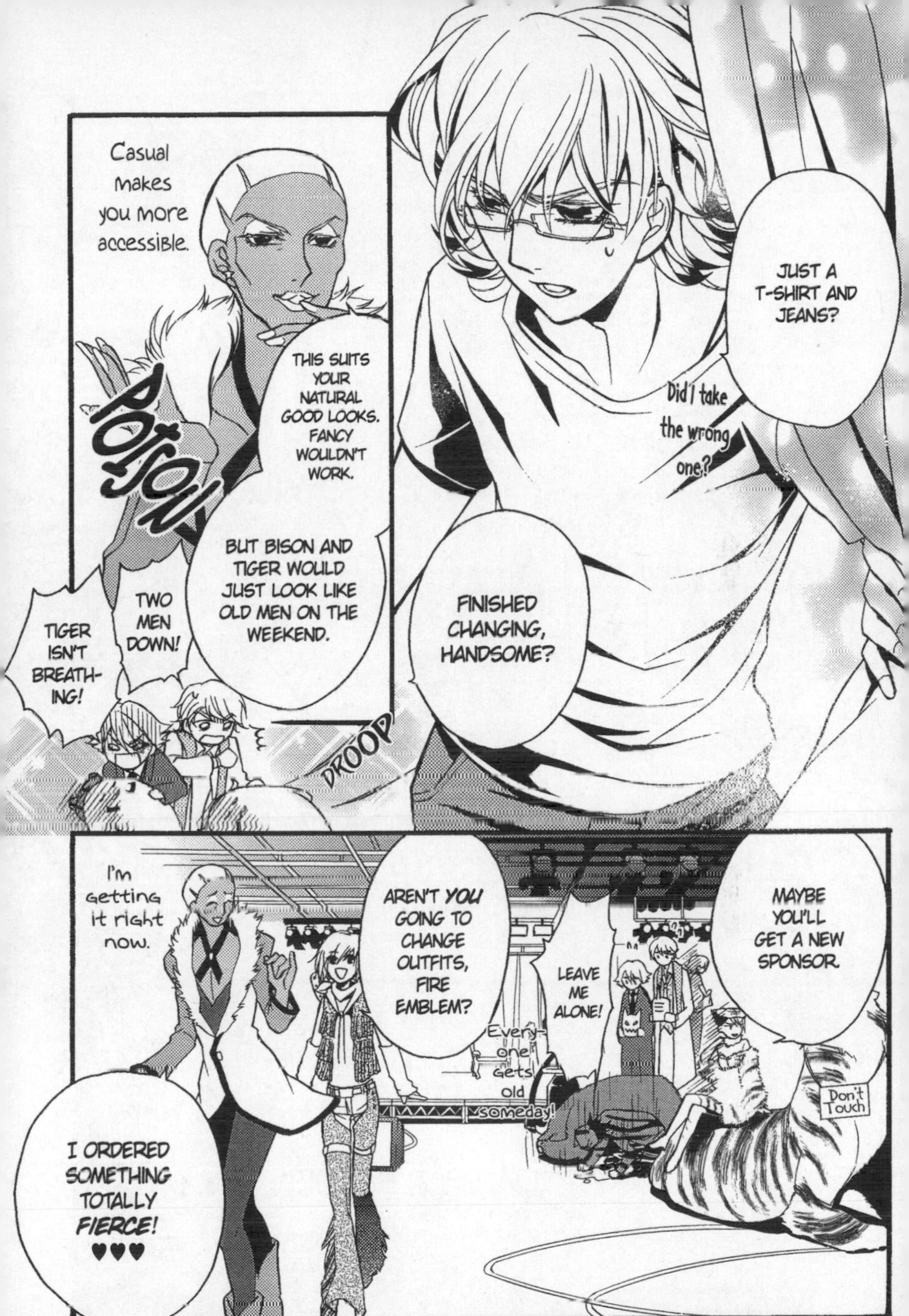
JUST A T-SHIRT AND JEANS?
Did I take the wrong one?
FINISHED CHANGING, HANDSOME?
Casual makes you more accessible.
THIS SUITS YOUR NATURAL GOOD LOOKS. FANCY WOULDN'T WORK.
POISON
BUT BISON AND TIGER WOULD JUST LOOK LIKE OLD MEN ON THE WEEKEND.
TWO MEN DOWN!
TIGER ISN'T BREATH-ING!
DROOP
MAYBE YOU'LL GET A NEW SPONSOR.
Don't Touch
LEAVE ME ALONE!
Every-one gets old someday!
AREN'T *YOU* GOING TO CHANGE OUTFITS, FIRE EMBLEM?
I'm getting it right now.
I ORDERED SOMETHING TOTALLY *FIERCE!* ♥♥♥

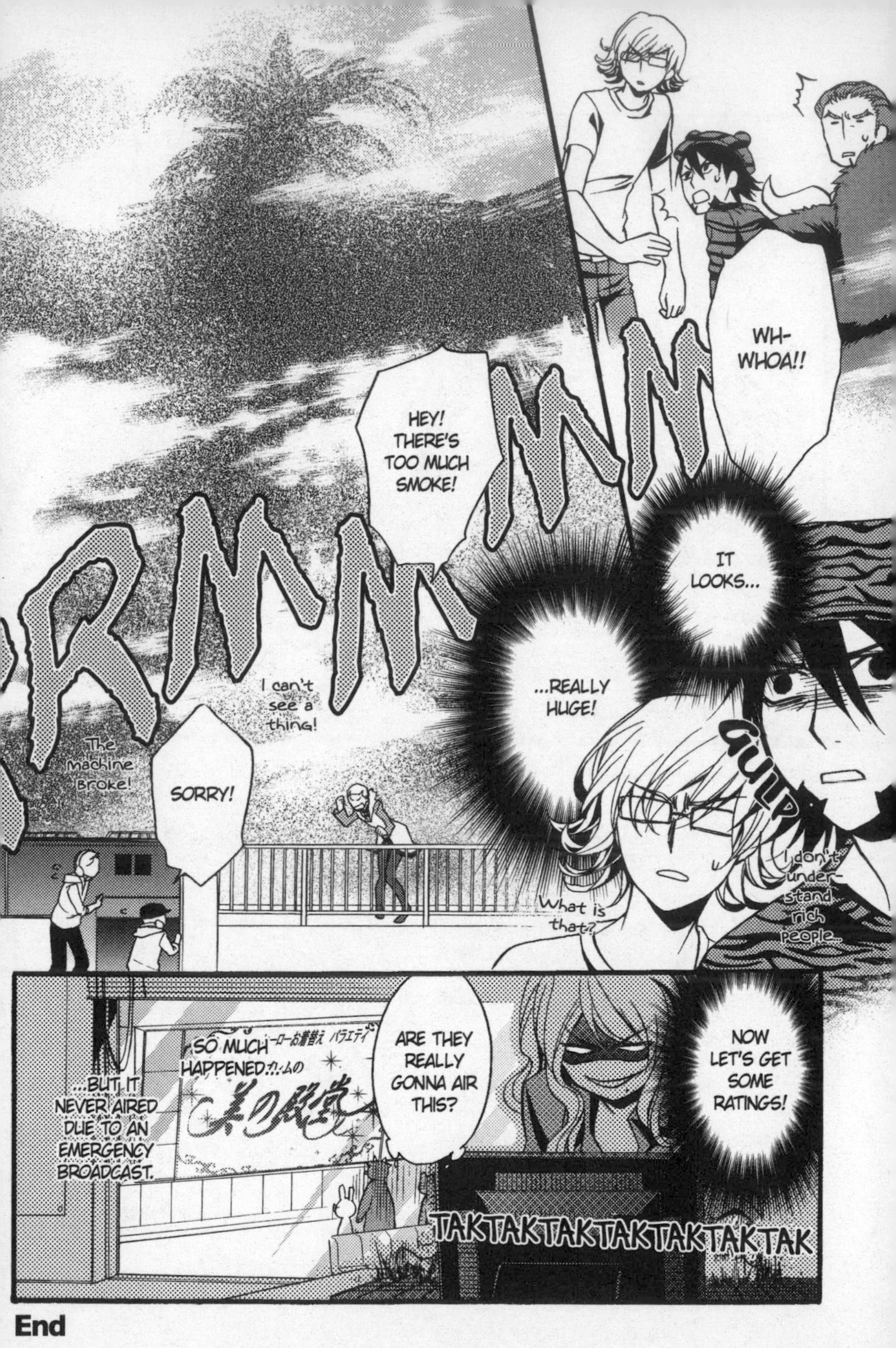
WH-WHOA!!
HEY! THERE'S TOO MUCH SMOKE!
RMMMM
I can't see a thing!
The machine broke!
SORRY!
IT LOOKS...
...REALLY HUGE!
GULP
I don't understand rich people...
What is that?
NOW LET'S GET SOME RATINGS!
ARE THEY REALLY GONNA AIR THIS?
SO MUCH HAPPENED
...BUT IT NEVER AIRED DUE TO AN EMERGENCY BROADCAST.
TAKTAKTAKTAKTAKTAKTAK

End

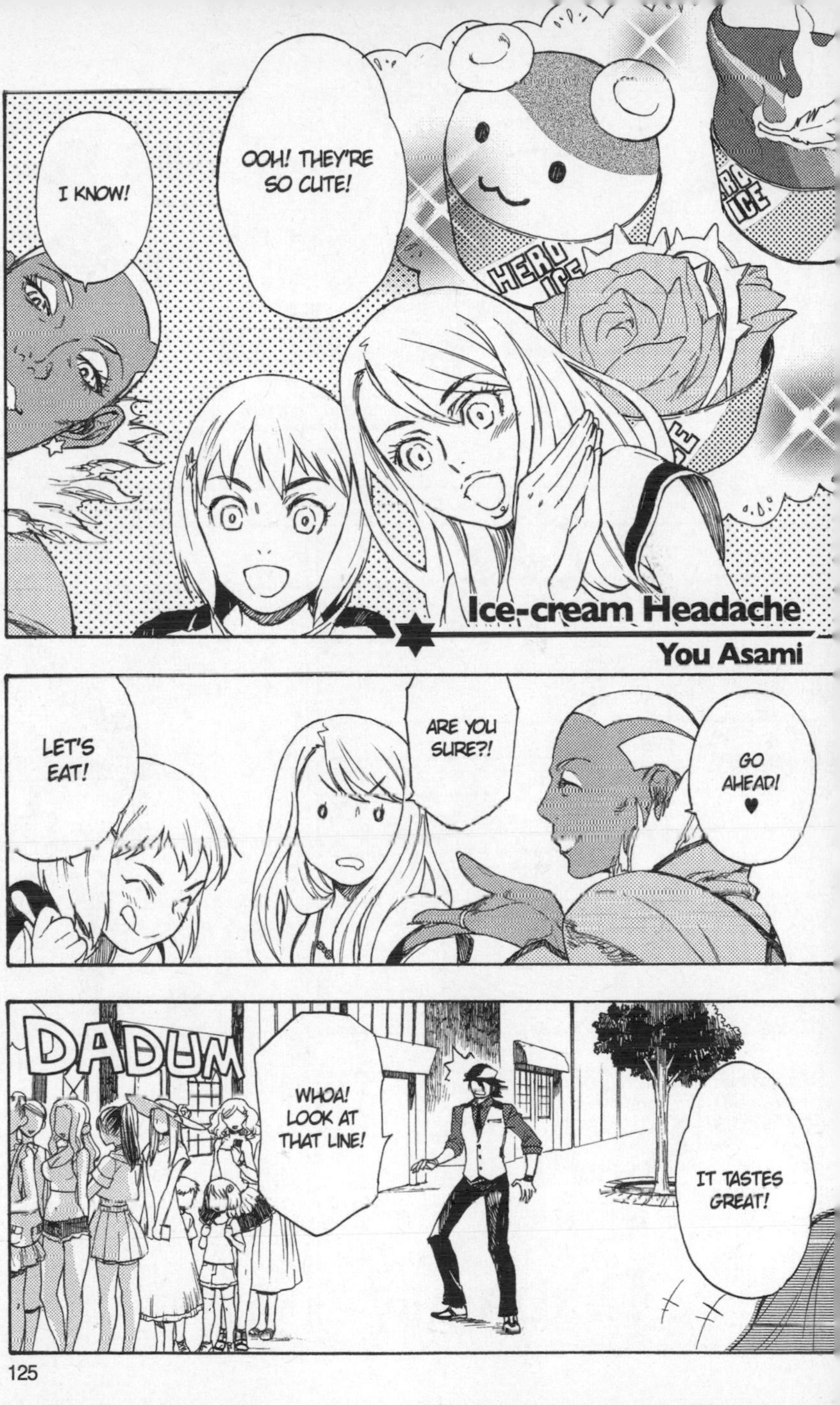
HERO ICE
OOH! THEY'RE SO CUTE!
I KNOW!
Ice-cream Headache
You Asami
GO AHEAD! ♥
ARE YOU SURE?!
LET'S EAT!
IT TASTES GREAT!
WHOA! LOOK AT THAT LINE!
DADUM

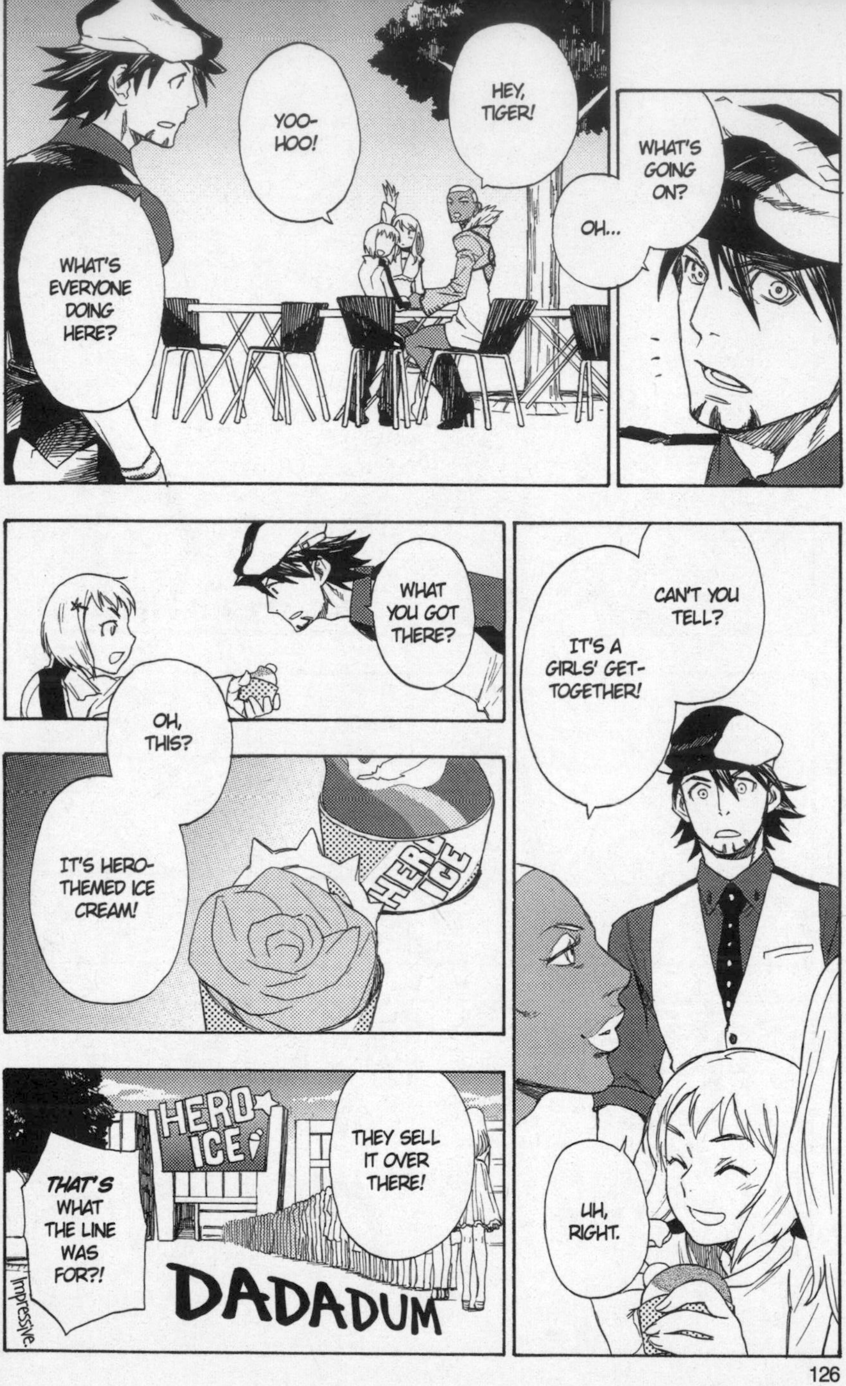
WHAT'S GOING ON?
OH...
HEY, TIGER!
YOO-HOO!
WHAT'S EVERYONE DOING HERE?
CAN'T YOU TELL?
IT'S A GIRLS' GET-TOGETHER!
UH, RIGHT.
WHAT YOU GOT THERE?
OH, THIS?
IT'S HERO-THEMED ICE CREAM!
HERO ICE
HERO ICE
THEY SELL IT OVER THERE!
THAT'S WHAT THE LINE WAS FOR?!
DADADUM
Impressive.

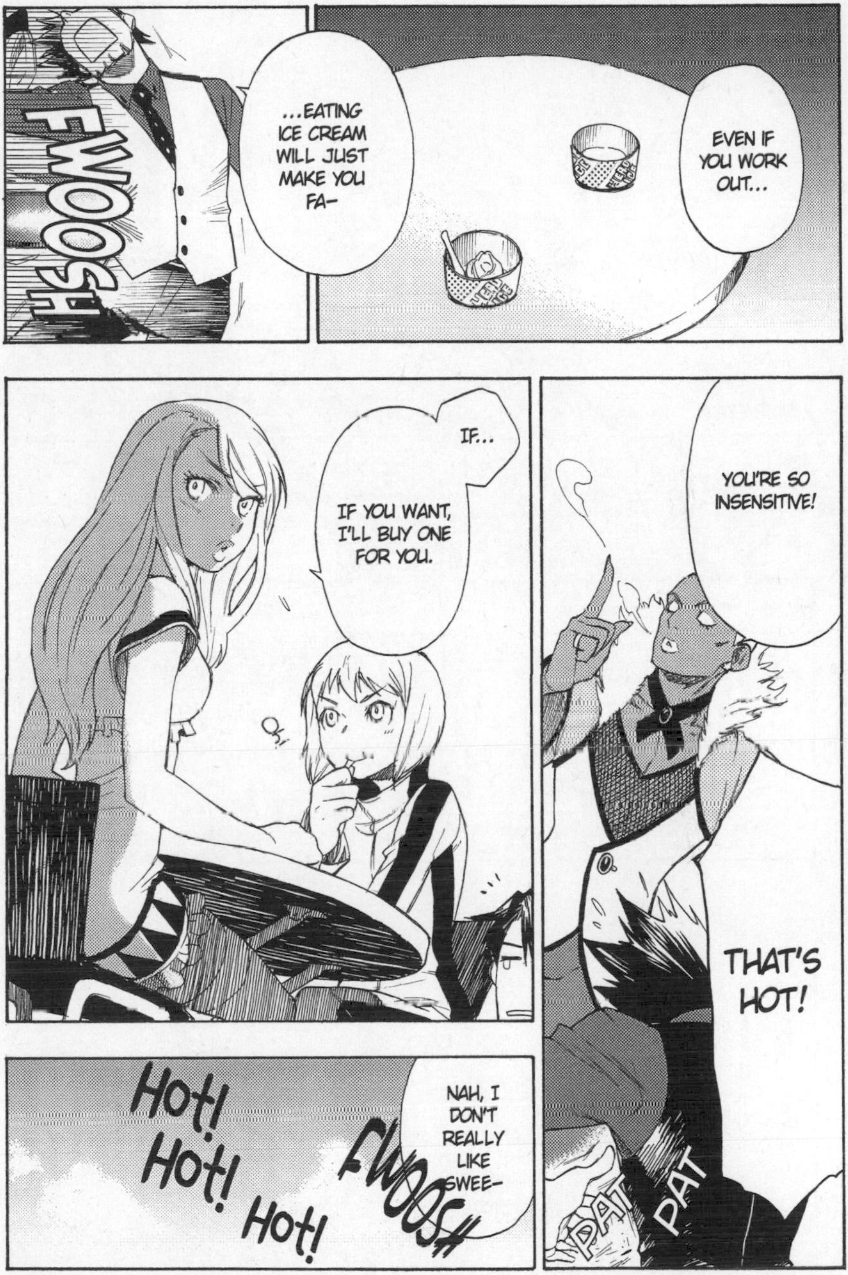
EVEN IF YOU WORK OUT...
...EATING ICE CREAM WILL JUST MAKE YOU FA-
FWOOSH
YOU'RE SO INSENSITIVE!
THAT'S HOT!
PAT
PAT
IF...
IF YOU WANT, I'LL BUY ONE FOR YOU.
NAH, I DON'T REALLY LIKE SWEE-
FWOOSH
Hot! Hot! Hot!

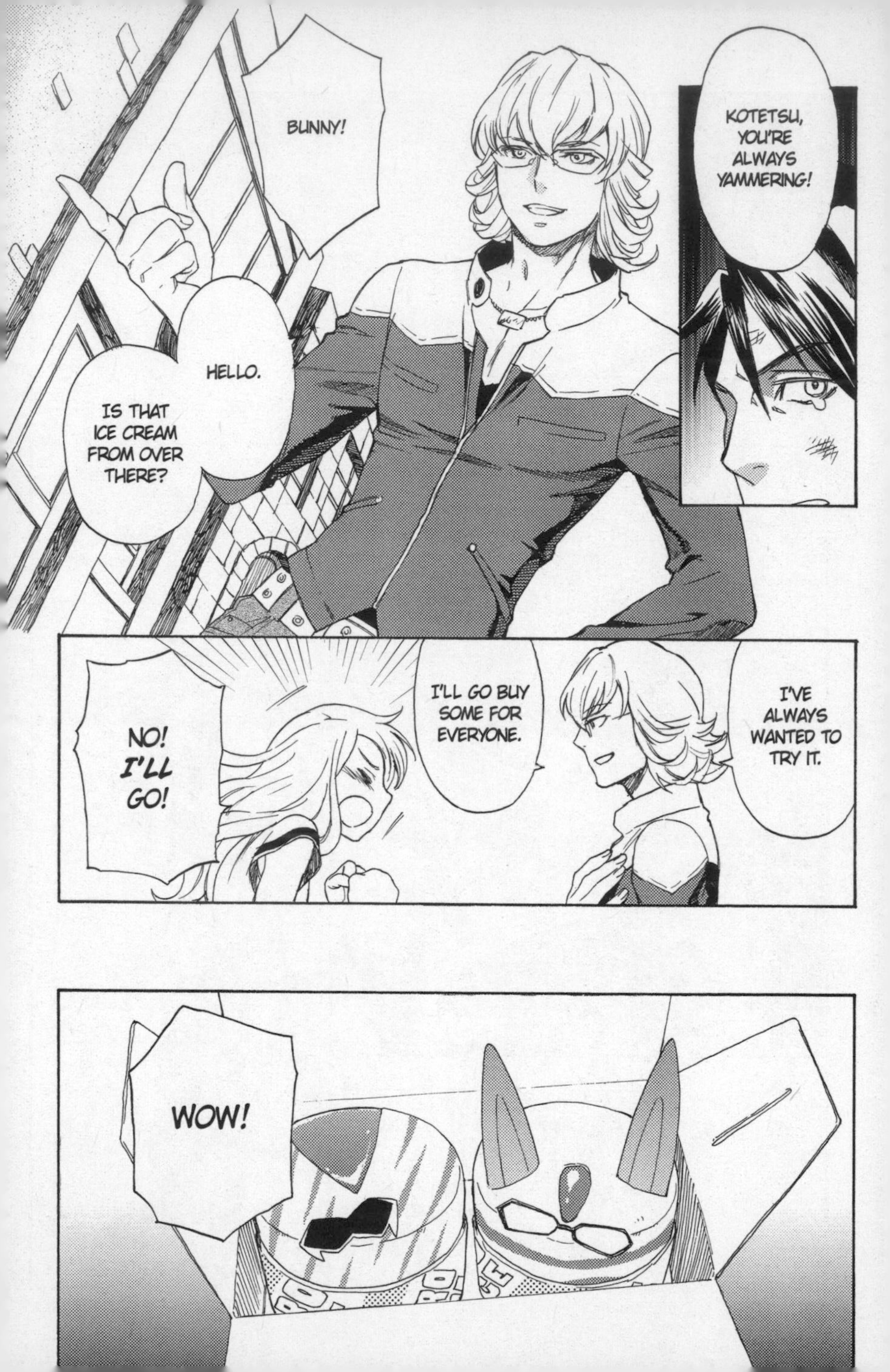
KOTETSU, YOU'RE ALWAYS YAMMERING!
BUNNY!
HELLO.
IS THAT ICE CREAM FROM OVER THERE?
I'VE ALWAYS WANTED TO TRY IT.
I'LL GO BUY SOME FOR EVERYONE.
NO! *I'LL* GO!
WOW!

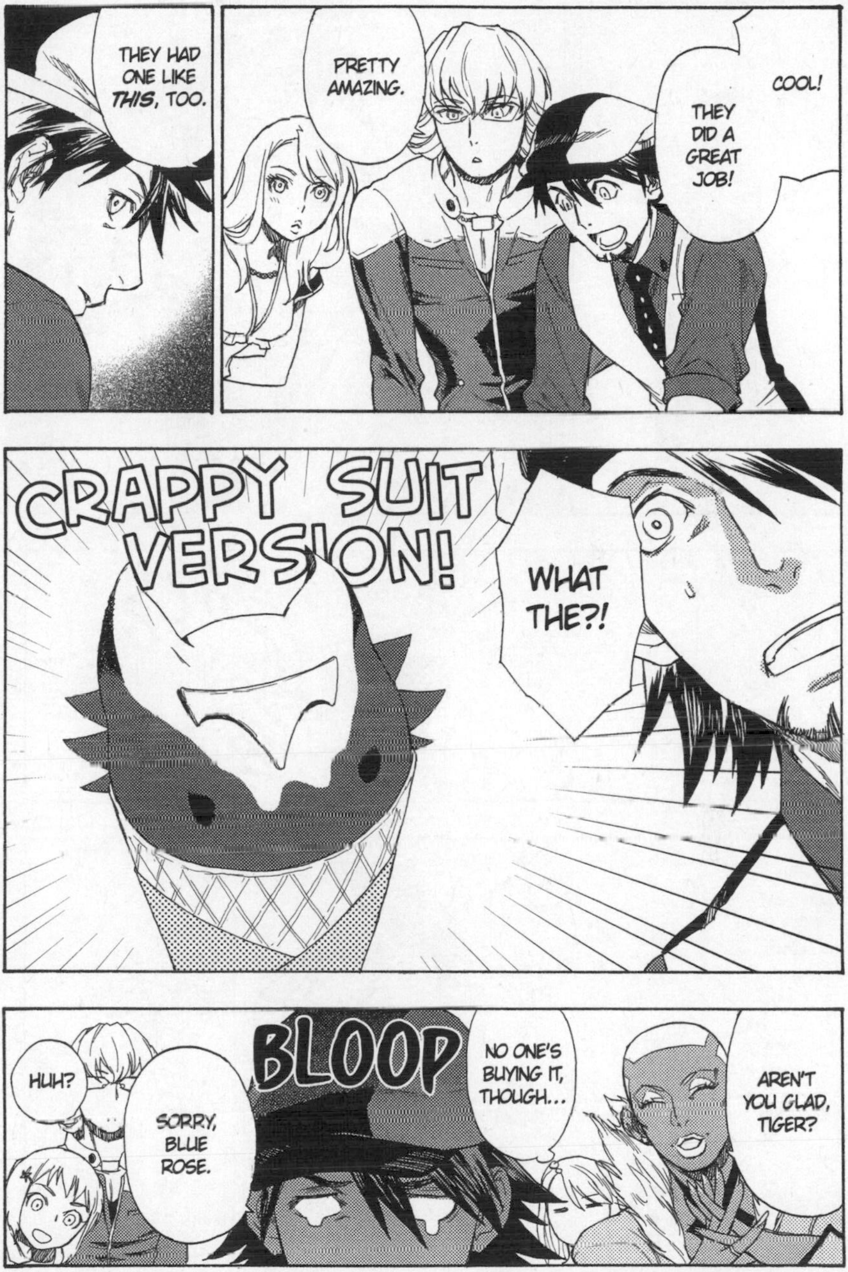
COOL!
THEY DID A GREAT JOB!
PRETTY AMAZING.
THEY HAD ONE LIKE *THIS*, TOO.
CRAPPY SUIT VERSION!
WHAT THE?!
AREN'T YOU GLAD, TIGER?
NO ONE'S BUYING IT, THOUGH...
BLOOP
SORRY, BLUE ROSE.
HUH?

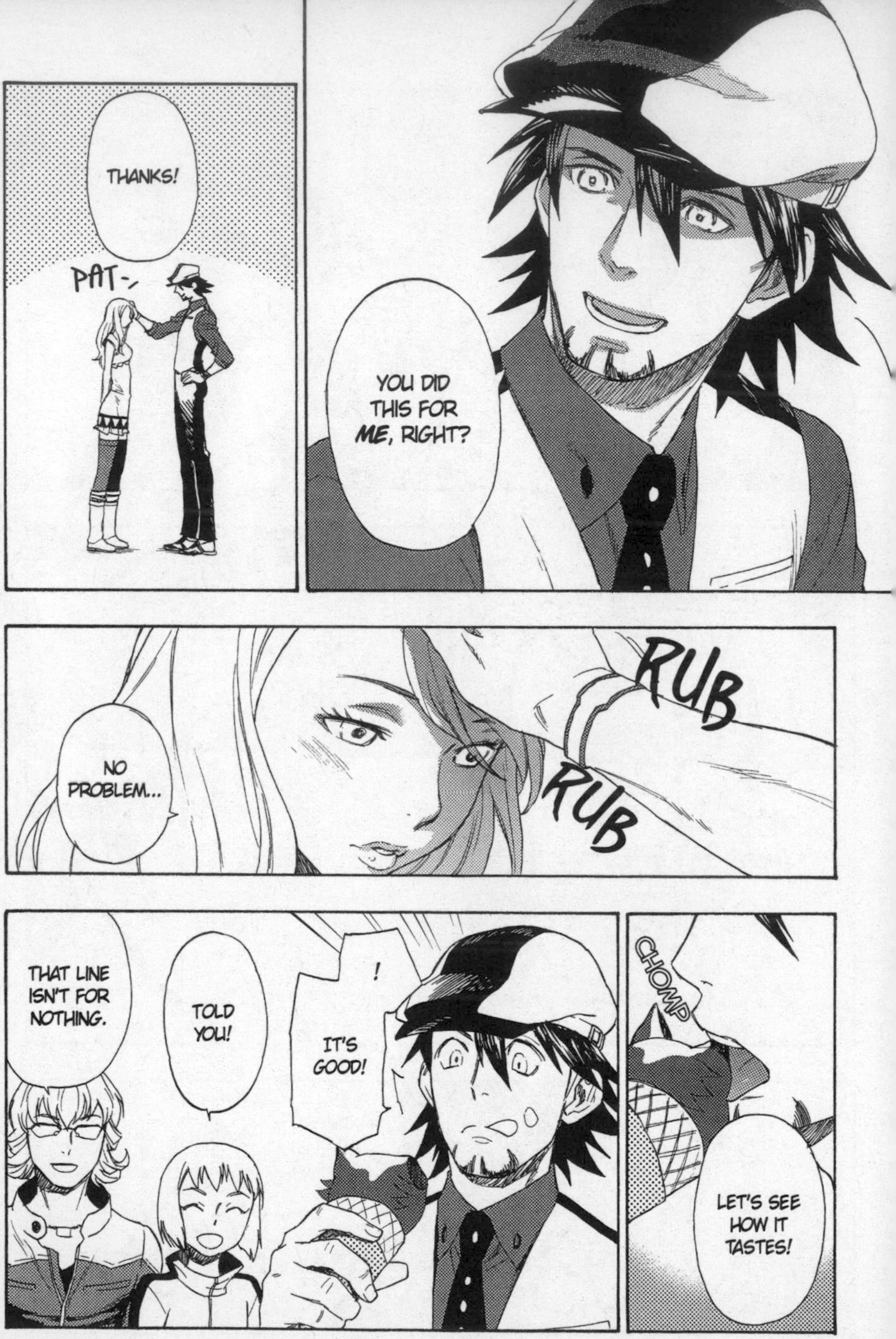
YOU DID THIS FOR *ME*, RIGHT?
THANKS!
PAT-
RUB
RUB
NO PROBLEM...
CHOMP
LET'S SEE HOW IT TASTES!
!
IT'S GOOD!
TOLD YOU!
THAT LINE ISN'T FOR NOTHING.

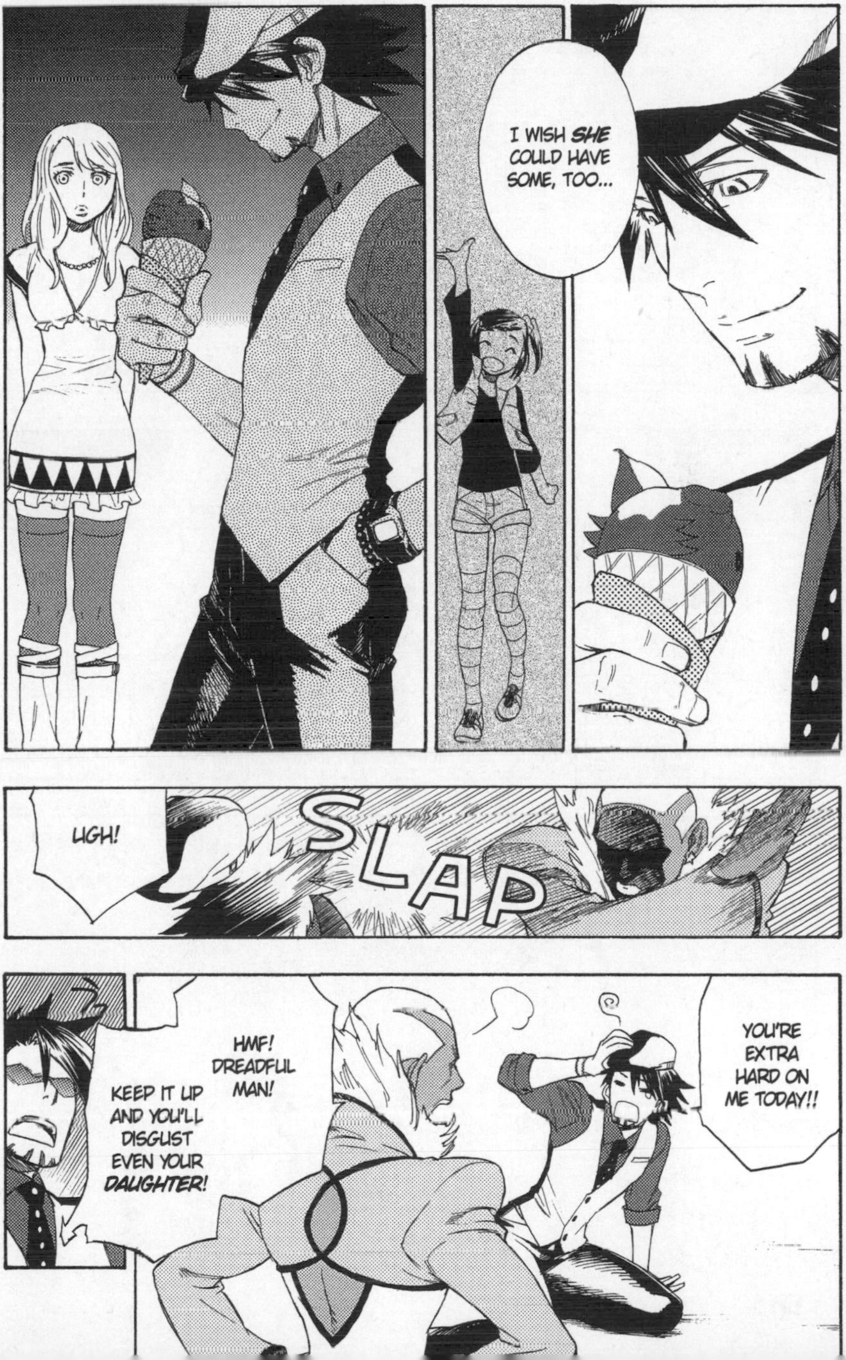
I WISH *SHE* COULD HAVE SOME, TOO...
SLAP
UGH!
YOU'RE EXTRA HARD ON ME TODAY!!
HMF! DREADFUL MAN!
KEEP IT UP AND YOU'LL DISGUST EVEN YOUR *DAUGHTER*!

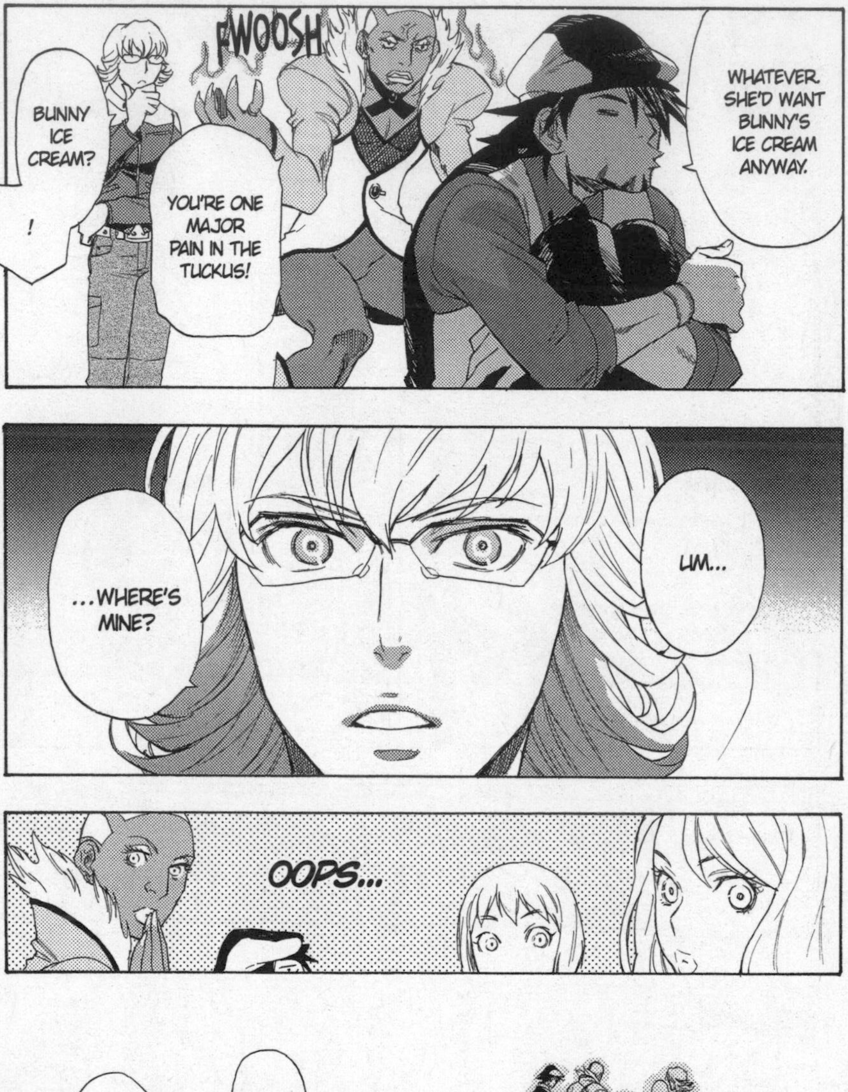
WHATEVER. SHE'D WANT BUNNY'S ICE CREAM ANYWAY.
FWOOSH
YOU'RE ONE MAJOR PAIN IN THE TUCKUS!
BUNNY ICE CREAM?
!
UM...
...WHERE'S MINE?
OOPS...
YUCK...
IT'S ALL MELTED...

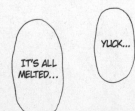

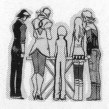

End

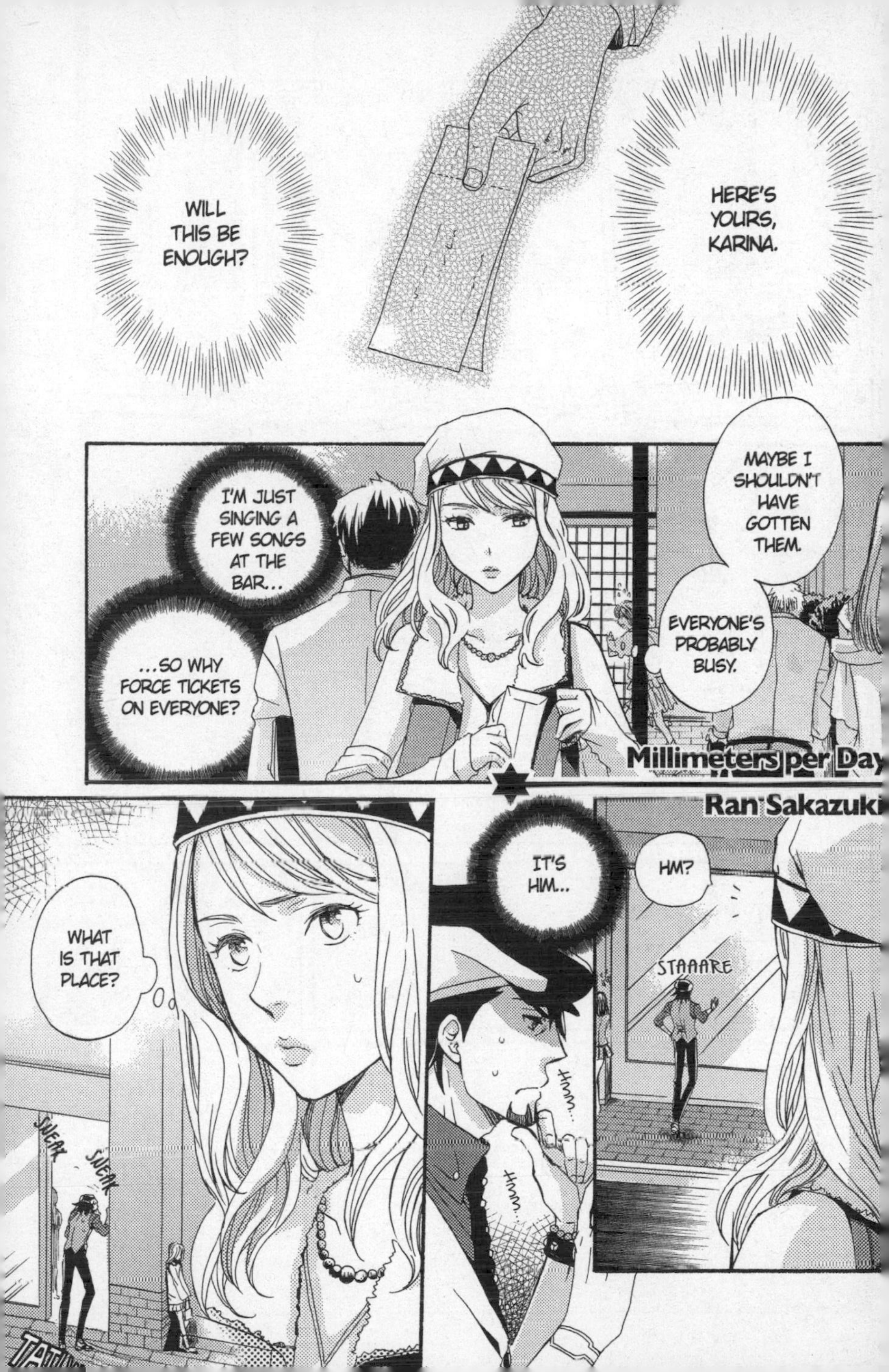
HERE'S YOURS, KARINA.
WILL THIS BE ENOUGH?
MAYBE I SHOULDN'T HAVE GOTTEN THEM.
EVERYONE'S PROBABLY BUSY.
I'M JUST SINGING A FEW SONGS AT THE BAR...
...SO WHY FORCE TICKETS ON EVERYONE?
Millimeters per Day
Ran Sakazuki
HM?
STAAARE
IT'S HIM...
Hmm...
Hmm...
WHAT IS THAT PLACE?
SNEAK
SNEAK

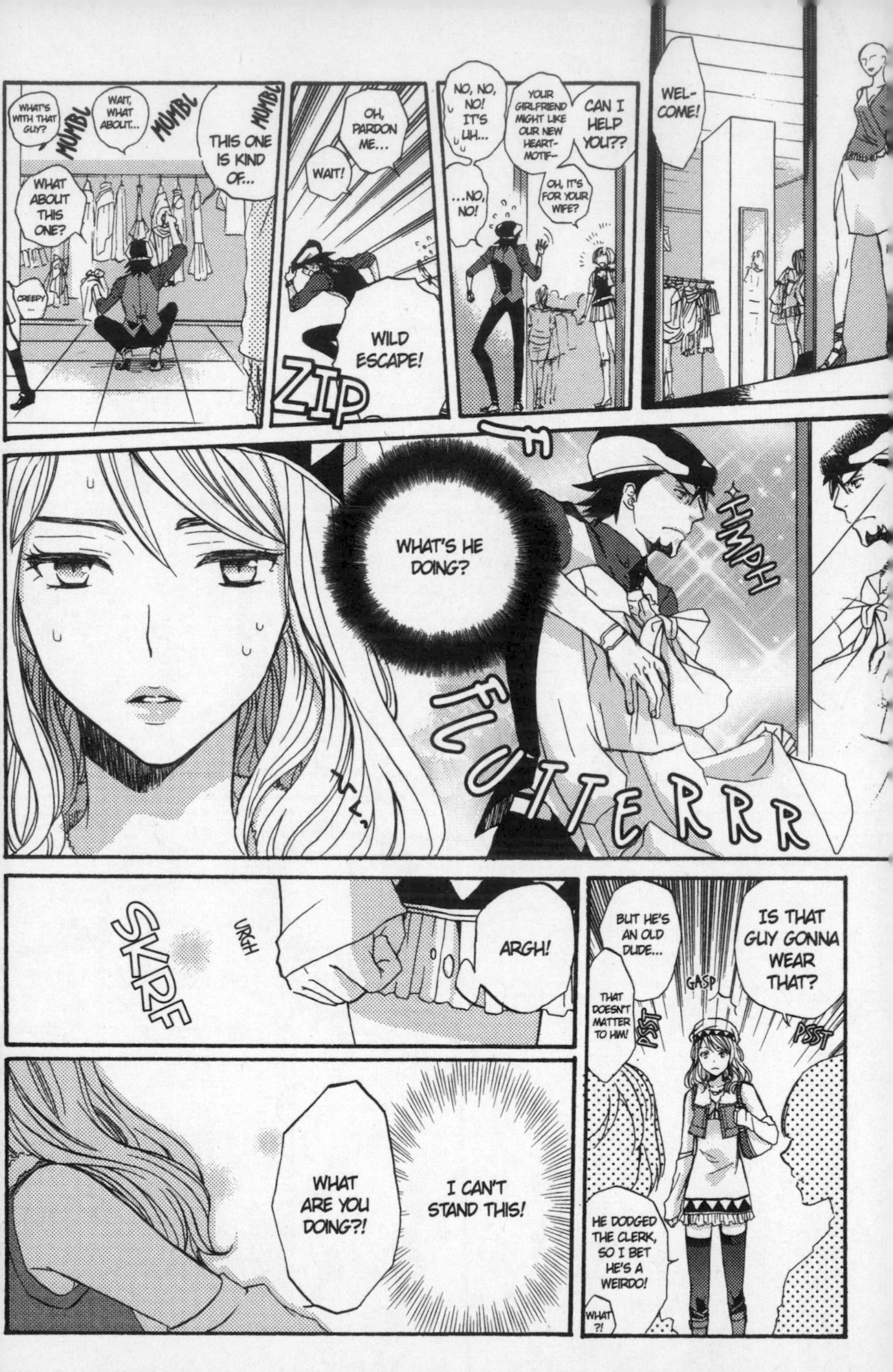
WEL-COME!
CAN I HELP YOU??
YOUR GIRLFRIEND MIGHT LIKE OUR NEW HEART-MOTIF-
NO, NO, NO! IT'S UH...
OH, IT'S FOR YOUR WIFE?
...NO, NO!
OH, PARDON ME...
WAIT!
WILD ESCAPE!
ZIP
MUMBL
THIS ONE IS KIND OF...
MUMBL
WAIT, WHAT ABOUT...
WHAT'S WITH THAT GUY?
MUMBL
WHAT ABOUT THIS ONE?
CREEPY...
HMPH
WHAT'S HE DOING?
FLUTTERRR
IS THAT GUY GONNA WEAR THAT?
BUT HE'S AN OLD DUDE...
GASP
PSST
PSST
THAT DOESN'T MATTER TO HIM!
HE DODGED THE CLERK, SO I BET HE'S A WEIRDO!
WHAT?!
ARGH!
URGH
SKRF
I CAN'T STAND THIS!
WHAT ARE YOU DOING?!

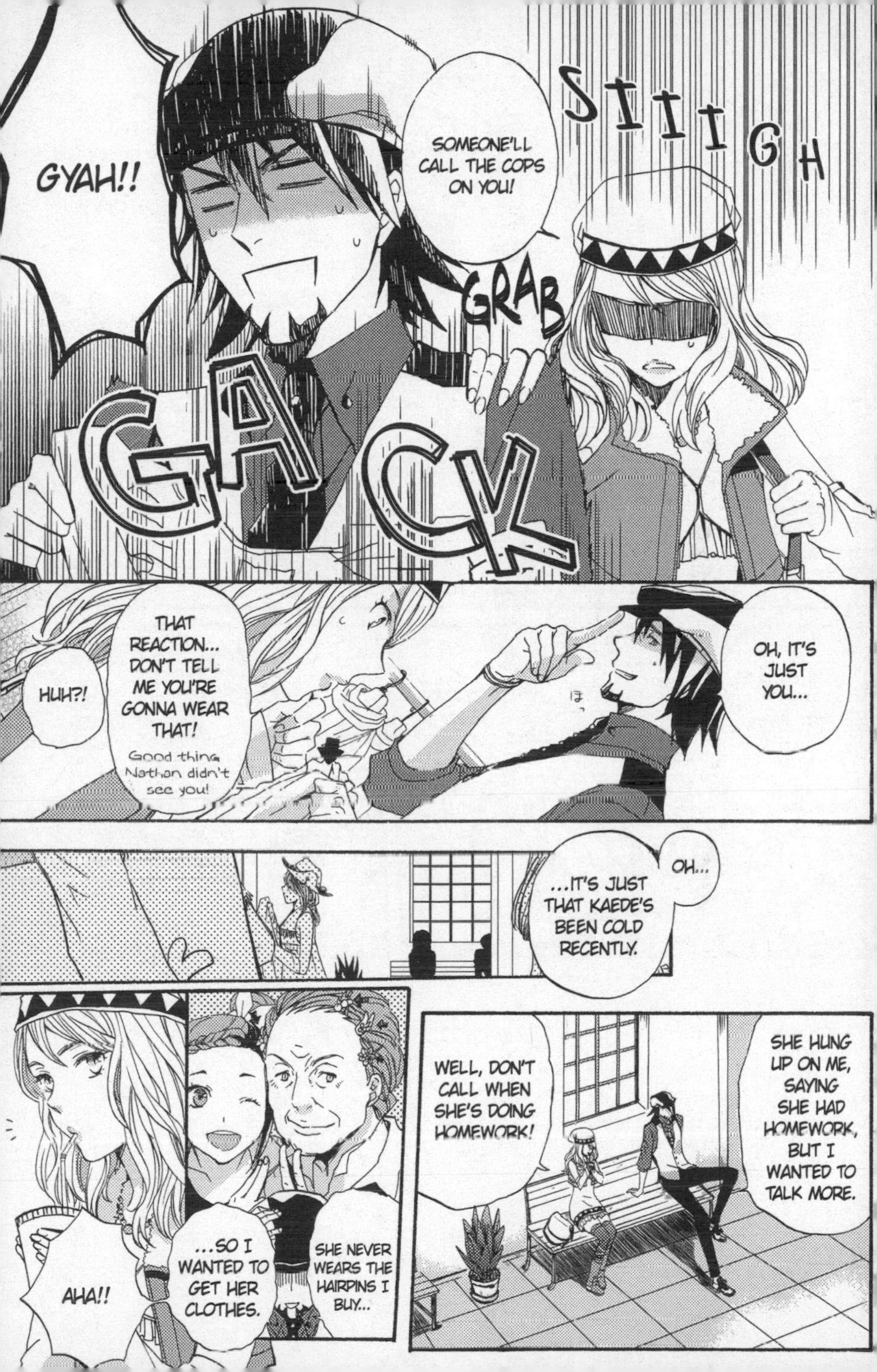
SIIIGH
SOMEONE'LL CALL THE COPS ON YOU!
GYAH!!
GRAB
GACK
OH, IT'S JUST YOU...
ほっ
THAT REACTION... DON'T TELL ME YOU'RE GONNA WEAR THAT!
Good thing Nathan didn't see you!
HUH?!
OH...
...IT'S JUST THAT KAEDE'S BEEN COLD RECENTLY.
SHE HUNG UP ON ME, SAYING SHE HAD HOMEWORK, BUT I WANTED TO TALK MORE.
WELL, DON'T CALL WHEN SHE'S DOING HOMEWORK!
SHE NEVER WEARS THE HAIRPINS I BUY...
...SO I WANTED TO GET HER CLOTHES.
AHA!!

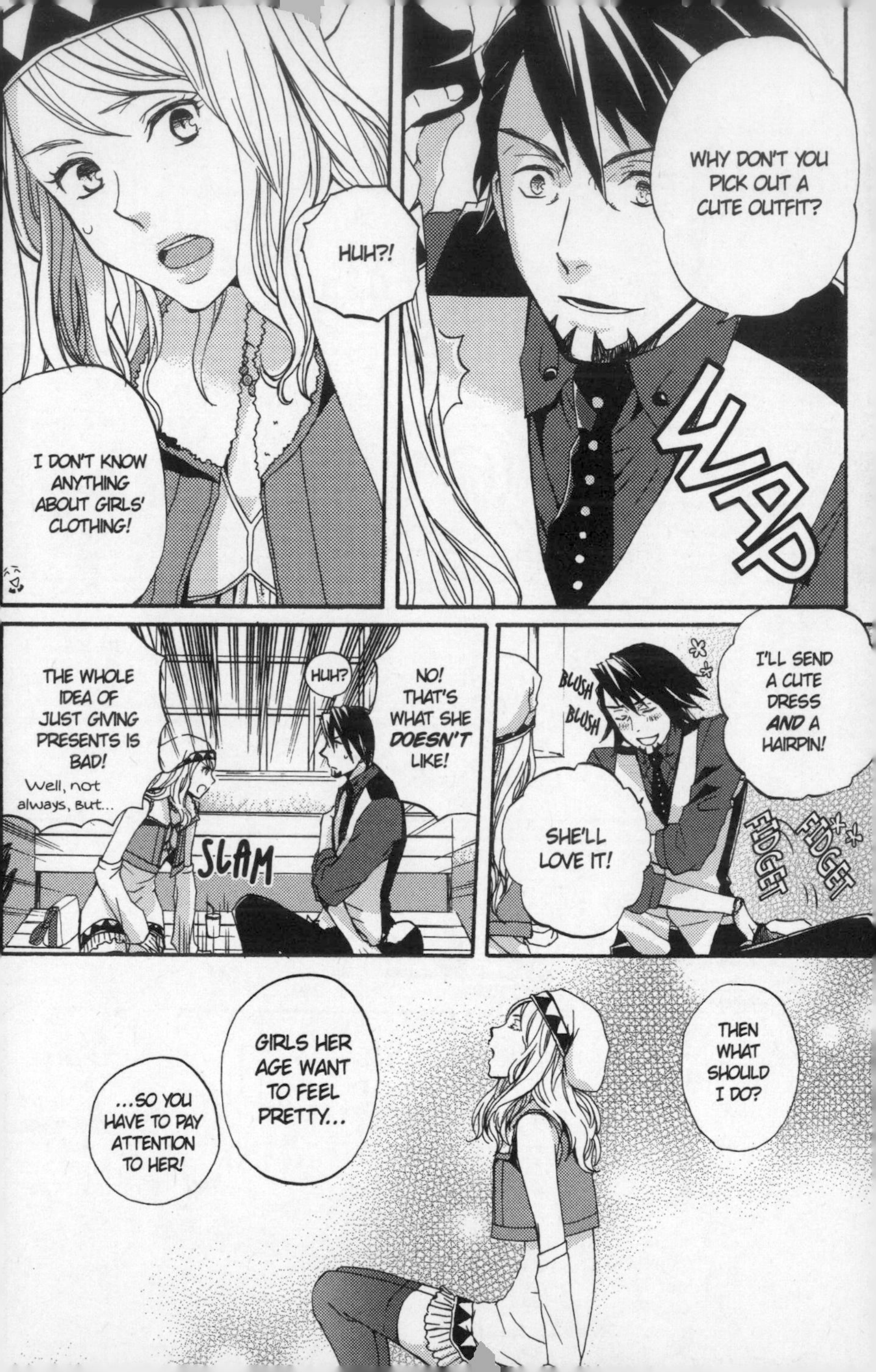
WHY DON'T YOU PICK OUT A CUTE OUTFIT?
WAP
HUH?!
I DON'T KNOW ANYTHING ABOUT GIRLS' CLOTHING!
I'LL SEND A CUTE DRESS AND A HAIRPIN!
BLUSH
BLUSH
FIDGET
FIDGET
SHE'LL LOVE IT!
NO! THAT'S WHAT SHE DOESN'T LIKE!
HUH?
THE WHOLE IDEA OF JUST GIVING PRESENTS IS BAD!
Well, not always, but...
SLAM
THEN WHAT SHOULD I DO?
GIRLS HER AGE WANT TO FEEL PRETTY...
...SO YOU HAVE TO PAY ATTENTION TO HER!

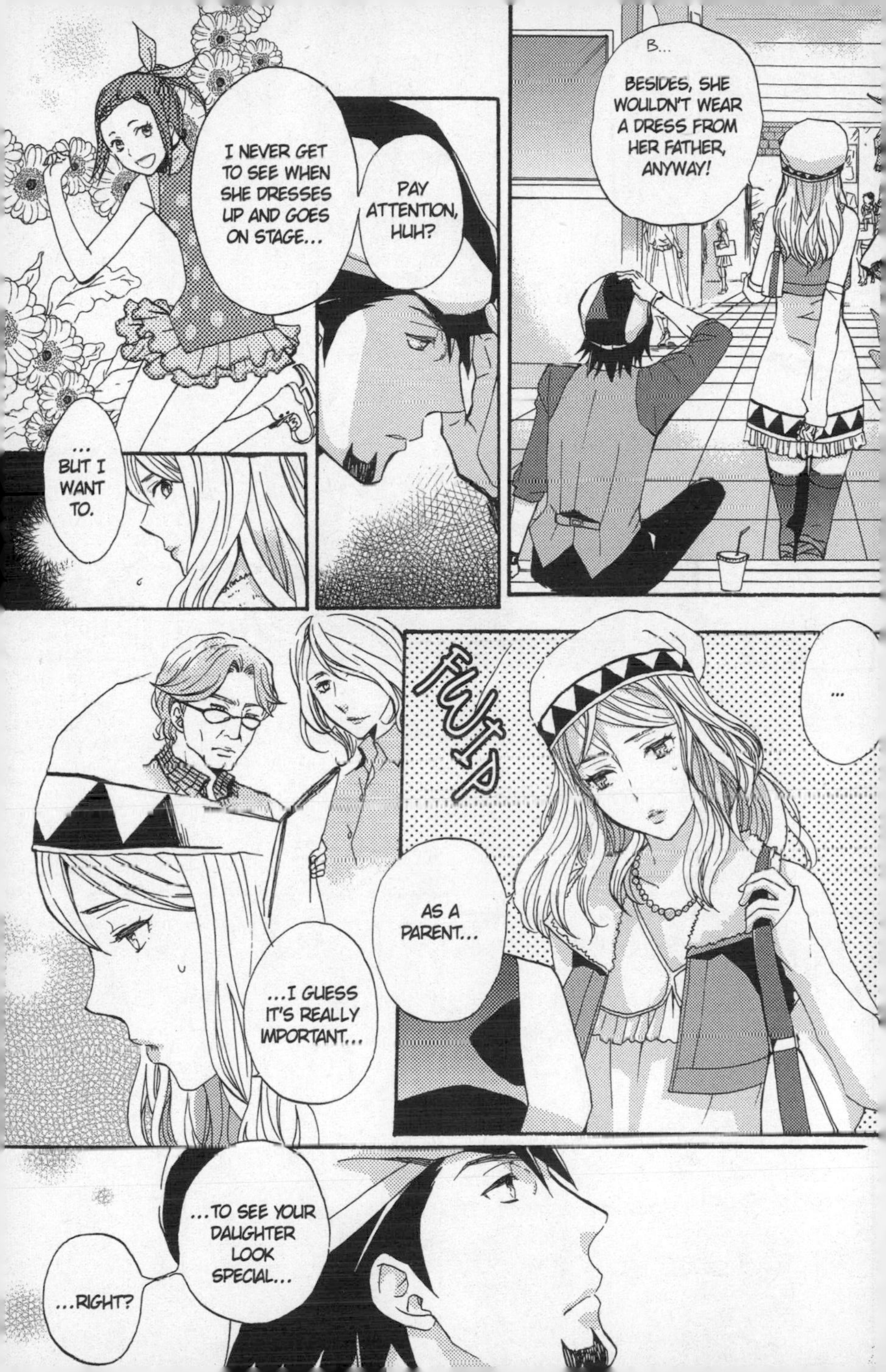
B...
BESIDES, SHE WOULDN'T WEAR A DRESS FROM HER FATHER, ANYWAY!
PAY ATTENTION, HUH?
I NEVER GET TO SEE WHEN SHE DRESSES UP AND GOES ON STAGE...
...BUT I WANT TO.
...
FLIP
AS A PARENT...
...I GUESS IT'S REALLY IMPORTANT...
...TO SEE YOUR DAUGHTER LOOK SPECIAL...
...RIGHT?

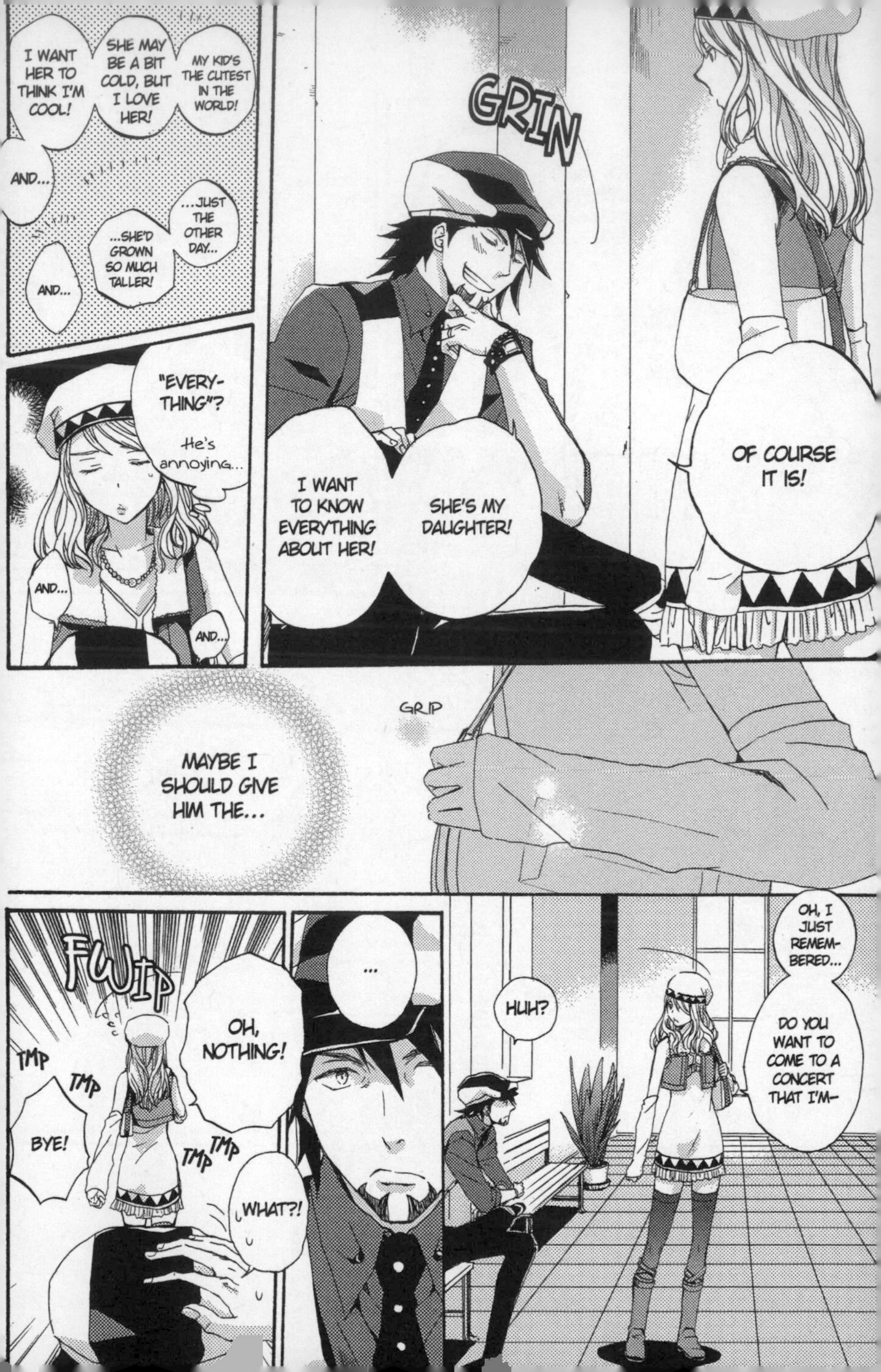
OF COURSE IT IS!
GRIN
SHE'S MY DAUGHTER!
I WANT TO KNOW EVERYTHING ABOUT HER!
MY KID'S THE CUTEST IN THE WORLD!
SHE MAY BE A BIT COLD, BUT I LOVE HER!
I WANT HER TO THINK I'M COOL!
AND...
...JUST THE OTHER DAY...
...SHE'D GROWN SO MUCH TALLER!
AND...
"EVERY-THING"?
He's annoying...
AND...
AND...
GRIP
MAYBE I SHOULD GIVE HIM THE...
OH, I JUST REMEMBERED...
DO YOU WANT TO COME TO A CONCERT THAT I'M-
HUH?
...
OH, NOTHING!
WHAT?!
FWIP
TMP
TMP
BYE!
TMP
TMP

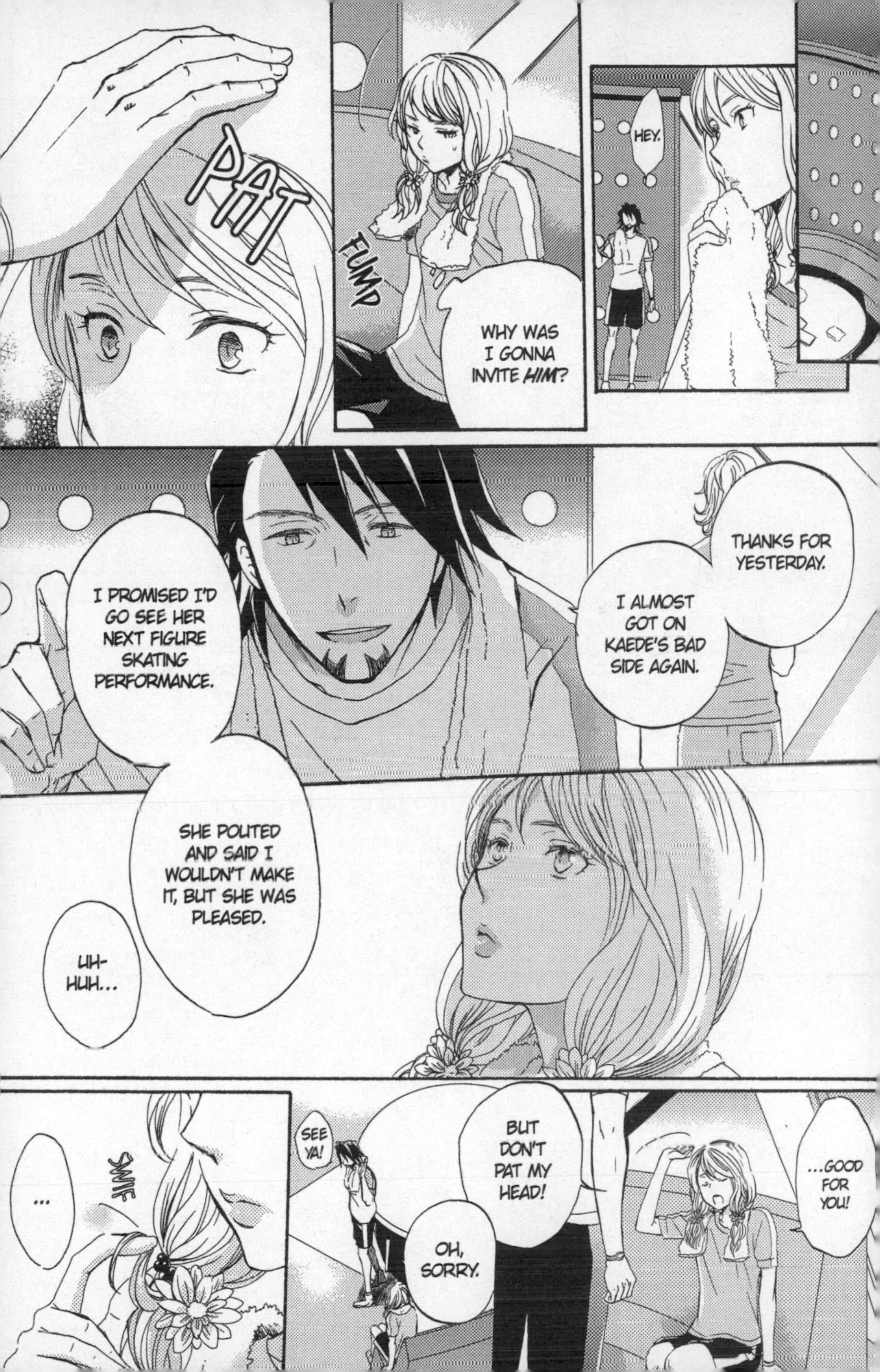
HEY.
FUMP
WHY WAS I GONNA INVITE *HIM*?
PAT
THANKS FOR YESTERDAY.
I ALMOST GOT ON KAEDE'S BAD SIDE AGAIN.
I PROMISED I'D GO SEE HER NEXT FIGURE SKATING PERFORMANCE.
SHE POUTED AND SAID I WOULDN'T MAKE IT, BUT SHE WAS PLEASED.
UH-HUH...
...GOOD FOR YOU!
BUT DON'T PAT MY HEAD!
OH, SORRY.
SEE YA!
SWIF
...

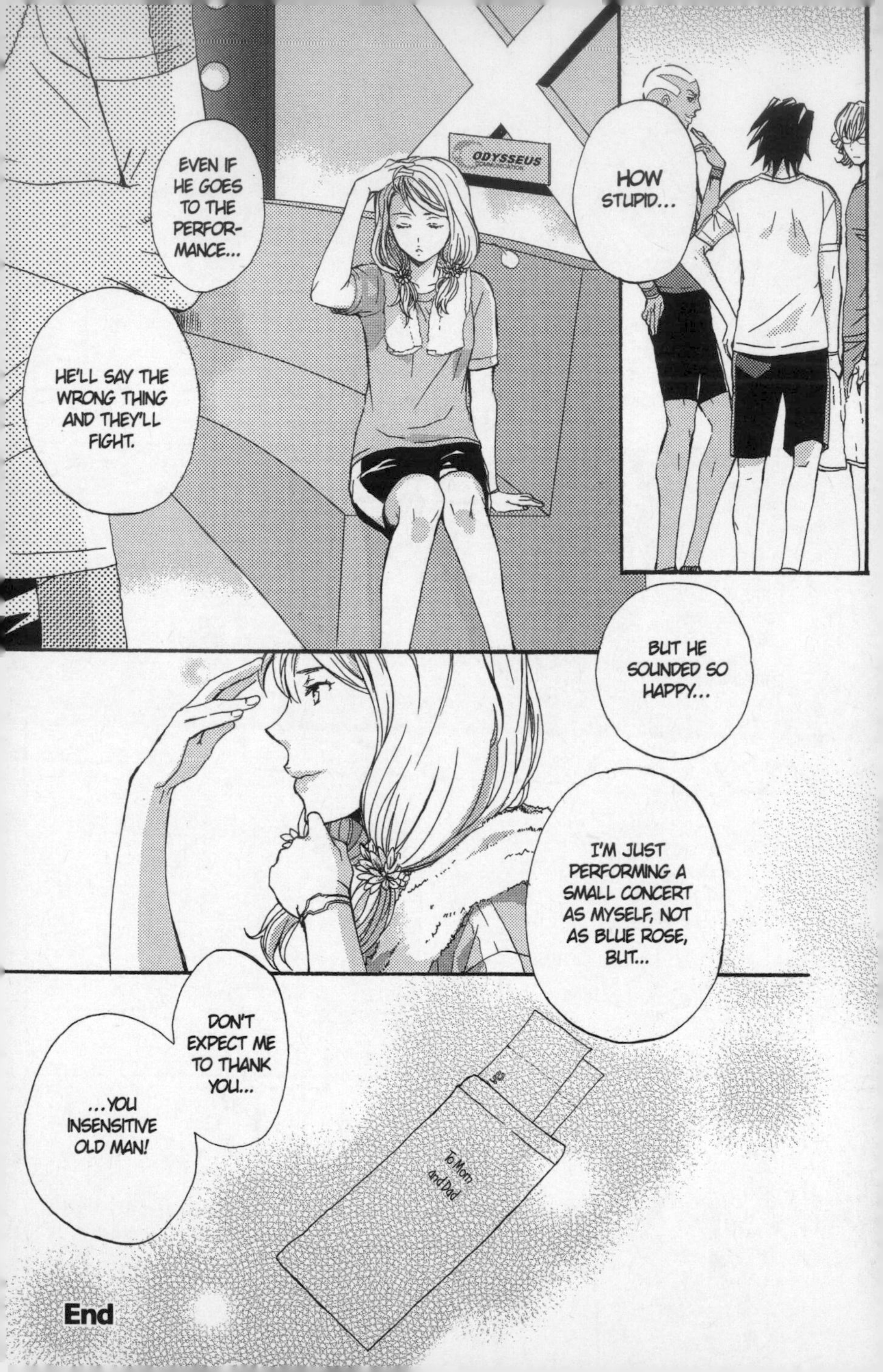
HOW STUPID...
EVEN IF HE GOES TO THE PERFOR-MANCE...
HE'LL SAY THE WRONG THING AND THEY'LL FIGHT.
ODYSSEUS
BUT HE SOUNDED SO HAPPY...
I'M JUST PERFORMING A SMALL CONCERT AS MYSELF, NOT AS BLUE ROSE, BUT...
DON'T EXPECT ME TO THANK YOU...
...YOU INSENSITIVE OLD MAN!
To Mom and Dad
End

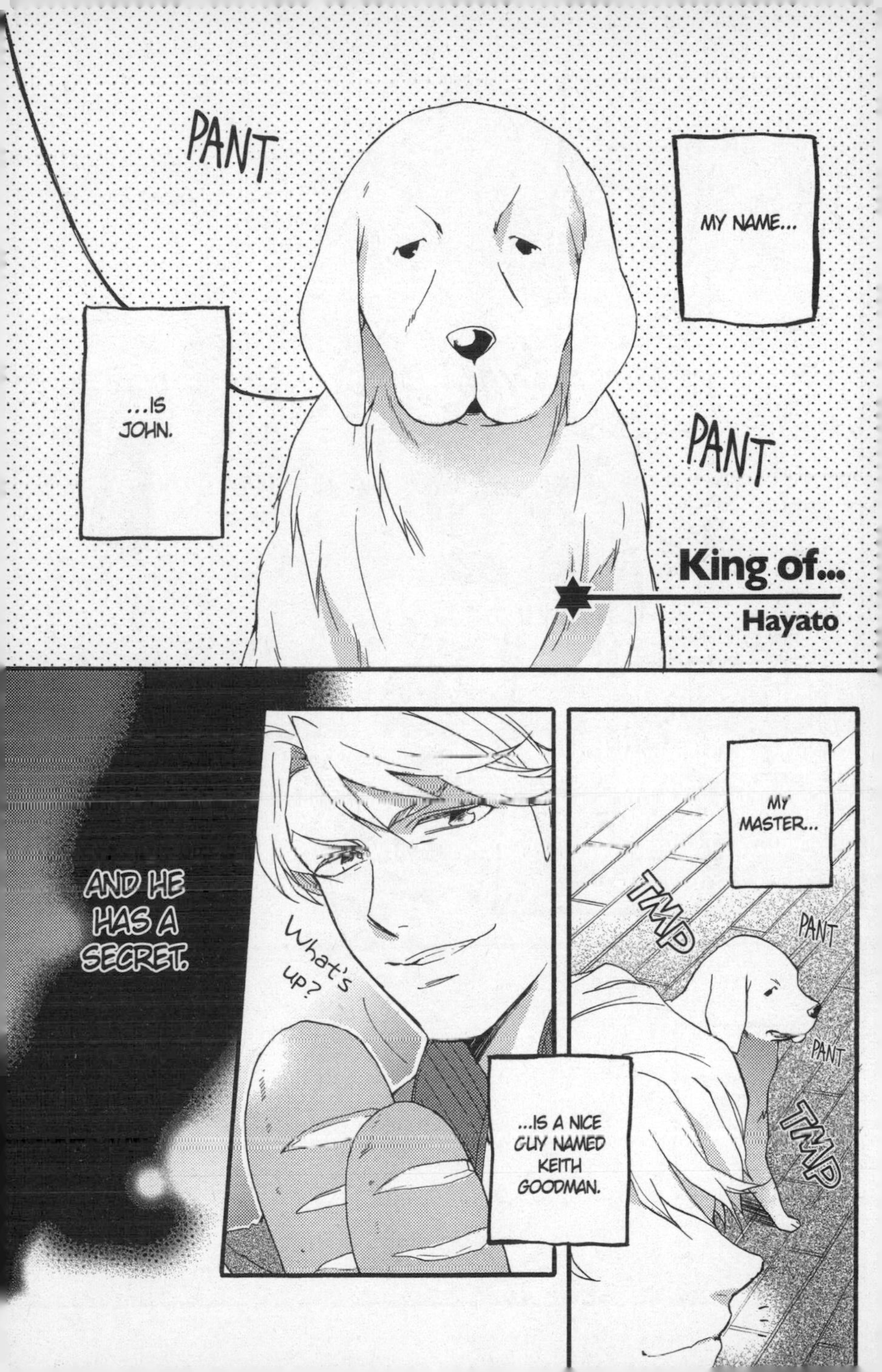
MY NAME...
PANT
...IS JOHN.
PANT
King of...
Hayato
MY MASTER...
TMP
PANT
PANT
TMP
...IS A NICE GUY NAMED KEITH GOODMAN.
What's up?
AND HE HAS A SECRET.

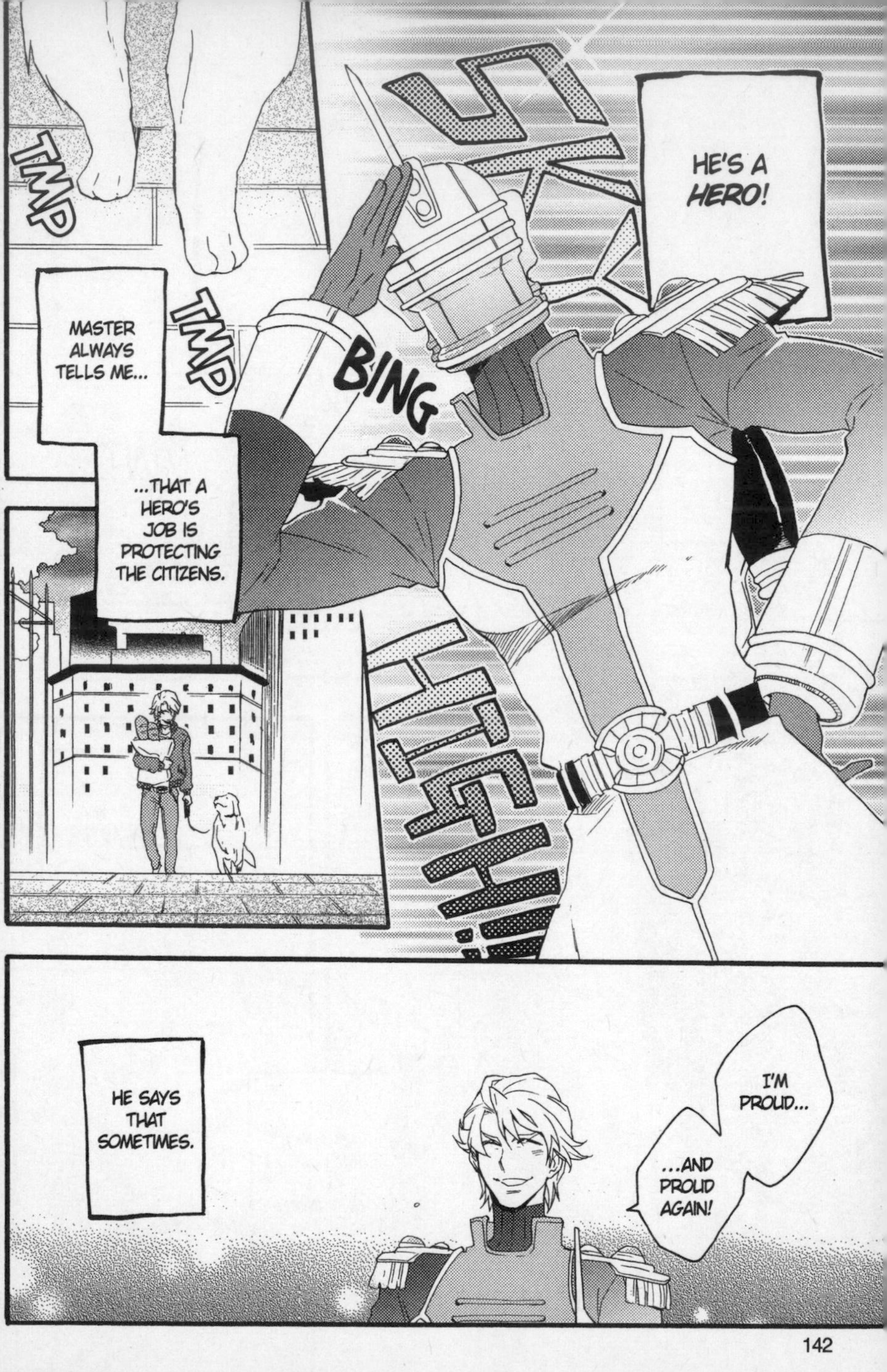
HE'S A HERO!
SKY
BING
TMP
TMP
MASTER ALWAYS TELLS ME...
...THAT A HERO'S JOB IS PROTECTING THE CITIZENS.
I'M PROUD...
...AND PROUD AGAIN!
HE SAYS THAT SOMETIMES.

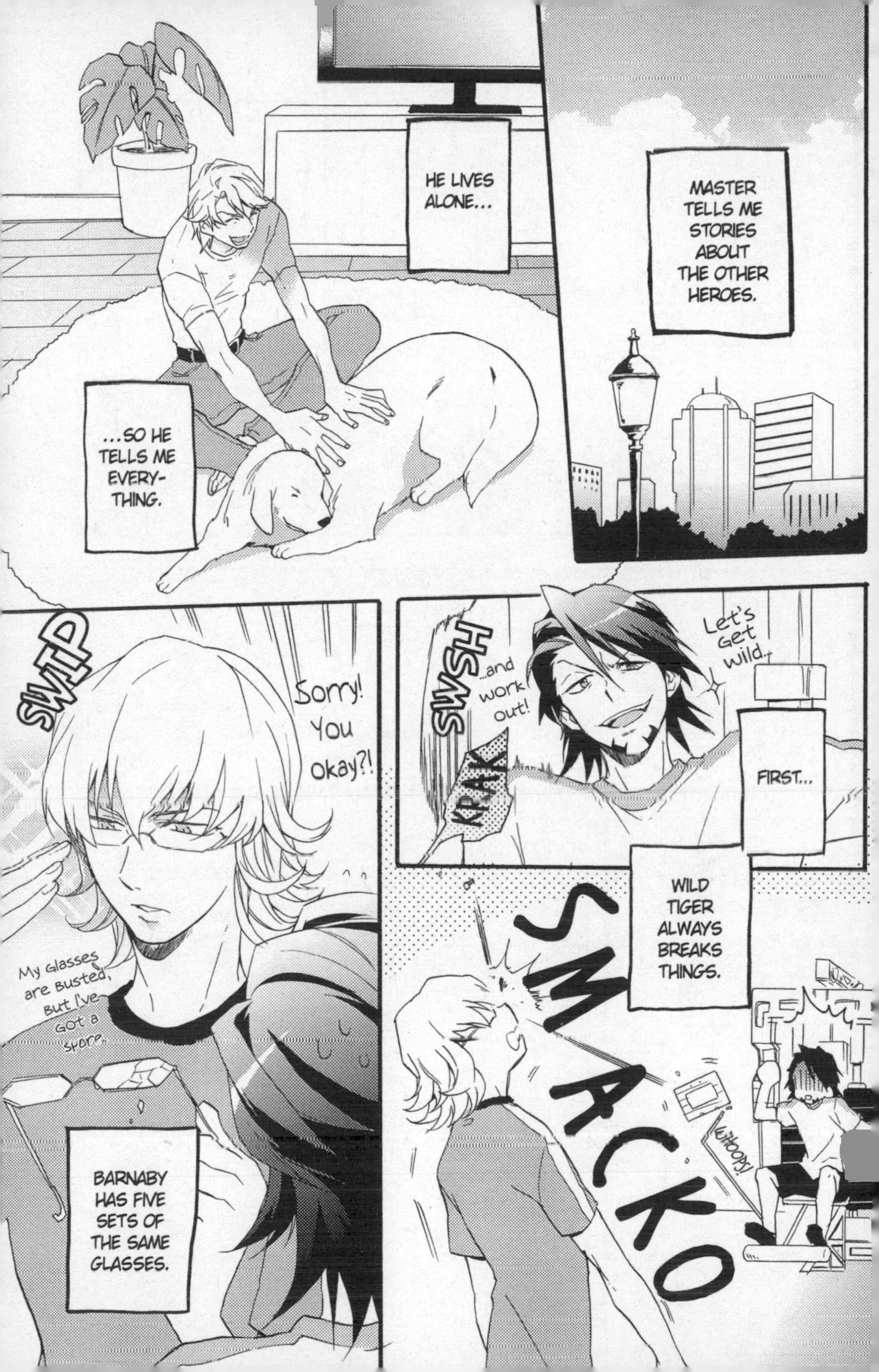
MASTER TELLS ME STORIES ABOUT THE OTHER HEROES.
HE LIVES ALONE...
...SO HE TELLS ME EVERY-THING.
FIRST...
Let's Get wild..
...and work out!
SWSH
KRAK
WILD TIGER ALWAYS BREAKS THINGS.
SMACKO
Whoops!
SWIP
Sorry! You okay?!
My Glasses are Busted, But I've Got a spare.
BARNABY HAS FIVE SETS OF THE SAME GLASSES.

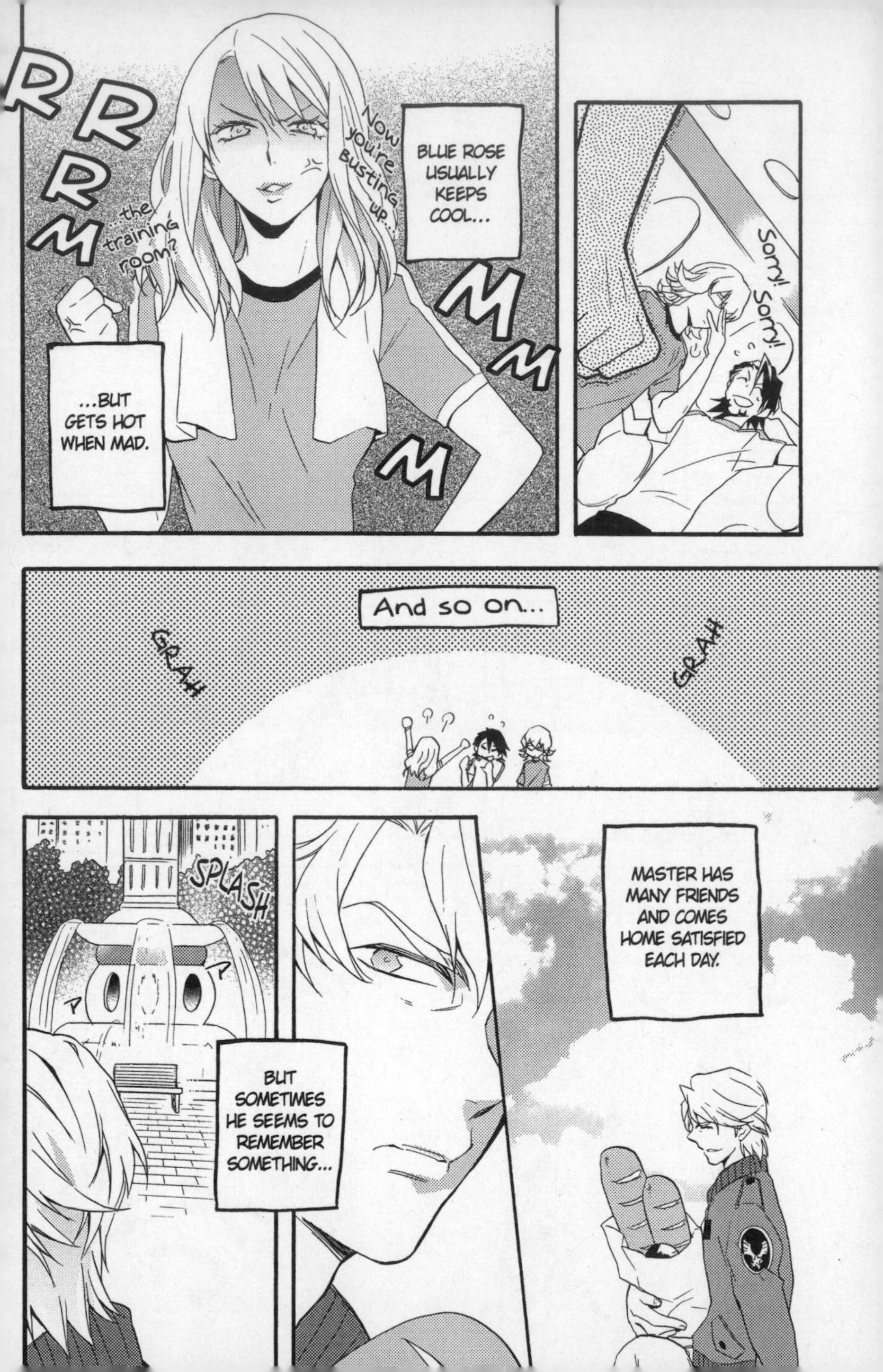
Sorry! Sorry! Sorry!
BLUE ROSE USUALLY KEEPS COOL...
Now you're busting up...
...the training room?
RRRRM
...BUT GETS HOT WHEN MAD.
MMMM
And so on...
GRAH
GRAH
MASTER HAS MANY FRIENDS AND COMES HOME SATISFIED EACH DAY.
BUT SOMETIMES HE SEEMS TO REMEMBER SOMETHING...
SPLASH

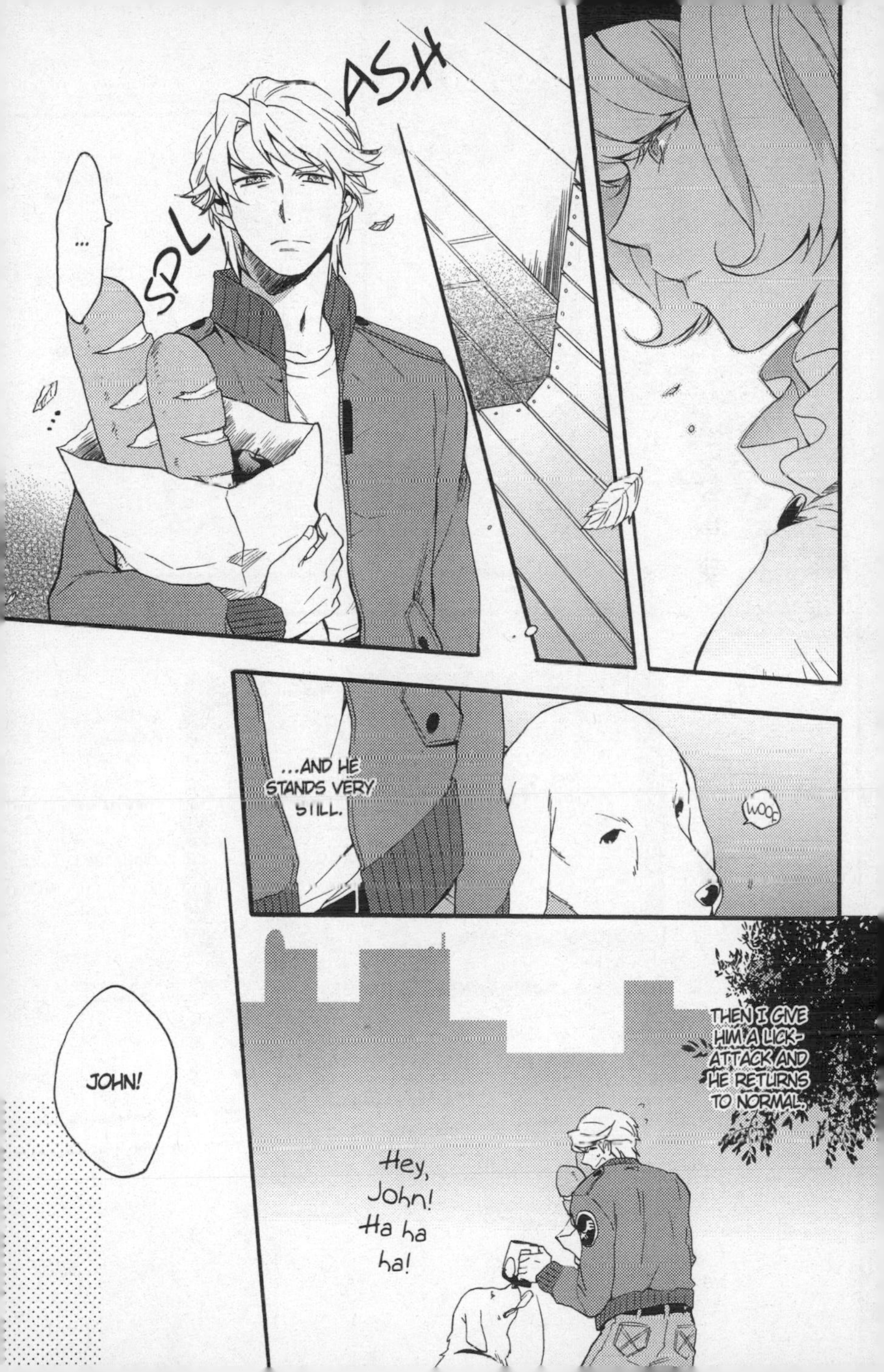

SPL
ASH
...
WOOF
...AND HE STANDS VERY STILL.
THEN I GIVE HIM A LICK-ATTACK AND HE RETURNS TO NORMAL.
Hey, John! Ha ha ha!
JOHN!

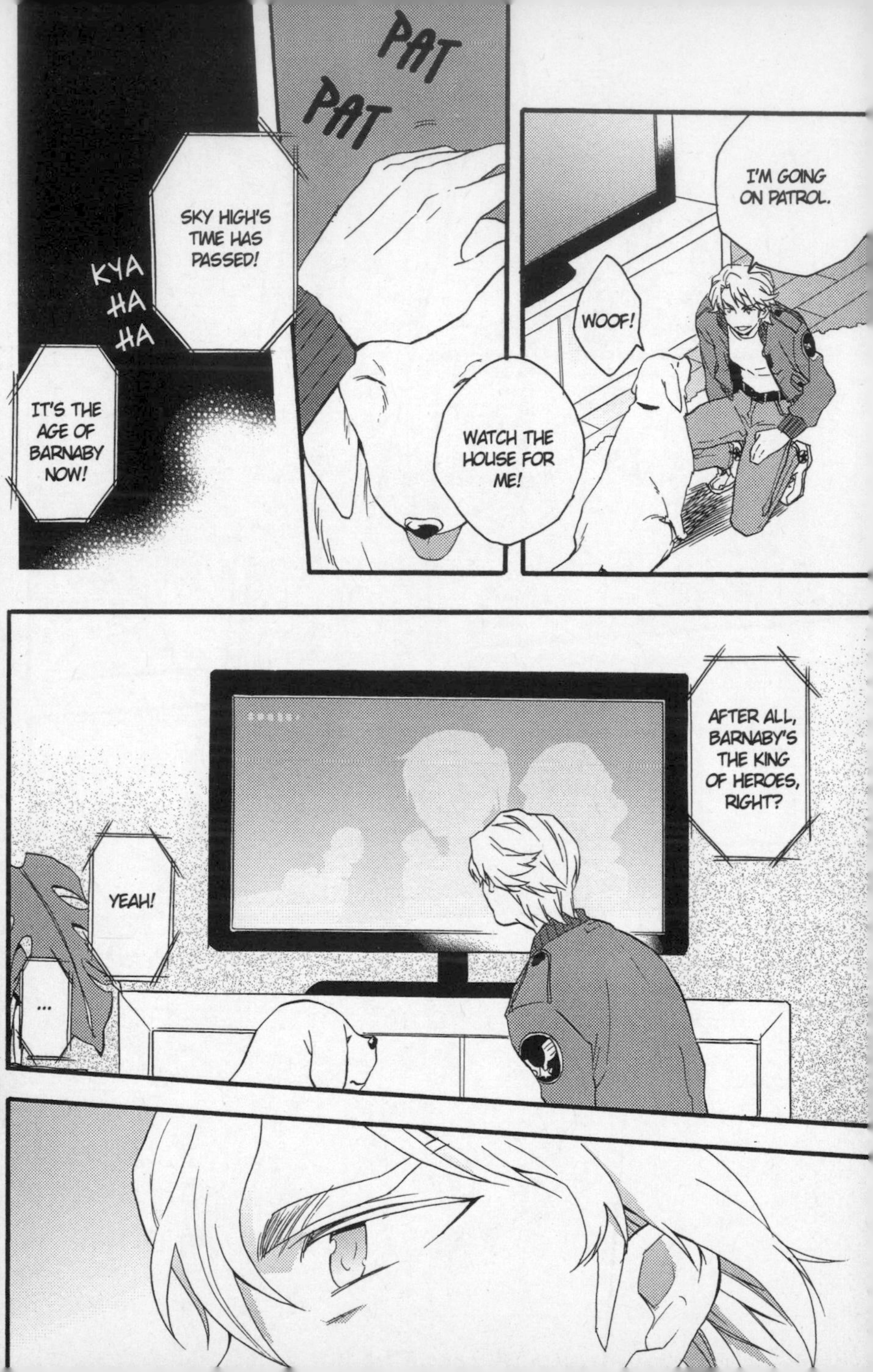
I'M GOING ON PATROL.
WOOF!
PAT PAT
WATCH THE HOUSE FOR ME!
SKY HIGH'S TIME HAS PASSED!
KYA HA HA
IT'S THE AGE OF BARNABY NOW!
AFTER ALL, BARNABY'S THE KING OF HEROES, RIGHT?
YEAH!
...

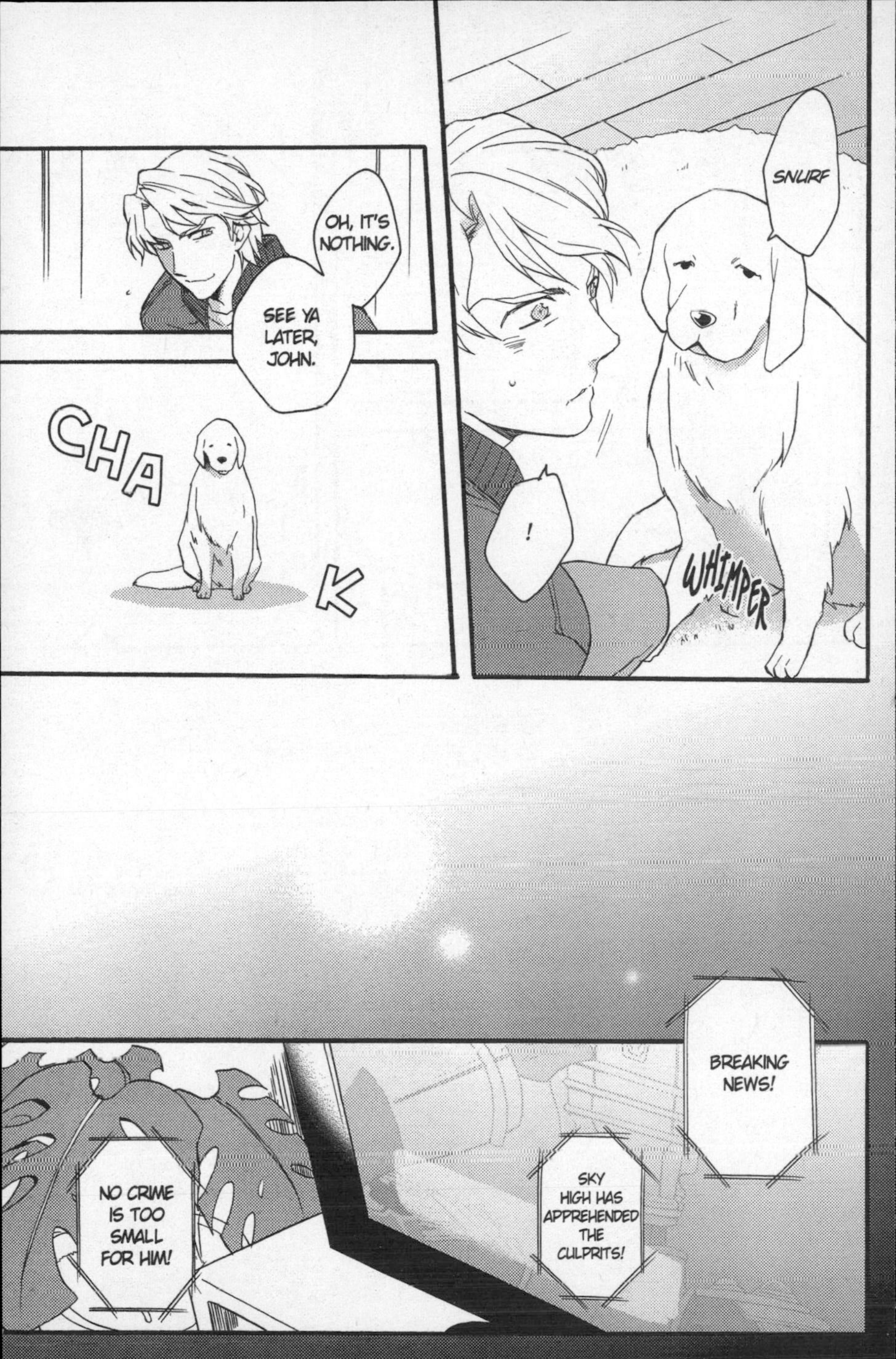
SNURF
!
WHIMPER
OH, IT'S NOTHING.
SEE YA LATER, JOHN.
CHA
K
BREAKING NEWS!
SKY HIGH HAS APPREHENDED THE CULPRITS!
NO CRIME IS TOO SMALL FOR HIM!

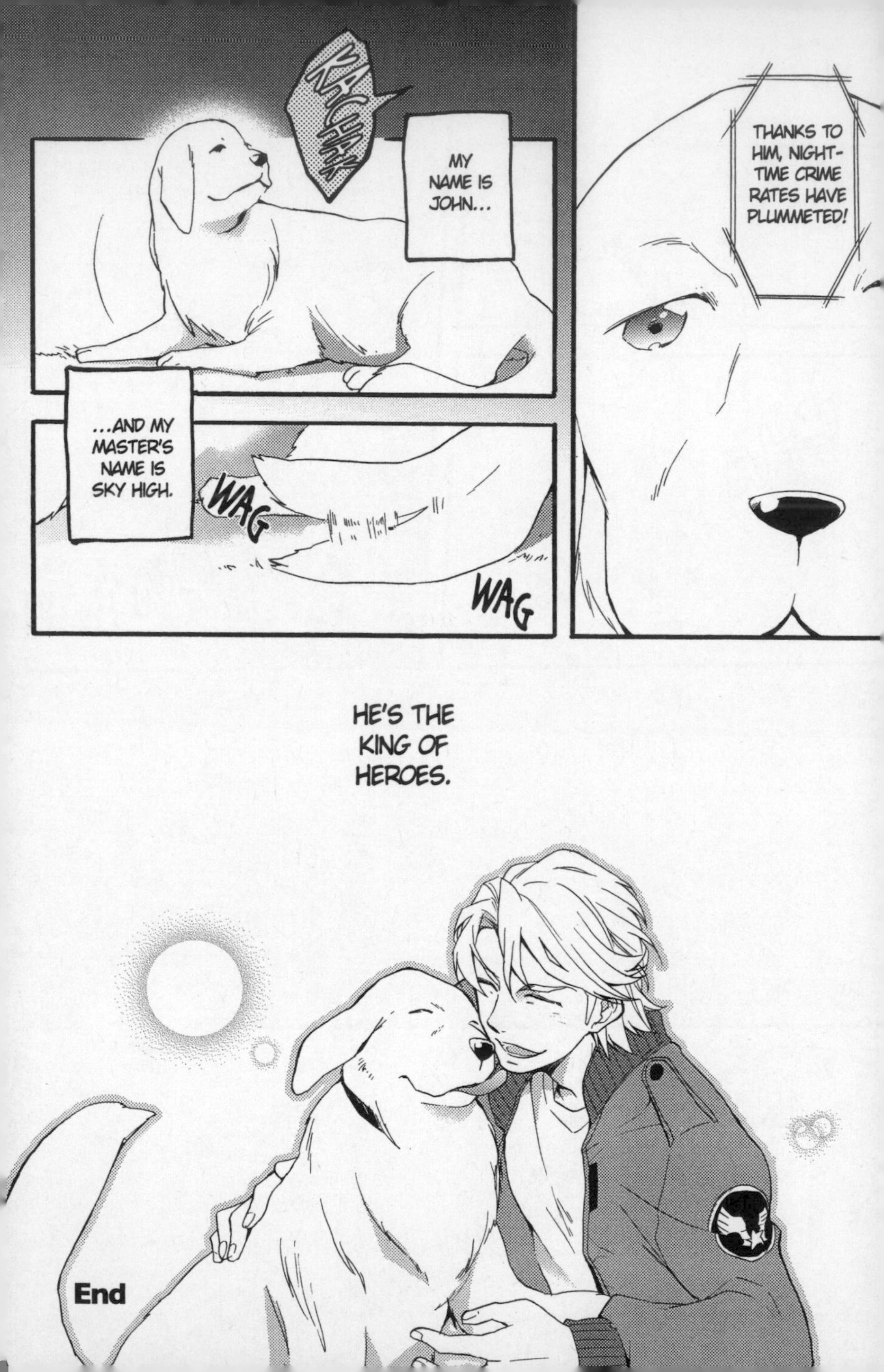
THANKS TO HIM, NIGHT-TIME CRIME RATES HAVE PLUMMETED!
KACHAK
MY NAME IS JOHN...
...AND MY MASTER'S NAME IS SKY HIGH.
WAG
WAG
HE'S THE KING OF HEROES.
End

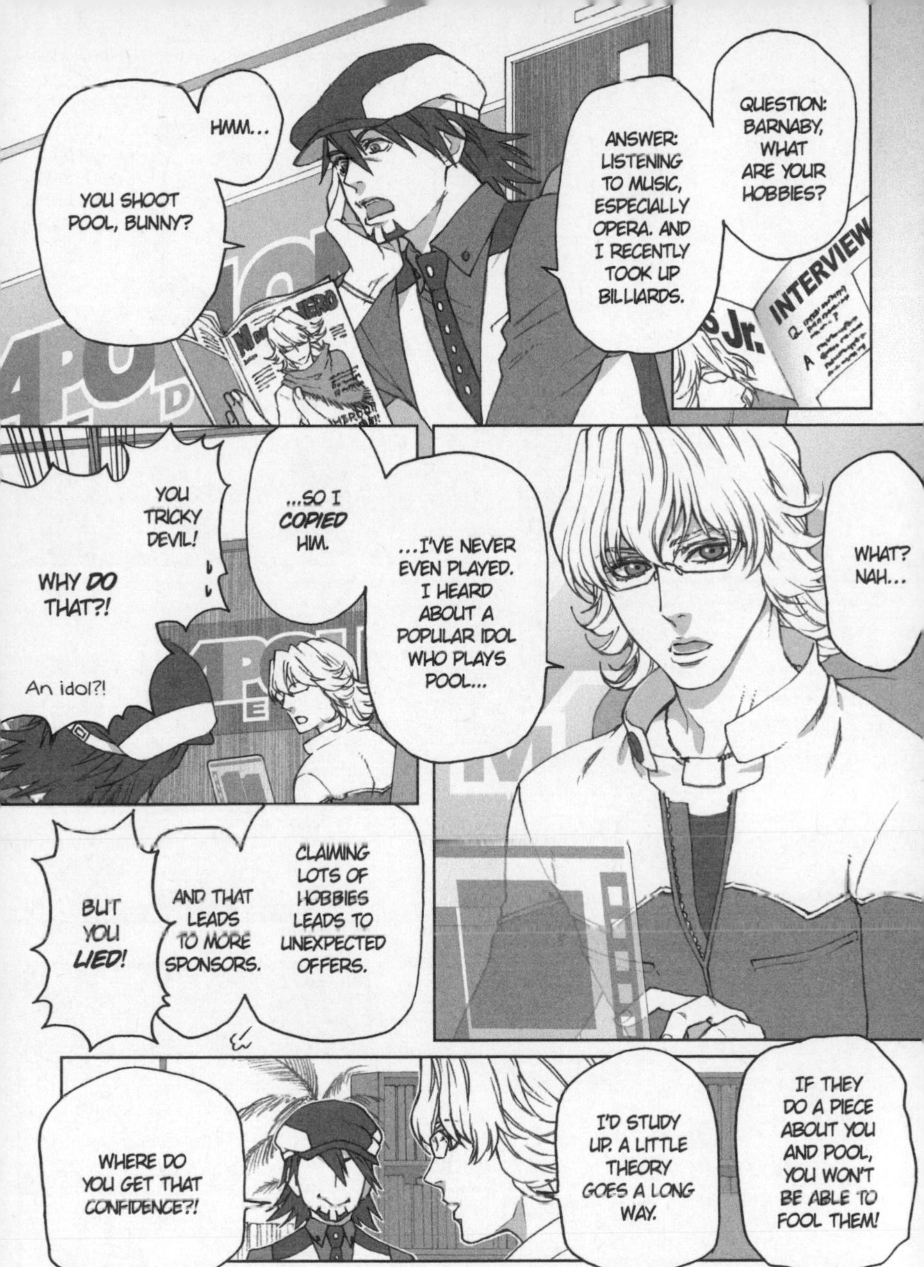
QUESTION: BARNABY, WHAT ARE YOUR HOBBIES?
INTERVIEW
ANSWER: LISTENING TO MUSIC, ESPECIALLY OPERA. AND I RECENTLY TOOK UP BILLIARDS.
HMM...
YOU SHOOT POOL, BUNNY?
WHAT? NAH...
...I'VE NEVER EVEN PLAYED. I HEARD ABOUT A POPULAR IDOL WHO PLAYS POOL...
...SO I *COPIED* HIM.
YOU TRICKY DEVIL!
WHY *DO* THAT?!
An idol?!
CLAIMING LOTS OF HOBBIES LEADS TO UNEXPECTED OFFERS.
AND THAT LEADS TO MORE SPONSORS.
BUT YOU *LIED!*
IF THEY DO A PIECE ABOUT YOU AND POOL, YOU WON'T BE ABLE TO FOOL THEM!
I'D STUDY UP. A LITTLE THEORY GOES A LONG WAY.
WHERE DO YOU GET THAT CONFIDENCE?!

THE BELIEVED CHOICE.

Tomo

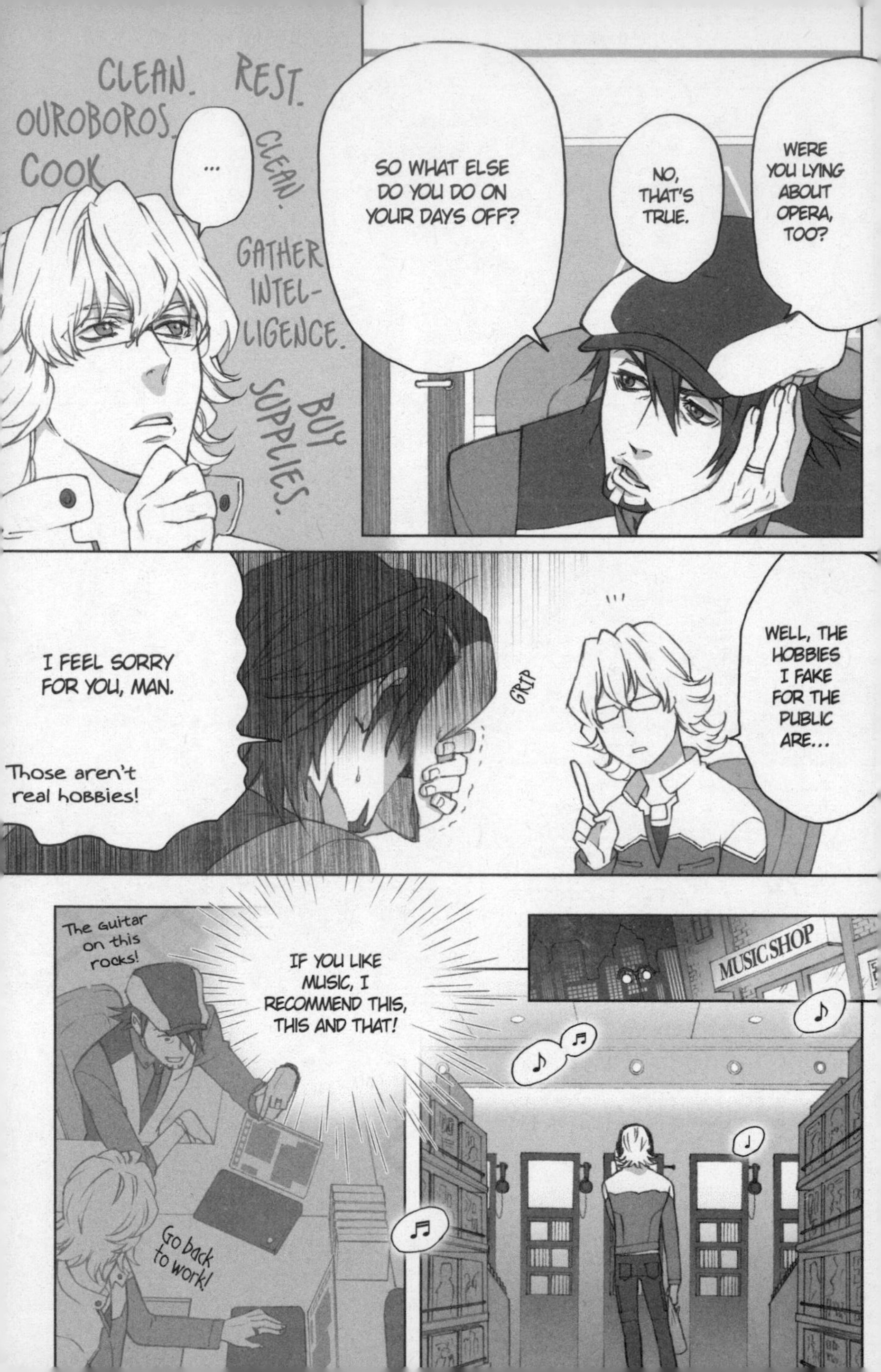
WERE YOU LYING ABOUT OPERA, TOO?
NO, THAT'S TRUE.
SO WHAT ELSE DO YOU DO ON YOUR DAYS OFF?
...
REST.
CLEAN.
OUROBOROS.
COOK
CLEAN.
GATHER INTEL-LIGENCE.
BUY SUPPLIES.
WELL, THE HOBBIES I FAKE FOR THE PUBLIC ARE...
GRIP
I FEEL SORRY FOR YOU, MAN.
Those aren't real hobbies!
MUSIC SHOP
IF YOU LIKE MUSIC, I RECOMMEND THIS, THIS AND THAT!
The guitar on this rocks!
Go back to work!

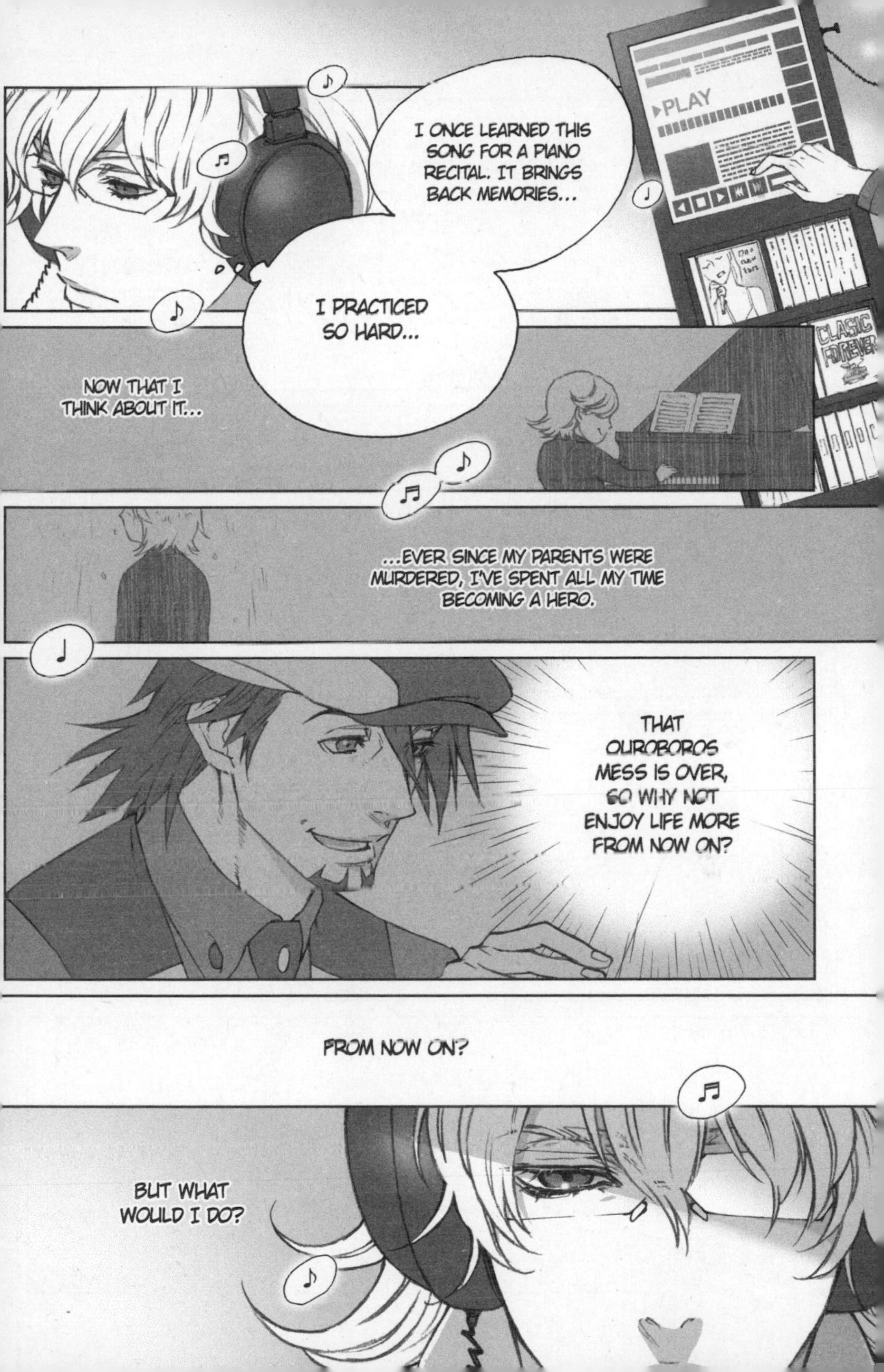

PLAY
I ONCE LEARNED THIS SONG FOR A PIANO RECITAL. IT BRINGS BACK MEMORIES...
I PRACTICED SO HARD...
CLASIC FOREVER
NOW THAT I THINK ABOUT IT...
...EVER SINCE MY PARENTS WERE MURDERED, I'VE SPENT ALL MY TIME BECOMING A HERO.
THAT OUROBOROS MESS IS OVER, SO WHY NOT ENJOY LIFE MORE FROM NOW ON?
FROM NOW ON?
BUT WHAT WOULD I DO?

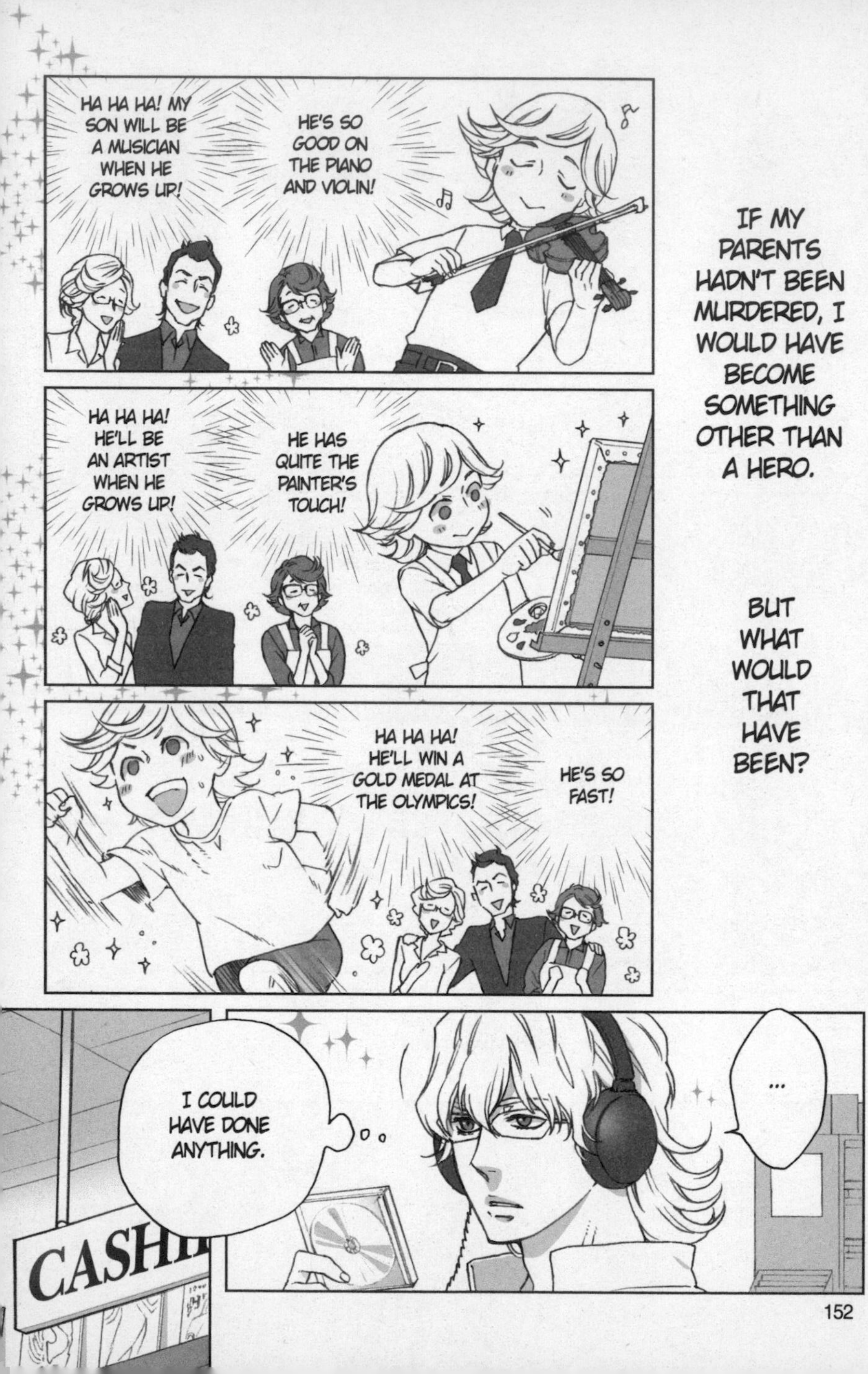

IF MY PARENTS HADN'T BEEN MURDERED, I WOULD HAVE BECOME SOMETHING OTHER THAN A HERO.
BUT WHAT WOULD THAT HAVE BEEN?
HE'S SO GOOD ON THE PIANO AND VIOLIN!
HA HA HA! MY SON WILL BE A MUSICIAN WHEN HE GROWS UP!
HE HAS QUITE THE PAINTER'S TOUCH!
HA HA HA! HE'LL BE AN ARTIST WHEN HE GROWS UP!
HE'S SO FAST!
HA HA HA! HE'LL WIN A GOLD MEDAL AT THE OLYMPICS!
...
I COULD HAVE DONE ANYTHING.

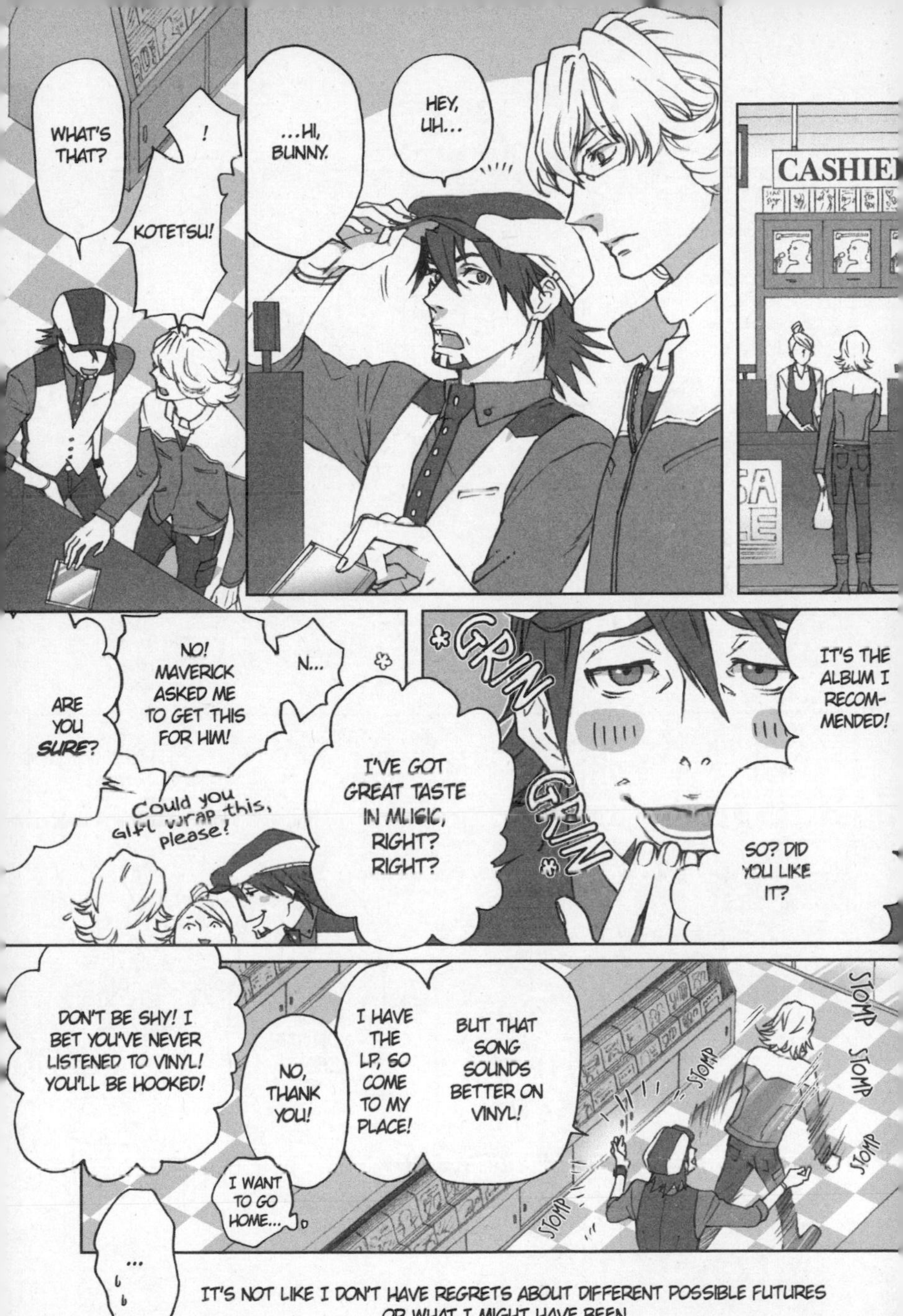
CASHIER
HEY, UH...
...HI, BUNNY.
!
KOTETSU!
WHAT'S THAT?
IT'S THE ALBUM I RECOMMENDED!
GRIN GRIN
SO? DID YOU LIKE IT?
I'VE GOT GREAT TASTE IN MUSIC, RIGHT? RIGHT?
N...
NO! MAVERICK ASKED ME TO GET THIS FOR HIM!
ARE YOU *SURE*?
Could you gift wrap this, please!
STOMP STOMP STOMP
BUT THAT SONG SOUNDS BETTER ON VINYL!
I HAVE THE LP, SO COME TO MY PLACE!
NO, THANK YOU!
DON'T BE SHY! I BET YOU'VE NEVER LISTENED TO VINYL! YOU'LL BE HOOKED!
STOMP STOMP
I WANT TO GO HOME...
...
IT'S NOT LIKE I DON'T HAVE REGRETS ABOUT DIFFERENT POSSIBLE FUTURES OR WHAT I MIGHT HAVE BEEN...

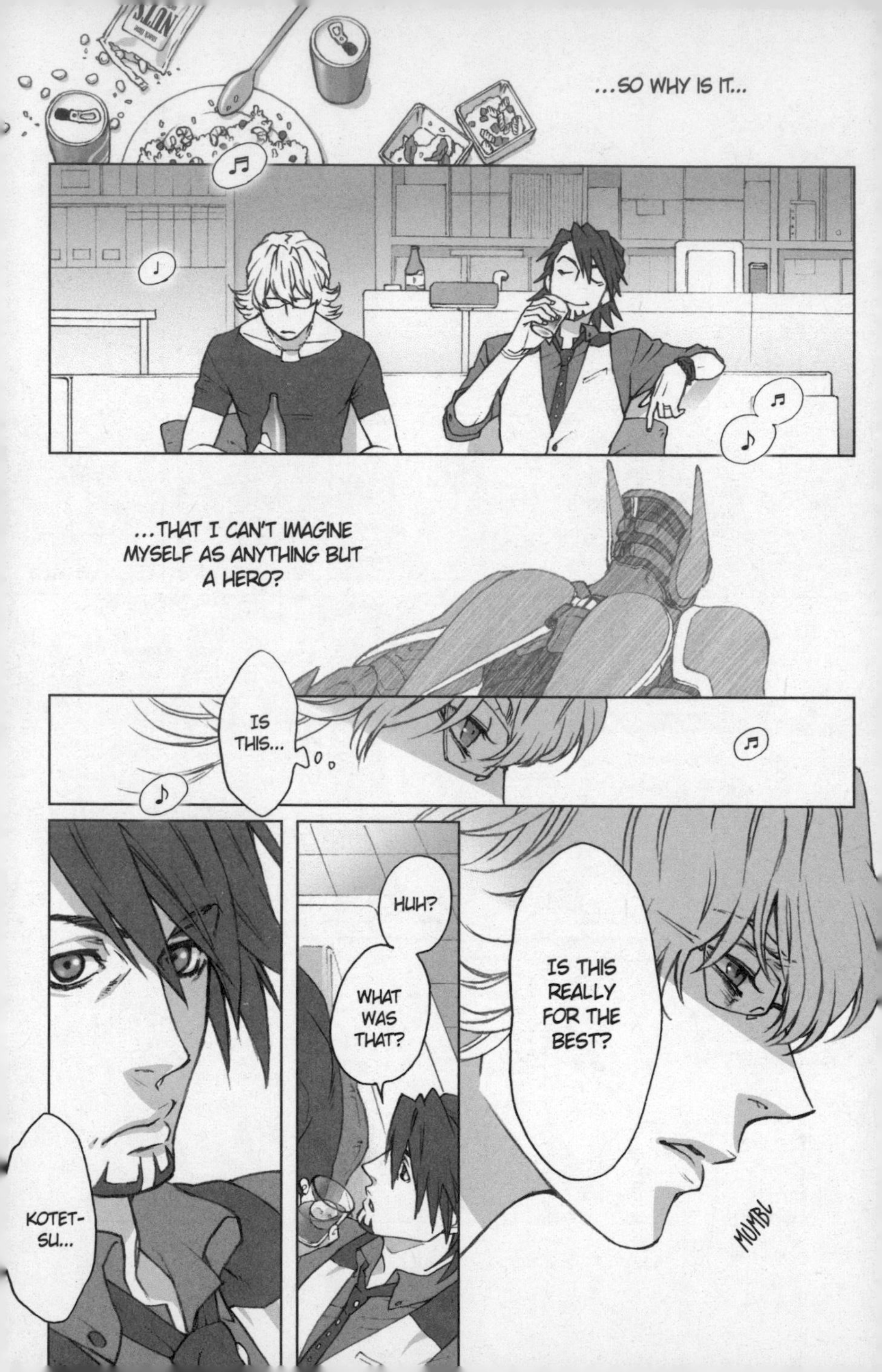
...SO WHY IS IT...
...THAT I CAN'T IMAGINE MYSELF AS ANYTHING BUT A HERO?
IS THIS...
IS THIS REALLY FOR THE BEST?
MUMBL
HUH?
WHAT WAS THAT?
KOTET-SU...

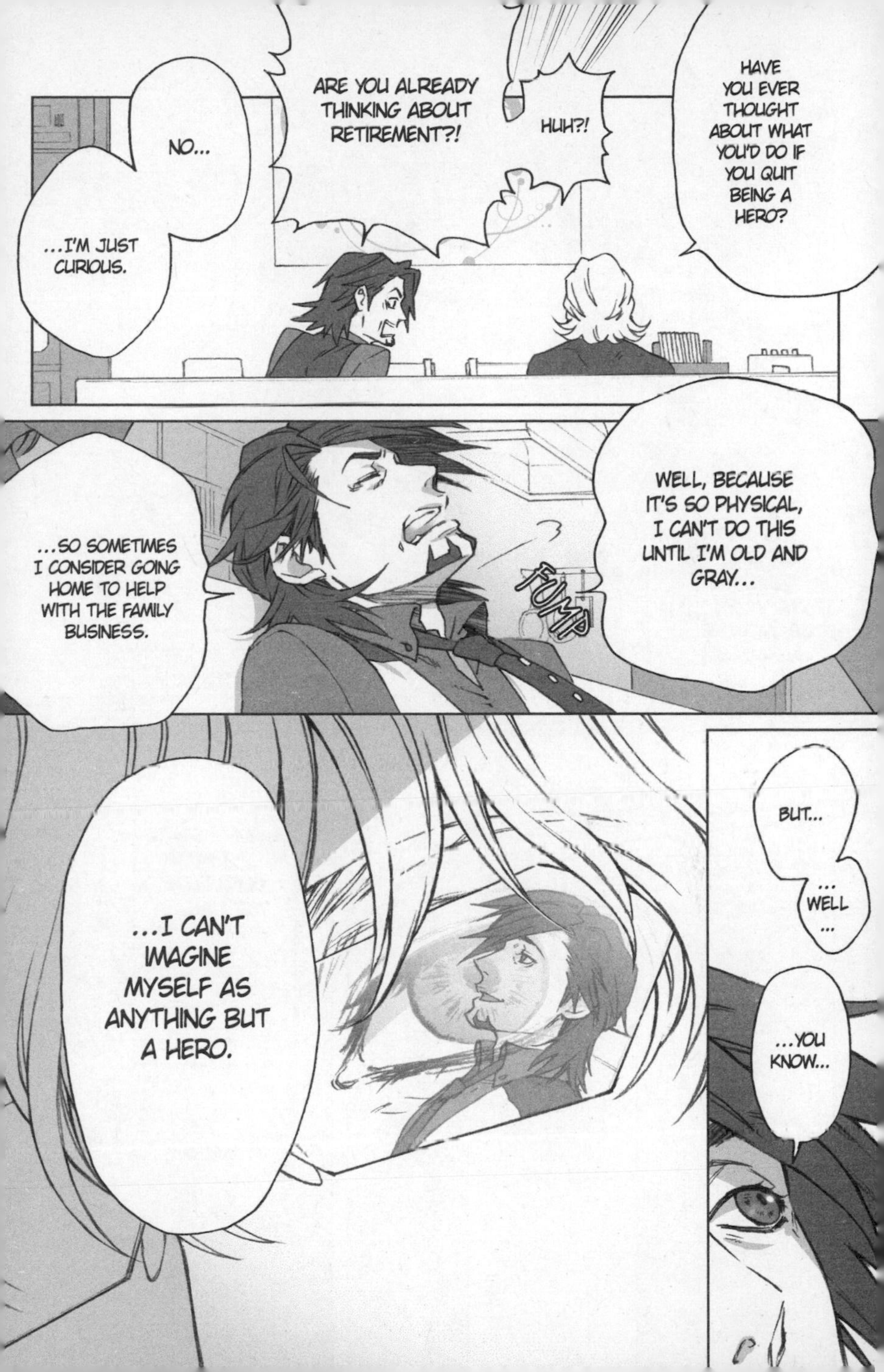
HAVE YOU EVER THOUGHT ABOUT WHAT YOU'D DO IF YOU QUIT BEING A HERO?
HUH?!
ARE YOU ALREADY THINKING ABOUT RETIREMENT?!
NO...
...I'M JUST CURIOUS.
WELL, BECAUSE IT'S SO PHYSICAL, I CAN'T DO THIS UNTIL I'M OLD AND GRAY...
FUMP
...SO SOMETIMES I CONSIDER GOING HOME TO HELP WITH THE FAMILY BUSINESS.
BUT...
...WELL...
...YOU KNOW...
...I CAN'T IMAGINE MYSELF AS ANYTHING BUT A HERO.

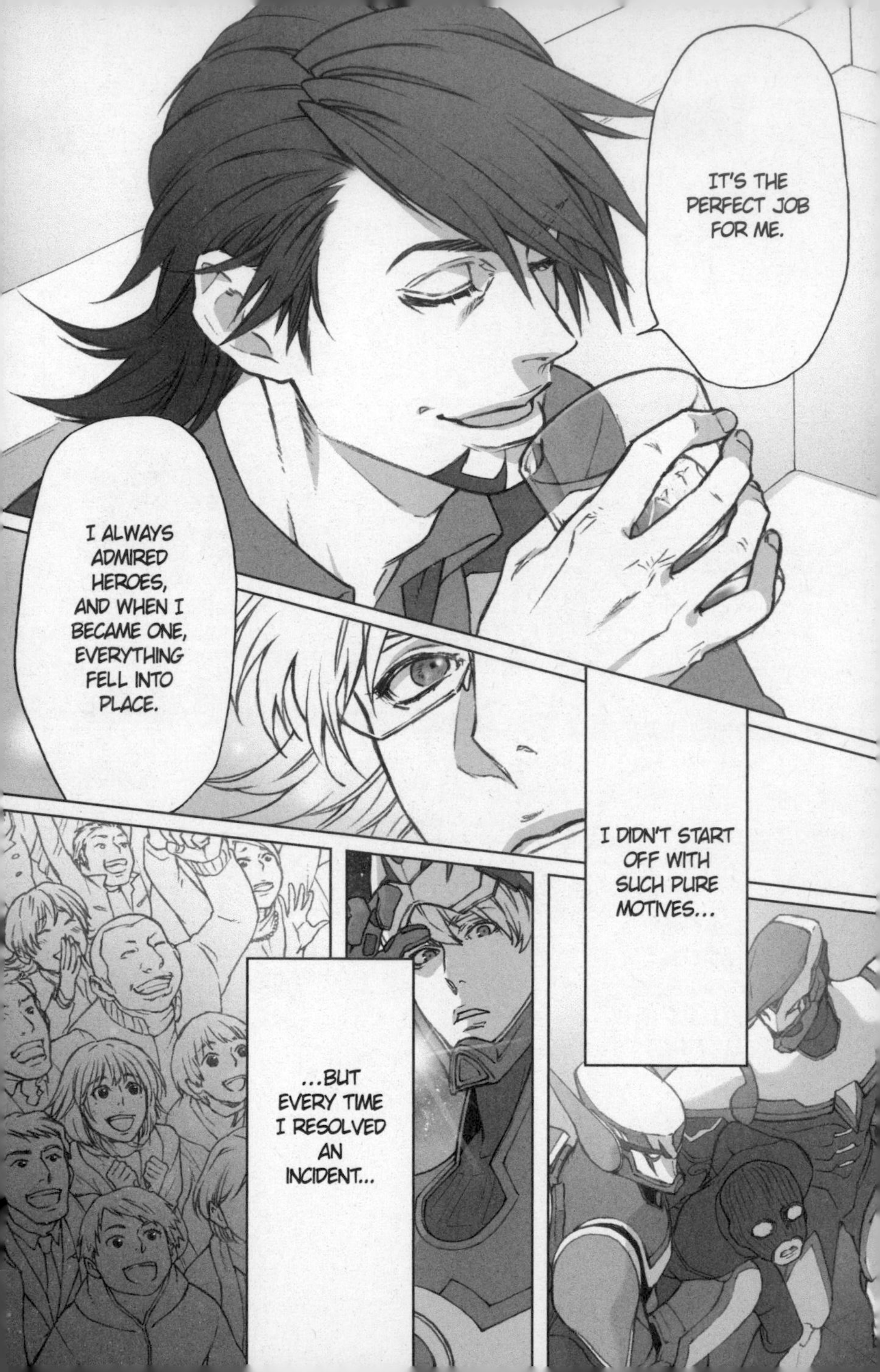
IT'S THE PERFECT JOB FOR ME.
I ALWAYS ADMIRED HEROES, AND WHEN I BECAME ONE, EVERYTHING FELL INTO PLACE.
I DIDN'T START OFF WITH SUCH PURE MOTIVES...
...BUT EVERY TIME I RESOLVED AN INCIDENT...

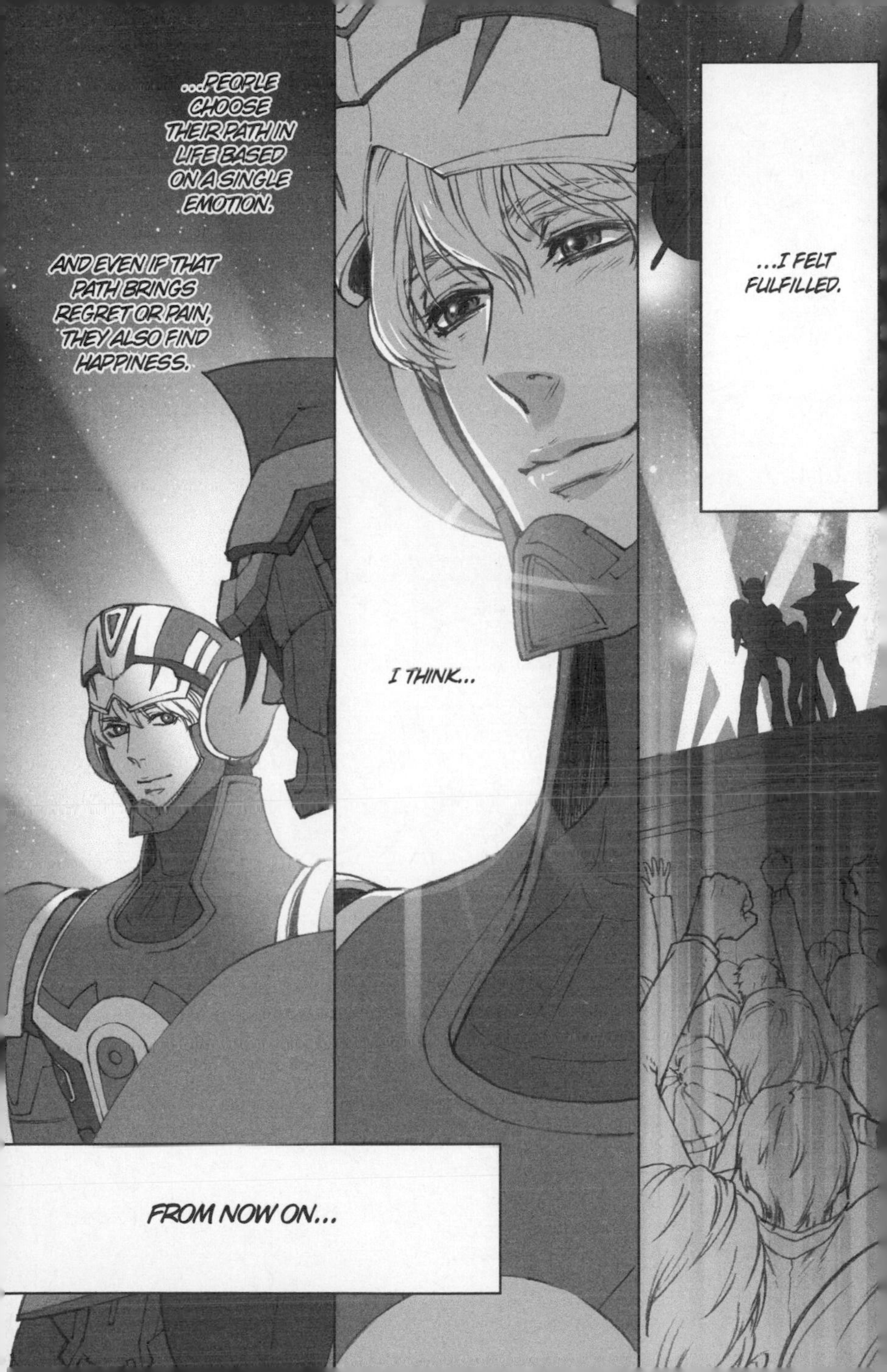
...I FELT FULFILLED.
I THINK...
...PEOPLE CHOOSE THEIR PATH IN LIFE BASED ON A SINGLE EMOTION.
AND EVEN IF THAT PATH BRINGS REGRET OR PAIN, THEY ALSO FIND HAPPINESS.
FROM NOW ON...

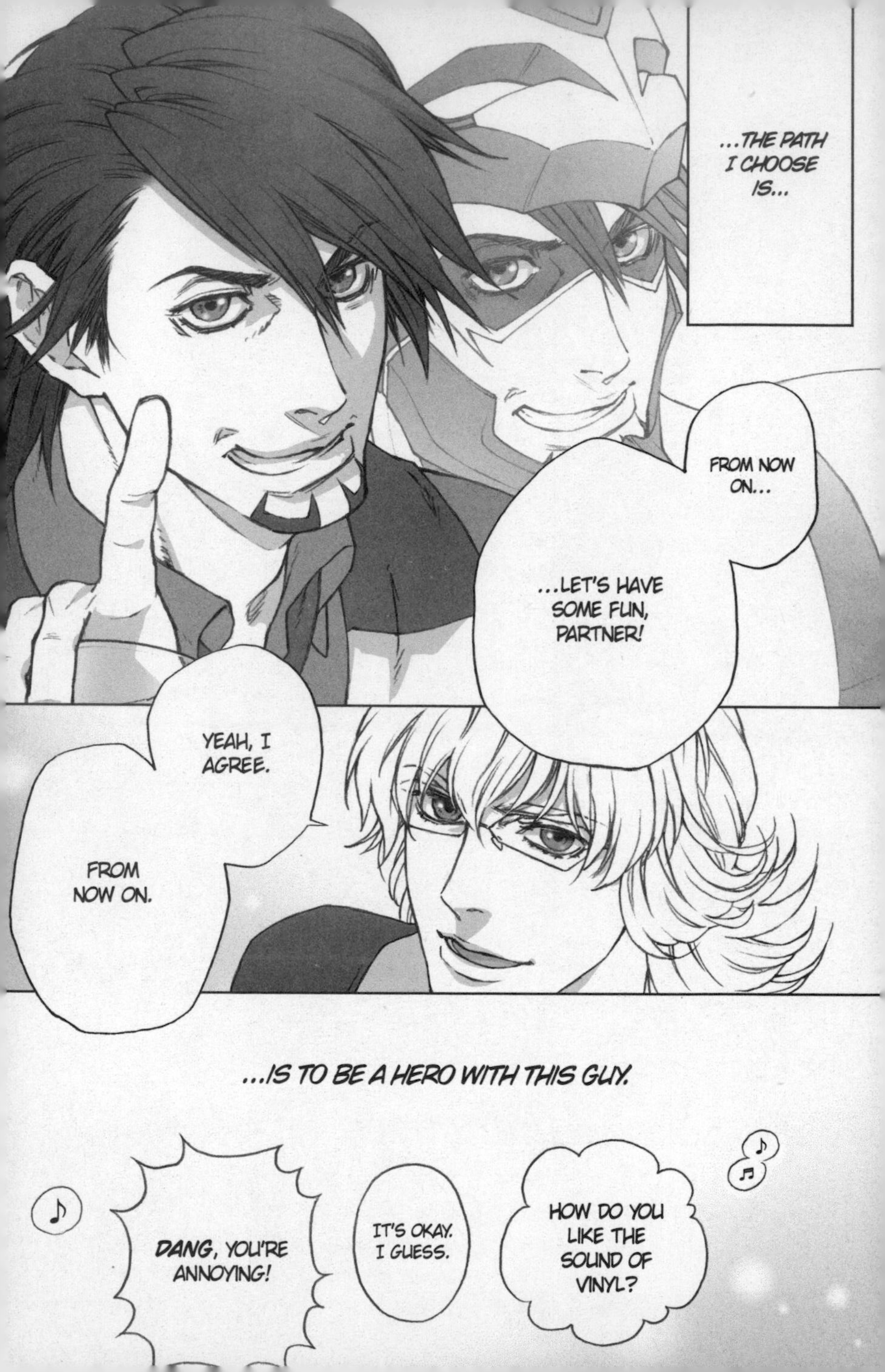
...THE PATH I CHOOSE IS...
FROM NOW ON...
...LET'S HAVE SOME FUN, PARTNER!
YEAH, I AGREE.
FROM NOW ON.
...IS TO BE A HERO WITH THIS GUY.
HOW DO YOU LIKE THE SOUND OF VINYL?
IT'S OKAY. I GUESS.
DANG, YOU'RE ANNOYING!

TIGER & BUNNY OFFICIAL COMIC ANTHOLOGY #01

It takes two to make a quarrel.

COMMENT

WE RESPECT TIGER & BUNNY

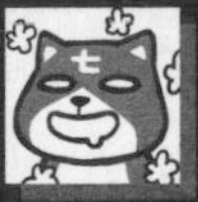

Nanao Yamashita

Since getting hooked on *Tiger & Bunny*, I've always felt like I'm floating five centimeters off the ground. I had forgotten that feeling for a long time! I can't thank the people who created *Tiger & Bunny* enough!

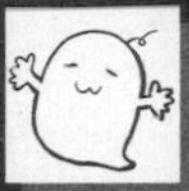

Suzuka Oda

Every week, I check to see if Origami is in the background. At first, I only wanted to draw Ivan, but the number of characters kept increasing, making it really hard work! It sure was fun, though!

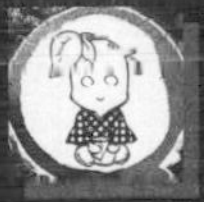

Ichimiya

Hello! My name is Ichimiya! The characters of *Tiger & Bunny* are all so appealing and cool and cute. Watching them every episode is awesome. It was fun drawing them, too! Thank you very much for this opportunity!

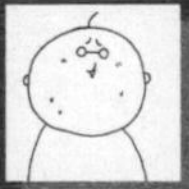

Kuro Nijo

Hi! I'm Kuro Nijo. I love, love, love *Tiger & Bunny*! I'm so happy that I get to be a part of this anthology! And I'm so glad that I got to draw Ivan and Huang! Thank you very much!

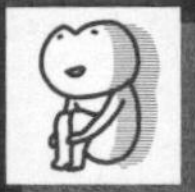

Min Sakusaka

Thank you for inviting me to do this! I'm so happy that I was able to draw Bunny and the old man!

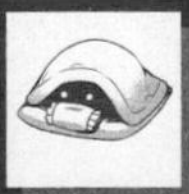

Ayumi Karino

About the story with Blue Rose on a diet...I actually like it when girls have slightly thicker legs. I'm sure all girls on a diet will hear the voice of Thanatos when they see how thin Barnaby and Kotetsu's legs are!

WE RESPECT TIGER & BUNNY

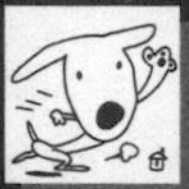

Pochi

I can't wait to find out what will be happening in the series by the time this book comes out! I love all the characters, but I especially like Rock Bison and Saito! Thank you again for giving me this opportunity!

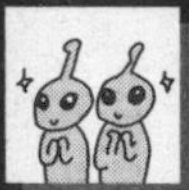

Miki Maki

It's so cute seeing the heroes each do their thing! There was a time when I wished that I myself had the Hundred Power!

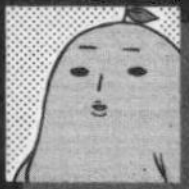

Uka Nagao

It was fun drawing a comic for Tiger & Bunny because I love it so much. I like Kotetsu the best, but I'm starting to take an interest in the girls, too. Just seeing the three of them have fun over tea makes me want to stare at them all day!

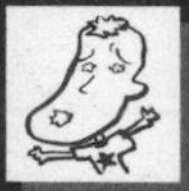

Tsutomu Ohno

I felt very out of place here, but I was still happy to be a part of it!

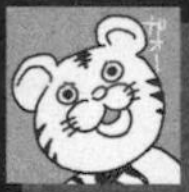

Yoko Fujioka

When Karina was covered head-to-toe in tiger items, she looked like a Hanshin Tigers fan! That's weird, since it wasn't intentional...

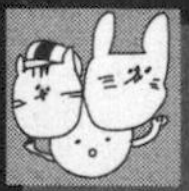

Harara Fuji

I loved Bunny's English pronunciation every single time!

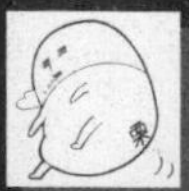

Renshi Kuriyama

I thought about making Kotetsu eat that burger, too, but it was already slopping all over the place with gobs of mayo, so it would have been horrible! By the way, I really like stale potato chips!

TIGER & BUNNY COMIC ANTHOLOGY 2

First, Catch Your Hare

COMMENT

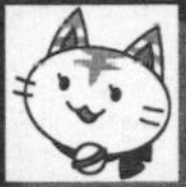

Toru Tegoshihara

I love Sky High! I once dreamed of him going headfirst into a wall, so seeing that in Episode 15 made my life complete! Thanks and thanks again!

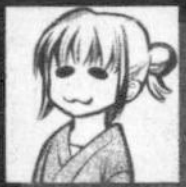

Mamika Mitsushio

This was my first time to be a part of an anthology—and it was stellar! I want to try getting the same hairstyle as Barnaby...

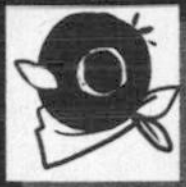

Hazuki Matsuo

I loved seeing the heroes be such good friends. I get 30% happier every time I see Fire Emblem.

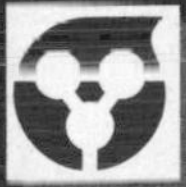

Yo Asami

The heroes are such great friends, and those life-sized characters are so cute! Cute and cute again!

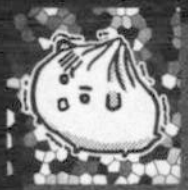

Ran Sakazuki

Hi there! The girls and boys of *Tiger & Bunny* are so cute! I don't know who I'm the biggest fan of anymore. I hope Yuri turns around... I want Sky High to take me up high, high in the sky!

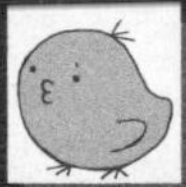

Hayato

Thank you for inviting me! The two seasons went by so fast. I'm happy that I was a part of this and I want to share that happiness with others!

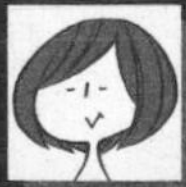

Tomo

I gained immense peace of mind being able to draw my two favorite characters so much. Thanks a million for helping my heart to burn with passion!

TIGER & BUNNY

COMIC ANTHOLOGY

END | Volume 1

TIGER & BUNNY

COMIC ANTHOLOGY

2

First, Catch Your Hare

EDITED BY: **Asuka Henshubu** | PRODUCTION: **SUNRISE**

TIGER & BUNNY COMIC ANTHOLOGY 2

First, Catch Your Hare

CONTENTS

WE RESPECT TIGER & BUNNY

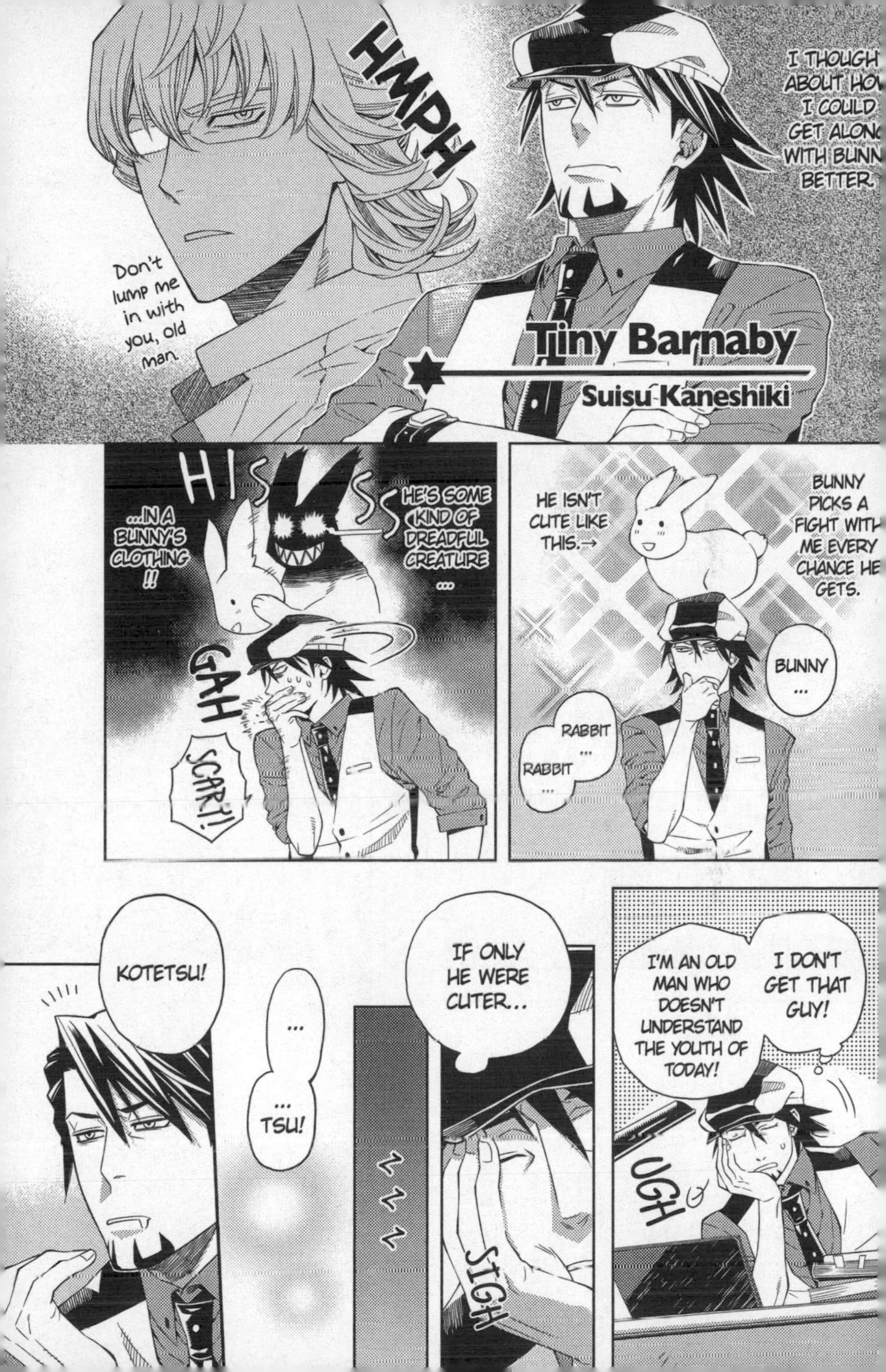
I THOUGH ABOUT HOW I COULD GET ALONG WITH BUNN BETTER.
HMPH
Don't lump me in with you, old man.
Tiny Barnaby
Suisu Kaneshiki
BUNNY PICKS A FIGHT WITH ME EVERY CHANCE HE GETS.
HE ISN'T CUTE LIKE THIS.→
BUNNY ...
RABBIT ...
RABBIT ...
HISSS
HE'S SOME KIND OF DREADFUL CREATURE ...
...IN A BUNNY'S CLOTHING !!
GAH
SCAR!!
I DON'T GET THAT GUY!
I'M AN OLD MAN WHO DOESN'T UNDERSTAND THE YOUTH OF TODAY!
UGH
IF ONLY HE WERE CUTER...
SIGH
KOTETSU!
...
... TSU!

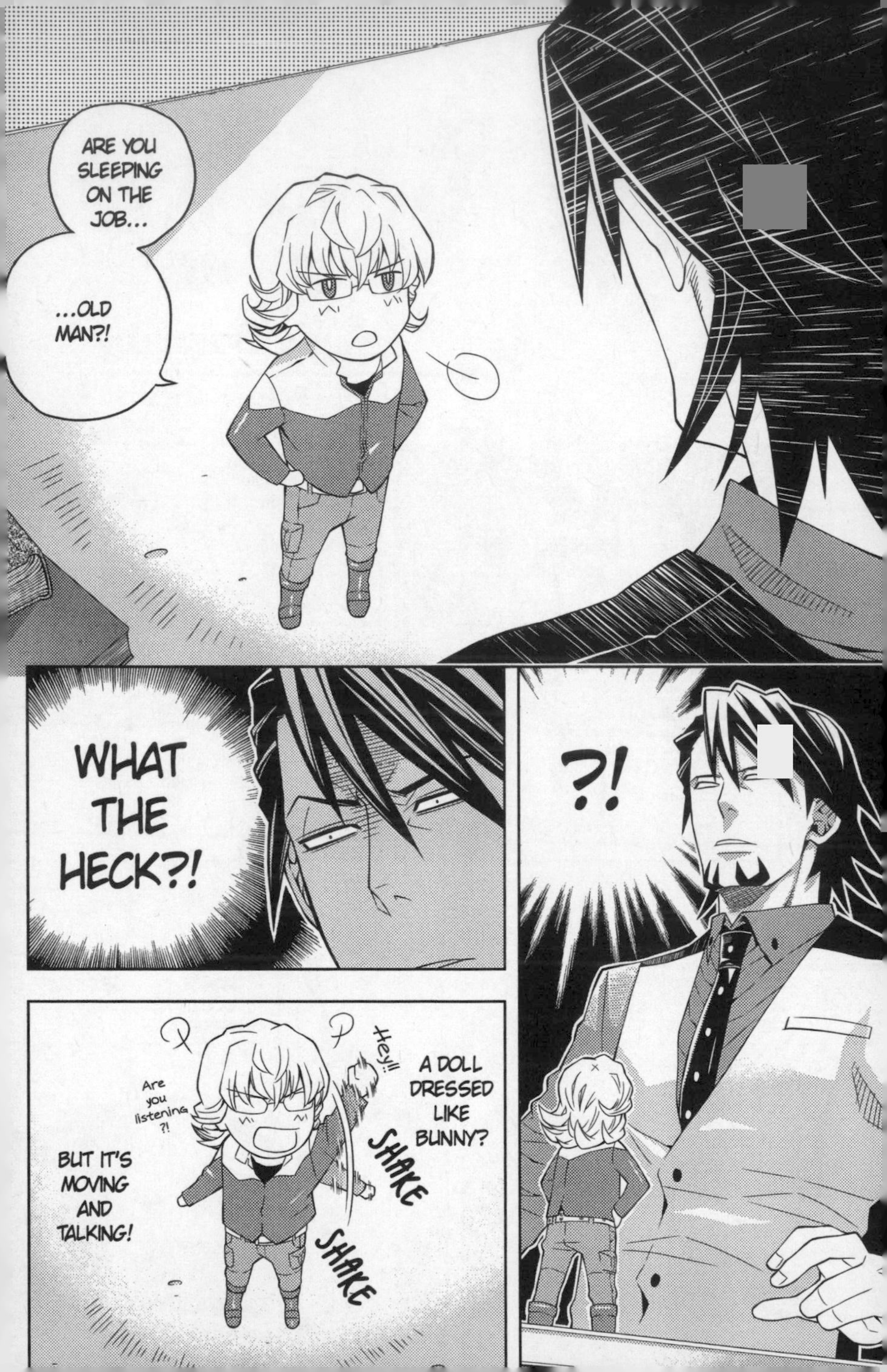
ARE YOU SLEEPING ON THE JOB...
...OLD MAN?!
?!
WHAT THE HECK?!
A DOLL DRESSED LIKE BUNNY?
Hey!!
Are you listening ?!
SHAKE
SHAKE
BUT IT'S MOVING AND TALKING!

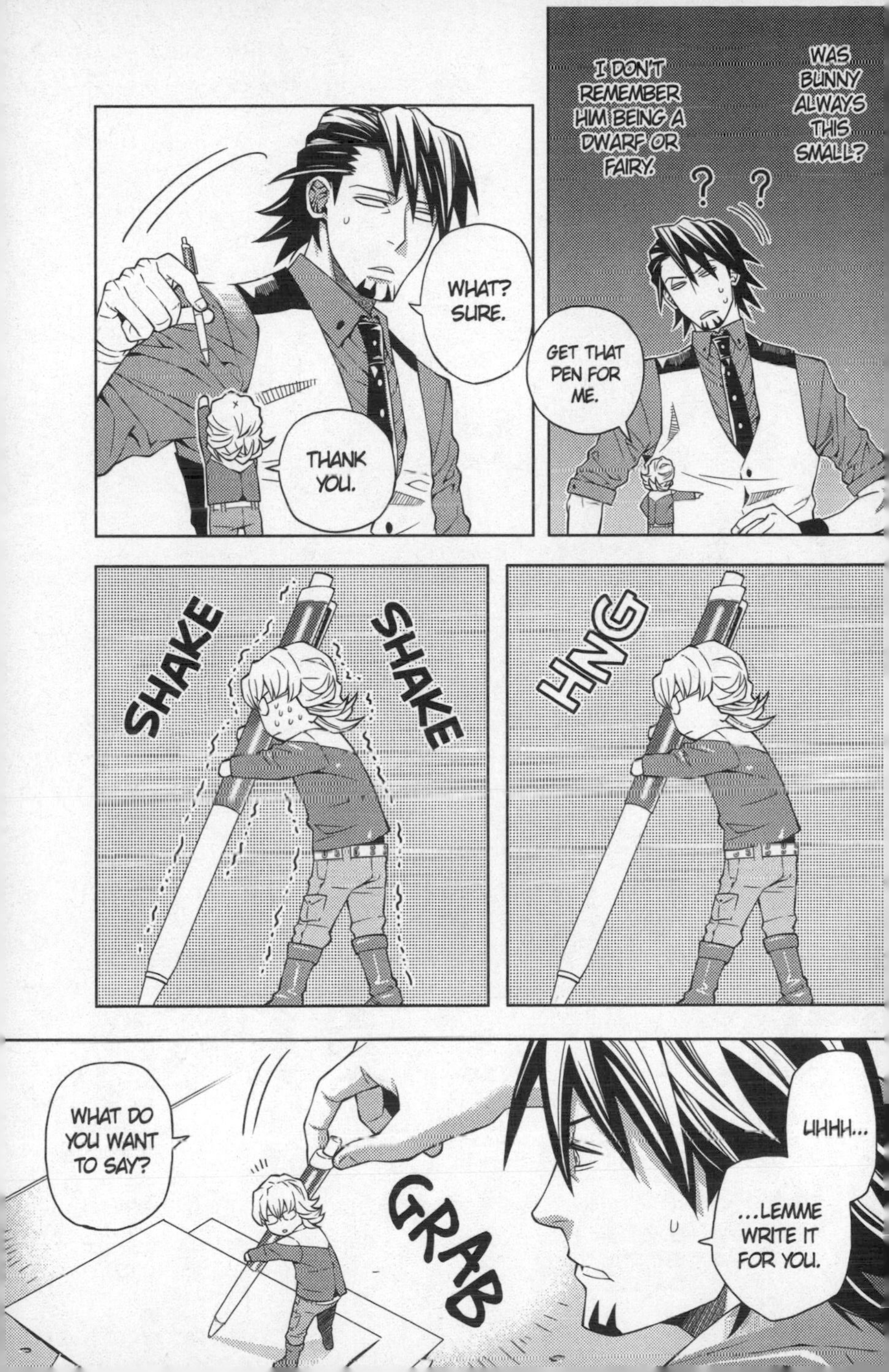
WAS BUNNY ALWAYS THIS SMALL?
I DON'T REMEMBER HIM BEING A DWARF OR FAIRY.
GET THAT PEN FOR ME.
WHAT? SURE.
THANK YOU.
HNG
SHAKE
SHAKE
UHHH...
WHAT DO YOU WANT TO SAY?
...LEMME WRITE IT FOR YOU.
GRAB

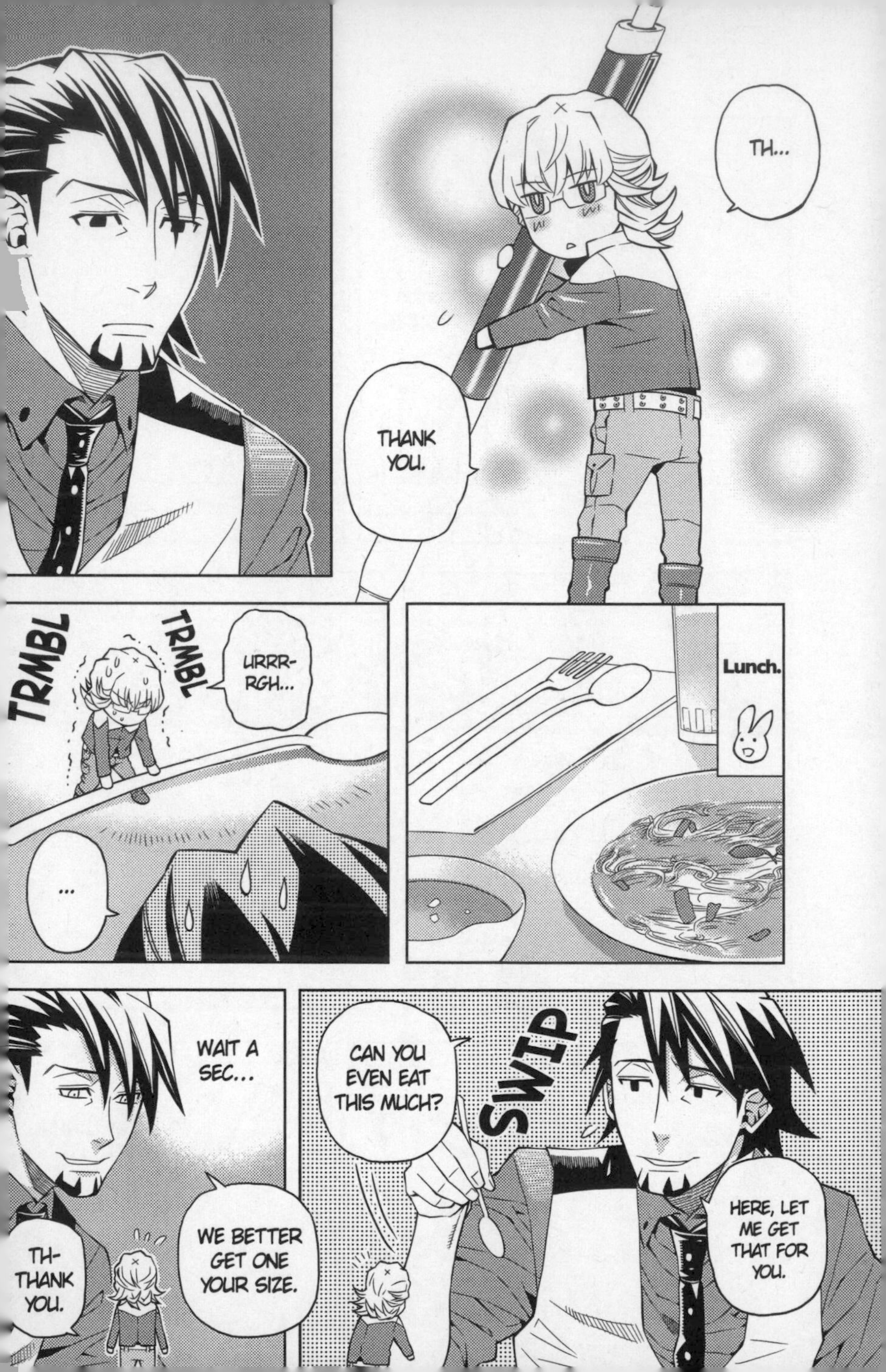
TH...
THANK YOU.
Lunch.
TRMBL
TRMBL
URRR-RGH...
...
SWIP
CAN YOU EVEN EAT THIS MUCH?
HERE, LET ME GET THAT FOR YOU.
WAIT A SEC...
WE BETTER GET ONE YOUR SIZE.
TH-THANK YOU.

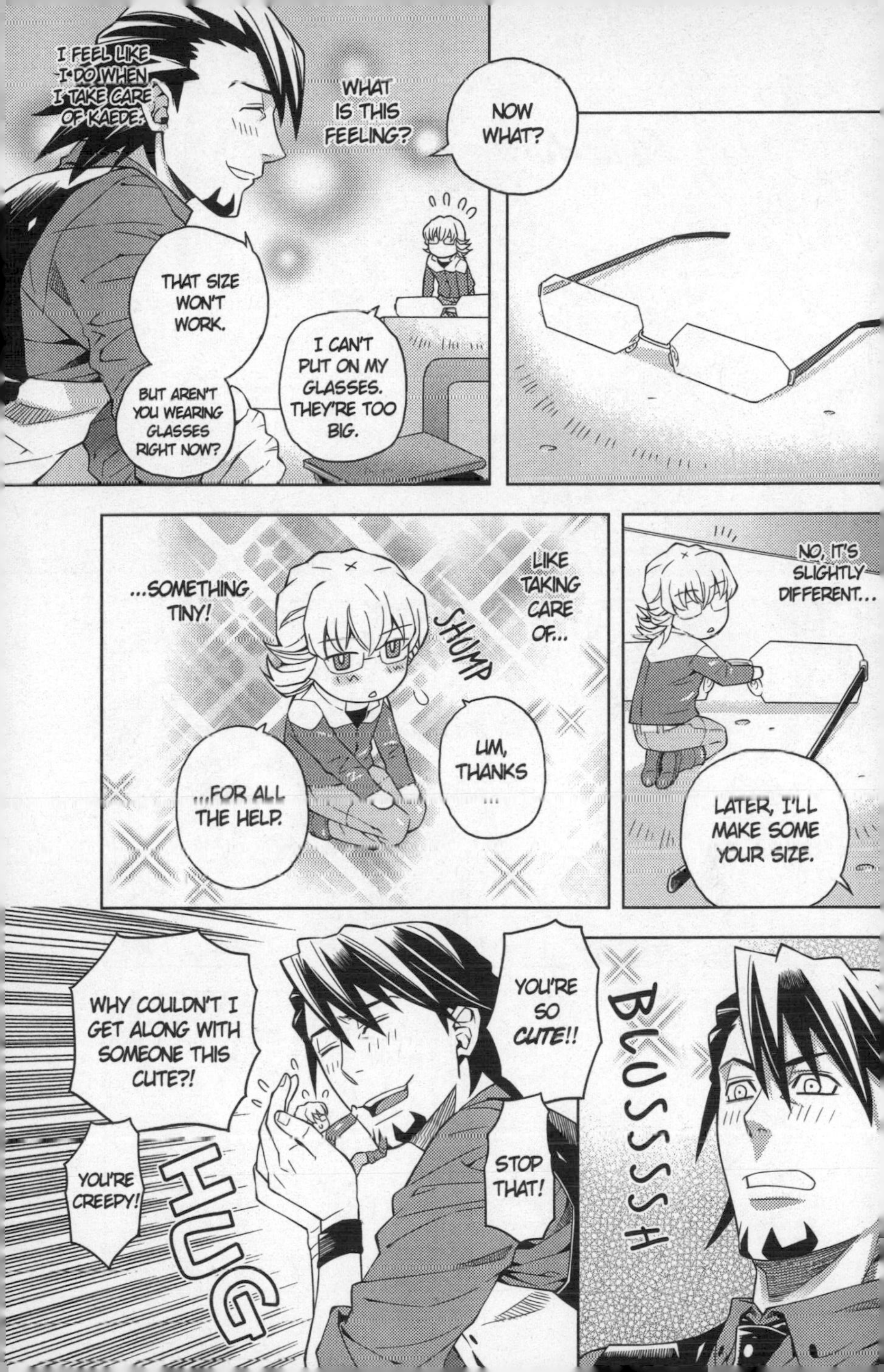
NOW WHAT?
WHAT IS THIS FEELING?
I FEEL LIKE I DO WHEN I TAKE CARE OF KAEDE.
I CAN'T PUT ON MY GLASSES. THEY'RE TOO BIG.
THAT SIZE WON'T WORK.
BUT AREN'T YOU WEARING GLASSES RIGHT NOW?
NO, IT'S SLIGHTLY DIFFERENT...
LATER, I'LL MAKE SOME YOUR SIZE.
LIKE TAKING CARE OF...
...SOMETHING TINY!
SHUMP
UM, THANKS ...
...FOR ALL THE HELP.
BUSSSSH
YOU'RE SO CUTE!!
WHY COULDN'T I GET ALONG WITH SOMEONE THIS CUTE?!
STOP THAT!
YOU'RE CREEPY!
HUG

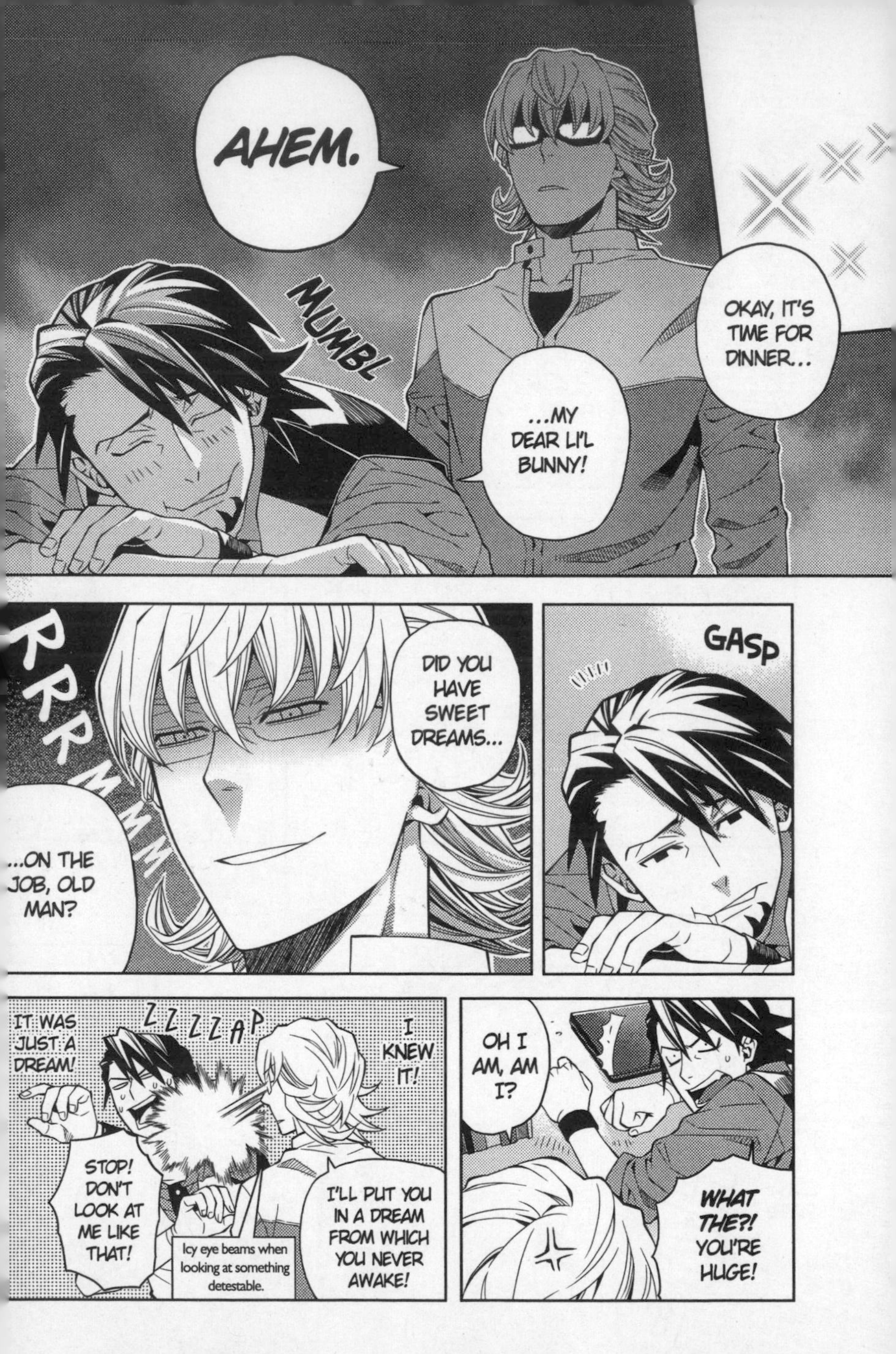
OKAY, IT'S TIME FOR DINNER...
...MY DEAR LI'L BUNNY!
MUMBL
AHEM.
GASP
DID YOU HAVE SWEET DREAMS...
RRRMMMM
...ON THE JOB, OLD MAN?
WHAT THE?! YOU'RE HUGE!
OH I AM, AM I?
IT WAS JUST A DREAM!
I KNEW IT!
ZZZZAP
STOP! DON'T LOOK AT ME LIKE THAT!
I'LL PUT YOU IN A DREAM FROM WHICH YOU NEVER AWAKE!
Icy eye beams when looking at something detestable.

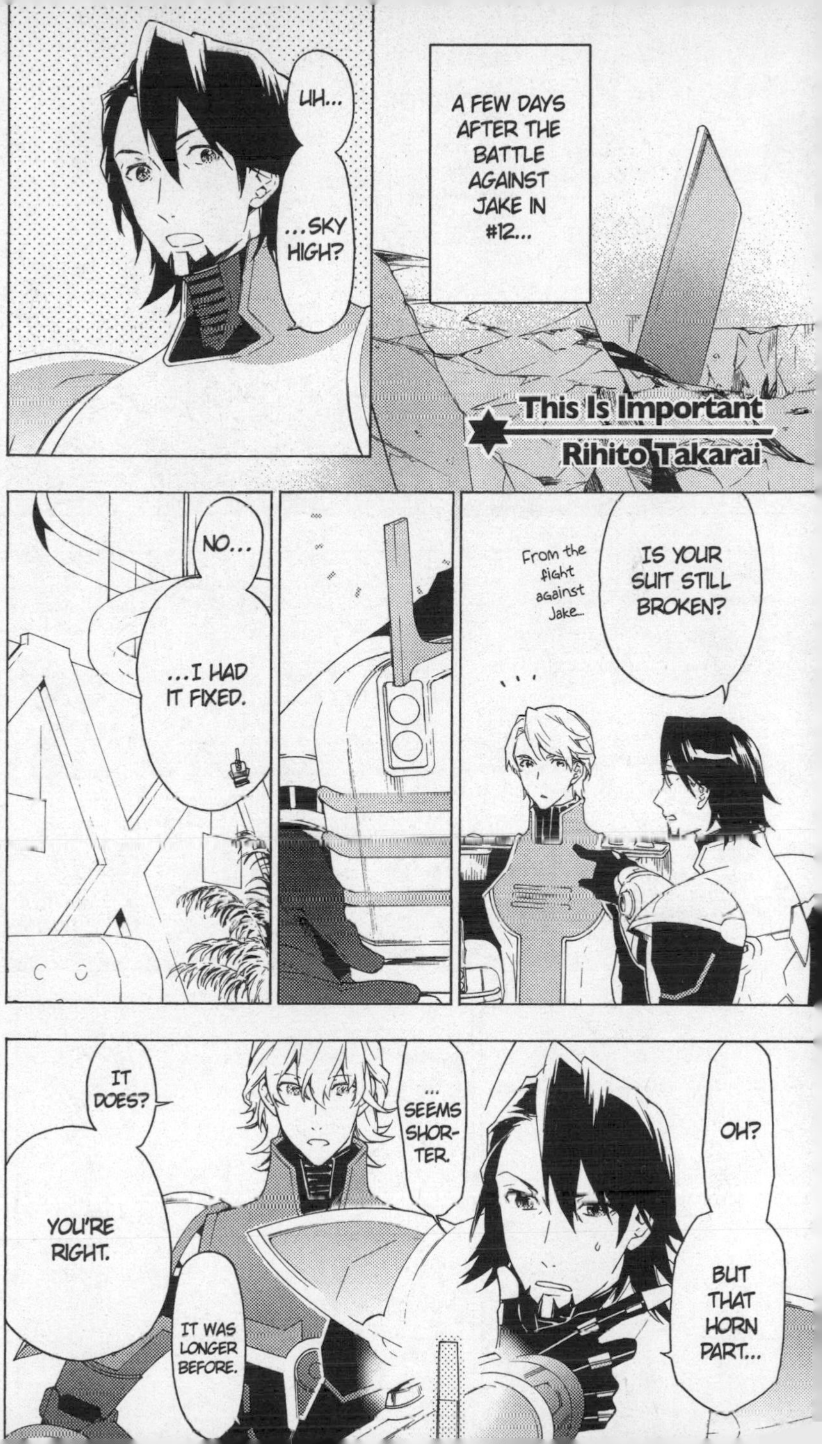
A FEW DAYS AFTER THE BATTLE AGAINST JAKE IN #12...
This Is Important
Rihito Takarai
UH...
...SKY HIGH?
From the fight against Jake...
IS YOUR SUIT STILL BROKEN?
...
NO...
...I HAD IT FIXED.
OH?
BUT THAT HORN PART...
...SEEMS SHORTER.
IT DOES?
YOU'RE RIGHT.
IT WAS LONGER BEFORE.

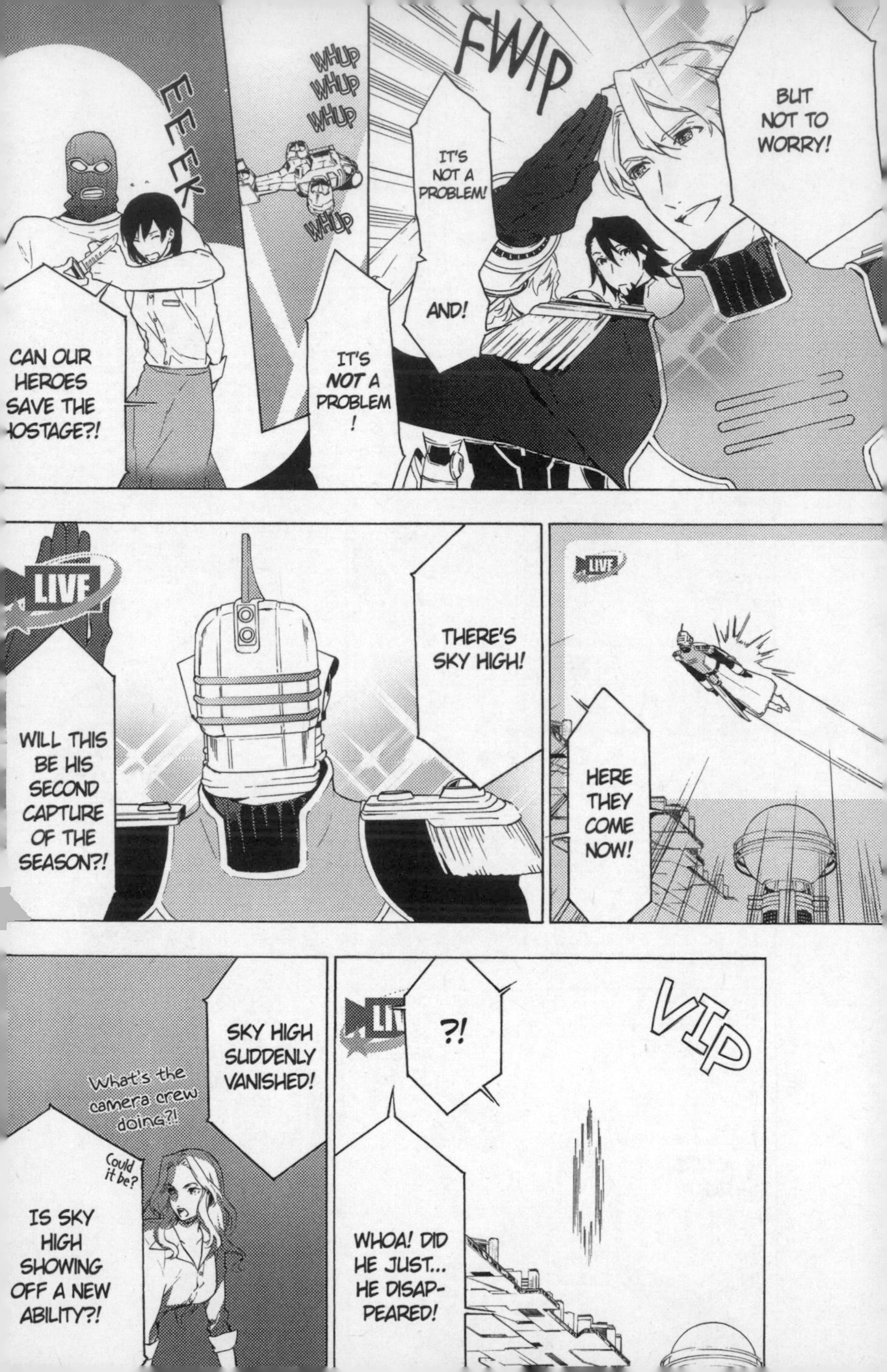
FWIP
BUT NOT TO WORRY!
IT'S NOT A PROBLEM!
AND!
IT'S *NOT* A PROBLEM!
WHUP WHUP WHUP
WHUP
EEEK
CAN OUR HEROES SAVE THE HOSTAGE?!
LIVE
HERE THEY COME NOW!
LIVE
THERE'S SKY HIGH!
WILL THIS BE HIS SECOND CAPTURE OF THE SEASON?!
VIP
?!
WHOA! DID HE JUST... HE DISAP-PEARED!
SKY HIGH SUDDENLY VANISHED!
What's the camera crew doing?!
Could it be?
IS SKY HIGH SHOWING OFF A NEW ABILITY?!

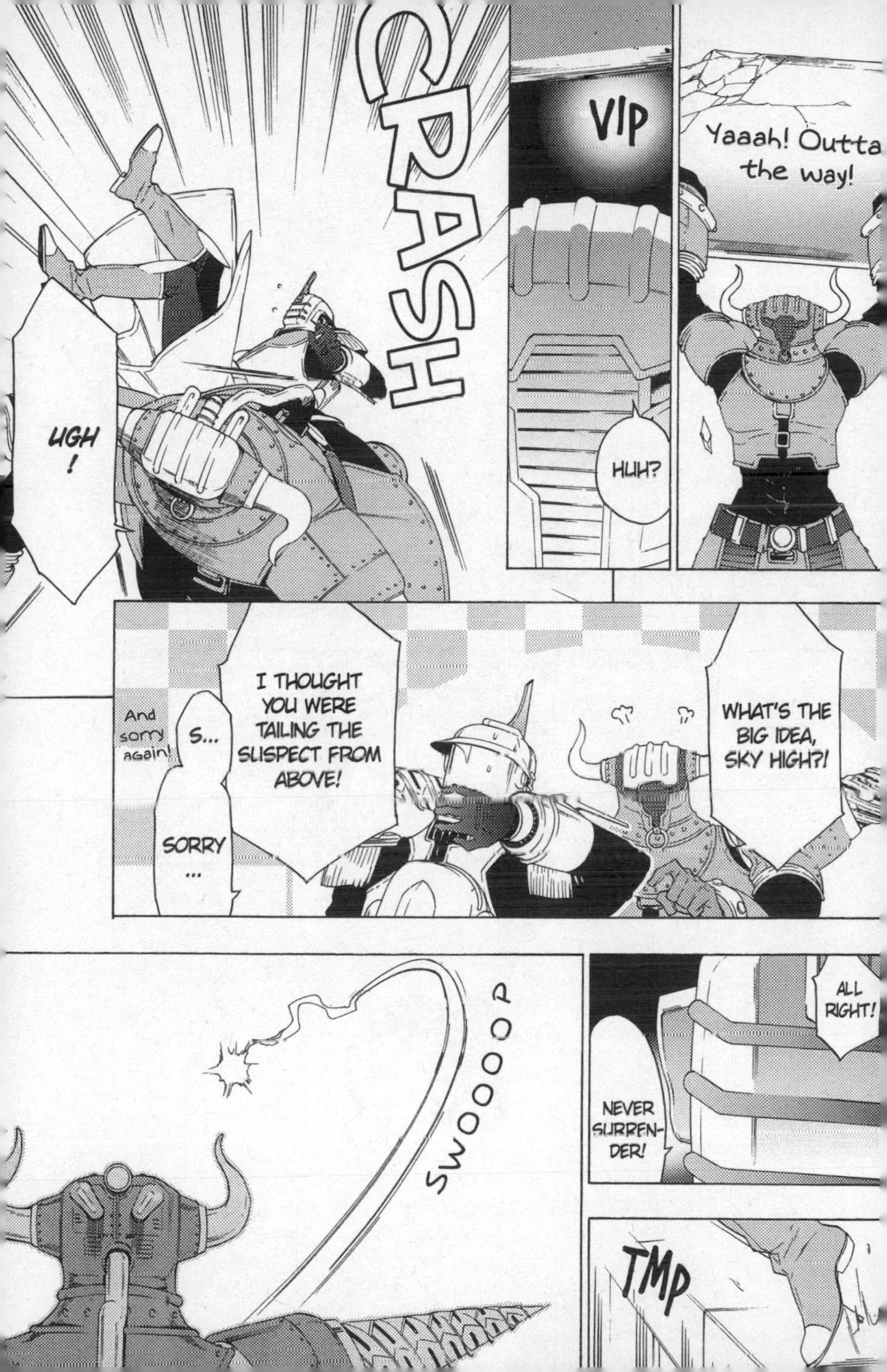
Yaaah! Outta the way!
VIP
HUH?
CRASH
UGH!
WHAT'S THE BIG IDEA, SKY HIGH?!
I THOUGHT YOU WERE TAILING THE SUSPECT FROM ABOVE!
S...
SORRY...
And sorry again!
ALL RIGHT!
NEVER SURREN-DER!
TMP
SWOOOOP

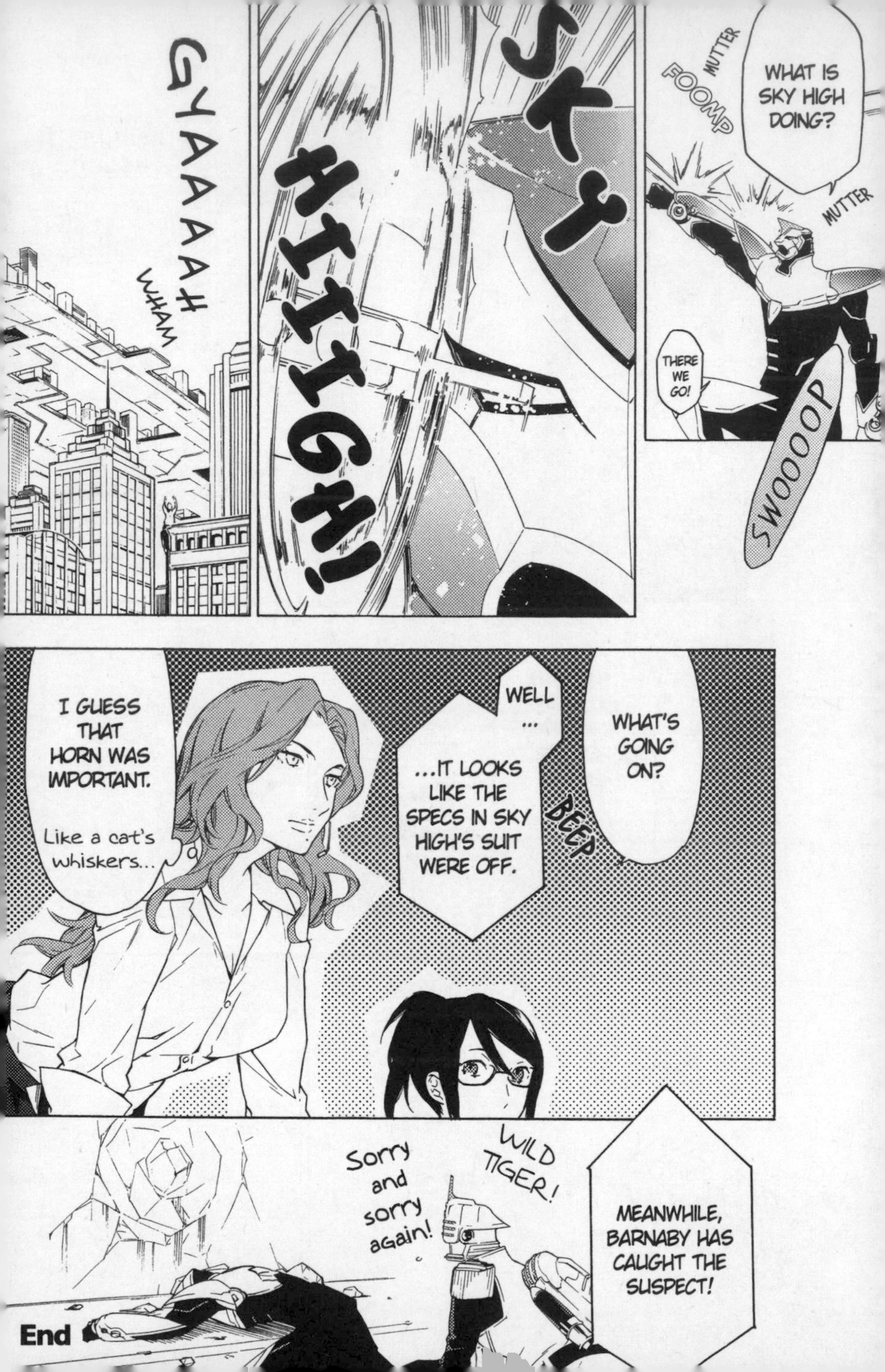

WHAT IS SKY HIGH DOING?
MUTTER
FOOMP
MUTTER
THERE WE GO!
SWOOOOP
SKY HIIIGH!
GYAAAAAH
WHAM
WHAT'S GOING ON?
BEEP
WELL ...
...IT LOOKS LIKE THE SPECS IN SKY HIGH'S SUIT WERE OFF.
I GUESS THAT HORN WAS IMPORTANT.
Like a cat's whiskers...
MEANWHILE, BARNABY HAS CAUGHT THE SUSPECT!
WILD TIGER!
Sorry and sorry again!
End

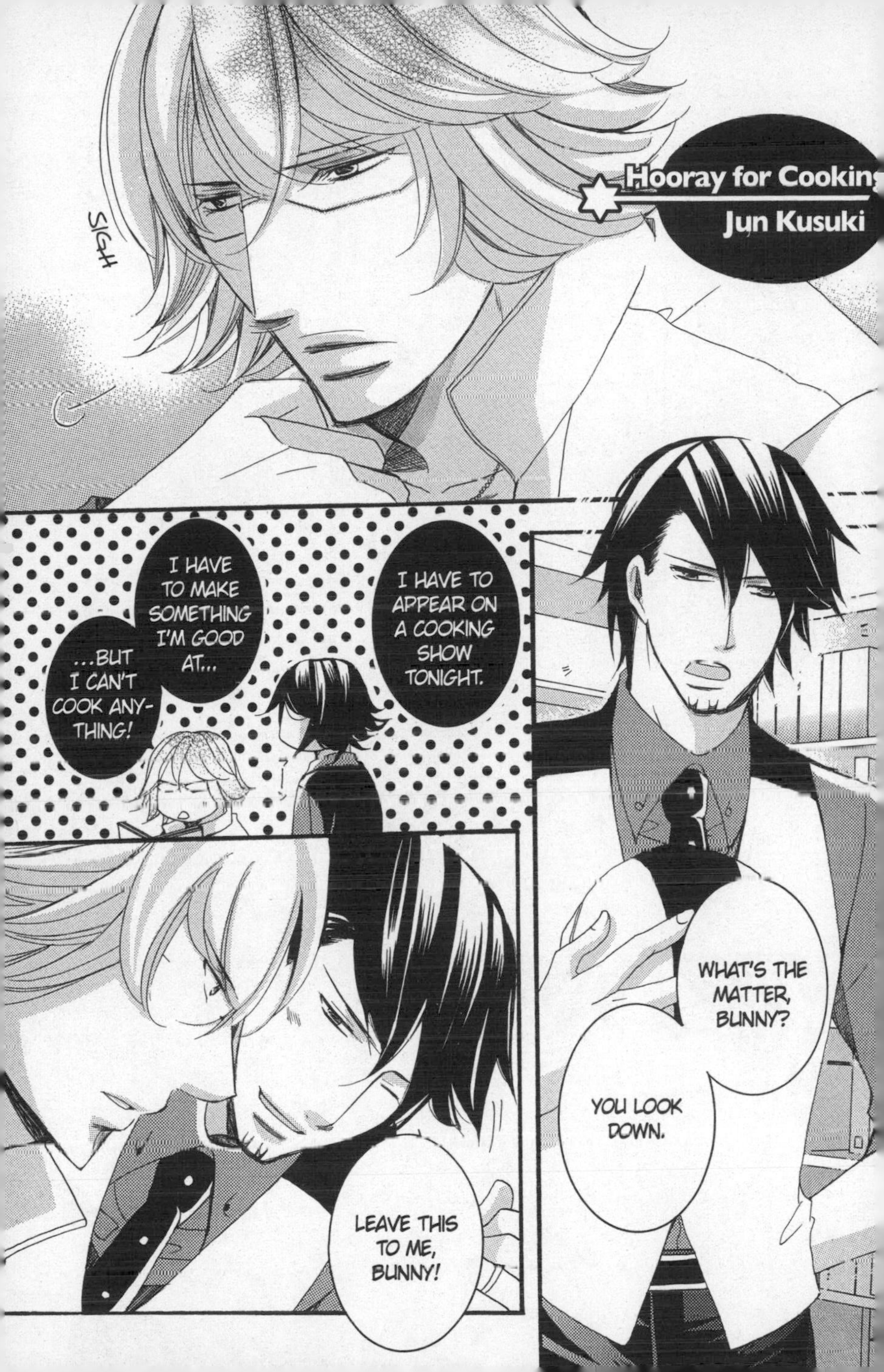
Hooray for Cooking
Jun Kusuki
SIGH
WHAT'S THE MATTER, BUNNY?
YOU LOOK DOWN.
I HAVE TO APPEAR ON A COOKING SHOW TONIGHT.
I HAVE TO MAKE SOMETHING I'M GOOD AT...
...BUT I CAN'T COOK ANYTHING!
LEAVE THIS TO ME, BUNNY!

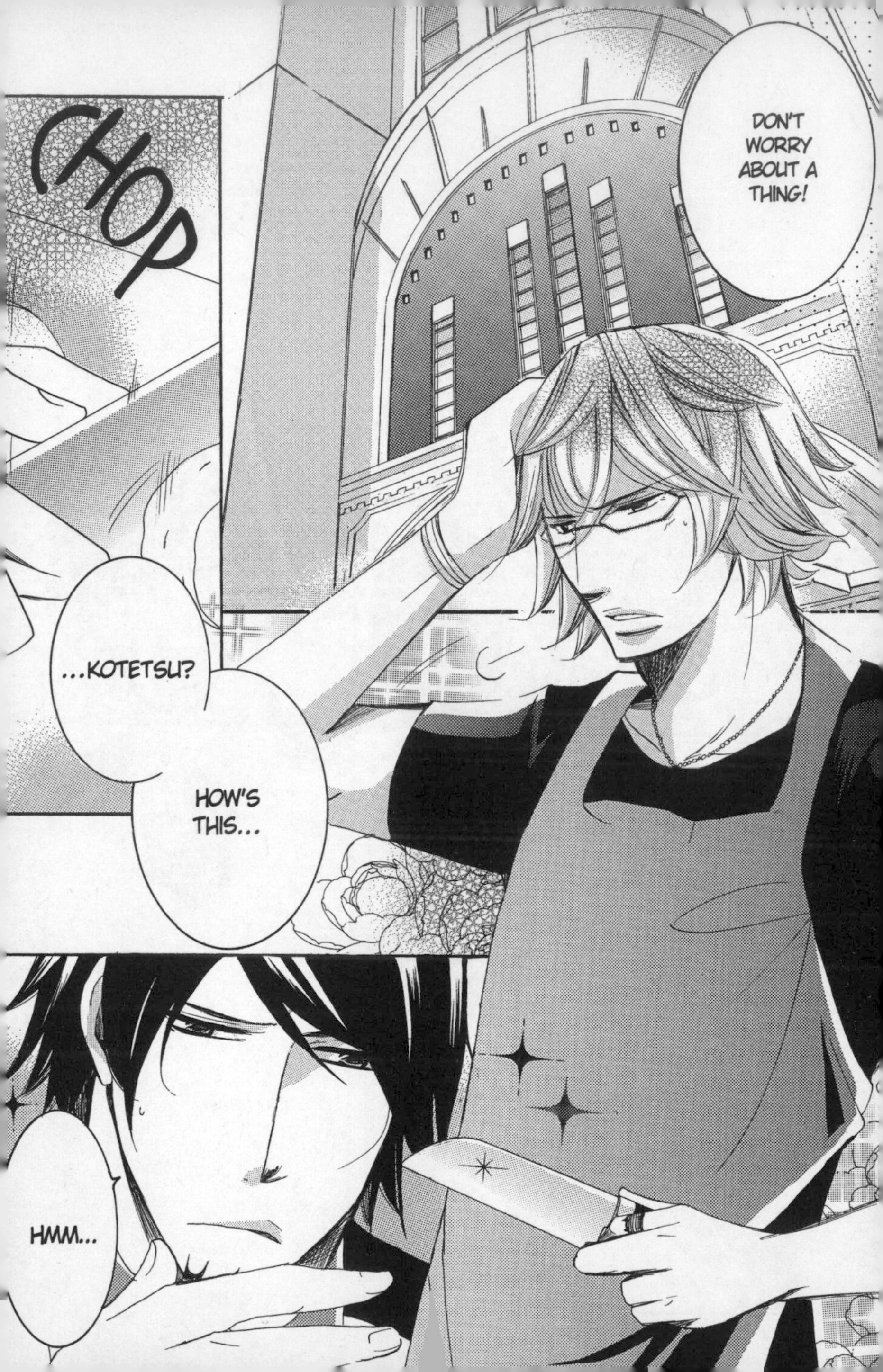
DON'T WORRY ABOUT A THING!
CHOP
...KOTETSU?
HOW'S THIS...
HMM...

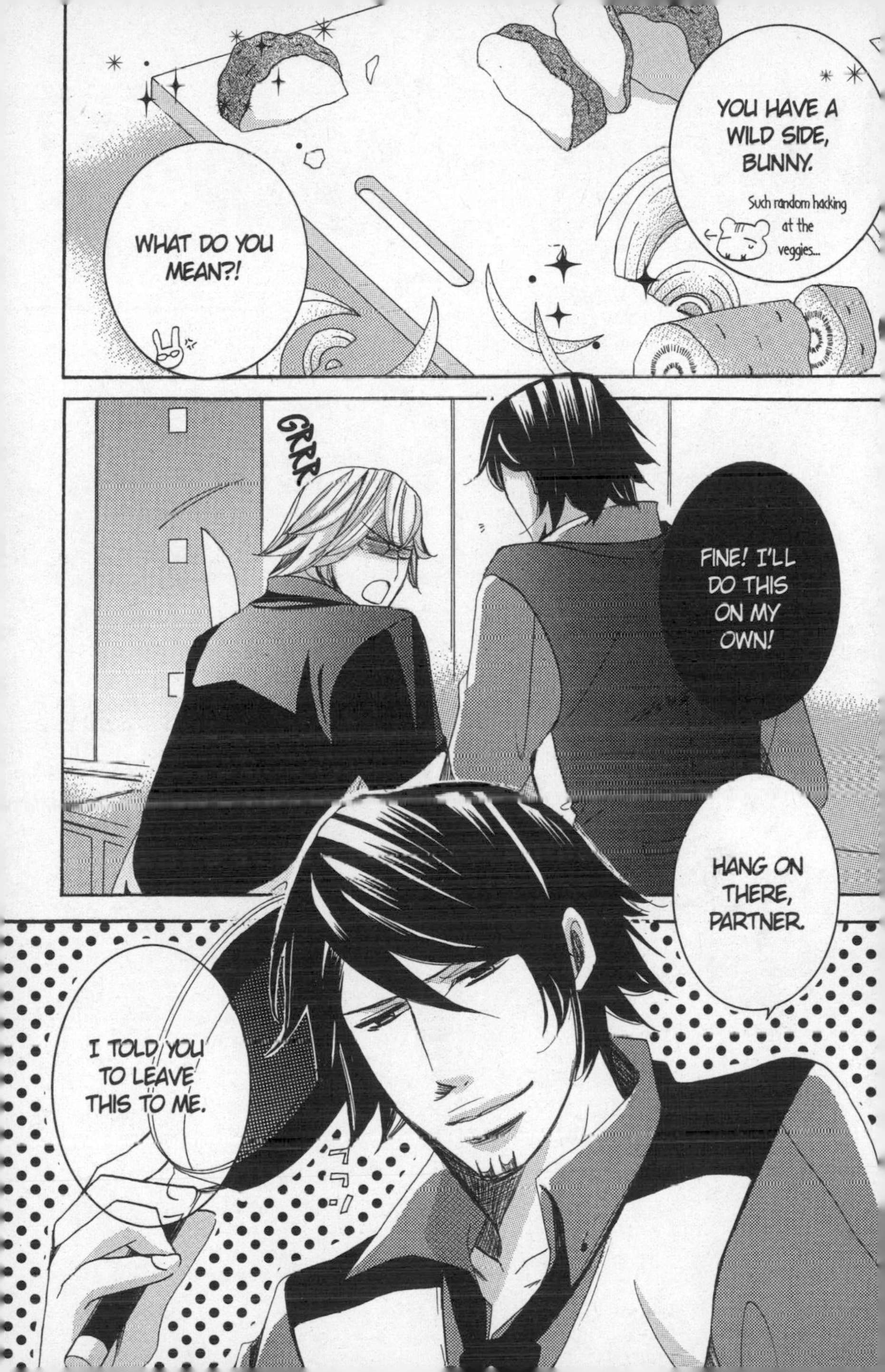
YOU HAVE A WILD SIDE, BUNNY.
Such random hacking at the veggies...
WHAT DO YOU MEAN?!
FINE! I'LL DO THIS ON MY OWN!
GRRR
HANG ON THERE, PARTNER.
I TOLD YOU TO LEAVE THIS TO ME.

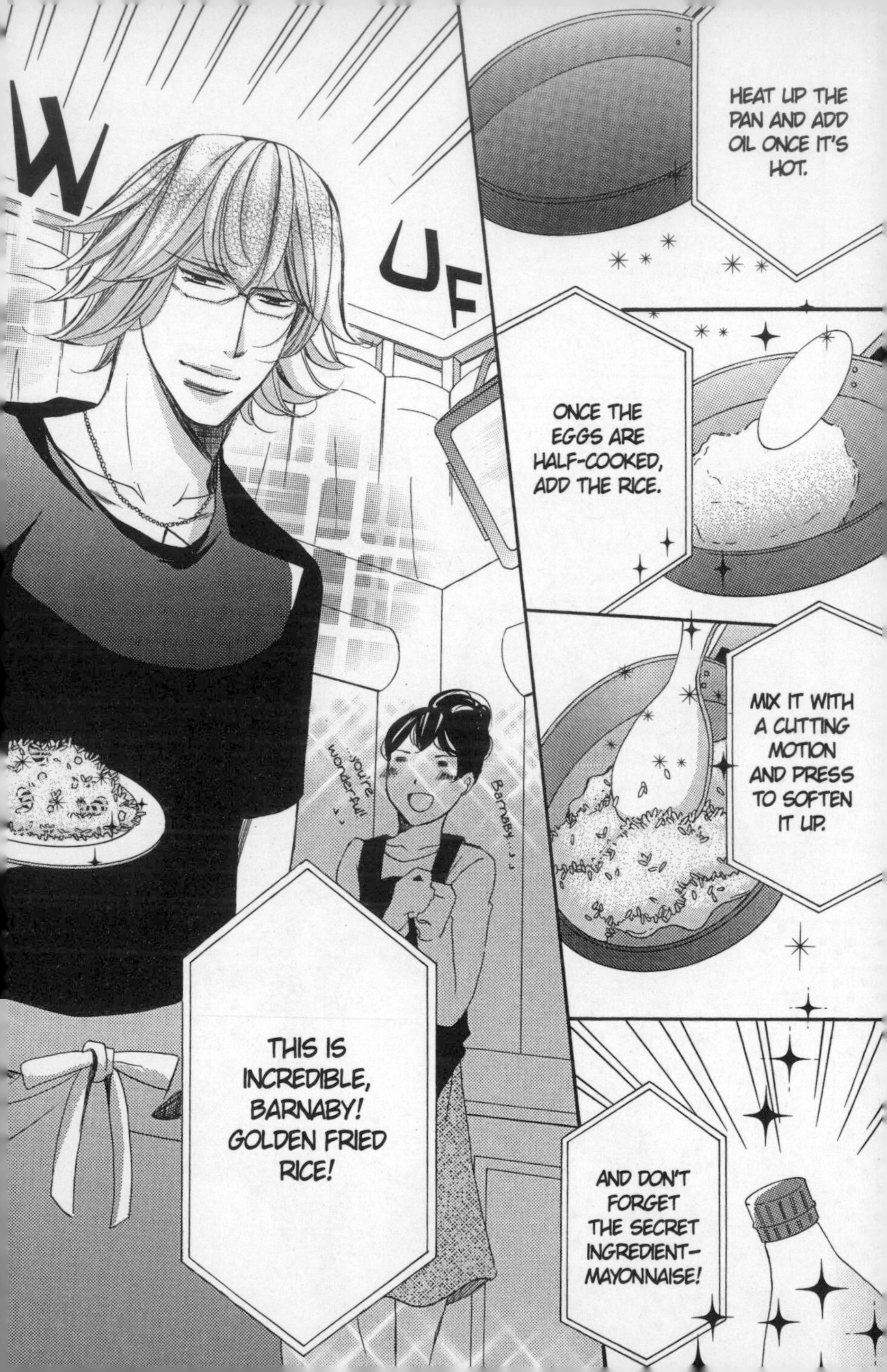
HEAT UP THE PAN AND ADD OIL ONCE IT'S HOT.
ONCE THE EGGS ARE HALF-COOKED, ADD THE RICE.
MIX IT WITH A CUTTING MOTION AND PRESS TO SOFTEN IT UP.
AND DON'T FORGET THE SECRET INGREDIENT–MAYONNAISE!
W UF
Barnaby...
...you're wonderful...
THIS IS INCREDIBLE, BARNABY! GOLDEN FRIED RICE!

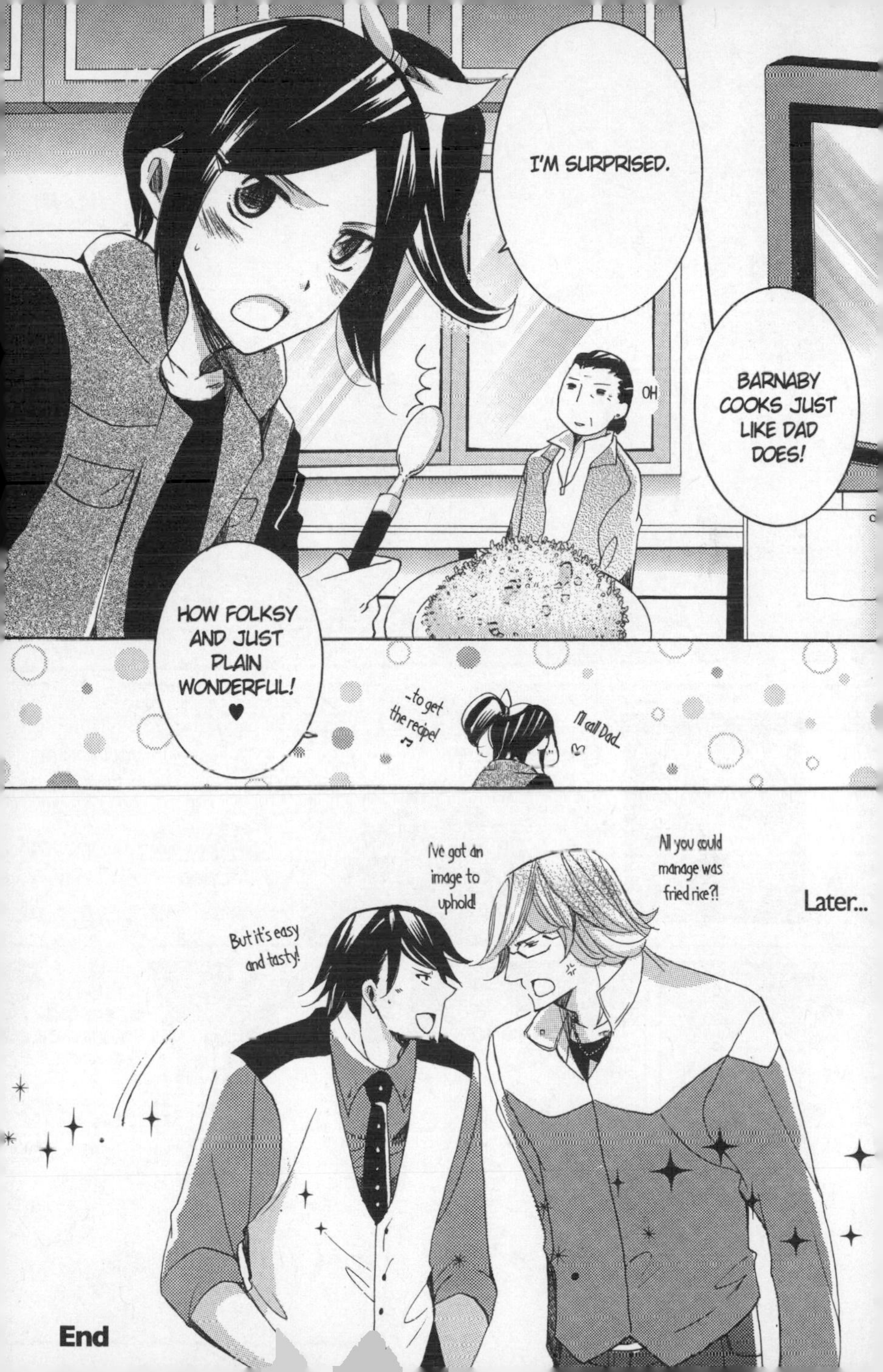
I'M SURPRISED.
BARNABY COOKS JUST LIKE DAD DOES!
OH
HOW FOLKSY AND JUST PLAIN WONDERFUL! ♥
I'll call Dad
...to get the recipe! ♪
Later...
All you could manage was fried rice?!
I've got an image to uphold!
But it's easy and tasty!
End

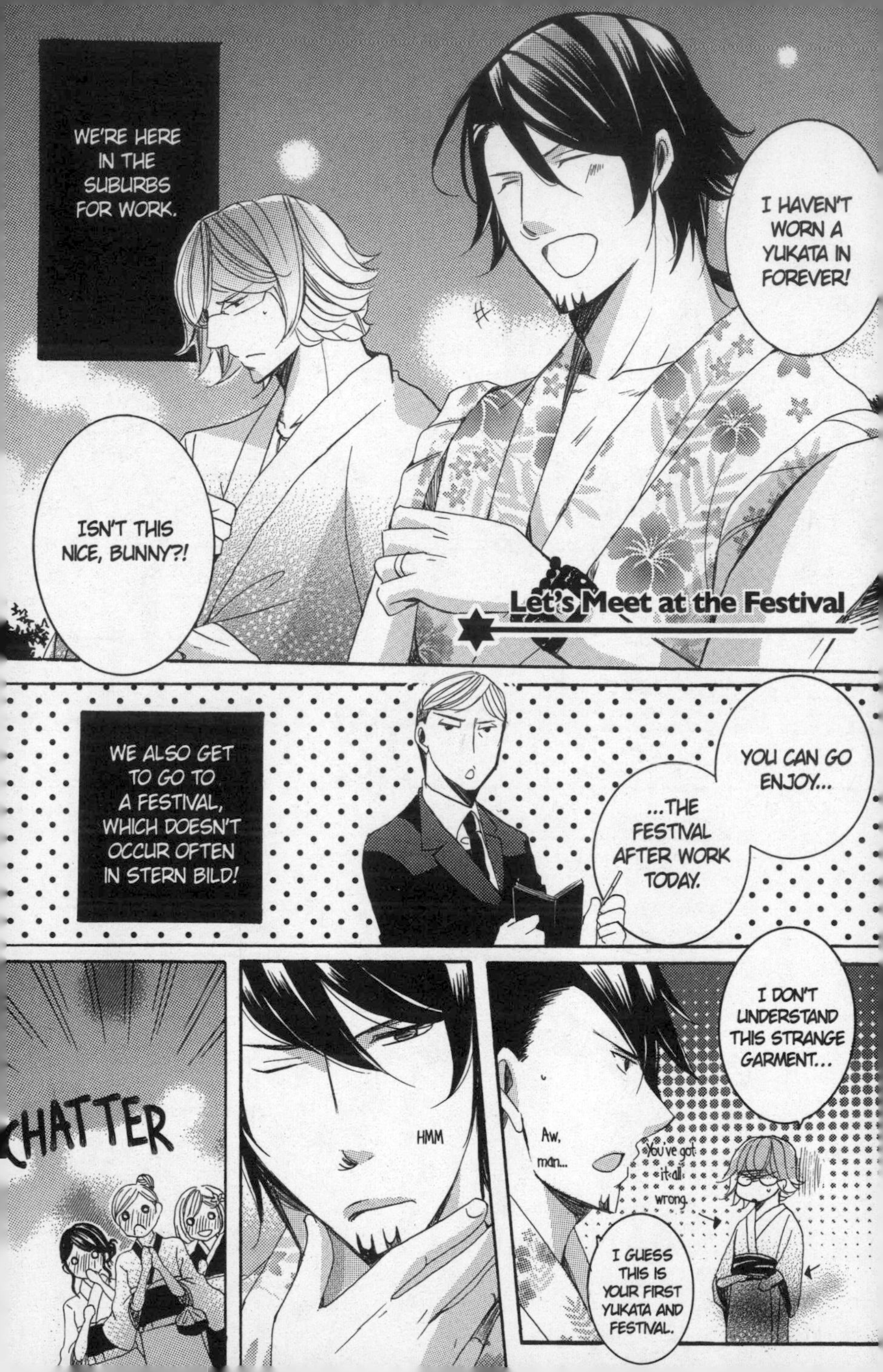
I HAVEN'T WORN A YUKATA IN FOREVER!
WE'RE HERE IN THE SUBURBS FOR WORK.
ISN'T THIS NICE, BUNNY?!
Let's Meet at the Festival
YOU CAN GO ENJOY...
...THE FESTIVAL AFTER WORK TODAY.
WE ALSO GET TO GO TO A FESTIVAL, WHICH DOESN'T OCCUR OFTEN IN STERN BILD!
I DON'T UNDERSTAND THIS STRANGE GARMENT...
Aw, man...
You've got it all wrong.
I GUESS THIS IS YOUR FIRST YUKATA AND FESTIVAL.
HMM
CHATTER

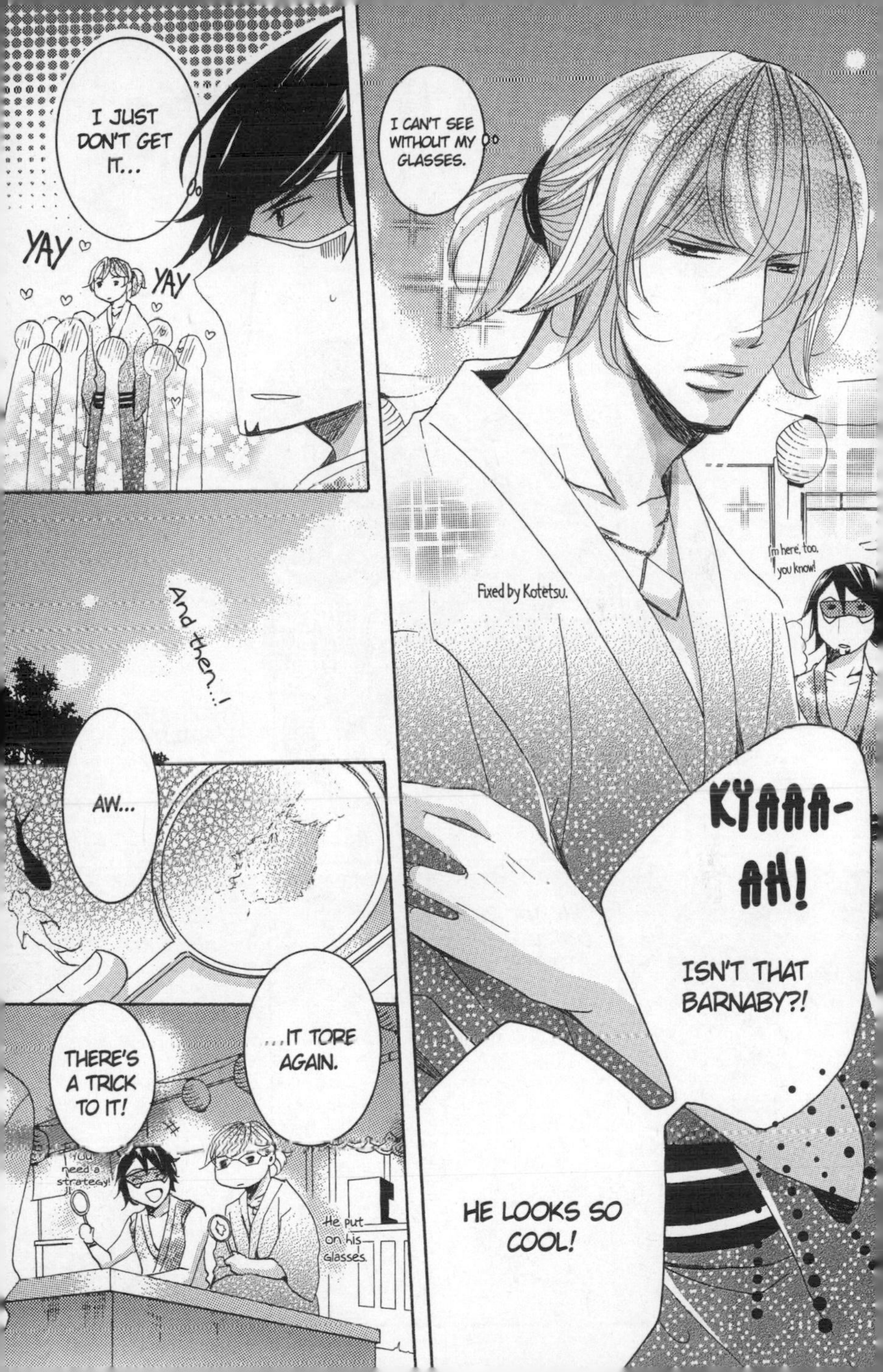
I CAN'T SEE WITHOUT MY GLASSES.
Fixed by Kotetsu.
I'm here, too, you know!
KYAAA-AH!
ISN'T THAT BARNABY?!
HE LOOKS SO COOL!
I JUST DON'T GET IT...
YAY
YAY
And then...!
AW...
...IT TORE AGAIN.
THERE'S A TRICK TO IT!
You need a strategy!
He put on his glasses.

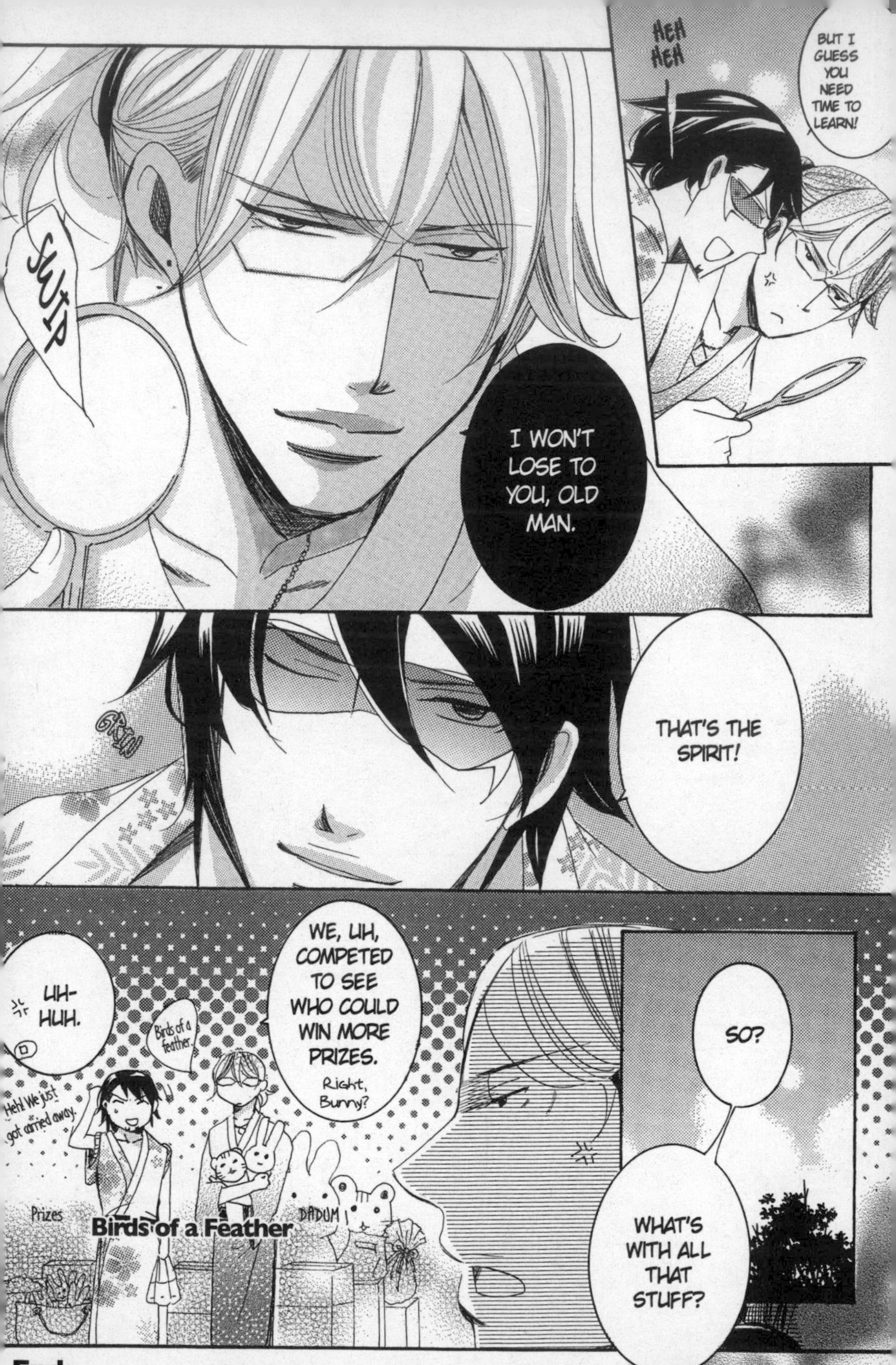
HEH HEH
BUT I GUESS YOU NEED TIME TO LEARN!
SWIP
I WON'T LOSE TO YOU, OLD MAN.
THAT'S THE SPIRIT!
GRIN
SO?
WHAT'S WITH ALL THAT STUFF?
WE, UH, COMPETED TO SEE WHO COULD WIN MORE PRIZES.
Right, Bunny?
UH-HUH.
Birds of a feather.
Heh! We just got carried away.
Prizes
DADUM
Birds of a Feather

End

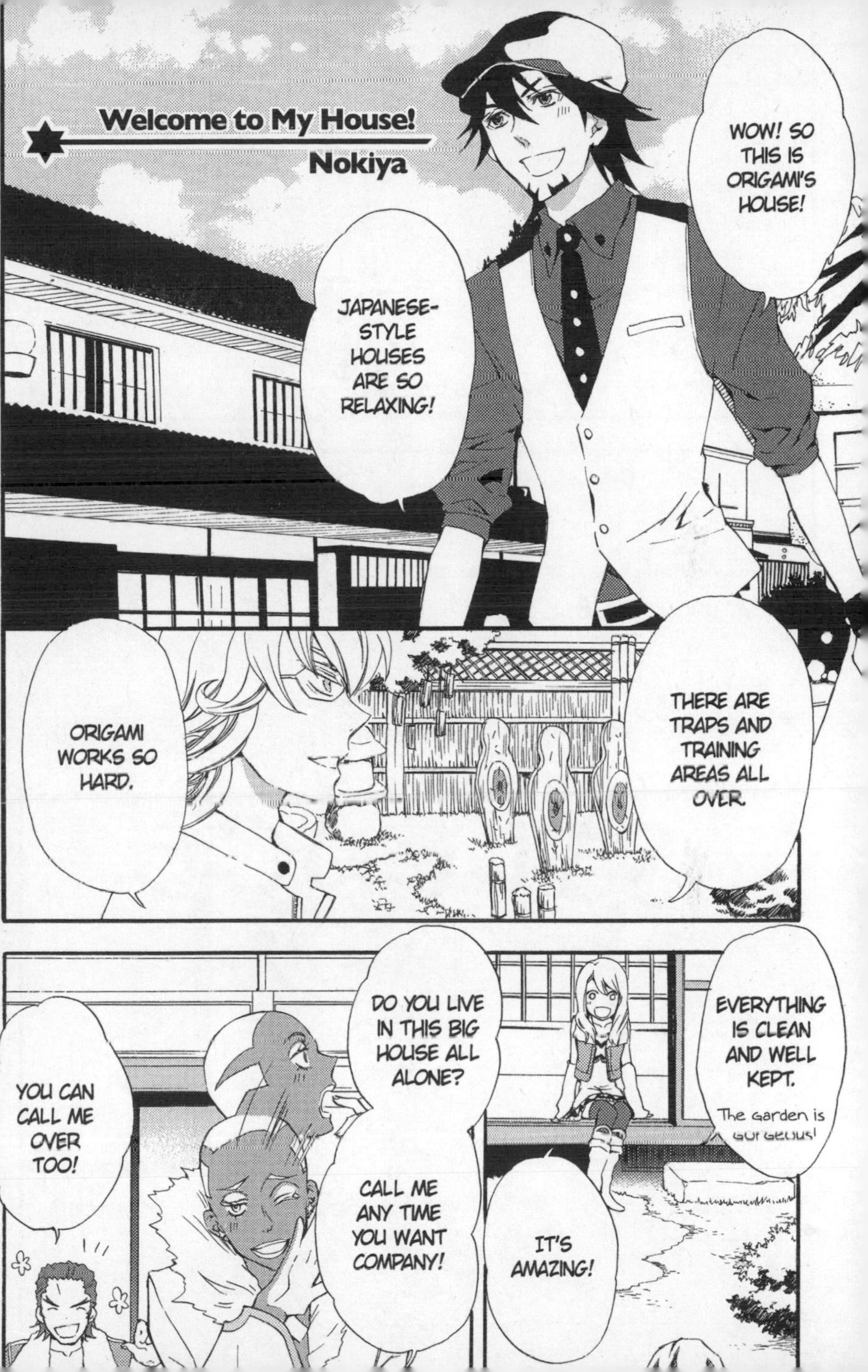
Welcome to My House!
Nokiya
WOW! SO THIS IS ORIGAMI'S HOUSE!
JAPANESE-STYLE HOUSES ARE SO RELAXING!
THERE ARE TRAPS AND TRAINING AREAS ALL OVER.
ORIGAMI WORKS SO HARD.
EVERYTHING IS CLEAN AND WELL KEPT.
The garden is gorgeous!
IT'S AMAZING!
DO YOU LIVE IN THIS BIG HOUSE ALL ALONE?
CALL ME ANY TIME YOU WANT COMPANY!
YOU CAN CALL ME OVER TOO!

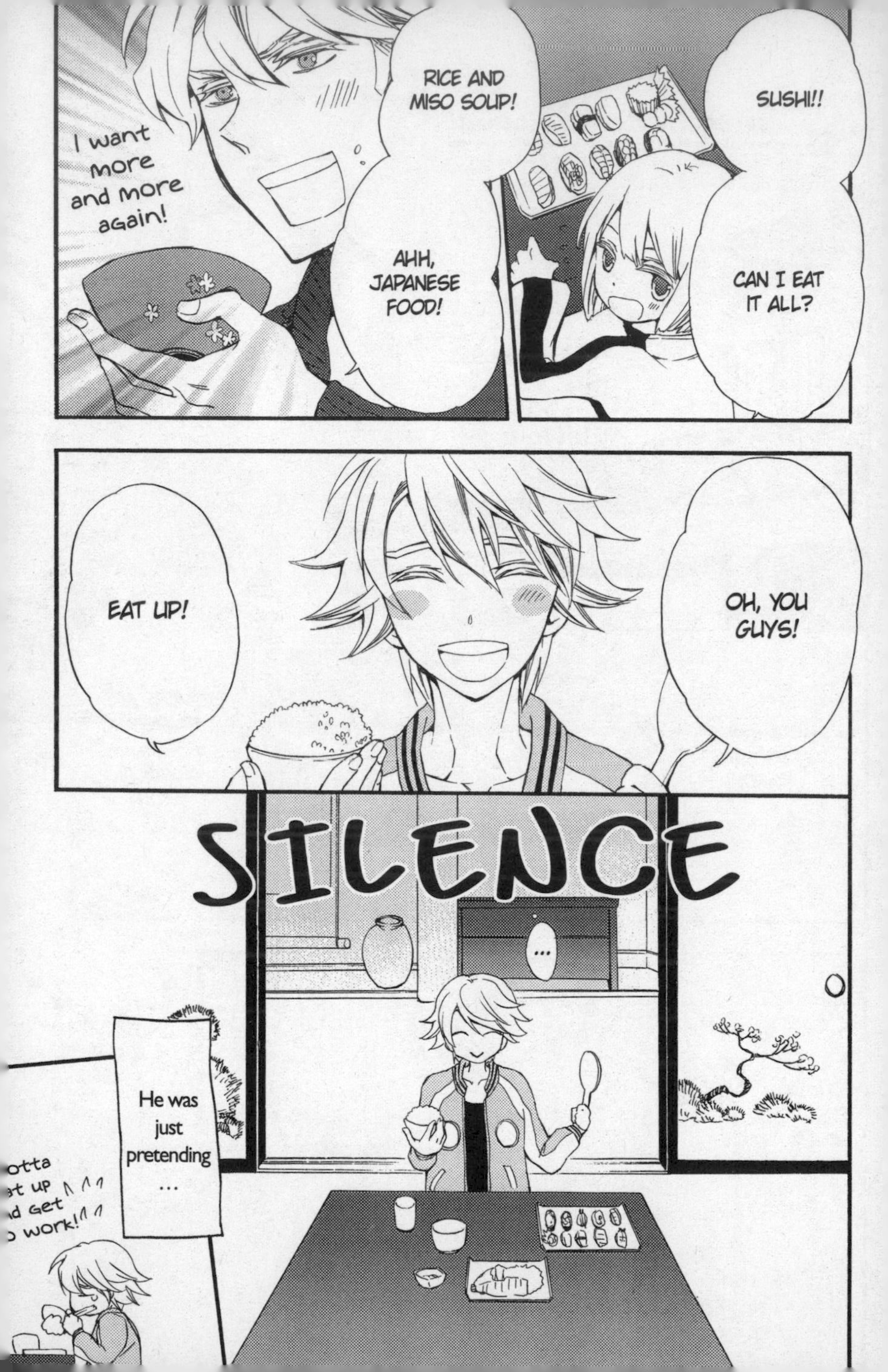
SUSHI!!
CAN I EAT IT ALL?
RICE AND MISO SOUP!
AHH, JAPANESE FOOD!
I want more and more again!
OH, YOU GUYS!
EAT UP!
SILENCE
...
He was just pretending...

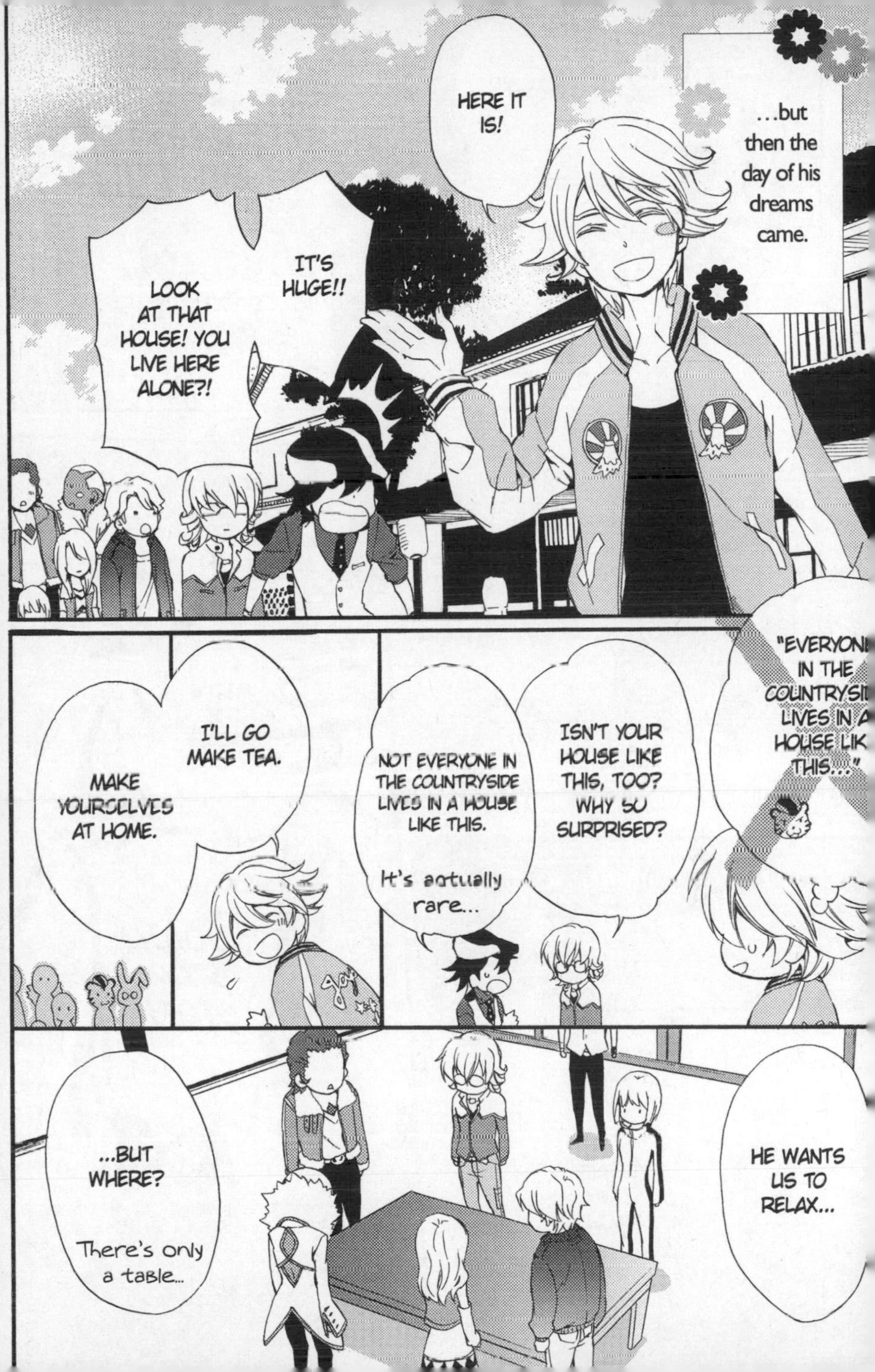
...but then the day of his dreams came.
HERE IT IS!
IT'S HUGE!!
LOOK AT THAT HOUSE! YOU LIVE HERE ALONE?!
"EVERYON IN THE COUNTRYSI LIVES IN A HOUSE LIK THIS..."
ISN'T YOUR HOUSE LIKE THIS, TOO? WHY SO SURPRISED?
NOT EVERYONE IN THE COUNTRYSIDE LIVES IN A HOUSE LIKE THIS.
It's actually rare...
I'LL GO MAKE TEA.
MAKE YOURSELVES AT HOME.
HE WANTS US TO RELAX...
...BUT WHERE?
There's only a table...

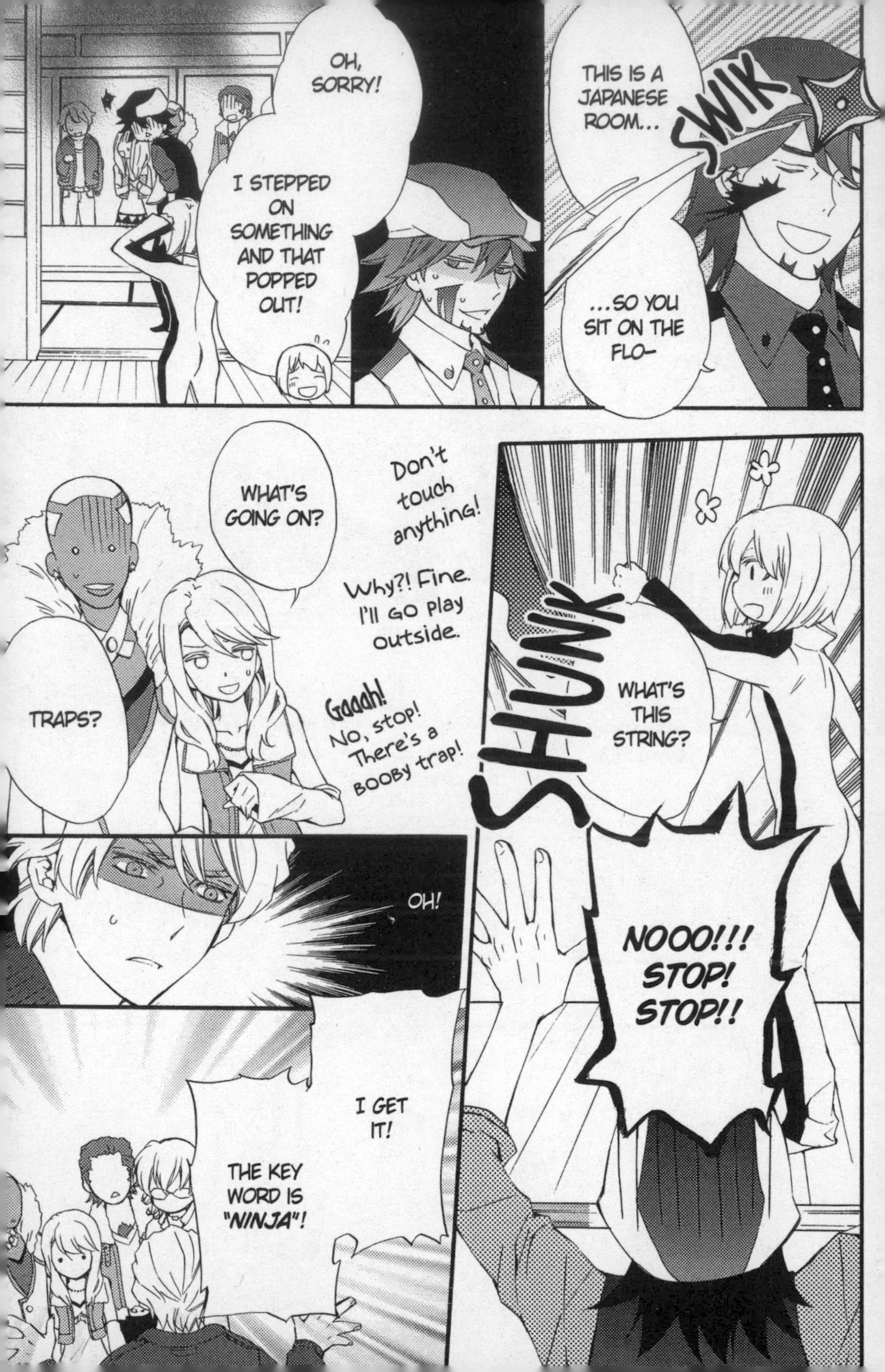
THIS IS A JAPANESE ROOM...
SWIK
...SO YOU SIT ON THE FLO–
OH, SORRY!
I STEPPED ON SOMETHING AND THAT POPPED OUT!
WHAT'S THIS STRING?
SHUNK
NOOO!!! STOP! STOP!!
WHAT'S GOING ON?
Don't touch anything!
Why?! Fine. I'll GO play outside.
Gaaah! No, stop! There's a BOOBY trap!
TRAPS?
OH!
I GET IT!
THE KEY WORD IS "NINJA"!

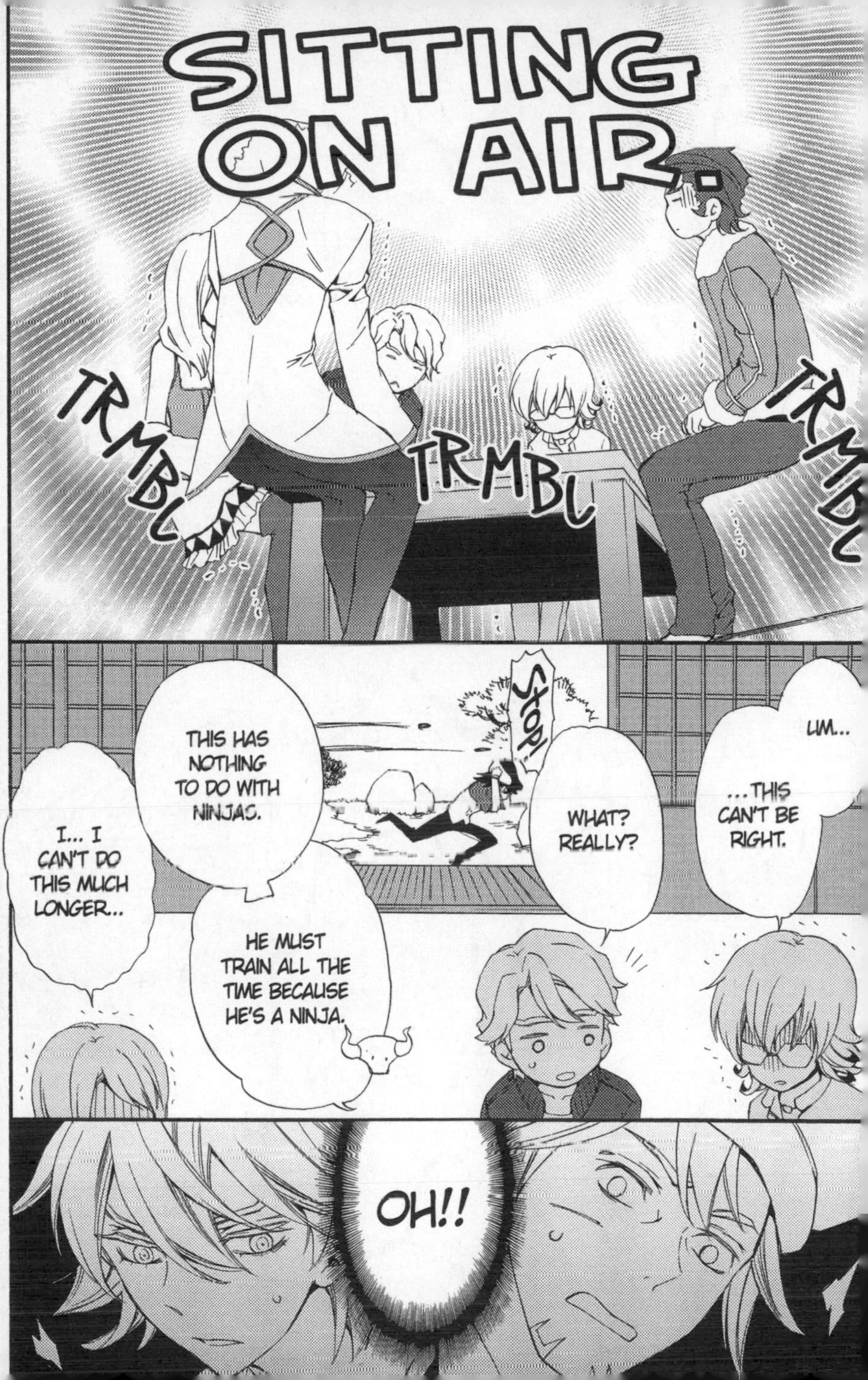
SITTING ON AIR.
TRMBL
TRMBL
TRMBL
UM...
...THIS CAN'T BE RIGHT.
STOP!
WHAT? REALLY?
THIS HAS NOTHING TO DO WITH NINJAS.
I... I CAN'T DO THIS MUCH LONGER...
HE MUST TRAIN ALL THE TIME BECAUSE HE'S A NINJA.
OH!!

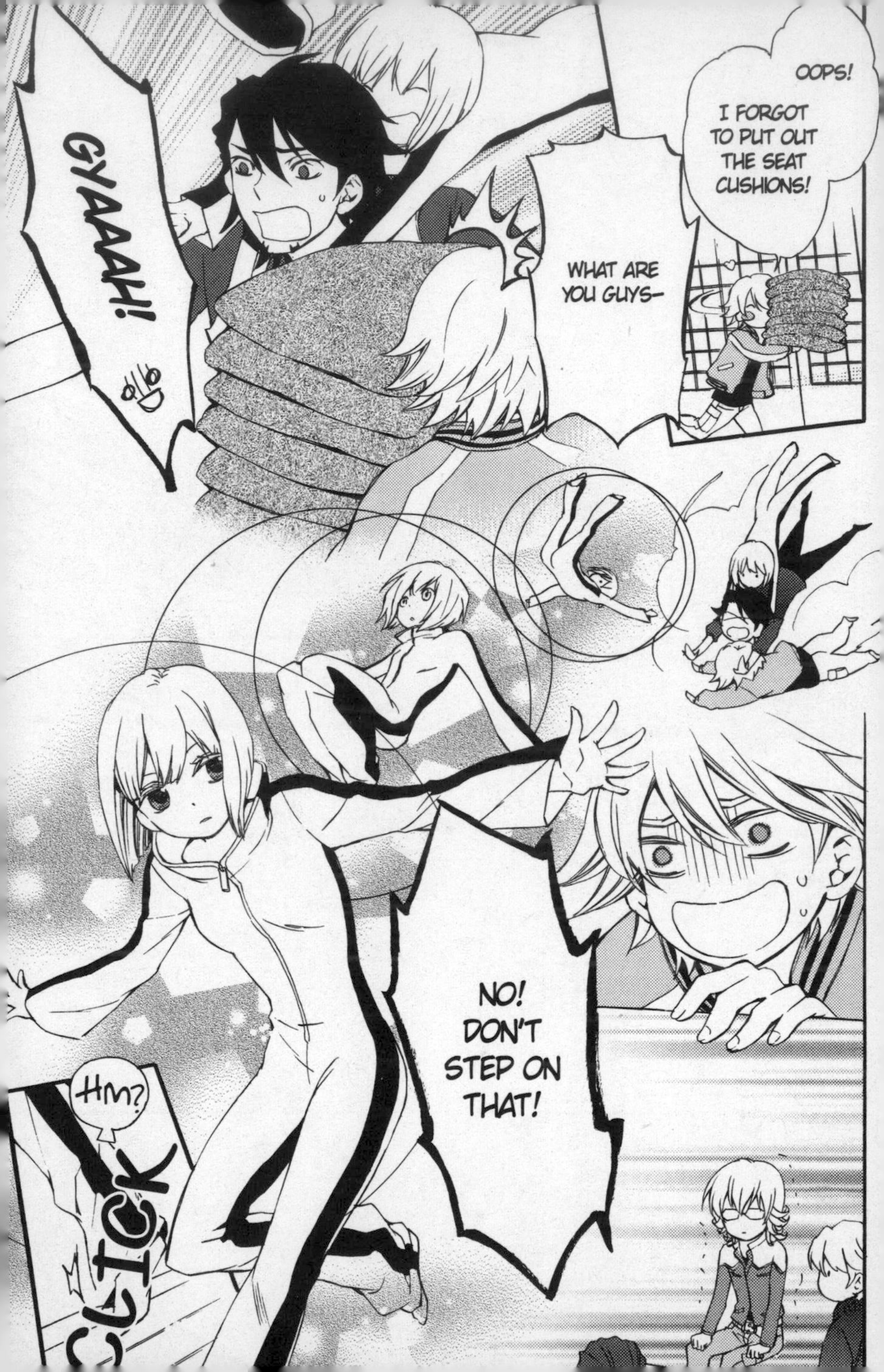
OOPS!
I FORGOT TO PUT OUT THE SEAT CUSHIONS!
WHAT ARE YOU GUYS–
GYAAAH!
NO! DON'T STEP ON THAT!
Hm?
CLICK

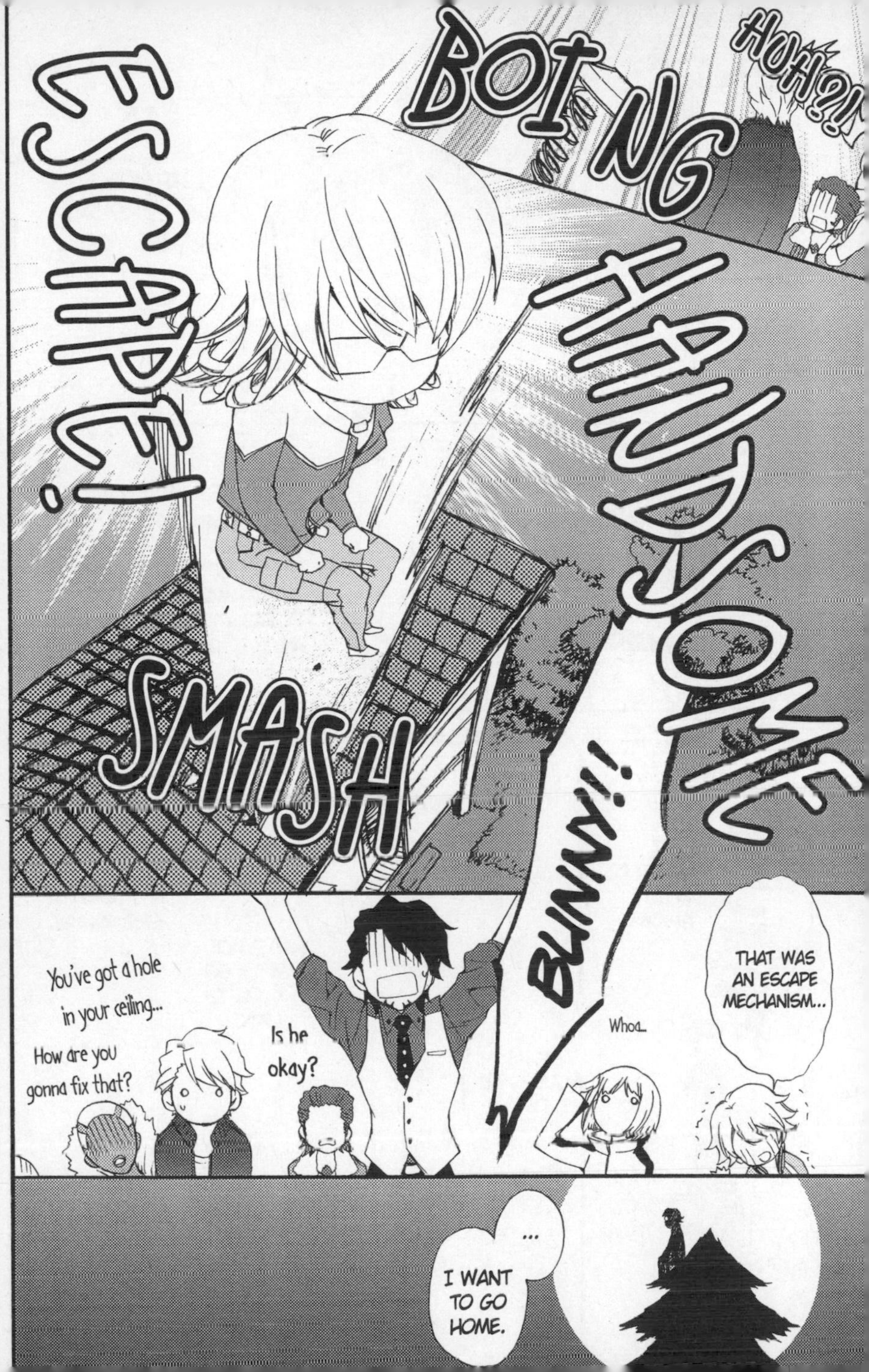
HUH?!!
BOING
HANDSOME
ESCAPE!
SMASH
BUNNY!!
THAT WAS AN ESCAPE MECHANISM...
Whoa
Is he okay?
You've got a hole in your ceiling...
How are you gonna fix that?
...
I WANT TO GO HOME.

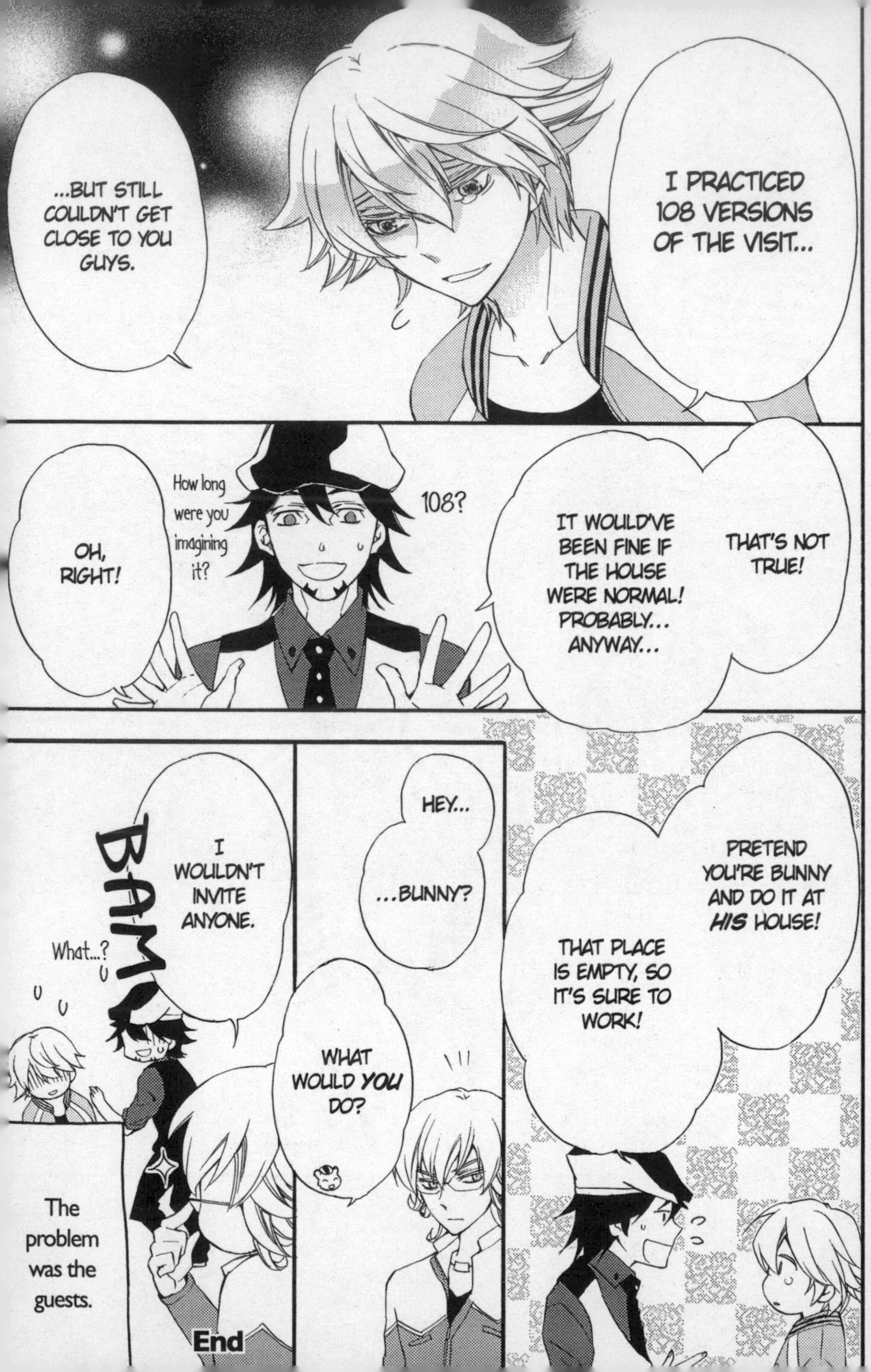
I PRACTICED 108 VERSIONS OF THE VISIT...
...BUT STILL COULDN'T GET CLOSE TO YOU GUYS.
THAT'S NOT TRUE!
IT WOULD'VE BEEN FINE IF THE HOUSE WERE NORMAL! PROBABLY... ANYWAY...
108?
How long were you imagining it?
OH, RIGHT!
PRETEND YOU'RE BUNNY AND DO IT AT *HIS* HOUSE!
THAT PLACE IS EMPTY, SO IT'S SURE TO WORK!
HEY...
...BUNNY?
WHAT WOULD *YOU* DO?
I WOULDN'T INVITE ANYONE.
BAM
What...?
The problem was the guests.
End

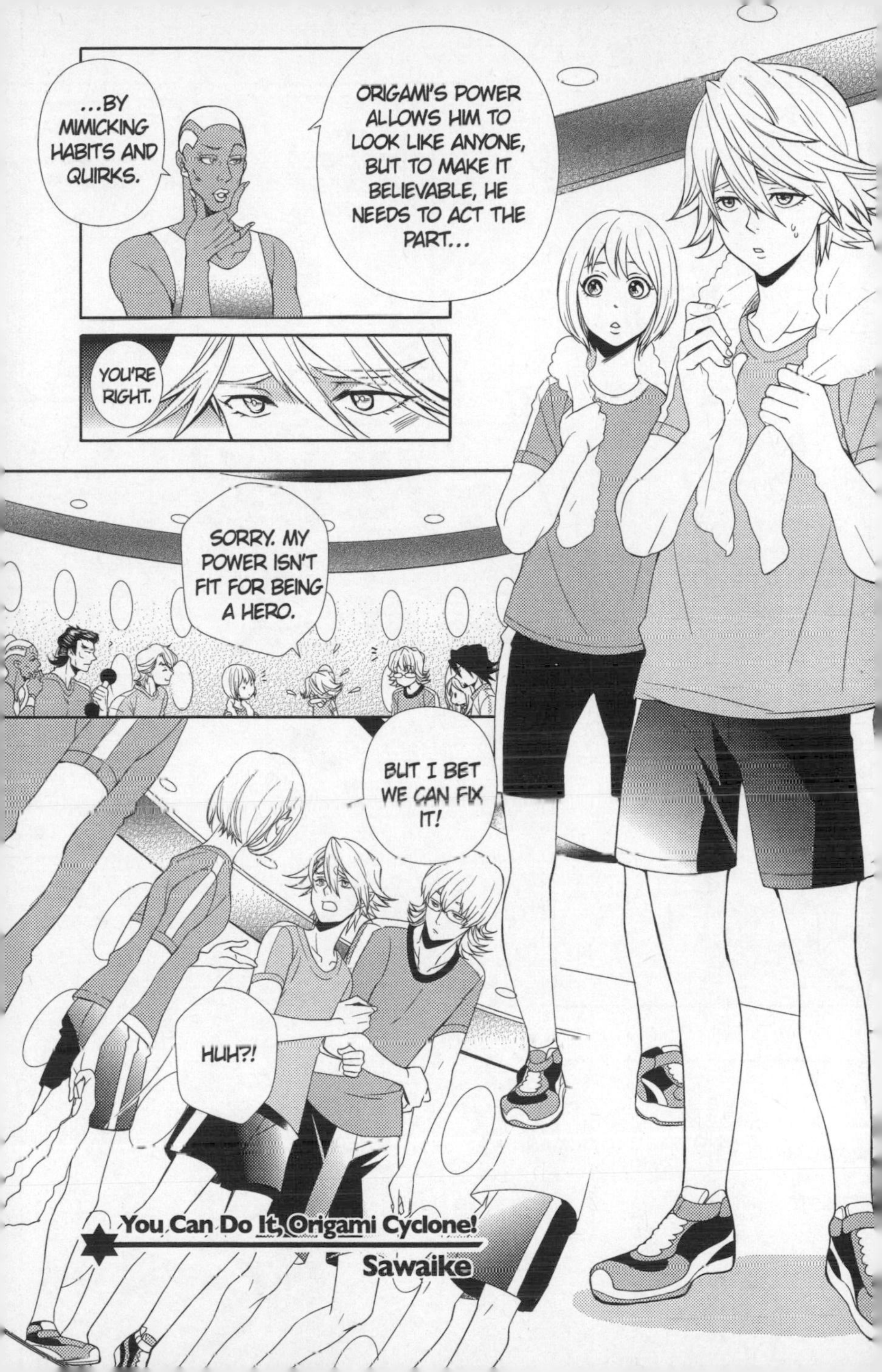
ORIGAMI'S POWER ALLOWS HIM TO LOOK LIKE ANYONE, BUT TO MAKE IT BELIEVABLE, HE NEEDS TO ACT THE PART...
...BY MIMICKING HABITS AND QUIRKS.
YOU'RE RIGHT.
SORRY. MY POWER ISN'T FIT FOR BEING A HERO.
BUT I BET WE CAN FIX IT!
HUH?!
You Can Do It, Origami Cyclone!
Sawaike

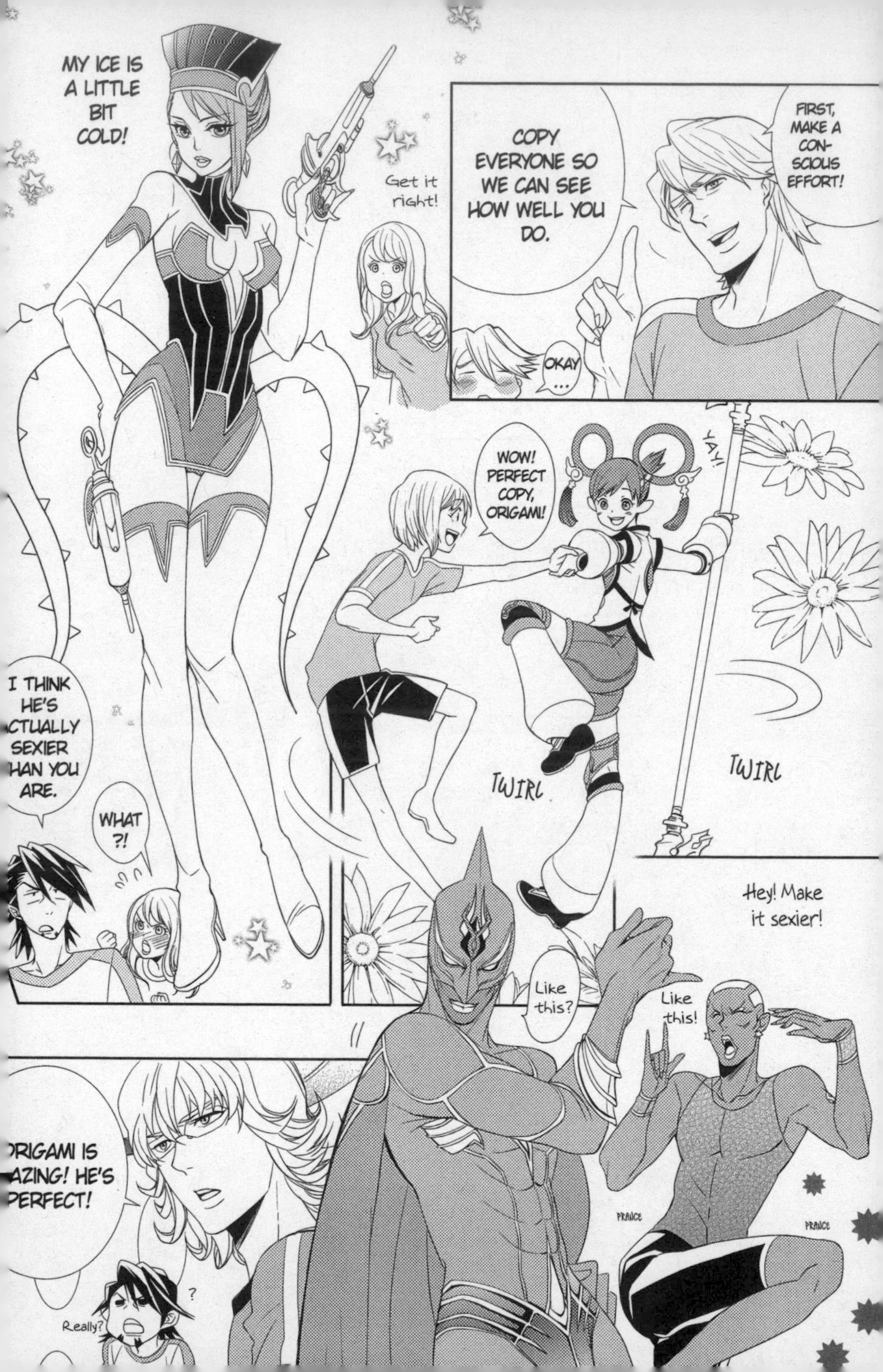
FIRST, MAKE A CON-SCIOUS EFFORT!
COPY EVERYONE SO WE CAN SEE HOW WELL YOU DO.
OKAY ...
YAY!
WOW! PERFECT COPY, ORIGAMI!
TWIRL
TWIRL
MY ICE IS A LITTLE BIT COLD!
Get it right!
I THINK HE'S CTUALLY SEXIER HAN YOU ARE.
WHAT ?!
Hey! Make it sexier!
Like this!
Like this?
PRANCE
PRANCE
ORIGAMI IS AZING! HE'S PERFECT!
?
Really?

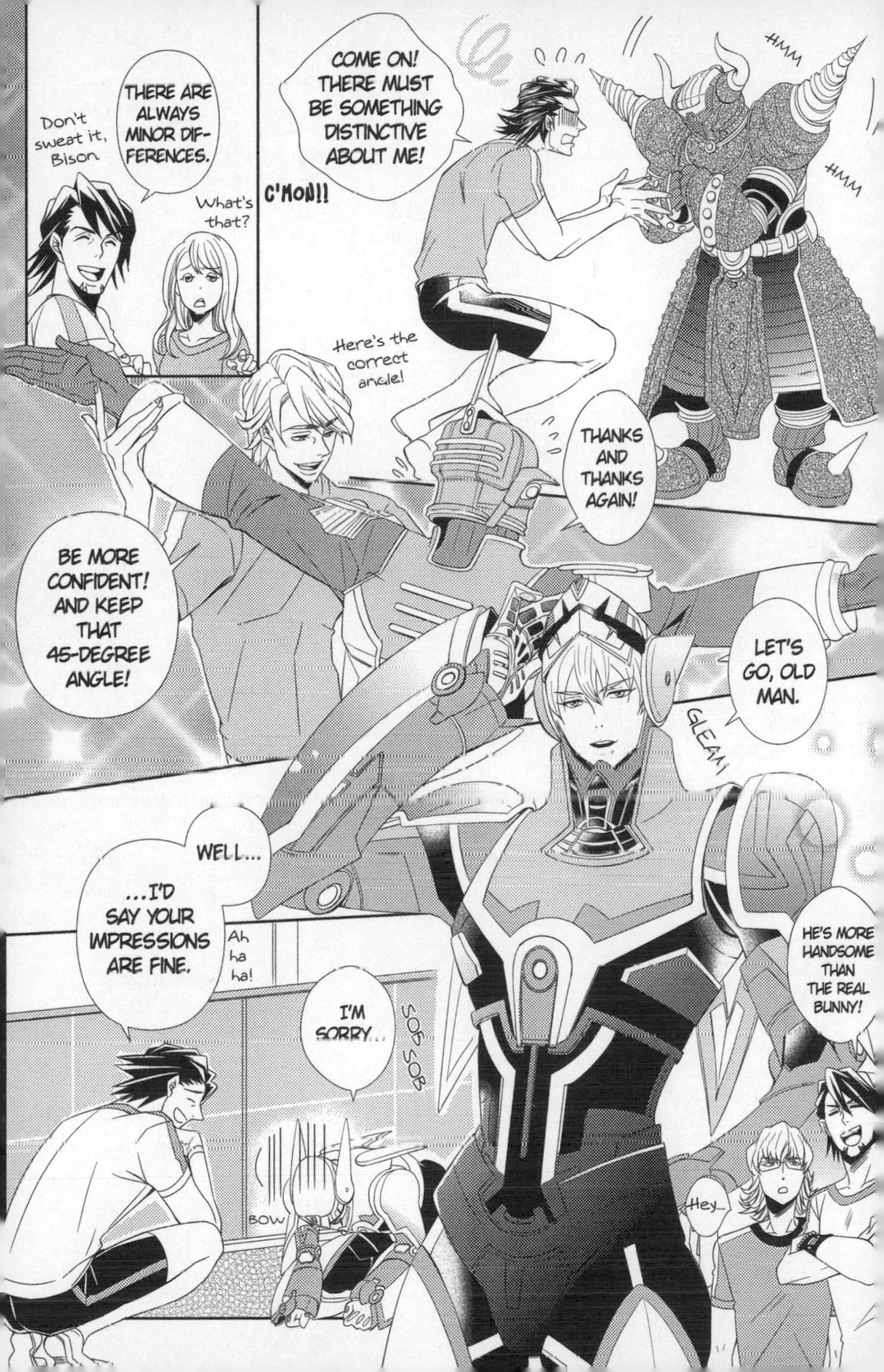
HMM
HMM
COME ON! THERE MUST BE SOMETHING DISTINCTIVE ABOUT ME!
C'MON!!
THERE ARE ALWAYS MINOR DIF-FERENCES.
Don't sweat it, Bison.
What's that?
THANKS AND THANKS AGAIN!
Here's the correct angle!
BE MORE CONFIDENT! AND KEEP THAT 45-DEGREE ANGLE!
LET'S GO, OLD MAN.
GLEAM
HE'S MORE HANDSOME THAN THE REAL BUNNY!
Hey...
SOB SOB
I'M SORRY...
BOW
WELL...
...I'D SAY YOUR IMPRESSIONS ARE FINE.
Ah ha ha!

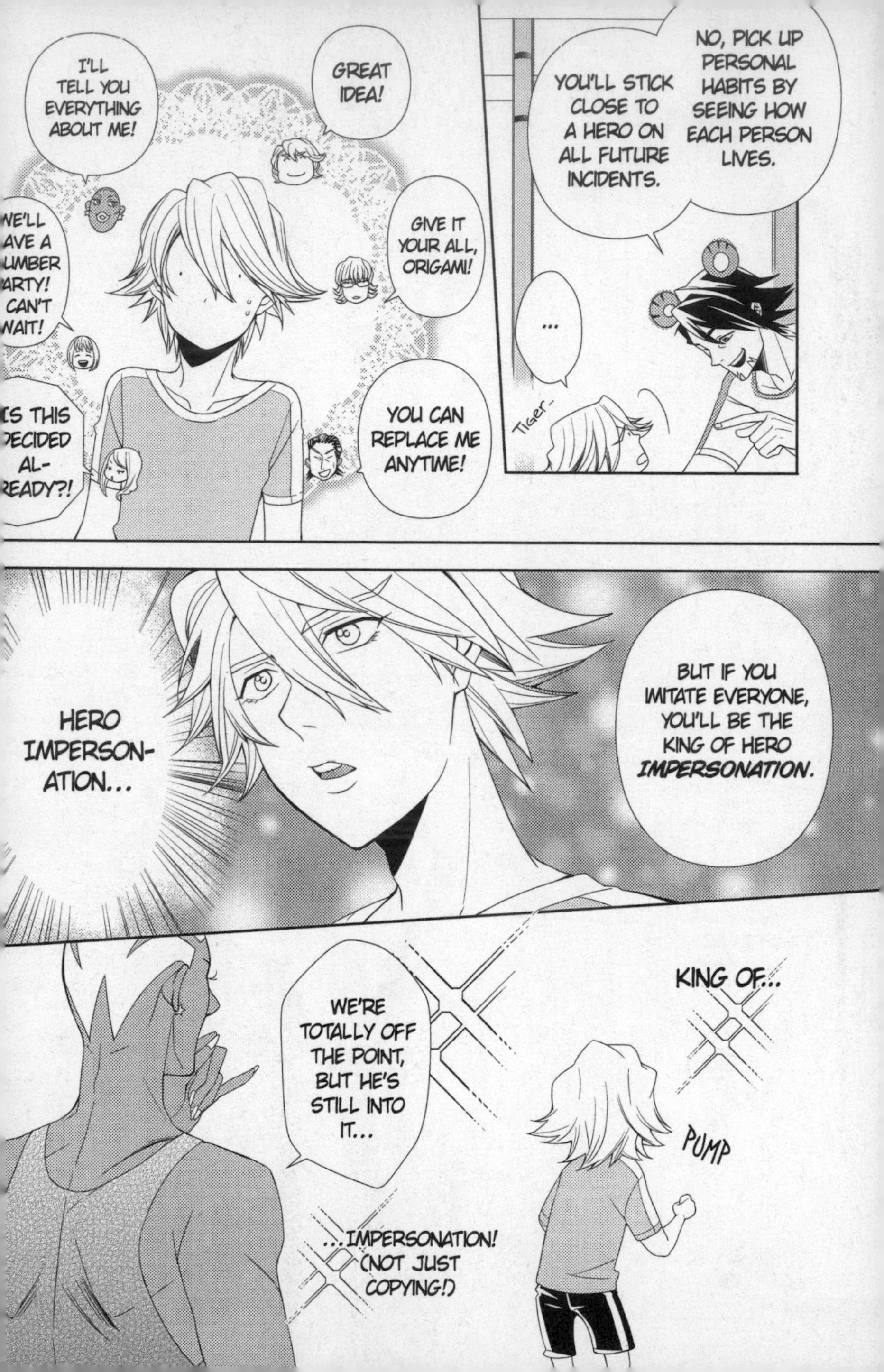
NO, PICK UP PERSONAL HABITS BY SEEING HOW EACH PERSON LIVES.
YOU'LL STICK CLOSE TO A HERO ON ALL FUTURE INCIDENTS.
...
Tiger...
GREAT IDEA!
GIVE IT YOUR ALL, ORIGAMI!
I'LL TELL YOU EVERYTHING ABOUT ME!
YOU CAN REPLACE ME ANYTIME!
NE'LL AVE A LUMBER ARTY! CAN'T NAIT!
IS THIS ECIDED AL- READY?!
BUT IF YOU IMITATE EVERYONE, YOU'LL BE THE KING OF HERO ***IMPERSONATION***.
HERO IMPERSON- ATION...
KING OF...
PUMP
...IMPERSONATION! (NOT JUST COPYING!)
WE'RE TOTALLY OFF THE POINT, BUT HE'S STILL INTO IT...

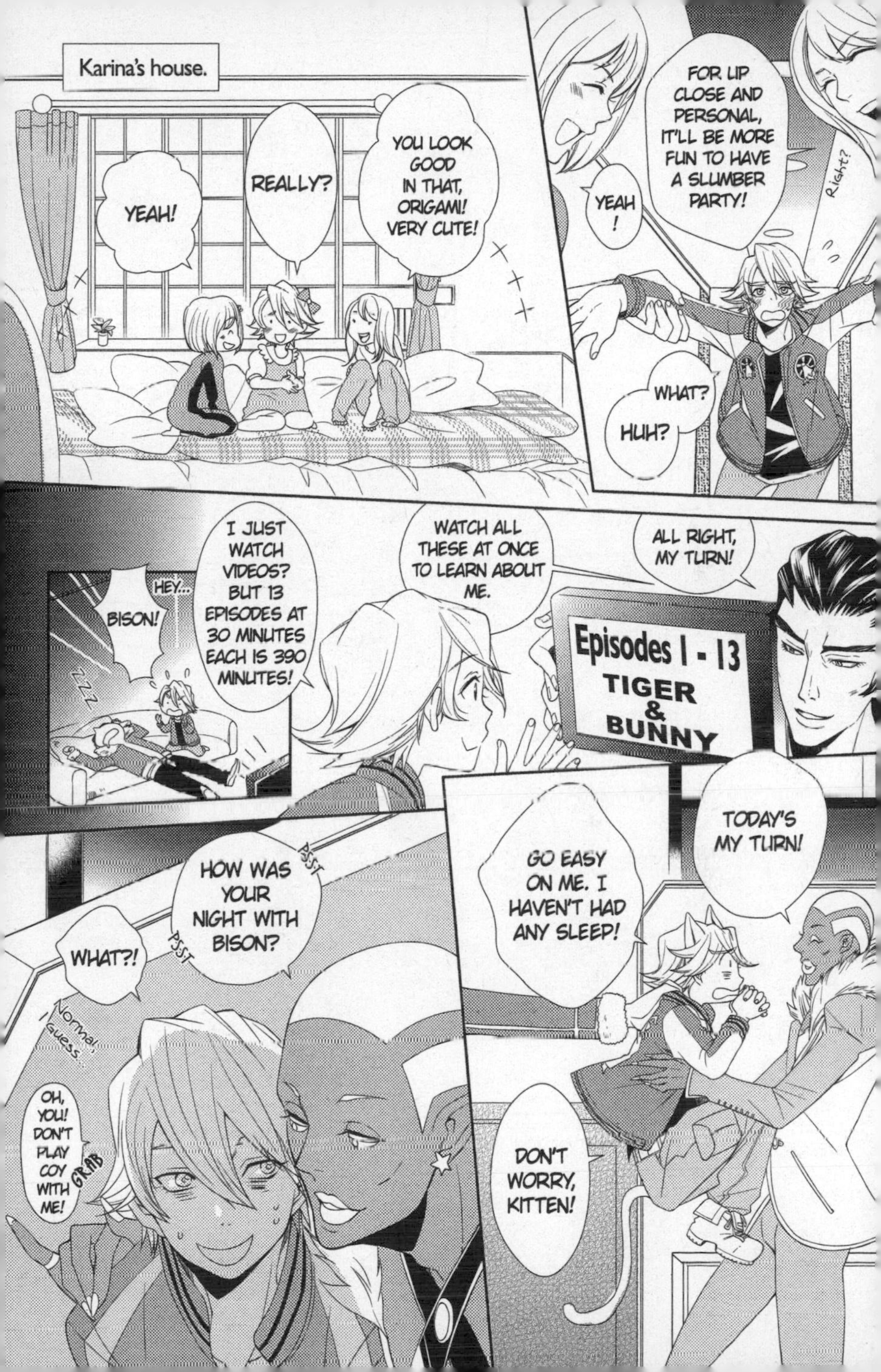
FOR UP CLOSE AND PERSONAL, IT'LL BE MORE FUN TO HAVE A SLUMBER PARTY!
Right?
YEAH!
WHAT?
HUH?
Karina's house.
YOU LOOK GOOD IN THAT, ORIGAMI! VERY CUTE!
REALLY?
YEAH!
ALL RIGHT, MY TURN!
WATCH ALL THESE AT ONCE TO LEARN ABOUT ME.
Episodes 1 - 13
TIGER & BUNNY
I JUST WATCH VIDEOS? BUT 13 EPISODES AT 30 MINUTES EACH IS 390 MINUTES!
HEY...
BISON!
ZZZ
TODAY'S MY TURN!
GO EASY ON ME. I HAVEN'T HAD ANY SLEEP!
DON'T WORRY, KITTEN!
PSST
HOW WAS YOUR NIGHT WITH BISON?
PSST
WHAT?!
Normal, I guess...
OH, YOU! DON'T PLAY COY WITH ME!
GRAB

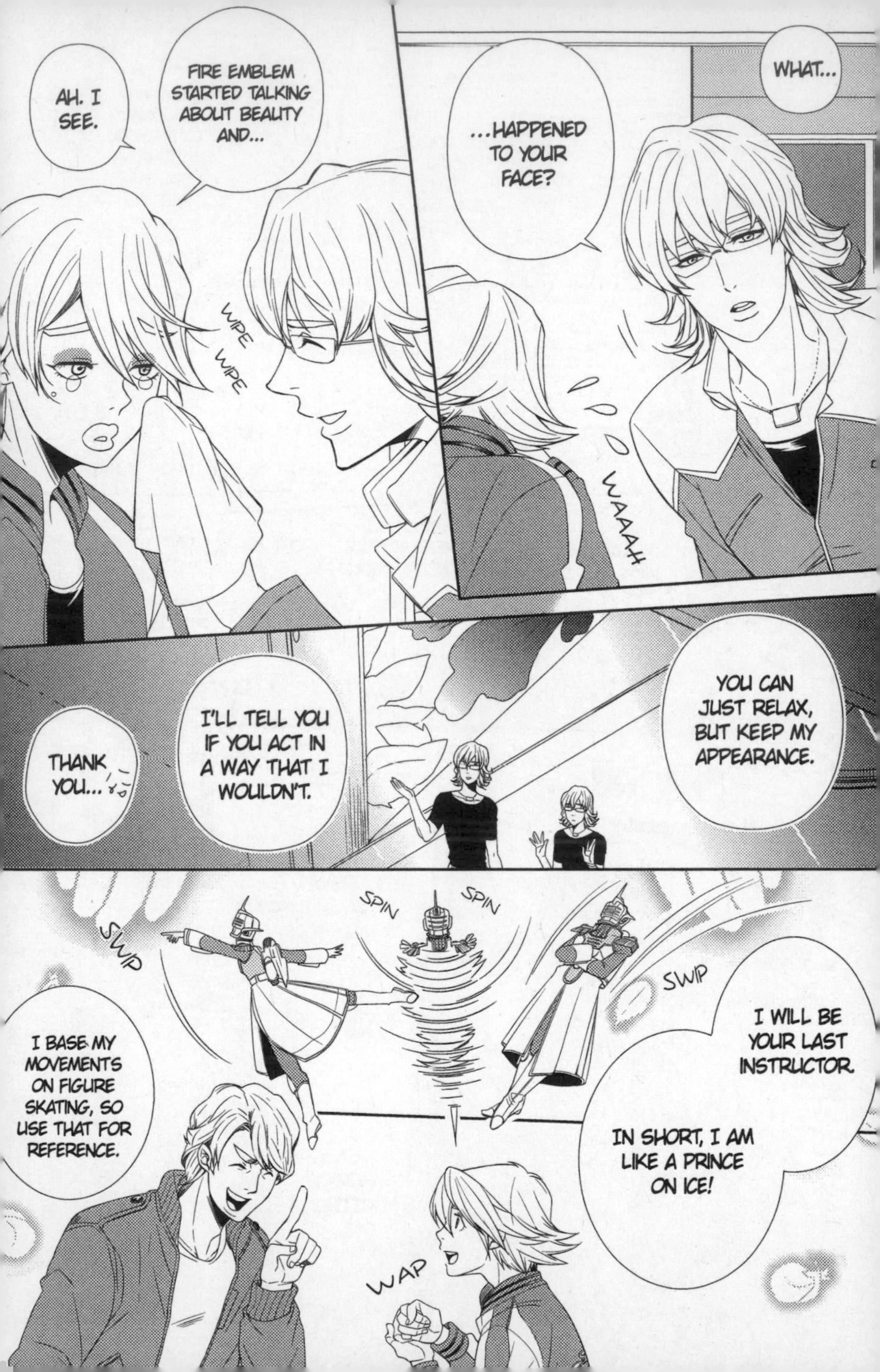
WHAT...
...HAPPENED TO YOUR FACE?
WAAAAH
FIRE EMBLEM STARTED TALKING ABOUT BEAUTY AND...
AH. I SEE.
WIPE WIPE
YOU CAN JUST RELAX, BUT KEEP MY APPEARANCE.
I'LL TELL YOU IF YOU ACT IN A WAY THAT I WOULDN'T.
THANK YOU...
SWP
SPIN SPIN
SWP
I WILL BE YOUR LAST INSTRUCTOR.
IN SHORT, I AM LIKE A PRINCE ON ICE!
I BASE MY MOVEMENTS ON FIGURE SKATING, SO USE THAT FOR REFERENCE.
WAP

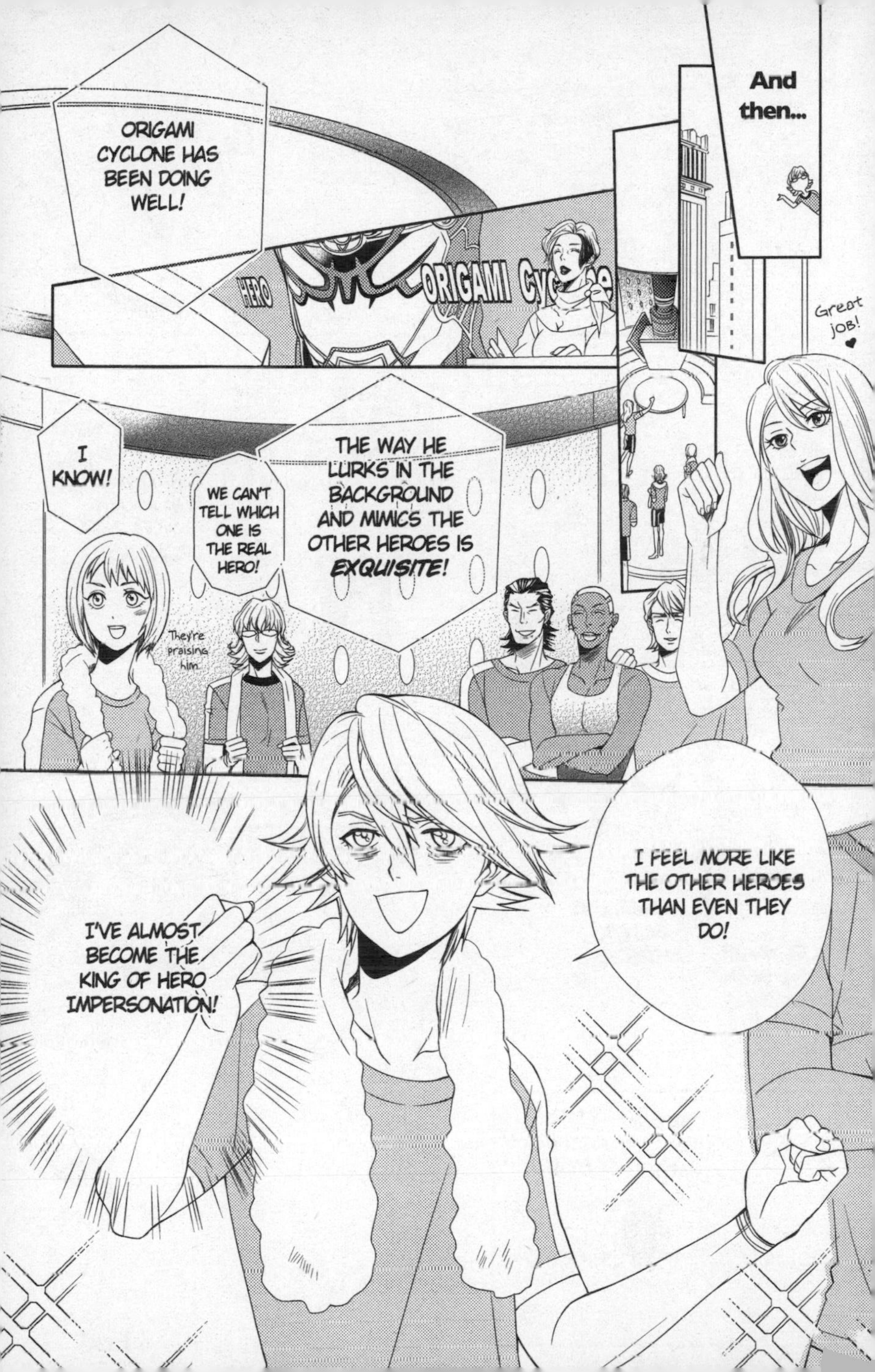
And then...
ORIGAMI CYCLONE HAS BEEN DOING WELL!
HERO
ORIGAMI Cyclone
Great job! ♥
THE WAY HE LURKS IN THE BACKGROUND AND MIMICS THE OTHER HEROES IS *EXQUISITE*!
WE CAN'T TELL WHICH ONE IS THE REAL HERO!
I KNOW!
They're praising him.
I FEEL MORE LIKE THE OTHER HEROES THAN EVEN THEY DO!
I'VE ALMOST BECOME THE KING OF HERO IMPERSONATION!

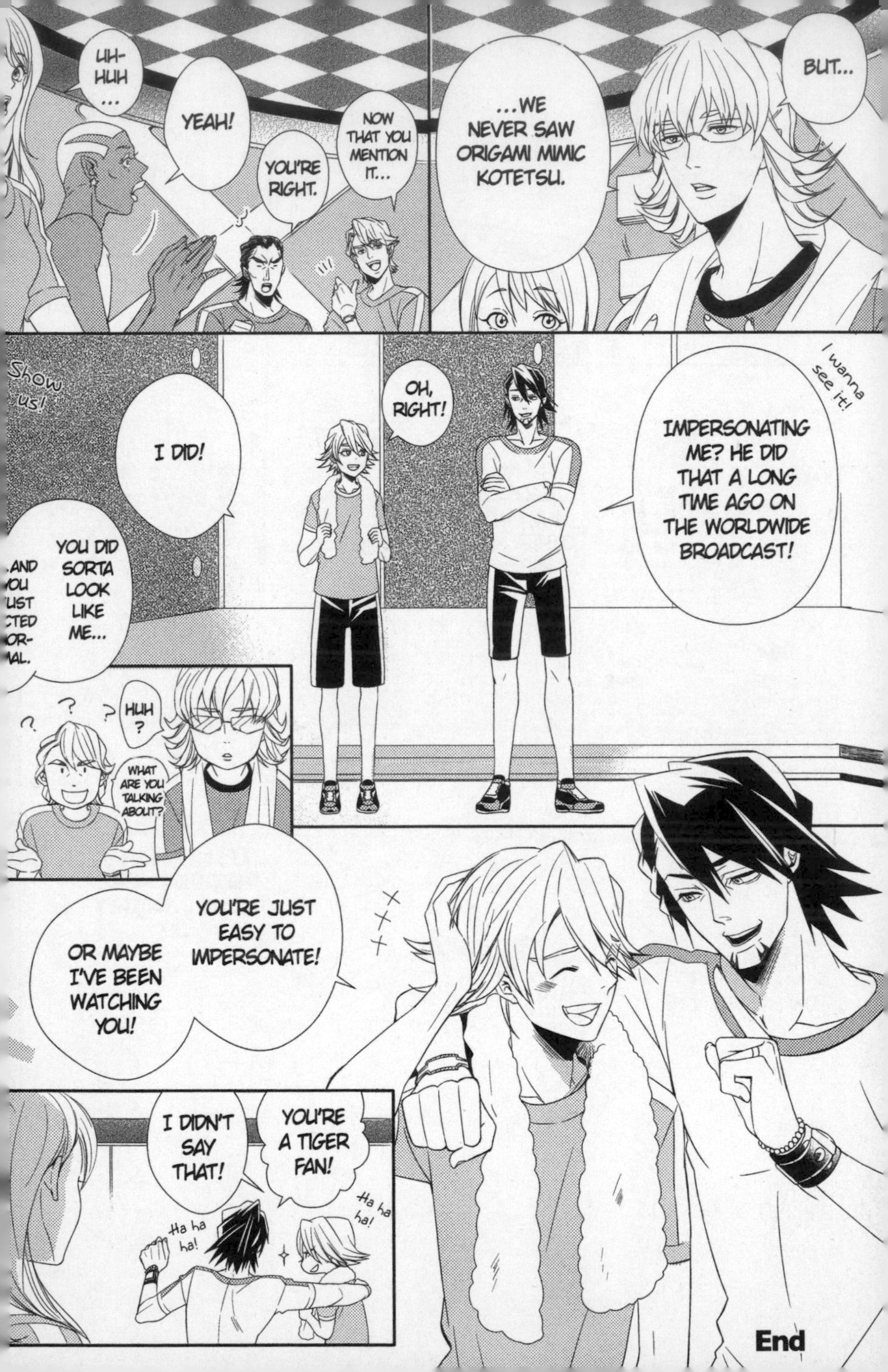
BUT...
...WE NEVER SAW ORIGAMI MIMIC KOTETSU.
NOW THAT YOU MENTION IT...
YOU'RE RIGHT.
YEAH!
UH-HUH...
I wanna see it!
IMPERSONATING ME? HE DID THAT A LONG TIME AGO ON THE WORLDWIDE BROADCAST!
OH, RIGHT!
I DID!
Show us!
YOU DID SORTA LOOK LIKE ME...
.AND YOU UST CTED ORM- AL.
HUH?
WHAT ARE YOU TALKING ABOUT?
YOU'RE JUST EASY TO IMPERSONATE!
OR MAYBE I'VE BEEN WATCHING YOU!
YOU'RE A TIGER FAN!
I DIDN'T SAY THAT!
Ha ha ha!
Ha ha ha!
End

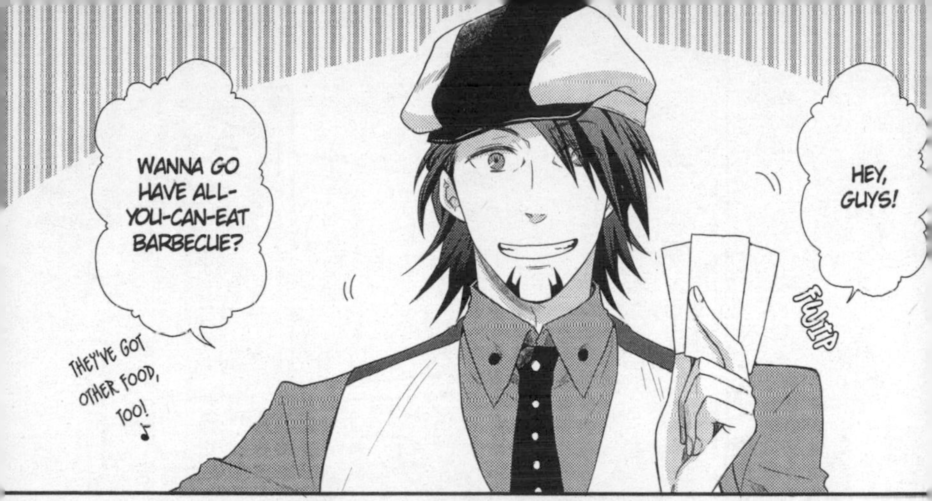
HEY, GUYS!
FLIP
WANNA GO HAVE ALL-YOU-CAN-EAT BARBECUE?
THEY'VE GOT OTHER FOOD, TOO! ♪

The Heroes Have BBQ

Uka Nagao

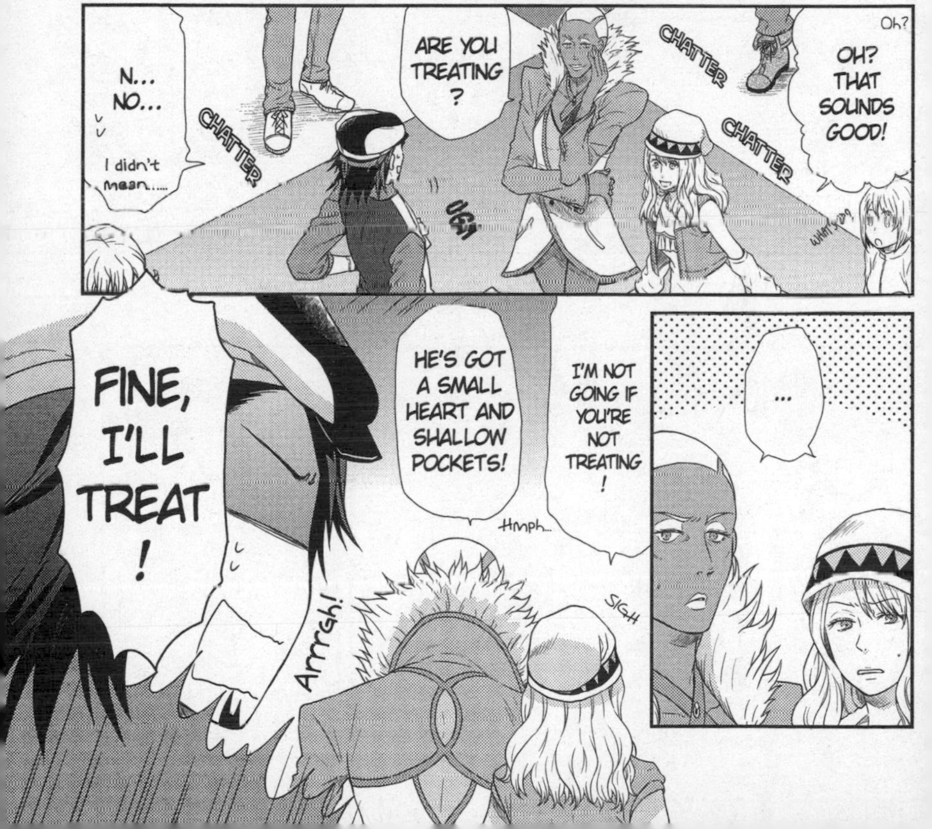
Oh?
OH? THAT SOUNDS GOOD!
CHATTER
CHATTER
ARE YOU TREATING?
UGH
CHATTER
N... NO...
I didn't mean......
...
I'M NOT GOING IF YOU'RE NOT TREATING!
HE'S GOT A SMALL HEART AND SHALLOW POCKETS!
SIGH
Hmph...
FINE, I'LL TREAT!
Arrrgh!

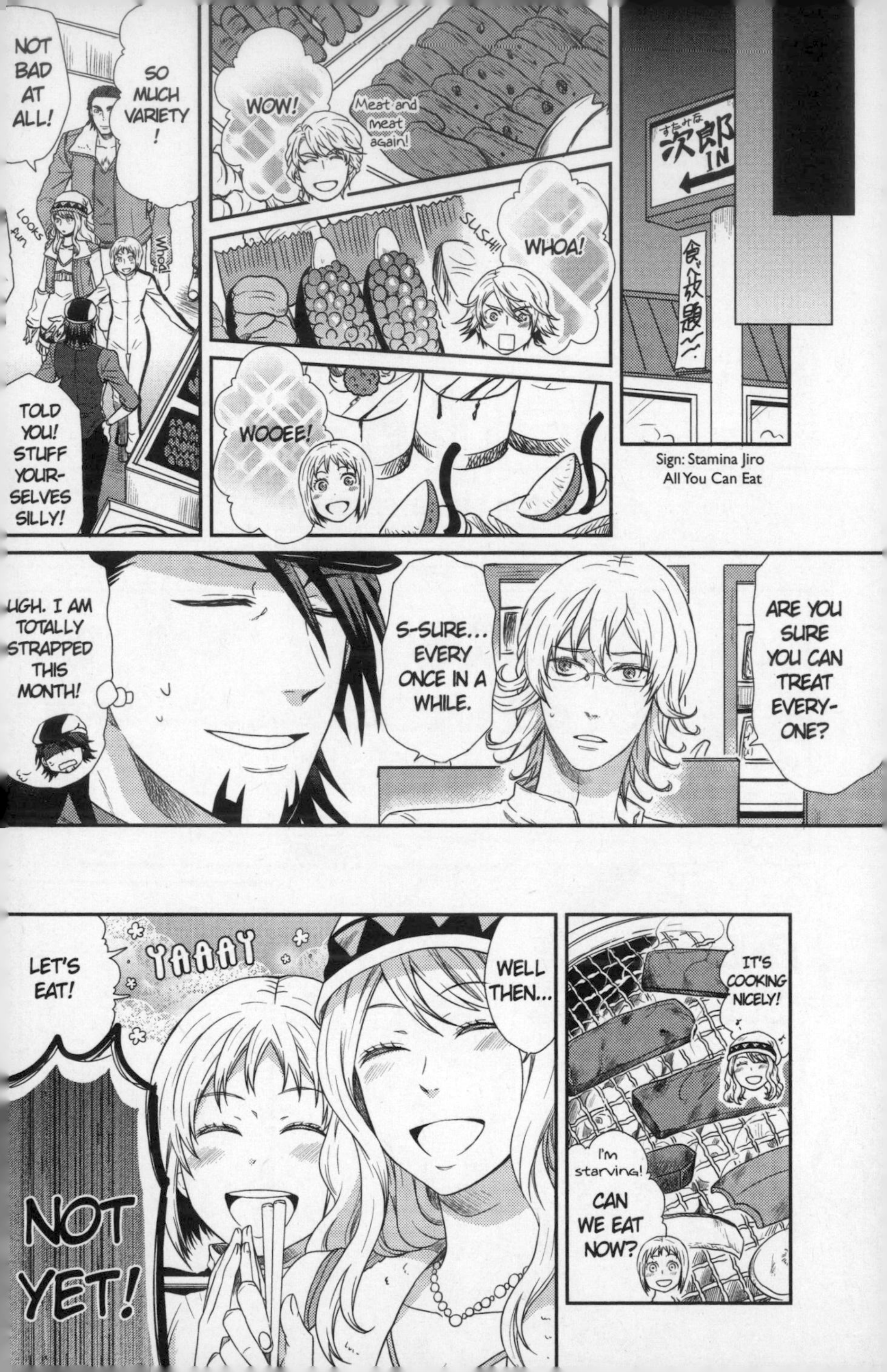

すたみな
次郎
IN
食べ放題～
Sign: Stamina Jiro
All You Can Eat
WOW!
Meat and meat again!
SUSHI!
WHOA!
WOOEE!
SO MUCH VARIETY!
NOT BAD AT ALL!
Whoa!
Looks fun.
TOLD YOU! STUFF YOURSELVES SILLY!
ARE YOU SURE YOU CAN TREAT EVERYONE?
S-SURE... EVERY ONCE IN A WHILE.
UGH. I AM TOTALLY STRAPPED THIS MONTH!
IT'S COOKING NICELY!
I'm starving!
CAN WE EAT NOW?
WELL THEN...
YAAAY
LET'S EAT!
NOT YET!

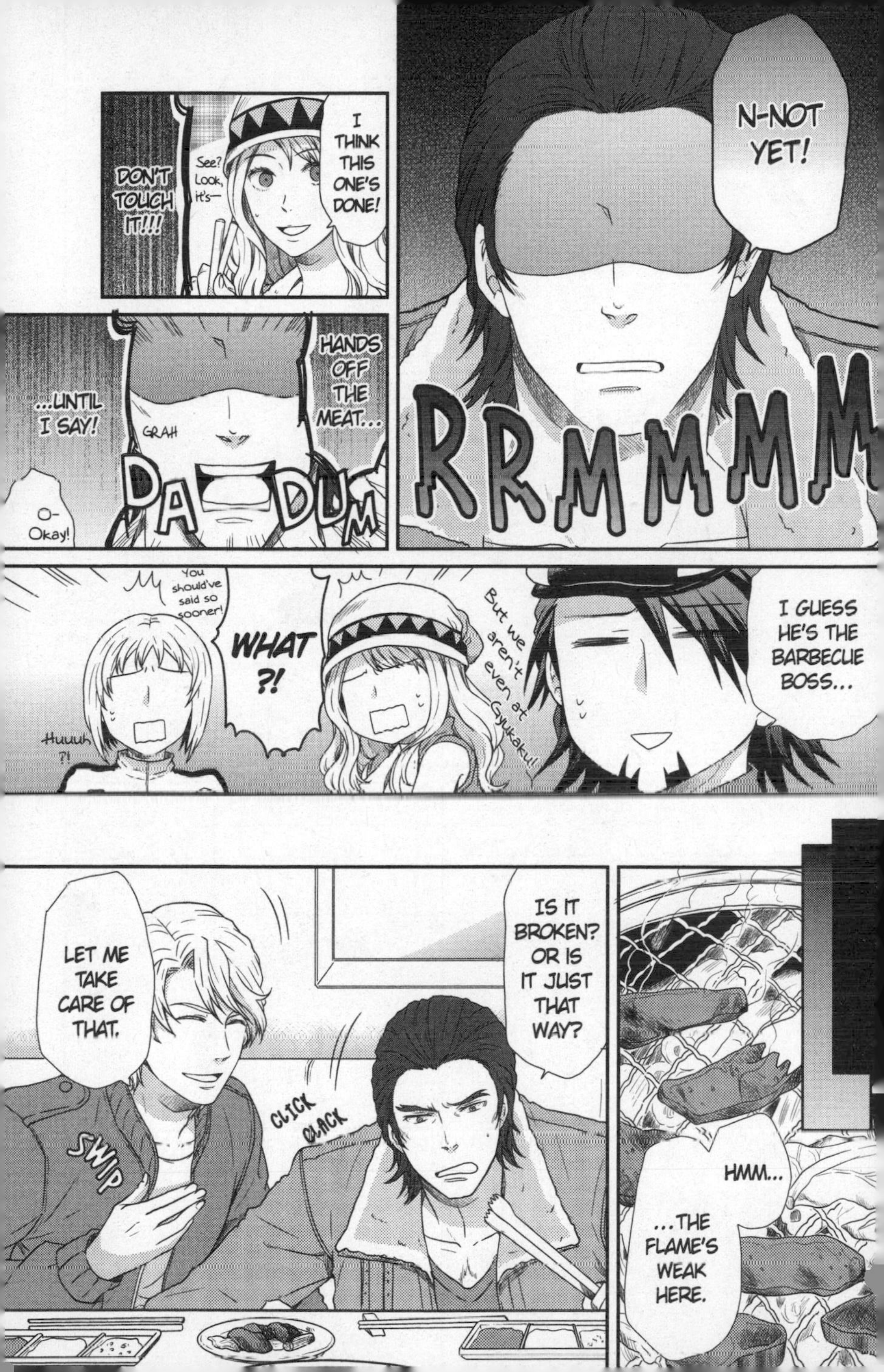
N-NOT YET!
RRMMMM
I THINK THIS ONE'S DONE!
See? Look, it's—
DON'T TOUCH IT!!!
HANDS OFF THE MEAT...
GRAH
...UNTIL I SAY!
DA DUM
O-Okay!
I GUESS HE'S THE BARBECUE BOSS...
But we aren't even at Gyukaku!
WHAT?!
You should've said so sooner!
Huuuh?!
HMM...
...THE FLAME'S WEAK HERE.
IS IT BROKEN? OR IS IT JUST THAT WAY?
CLICK CLACK
LET ME TAKE CARE OF THAT.
SWIP

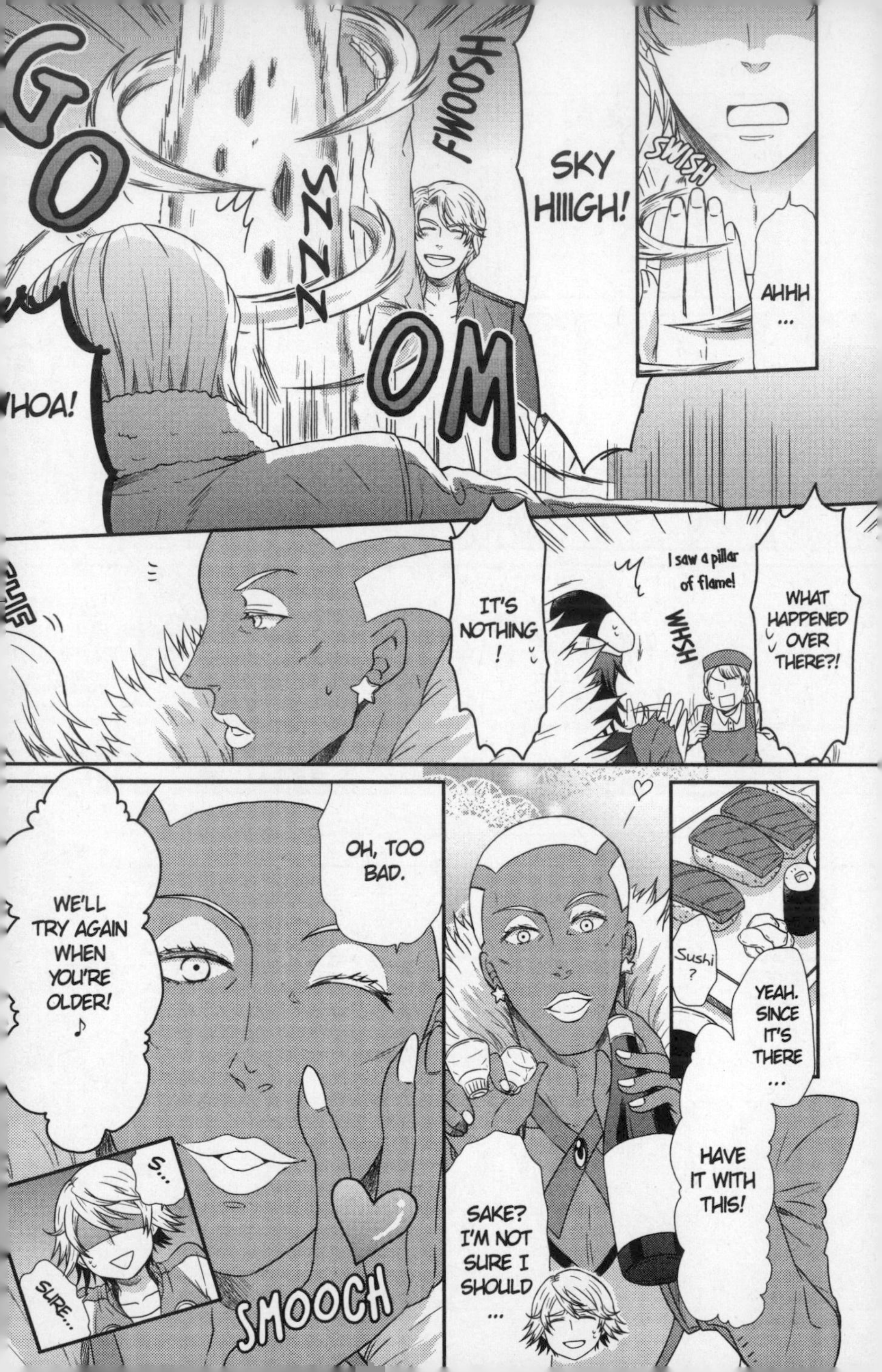
SWISH
AHHH ...
SKY HIIIGH!
FWOOSH
GO
OM
WHOA!
WHAT HAPPENED OVER THERE?!
I saw a pillar of flame!
WHSH
IT'S NOTHING!
Sushi?
YEAH. SINCE IT'S THERE ...
HAVE IT WITH THIS!
SAKE? I'M NOT SURE I SHOULD ...
OH, TOO BAD.
WE'LL TRY AGAIN WHEN YOU'RE OLDER! ♪
S...
SURE...
SMOOCH

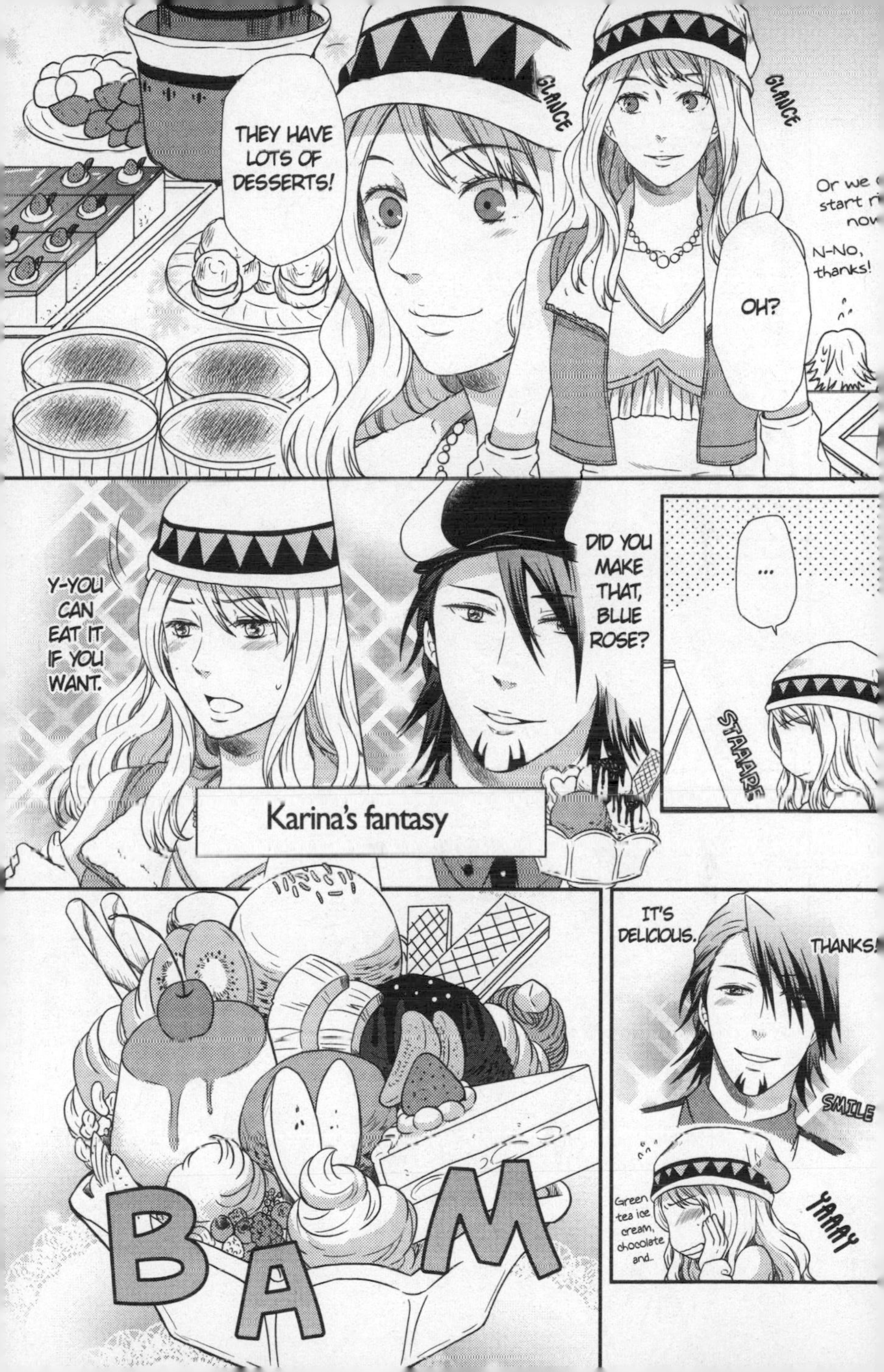
GLANCE
GLANCE
Or we c
start ri
now
N-No, thanks!
OH?
THEY HAVE LOTS OF DESSERTS!
...
STAAARE
DID YOU MAKE THAT, BLUE ROSE?
Y-YOU CAN EAT IT IF YOU WANT.
Karina's fantasy
IT'S DELICIOUS.
THANKS!
SMILE
YAAAY
Green tea ice cream, chocolate and...
BAM

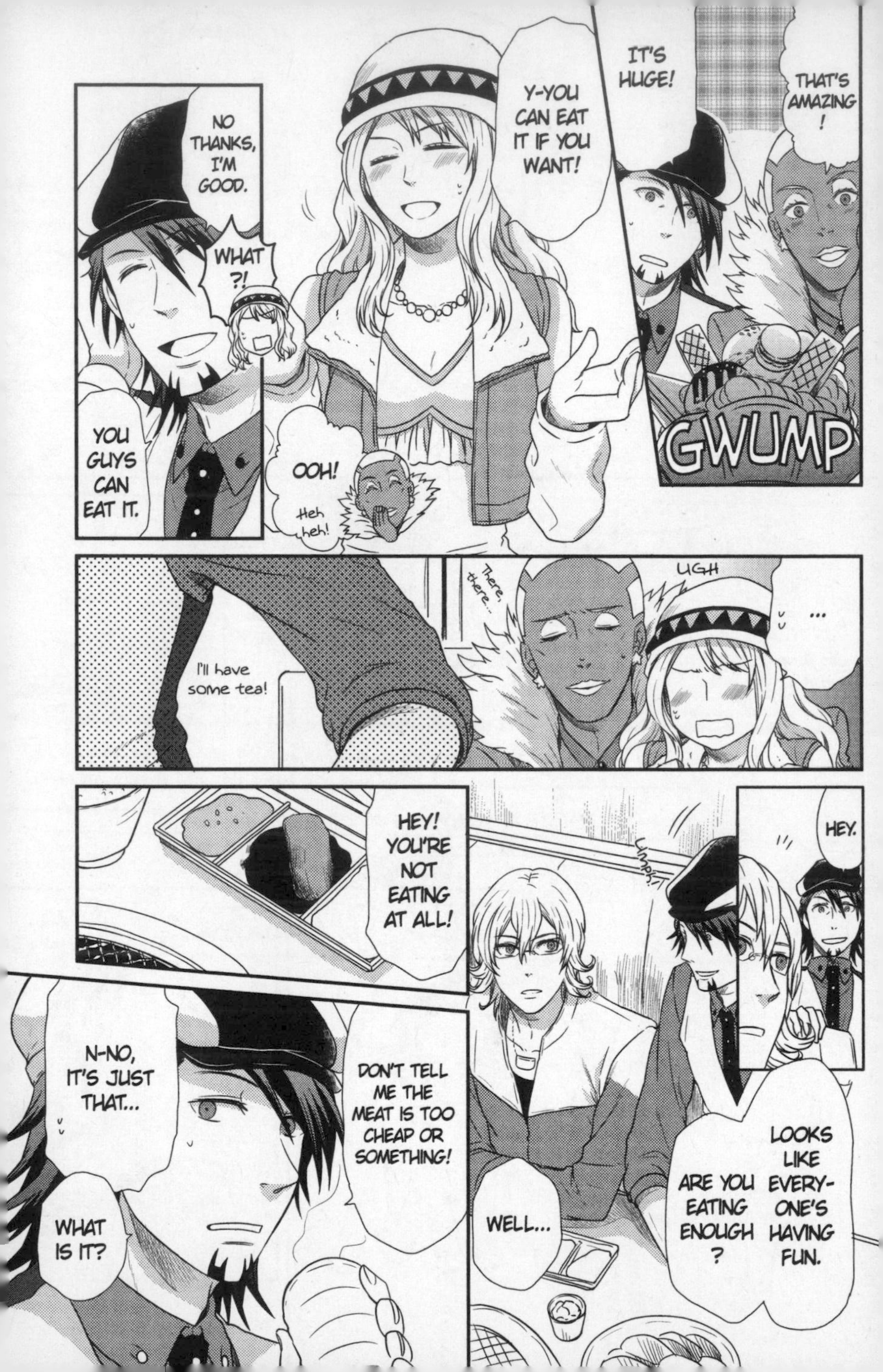
THAT'S AMAZING!
IT'S HUGE!
GWUMP
Y-YOU CAN EAT IT IF YOU WANT!
NO THANKS, I'M GOOD.
WHAT ?!
OOH!
Heh heh!
YOU GUYS CAN EAT IT.
...
UGH
There, there...
I'll have some tea!
HEY.
Umph!
HEY! YOU'RE NOT EATING AT ALL!
LOOKS LIKE EVERY-ONE'S HAVING FUN.
ARE YOU EATING ENOUGH ?
WELL...
DON'T TELL ME THE MEAT IS TOO CHEAP OR SOMETHING!
N-NO, IT'S JUST THAT...
WHAT IS IT?

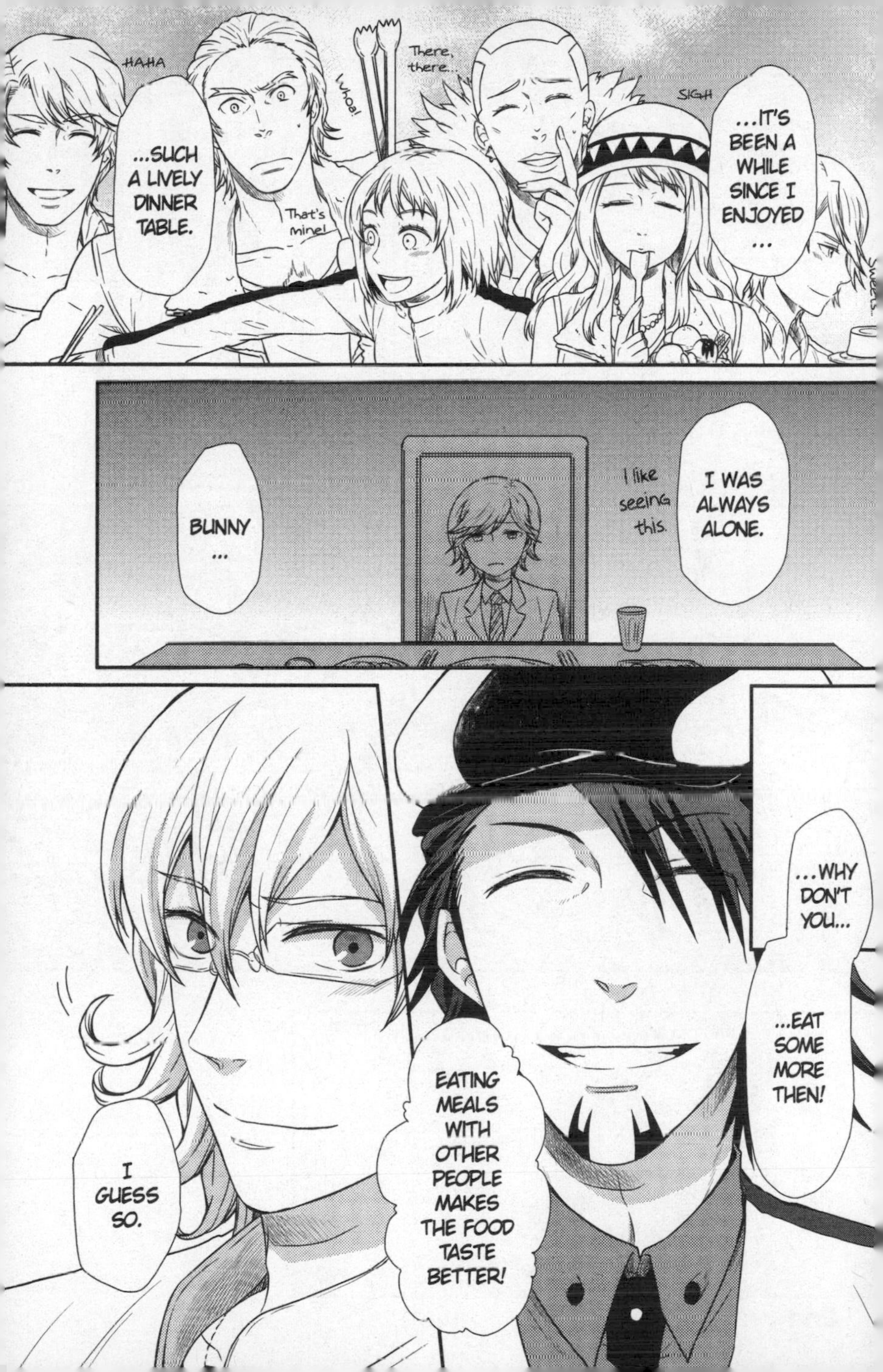
...IT'S BEEN A WHILE SINCE I ENJOYED ...
Sweets.
SIGH
There, there...
Whoa!
That's mine!
...SUCH A LIVELY DINNER TABLE.
HAHA
I WAS ALWAYS ALONE.
I like seeing this.
BUNNY ...
...WHY DON'T YOU...
...EAT SOME MORE THEN!
EATING MEALS WITH OTHER PEOPLE MAKES THE FOOD TASTE BETTER!
I GUESS SO.

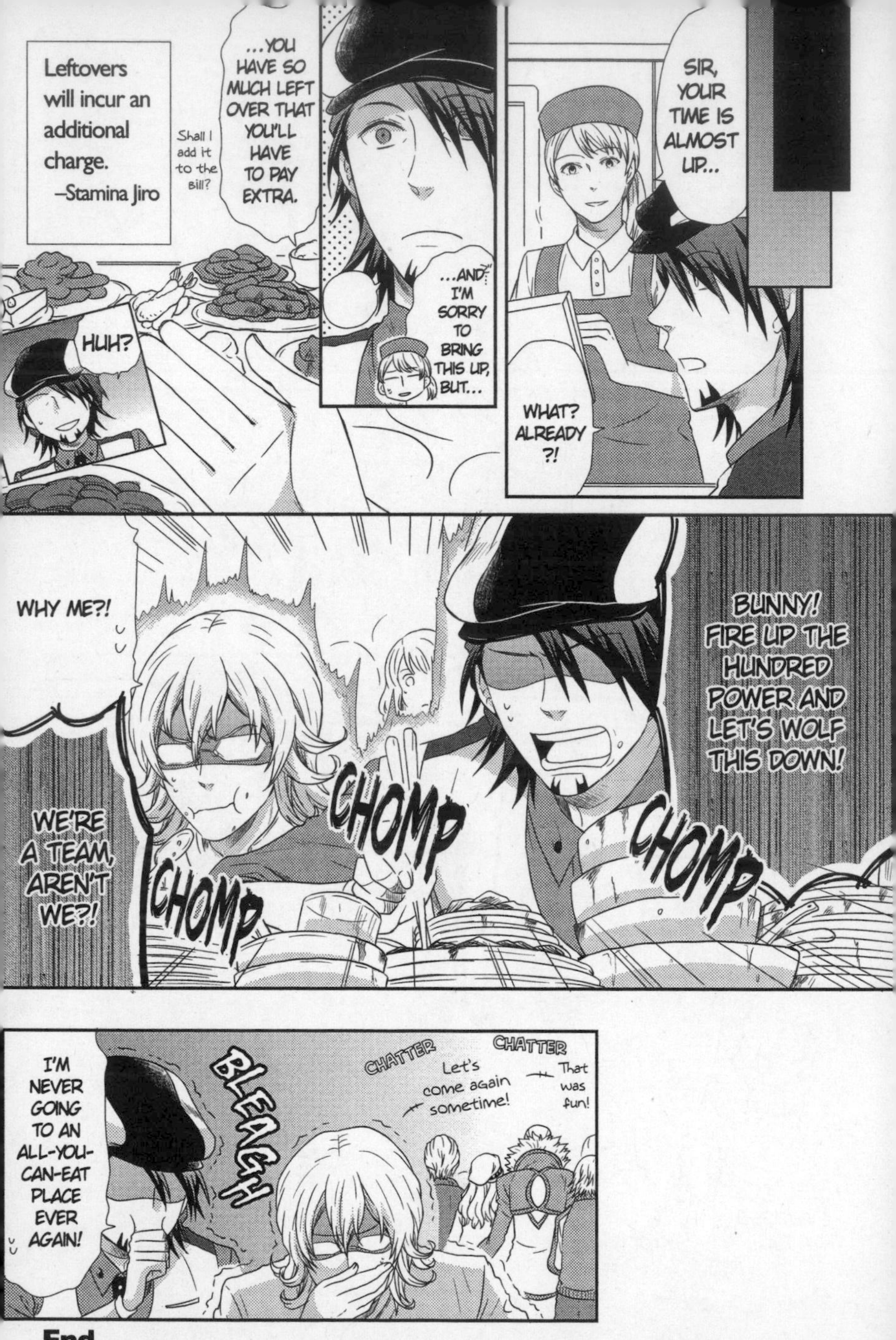
SIR, YOUR TIME IS ALMOST UP...
WHAT? ALREADY?!
...AND I'M SORRY TO BRING THIS UP, BUT...
...YOU HAVE SO MUCH LEFT OVER THAT YOU'LL HAVE TO PAY EXTRA.
Shall I add it to the bill?
Leftovers will incur an additional charge. –Stamina Jiro
HUH?
BUNNY! FIRE UP THE HUNDRED POWER AND LET'S WOLF THIS DOWN!
CHOMP
CHOMP
WHY ME?!
WE'RE A TEAM, AREN'T WE?!
CHOMP
CHATTER
That was fun!
CHATTER
Let's come again sometime!
BLEAGH
I'M NEVER GOING TO AN ALL-YOU-CAN-EAT PLACE EVER AGAIN!

End

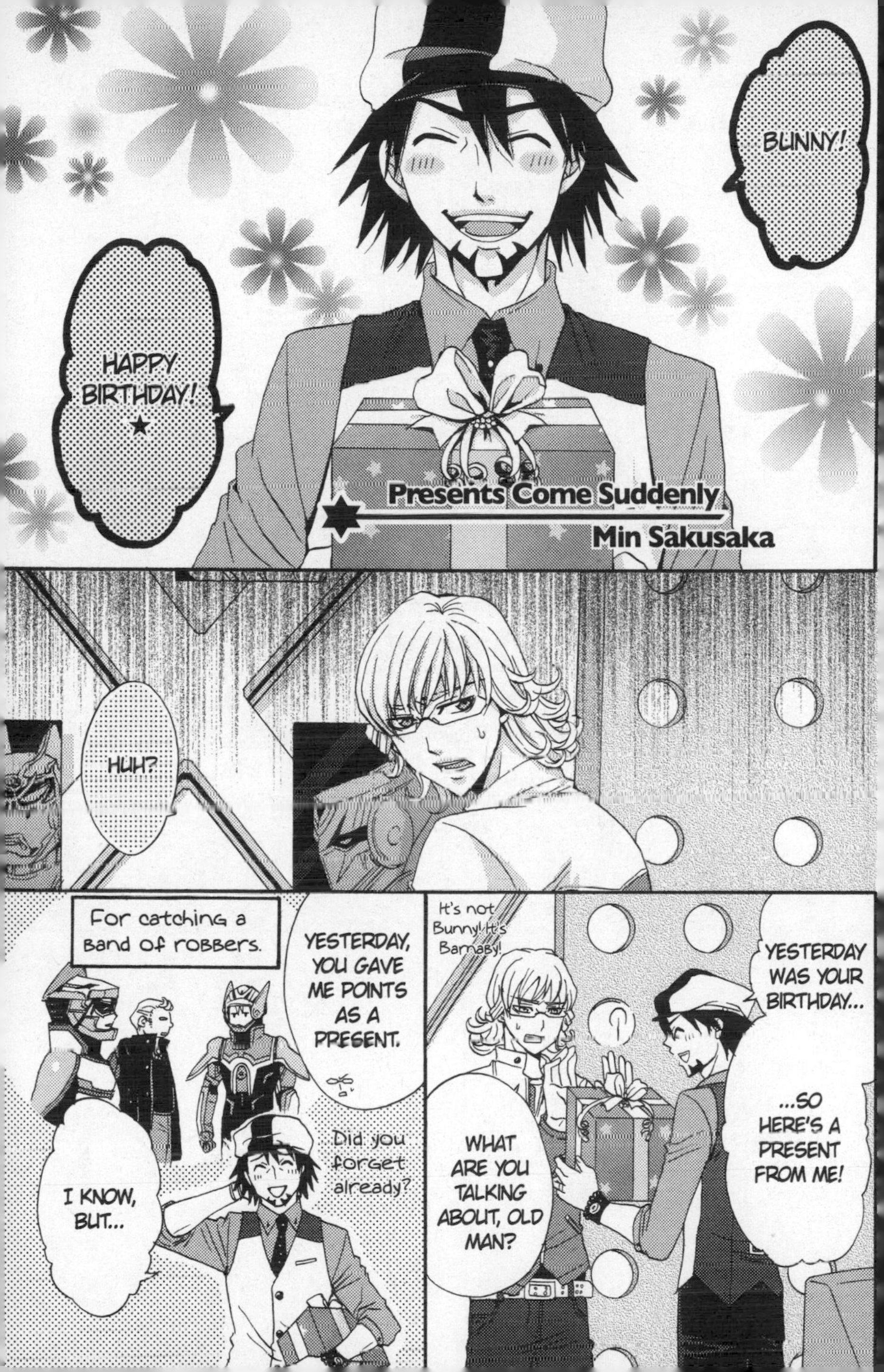
BUNNY!
HAPPY BIRTHDAY! ★
Presents Come Suddenly
Min Sakusaka
HUH?
YESTERDAY WAS YOUR BIRTHDAY...
It's not Bunny! It's Barnaby!
...SO HERE'S A PRESENT FROM ME!
WHAT ARE YOU TALKING ABOUT, OLD MAN?
YESTERDAY, YOU GAVE ME POINTS AS A PRESENT.
For catching a band of robbers.
Did you forget already?
I KNOW, BUT...

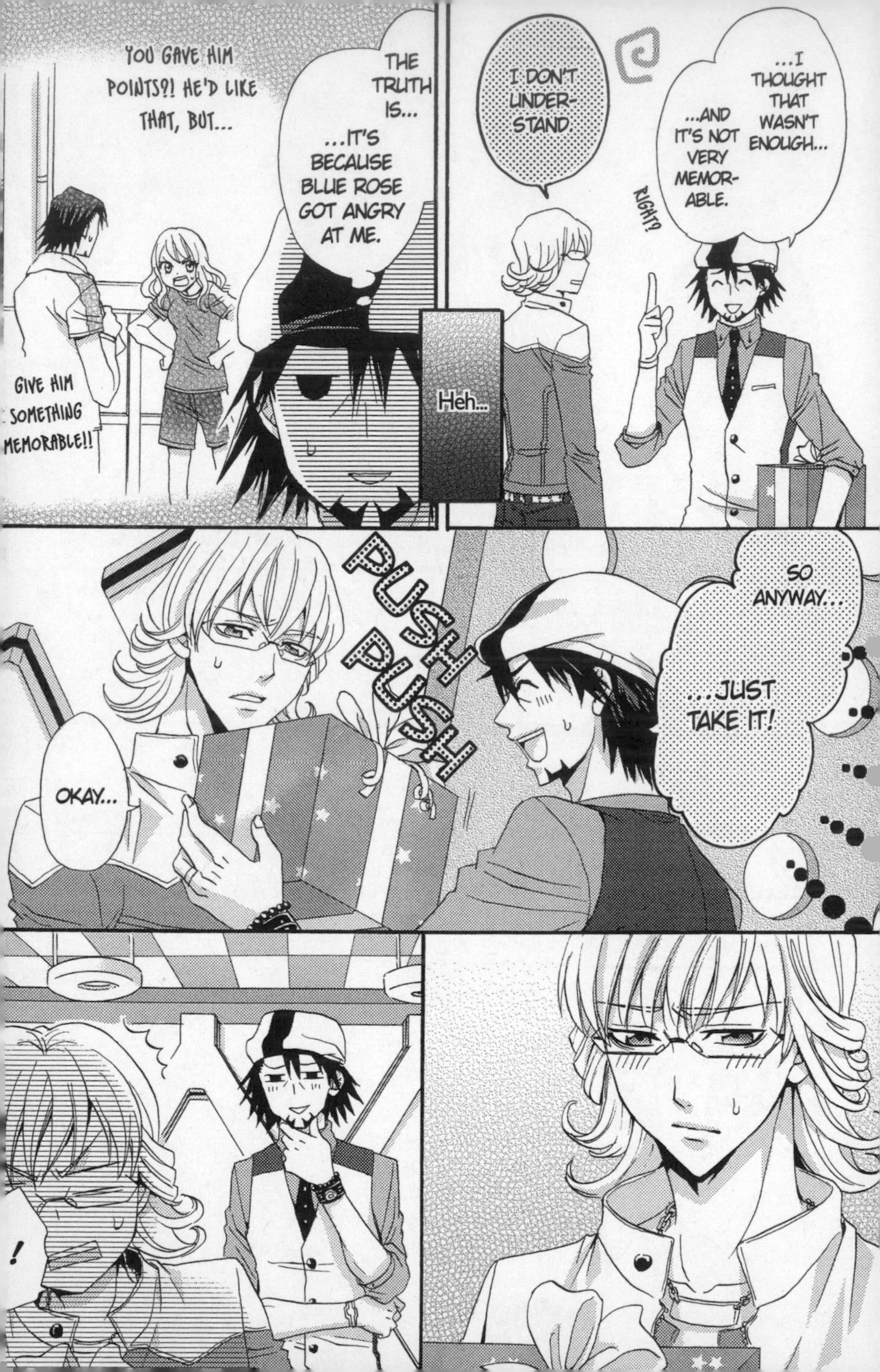
...I THOUGHT THAT WASN'T ENOUGH...
...AND IT'S NOT VERY MEMORABLE.
RIGHT?
I DON'T UNDERSTAND.
THE TRUTH IS...
...IT'S BECAUSE BLUE ROSE GOT ANGRY AT ME.
Heh...
YOU GAVE HIM POINTS?! HE'D LIKE THAT, BUT...
GIVE HIM SOMETHING MEMORABLE!!
SO ANYWAY...
...JUST TAKE IT!
PUSH PUSH
OKAY...
!

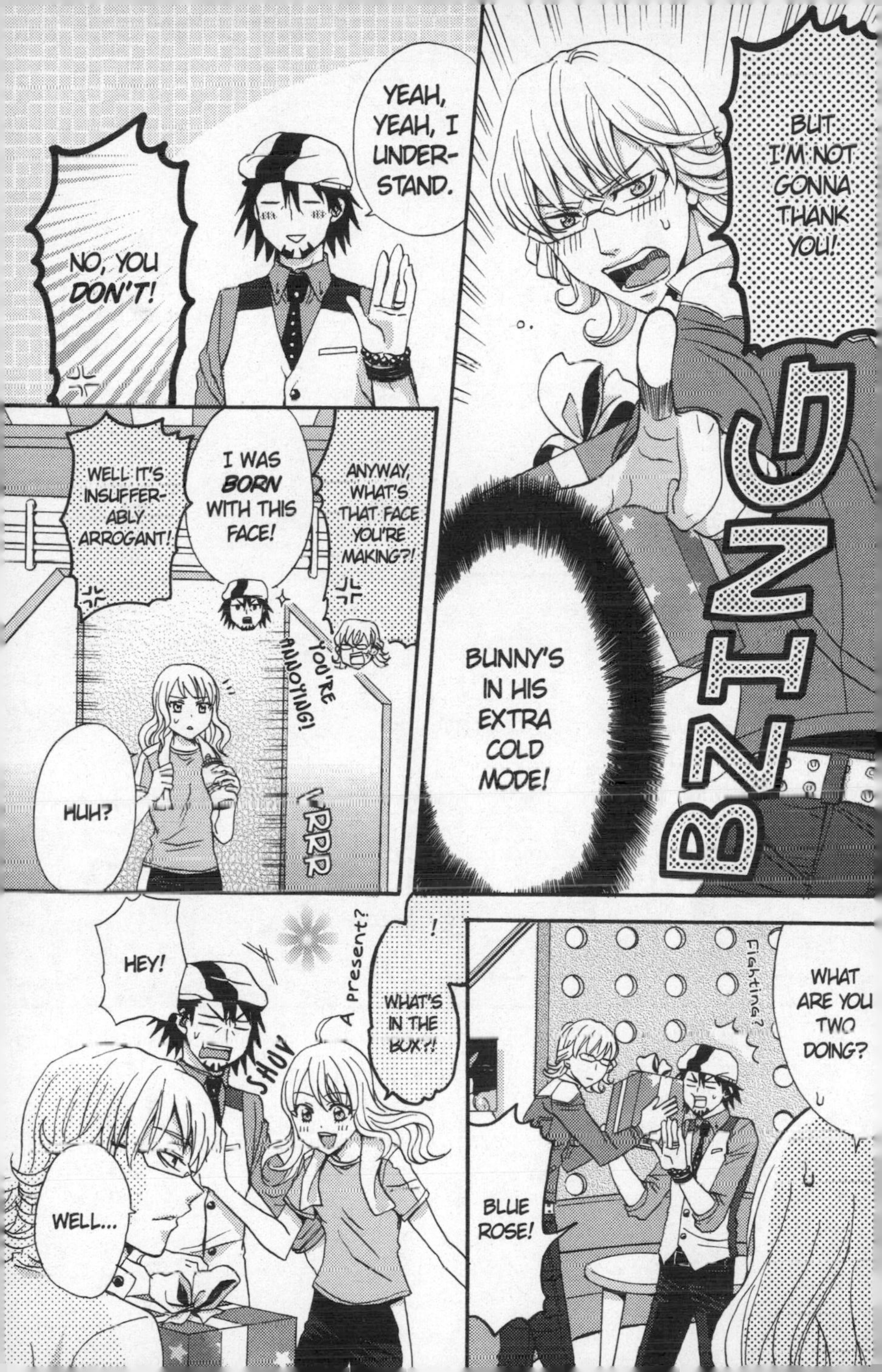
BUT I'M NOT GONNA THANK YOU!
BZING
BUNNY'S IN HIS EXTRA COLD MODE!
YEAH, YEAH, I UNDER-STAND.
NO, YOU DON'T!
ANYWAY, WHAT'S THAT FACE YOU'RE MAKING?!
I WAS BORN WITH THIS FACE!
WELL IT'S INSUFFER-ABLY ARROGANT!
YOU'RE ANNOYING!
VRRR
HUH?
WHAT ARE YOU TWO DOING?
Fighting?
BLUE ROSE!
!
WHAT'S IN THE BOX?!
A present?
HEY!
SHOV
WELL...

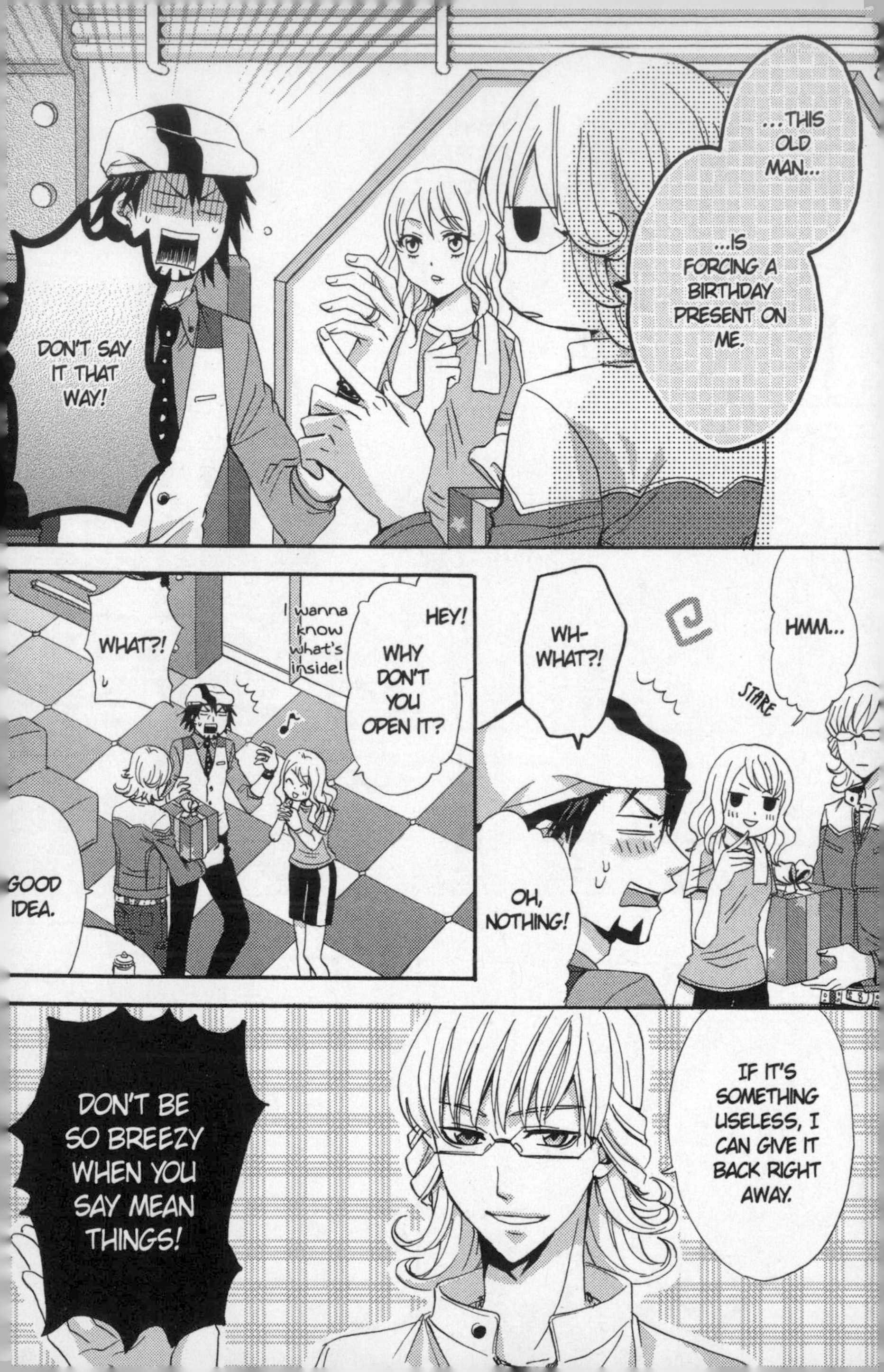
...THIS OLD MAN...
...IS FORCING A BIRTHDAY PRESENT ON ME.
DON'T SAY IT THAT WAY!
HMM...
STARE
WH-WHAT?!
OH, NOTHING!
HEY!
WHY DON'T YOU OPEN IT?
I wanna know what's inside!
WHAT?!
GOOD IDEA.
IF IT'S SOMETHING USELESS, I CAN GIVE IT BACK RIGHT AWAY.
DON'T BE SO BREEZY WHEN YOU SAY MEAN THINGS!

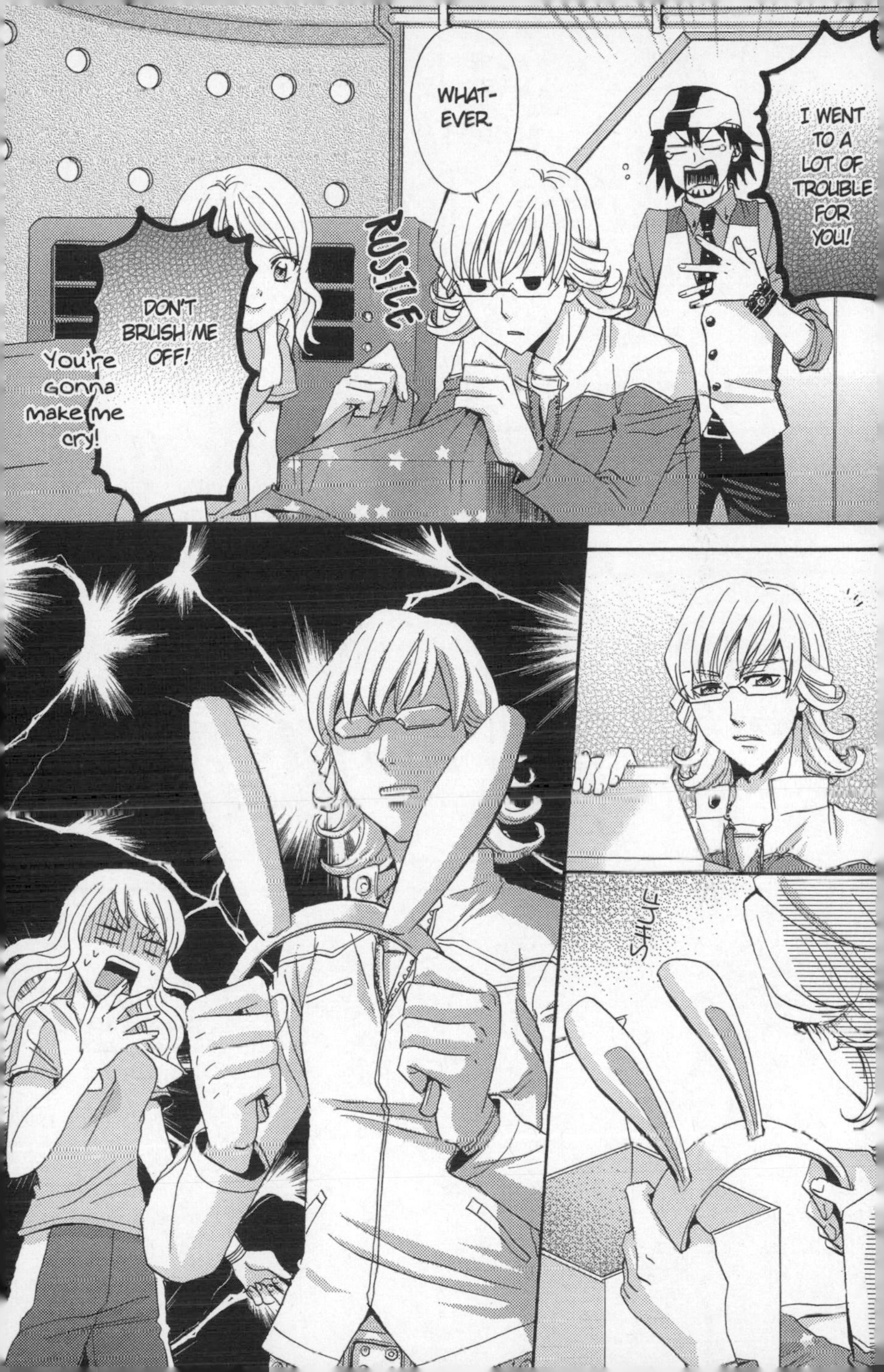
I WENT TO A LOT OF TROUBLE FOR YOU!
WHAT-EVER.
RUSTLE
DON'T BRUSH ME OFF!
You're gonna make me cry!
SHUF

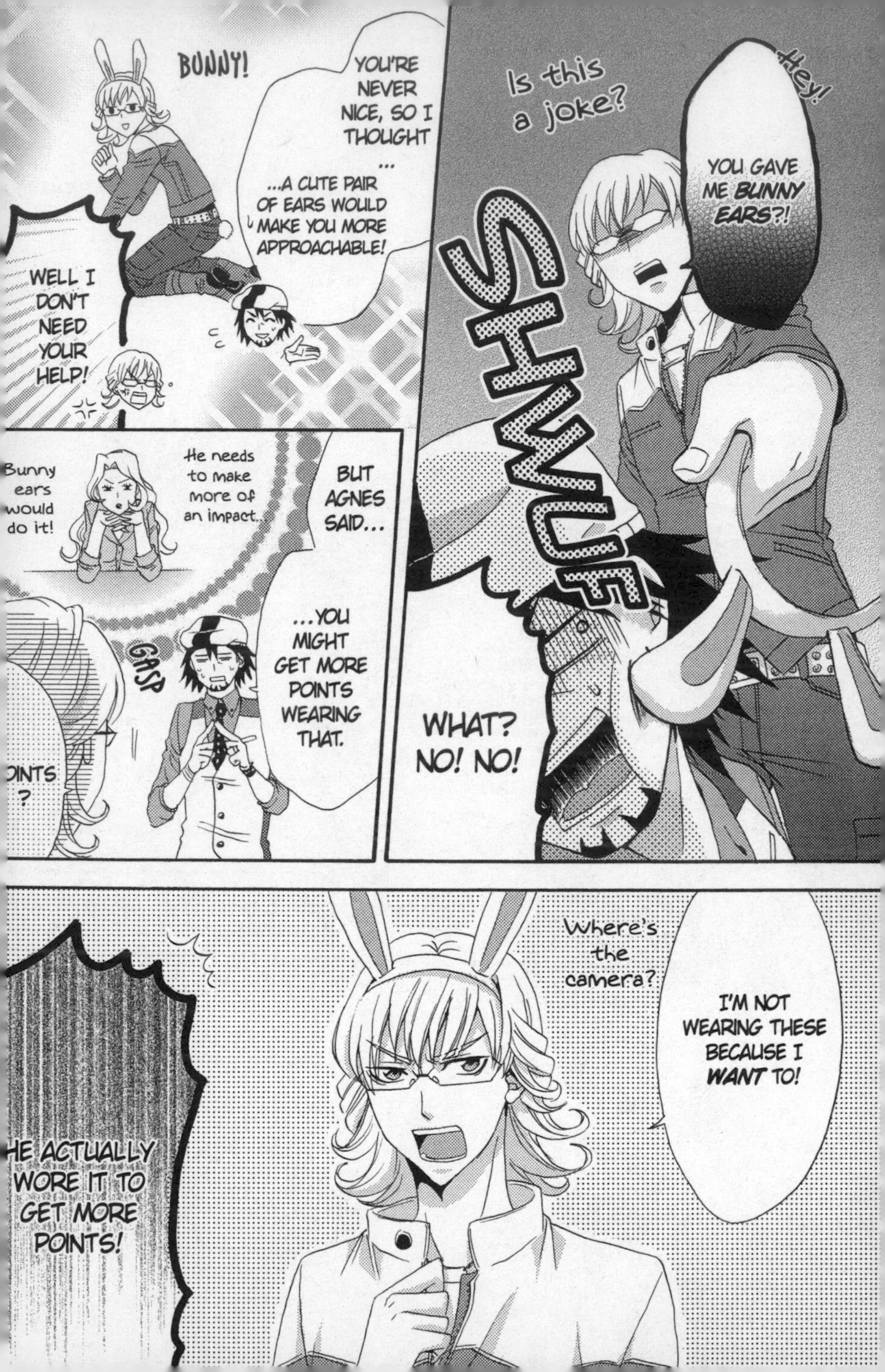
Hey!
Is this a joke?
YOU GAVE ME BUNNY EARS?!
SHWUF
WHAT? NO! NO!
YOU'RE NEVER NICE, SO I THOUGHT ...
...A CUTE PAIR OF EARS WOULD MAKE YOU MORE APPROACHABLE!
BUNNY!
WELL I DON'T NEED YOUR HELP!
BUT AGNES SAID...
He needs to make more of an impact..
Bunny ears would do it!
...YOU MIGHT GET MORE POINTS WEARING THAT.
GASP
OINTS ?
Where's the camera?
I'M NOT WEARING THESE BECAUSE I WANT TO!
HE ACTUALLY WORE IT TO GET MORE POINTS!

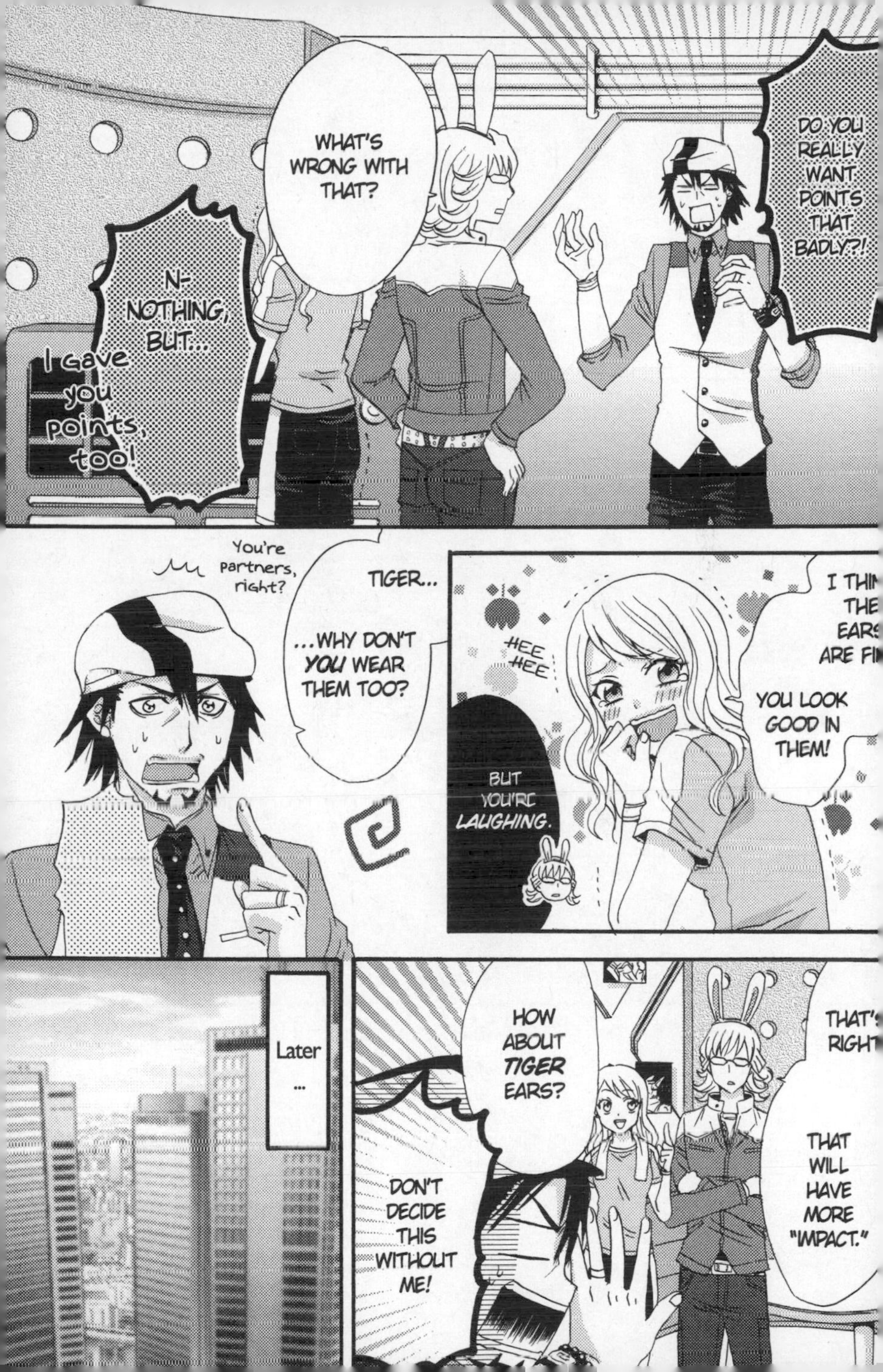
DO YOU REALLY WANT POINTS THAT BADLY?!
WHAT'S WRONG WITH THAT?
N-NOTHING, BUT...
I gave you points, too!
I THIN THE EARS ARE FI
YOU LOOK GOOD IN THEM!
HEE HEE
BUT YOU'RE LAUGHING.
TIGER...
...WHY DON'T YOU WEAR THEM TOO?
You're partners, right?
THAT'S RIGHT
THAT WILL HAVE MORE "IMPACT."
HOW ABOUT TIGER EARS?
DON'T DECIDE THIS WITHOUT ME!
Later ...

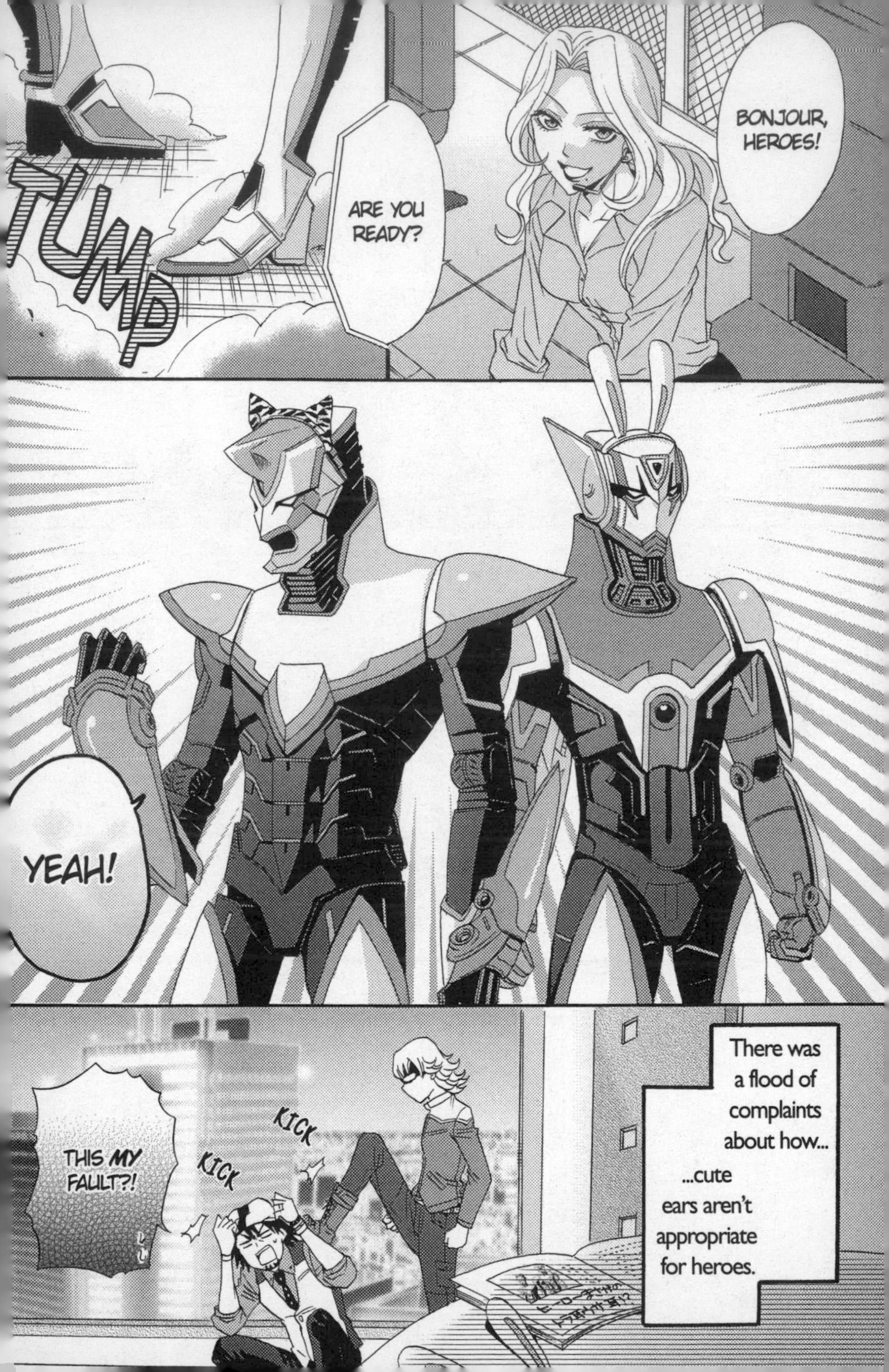
BONJOUR, HEROES!
ARE YOU READY?
TUMP
YEAH!
There was a flood of complaints about how...
...cute ears aren't appropriate for heroes.
KICK
KICK
THIS MY FAULT?!

Ivan, You Foo

Suzu Kohn

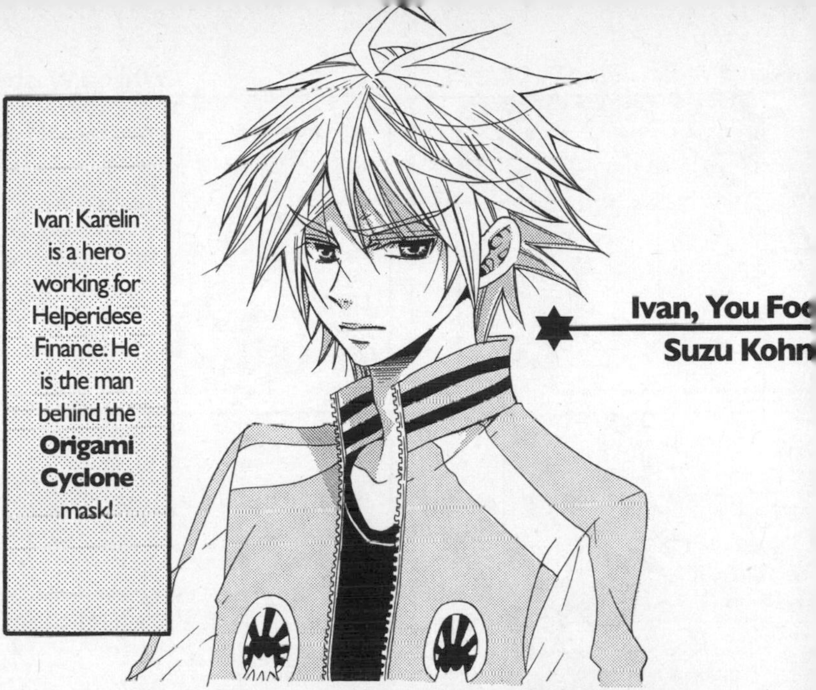
Ivan Karelin is a hero working for Helperidese Finance. He is the man behind the **Origami Cyclone** mask!

A Man of Japanese Culture

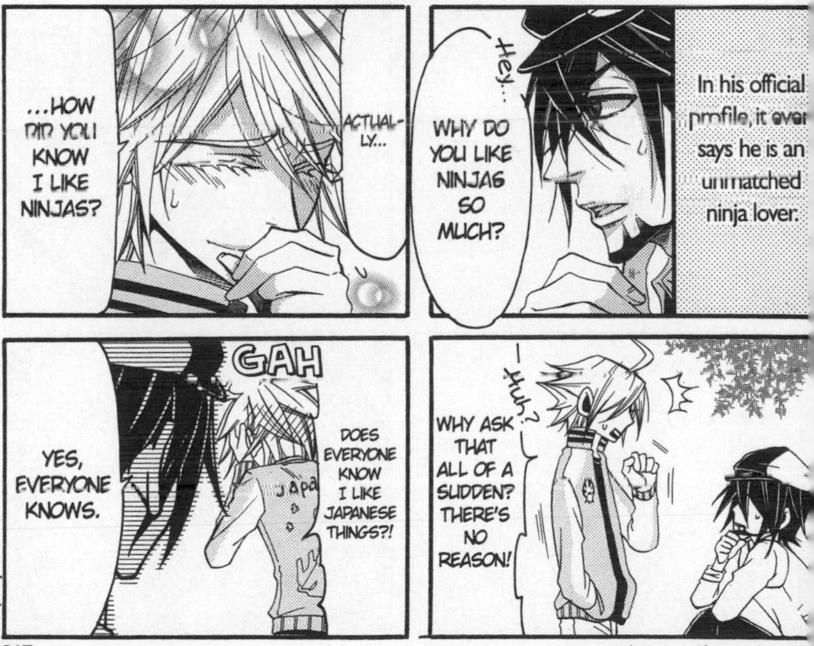
In his official profile, it even says he is an unmatched ninja lover.
Hey...
WHY DO YOU LIKE NINJAS SO MUCH?
ACTUALLY...
...HOW DID YOU KNOW I LIKE NINJAS?
Huh?
WHY ASK THAT ALL OF A SUDDEN? THERE'S NO REASON!
GAH
DOES EVERYONE KNOW I LIKE JAPANESE THINGS?!
Japa
YES, EVERYONE KNOWS.

It says so on your back...

What a Waste!

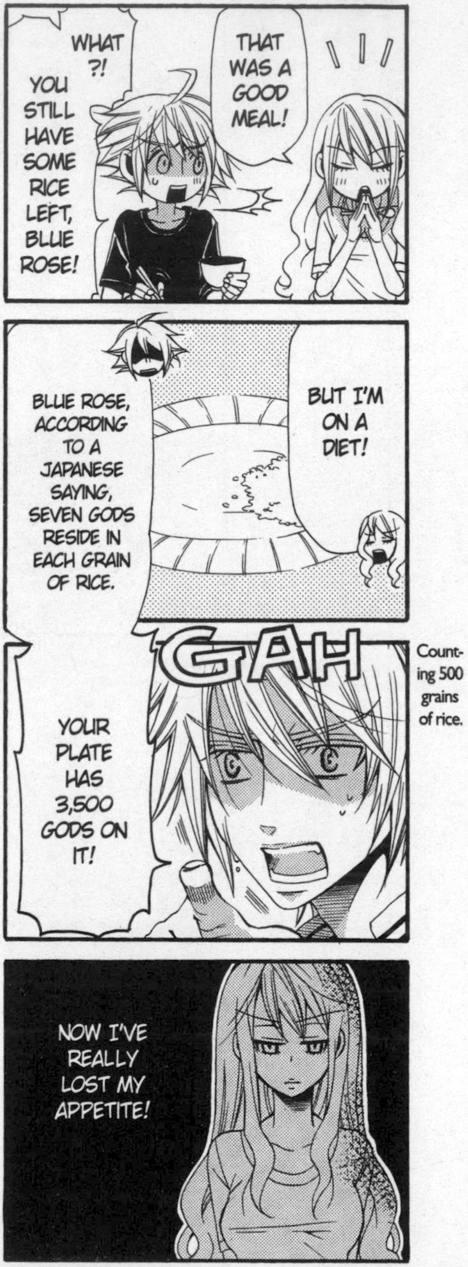
THAT WAS A GOOD MEAL!
WHAT ?! YOU STILL HAVE SOME RICE LEFT, BLUE ROSE!
BUT I'M ON A DIET!
BLUE ROSE, ACCORDING TO A JAPANESE SAYING, SEVEN GODS RESIDE IN EACH GRAIN OF RICE.
Counting 500 grains of rice.
GAH
YOUR PLATE HAS 3,500 GODS ON IT!
NOW I'VE REALLY LOST MY APPETITE!

I Would Wear a Monk's Clothes

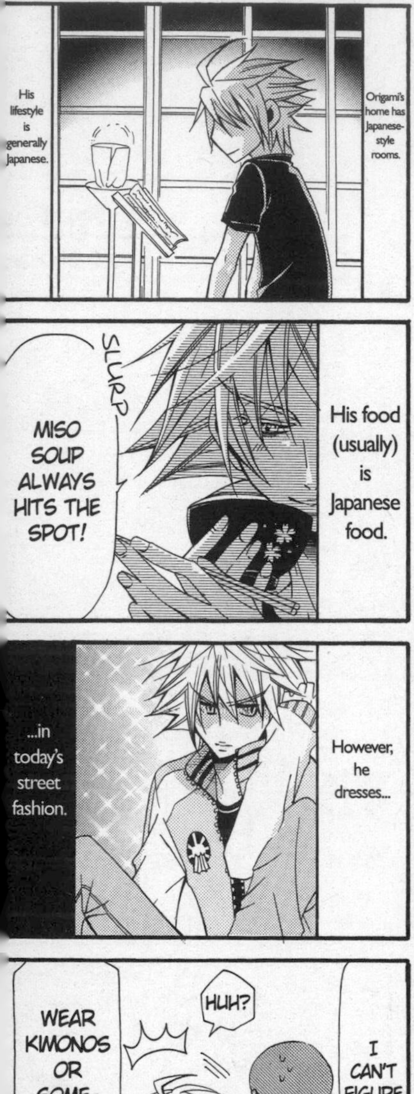
Origami's home has Japanese-style rooms.
His lifestyle is generally Japanese.
His food (usually) is Japanese food.
SLURP
MISO SOUP ALWAYS HITS THE SPOT!
However, he dresses...
...in today's street fashion.
I CAN'T FIGURE YOU OUT...
HUH?
WEAR KIMONOS OR SOME-THING!
HUH ?!
Japan

I'm Younger Than Barnab

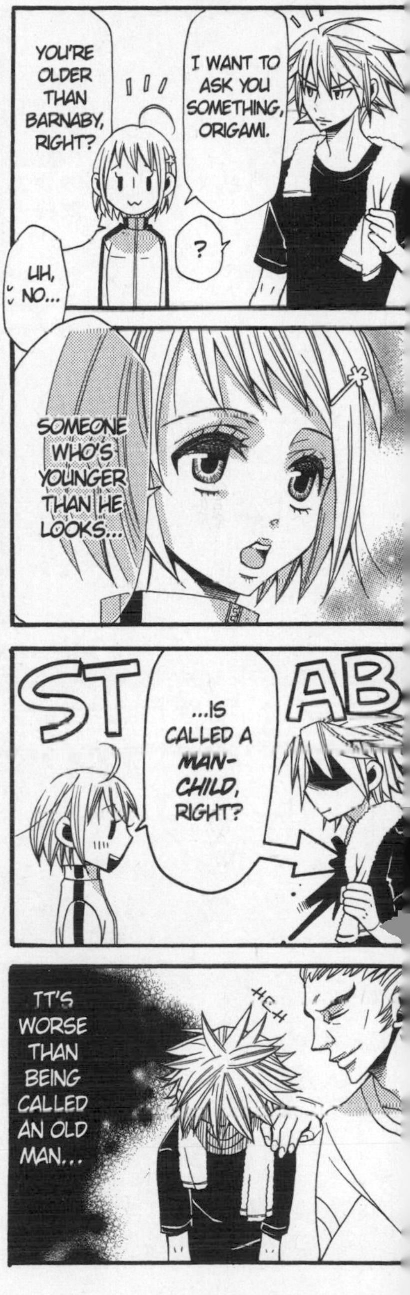
I WANT TO ASK YOU SOMETHING, ORIGAMI.
?
YOU'RE OLDER THAN BARNABY, RIGHT?
UH, NO...
SOMEONE WHO'S YOUNGER THAN HE LOOKS...
STAB
...IS CALLED A MAN-CHILD, RIGHT?
IT'S WORSE THAN BEING CALLED AN OLD MAN...

All the Old Men Love Her

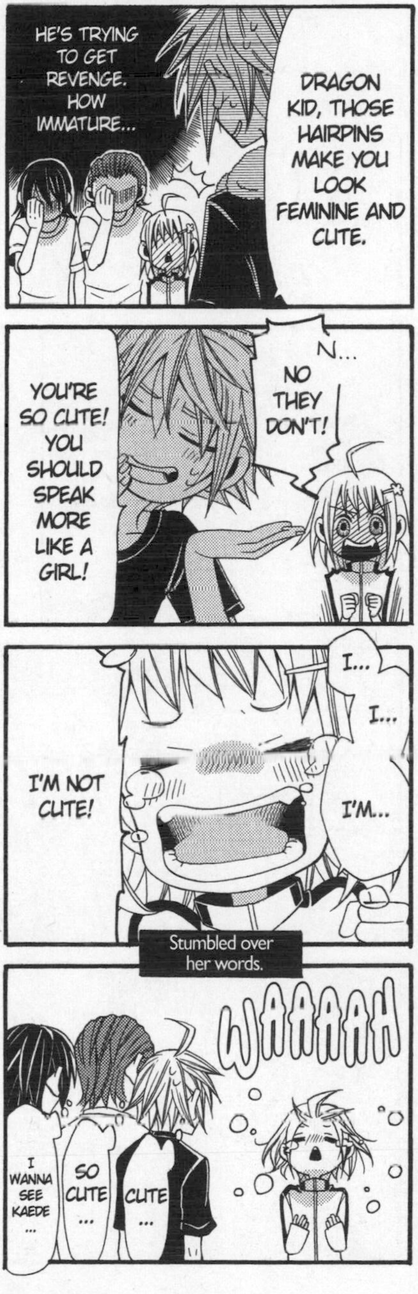
DRAGON KID, THOSE HAIRPINS MAKE YOU LOOK FEMININE AND CUTE.
HE'S TRYING TO GET REVENGE. HOW IMMATURE...
N... NO THEY DON'T!
YOU'RE SO CUTE! YOU SHOULD SPEAK MORE LIKE A GIRL!
I...
I...
I'M...
I'M NOT CUTE!
Stumbled over her words.
WAAAAH
CUTE...
SO CUTE...
I WANNA SEE KAEDE...

The Many Faces of Heroes

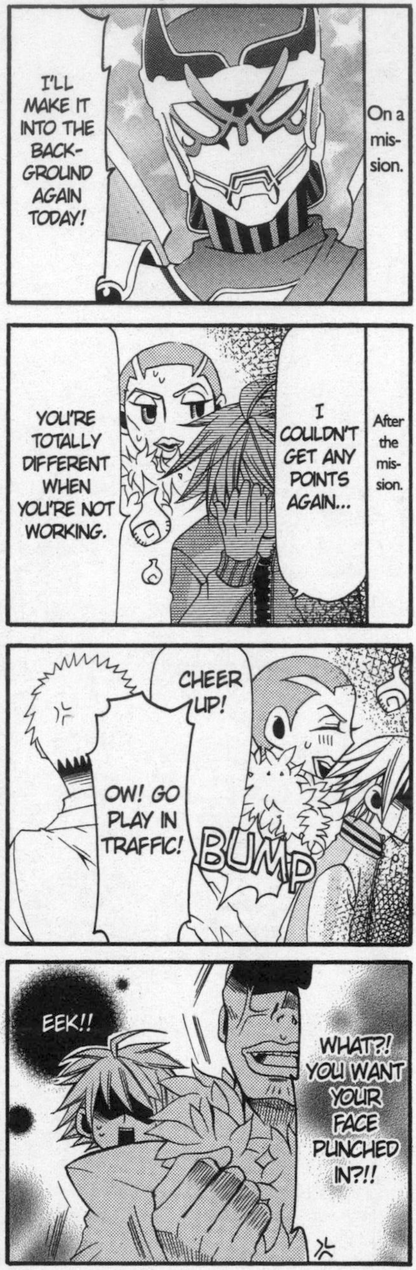
On a mission.
I'LL MAKE IT INTO THE BACKGROUND AGAIN TODAY!
After the mission.
I COULDN'T GET ANY POINTS AGAIN...
YOU'RE TOTALLY DIFFERENT WHEN YOU'RE NOT WORKING.
CHEER UP!
BUMP
OW! GO PLAY IN TRAFFIC!
WHAT?! YOU WANT YOUR FACE PUNCHED IN?!!
EEK!!

In the Background...or Not.

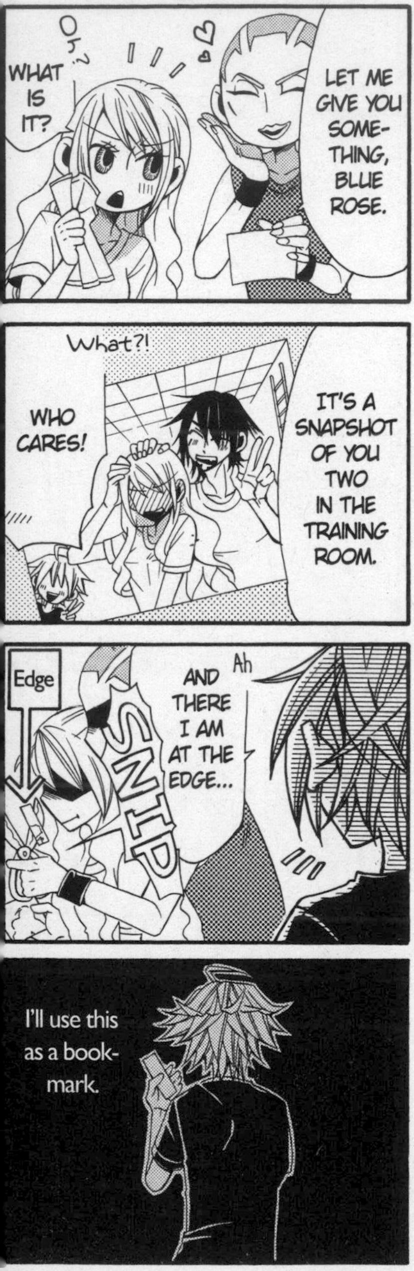
LET ME GIVE YOU SOMETHING, BLUE ROSE.
WHAT IS IT?
IT'S A SNAPSHOT OF YOU TWO IN THE TRAINING ROOM.
What?!
WHO CARES!
Ah
AND THERE I AM AT THE EDGE...
SNIP
Edge
I'll use this as a bookmark.

Hero < Japanese Culture Researcher

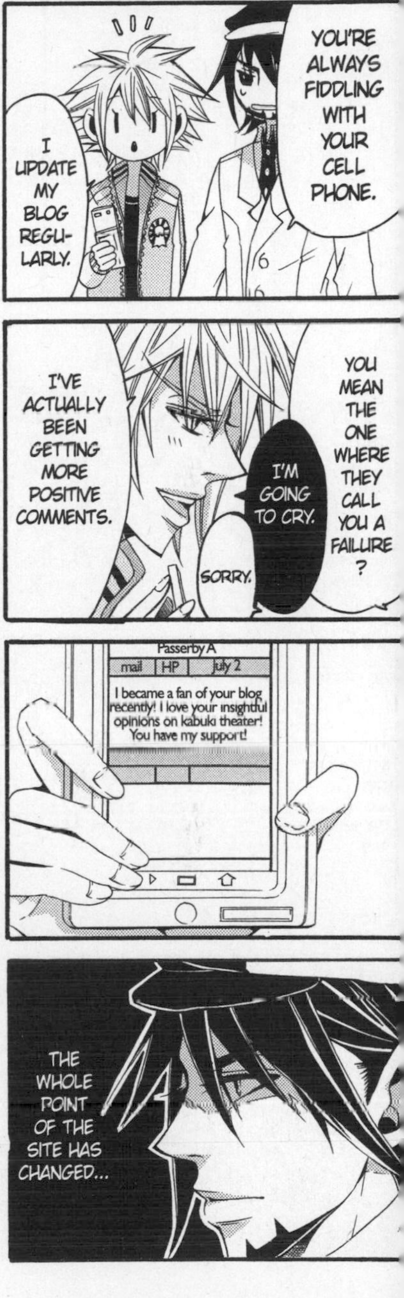
YOU'RE ALWAYS FIDDLING WITH YOUR CELL PHONE.
I UPDATE MY BLOG REGULARLY.
YOU MEAN THE ONE WHERE THEY CALL YOU A FAILURE?
I'M GOING TO CRY.
SORRY.
I'VE ACTUALLY BEEN GETTING MORE POSITIVE COMMENTS.
Passerby A
mail HP july 2
I became a fan of your blog recently! I love your insightful opinions on kabuki theater! You have my support!
THE WHOLE POINT OF THE SITE HAS CHANGED...

He Doesn't Know He's Getting Flamed

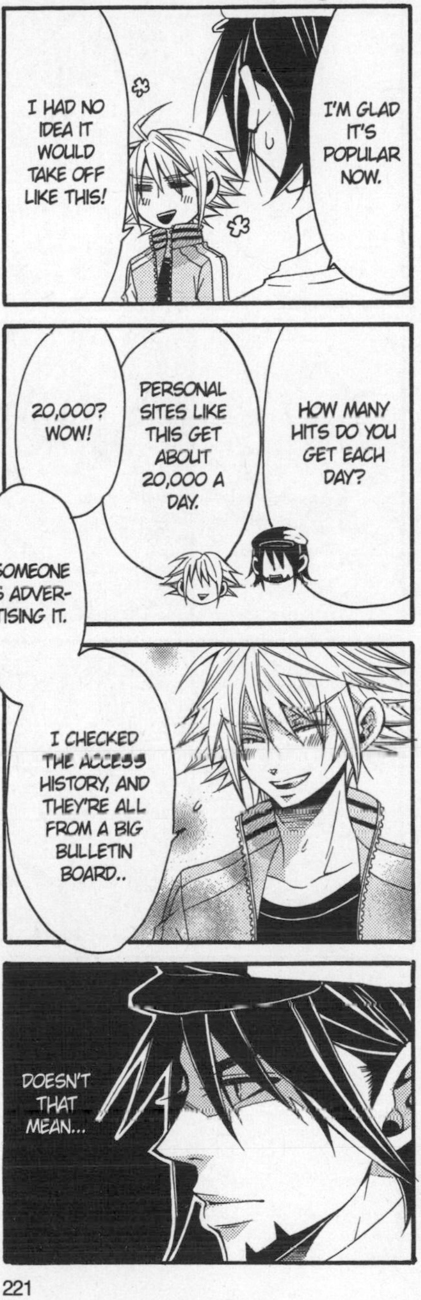
I'M GLAD IT'S POPULAR NOW.
I HAD NO IDEA IT WOULD TAKE OFF LIKE THIS!
HOW MANY HITS DO YOU GET EACH DAY?
PERSONAL SITES LIKE THIS GET ABOUT 20,000 A DAY.
20,000? WOW!
SOMEONE IS ADVERTISING IT.
I CHECKED THE ACCESS HISTORY, AND THEY'RE ALL FROM A BIG BULLETIN BOARD..
DOESN'T THAT MEAN...

I Felt Like I Won

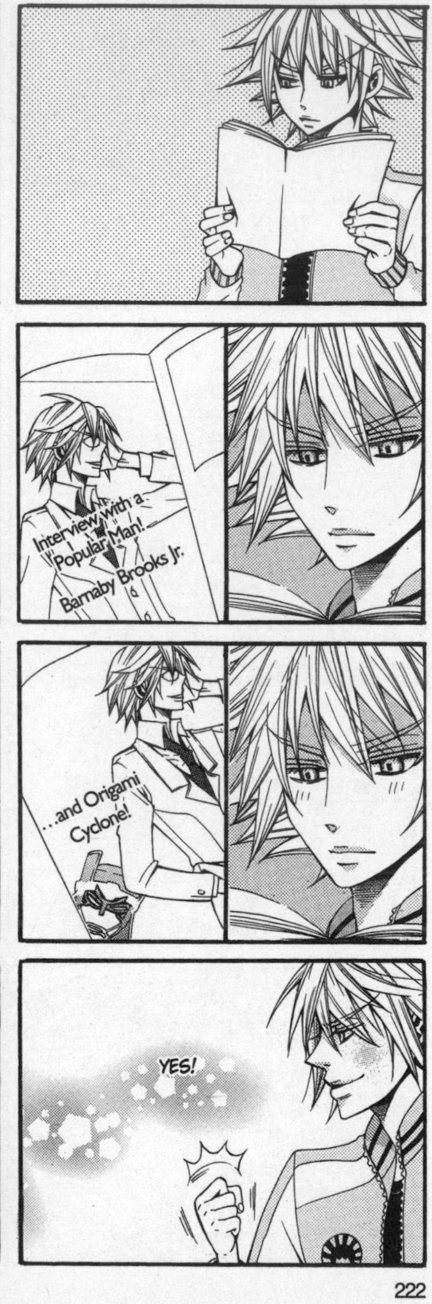
Interview with a Popular Man! Barnaby Brooks Jr.
...and Origami Cyclone!
YES!

I Felt Like I Lost

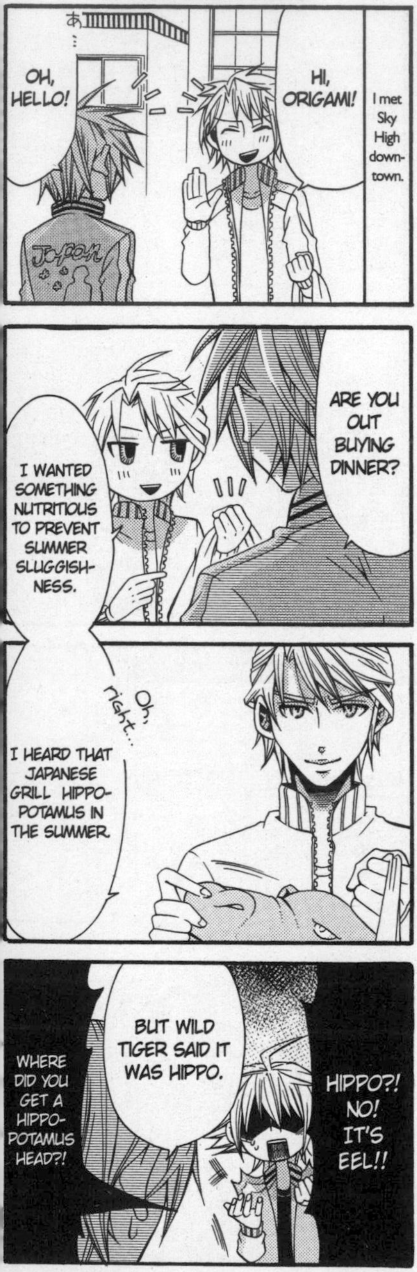
I met Sky High downtown.
HI, ORIGAMI!
あ…
OH, HELLO!
ARE YOU OUT BUYING DINNER?
I WANTED SOMETHING NUTRITIOUS TO PREVENT SUMMER SLUGGISH-NESS.
Oh, right...
I HEARD THAT JAPANESE GRILL HIPPO-POTAMUS IN THE SUMMER.
HIPPO?! NO! IT'S EEL!!
BUT WILD TIGER SAID IT WAS HIPPO.
WHERE DID YOU GET A HIPPO-POTAMUS HEAD?!

Depression from Seeing a Friend in a Suit on Monday

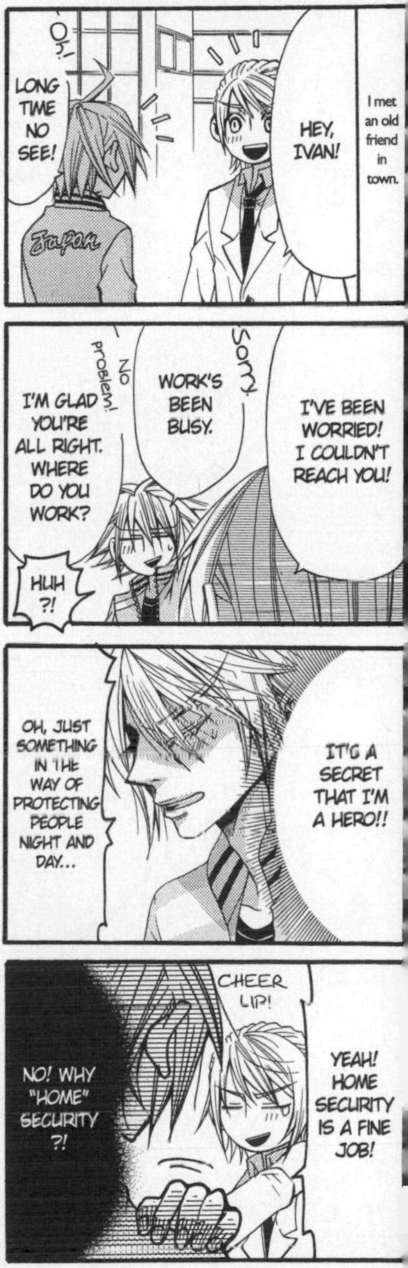
I met an old friend in town.
HEY, IVAN!
Oh!
LONG TIME NO SEE!
I'VE BEEN WORRIED! I COULDN'T REACH YOU!
Sorry.
WORK'S BEEN BUSY.
No problem!
I'M GLAD YOU'RE ALL RIGHT. WHERE DO YOU WORK?
HUH?!
IT'S A SECRET THAT I'M A HERO!!
OH, JUST SOMETHING IN THE WAY OF PROTECTING PEOPLE NIGHT AND DAY...
YEAH! HOME SECURITY IS A FINE JOB!
CHEER UP!
NO! WHY "HOME" SECURITY?!

It Seems That Way

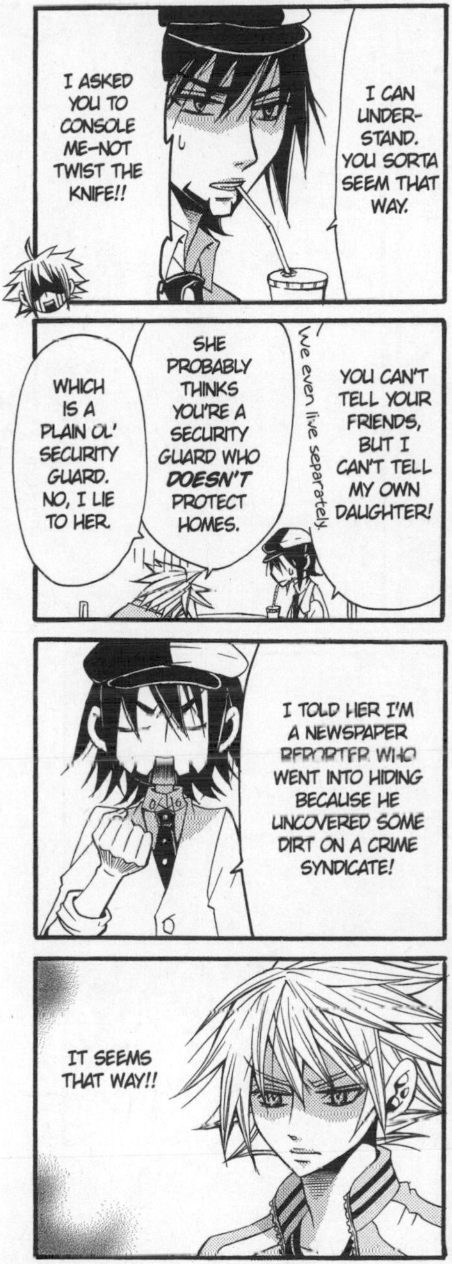
I CAN UNDERSTAND. YOU SORTA SEEM THAT WAY.
I ASKED YOU TO CONSOLE ME—NOT TWIST THE KNIFE!!
YOU CAN'T TELL YOUR FRIENDS, BUT I CAN'T TELL MY OWN DAUGHTER!
We even live separately.
SHE PROBABLY THINKS YOU'RE A SECURITY GUARD WHO ***DOESN'T*** PROTECT HOMES.
WHICH IS A PLAIN OL' SECURITY GUARD. NO, I LIE TO HER.
I TOLD HER I'M A NEWSPAPER REPORTER WHO WENT INTO HIDING BECAUSE HE UNCOVERED SOME DIRT ON A CRIME SYNDICATE!
IT SEEMS THAT WAY!!

I Make the Toy Ninja Stars They Sell at Dollar Stores

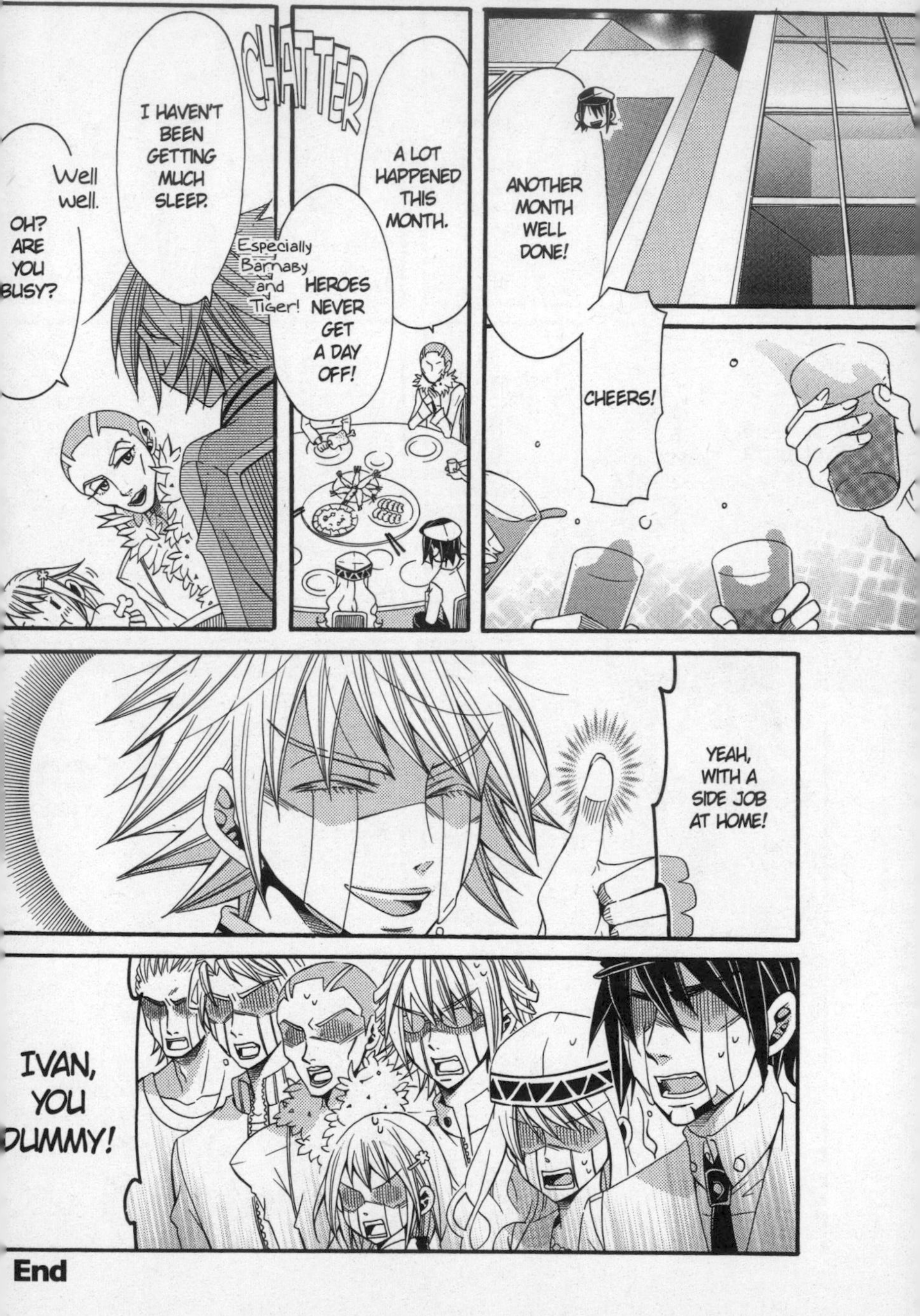
ANOTHER MONTH WELL DONE!
CHEERS!
CHATTER
A LOT HAPPENED THIS MONTH.
HEROES NEVER GET A DAY OFF!
Especially Barnaby and Tiger!
I HAVEN'T BEEN GETTING MUCH SLEEP.
Well well.
OH? ARE YOU BUSY?
YEAH, WITH A SIDE JOB AT HOME!
IVAN, YOU DUMMY!

End

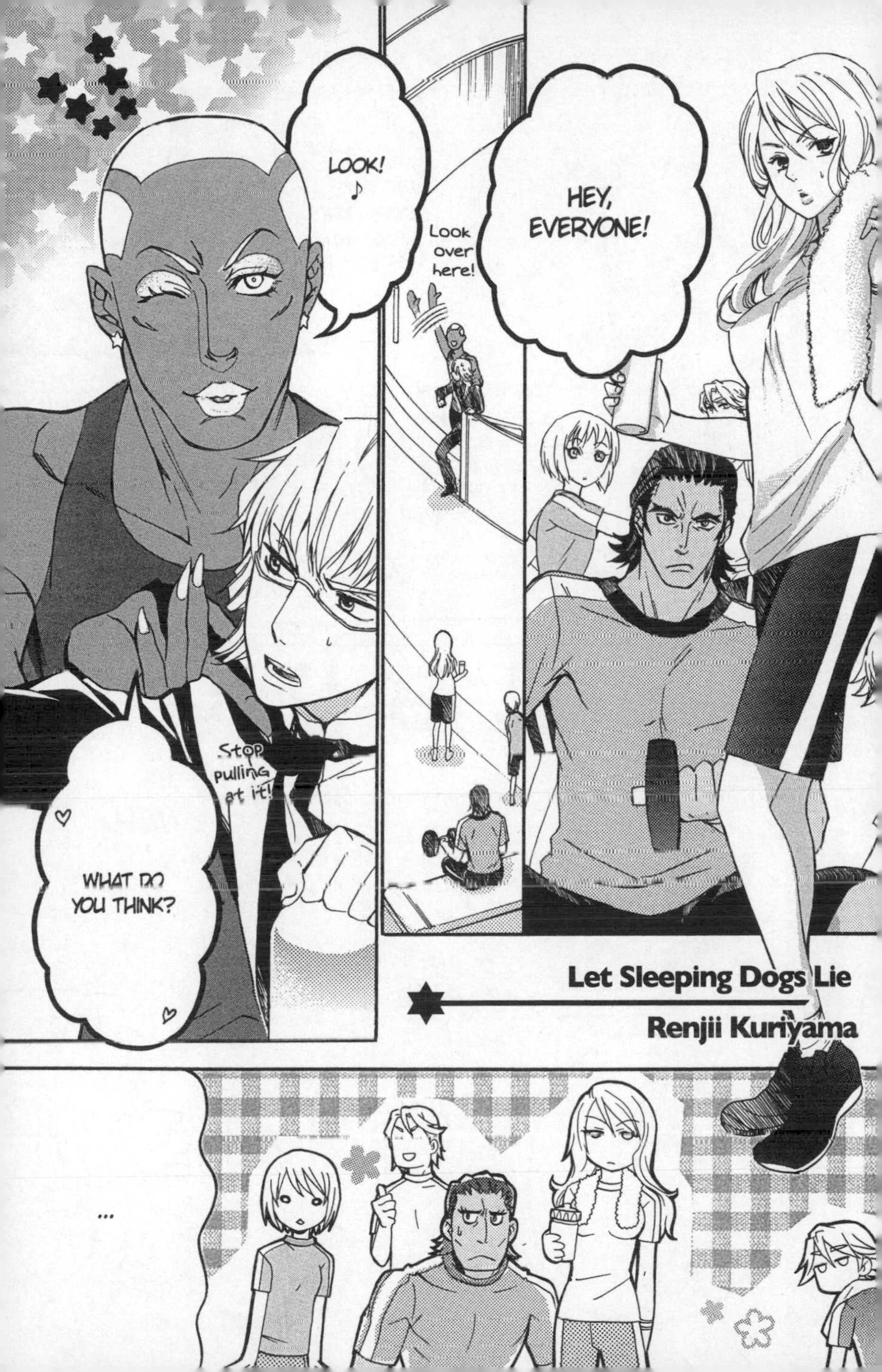
HEY, EVERYONE!
Look over here!
LOOK! ♪
WHAT DO YOU THINK?
Stop pulling at it!
Let Sleeping Dogs Lie
Renjii Kuriyama
...

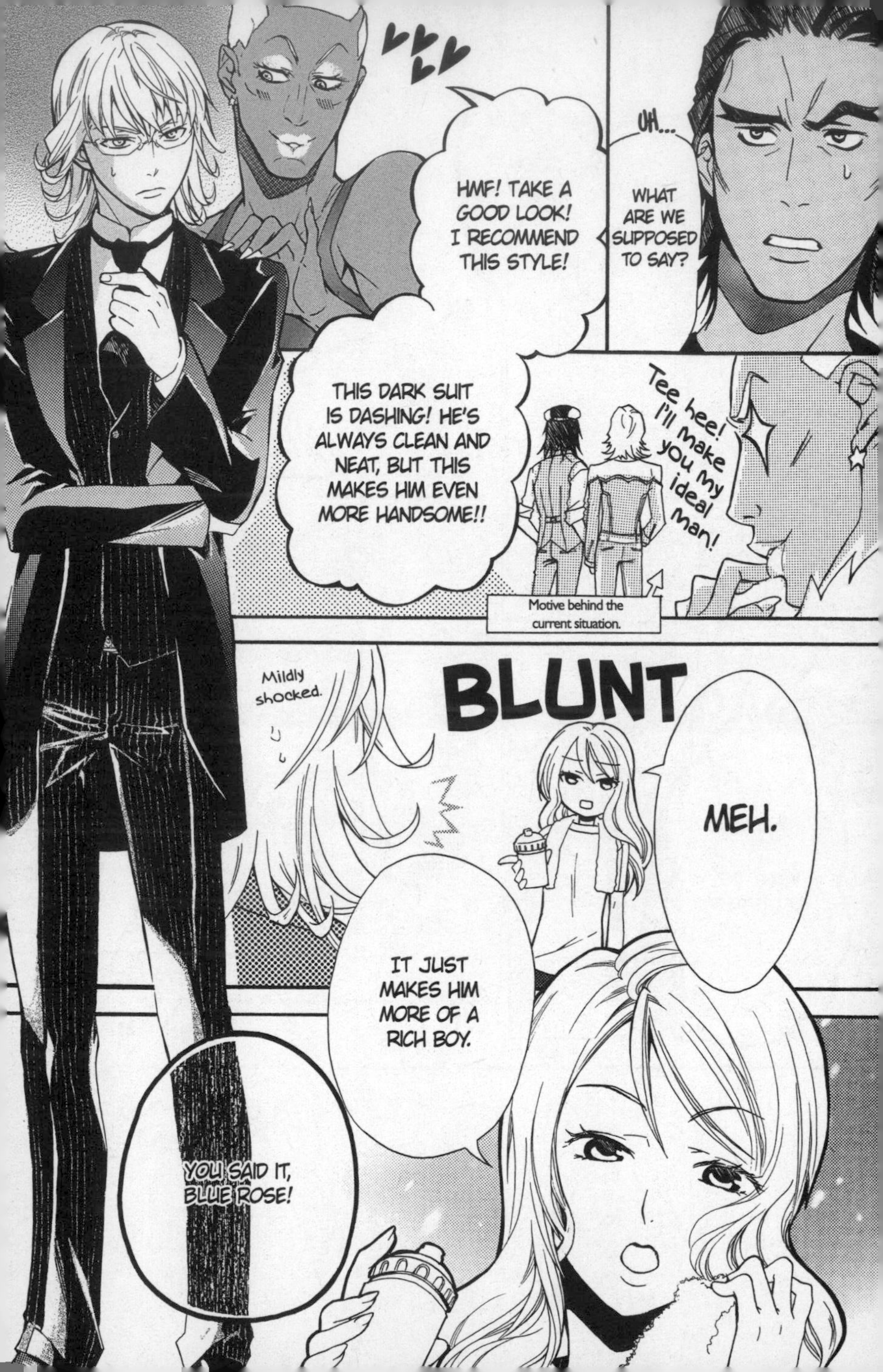
UH...
WHAT ARE WE SUPPOSED TO SAY?
HMF! TAKE A GOOD LOOK! I RECOMMEND THIS STYLE!
THIS DARK SUIT IS DASHING! HE'S ALWAYS CLEAN AND NEAT, BUT THIS MAKES HIM EVEN MORE HANDSOME!!
Tee hee! I'll make you my ideal man!
Motive behind the current situation.
BLUNT
MEH.
Mildly shocked.
IT JUST MAKES HIM MORE OF A RICH BOY.
YOU SAID IT, BLUE ROSE!

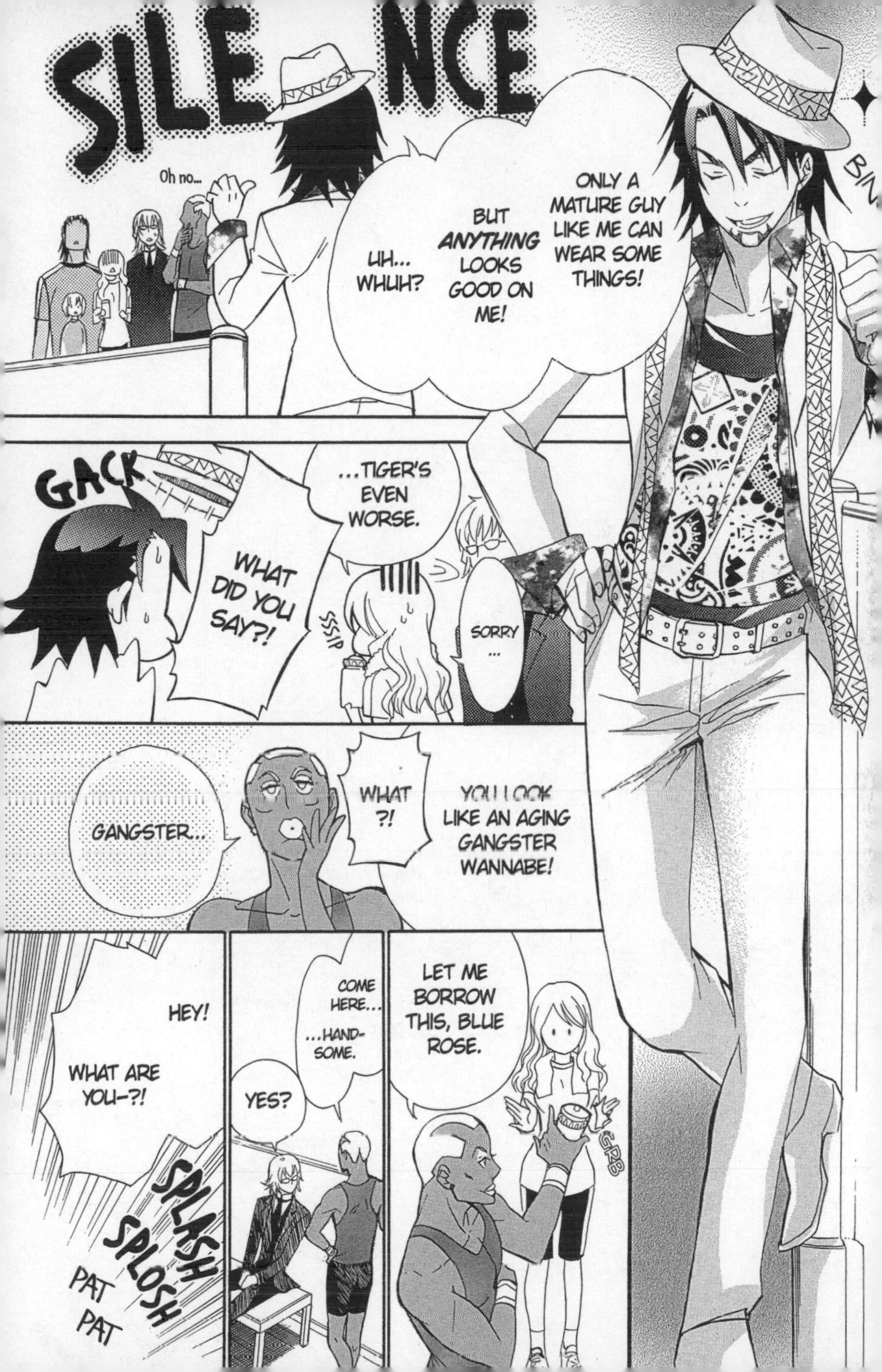

BIN
ONLY A MATURE GUY LIKE ME CAN WEAR SOME THINGS!
BUT *ANYTHING* LOOKS GOOD ON ME!
SILENCE
UH... WHUH?
Oh no...
...TIGER'S EVEN WORSE.
SORRY...
SSSIP
WHAT DID YOU SAY?!
GACK
YOU LOOK LIKE AN AGING GANGSTER WANNABE!
WHAT?!
GANGSTER...
LET ME BORROW THIS, BLUE ROSE.
GRAB
COME HERE... ...HANDSOME.
YES?
HEY!
WHAT ARE YOU-?!
SPLASH
SPLOSH
PAT PAT

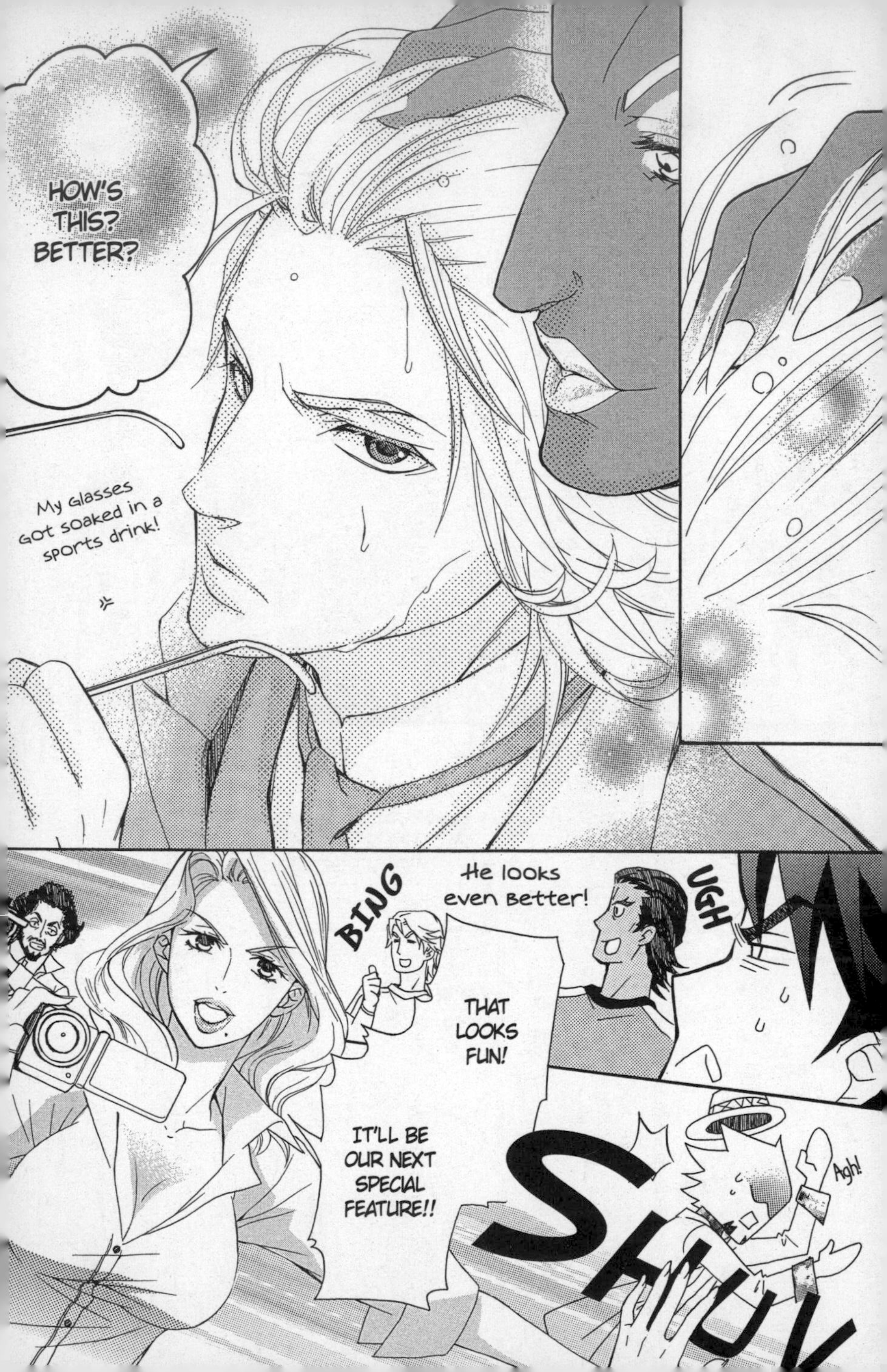
HOW'S THIS? BETTER?
My Glasses Got soaked in a sports drink!
UGH
He looks even Better!
BING
THAT LOOKS FUN!
Agh!
SHUV
IT'LL BE OUR NEXT SPECIAL FEATURE!!

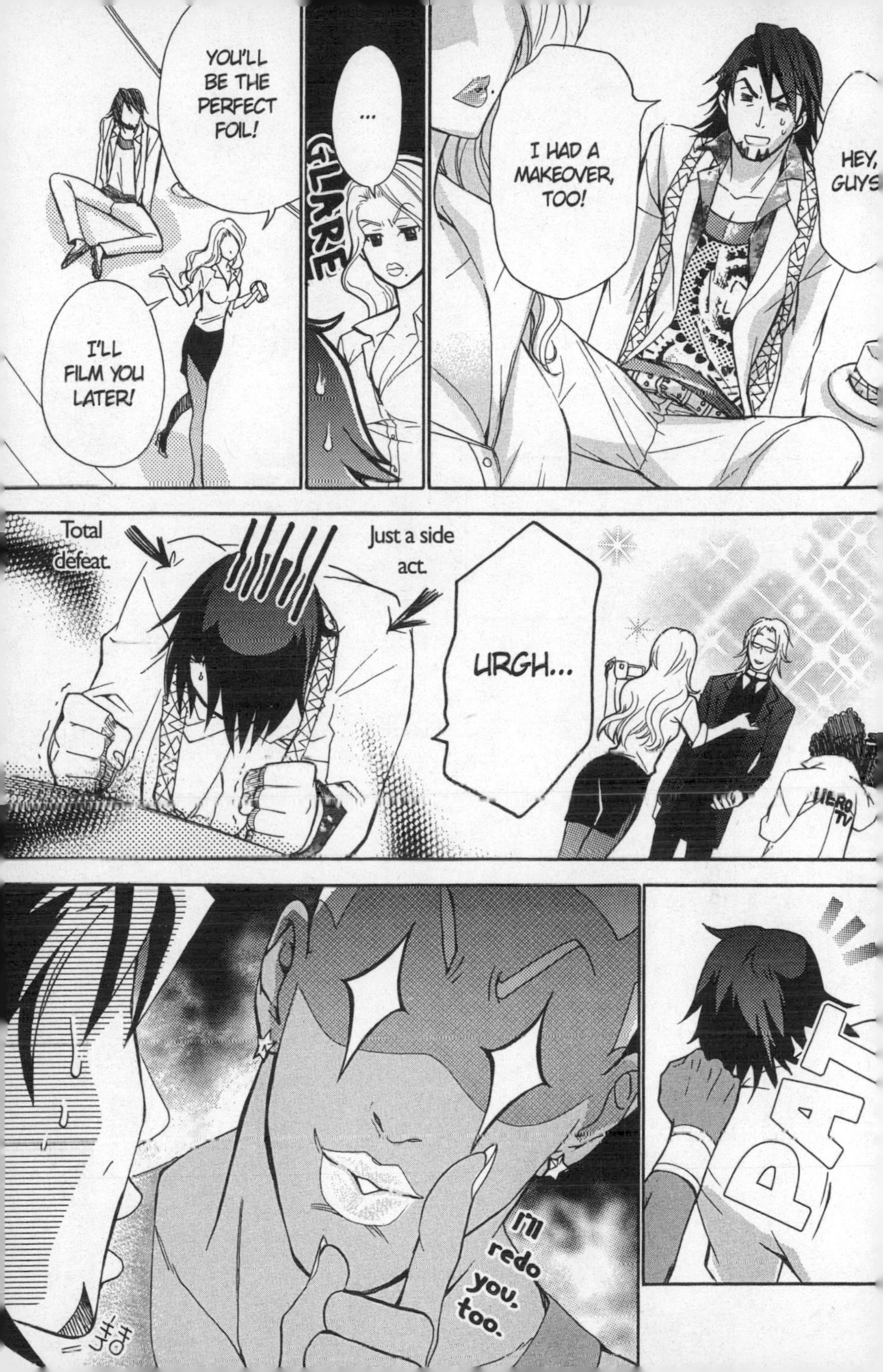
HEY, GUYS
I HAD A MAKEOVER, TOO!
...
GLARE
YOU'LL BE THE PERFECT FOIL!
I'LL FILM YOU LATER!
URGH...
Just a side act.
Total defeat.
PAT
I'll redo you, too.

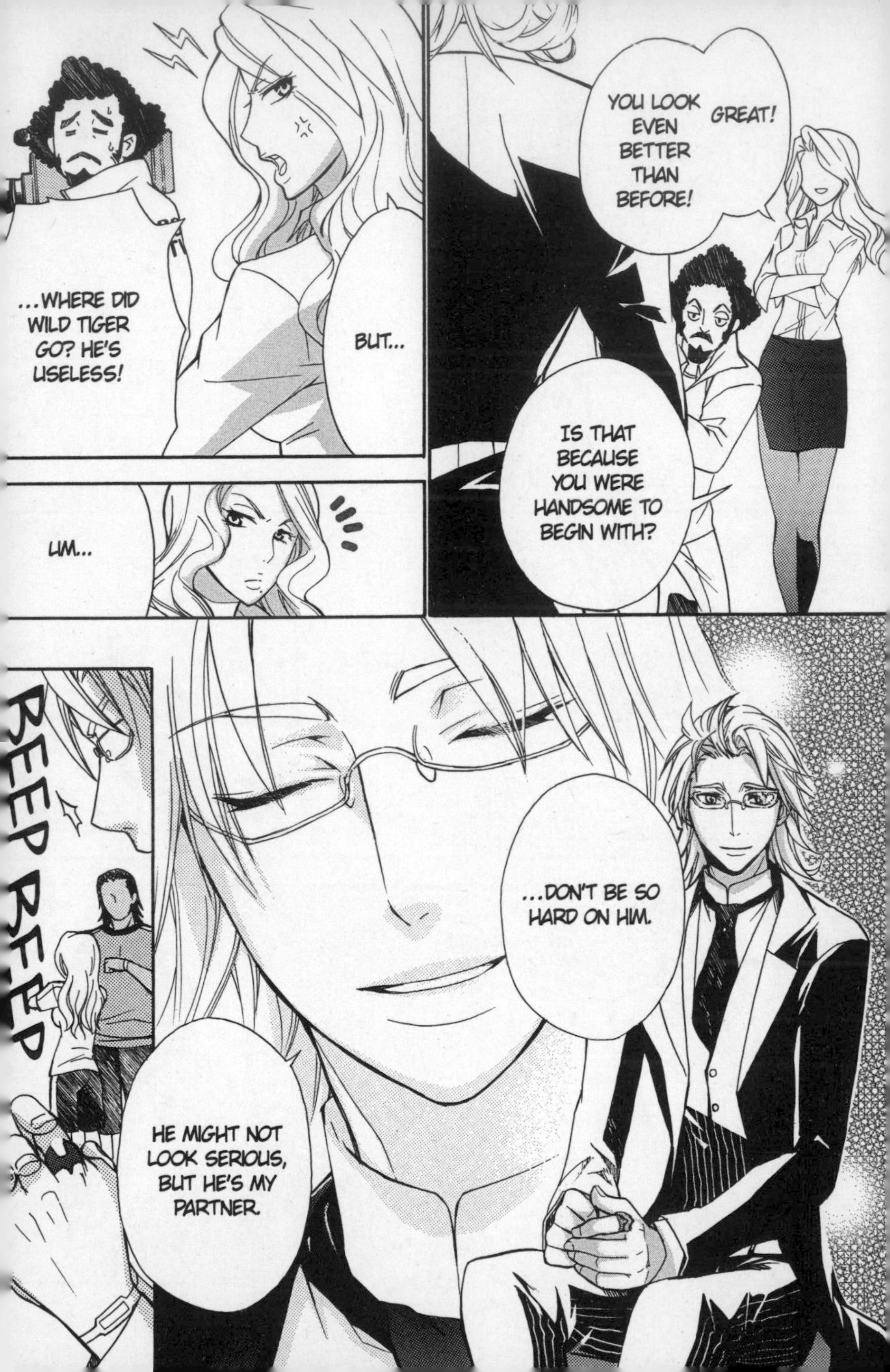
GREAT! YOU LOOK EVEN BETTER THAN BEFORE!
IS THAT BECAUSE YOU WERE HANDSOME TO BEGIN WITH?
BUT...
...WHERE DID WILD TIGER GO? HE'S USELESS!
UM...
...DON'T BE SO HARD ON HIM.
HE MIGHT NOT LOOK SERIOUS, BUT HE'S MY PARTNER.
BEEP BEEP

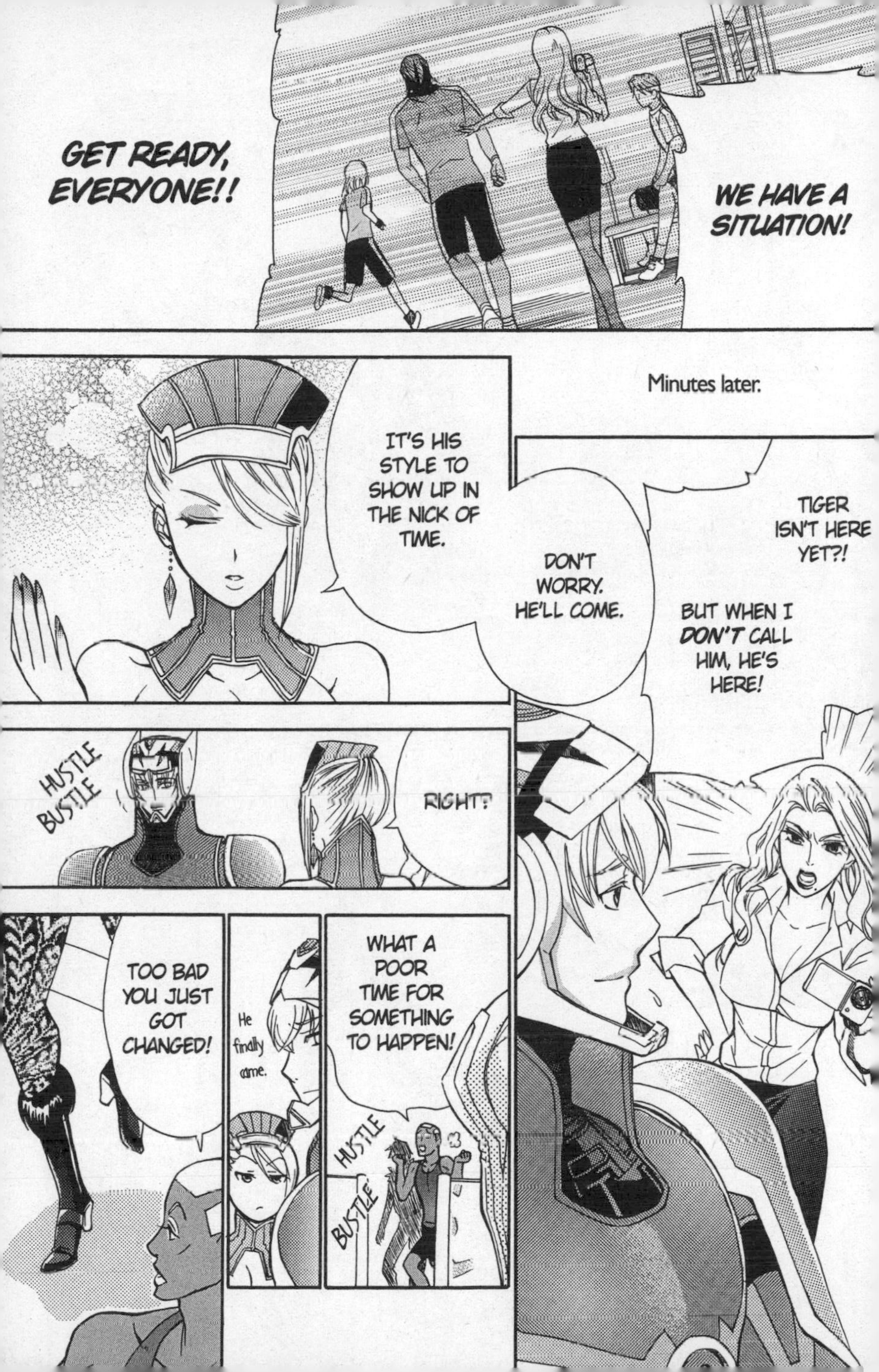
WE HAVE A SITUATION!
GET READY, EVERYONE!!
Minutes later.
TIGER ISN'T HERE YET?!
DON'T WORRY. HE'LL COME.
BUT WHEN I DON'T CALL HIM, HE'S HERE!
IT'S HIS STYLE TO SHOW UP IN THE NICK OF TIME.
HUSTLE BUSTLE
RIGHT?
WHAT A POOR TIME FOR SOMETHING TO HAPPEN!
HUSTLE BUSTLE
He finally came.
TOO BAD YOU JUST GOT CHANGED!

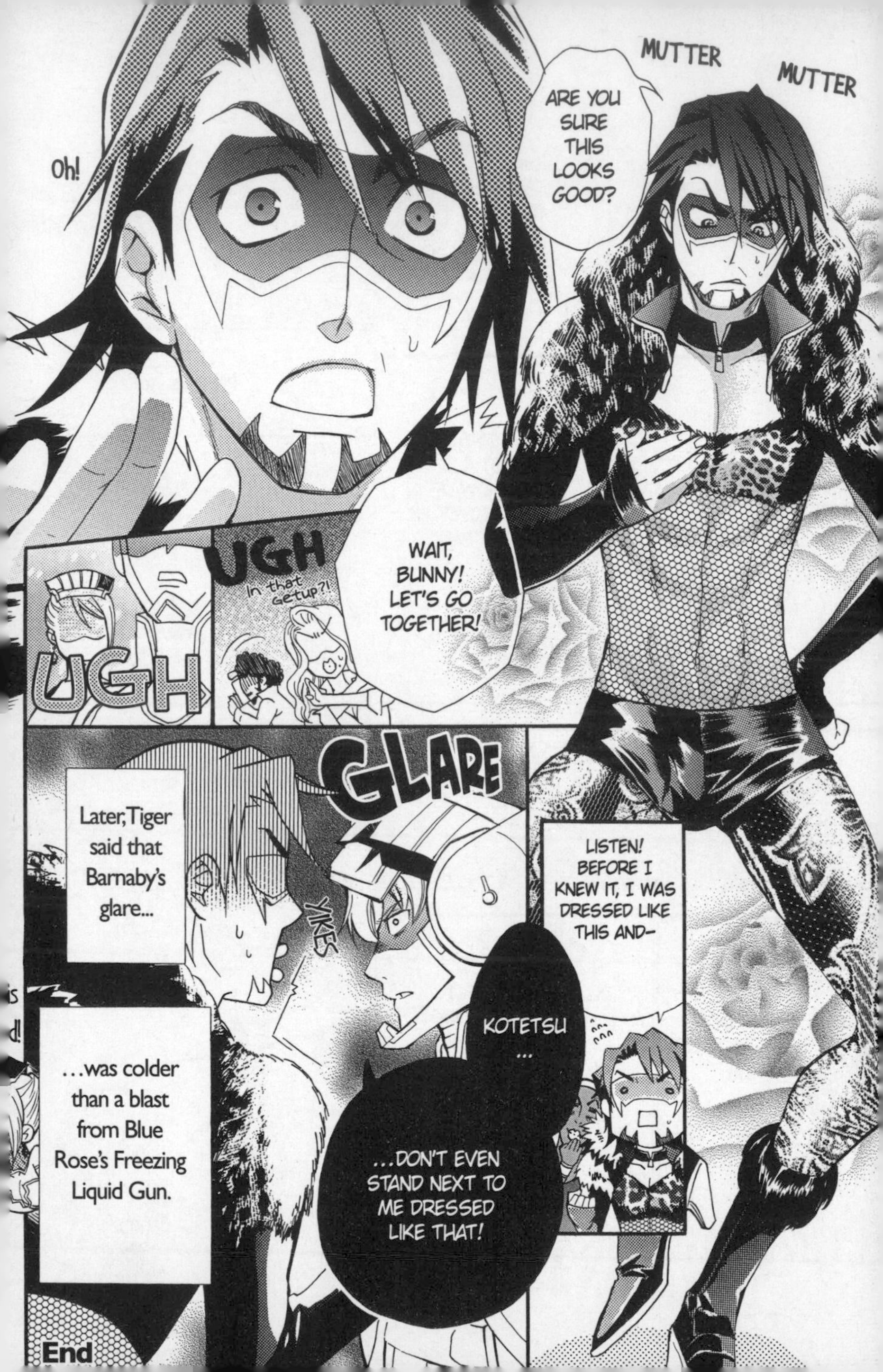
MUTTER
MUTTER
ARE YOU SURE THIS LOOKS GOOD?
Oh!
WAIT, BUNNY! LET'S GO TOGETHER!
UGH
In that getup?!
UGH
LISTEN! BEFORE I KNEW IT, I WAS DRESSED LIKE THIS AND–
GLARE
YIKES
Later,Tiger said that Barnaby's glare...
KOTETSU ...
...DON'T EVEN STAND NEXT TO ME DRESSED LIKE THAT!
...was colder than a blast from Blue Rose's Freezing Liquid Gun.
End

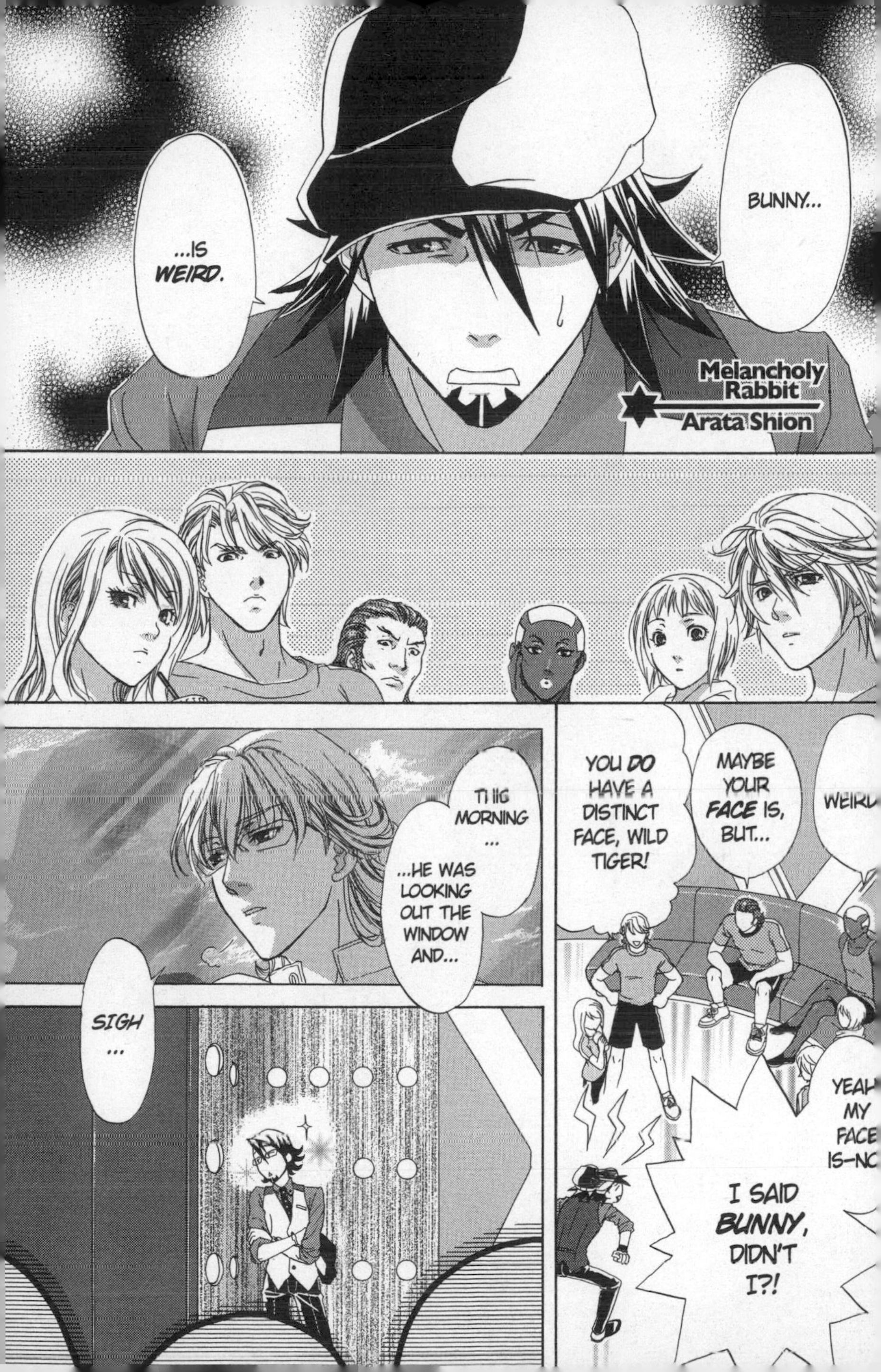
BUNNY...
...IS WEIRD.
Melancholy Rabbit
Arata Shion
WEIRD
MAYBE YOUR FACE IS, BUT...
YOU DO HAVE A DISTINCT FACE, WILD TIGER!
YEAH MY FACE IS—NO
I SAID BUNNY, DIDN'T I?!
THIS MORNING ...
...HE WAS LOOKING OUT THE WINDOW AND...
SIGH ...

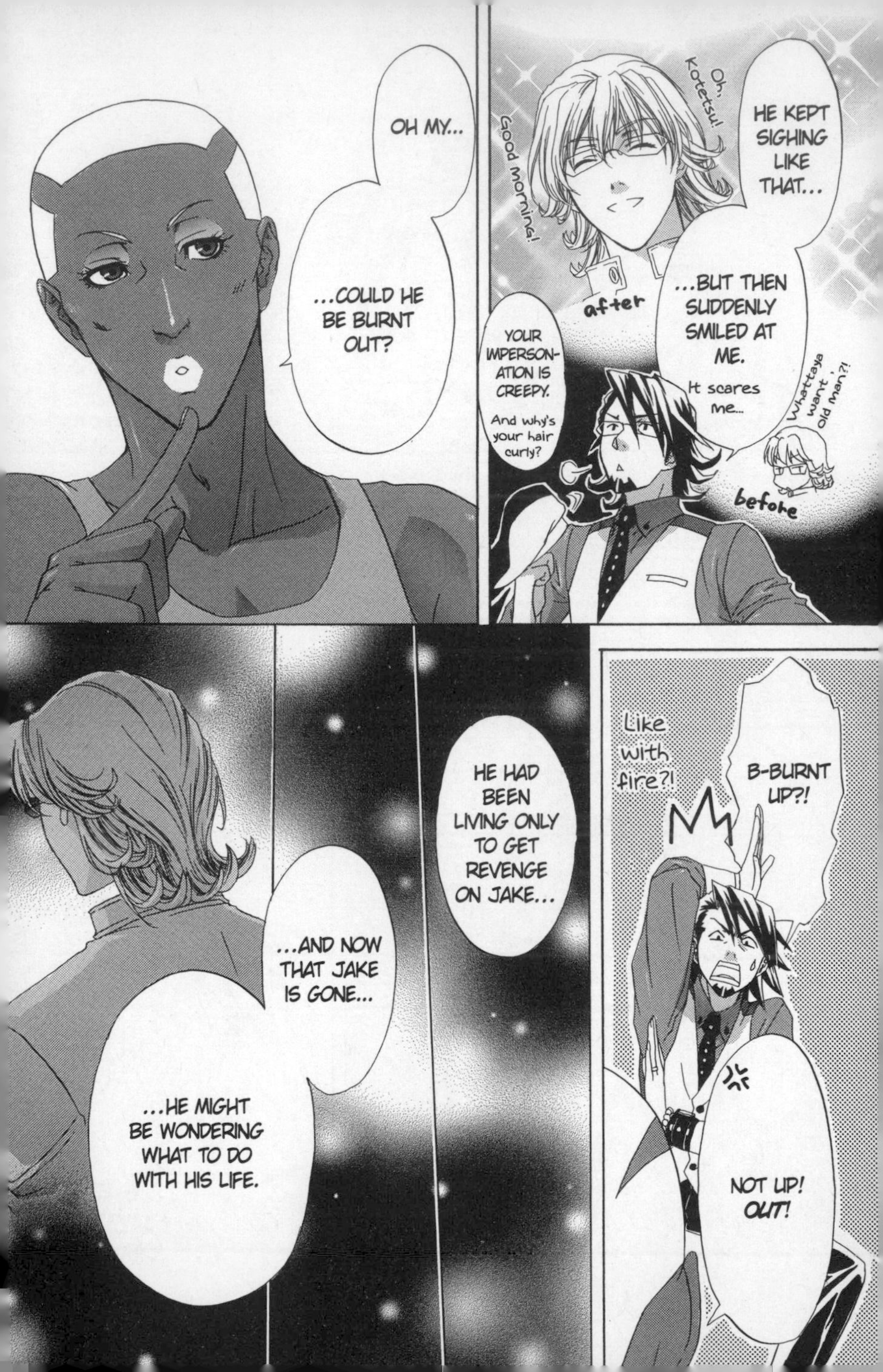
HE KEPT SIGHING LIKE THAT...
Oh, Kotetsu! Good morning!
after
...BUT THEN SUDDENLY SMILED AT ME.
It scares me...
Whattaya want, old man?!
before
YOUR IMPERSON-ATION IS CREEPY.
And why's your hair curly?
OH MY...
...COULD HE BE BURNT OUT?
B-BURNT UP?!
Like with fire?!
NOT UP! OUT!
HE HAD BEEN LIVING ONLY TO GET REVENGE ON JAKE...
...AND NOW THAT JAKE IS GONE...
...HE MIGHT BE WONDERING WHAT TO DO WITH HIS LIFE.

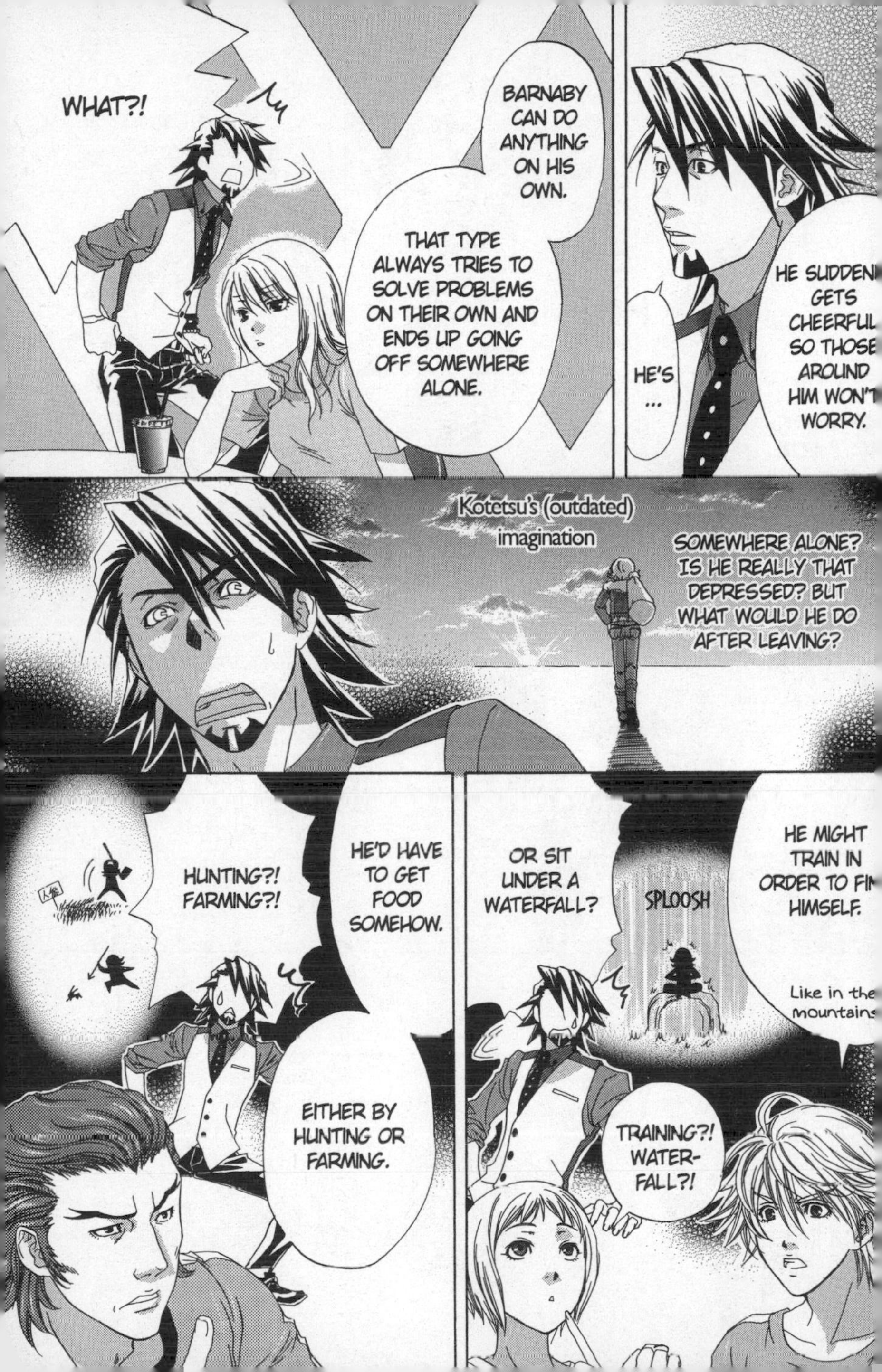
HE SUDDENL GETS CHEERFUL SO THOSE AROUND HIM WON'T WORRY.
HE'S ...
BARNABY CAN DO ANYTHING ON HIS OWN.
THAT TYPE ALWAYS TRIES TO SOLVE PROBLEMS ON THEIR OWN AND ENDS UP GOING OFF SOMEWHERE ALONE.
WHAT?!
Kotetsu's (outdated) imagination
SOMEWHERE ALONE? IS HE REALLY THAT DEPRESSED? BUT WHAT WOULD HE DO AFTER LEAVING?
HE MIGHT TRAIN IN ORDER TO FIN HIMSELF.
Like in the mountains
SPLOOSH
OR SIT UNDER A WATERFALL?
TRAINING?! WATER-FALL?!
HE'D HAVE TO GET FOOD SOMEHOW.
HUNTING?! FARMING?!
EITHER BY HUNTING OR FARMING.

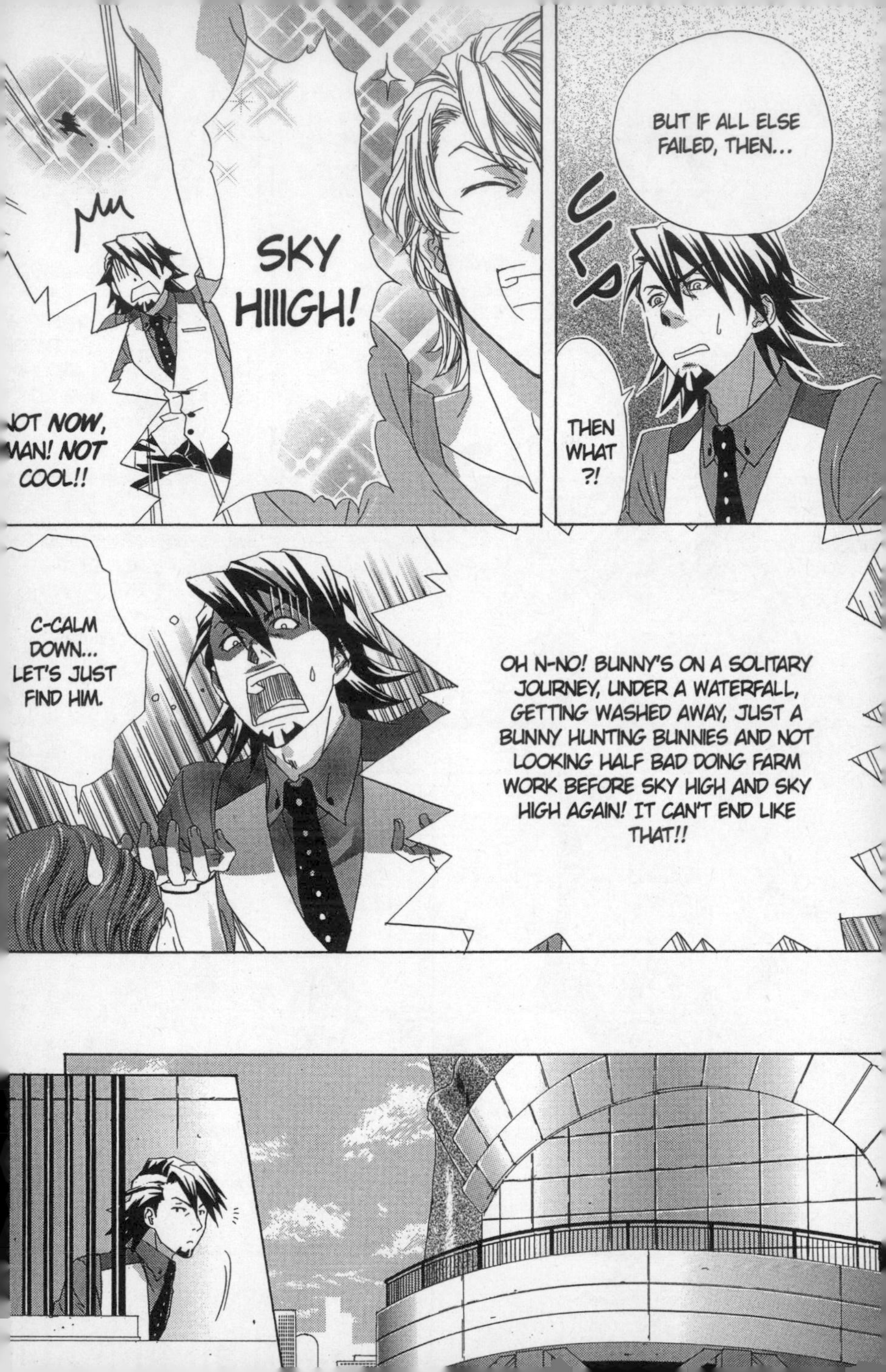
BUT IF ALL ELSE FAILED, THEN...
ULP
THEN WHAT ?!
SKY HIIIGH!
NOT NOW, MAN! NOT COOL!!
OH N-NO! BUNNY'S ON A SOLITARY JOURNEY, UNDER A WATERFALL, GETTING WASHED AWAY, JUST A BUNNY HUNTING BUNNIES AND NOT LOOKING HALF BAD DOING FARM WORK BEFORE SKY HIGH AND SKY HIGH AGAIN! IT CAN'T END LIKE THAT!!
C-CALM DOWN... LET'S JUST FIND HIM.

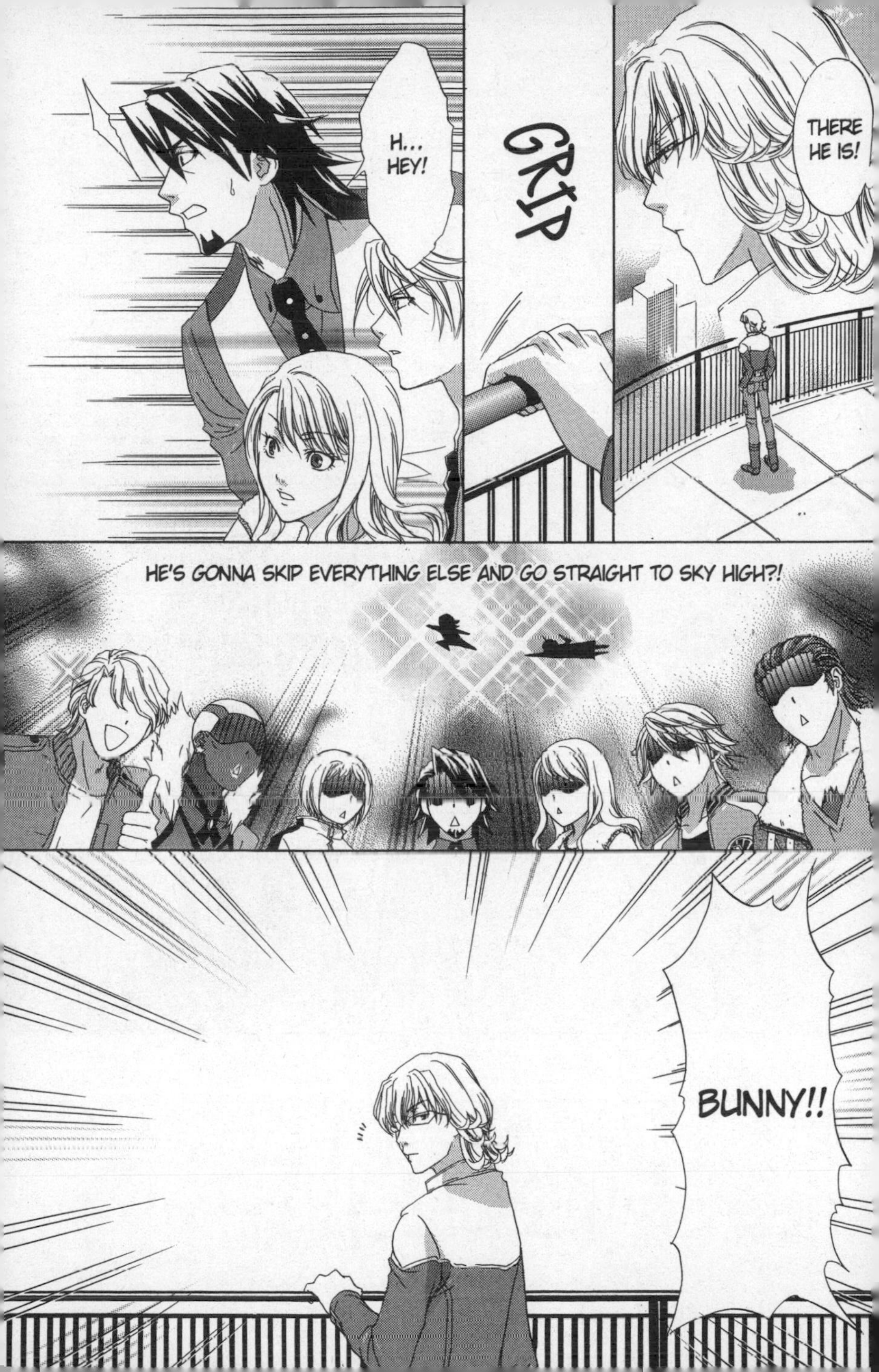
THERE HE IS!
GRIP
H... HEY!
HE'S GONNA SKIP EVERYTHING ELSE AND GO STRAIGHT TO SKY HIGH?!
BUNNY!!

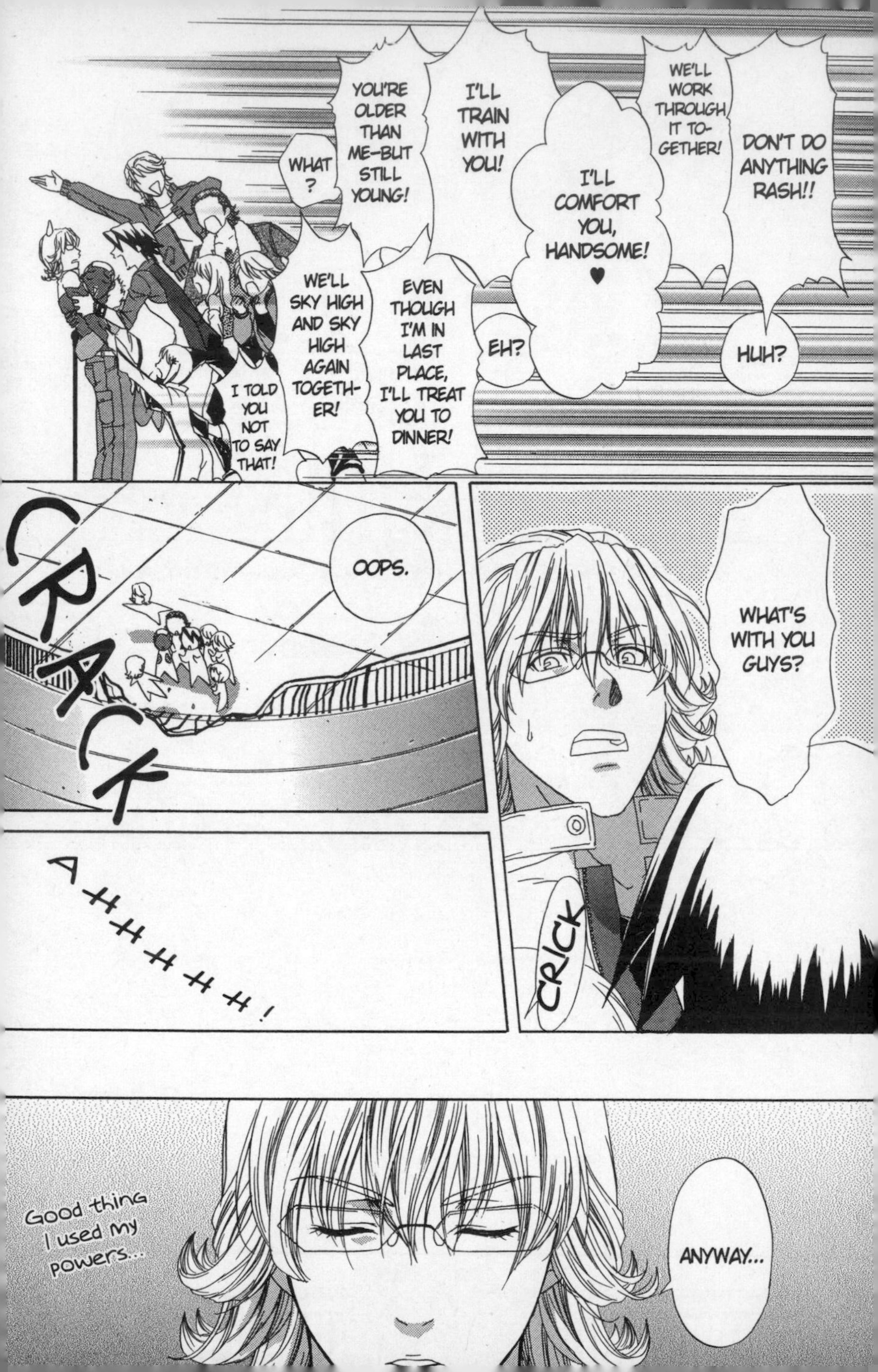
DON'T DO ANYTHING RASH!!
WE'LL WORK THROUGH IT TO-GETHER!
HUH?
I'LL COMFORT YOU, HANDSOME! ♥
EH?
I'LL TRAIN WITH YOU!
YOU'RE OLDER THAN ME—BUT STILL YOUNG!
WHAT?
EVEN THOUGH I'M IN LAST PLACE, I'LL TREAT YOU TO DINNER!
WE'LL SKY HIGH AND SKY HIGH AGAIN TOGETH-ER!
I TOLD YOU NOT TO SAY THAT!
WHAT'S WITH YOU GUYS?
CRICK
OOPS.
CRACK
AHHHHHH!
ANYWAY...
Good thing I used my powers...

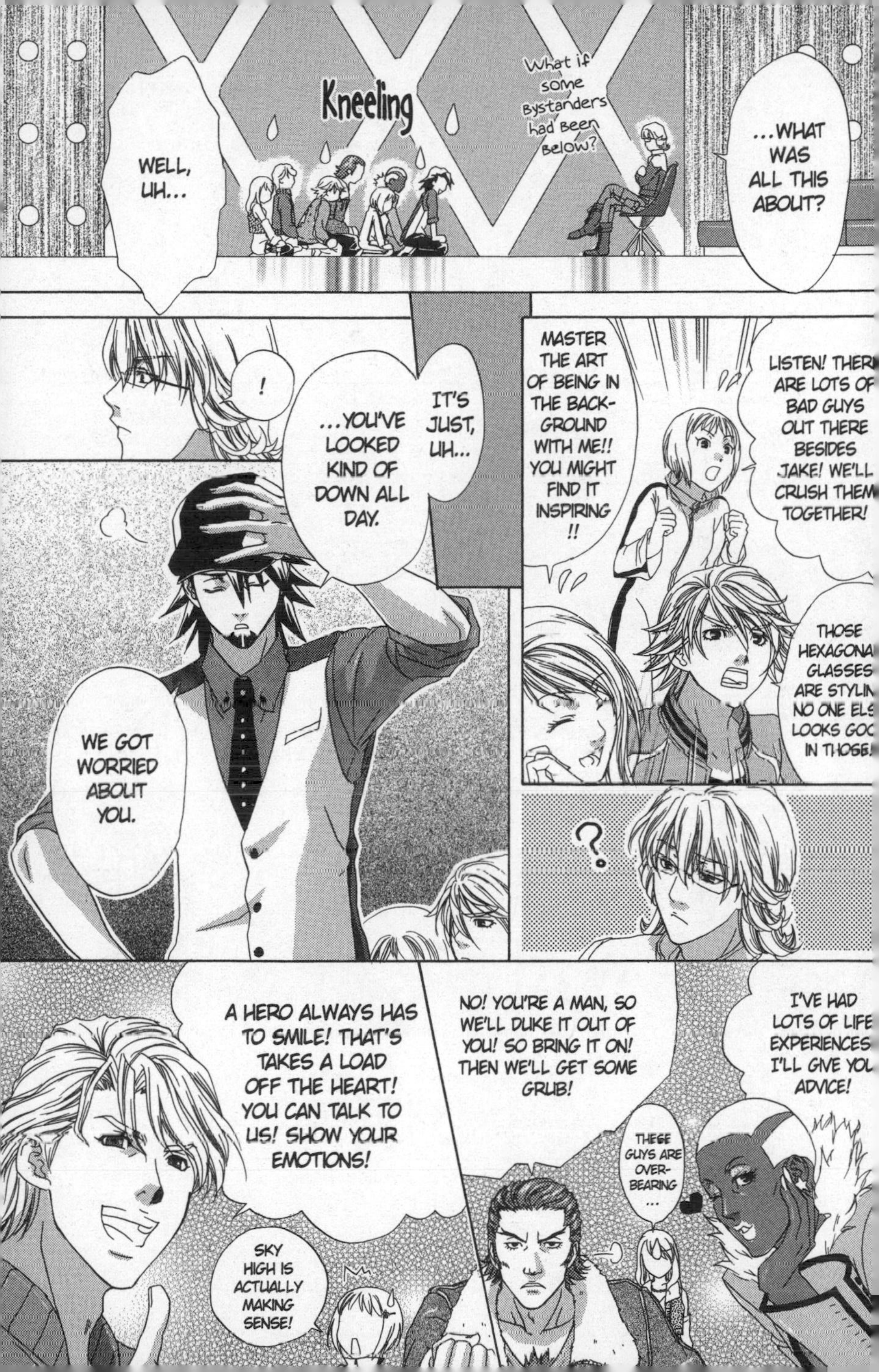
...WHAT WAS ALL THIS ABOUT?
What if some Bystanders had Been Below?
Kneeling
WELL, UH...
LISTEN! THER ARE LOTS OF BAD GUYS OUT THERE BESIDES JAKE! WE'LL CRUSH THEM TOGETHER!
MASTER THE ART OF BEING IN THE BACK-GROUND WITH ME!! YOU MIGHT FIND IT INSPIRING !!
THOSE HEXAGONA GLASSES ARE STYLIN NO ONE ELS LOOKS GOO IN THOSE!
?
!
IT'S JUST, UH...
...YOU'VE LOOKED KIND OF DOWN ALL DAY.
WE GOT WORRIED ABOUT YOU.
I'VE HAD LOTS OF LIFE EXPERIENCES I'LL GIVE YOU ADVICE!
THESE GUYS ARE OVER-BEARING ...
NO! YOU'RE A MAN, SO WE'LL DUKE IT OUT OF YOU! SO BRING IT ON! THEN WE'LL GET SOME GRUB!
A HERO ALWAYS HAS TO SMILE! THAT'S TAKES A LOAD OFF THE HEART! YOU CAN TALK TO US! SHOW YOUR EMOTIONS!
SKY HIGH IS ACTUALLY MAKING SENSE!

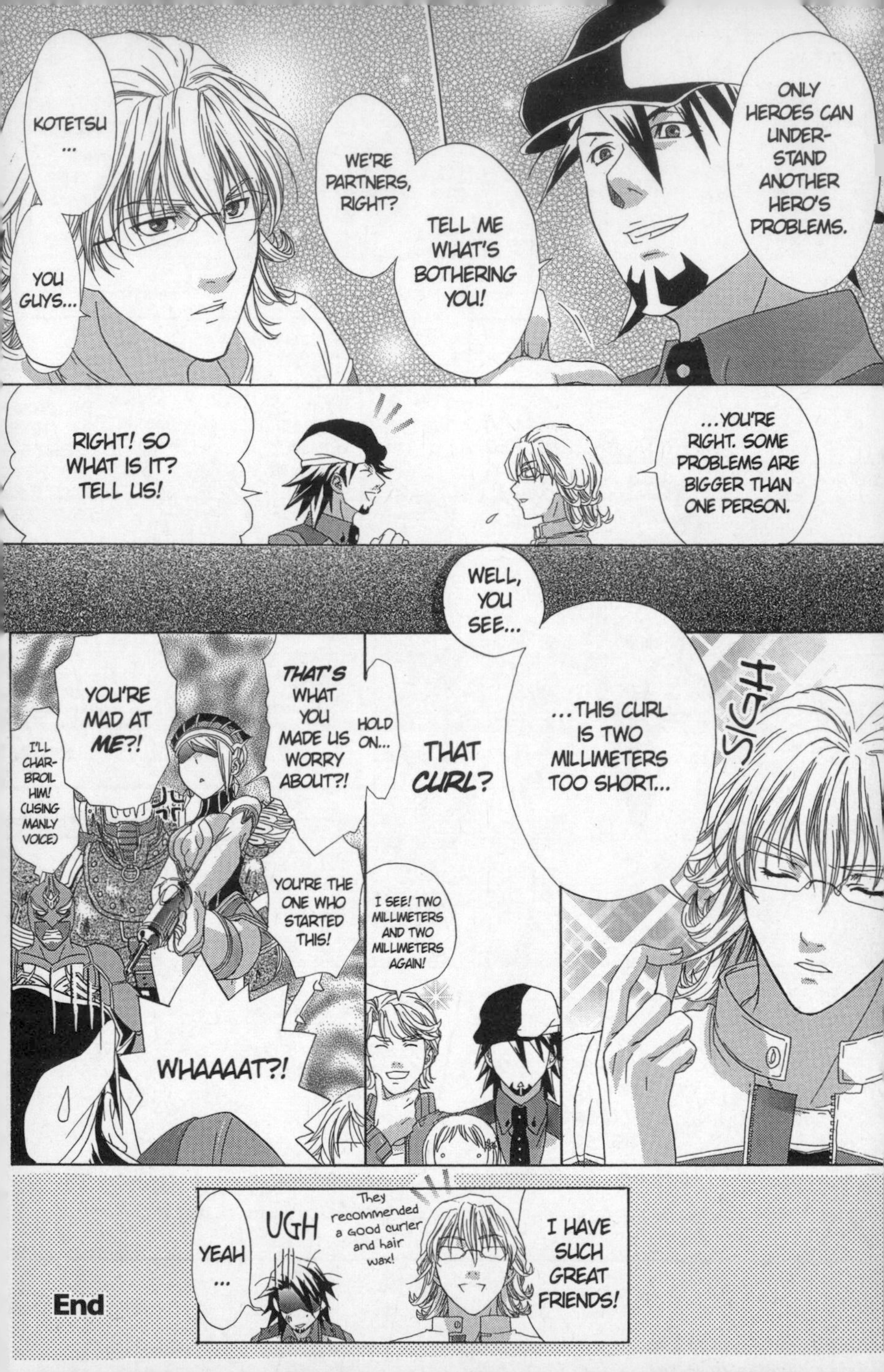
ONLY HEROES CAN UNDER-STAND ANOTHER HERO'S PROBLEMS.
WE'RE PARTNERS, RIGHT?
TELL ME WHAT'S BOTHERING YOU!
KOTETSU ...
YOU GUYS...
...YOU'RE RIGHT. SOME PROBLEMS ARE BIGGER THAN ONE PERSON.
RIGHT! SO WHAT IS IT? TELL US!
WELL, YOU SEE...
SIGH
...THIS CURL IS TWO MILLIMETERS TOO SHORT...
THAT CURL?
I SEE! TWO MILLIMETERS AND TWO MILLIMETERS AGAIN!
HOLD ON...
THAT'S WHAT YOU MADE US WORRY ABOUT?!
YOU'RE MAD AT ME?!
I'LL CHAR-BROIL HIM! (USING MANLY VOICE)
YOU'RE THE ONE WHO STARTED THIS!
WHAAAAT?!
I HAVE SUCH GREAT FRIENDS!
They recommended a good curler and hair wax!
UGH
YEAH ...
End

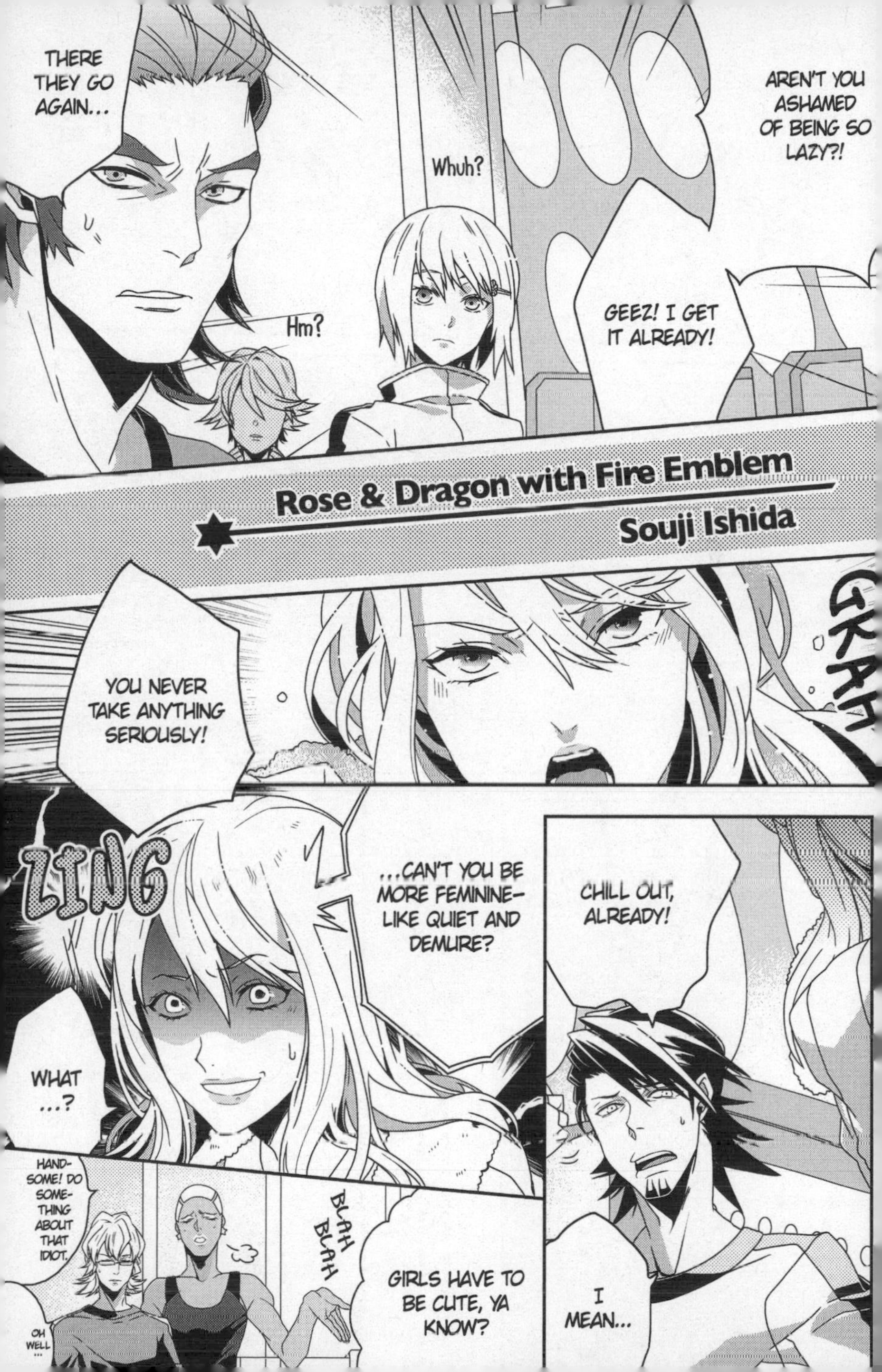
AREN'T YOU ASHAMED OF BEING SO LAZY?!
GEEZ! I GET IT ALREADY!
Whuh?
Hm?
THERE THEY GO AGAIN...
Rose & Dragon with Fire Emblem
Souji Ishida
GRAH
YOU NEVER TAKE ANYTHING SERIOUSLY!
CHILL OUT, ALREADY!
I MEAN...
ZING
...CAN'T YOU BE MORE FEMININE-LIKE QUIET AND DEMURE?
WHAT ...?
GIRLS HAVE TO BE CUTE, YA KNOW?
BLAH BLAH
HAND-SOME! DO SOME-THING ABOUT THAT IDIOT.
OH WELL ...

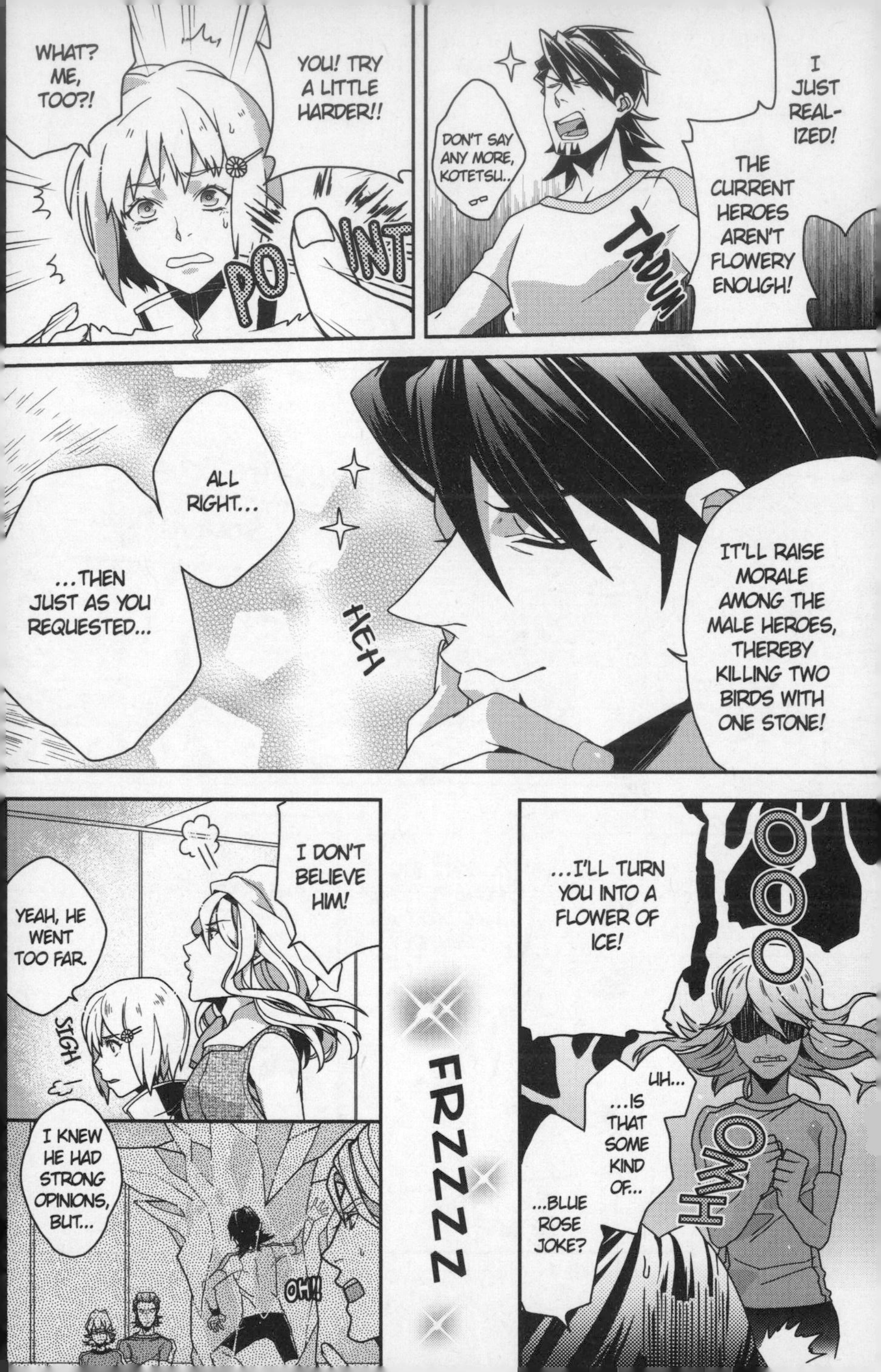
I JUST REAL-IZED!
THE CURRENT HEROES AREN'T FLOWERY ENOUGH!
DON'T SAY ANY MORE, KOTETSU...
TADUM
YOU! TRY A LITTLE HARDER!!
WHAT? ME, TOO?!
POINT
IT'LL RAISE MORALE AMONG THE MALE HEROES, THEREBY KILLING TWO BIRDS WITH ONE STONE!
HEH
ALL RIGHT...
...THEN JUST AS YOU REQUESTED...
...I'LL TURN YOU INTO A FLOWER OF ICE!
OOOO
UH...
...IS THAT SOME KIND OF...
...BLUE ROSE JOKE?
FRZZZ
I DON'T BELIEVE HIM!
YEAH, HE WENT TOO FAR.
SIGH
I KNEW HE HAD STRONG OPINIONS, BUT...
OH!!

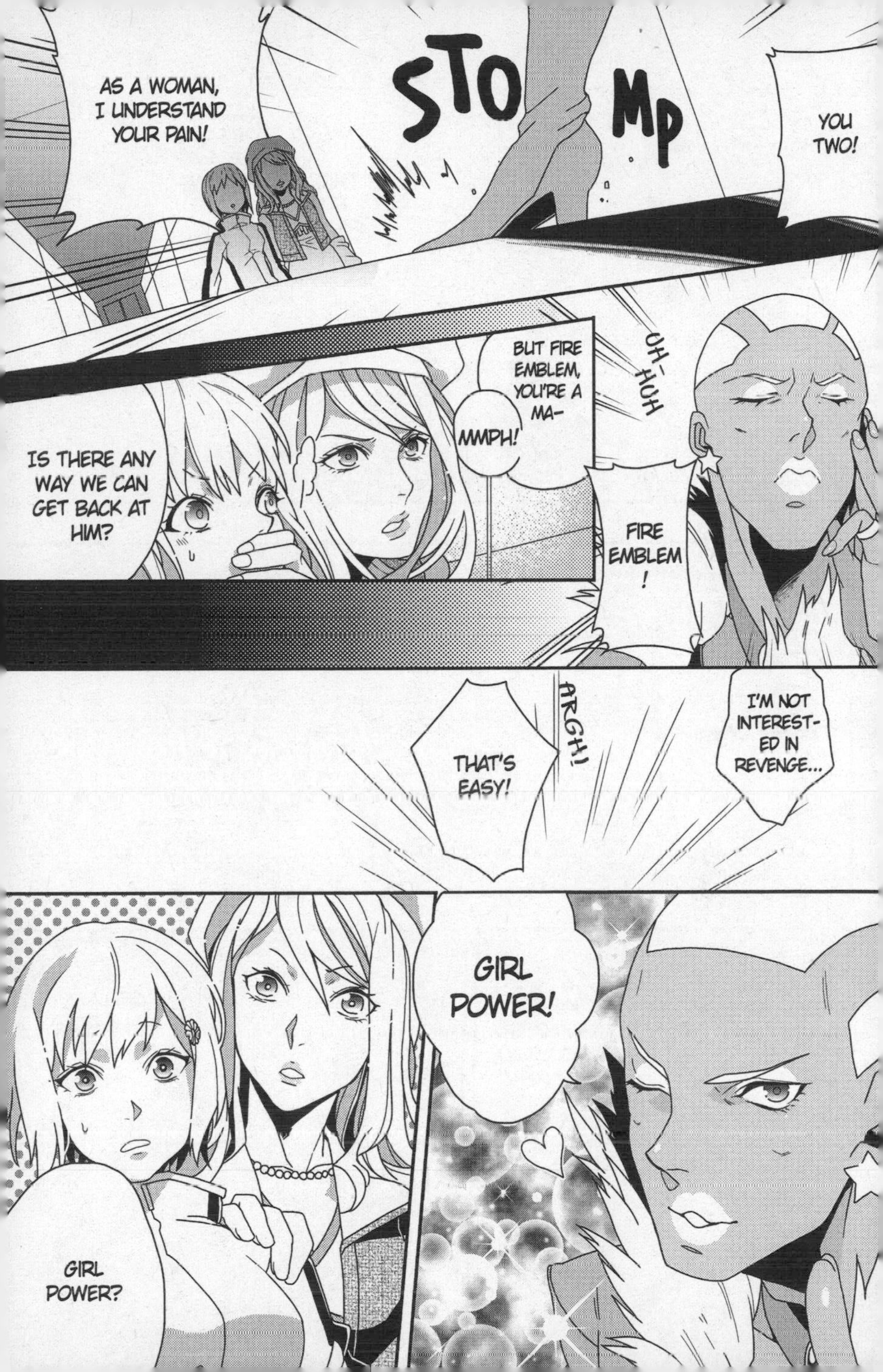
YOU TWO!
STOMP
AS A WOMAN, I UNDERSTAND YOUR PAIN!
UH-HUH
BUT FIRE EMBLEM, YOU'RE A MA-
MMPH!
FIRE EMBLEM!
IS THERE ANY WAY WE CAN GET BACK AT HIM?
I'M NOT INTEREST-ED IN REVENGE...
ARGH!
THAT'S EASY!
GIRL POWER!
GIRL POWER?

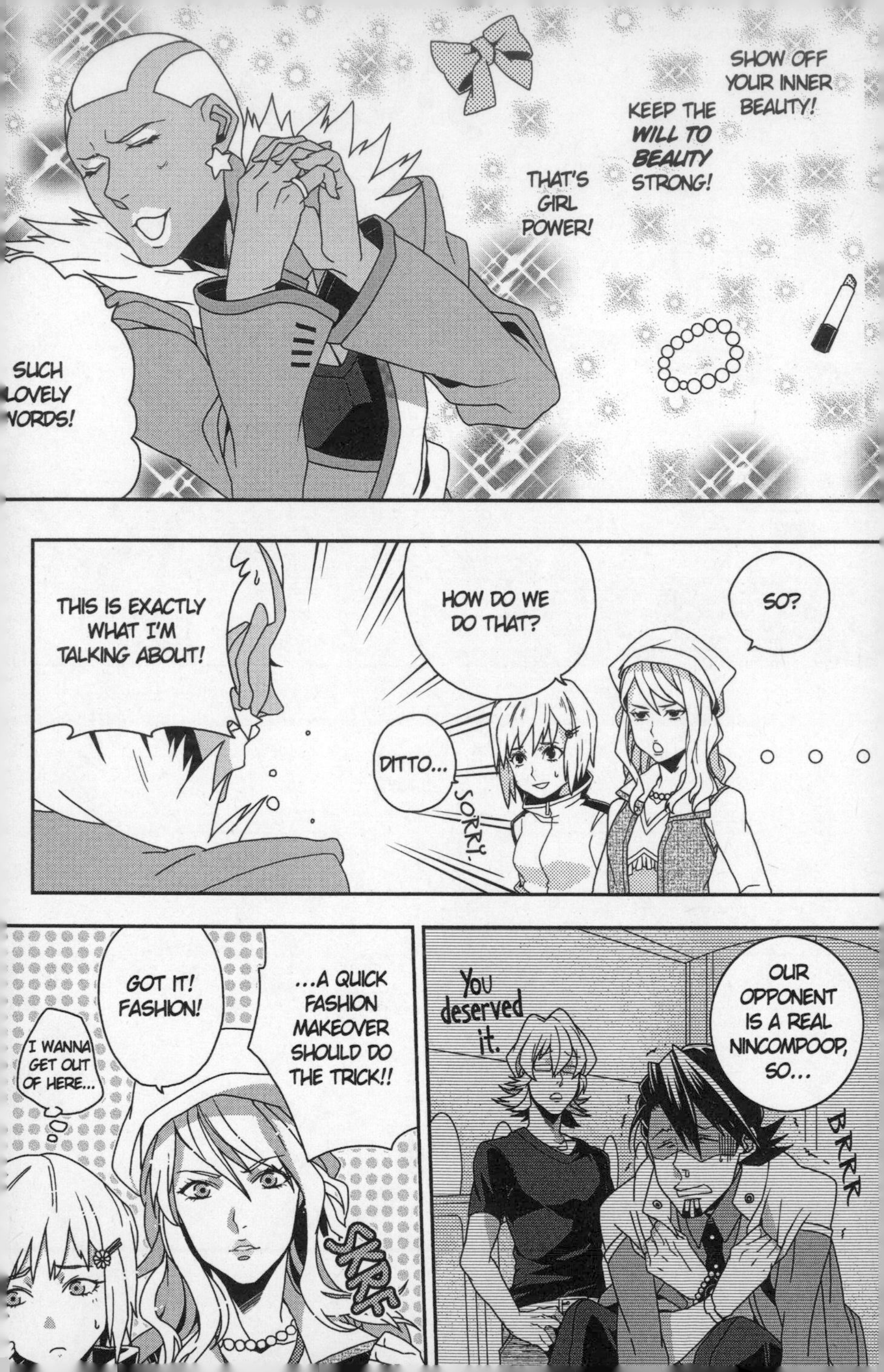
SHOW OFF YOUR INNER BEAUTY!
KEEP THE **WILL TO BEAUTY** STRONG!
THAT'S GIRL POWER!
SUCH LOVELY WORDS!
SO?
HOW DO WE DO THAT?
DITTO...
SORRY.
THIS IS EXACTLY WHAT I'M TALKING ABOUT!
OUR OPPONENT IS A REAL NINCOMPOOP, SO...
BRRR
You deserved it.
...A QUICK FASHION MAKEOVER SHOULD DO THE TRICK!!
GOT IT! FASHION!
I WANNA GET OUT OF HERE...
SKRF

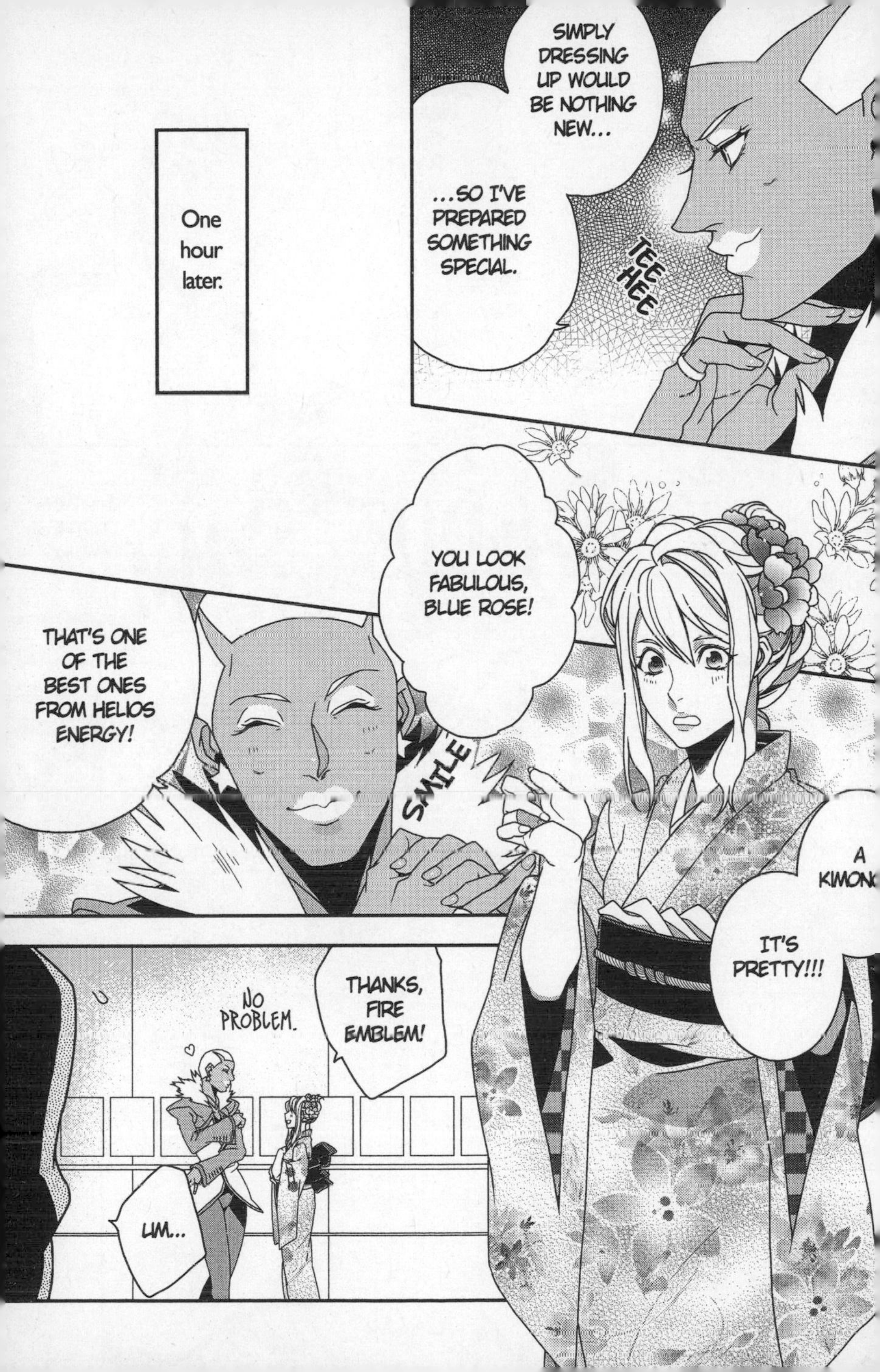
SIMPLY DRESSING UP WOULD BE NOTHING NEW...
...SO I'VE PREPARED SOMETHING SPECIAL.
TEE HEE
One hour later.
A KIMON
IT'S PRETTY!!!
YOU LOOK FABULOUS, BLUE ROSE!
THAT'S ONE OF THE BEST ONES FROM HELIOS ENERGY!
SMILE
THANKS, FIRE EMBLEM!
NO PROBLEM.
UM...

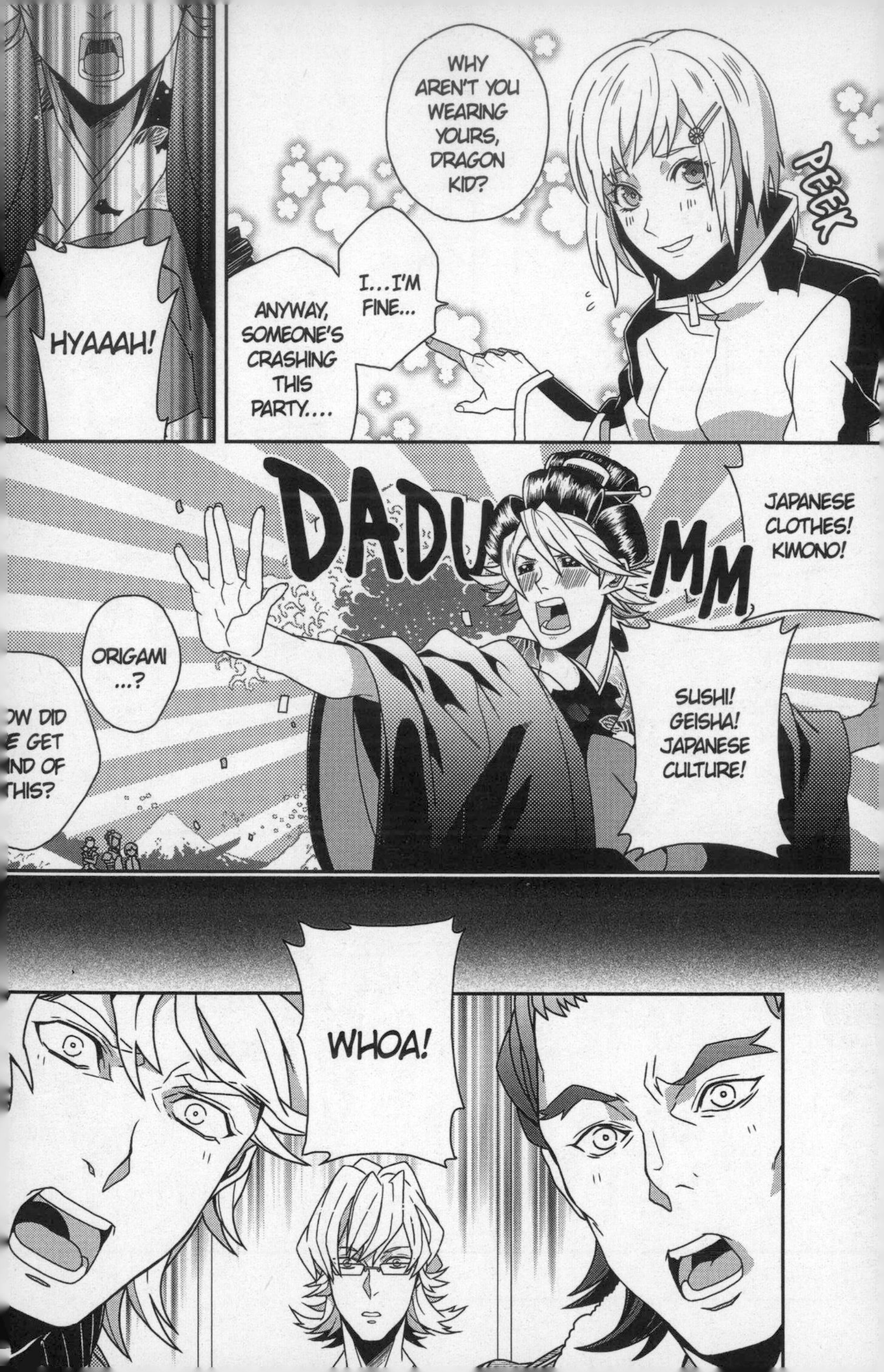
PEEK
WHY AREN'T YOU WEARING YOURS, DRAGON KID?
I...I'M FINE...
ANYWAY, SOMEONE'S CRASHING THIS PARTY....
HYAAAH!
DADUMMM
JAPANESE CLOTHES! KIMONO!
SUSHI! GEISHA! JAPANESE CULTURE!
ORIGAMI ...?
OW DID E GET IND OF THIS?
WHOA!

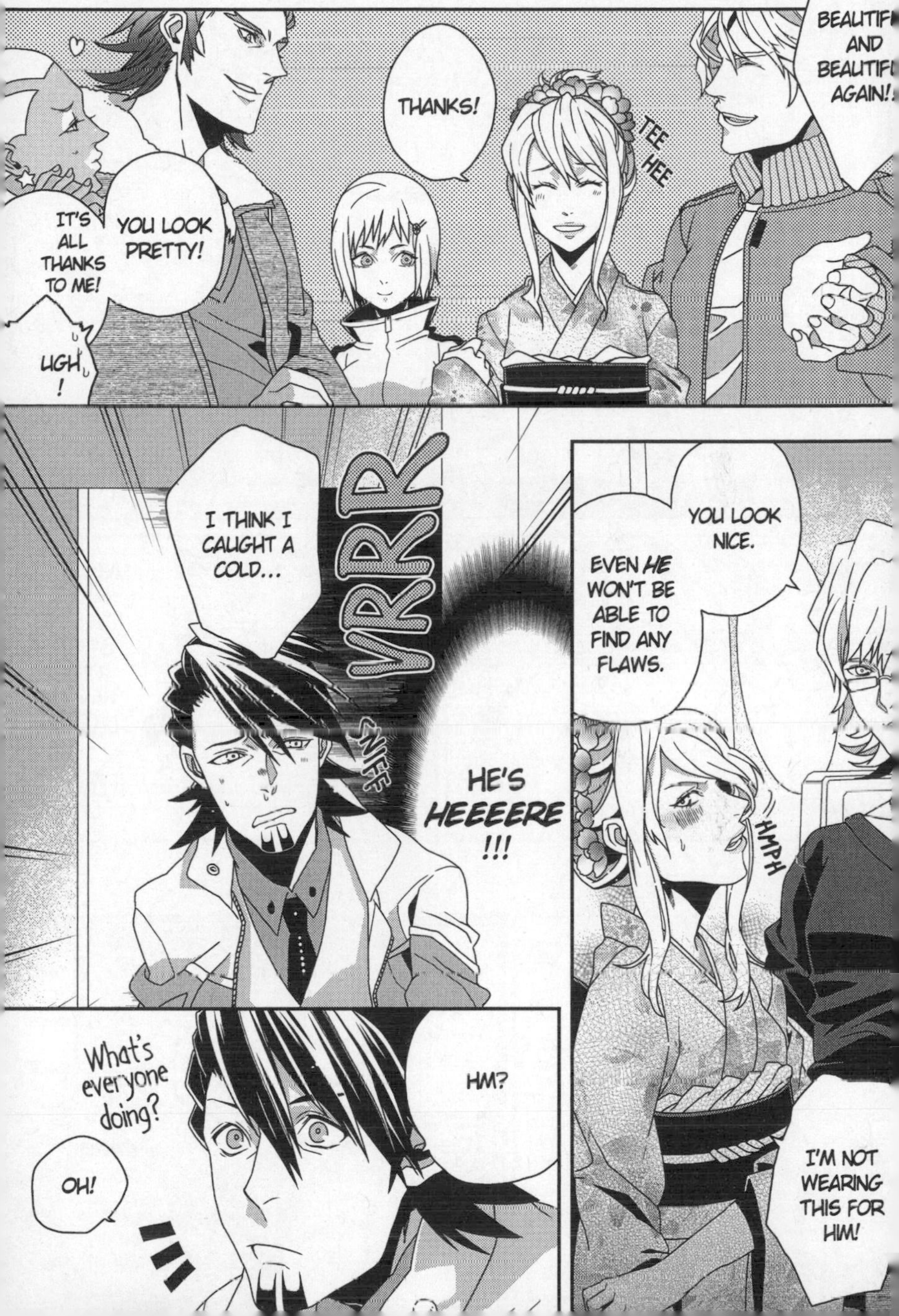
BEAUTIF AND BEAUTIF AGAIN!
TEE HEE
THANKS!
YOU LOOK PRETTY!
IT'S ALL THANKS TO ME!
UGH!
YOU LOOK NICE.
EVEN *HE* WON'T BE ABLE TO FIND ANY FLAWS.
HMPH
I'M NOT WEARING THIS FOR HIM!
I THINK I CAUGHT A COLD...
VRRR
SNIFF
HE'S *HEEEEERE*!!!
HM?
What's everyone doing?
OH!

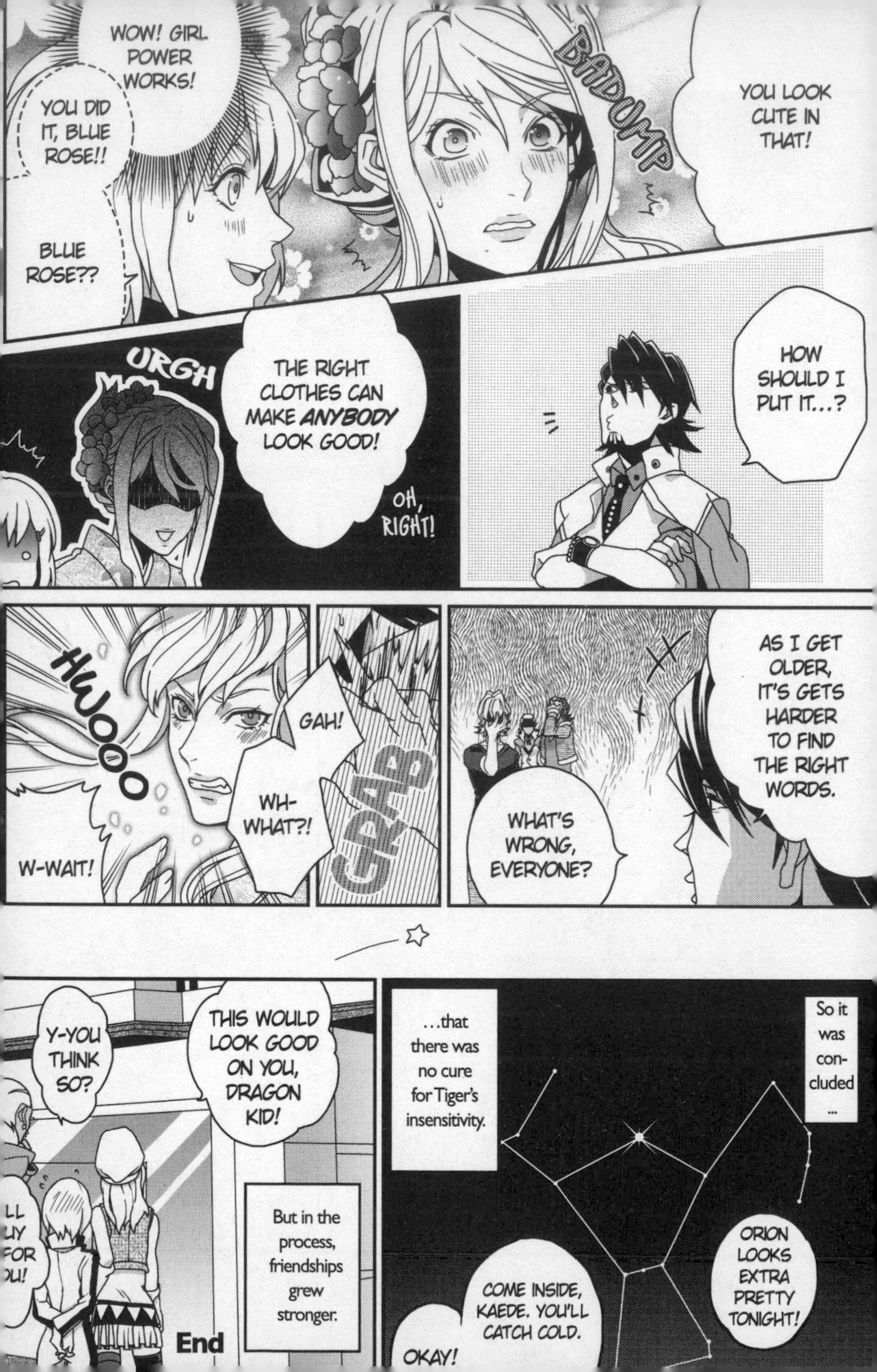
YOU LOOK CUTE IN THAT!
BADUMP
WOW! GIRL POWER WORKS!
YOU DID IT, BLUE ROSE!!
BLUE ROSE??
HOW SHOULD I PUT IT...?
THE RIGHT CLOTHES CAN MAKE *ANYBODY* LOOK GOOD!
URGH
OH, RIGHT!
AS I GET OLDER, IT'S GETS HARDER TO FIND THE RIGHT WORDS.
WHAT'S WRONG, EVERYONE?
GAH!
GRAB
WH-WHAT?!
HWOOO
W-WAIT!
So it was concluded ...
...that there was no cure for Tiger's insensitivity.
ORION LOOKS EXTRA PRETTY TONIGHT!
COME INSIDE, KAEDE. YOU'LL CATCH COLD.
OKAY!
THIS WOULD LOOK GOOD ON YOU, DRAGON KID!
Y-YOU THINK SO?
But in the process, friendships grew stronger.
End

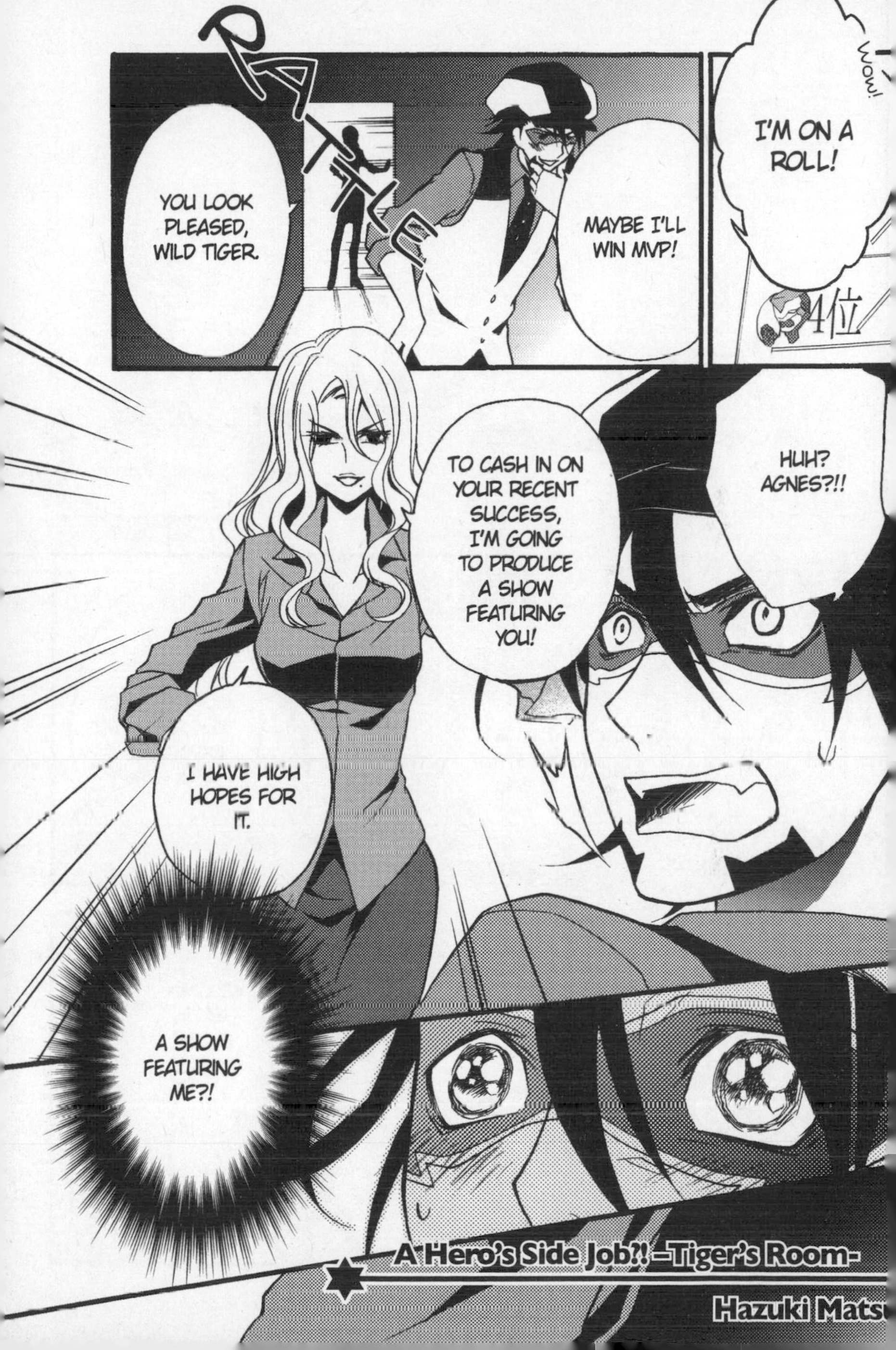
WOW!
I'M ON A ROLL!
4位
MAYBE I'LL WIN MVP!
RATTLE
YOU LOOK PLEASED, WILD TIGER.
HUH? AGNES?!!
TO CASH IN ON YOUR RECENT SUCCESS, I'M GOING TO PRODUCE A SHOW FEATURING YOU!
I HAVE HIGH HOPES FOR IT.
A SHOW FEATURING ME?!
A Hero's Side Job?! -Tiger's Room-
Hazuki Matsu

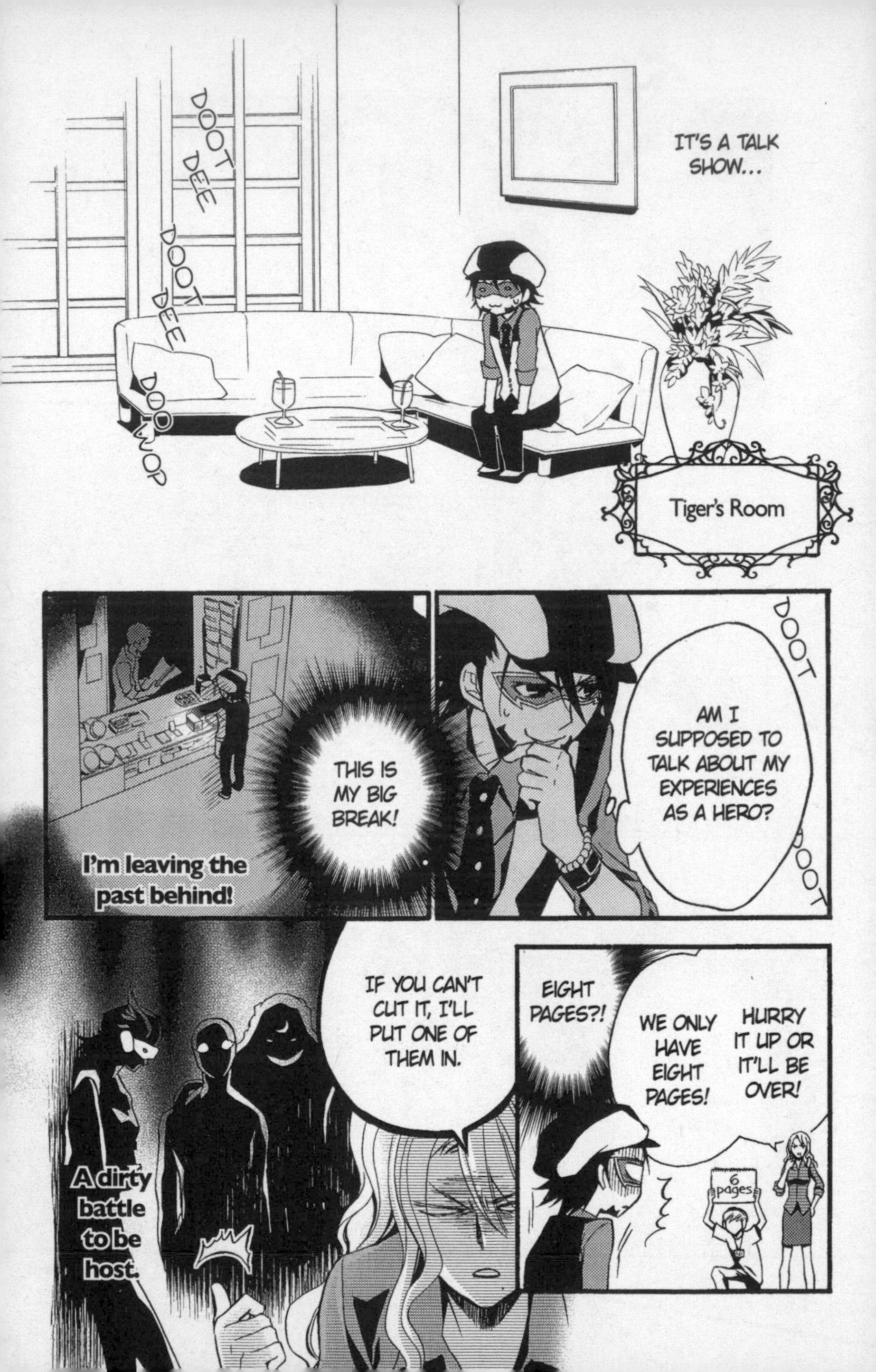
IT'S A TALK SHOW...
DOOT DEE
DOOT DEE
DOO WOP
Tiger's Room
DOOT
AM I SUPPOSED TO TALK ABOUT MY EXPERIENCES AS A HERO?
DOOT
THIS IS MY BIG BREAK!
I'm leaving the past behind!
HURRY IT UP OR IT'LL BE OVER!
WE ONLY HAVE EIGHT PAGES!
EIGHT PAGES?!
6 pages
IF YOU CAN'T CUT IT, I'LL PUT ONE OF THEM IN.
A dirty battle to be host.

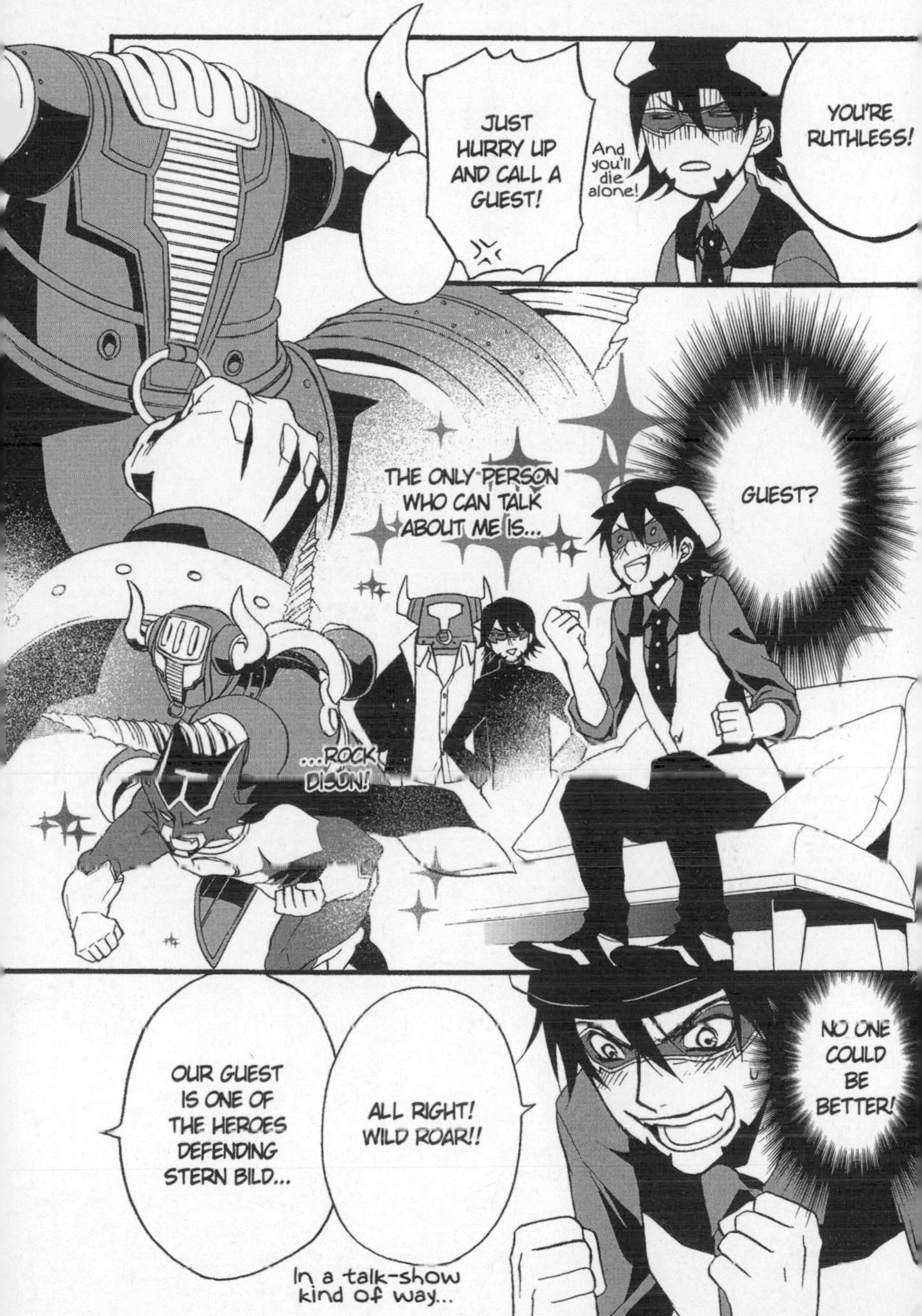
YOU'RE RUTHLESS!
And you'll die alone!
JUST HURRY UP AND CALL A GUEST!
GUEST?
THE ONLY PERSON WHO CAN TALK ABOUT ME IS...
...ROCK DISON!
NO ONE COULD BE BETTER!
ALL RIGHT! WILD ROAR!!
OUR GUEST IS ONE OF THE HEROES DEFENDING STERN BILD...
In a talk-show kind of way...

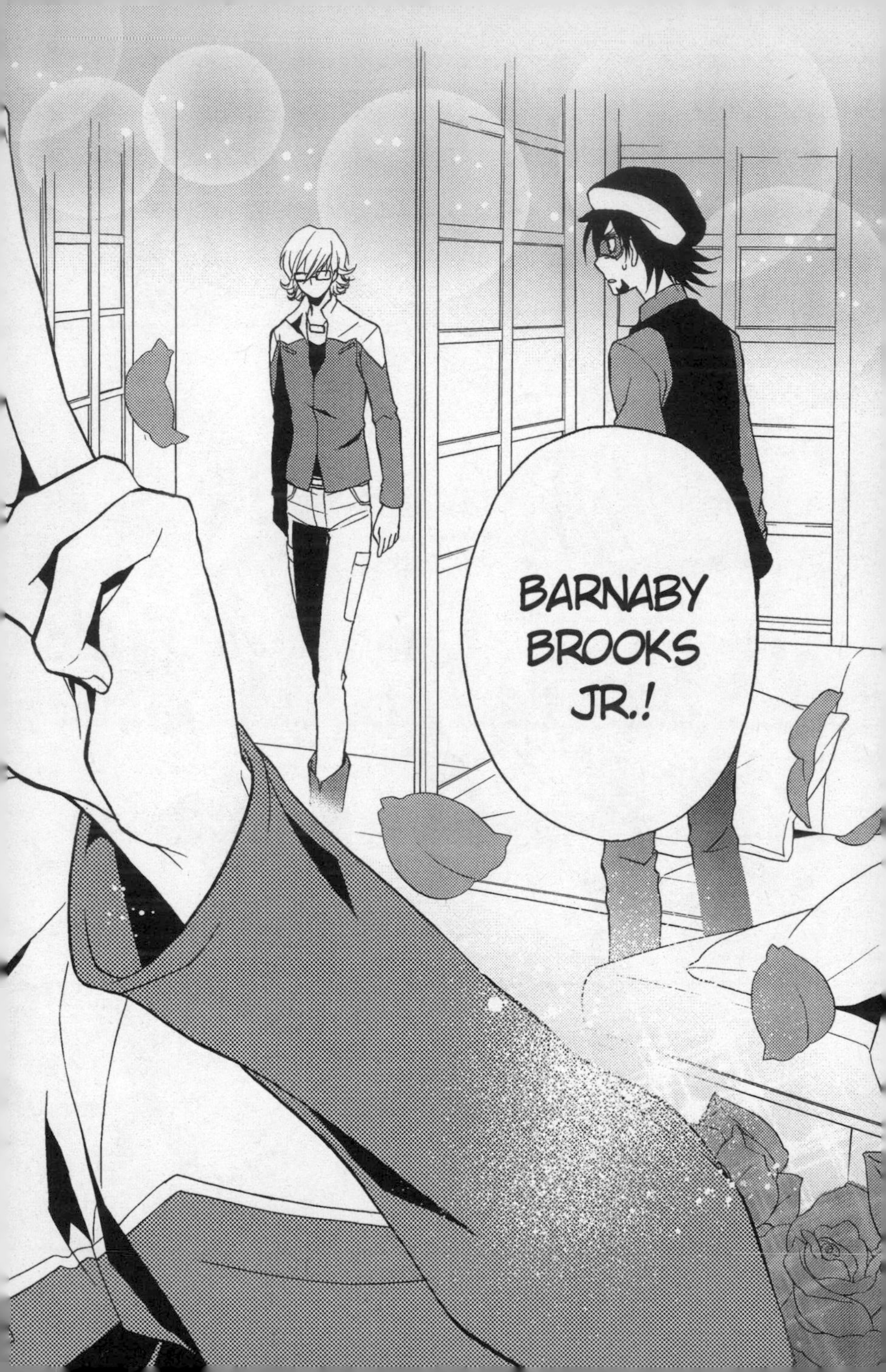
BARNABY BROOKS JR.!

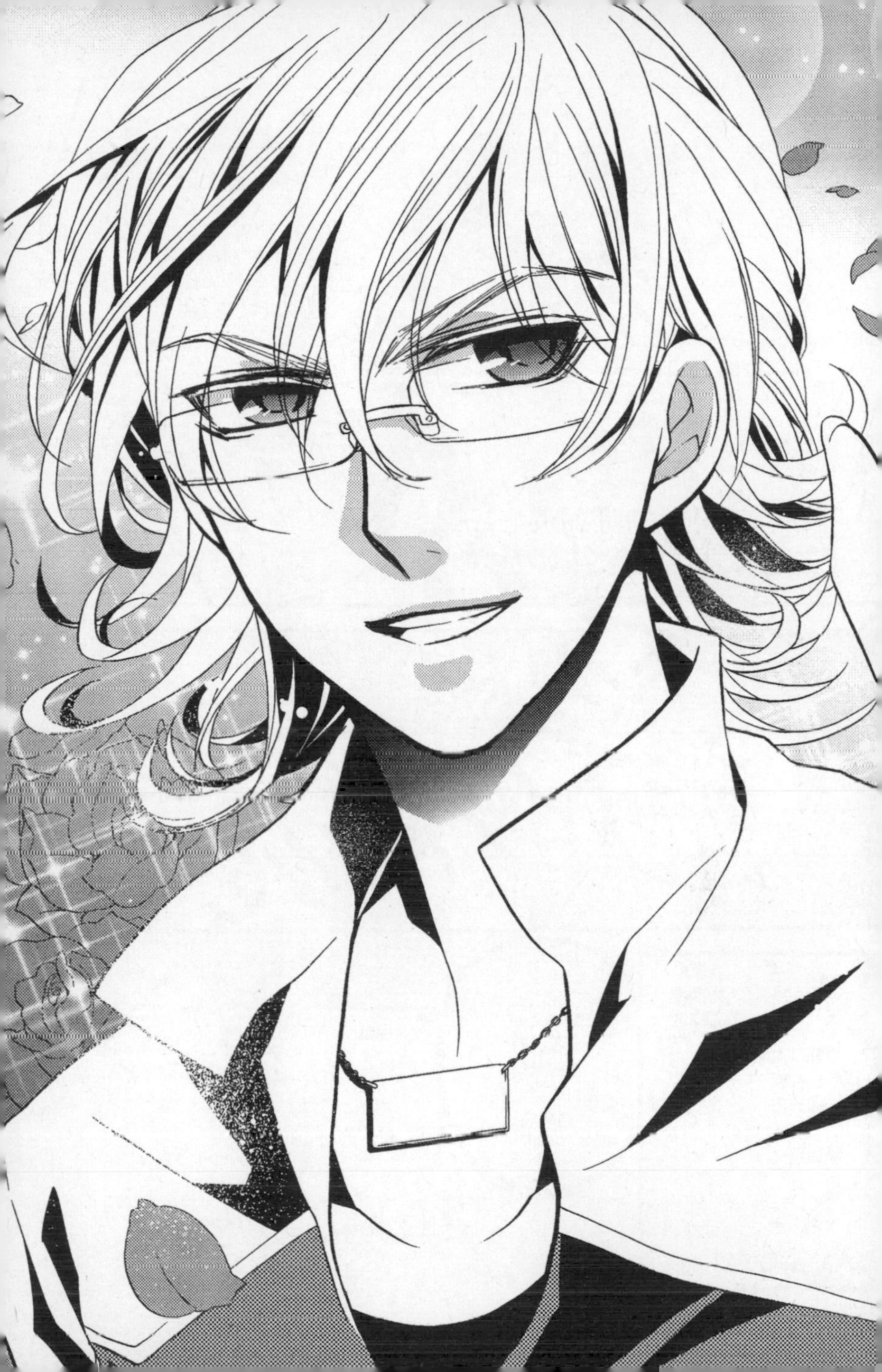

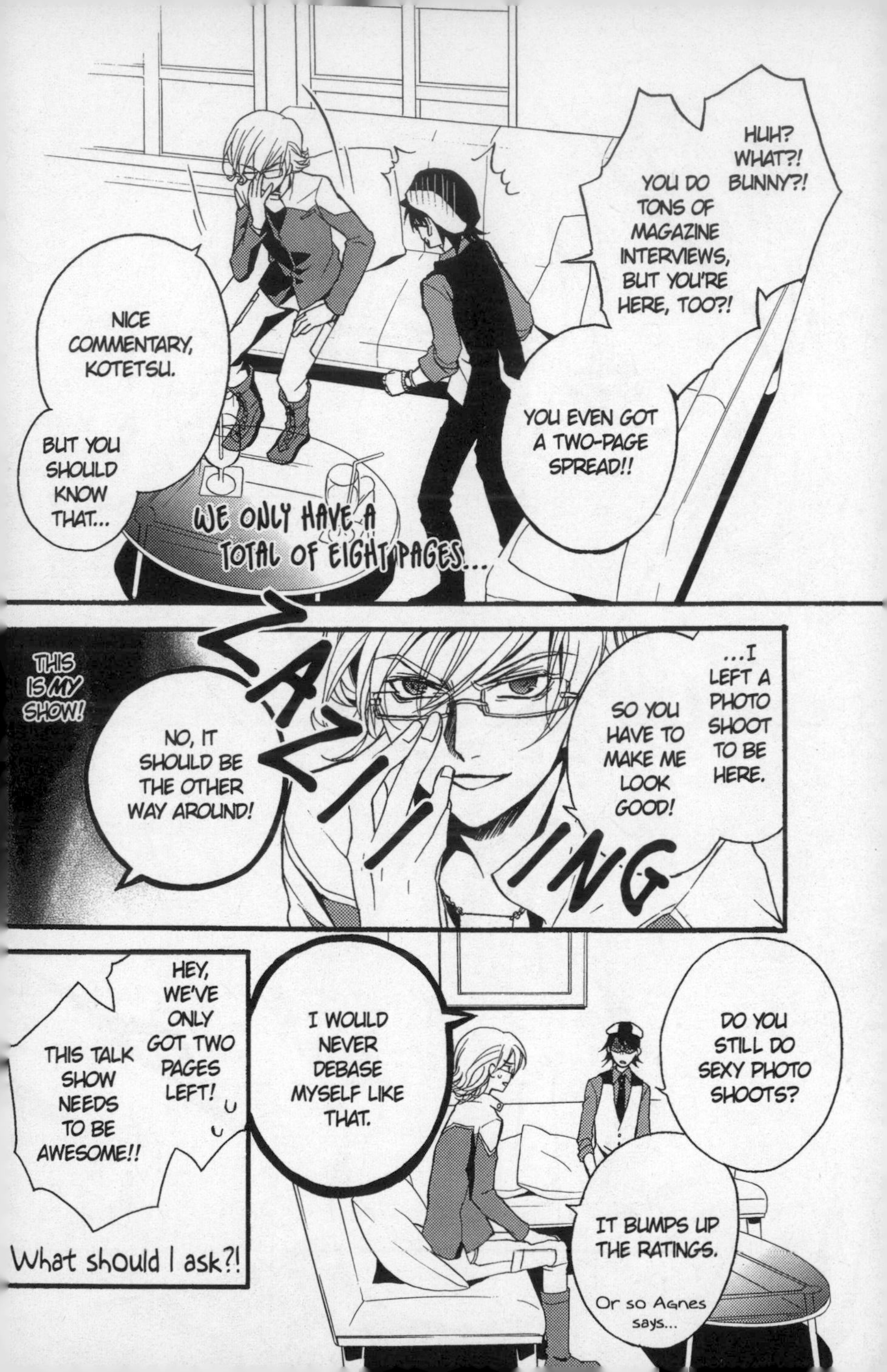
HUH? WHAT?! BUNNY?!
YOU DO TONS OF MAGAZINE INTERVIEWS, BUT YOU'RE HERE, TOO?!
YOU EVEN GOT A TWO-PAGE SPREAD!!
NICE COMMENTARY, KOTETSU.
BUT YOU SHOULD KNOW THAT...
WE ONLY HAVE A TOTAL OF EIGHT PAGES...
...I LEFT A PHOTO SHOOT TO BE HERE.
SO YOU HAVE TO MAKE ME LOOK GOOD!
ZAZIIING
NO, IT SHOULD BE THE OTHER WAY AROUND!
THIS IS MY SHOW!
DO YOU STILL DO SEXY PHOTO SHOOTS?
IT BUMPS UP THE RATINGS.
Or so Agnes says...
I WOULD NEVER DEBASE MYSELF LIKE THAT.
HEY, WE'VE ONLY GOT TWO PAGES LEFT!
THIS TALK SHOW NEEDS TO BE AWESOME!!
What should I ask?!

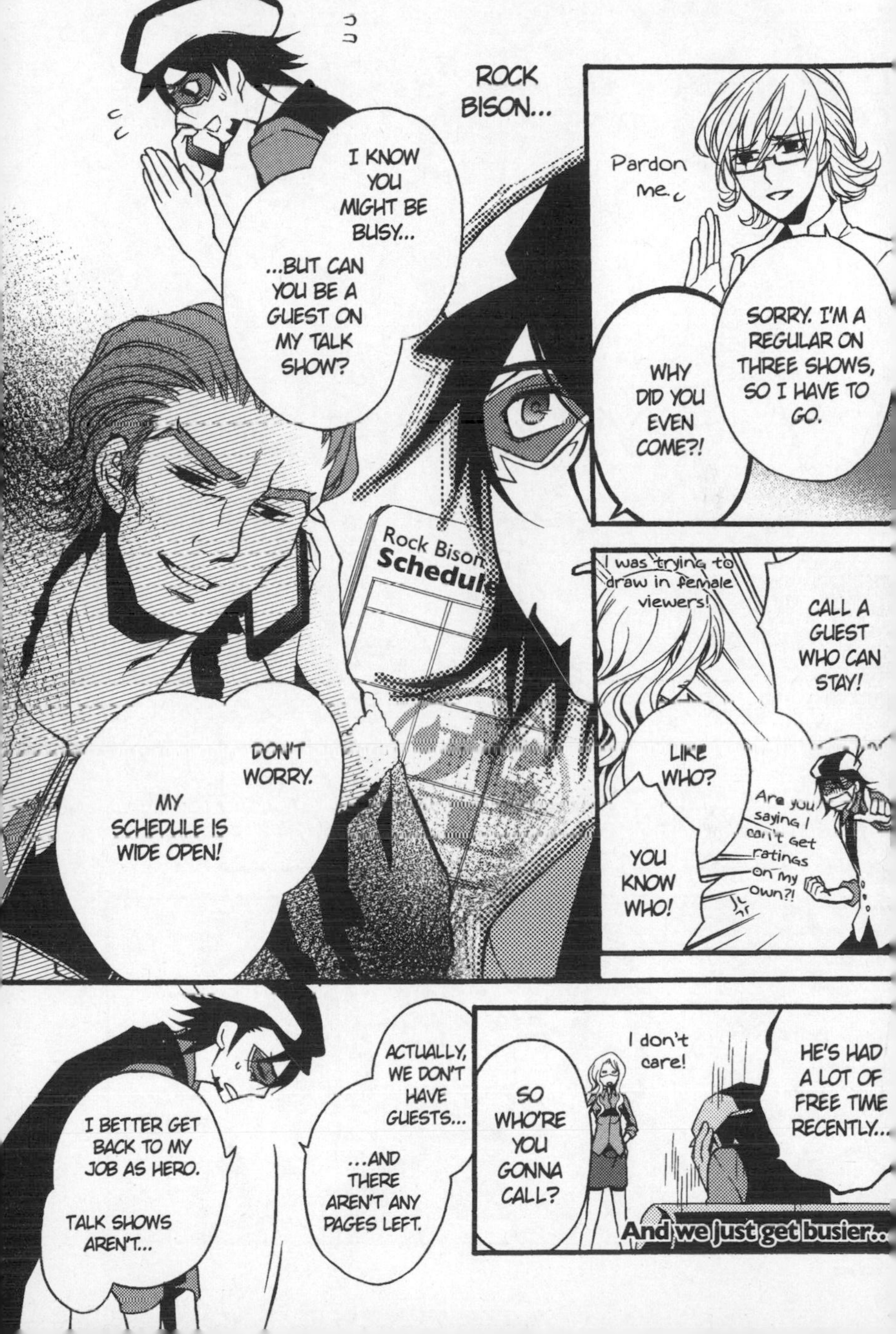
Pardon me.
SORRY. I'M A REGULAR ON THREE SHOWS, SO I HAVE TO GO.
WHY DID YOU EVEN COME?!
I was trying to draw in female viewers!
CALL A GUEST WHO CAN STAY!
LIKE WHO?
YOU KNOW WHO!
Are you saying I can't get ratings on my own?!
ROCK BISON...
I KNOW YOU MIGHT BE BUSY...
...BUT CAN YOU BE A GUEST ON MY TALK SHOW?
Rock Bison Schedule
DON'T WORRY.
MY SCHEDULE IS WIDE OPEN!
HE'S HAD A LOT OF FREE TIME RECENTLY...
I don't care!
SO WHO'RE YOU GONNA CALL?
And we just get busier...
ACTUALLY, WE DON'T HAVE GUESTS...
...AND THERE AREN'T ANY PAGES LEFT.
I BETTER GET BACK TO MY JOB AS HERO.
TALK SHOWS AREN'T...

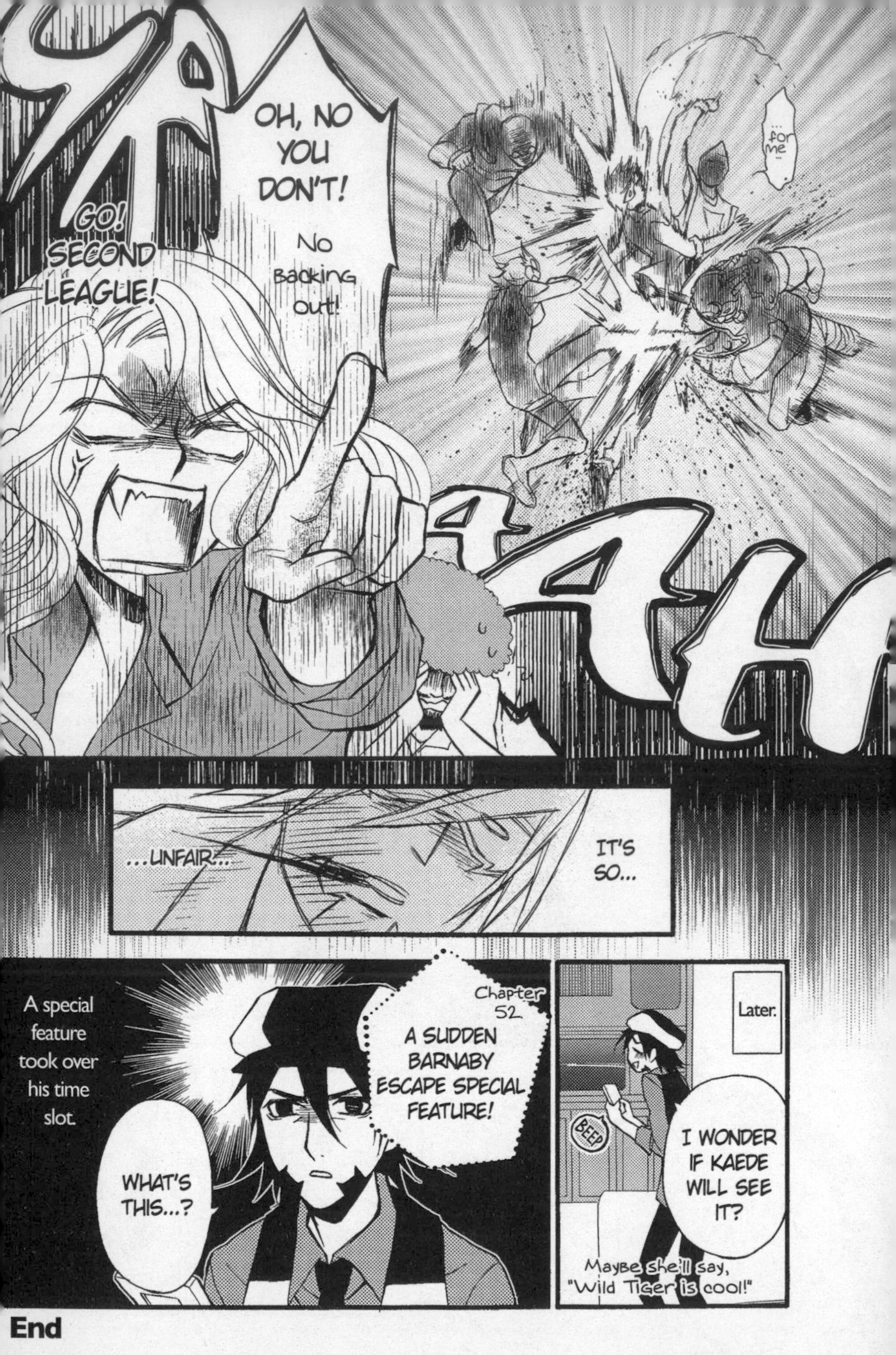
...for me...
OH, NO YOU DON'T!
No Backing out!
GO! SECOND LEAGUE!
IT'S SO...
...UNFAIR...
Later.
BEEP
I WONDER IF KAEDE WILL SEE IT?
Maybe she'll say, "Wild Tiger is cool!"
Chapter 52
A SUDDEN BARNABY ESCAPE SPECIAL FEATURE!
A special feature took over his time slot.
WHAT'S THIS...?

End

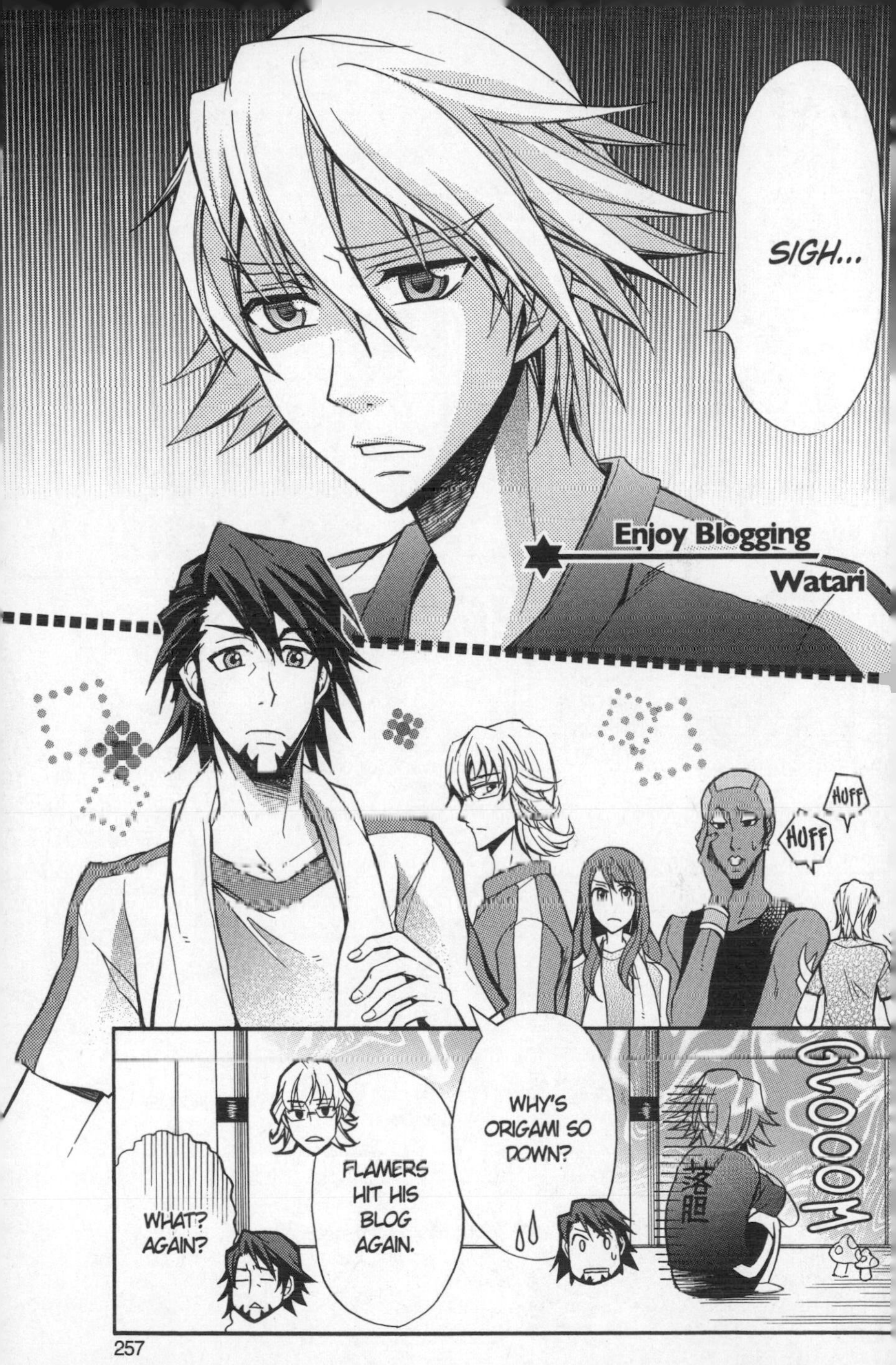
SIGH...
Enjoy Blogging
Watari
HUFF
HUFF
GLOOOM
落胆
WHY'S ORIGAMI SO DOWN?
FLAMERS HIT HIS BLOG AGAIN.
WHAT? AGAIN?

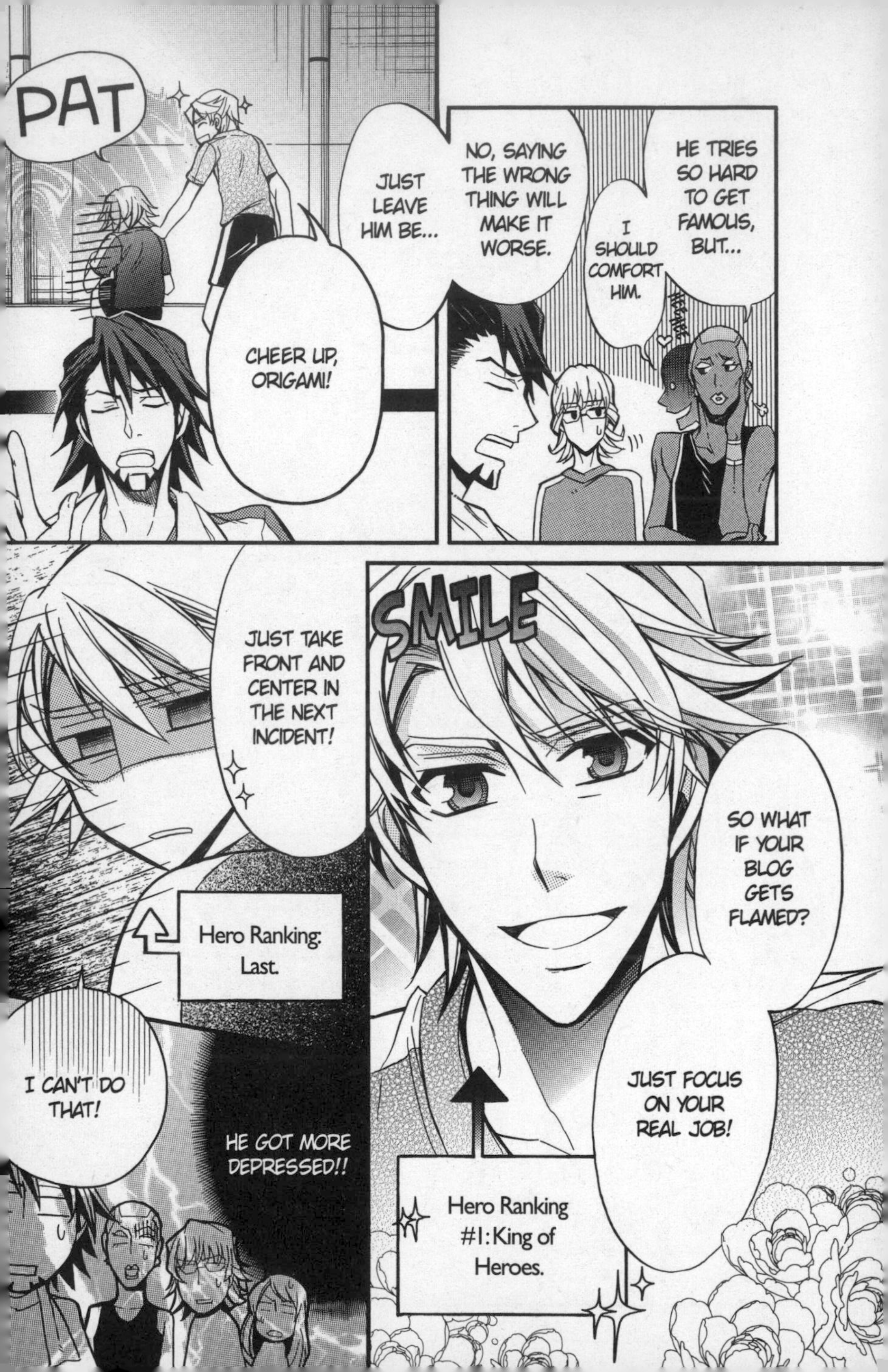
HE TRIES SO HARD TO GET FAMOUS, BUT...
I SHOULD COMFORT HIM.
NO, SAYING THE WRONG THING WILL MAKE IT WORSE.
JUST LEAVE HIM BE...
CHEER UP, ORIGAMI!
PAT
SMILE
SO WHAT IF YOUR BLOG GETS FLAMED?
JUST FOCUS ON YOUR REAL JOB!
Hero Ranking #1: King of Heroes.
JUST TAKE FRONT AND CENTER IN THE NEXT INCIDENT!
Hero Ranking: Last.
I CAN'T DO THAT!
HE GOT MORE DEPRESSED!!

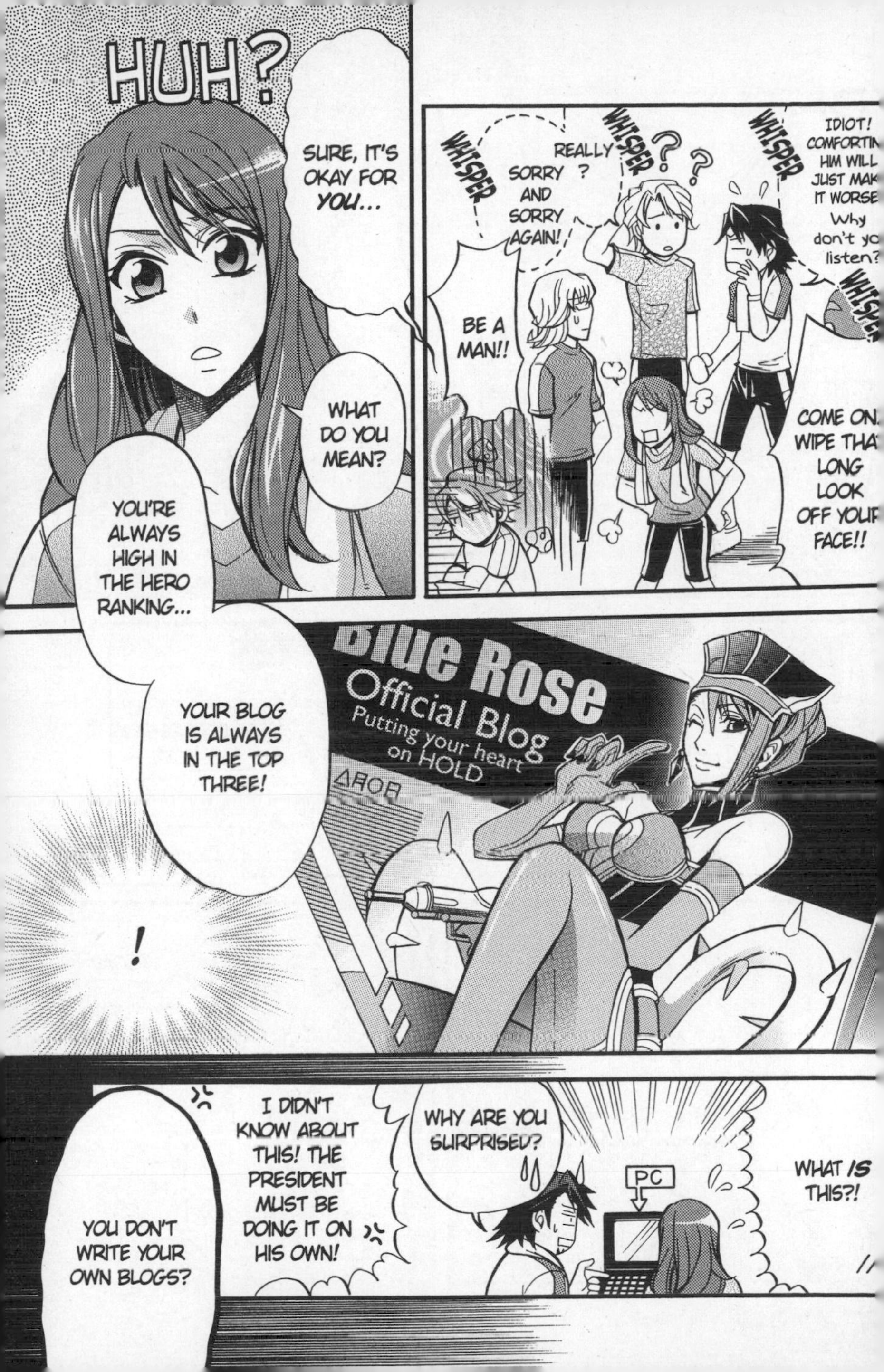
IDIOT! COMFORTIN HIM WILL JUST MAK IT WORSE
Why don't yo listen?
WHISPER
WHISPER
??
REALLY ?
WHISPER
SORRY AND SORRY AGAIN!
COME ON WIPE THA LONG LOOK OFF YOUF FACE!!
BE A MAN!!
HUH?
SURE, IT'S OKAY FOR *YOU*...
WHAT DO YOU MEAN?
YOU'RE ALWAYS HIGH IN THE HERO RANKING...
Blue Rose
Official Blog
Putting your heart on HOLD
YOUR BLOG IS ALWAYS IN THE TOP THREE!
!
WHAT *IS* THIS?!
PC
WHY ARE YOU SURPRISED?
I DIDN'T KNOW ABOUT THIS! THE PRESIDENT MUST BE DOING IT ON HIS OWN!
YOU DON'T WRITE YOUR OWN BLOGS?

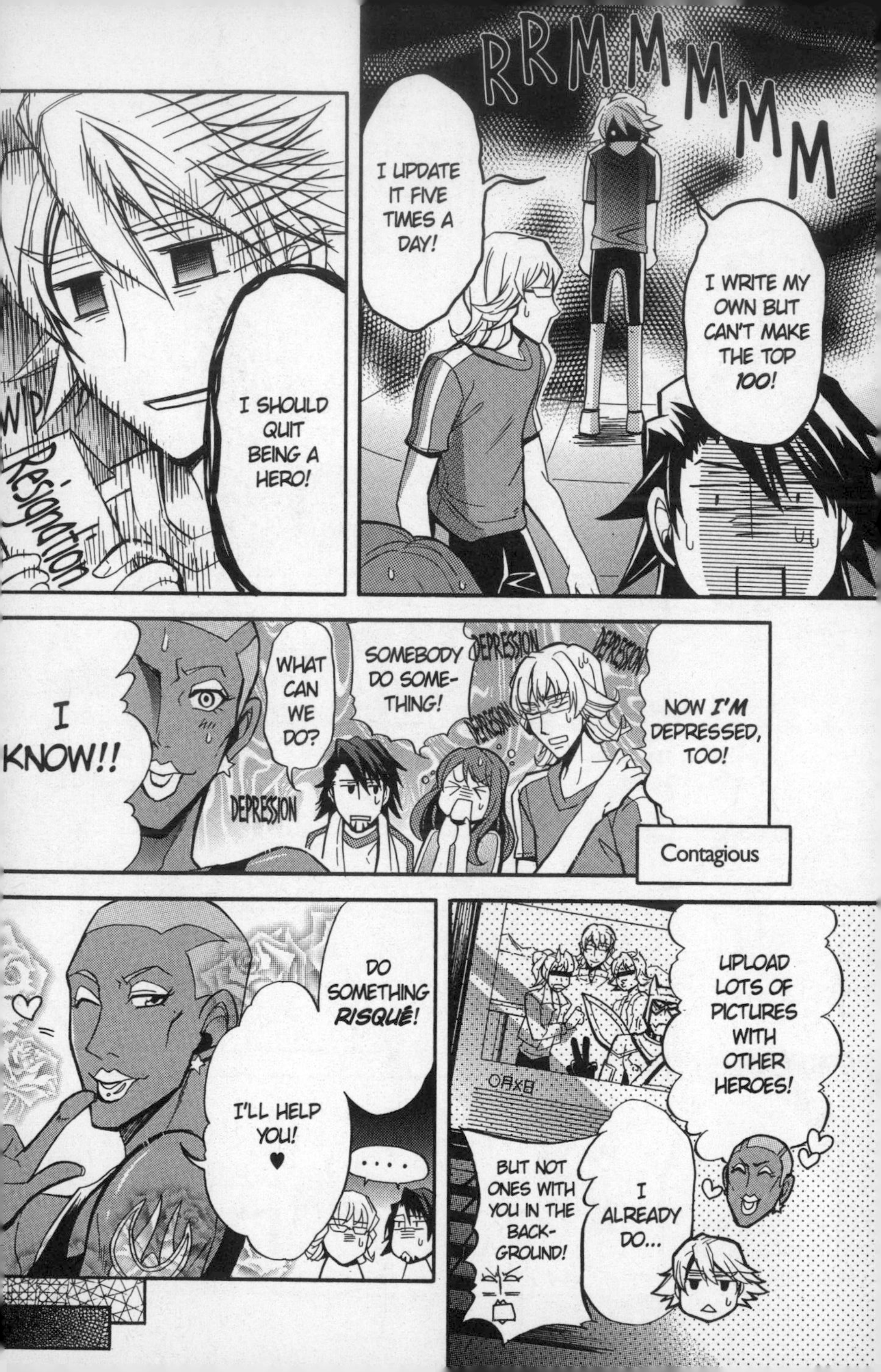

RRMMMMMM
I WRITE MY OWN BUT CAN'T MAKE THE TOP 100!
I UPDATE IT FIVE TIMES A DAY!
I SHOULD QUIT BEING A HERO!
Resignation
NOW *I'M* DEPRESSED, TOO!
Contagious
DEPRESSION
DEPRESSION
DEPRESSION
SOMEBODY DO SOME-THING!
WHAT CAN WE DO?
DEPRESSION
I KNOW!!
UPLOAD LOTS OF PICTURES WITH OTHER HEROES!
I ALREADY DO...
BUT NOT ONES WITH YOU IN THE BACK-GROUND!
DO SOMETHING ***RISQUÉ***!
I'LL HELP YOU! ♥
....

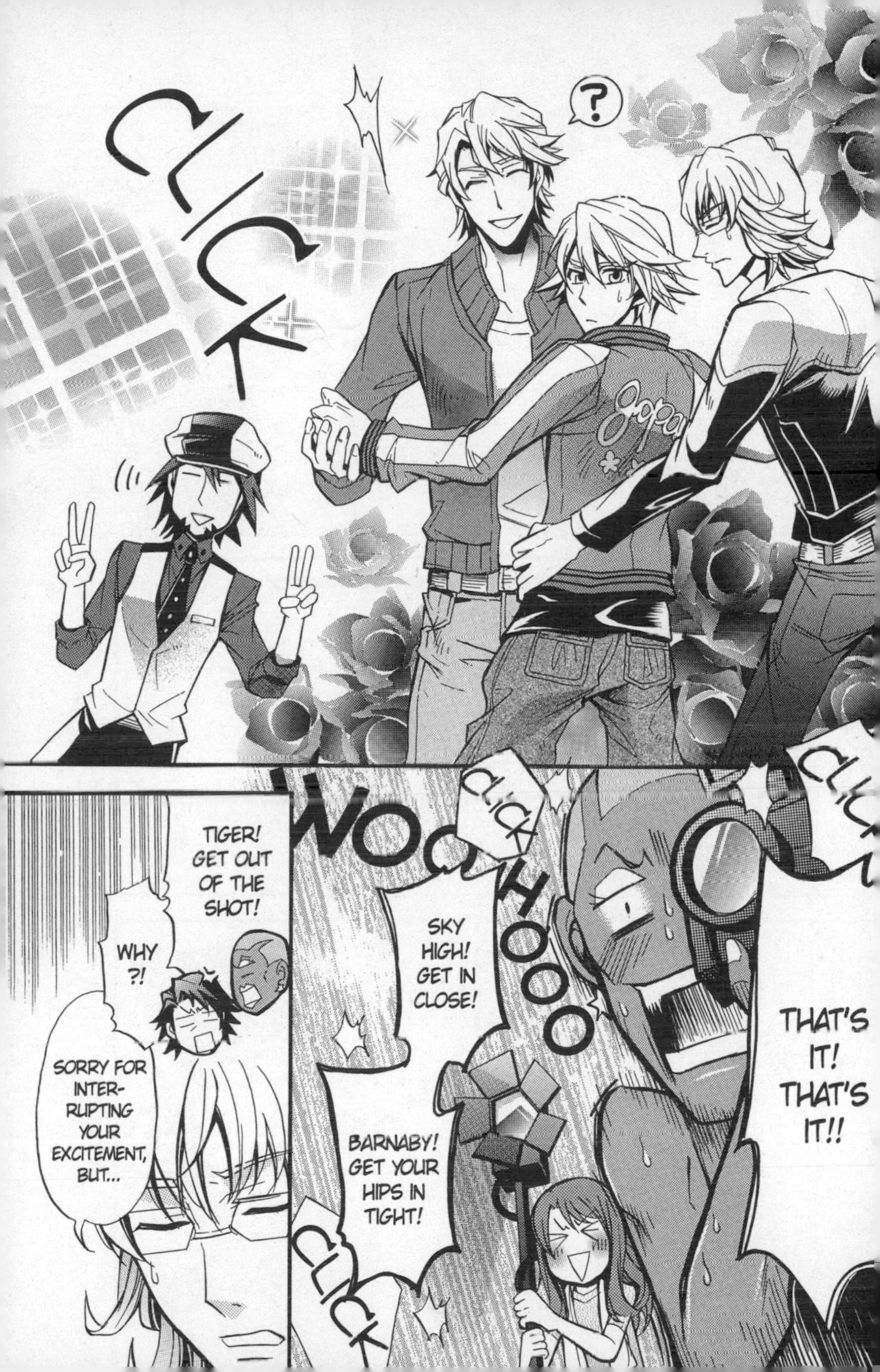

?
CLICK
CLICK
CLICK
WOOHOOOO
THAT'S IT! THAT'S IT!!
SKY HIGH! GET IN CLOSE!
BARNABY! GET YOUR HIPS IN TIGHT!
CLICK
TIGER! GET OUT OF THE SHOT!
WHY?!
SORRY FOR INTERRUPTING YOUR EXCITEMENT, BUT...

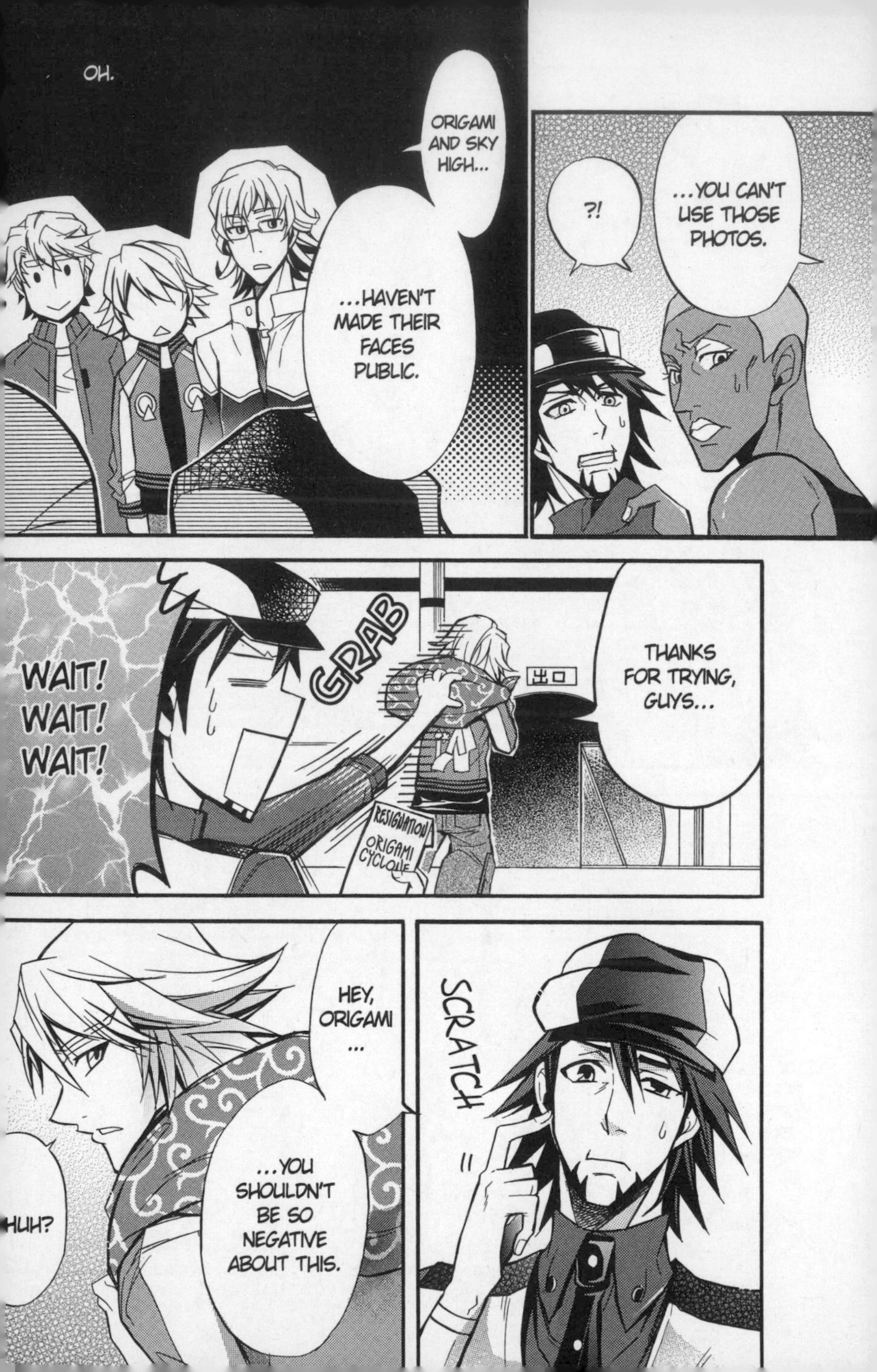
...YOU CAN'T USE THOSE PHOTOS.
?!
ORIGAMI AND SKY HIGH...
...HAVEN'T MADE THEIR FACES PUBLIC.
OH.
THANKS FOR TRYING, GUYS...
GRAB
出口
RESIGNATION ORIGAMI CYCLONE
WAIT! WAIT! WAIT!
SCRATCH
HEY, ORIGAMI ...
...YOU SHOULDN'T BE SO NEGATIVE ABOUT THIS.
HUH?

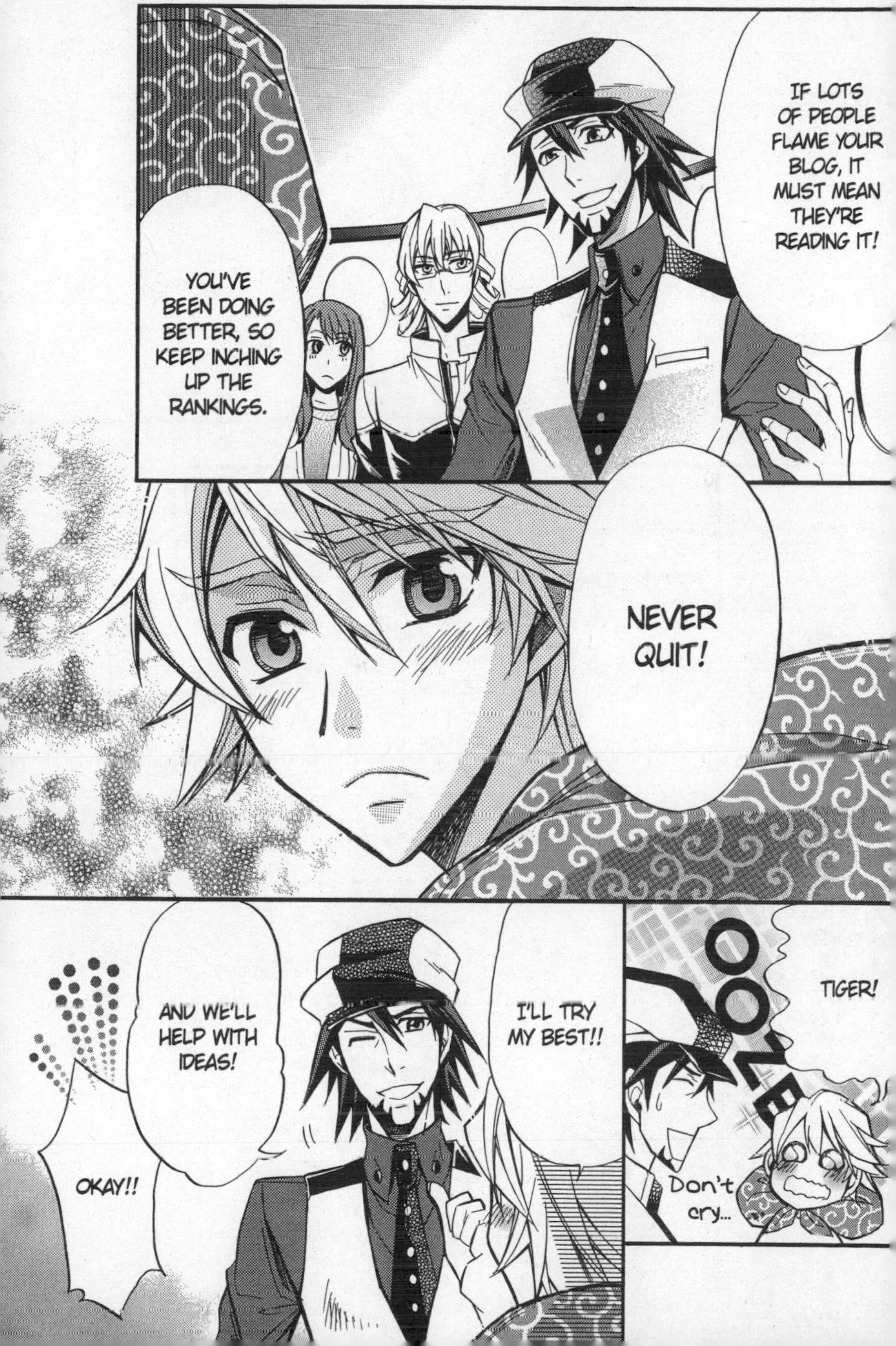
IF LOTS OF PEOPLE FLAME YOUR BLOG, IT MUST MEAN THEY'RE READING IT!
YOU'VE BEEN DOING BETTER, SO KEEP INCHING UP THE RANKINGS.
NEVER QUIT!
OOZE
TIGER!
Don't cry...
I'LL TRY MY BEST!!
AND WE'LL HELP WITH IDEAS!
OKAY!!

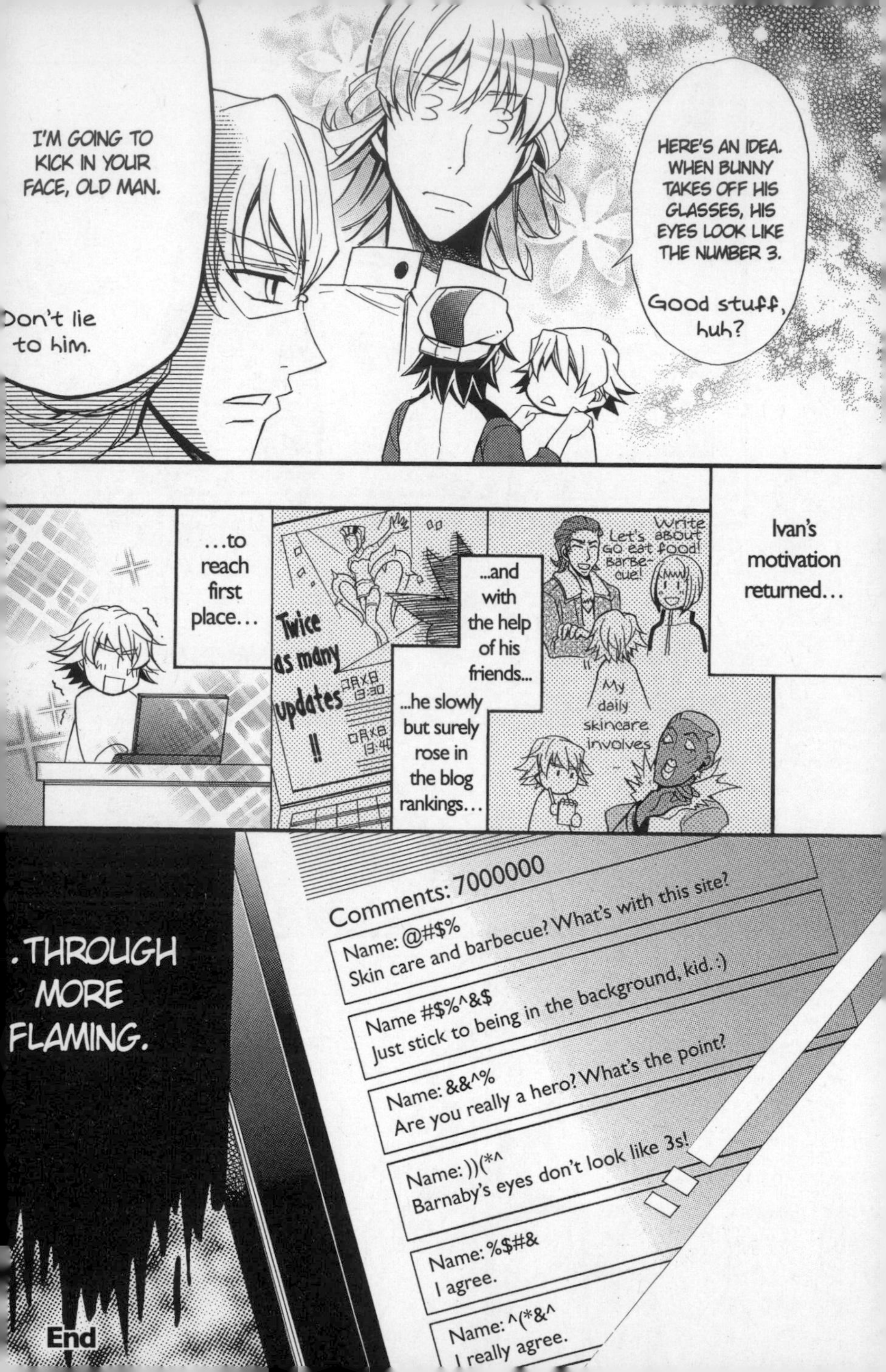
HERE'S AN IDEA. WHEN BUNNY TAKES OFF HIS GLASSES, HIS EYES LOOK LIKE THE NUMBER 3.
Good stuff, huh?
I'M GOING TO KICK IN YOUR FACE, OLD MAN.
Don't lie to him.
Ivan's motivation returned…
…and with the help of his friends…
Write about food!
Let's go eat barbecue!
My daily skincare involves
…he slowly but surely rose in the blog rankings…
Twice as many updates!!
…to reach first place…
Comments: 7000000
Name: @#$%
Skin care and barbecue? What's with this site?
Name #$%^&$
Just stick to being in the background, kid. :)
Name: &&^%
Are you really a hero? What's the point?
Name:))(*^
Barnaby's eyes don't look like 3s!
Name: %$#&
I agree.
Name: ^(*&^
I really agree.
.THROUGH MORE FLAMING.
End

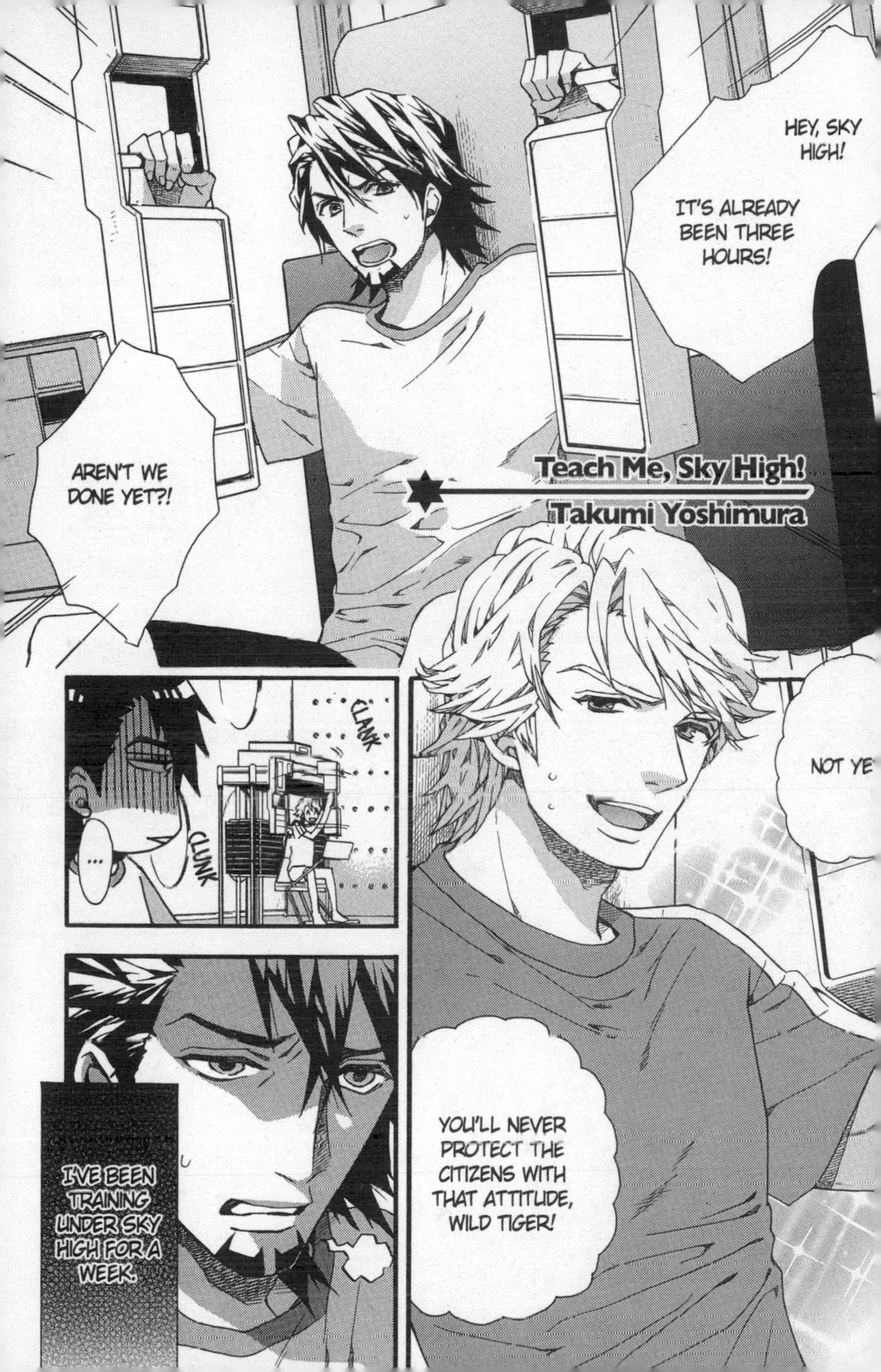
HEY, SKY HIGH!
IT'S ALREADY BEEN THREE HOURS!
AREN'T WE DONE YET?!
Teach Me, Sky High!
Takumi Yoshimura
NOT YE
YOU'LL NEVER PROTECT THE CITIZENS WITH THAT ATTITUDE, WILD TIGER!
CLANK
CLUNK
...
I'VE BEEN TRAINING UNDER SKY HIGH FOR A WEEK.

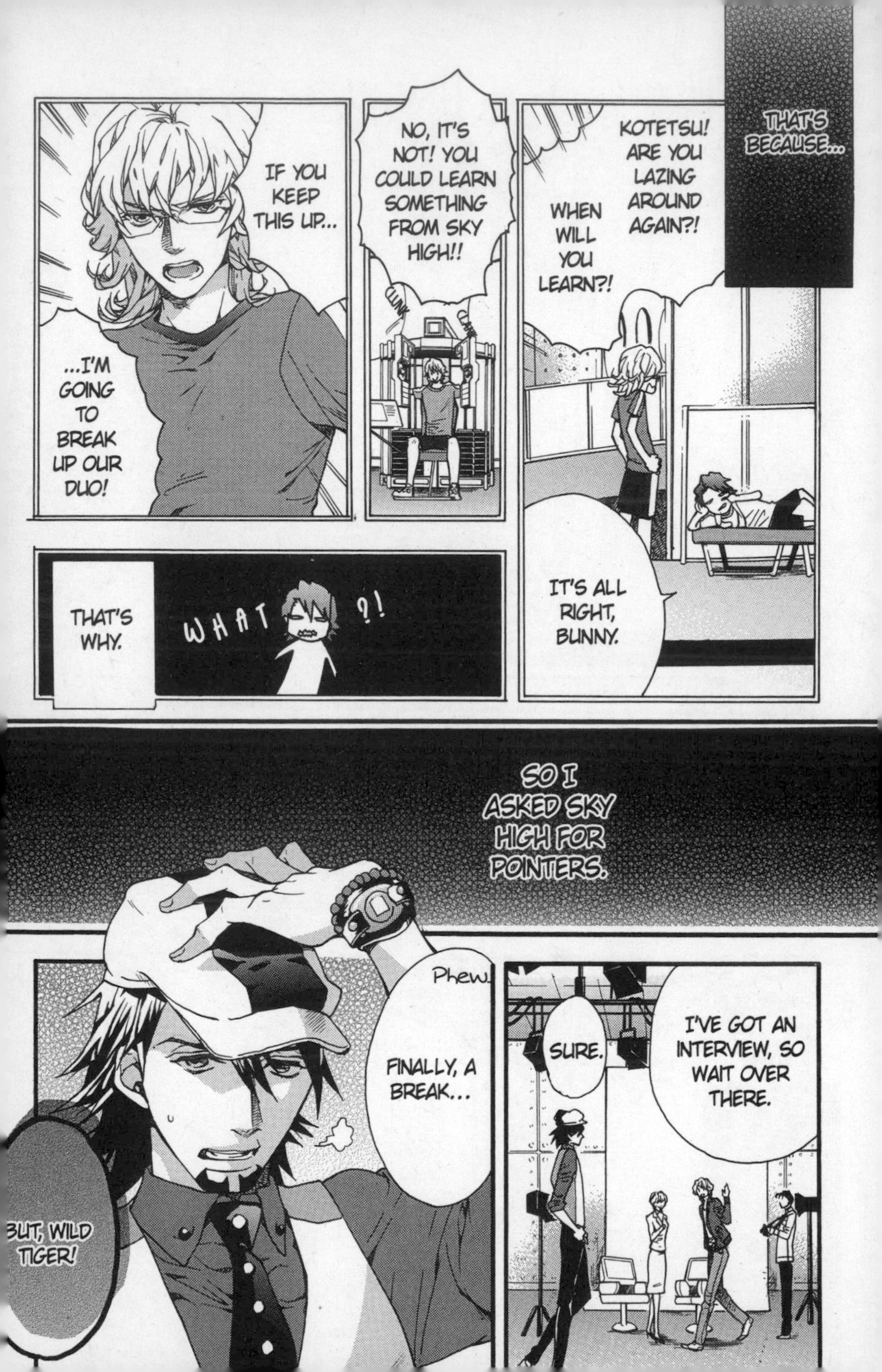
THAT'S BECAUSE...
KOTETSU! ARE YOU LAZING AROUND AGAIN?!
WHEN WILL YOU LEARN?!
IT'S ALL RIGHT, BUNNY.
NO, IT'S NOT! YOU COULD LEARN SOMETHING FROM SKY HIGH!!
IF YOU KEEP THIS UP...
...I'M GOING TO BREAK UP OUR DUO!
WHAT ?!
THAT'S WHY.
SO I ASKED SKY HIGH FOR POINTERS.
I'VE GOT AN INTERVIEW, SO WAIT OVER THERE.
SURE.
Phew.
FINALLY, A BREAK...
BUT, WILD TIGER!

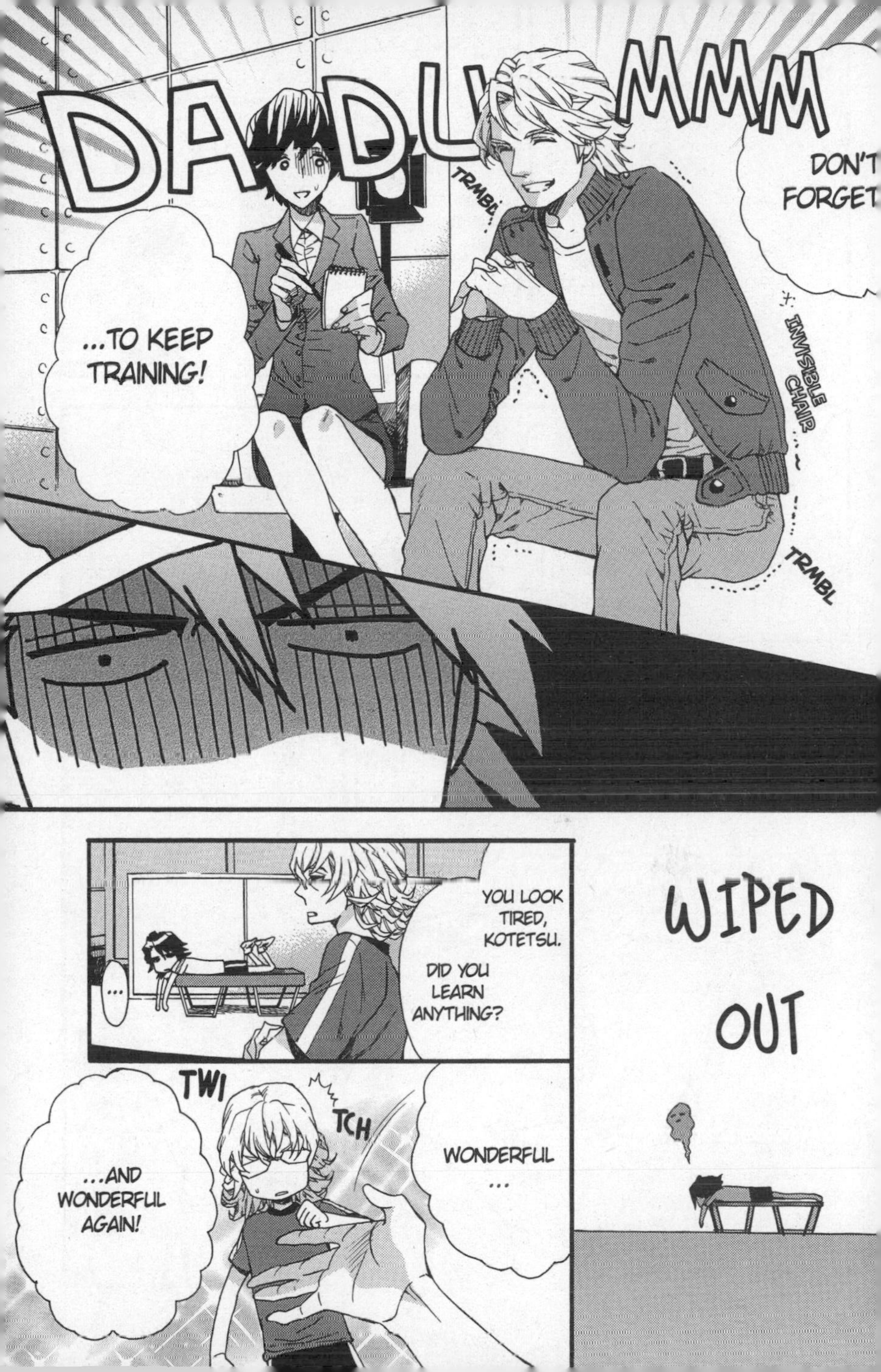
DA DU MMM
DON'T FORGET
TRMBL
...TO KEEP TRAINING!
INVISIBLE CHAIR
TRMBL
WIPED OUT
YOU LOOK TIRED, KOTETSU.
DID YOU LEARN ANYTHING?
...
WONDERFUL ...
TWI TCH
...AND WONDERFUL AGAIN!

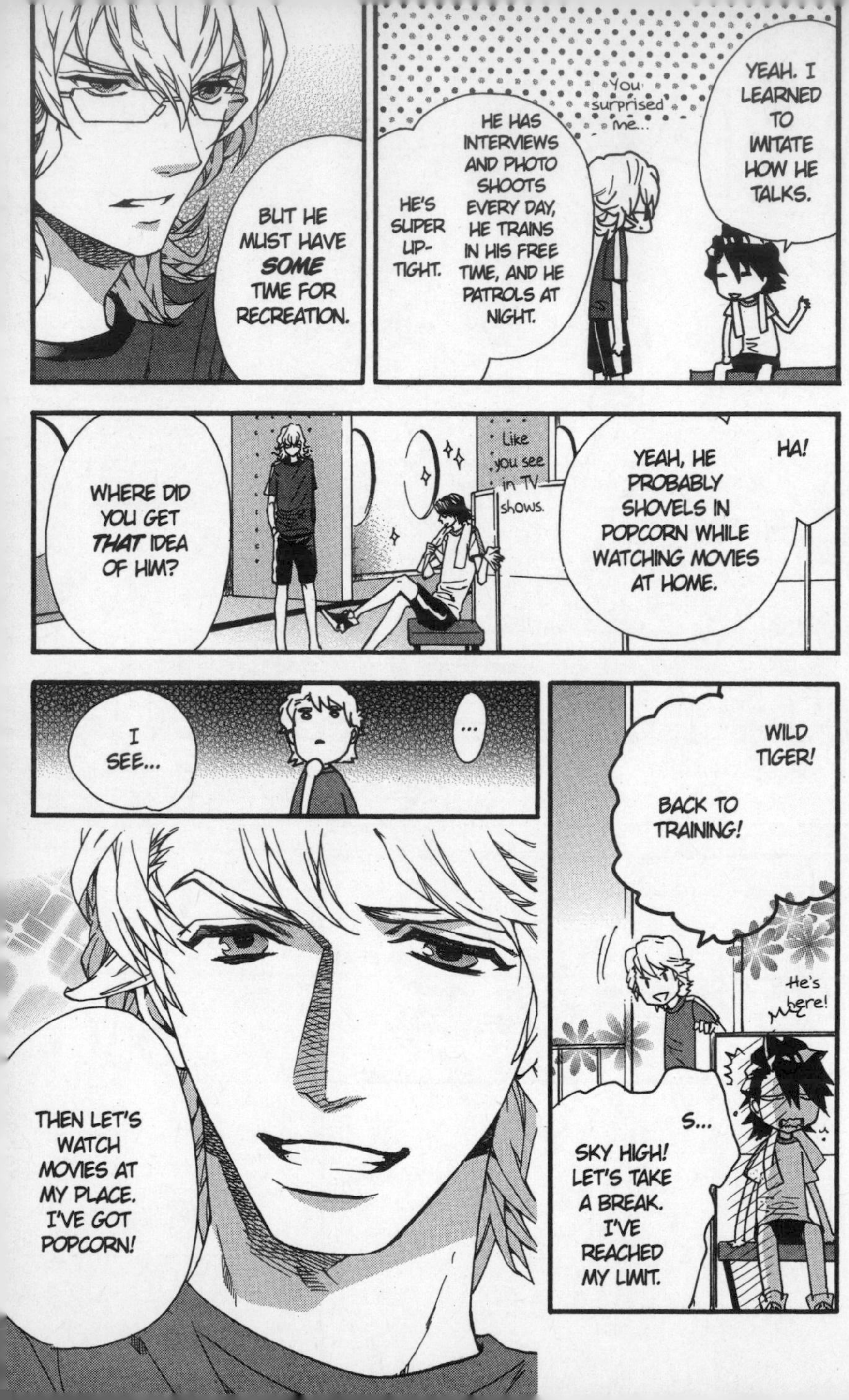
YEAH. I LEARNED TO IMITATE HOW HE TALKS.
You surprised me...
HE HAS INTERVIEWS AND PHOTO SHOOTS EVERY DAY, HE TRAINS IN HIS FREE TIME, AND HE PATROLS AT NIGHT.
HE'S SUPER UP-TIGHT.
BUT HE MUST HAVE *SOME* TIME FOR RECREATION.
HA!
YEAH, HE PROBABLY SHOVELS IN POPCORN WHILE WATCHING MOVIES AT HOME.
Like you see in TV shows.
WHERE DID YOU GET *THAT* IDEA OF HIM?
WILD TIGER!
BACK TO TRAINING!
He's here!
S...
SKY HIGH! LET'S TAKE A BREAK. I'VE REACHED MY LIMIT.
...
I SEE...
THEN LET'S WATCH MOVIES AT MY PLACE. I'VE GOT POPCORN!

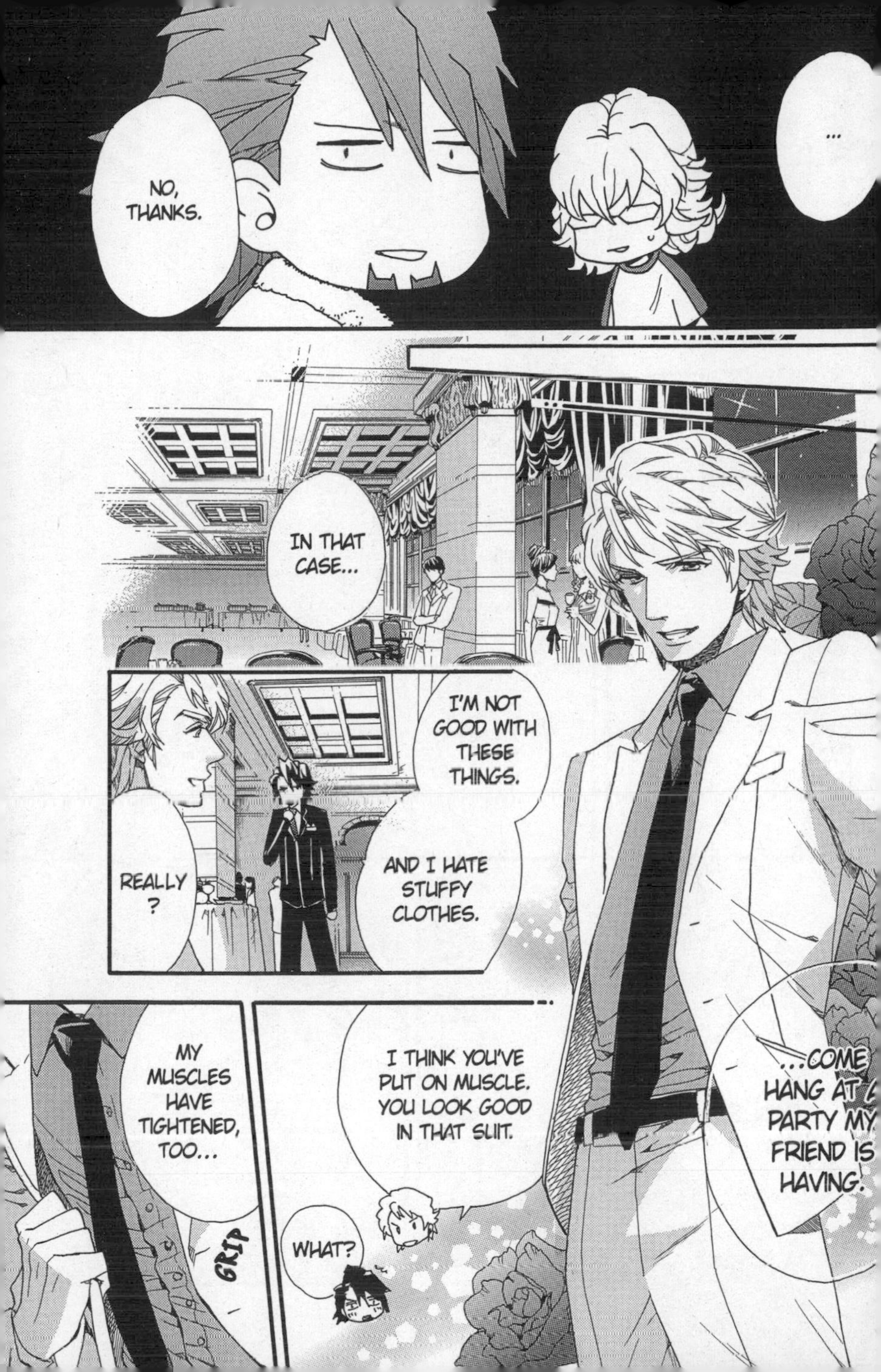
...
NO, THANKS.
IN THAT CASE...
...COME HANG AT A PARTY MY FRIEND IS HAVING.
I'M NOT GOOD WITH THESE THINGS.
AND I HATE STUFFY CLOTHES.
REALLY?
I THINK YOU'VE PUT ON MUSCLE. YOU LOOK GOOD IN THAT SUIT.
WHAT?
MY MUSCLES HAVE TIGHTENED, TOO...
GRIP

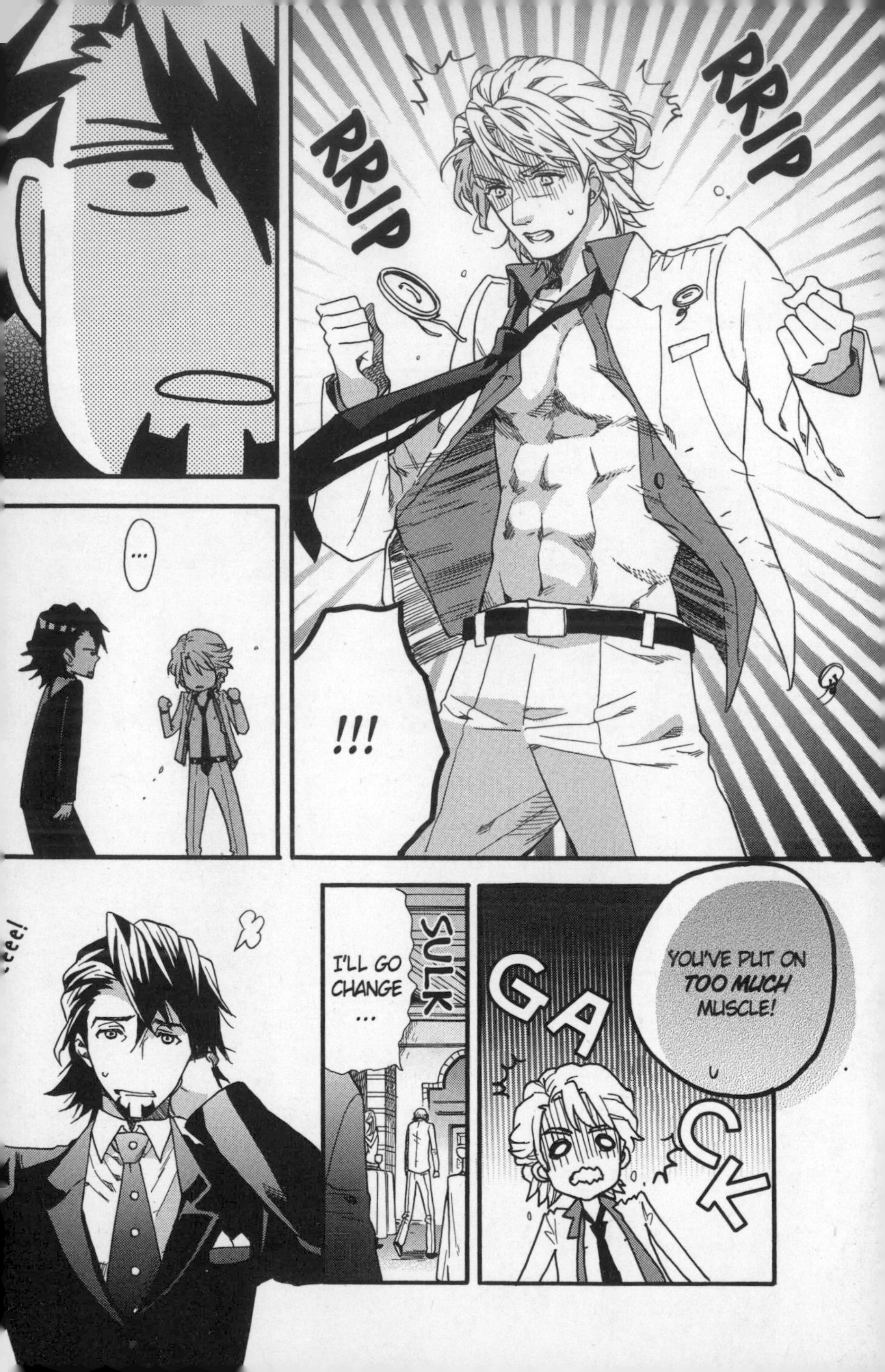
RRIP
RRIP
!!!
...
YOU'VE PUT ON TOO MUCH MUSCLE!
GACK
SULK
I'LL GO CHANGE ...

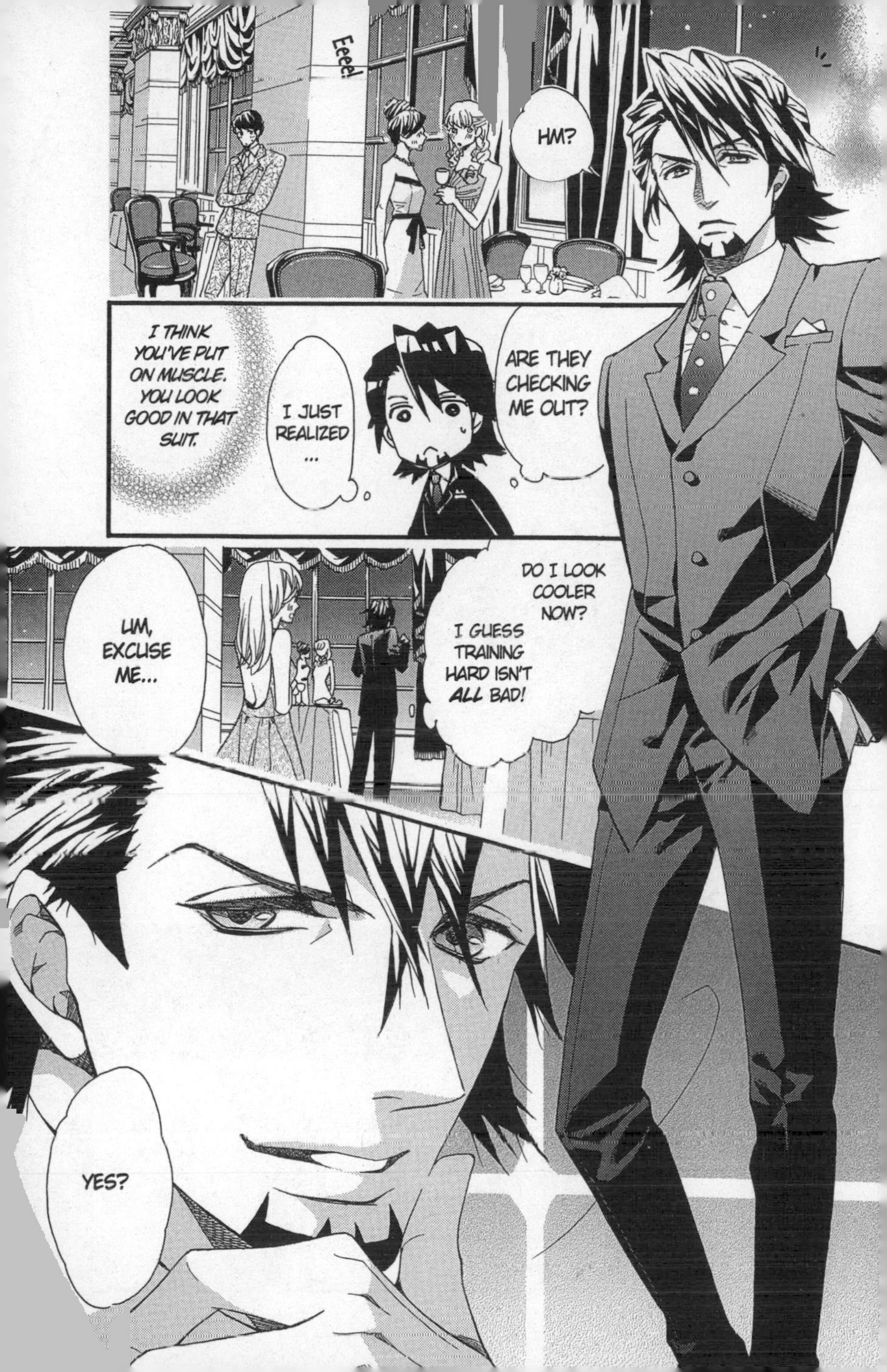
HM?
Eeee!
ARE THEY CHECKING ME OUT?
I JUST REALIZED ...
I THINK YOU'VE PUT ON MUSCLE. YOU LOOK GOOD IN THAT SUIT.
DO I LOOK COOLER NOW?
I GUESS TRAINING HARD ISN'T ALL BAD!
UM, EXCUSE ME...
YES?

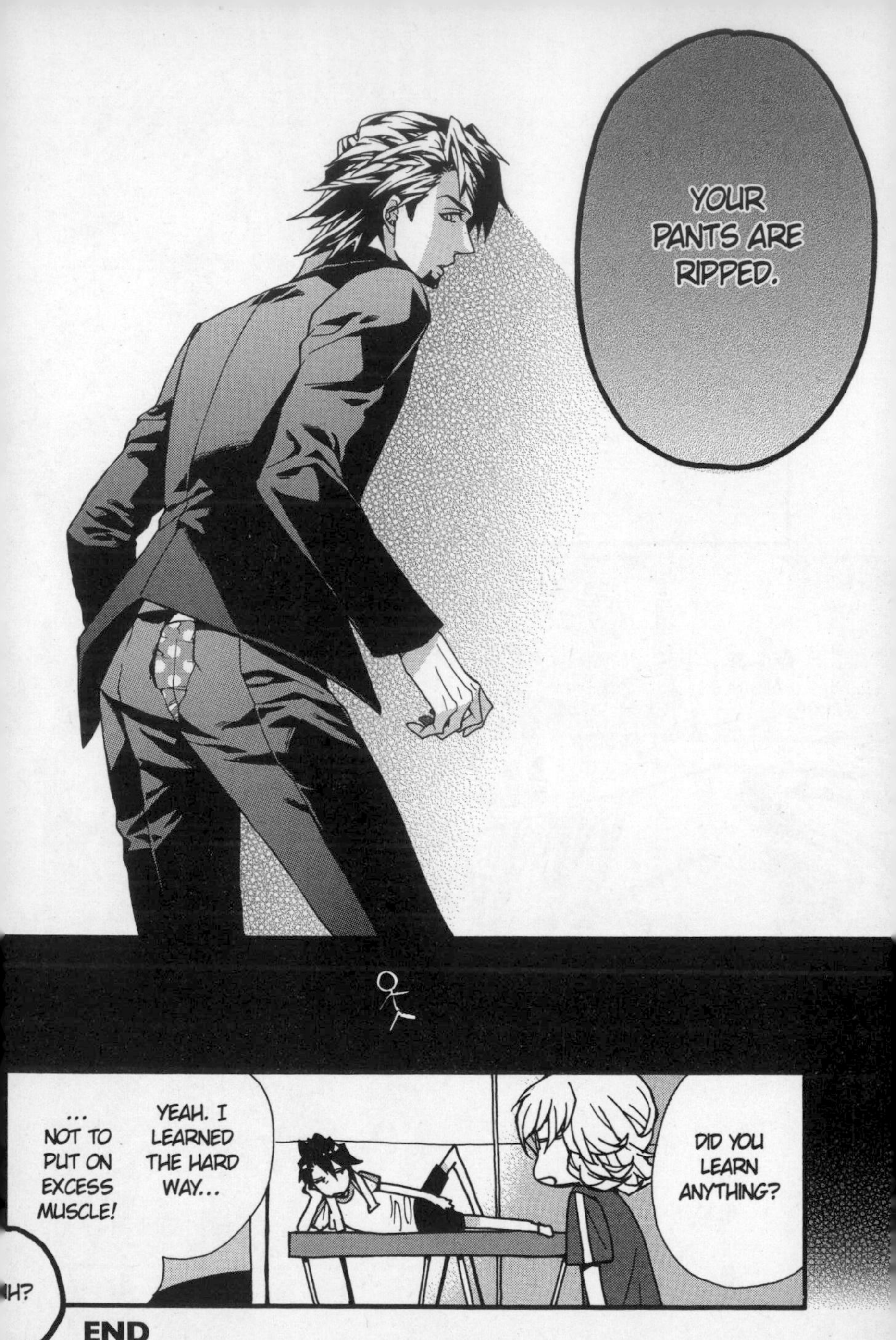
YOUR PANTS ARE RIPPED.
DID YOU LEARN ANYTHING?
YEAH. I LEARNED THE HARD WAY...
... NOT TO PUT ON EXCESS MUSCLE!

END

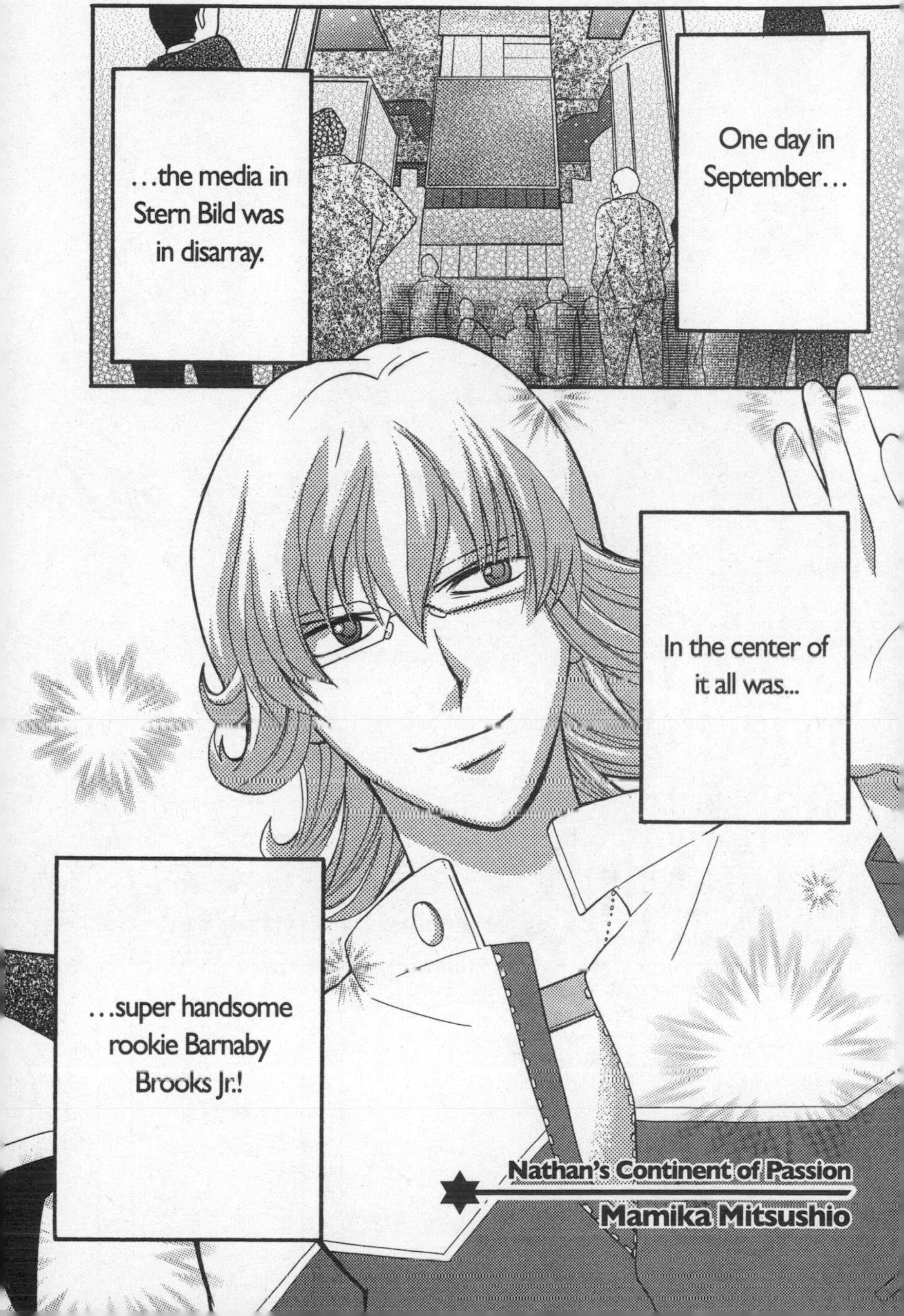
One day in September…
…the media in Stern Bild was in disarray.
In the center of it all was...
…super handsome rookie Barnaby Brooks Jr.!
Nathan's Continent of Passion
Mamika Mitsushio

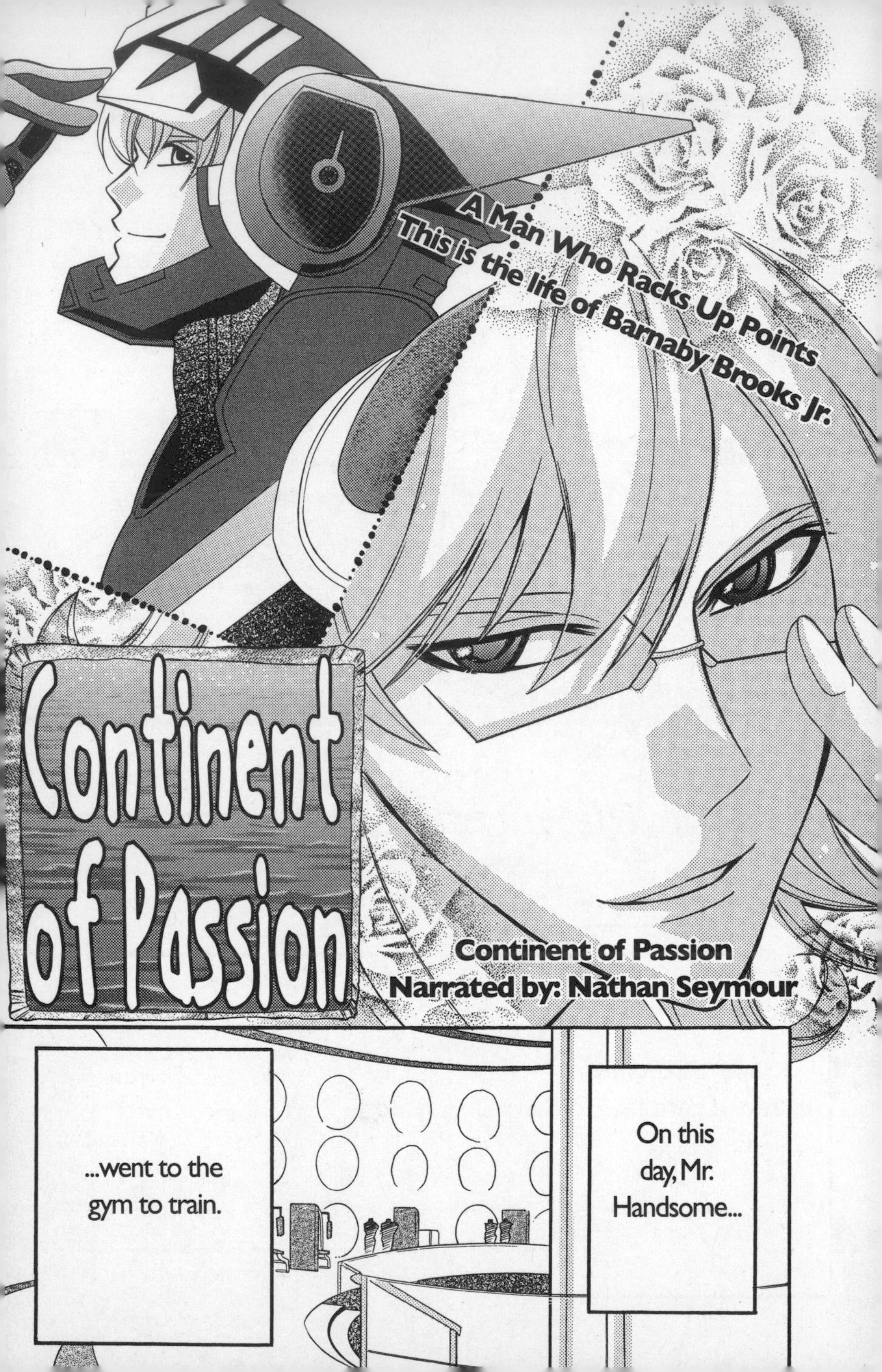
A Man Who Racks Up Points
This is the life of Barnaby Brooks Jr.
Continent of Passion
Continent of Passion
Narrated by: Nathan Seymour
On this day, Mr. Handsome...
...went to the gym to train.

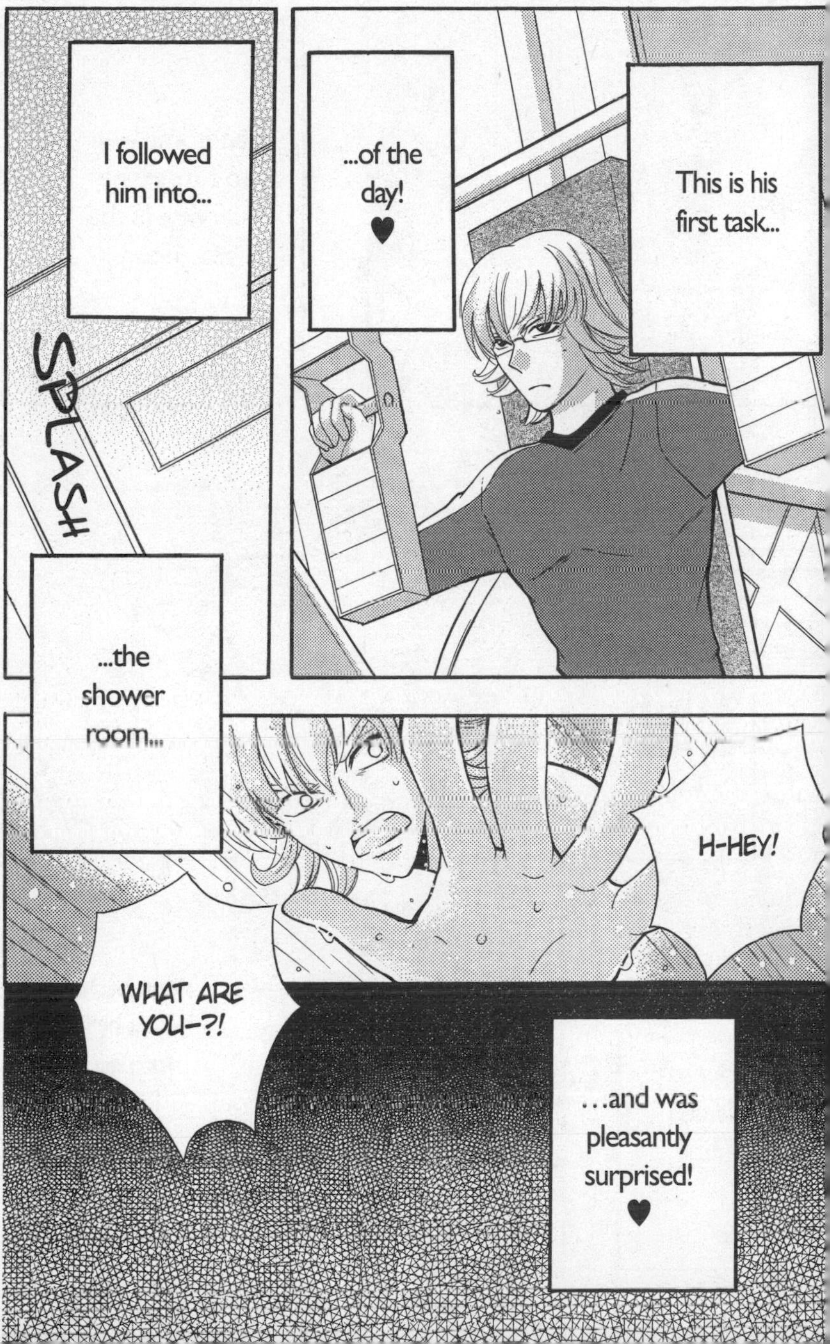
This is his first task...
...of the day! ♥
I followed him into...
SPLASH
...the shower room...
H-HEY!
WHAT ARE YOU-?!
. . .and was pleasantly surprised! ♥

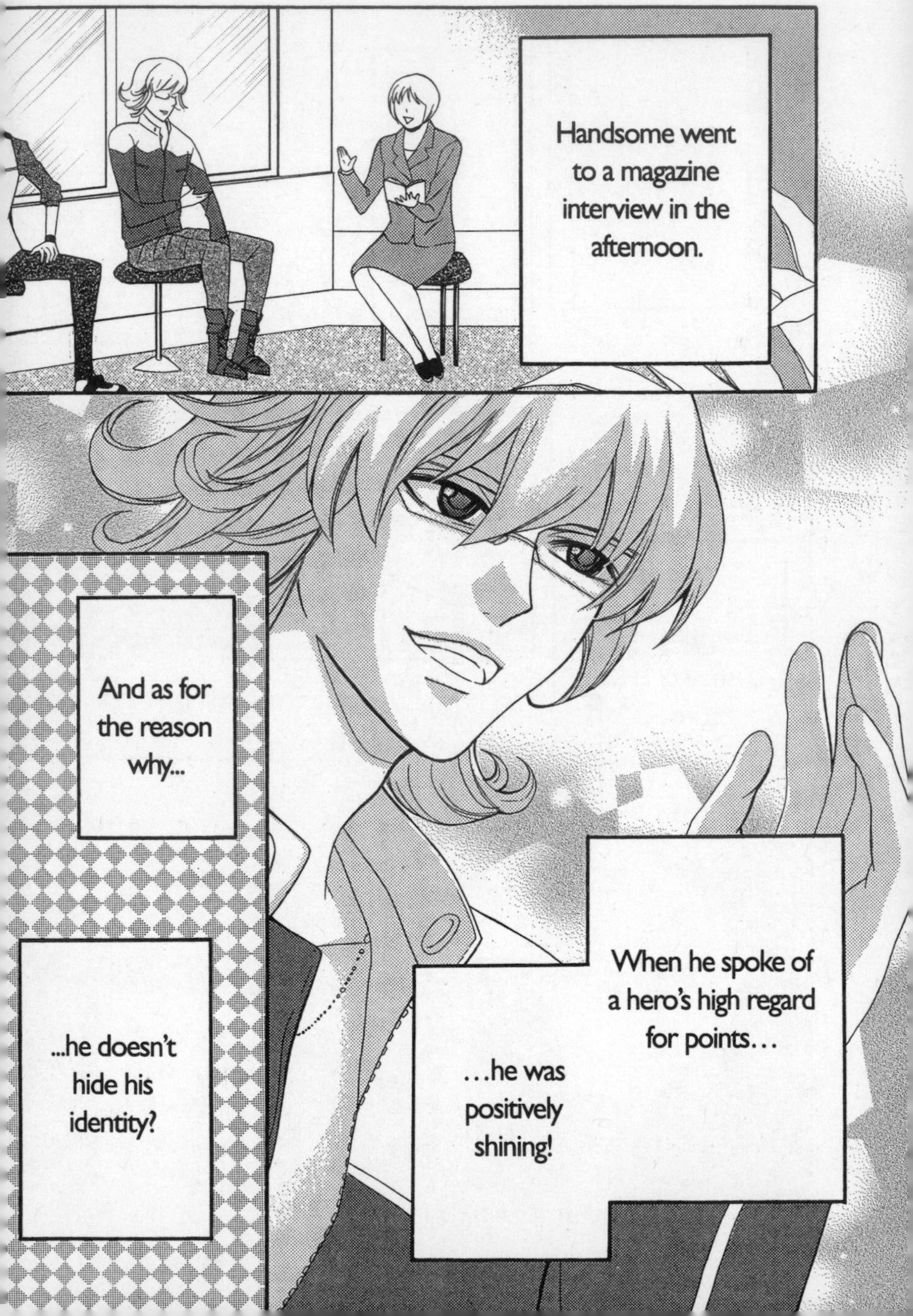
Handsome went to a magazine interview in the afternoon.
When he spoke of a hero's high regard for points…
…he was positively shining!
And as for the reason why...
...he doesn't hide his identity?

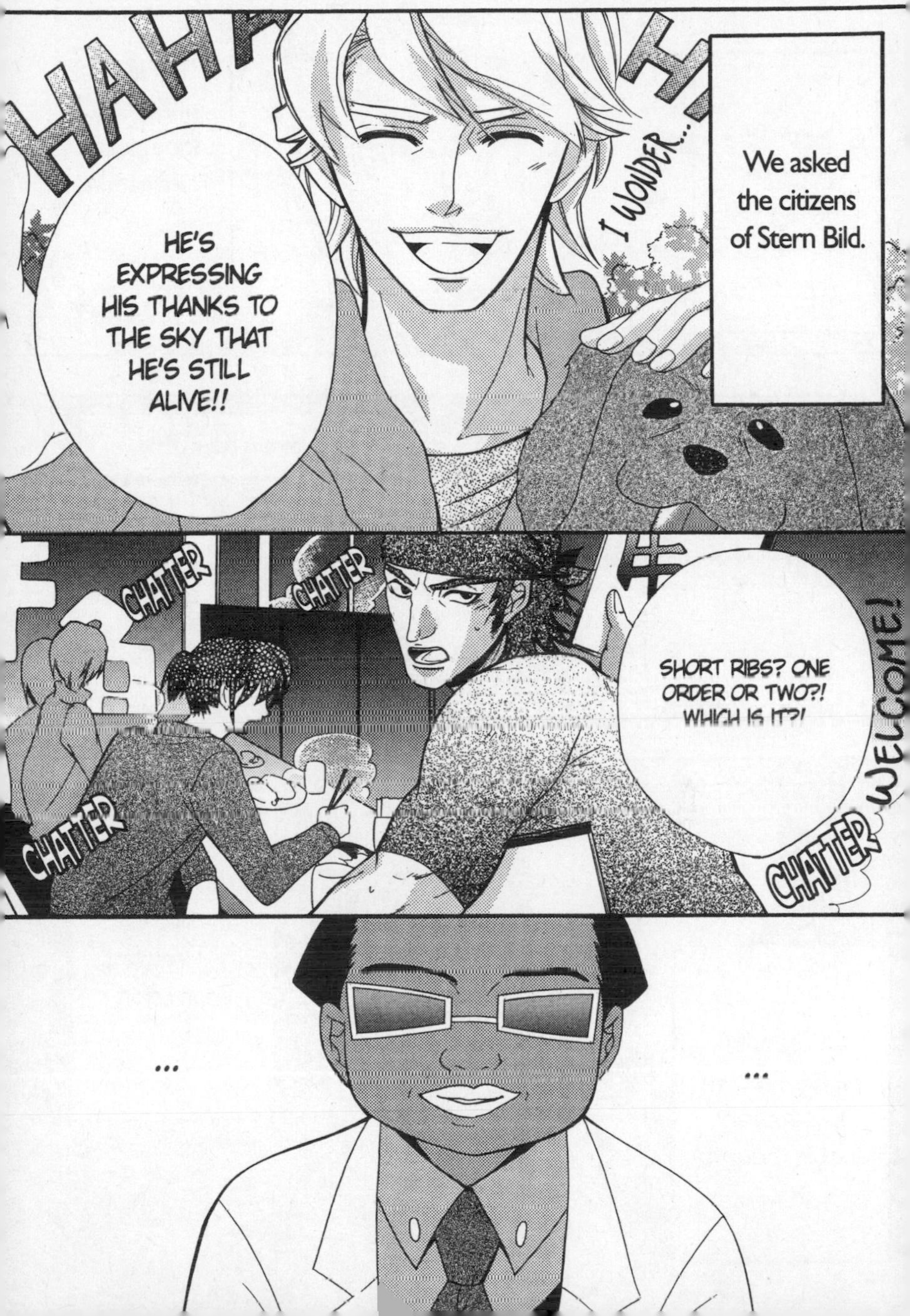
We asked the citizens of Stern Bild.
I WONDER...
HAHA
HE'S EXPRESSING HIS THANKS TO THE SKY THAT HE'S STILL ALIVE!!
WELCOME!
CHATTER
SHORT RIBS? ONE ORDER OR TWO?! WHICH IS IT?!
CHATTER
CHATTER
CHATTER
...
...

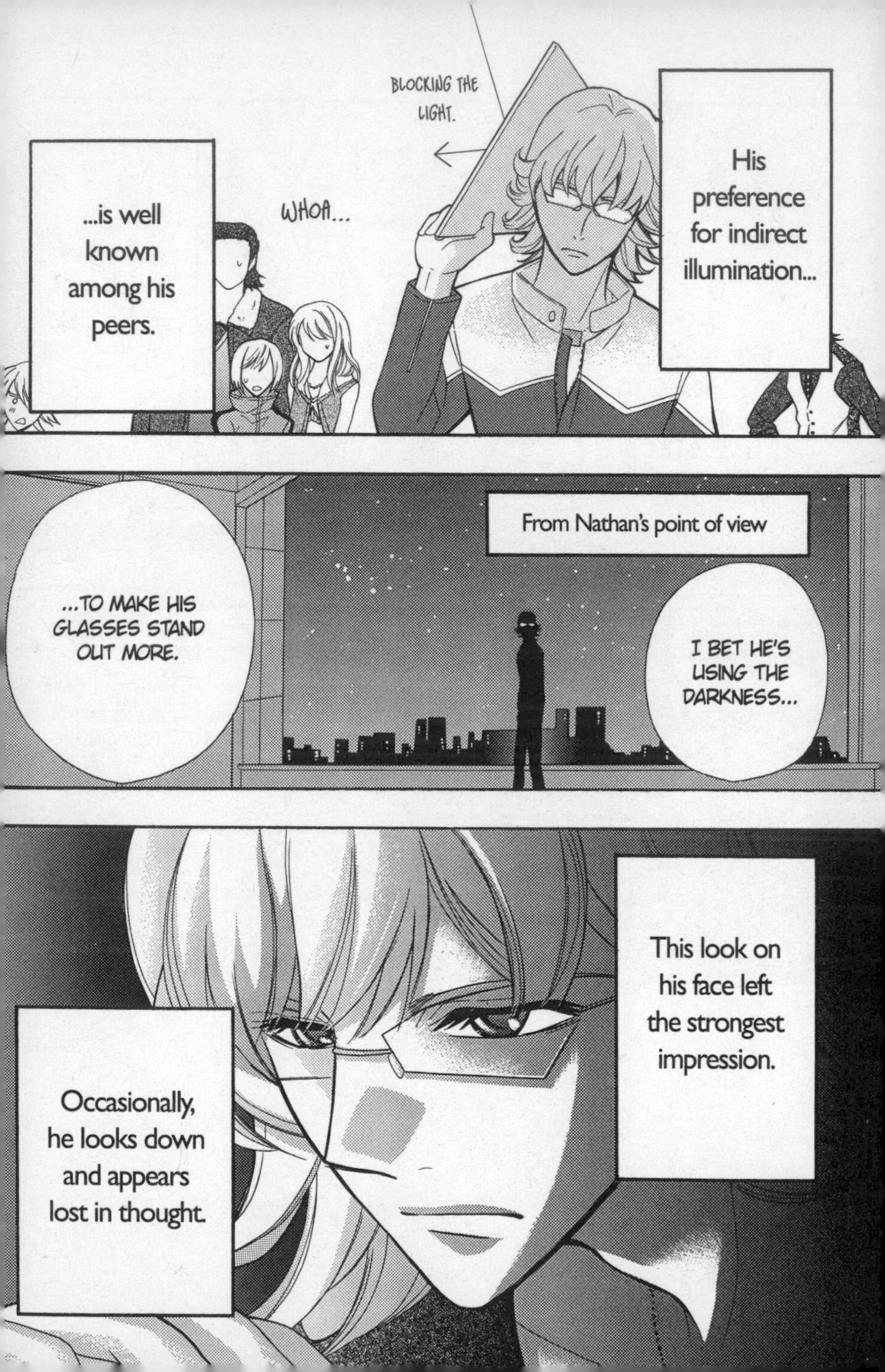
His preference for indirect illumination...
BLOCKING THE LIGHT.
WHOA...
...is well known among his peers.
From Nathan's point of view
I BET HE'S USING THE DARKNESS...
...TO MAKE HIS GLASSES STAND OUT MORE.
This look on his face left the strongest impression.
Occasionally, he looks down and appears lost in thought.

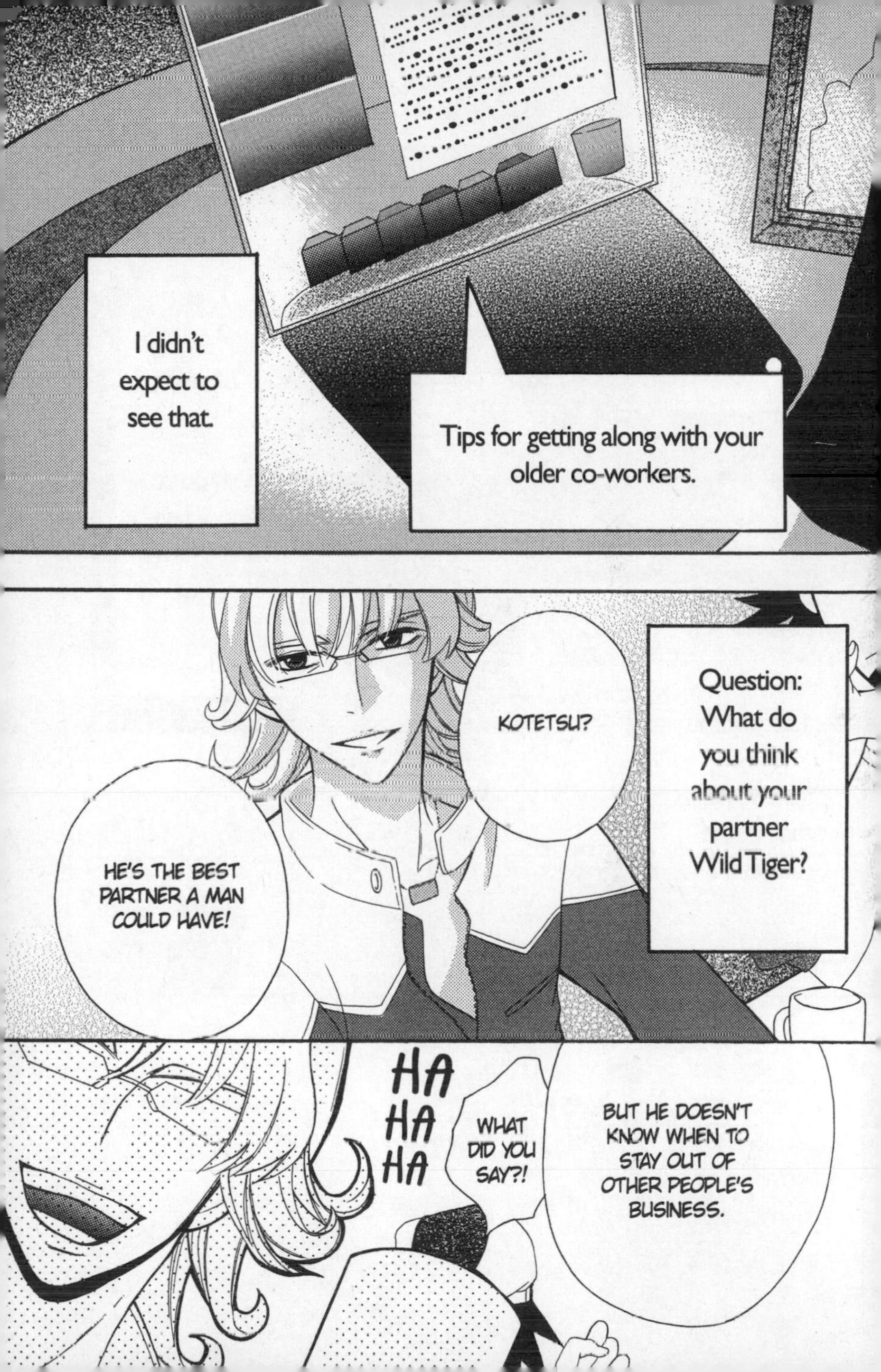

Tips for getting along with your older co-workers.
I didn't expect to see that.
Question: What do you think about your partner Wild Tiger?
KOTETSU?
HE'S THE BEST PARTNER A MAN COULD HAVE!
BUT HE DOESN'T KNOW WHEN TO STAY OUT OF OTHER PEOPLE'S BUSINESS.
WHAT DID YOU SAY?!
HA HA HA

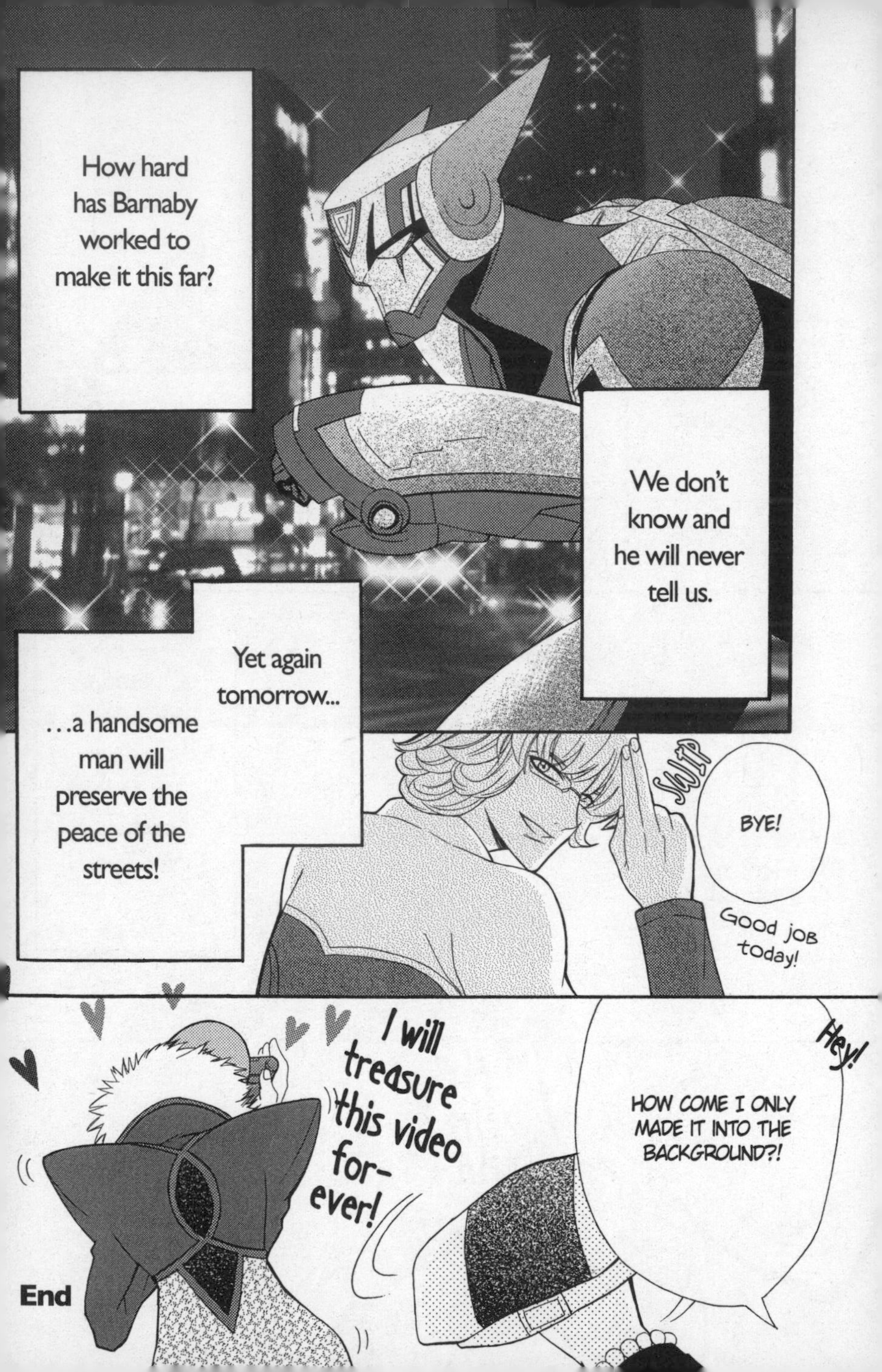

How hard has Barnaby worked to make it this far?
We don't know and he will never tell us.
Yet again tomorrow...
...a handsome man will preserve the peace of the streets!
SWIP
BYE!
Good job today!
I will treasure this video for-ever!
Hey!
HOW COME I ONLY MADE IT INTO THE BACKGROUND?!
End

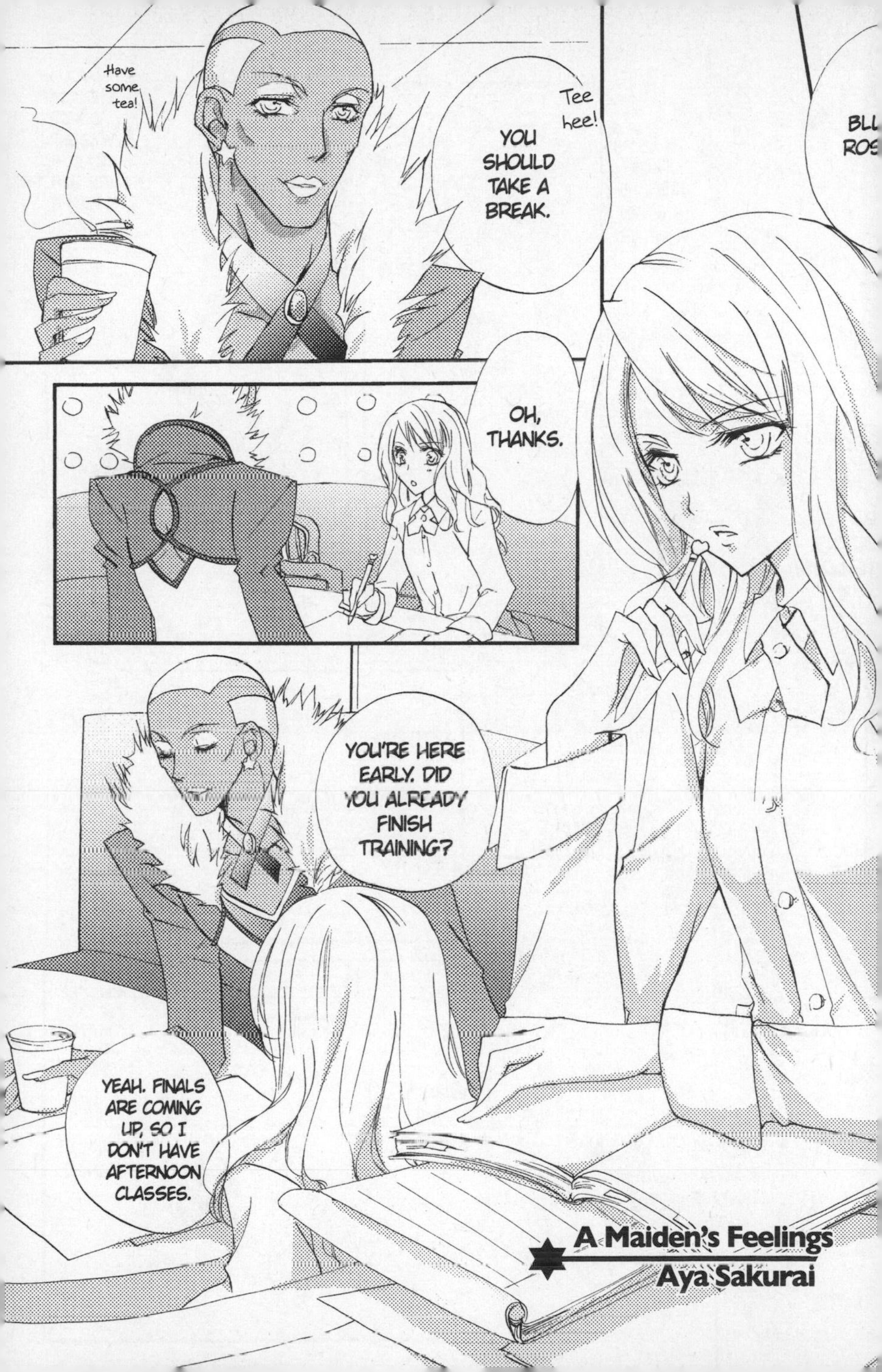
Tee hee!
YOU SHOULD TAKE A BREAK.
Have some tea!
OH, THANKS.
YOU'RE HERE EARLY. DID YOU ALREADY FINISH TRAINING?
YEAH. FINALS ARE COMING UP, SO I DON'T HAVE AFTERNOON CLASSES.
A Maiden's Feelings
Aya Sakurai

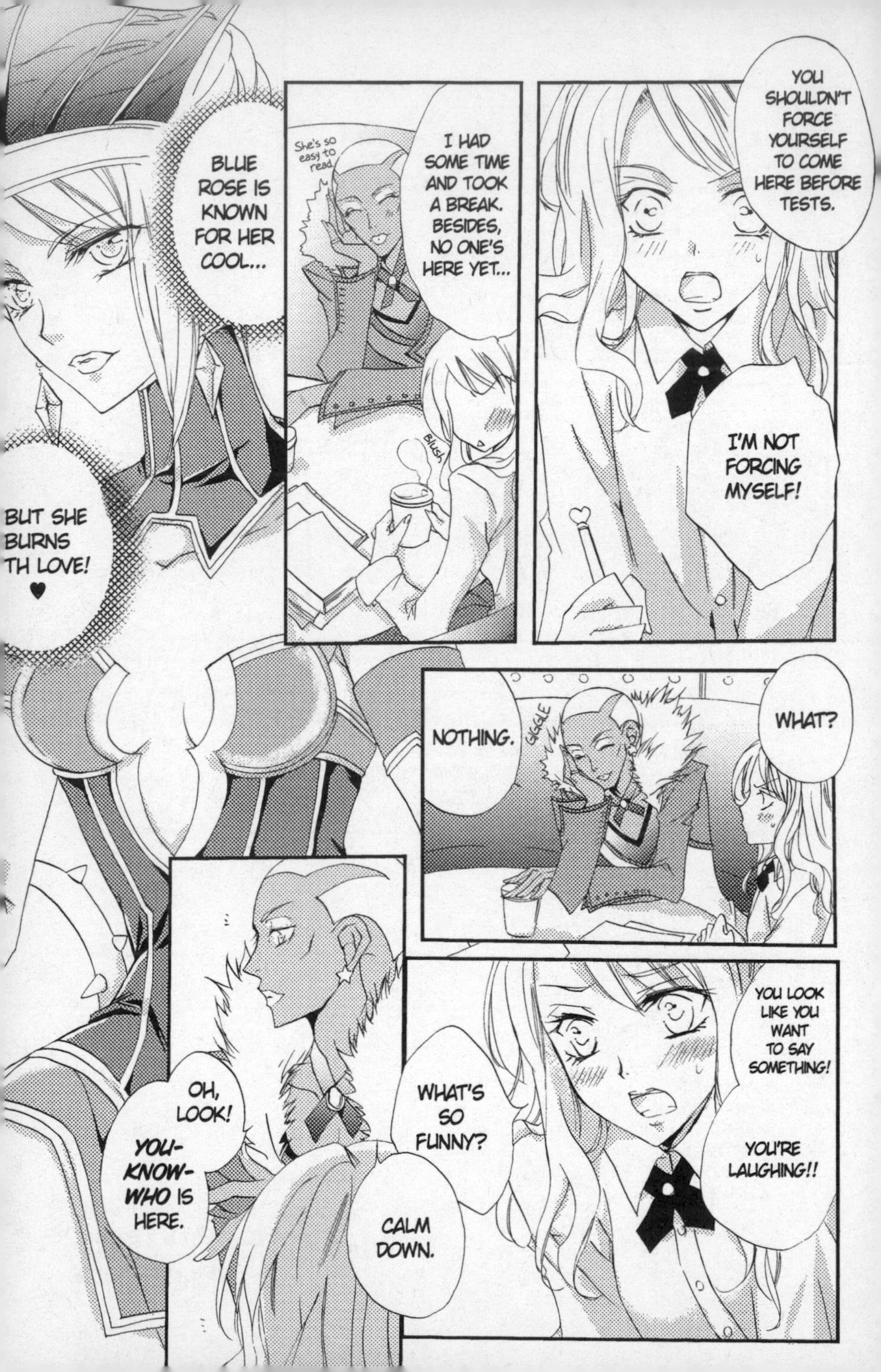
YOU SHOULDN'T FORCE YOURSELF TO COME HERE BEFORE TESTS.
I'M NOT FORCING MYSELF!
I HAD SOME TIME AND TOOK A BREAK. BESIDES, NO ONE'S HERE YET...
She's so easy to read
Blush
WHAT?
NOTHING.
GIGGLE
YOU LOOK LIKE YOU WANT TO SAY SOMETHING!
YOU'RE LAUGHING!!
WHAT'S SO FUNNY?
CALM DOWN.
OH, LOOK! *YOU-KNOW-WHO* IS HERE.
BLUE ROSE IS KNOWN FOR HER COOL...
BUT SHE BURNS TH LOVE! ♥

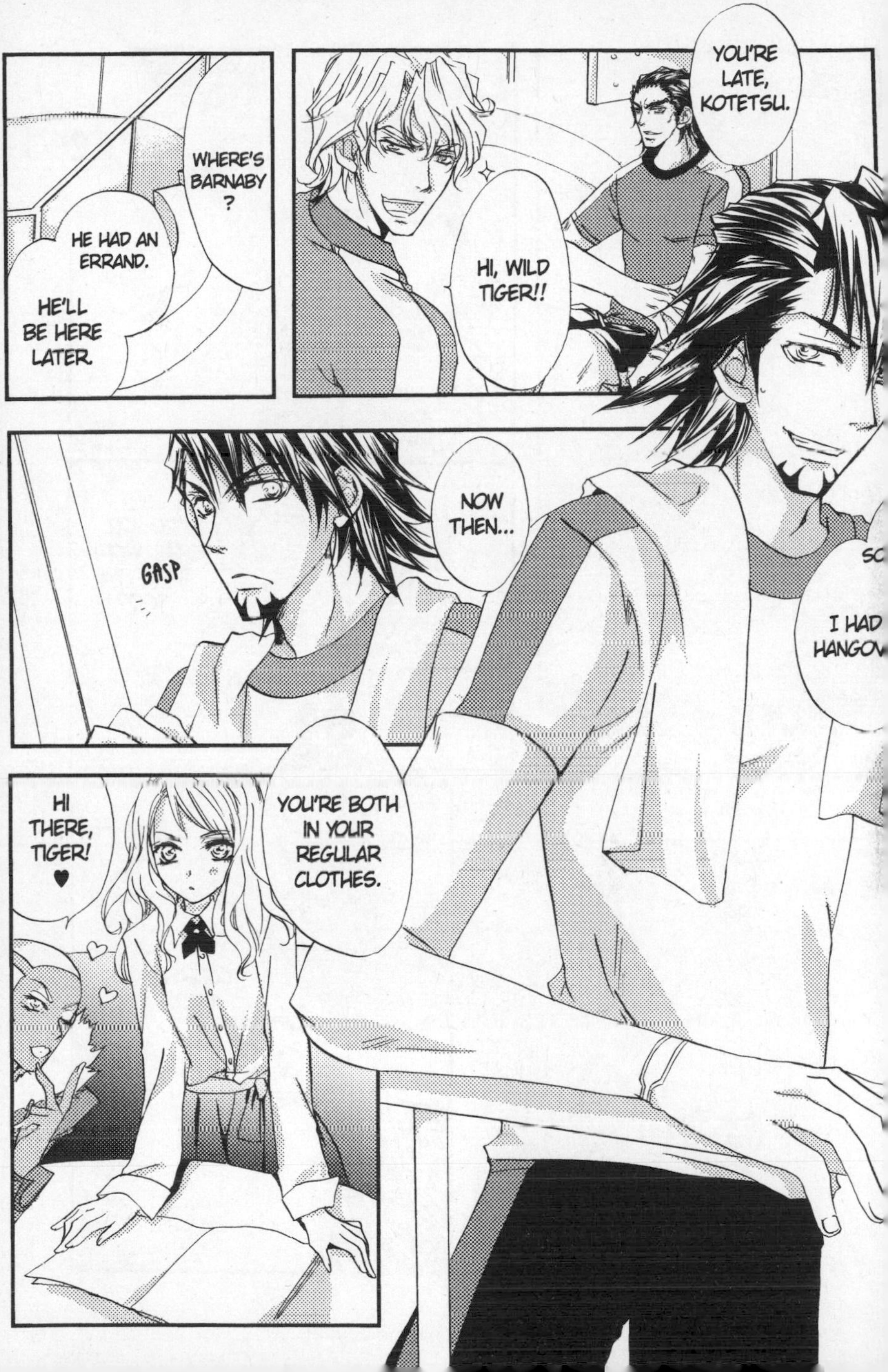
YOU'RE LATE, KOTETSU.
HI, WILD TIGER!!
WHERE'S BARNABY?
HE HAD AN ERRAND.
HE'LL BE HERE LATER.
I HAD
NOW THEN...
GASP
YOU'RE BOTH IN YOUR REGULAR CLOTHES.
HI THERE, TIGER! ♥

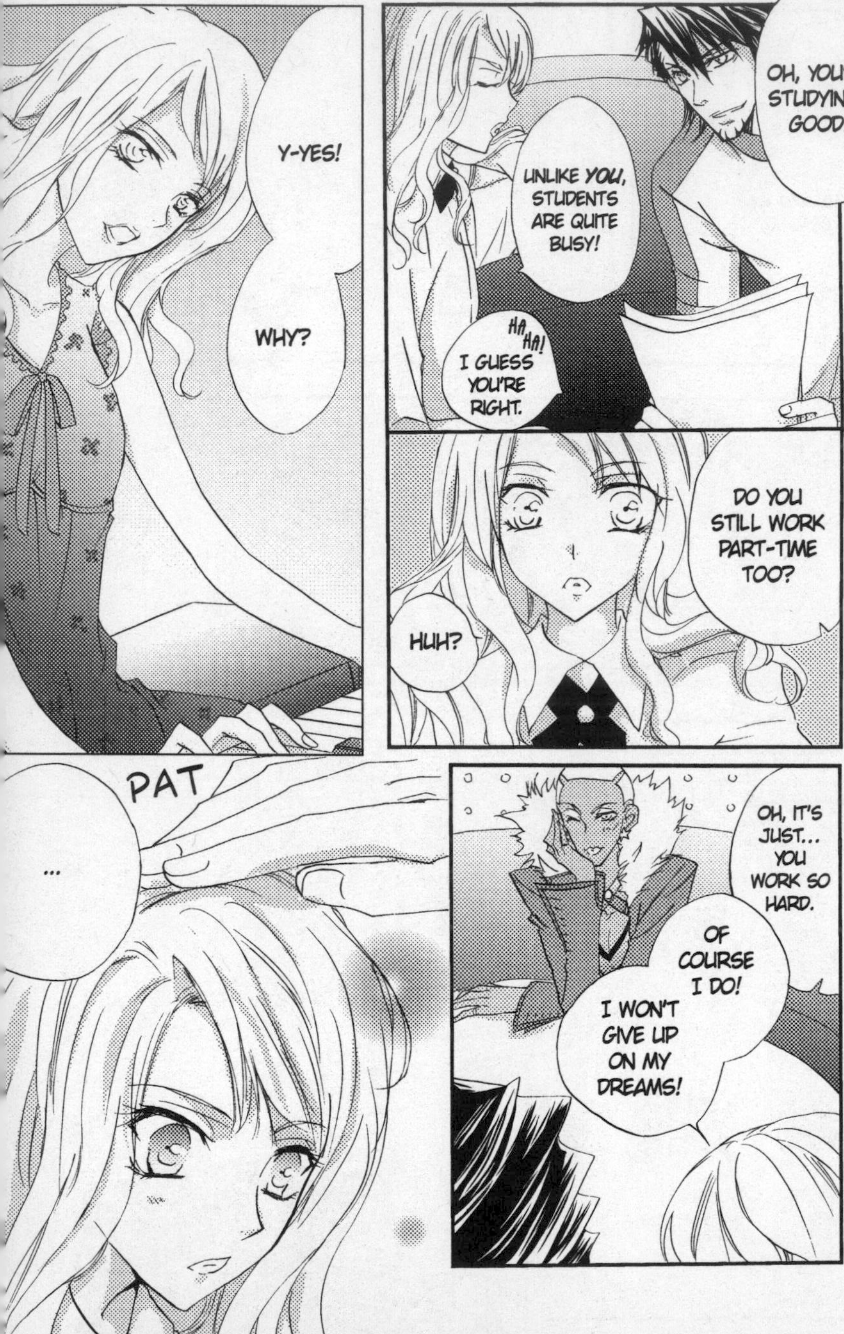
OH, YOU'RE STUDYING? GOOD!
UNLIKE YOU, STUDENTS ARE QUITE BUSY!
HA HA!
I GUESS YOU'RE RIGHT.
DO YOU STILL WORK PART-TIME TOO?
HUH?
Y-YES!
WHY?
OH, IT'S JUST... YOU WORK SO HARD.
OF COURSE I DO!
I WON'T GIVE UP ON MY DREAMS!
PAT
...

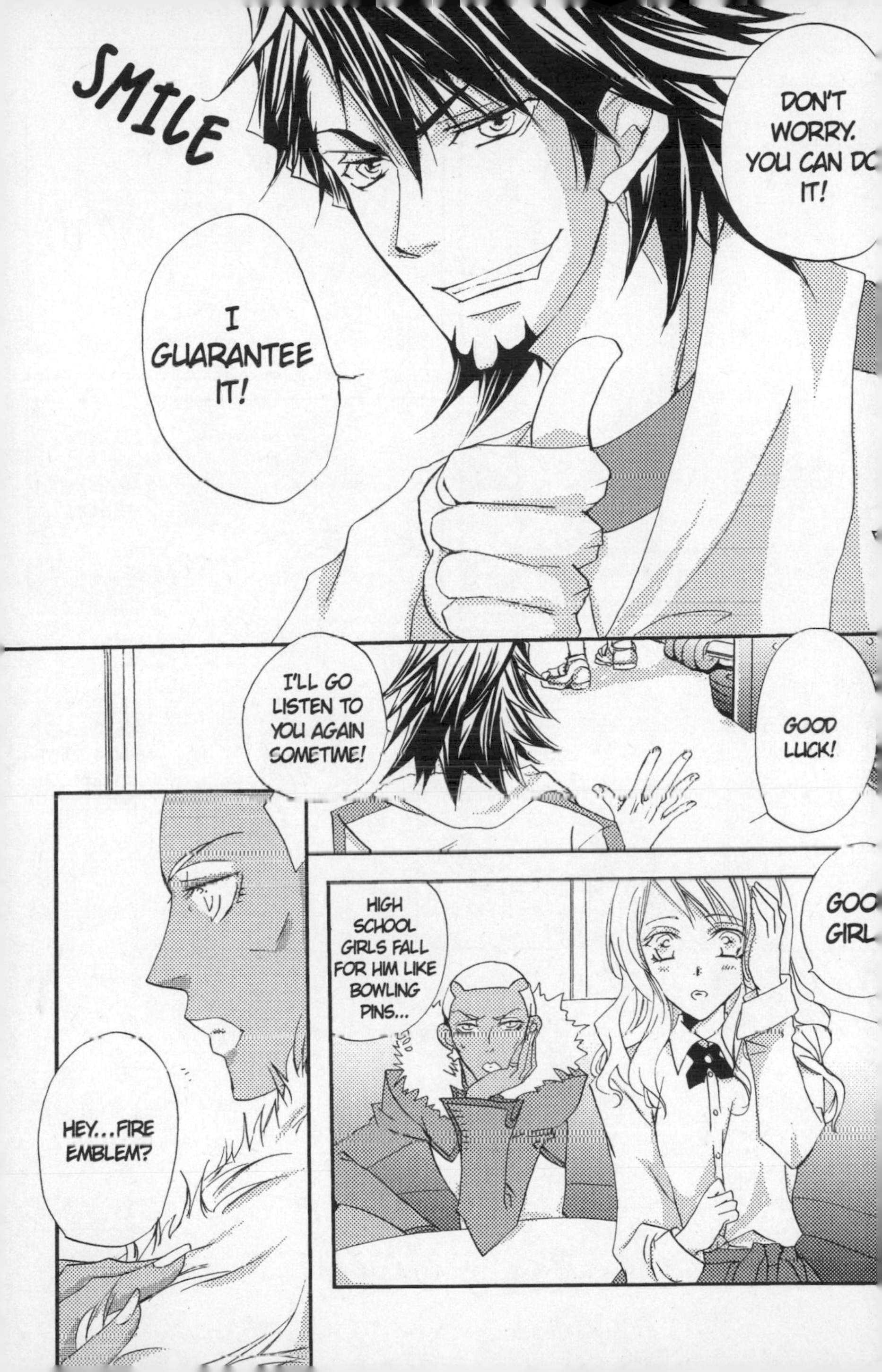
DON'T WORRY. YOU CAN DO IT!
SMILE
I GUARANTEE IT!
GOOD LUCK!
I'LL GO LISTEN TO YOU AGAIN SOMETIME!
GOO GIRL
HIGH SCHOOL GIRLS FALL FOR HIM LIKE BOWLING PINS...
HEY...FIRE EMBLEM?

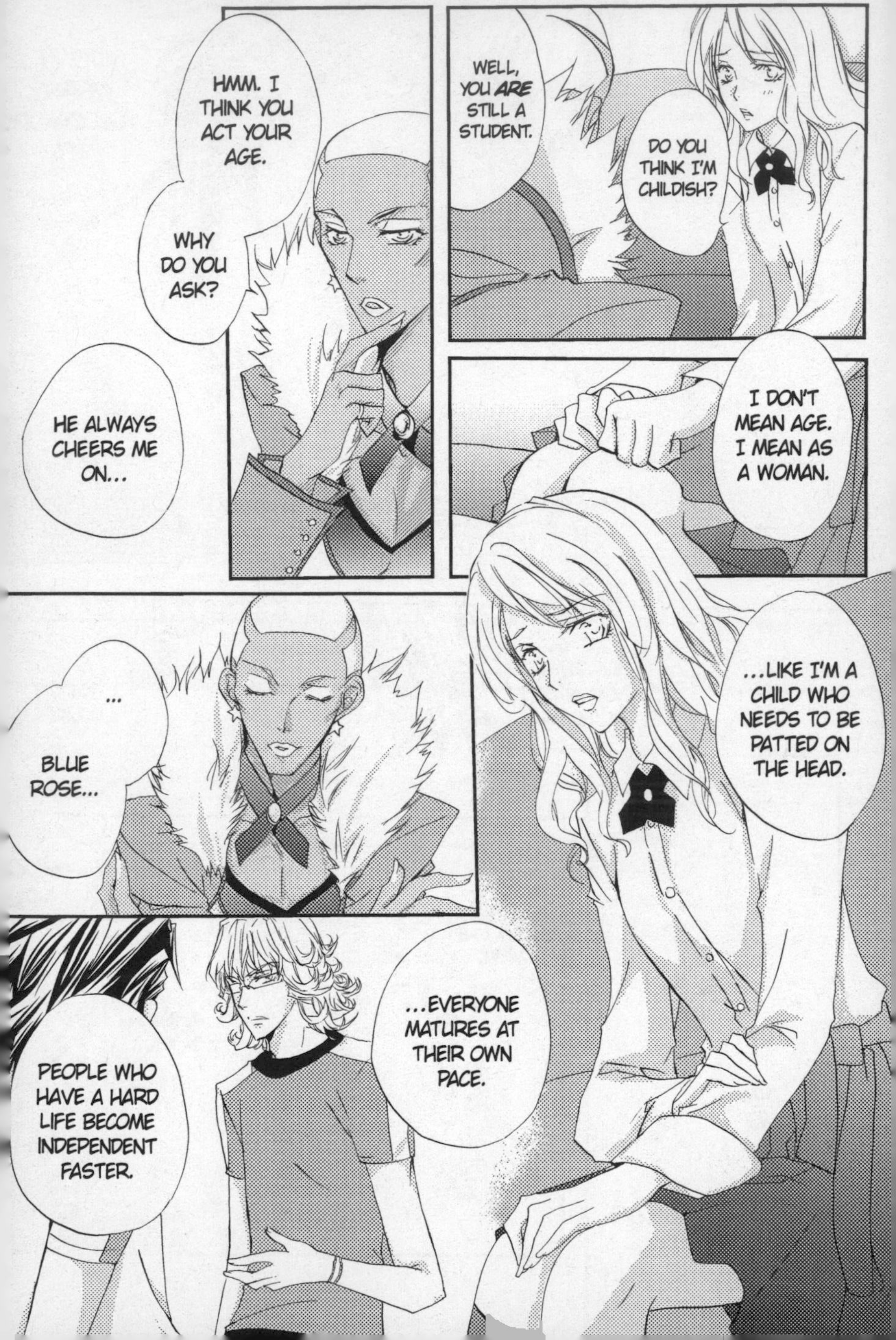
DO YOU THINK I'M CHILDISH?
WELL, YOU ***ARE*** STILL A STUDENT.
I DON'T MEAN AGE. I MEAN AS A WOMAN.
HMM. I THINK YOU ACT YOUR AGE.
WHY DO YOU ASK?
HE ALWAYS CHEERS ME ON...
...LIKE I'M A CHILD WHO NEEDS TO BE PATTED ON THE HEAD.
...
BLUE ROSE...
...EVERYONE MATURES AT THEIR OWN PACE.
PEOPLE WHO HAVE A HARD LIFE BECOME INDEPENDENT FASTER.

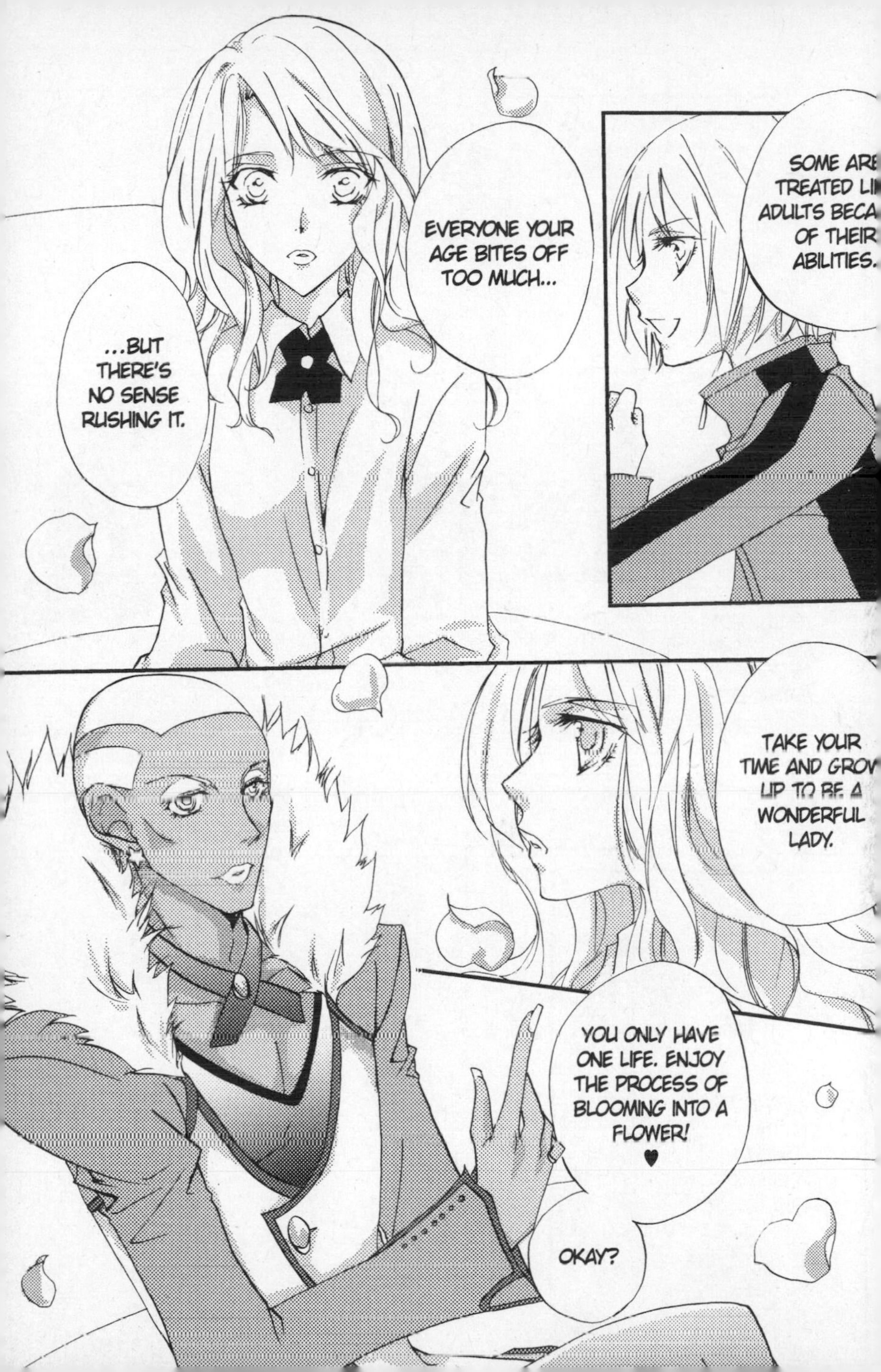
SOME ARE TREATED LI ADULTS BECA OF THEIR ABILITIES.
EVERYONE YOUR AGE BITES OFF TOO MUCH...
...BUT THERE'S NO SENSE RUSHING IT.
TAKE YOUR TIME AND GROW UP TO BE A WONDERFUL LADY.
YOU ONLY HAVE ONE LIFE. ENJOY THE PROCESS OF BLOOMING INTO A FLOWER! ♥
OKAY?

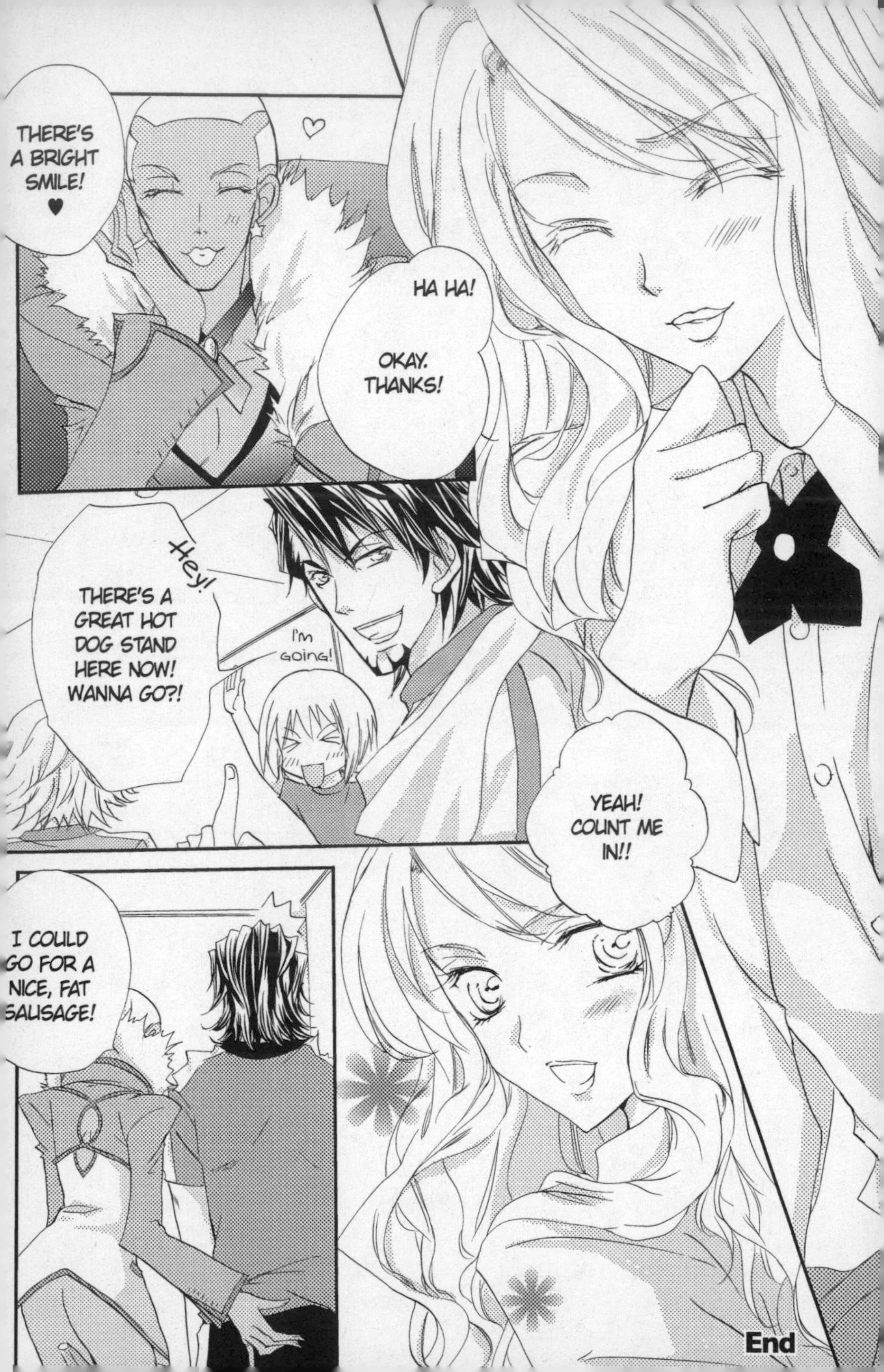
HA HA!
OKAY. THANKS!
THERE'S A BRIGHT SMILE! ♥
Hey!
THERE'S A GREAT HOT DOG STAND HERE NOW! WANNA GO?!
I'm going!
YEAH! COUNT ME IN!!
I COULD GO FOR A NICE, FAT SAUSAGE!
End

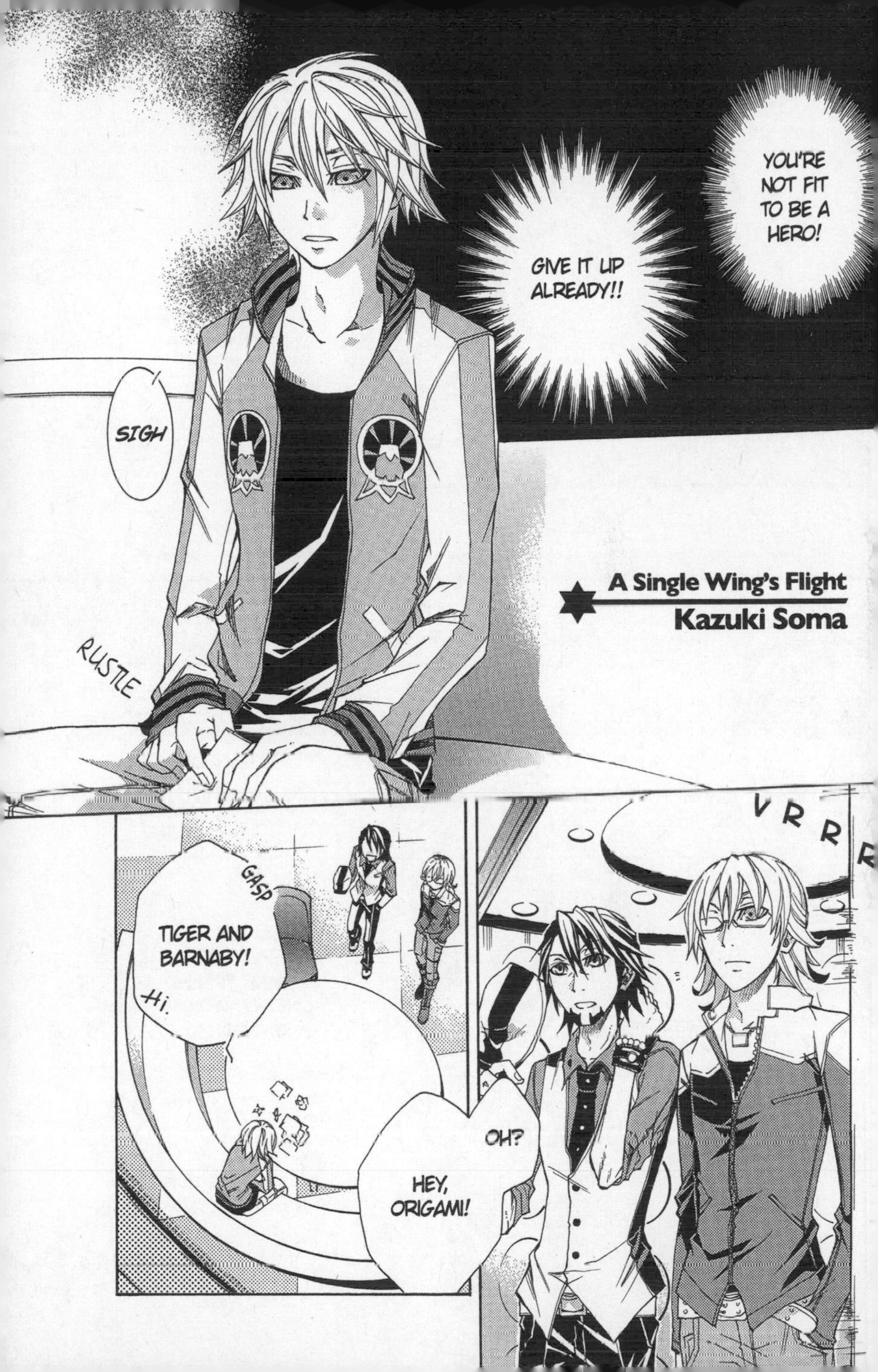
YOU'RE NOT FIT TO BE A HERO!
GIVE IT UP ALREADY!!
SIGH
A Single Wing's Flight
Kazuki Soma
RUSTLE
VRRR
OH?
HEY, ORIGAMI!
GASP
TIGER AND BARNABY!
HI.

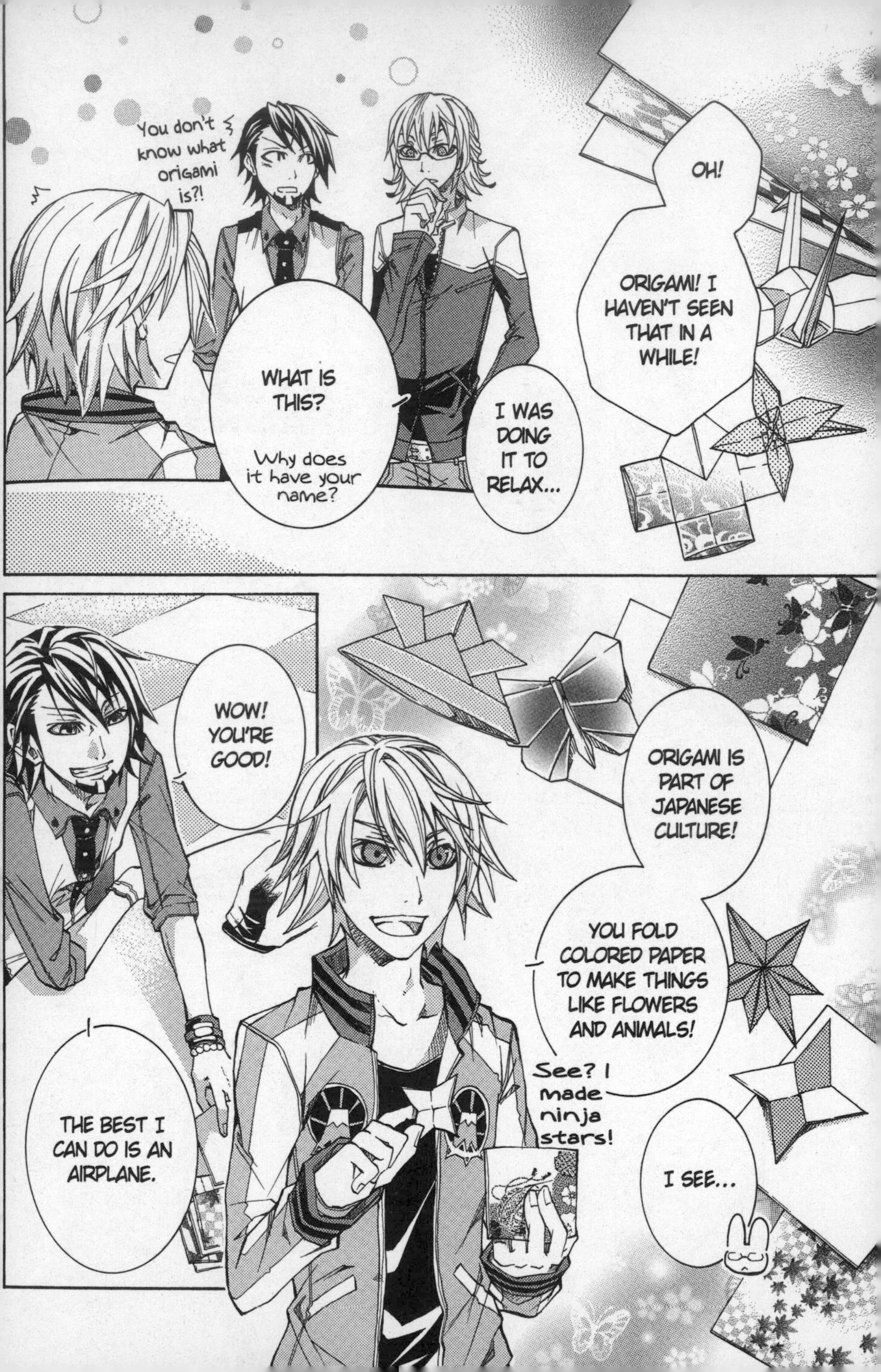
OH!
ORIGAMI! I HAVEN'T SEEN THAT IN A WHILE!
I WAS DOING IT TO RELAX...
WHAT IS THIS?
Why does it have your name?
You don't know what origami is?!
ORIGAMI IS PART OF JAPANESE CULTURE!
YOU FOLD COLORED PAPER TO MAKE THINGS LIKE FLOWERS AND ANIMALS!
See? I made ninja stars!
I SEE...
WOW! YOU'RE GOOD!
THE BEST I CAN DO IS AN AIRPLANE.

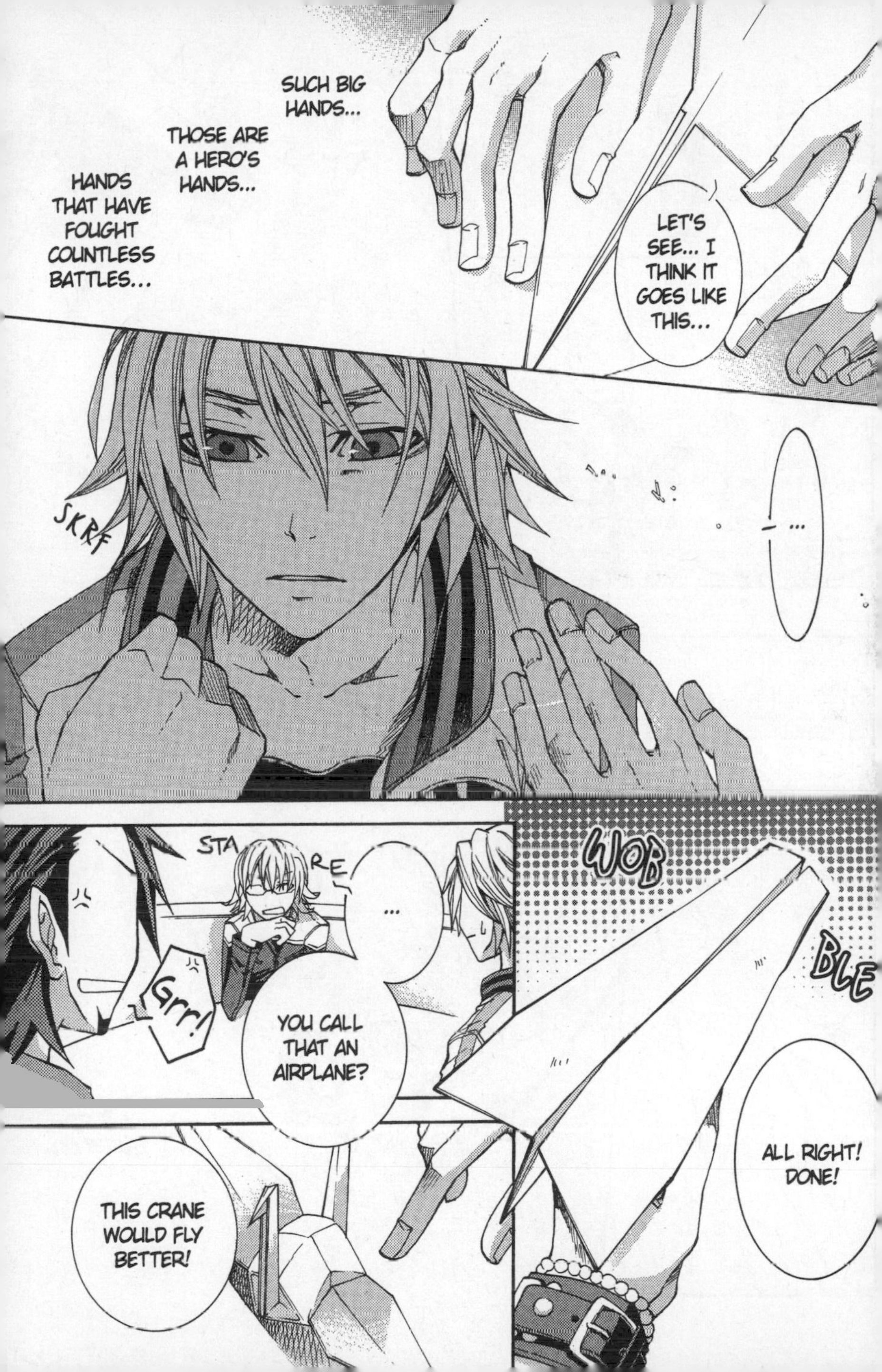
LET'S SEE... I THINK IT GOES LIKE THIS...
SUCH BIG HANDS...
THOSE ARE A HERO'S HANDS...
HANDS THAT HAVE FOUGHT COUNTLESS BATTLES...
—...
SKRF
WOB
BLE
ALL RIGHT! DONE!
STA
RE
...
YOU CALL THAT AN AIRPLANE?
Grr!
THIS CRANE WOULD FLY BETTER!

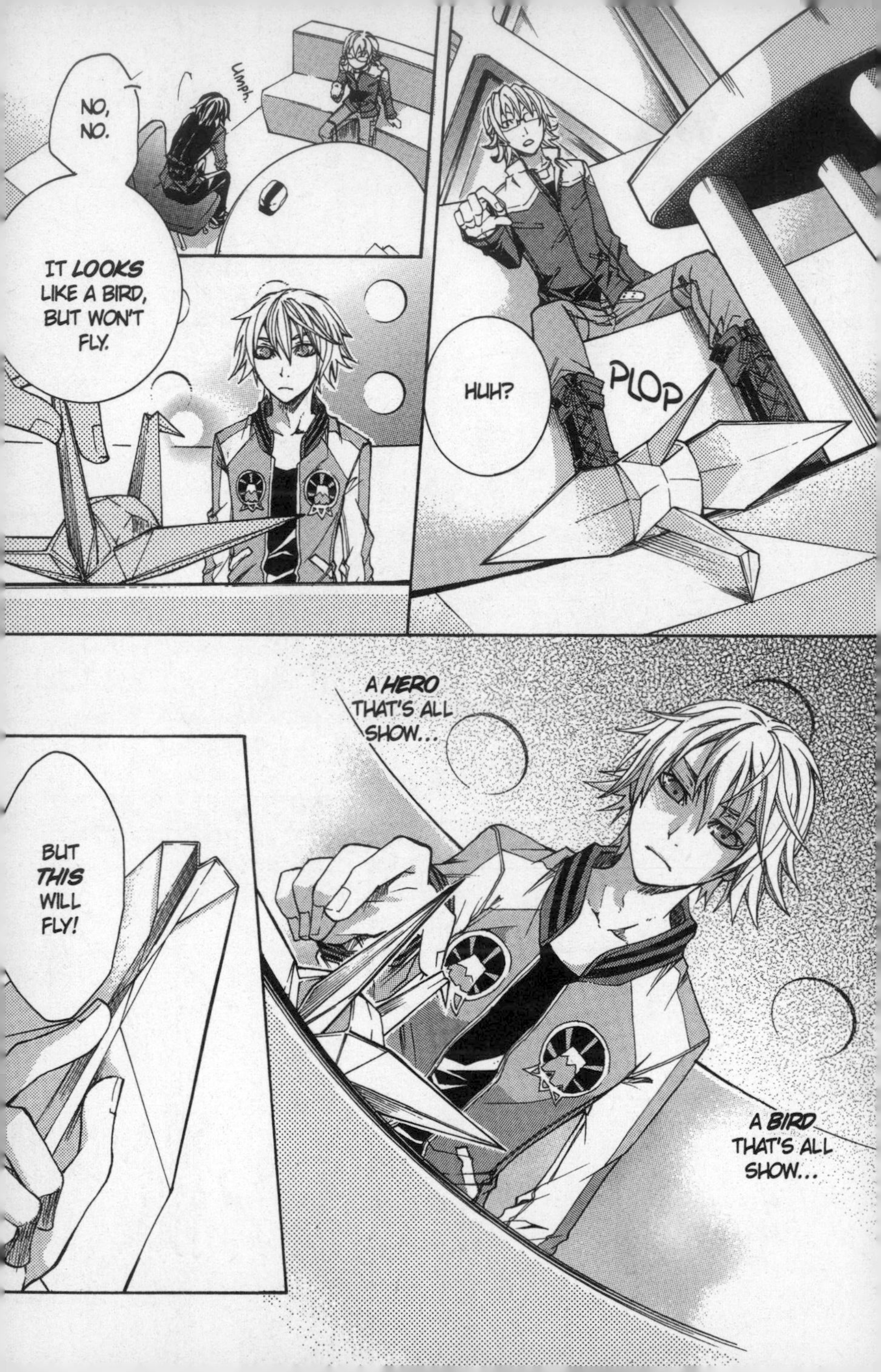
HUH?
PLOP
Umph.
NO, NO.
IT LOOKS LIKE A BIRD, BUT WON'T FLY.
A HERO THAT'S ALL SHOW...
A BIRD THAT'S ALL SHOW...
BUT THIS WILL FLY!

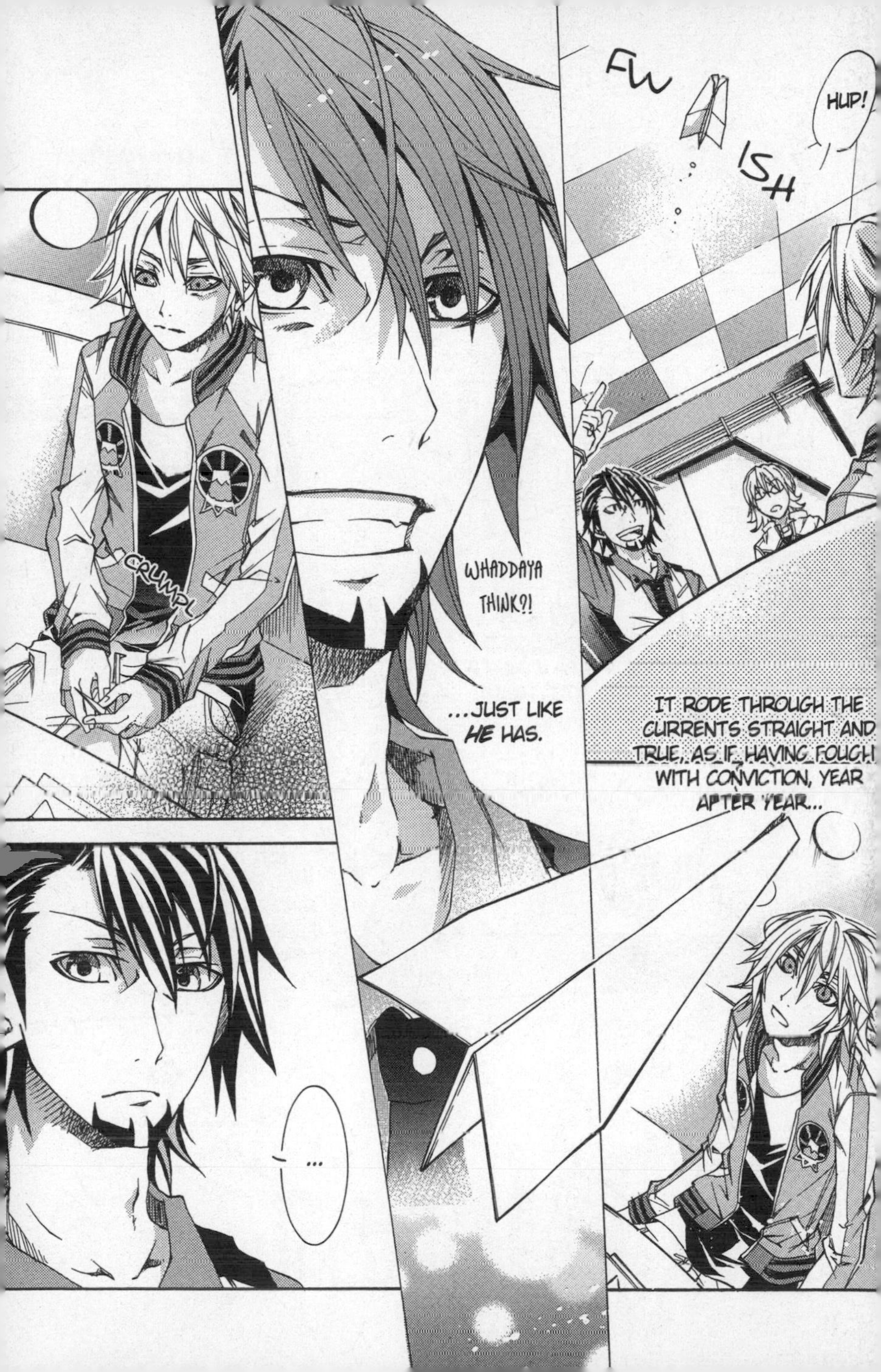
FW ISH
HUP!
IT RODE THROUGH THE CURRENTS STRAIGHT AND TRUE, AS IF HAVING FOUGHT WITH CONVICTION, YEAR AFTER YEAR...
WHADDAYA THINK?!
...JUST LIKE HE HAS.
CRUMPL
...

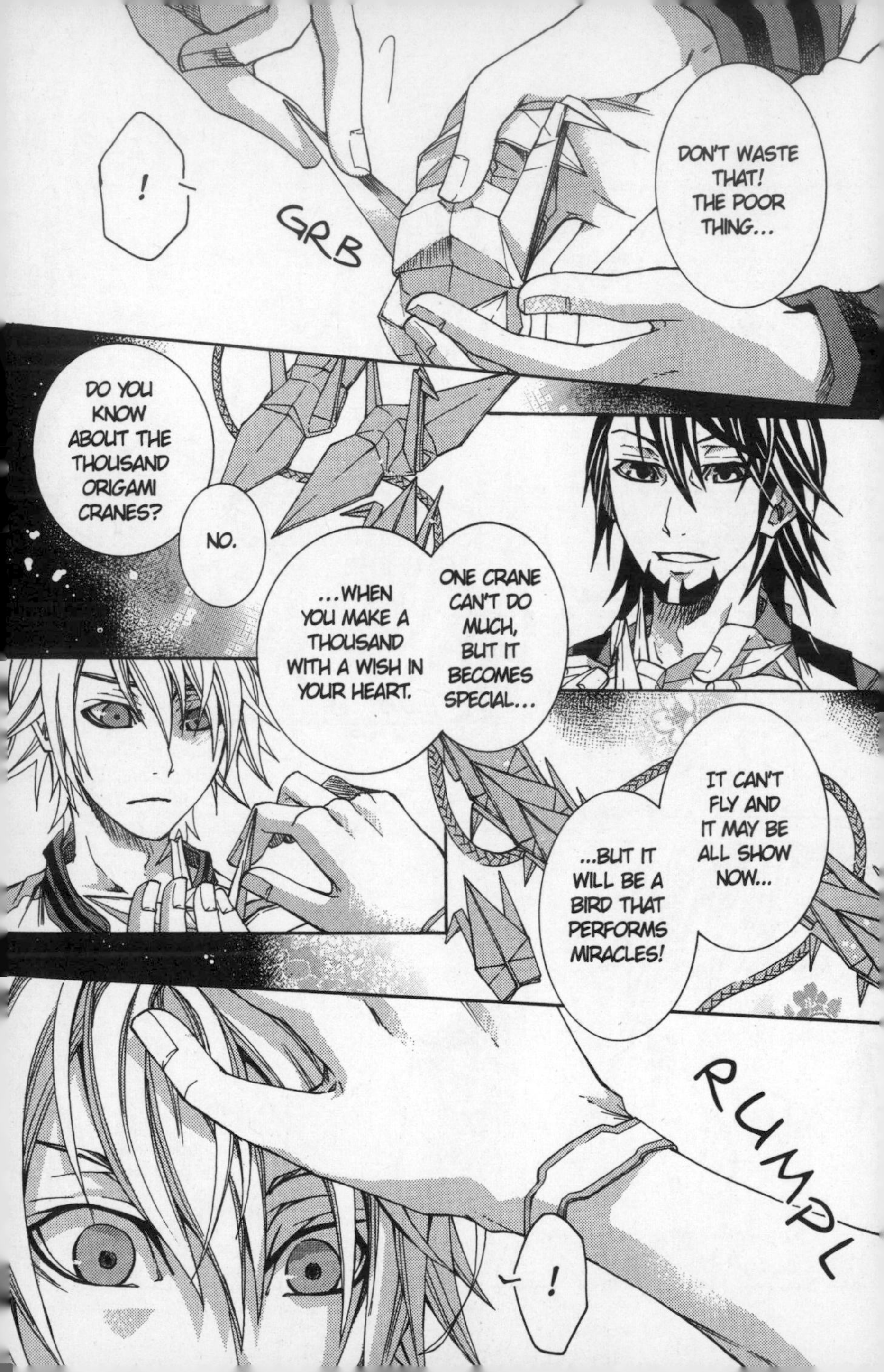
DON'T WASTE THAT! THE POOR THING...
GRB
!
DO YOU KNOW ABOUT THE THOUSAND ORIGAMI CRANES?
NO.
ONE CRANE CAN'T DO MUCH, BUT IT BECOMES SPECIAL...
...WHEN YOU MAKE A THOUSAND WITH A WISH IN YOUR HEART.
IT CAN'T FLY AND IT MAY BE ALL SHOW NOW...
...BUT IT WILL BE A BIRD THAT PERFORMS MIRACLES!
RUMPL
!

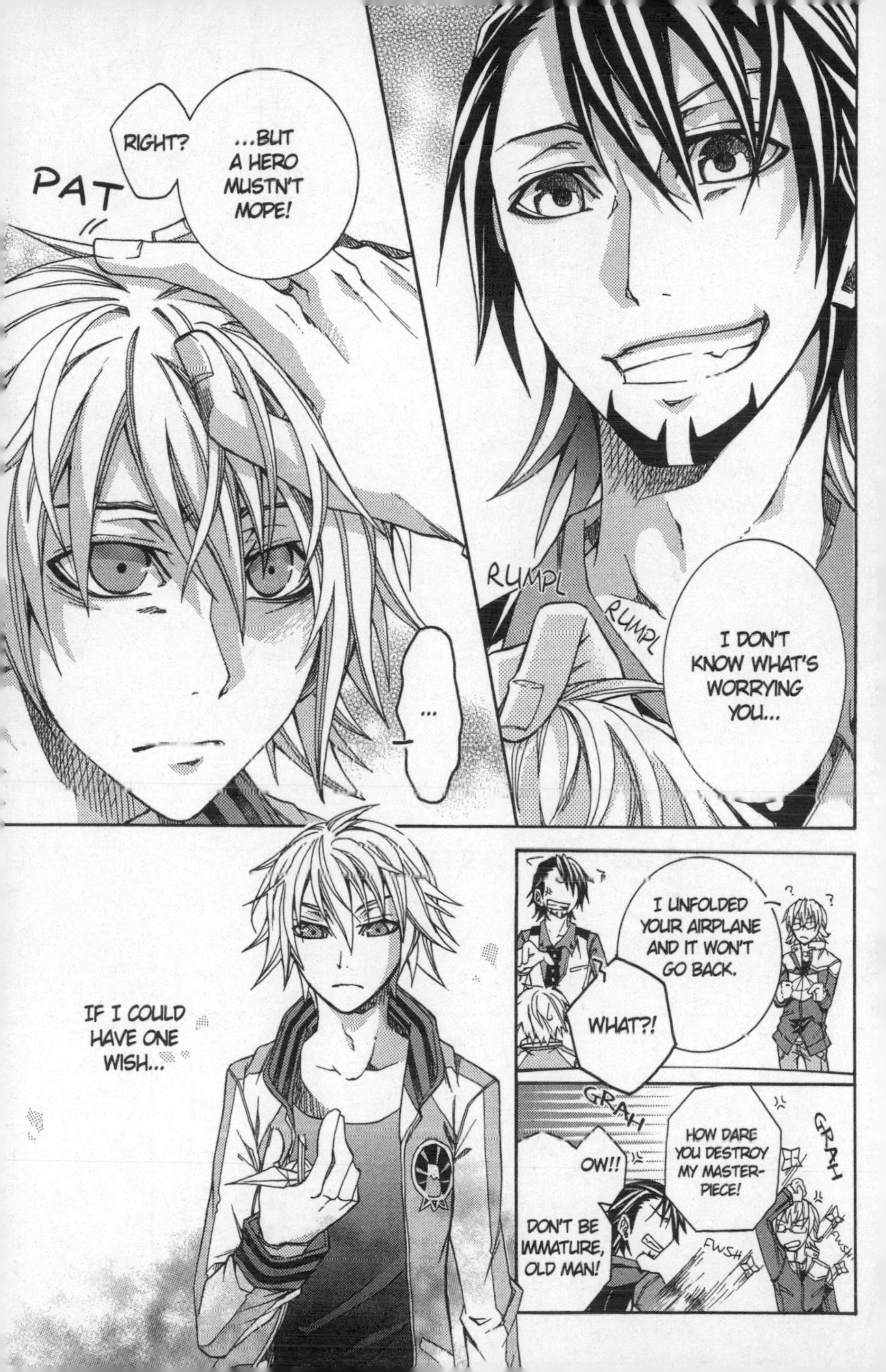
RUMPL
RUMPL
I DON'T KNOW WHAT'S WORRYING YOU...
...BUT A HERO MUSTN'T MOPE!
RIGHT?
PAT
...
I UNFOLDED YOUR AIRPLANE AND IT WON'T GO BACK.
WHAT?!
GRAH
HOW DARE YOU DESTROY MY MASTER-PIECE!
GRAH
OW!!
DON'T BE IMMATURE, OLD MAN!
FWSH
FWSH
IF I COULD HAVE ONE WISH...

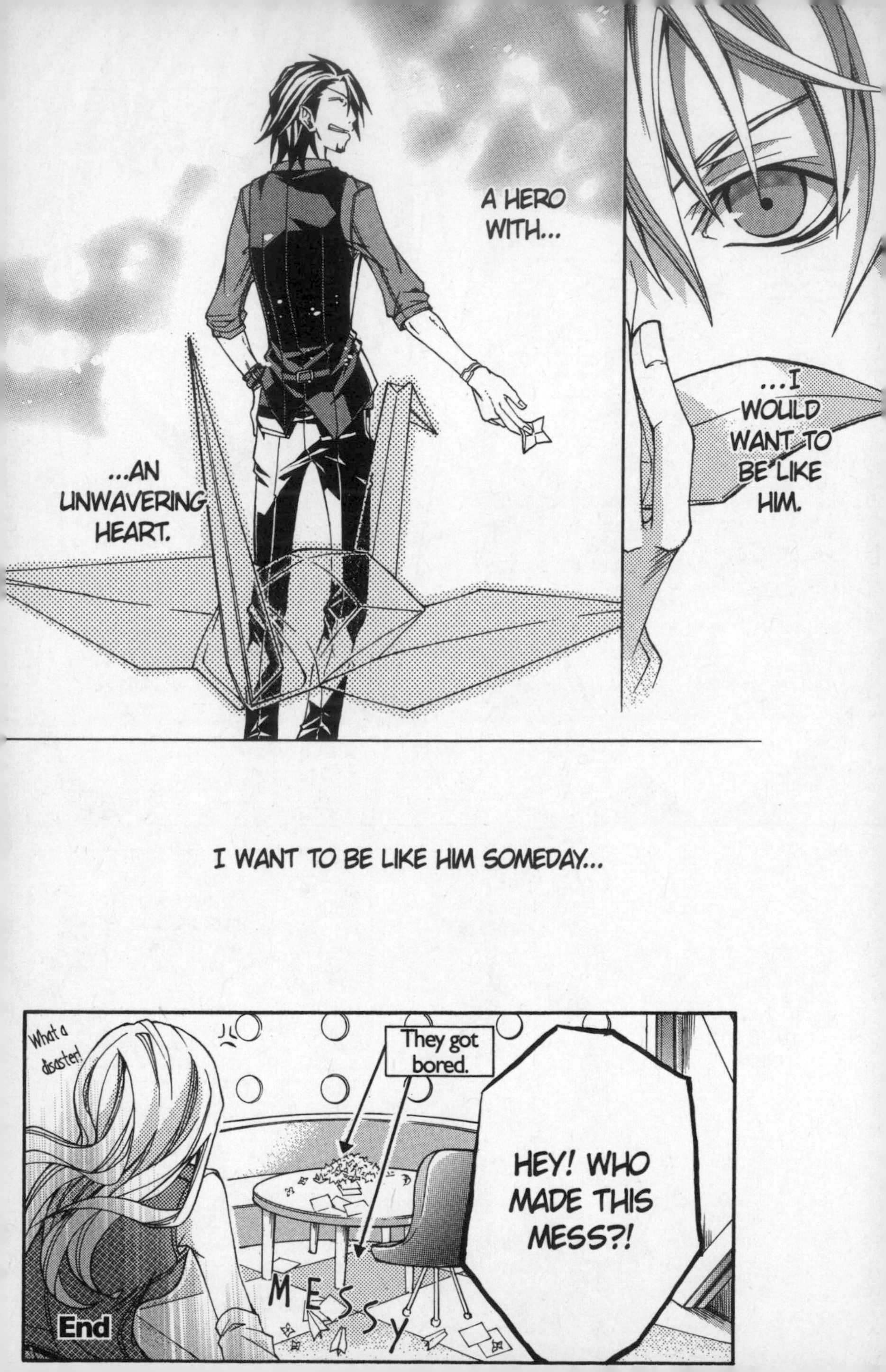
...I WOULD WANT TO BE LIKE HIM.
A HERO WITH...
...AN UNWAVERING HEART.
I WANT TO BE LIKE HIM SOMEDAY...
HEY! WHO MADE THIS MESS?!
They got bored.
MESSY
What a disaster!
End

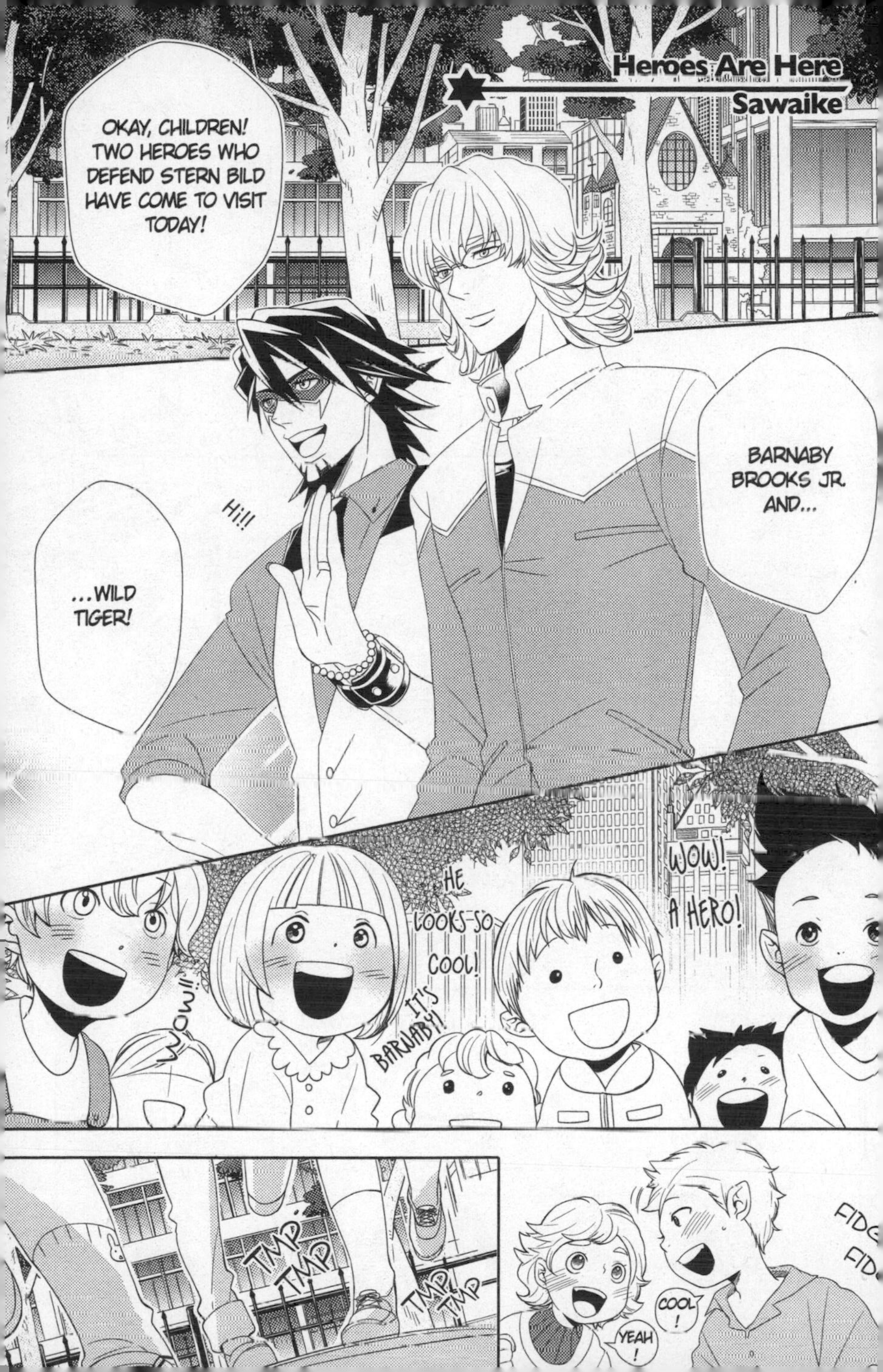
Heroes Are Here
Sawaike
OKAY, CHILDREN! TWO HEROES WHO DEFEND STERN BILD HAVE COME TO VISIT TODAY!
BARNABY BROOKS JR. AND...
HI!!
...WILD TIGER!
WOW! A HERO!
HE LOOKS SO COOL!
IT'S BARNABY!
WOW!!
FIDG
FID
COOL!
YEAH!
TMP TMP
TMP TMP

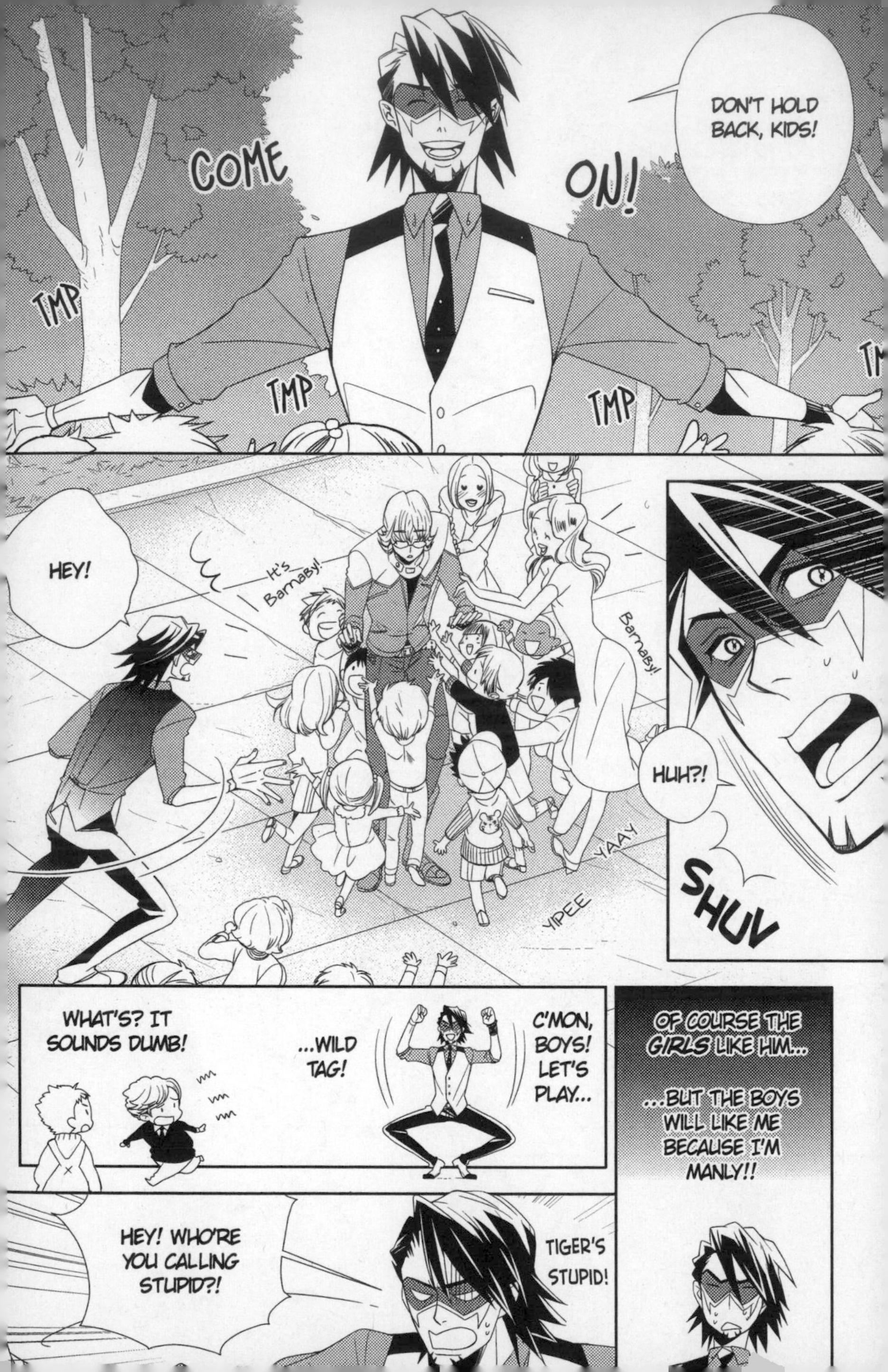
DON'T HOLD BACK, KIDS!
COME ON!
TMP
TMP
TMP
HUH?!
SHUV
Barnaby!
It's Barnaby!
HEY!
YAAY
YIPEE
OF COURSE THE GIRLS LIKE HIM...
...BUT THE BOYS WILL LIKE ME BECAUSE I'M MANLY!!
C'MON, BOYS! LET'S PLAY...
...WILD TAG!
WHAT'S? IT SOUNDS DUMB!
TIGER'S STUPID!
HEY! WHO'RE YOU CALLING STUPID?!

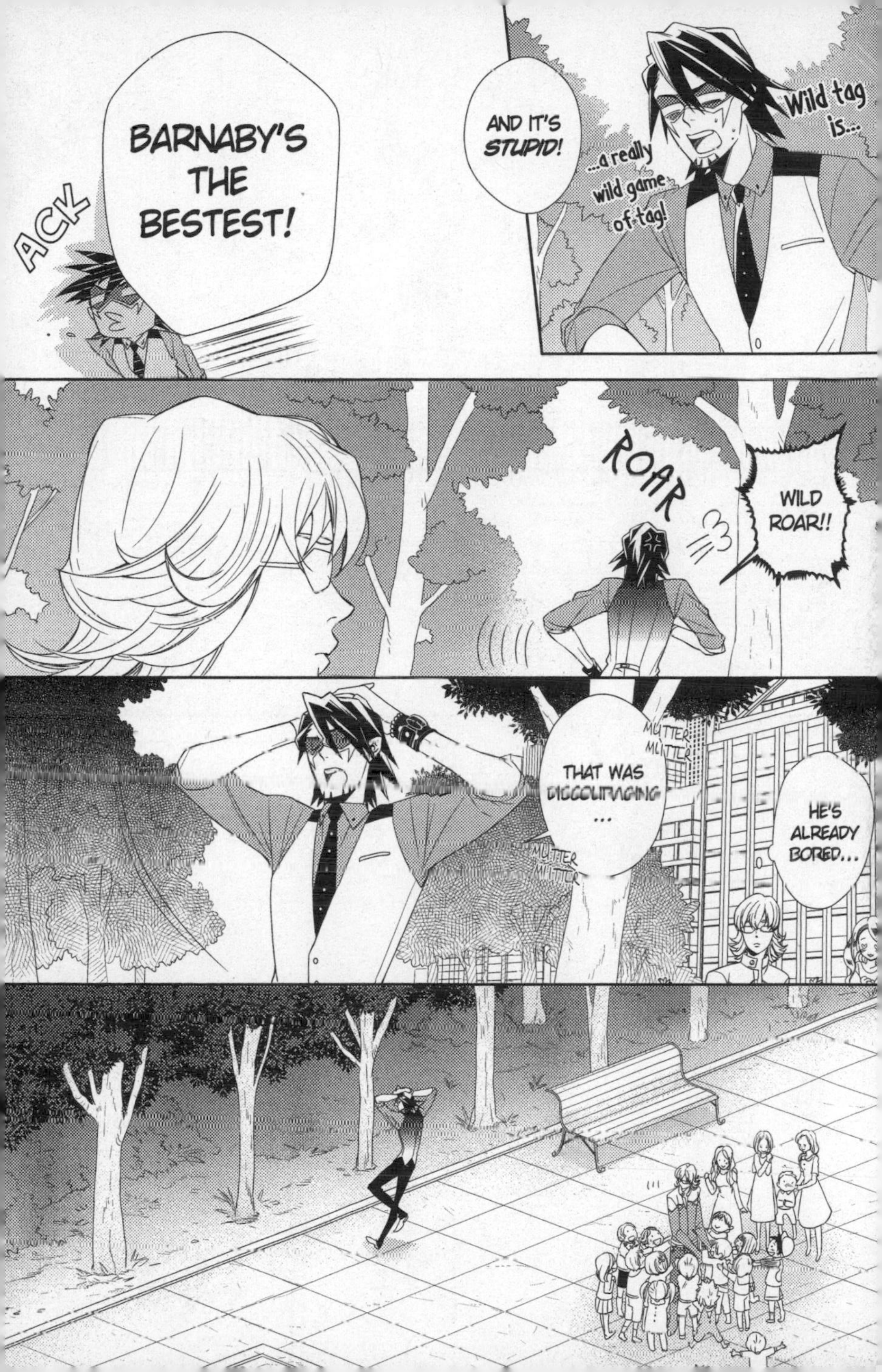
Wild tag is...
...a really wild game of tag!
AND IT'S STUPID!
BARNABY'S THE BESTEST!
ACK
WILD ROAR!!
ROAR
HE'S ALREADY BORED...
MUTTER MUTTER
THAT WAS DISCOURAGING...
MUTTER MUTTER

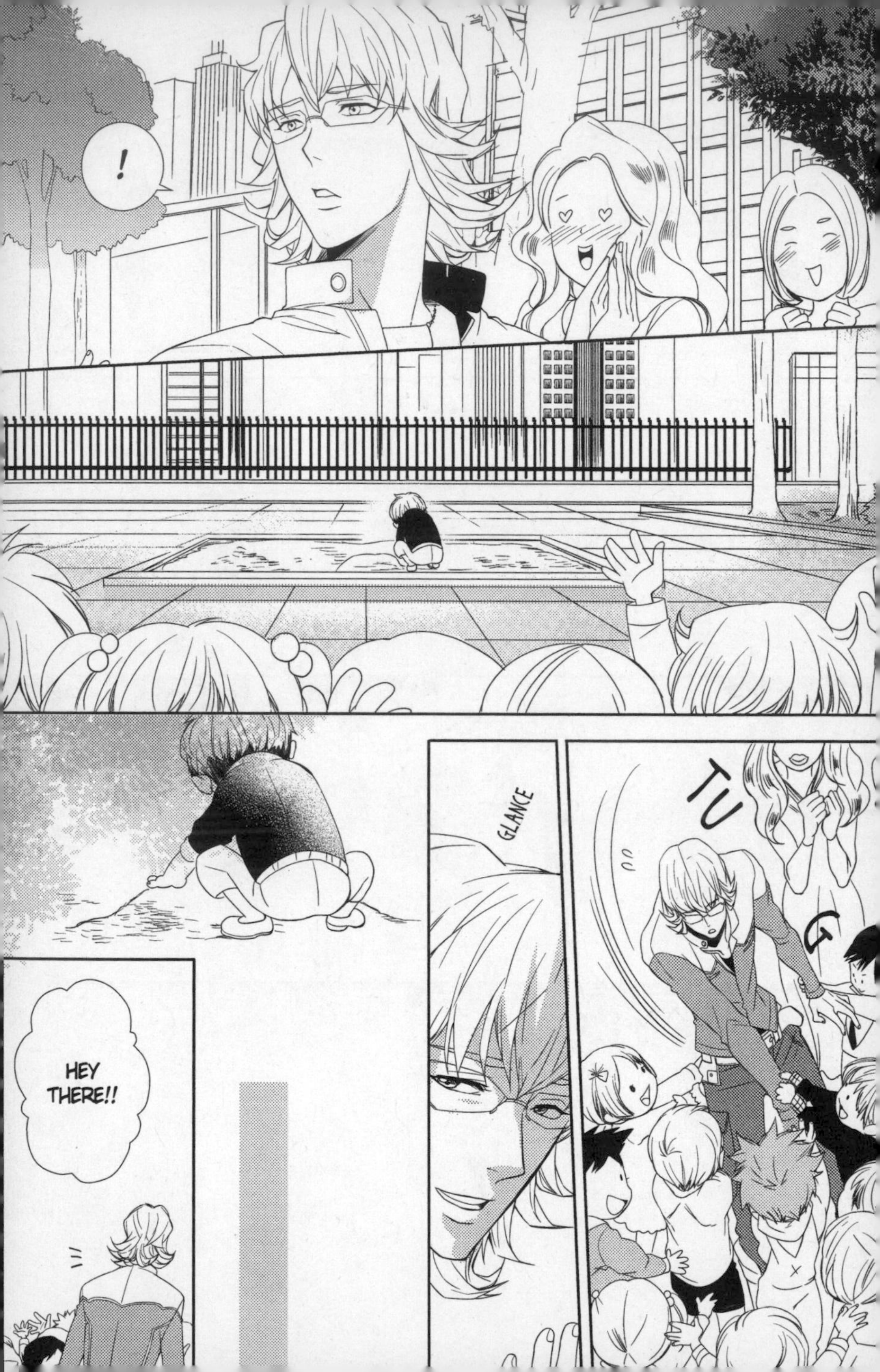
!
TUG
GLANCE
HEY THERE!!

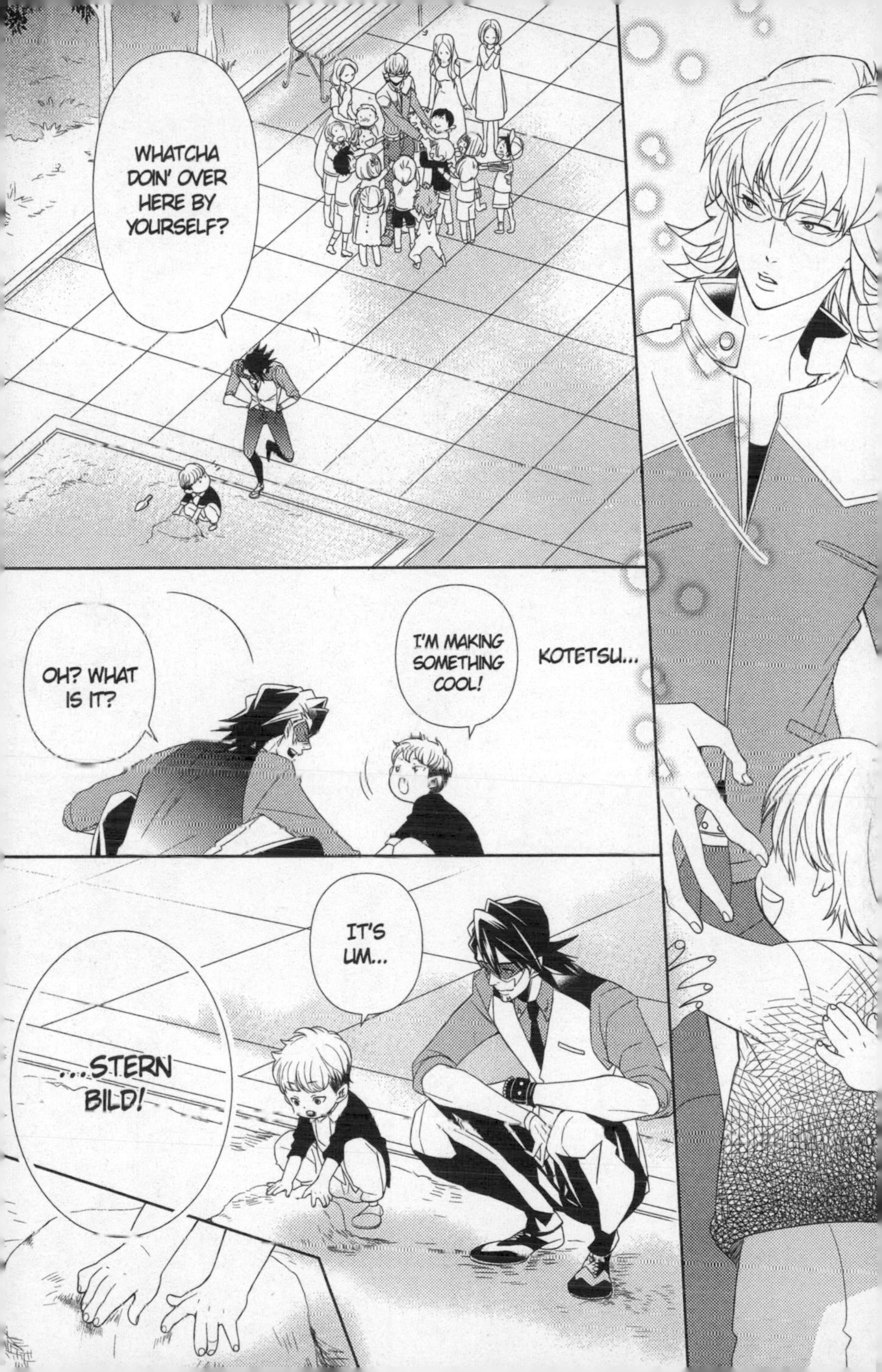
KOTETSU...
WHATCHA DOIN' OVER HERE BY YOURSELF?
I'M MAKING SOMETHING COOL!
OH? WHAT IS IT?
IT'S UM...
...STERN BILD!

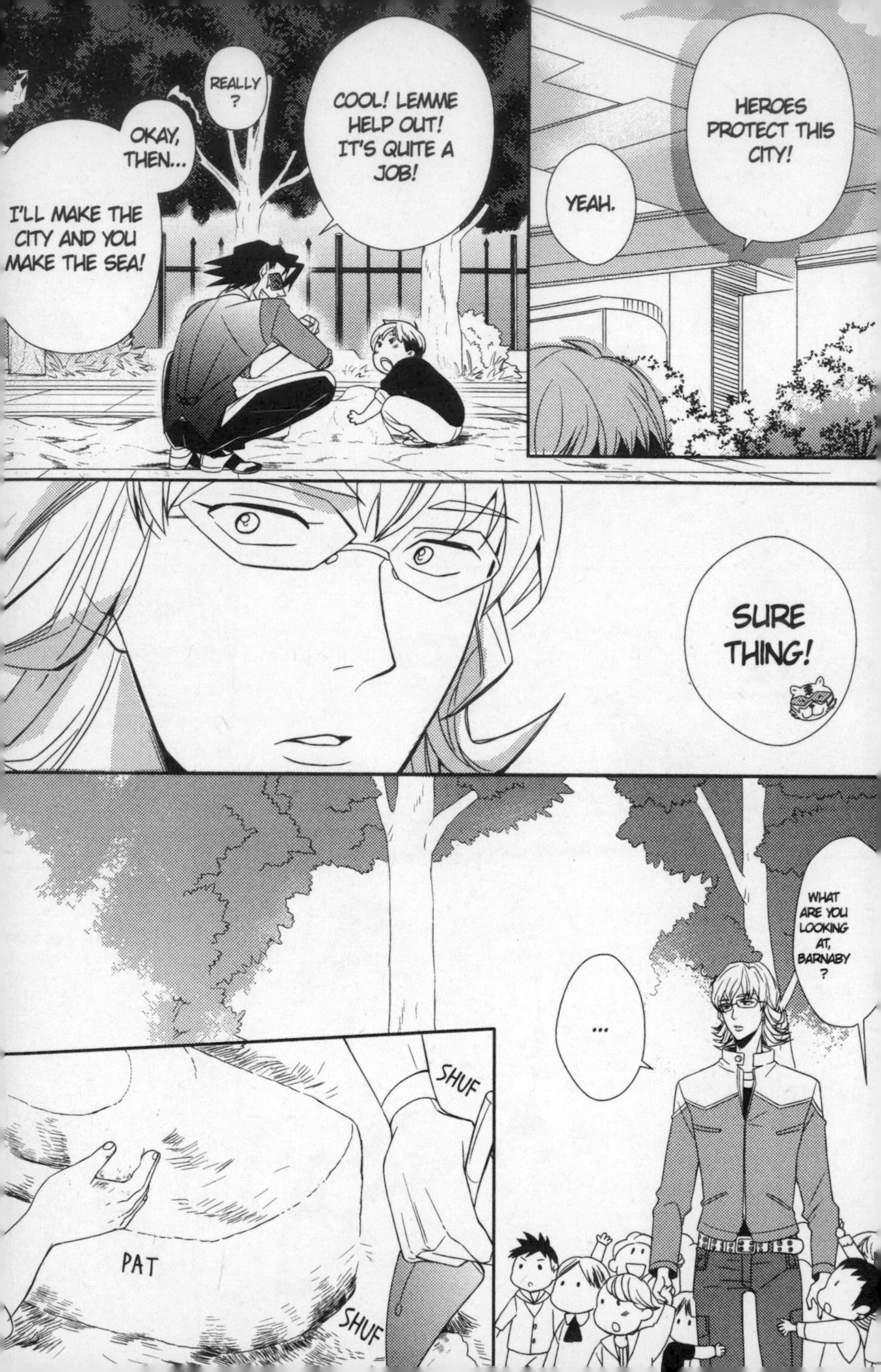
HEROES PROTECT THIS CITY!
YEAH.
COOL! LEMME HELP OUT! IT'S QUITE A JOB!
REALLY?
OKAY, THEN...
I'LL MAKE THE CITY AND YOU MAKE THE SEA!
SURE THING!
WHAT ARE YOU LOOKING AT, BARNABY?
...
SHUF
PAT
SHUF

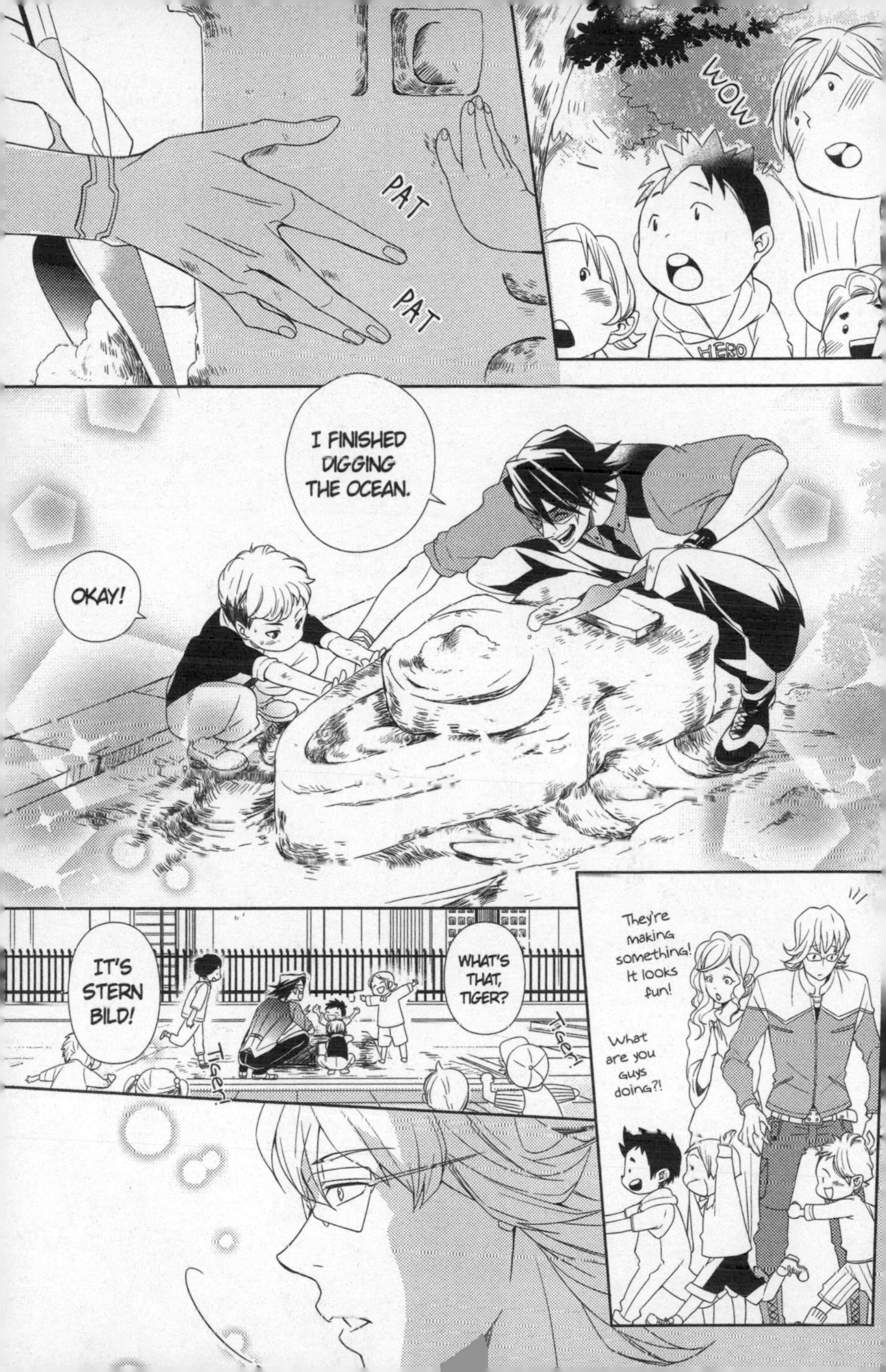
WOW
HERO
PAT
PAT
I FINISHED DIGGING THE OCEAN.
OKAY!
They're making something! It looks fun!
What are you guys doing?!
WHAT'S THAT, TIGER?
Tiger!
Tiger!
IT'S STERN BILD!

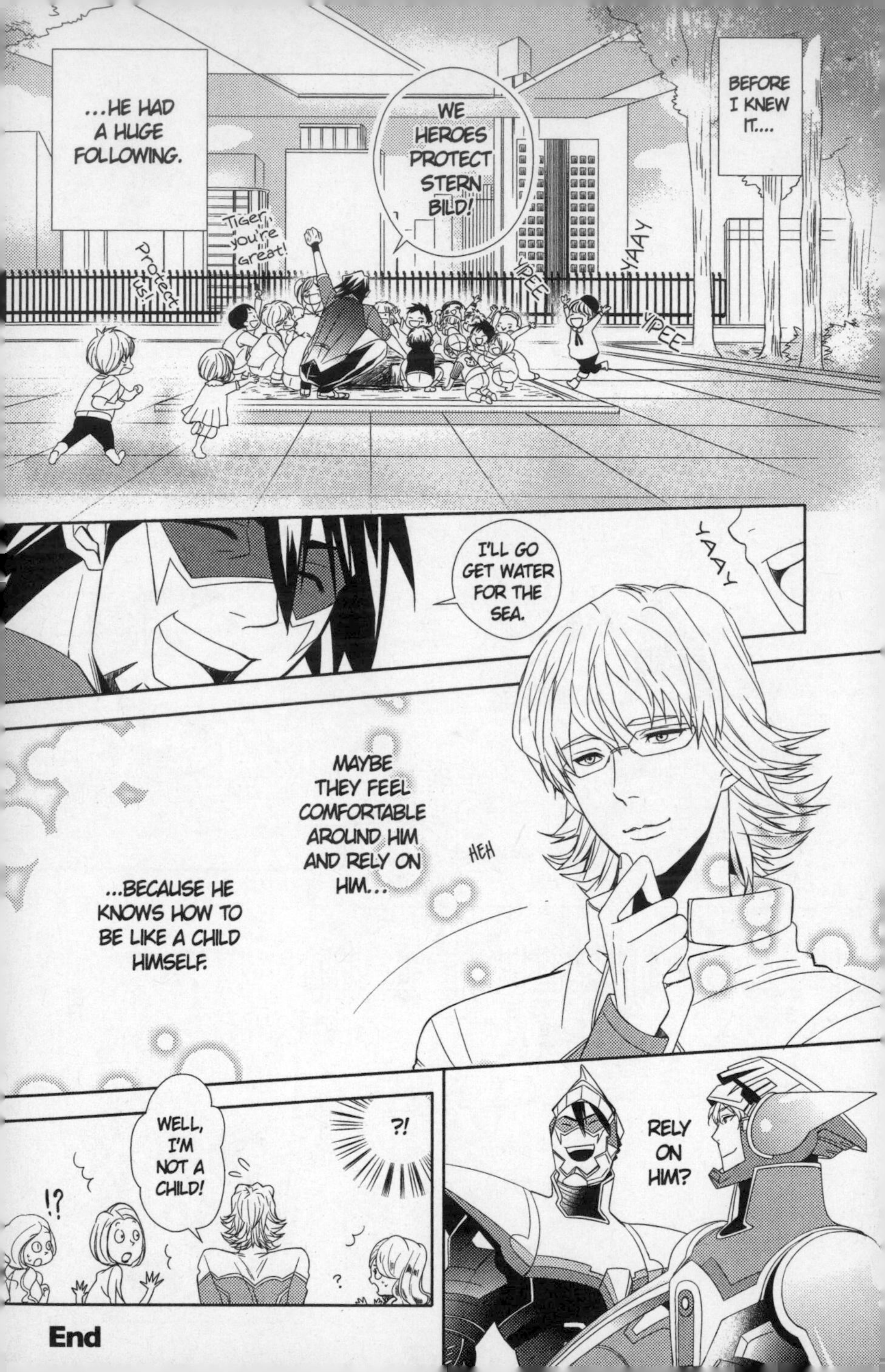
BEFORE I KNEW IT....
YAAY
YIPEE
WE HEROES PROTECT STERN BILD!
YIPEE
Tiger you're great!
Protect us!
...HE HAD A HUGE FOLLOWING.
YAAAY
I'LL GO GET WATER FOR THE SEA.
MAYBE THEY FEEL COMFORTABLE AROUND HIM AND RELY ON HIM...
HEH
...BECAUSE HE KNOWS HOW TO BE LIKE A CHILD HIMSELF.
RELY ON HIM?
?!
WELL, I'M NOT A CHILD!
!?
?
End

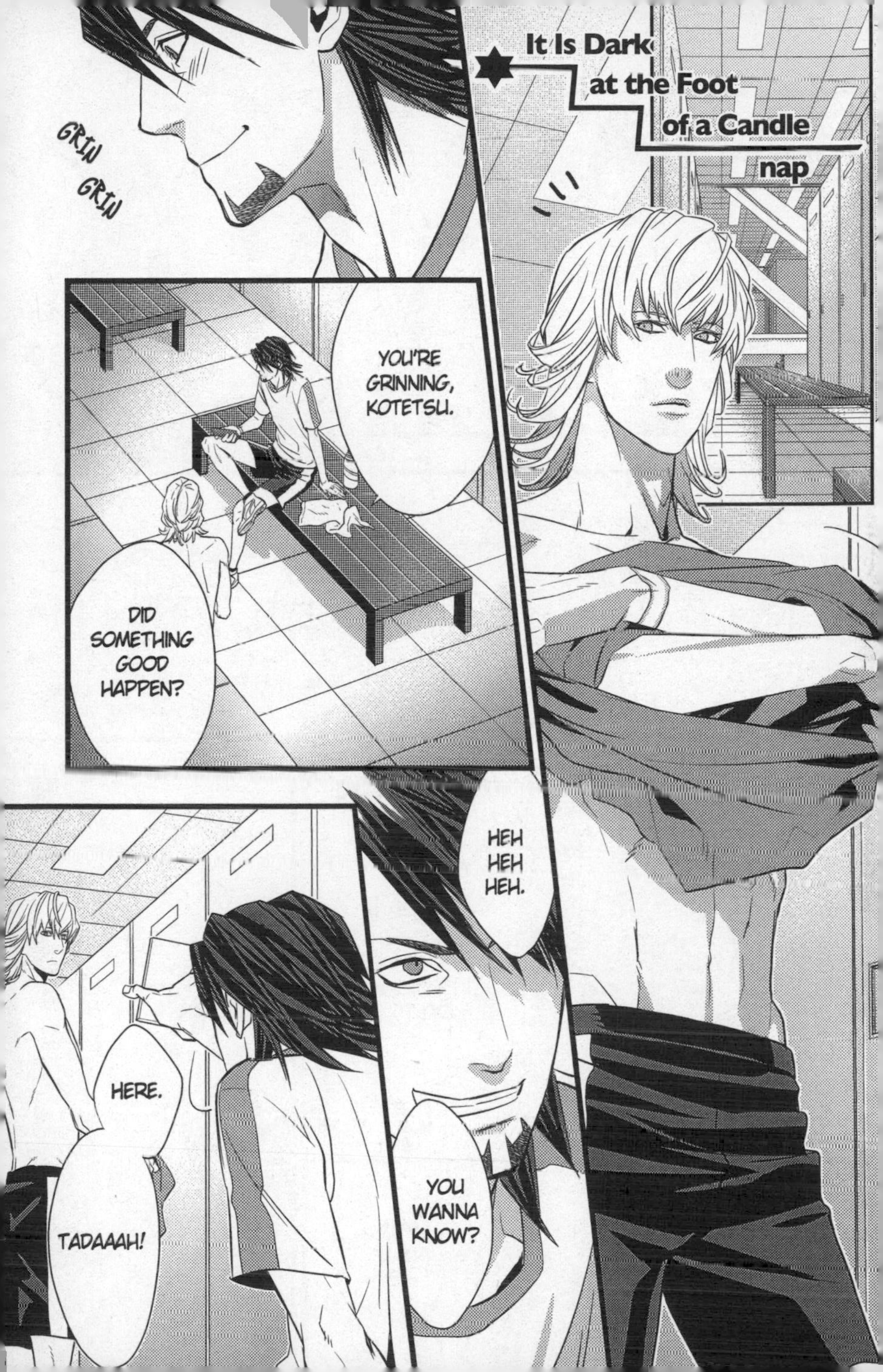
It Is Dark at the Foot of a Candle
nap
GRIN GRIN
YOU'RE GRINNING, KOTETSU.
DID SOMETHING GOOD HAPPEN?
HEH HEH HEH.
YOU WANNA KNOW?
HERE.
TADAAAH!

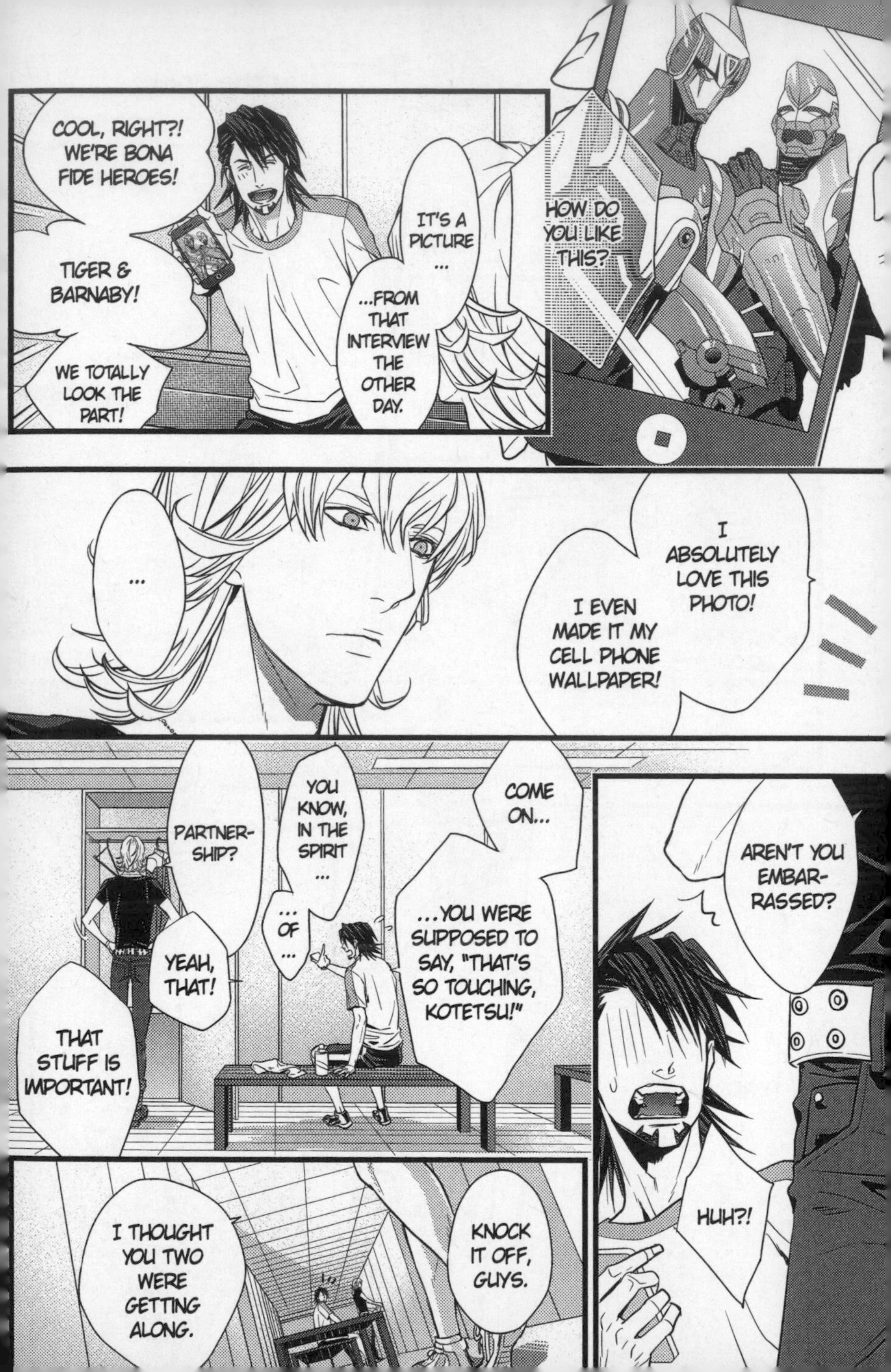
HOW DO YOU LIKE THIS?
IT'S A PICTURE ...
...FROM THAT INTERVIEW THE OTHER DAY.
COOL, RIGHT?! WE'RE BONA FIDE HEROES!
TIGER & BARNABY!
WE TOTALLY LOOK THE PART!
I ABSOLUTELY LOVE THIS PHOTO!
I EVEN MADE IT MY CELL PHONE WALLPAPER!
...
AREN'T YOU EMBARRASSED?
HUH?!
COME ON...
...YOU WERE SUPPOSED TO SAY, "THAT'S SO TOUCHING, KOTETSU!"
YOU KNOW, IN THE SPIRIT ...
... OF ...
PARTNERSHIP?
YEAH, THAT!
THAT STUFF IS IMPORTANT!
KNOCK IT OFF, GUYS.
I THOUGHT YOU TWO WERE GETTING ALONG.

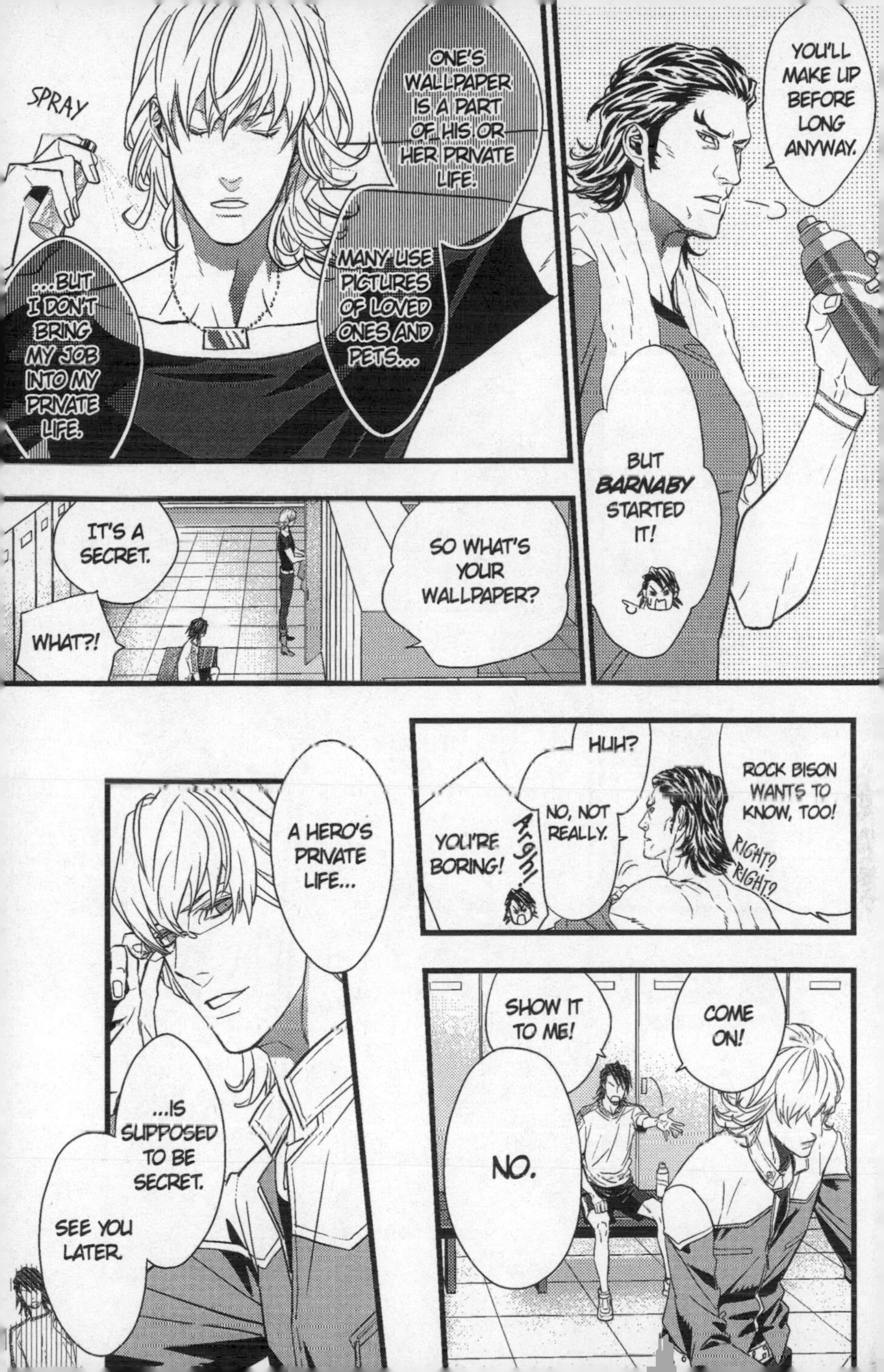
YOU'LL MAKE UP BEFORE LONG ANYWAY.
BUT BARNABY STARTED IT!
ONE'S WALLPAPER IS A PART OF HIS OR HER PRIVATE LIFE.
MANY USE PICTURES OF LOVED ONES AND PETS...
SPRAY
...BUT I DON'T BRING MY JOB INTO MY PRIVATE LIFE.
SO WHAT'S YOUR WALLPAPER?
IT'S A SECRET.
WHAT?!
HUH?
ROCK BISON WANTS TO KNOW, TOO!
RIGHT? RIGHT?
NO, NOT REALLY.
YOU'RE BORING!
Argh!
COME ON!
SHOW IT TO ME!
NO.
A HERO'S PRIVATE LIFE...
...IS SUPPOSED TO BE SECRET.
SEE YOU LATER.

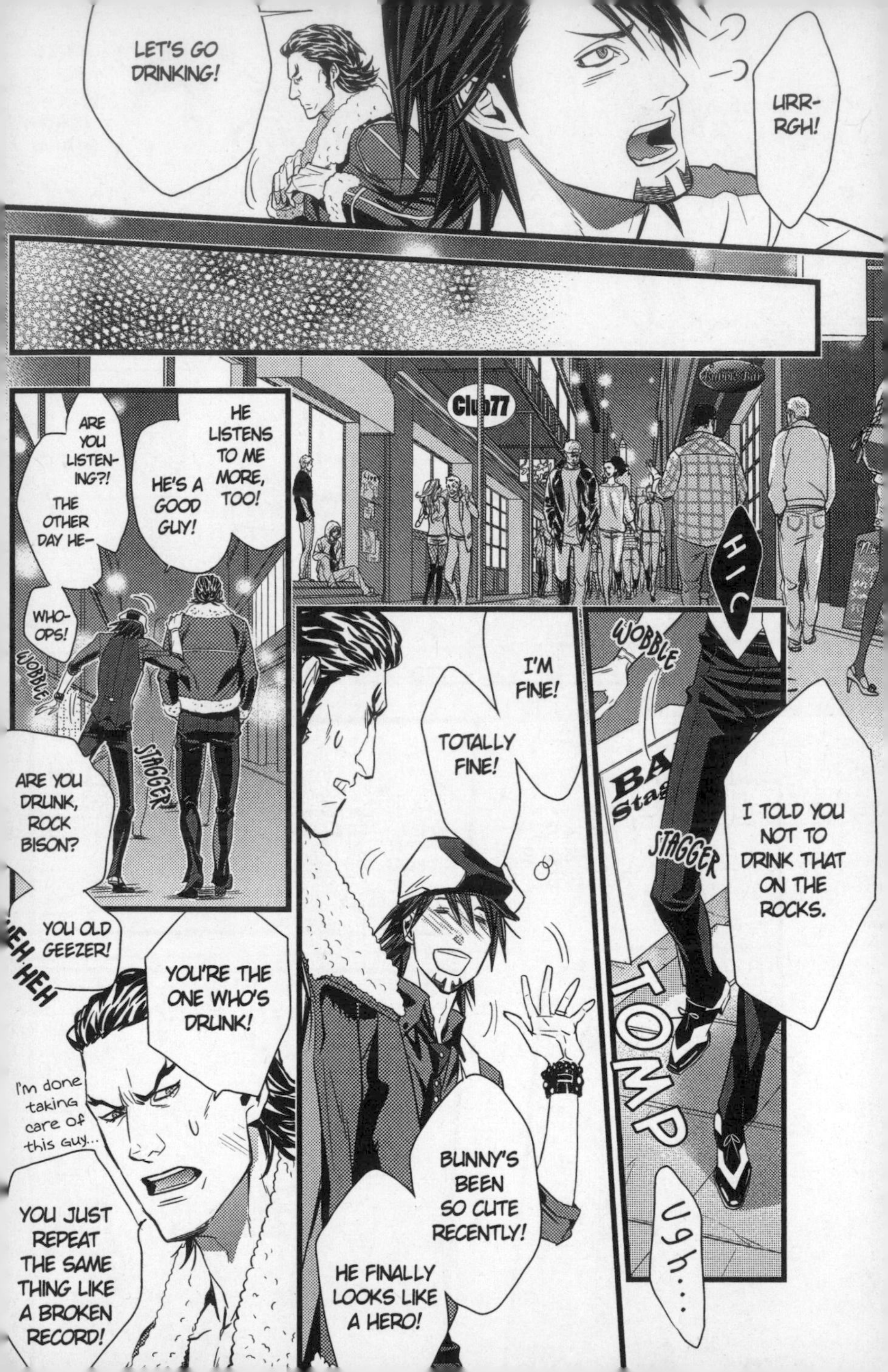

URRR-
RGH!
LET'S GO DRINKING!
Club77
HE LISTENS TO ME MORE, TOO!
HE'S A GOOD GUY!
ARE YOU LISTENING?!
THE OTHER DAY HE—
WHO-OPS!
WOBBLE
STAGGER
HIC
WOBBLE
STAGGER
I TOLD YOU NOT TO DRINK THAT ON THE ROCKS.
TOMP
Ugh...
I'M FINE!
TOTALLY FINE!
BUNNY'S BEEN SO CUTE RECENTLY!
HE FINALLY LOOKS LIKE A HERO!
ARE YOU DRUNK, ROCK BISON?
YOU OLD GEEZER!
HEH HEH
YOU'RE THE ONE WHO'S DRUNK!
I'm done taking care of this guy...
YOU JUST REPEAT THE SAME THING LIKE A BROKEN RECORD!

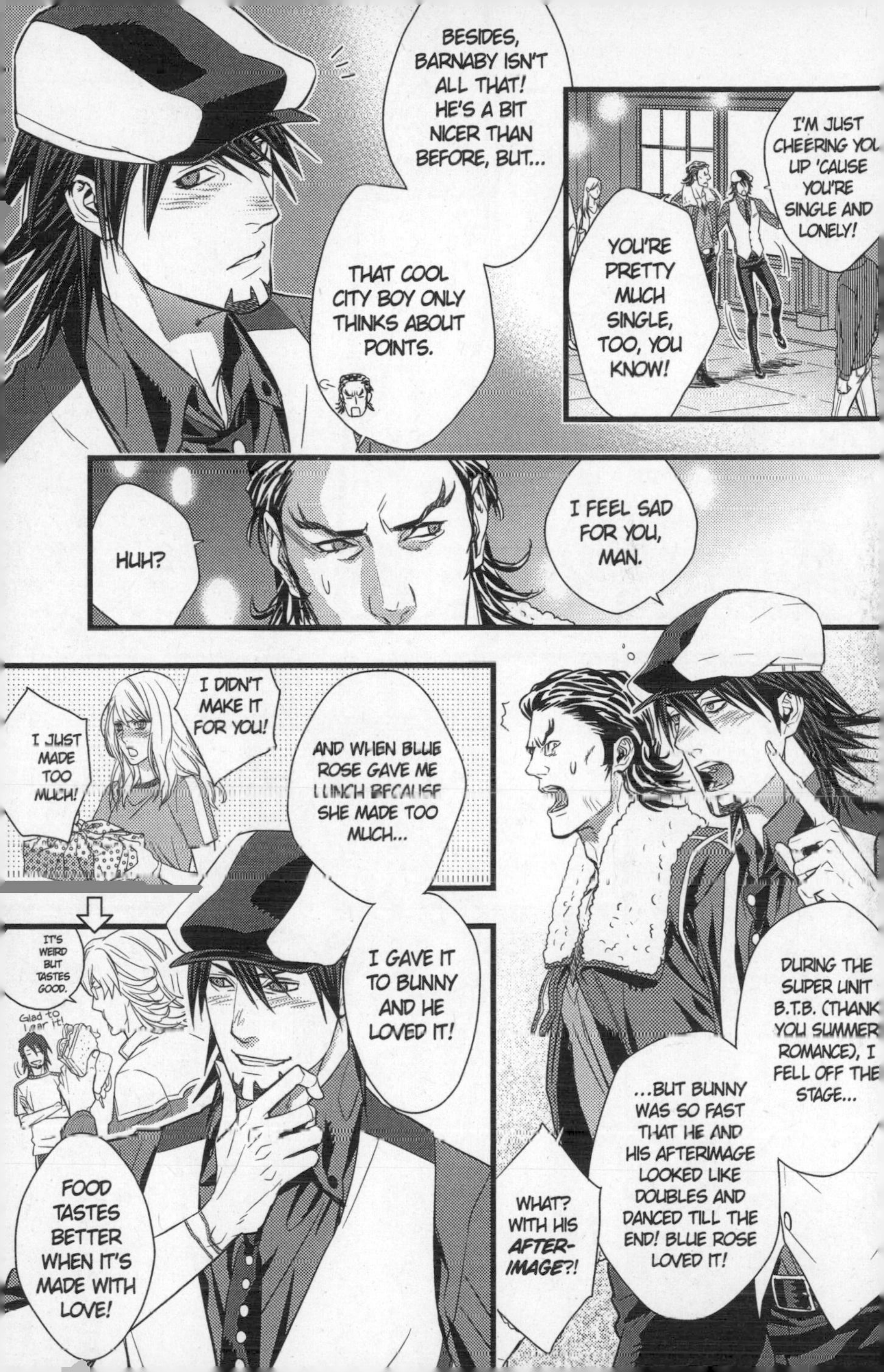
I'M JUST CHEERING YOU UP 'CAUSE YOU'RE SINGLE AND LONELY!
YOU'RE PRETTY MUCH SINGLE, TOO, YOU KNOW!
BESIDES, BARNABY ISN'T ALL THAT! HE'S A BIT NICER THAN BEFORE, BUT...
THAT COOL CITY BOY ONLY THINKS ABOUT POINTS.
I FEEL SAD FOR YOU, MAN.
HUH?
DURING THE SUPER UNIT B.T.B. (THANK YOU SUMMER ROMANCE), I FELL OFF THE STAGE...
...BUT BUNNY WAS SO FAST THAT HE AND HIS AFTERIMAGE LOOKED LIKE DOUBLES AND DANCED TILL THE END! BLUE ROSE LOVED IT!
WHAT? WITH HIS *AFTER-IMAGE*?!
AND WHEN BLUE ROSE GAVE ME LUNCH BECAUSE SHE MADE TOO MUCH...
I DIDN'T MAKE IT FOR YOU!
I JUST MADE TOO MUCH!
I GAVE IT TO BUNNY AND HE LOVED IT!
IT'S WEIRD BUT TASTES GOOD.
Glad to hear it!
FOOD TASTES BETTER WHEN IT'S MADE WITH LOVE!

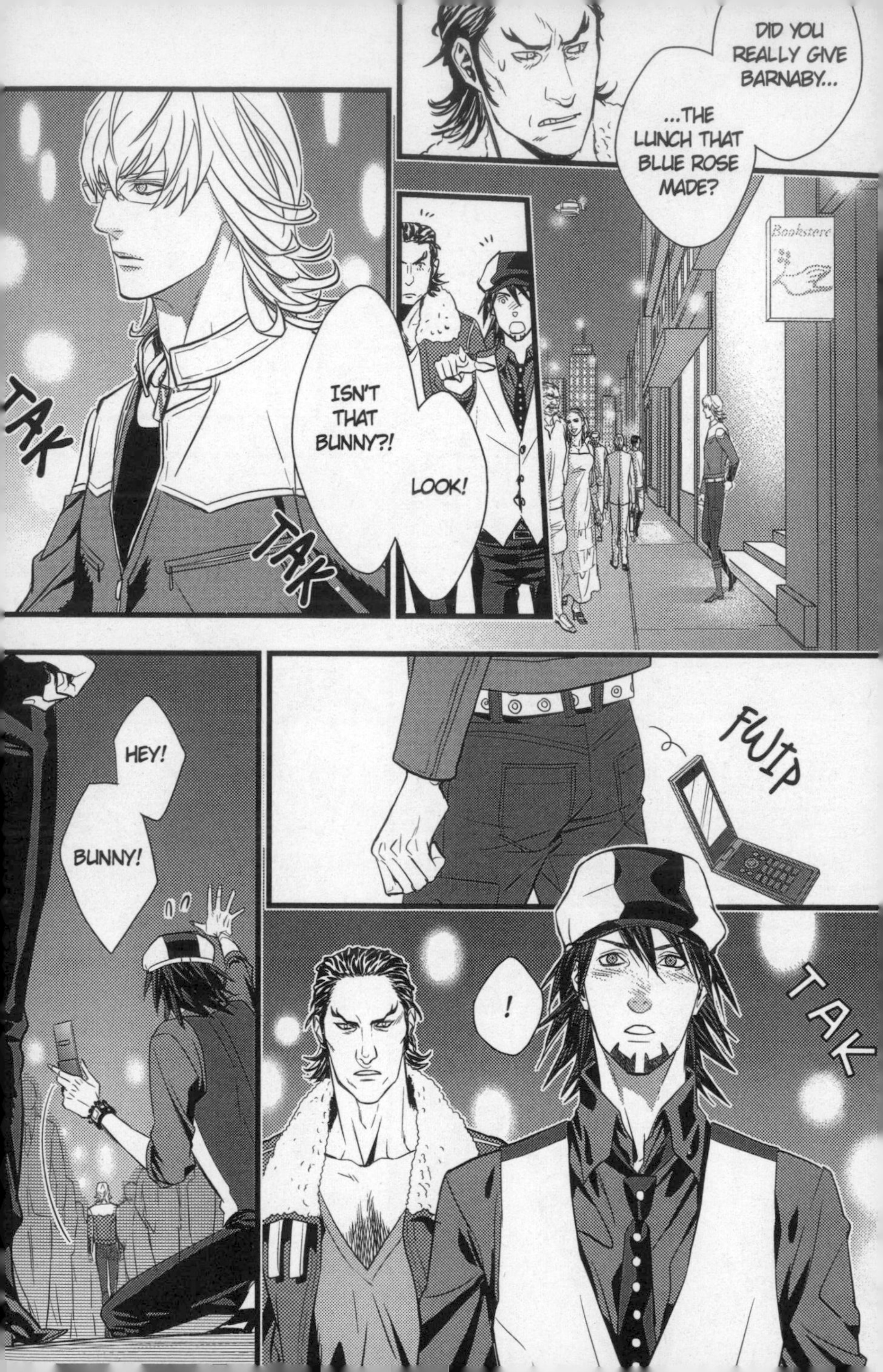
DID YOU REALLY GIVE BARNABY...
...THE LUNCH THAT BLUE ROSE MADE?
Bookstore
LOOK!
ISN'T THAT BUNNY?!
TAK
TAK
FWIP
TAK
!
HEY!
BUNNY!

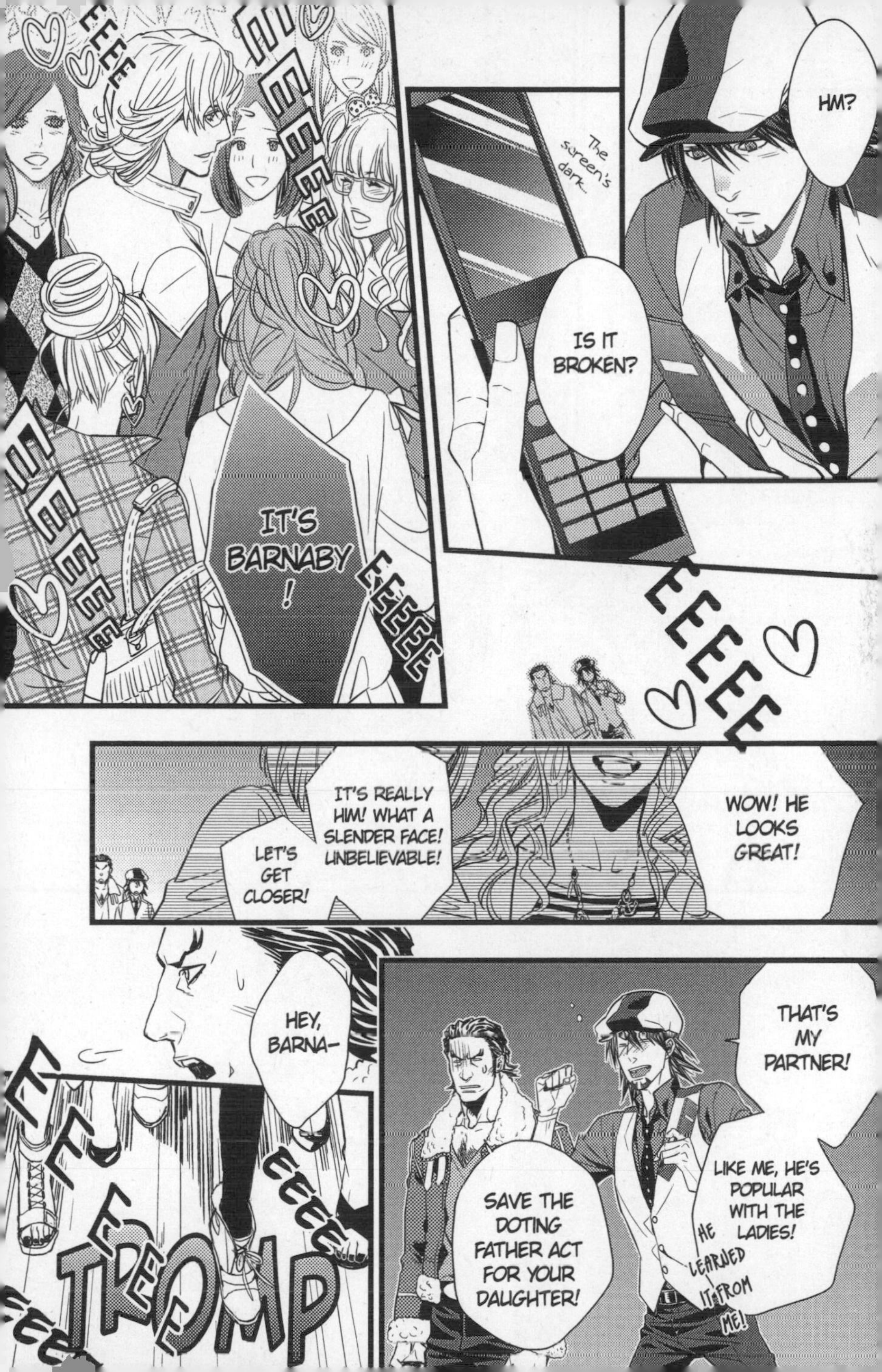
HM?
The screen's dark...
IS IT BROKEN?
EEEE
EEEEEEE
IT'S BARNABY!
EEEEE
EEEEE
EEEEE
WOW! HE LOOKS GREAT!
IT'S REALLY HIM! WHAT A SLENDER FACE! UNBELIEVABLE!
LET'S GET CLOSER!
THAT'S MY PARTNER!
LIKE ME, HE'S POPULAR WITH THE LADIES!
HE LEARNED IT FROM ME!
SAVE THE DOTING FATHER ACT FOR YOUR DAUGHTER!
HEY, BARNA-
EEEE
TROMP
EEEE

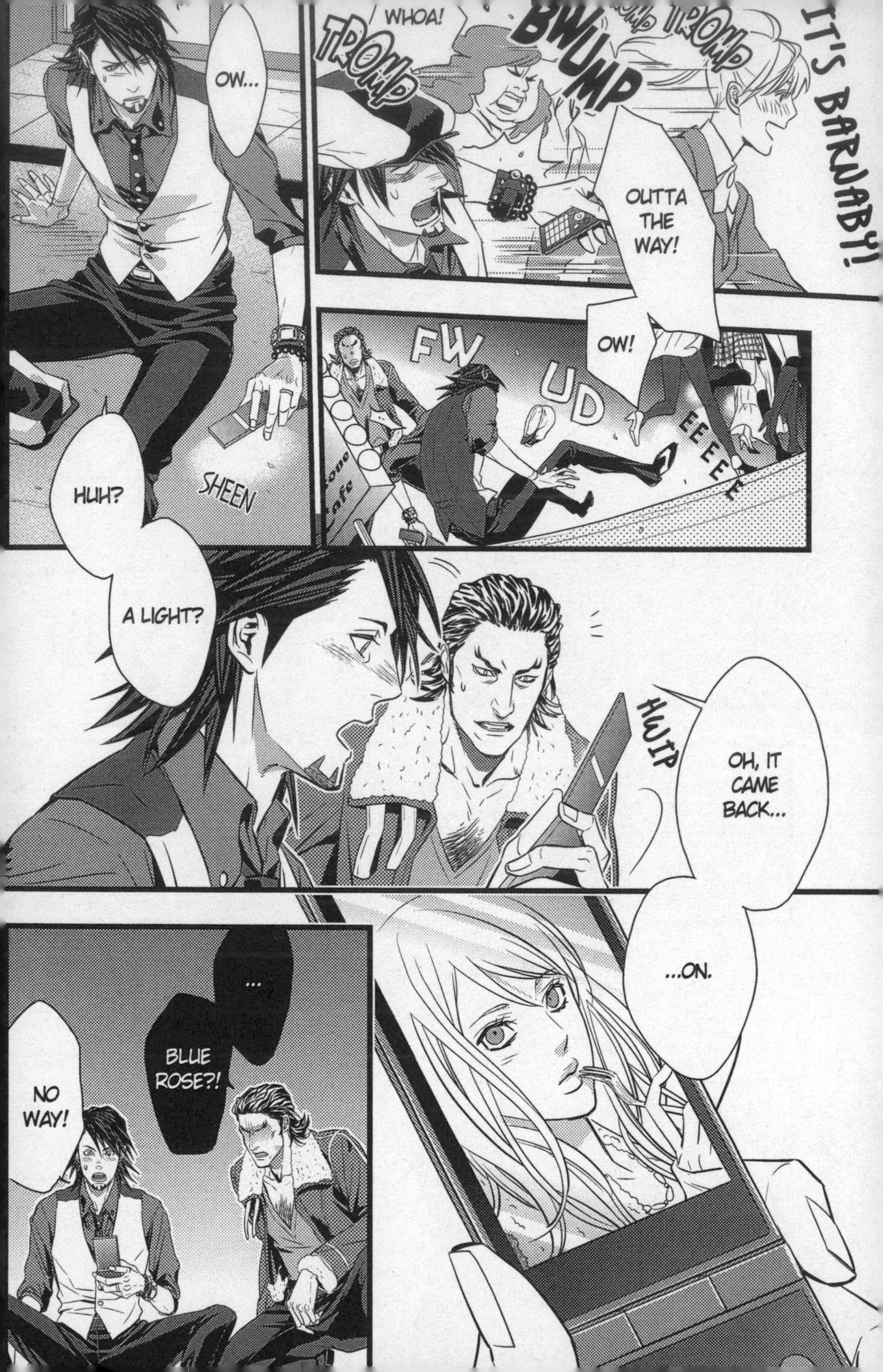
IT'S BARNABY!!
WHOA!
TROMP
BWUMP
TROMP TROMP
OUTTA THE WAY!
OW!
FW
UD
EEEEE
OW...
SHEEN
HUH?
OH, IT CAME BACK...
HWIP
A LIGHT?
...ON.
...
BLUE ROSE?!
NO WAY!

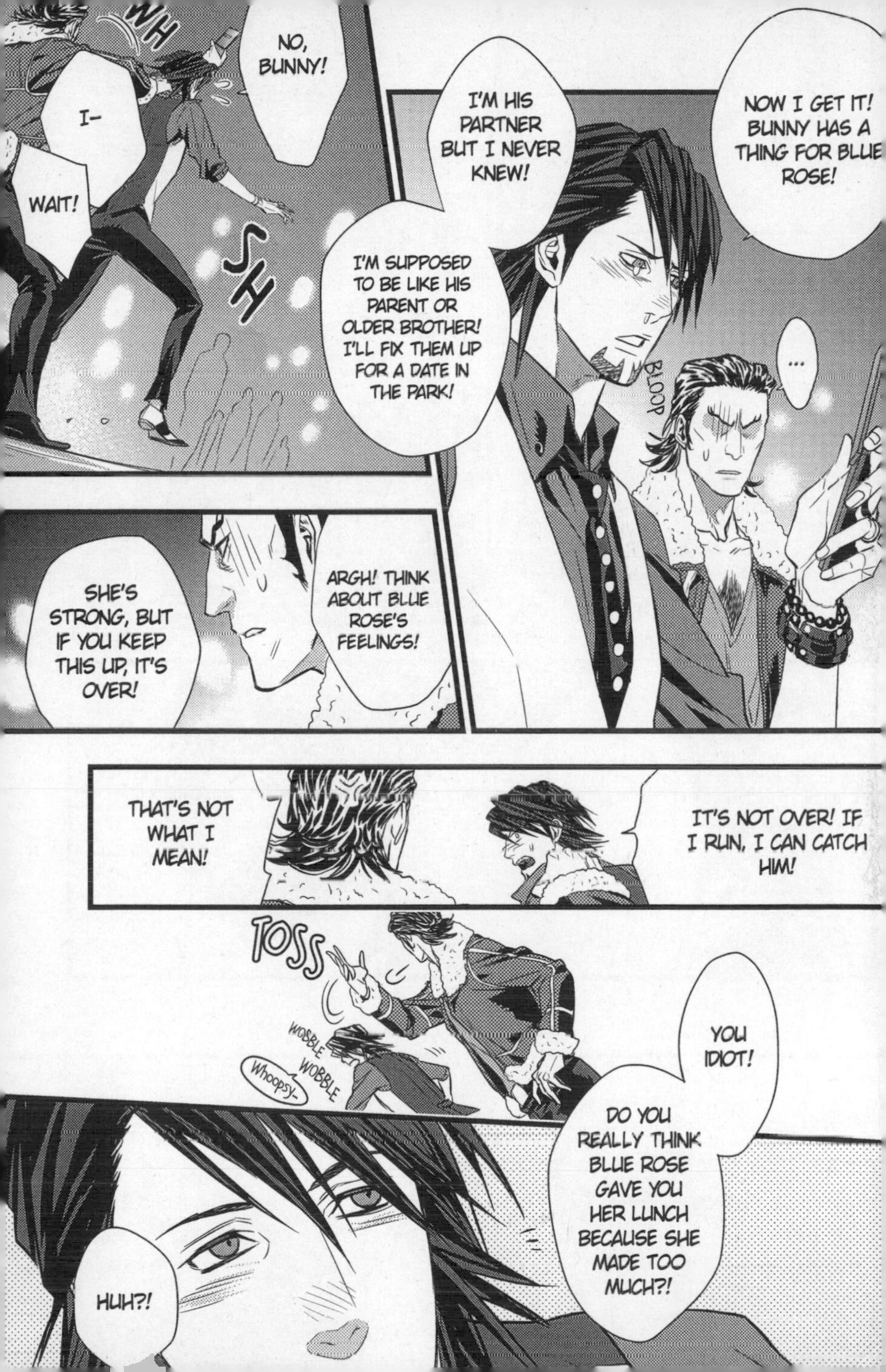
NOW I GET IT! BUNNY HAS A THING FOR BLUE ROSE!
I'M HIS PARTNER BUT I NEVER KNEW!
I'M SUPPOSED TO BE LIKE HIS PARENT OR OLDER BROTHER! I'LL FIX THEM UP FOR A DATE IN THE PARK!
...
BLOOP
NO, BUNNY!
WH
I-
WAIT!
SH
ARGH! THINK ABOUT BLUE ROSE'S FEELINGS!
SHE'S STRONG, BUT IF YOU KEEP THIS UP, IT'S OVER!
IT'S NOT OVER! IF I RUN, I CAN CATCH HIM!
THAT'S NOT WHAT I MEAN!
YOU IDIOT!
TOSS
WOBBLE WOBBLE
Whoopsy-
DO YOU REALLY THINK BLUE ROSE GAVE YOU HER LUNCH BECAUSE SHE MADE TOO MUCH?!
HUH?!

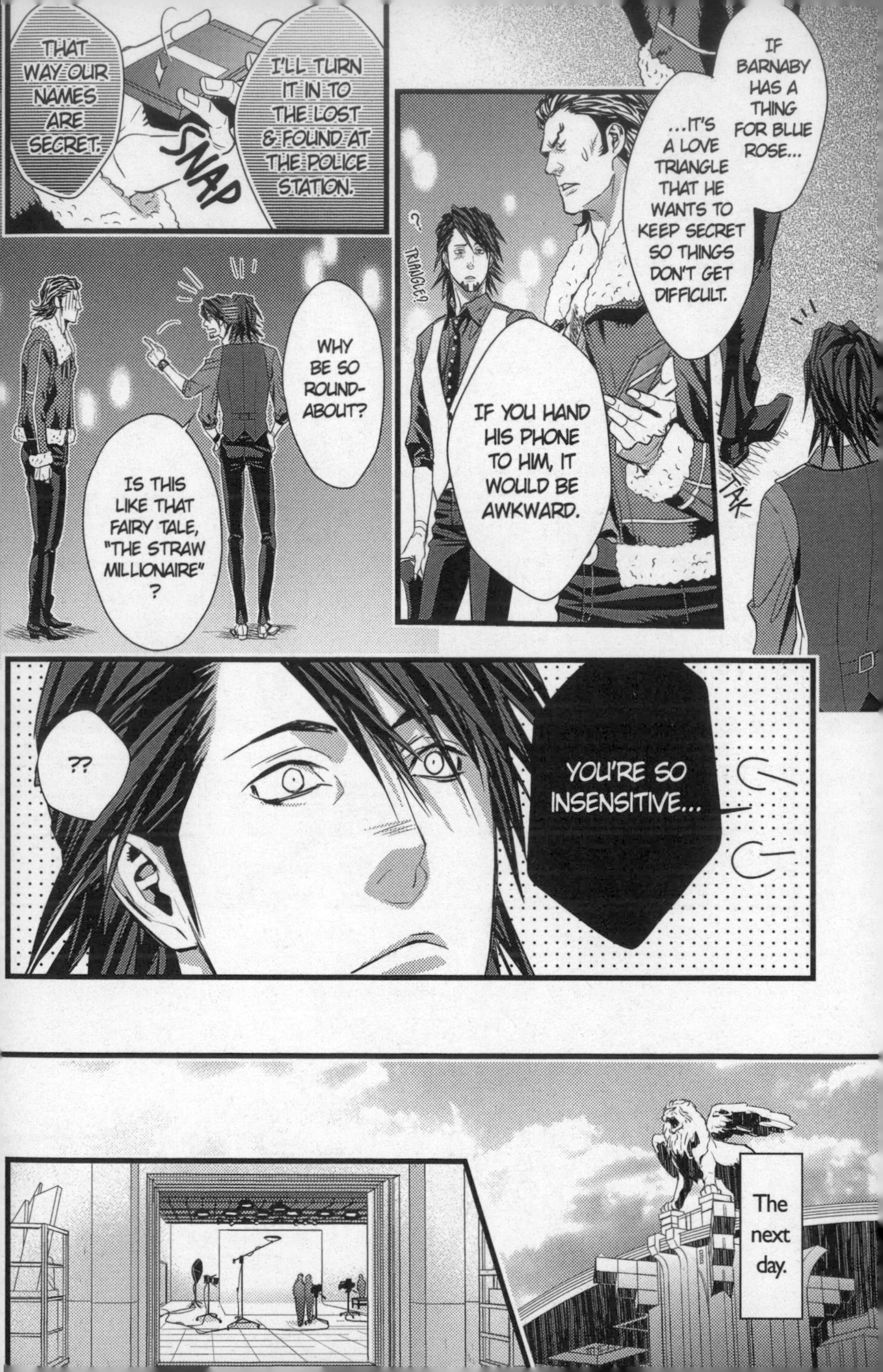
IF BARNABY HAS A THING FOR BLUE ROSE...
...IT'S A LOVE TRIANGLE THAT HE WANTS TO KEEP SECRET SO THINGS DON'T GET DIFFICULT.
TAK
IF YOU HAND HIS PHONE TO HIM, IT WOULD BE AWKWARD.
TRIANGLE?
I'LL TURN IT IN TO THE LOST & FOUND AT THE POLICE STATION.
THAT WAY OUR NAMES ARE SECRET.
SNAP
WHY BE SO ROUND-ABOUT?
IS THIS LIKE THAT FAIRY TALE, "THE STRAW MILLIONAIRE" ?
YOU'RE SO INSENSITIVE...
??
The next day.

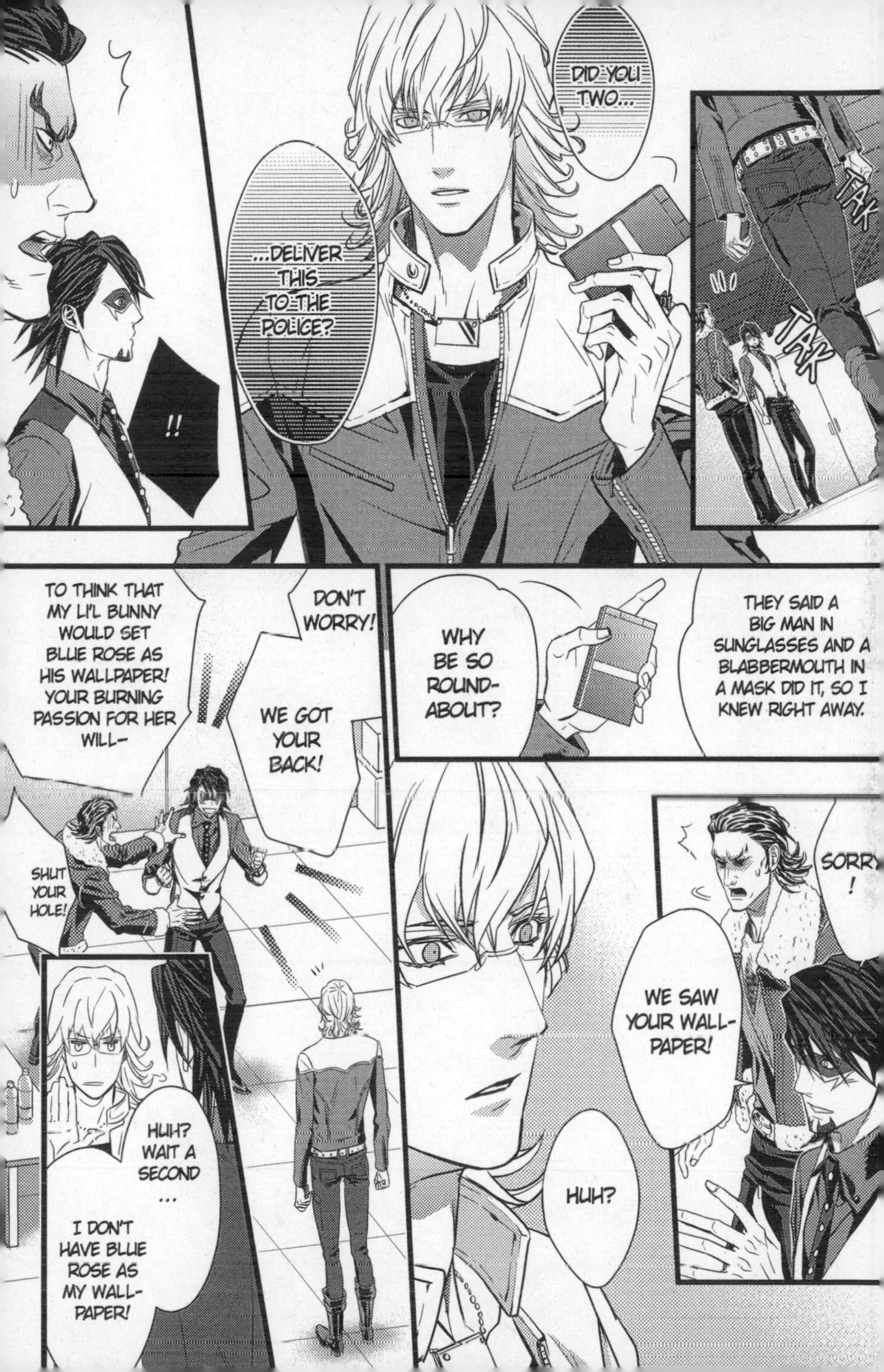
TAK
TAK
DID YOU TWO...
...DELIVER THIS TO THE POLICE?
!!
THEY SAID A BIG MAN IN SUNGLASSES AND A BLABBERMOUTH IN A MASK DID IT, SO I KNEW RIGHT AWAY.
WHY BE SO ROUND-ABOUT?
SORRY!
WE SAW YOUR WALL-PAPER!
HUH?
DON'T WORRY!
WE GOT YOUR BACK!
TO THINK THAT MY LI'L BUNNY WOULD SET BLUE ROSE AS HIS WALLPAPER! YOUR BURNING PASSION FOR HER WILL-
SHUT YOUR HOLE!
HUH? WAIT A SECOND ...
I DON'T HAVE BLUE ROSE AS MY WALL-PAPER!

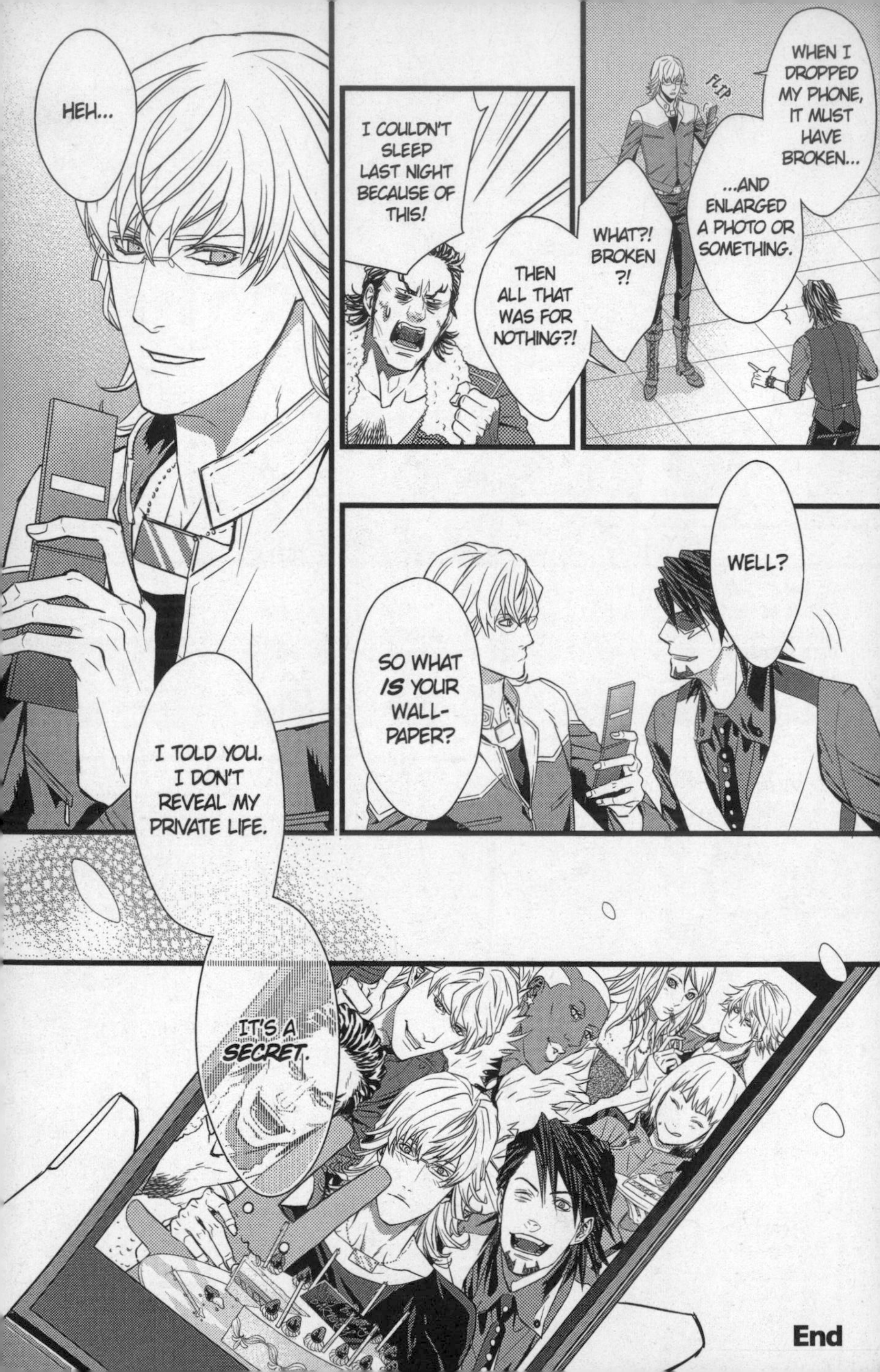
FLIP
WHEN I DROPPED MY PHONE, IT MUST HAVE BROKEN...
...AND ENLARGED A PHOTO OR SOMETHING.
WHAT?! BROKEN?!
I COULDN'T SLEEP LAST NIGHT BECAUSE OF THIS!
THEN ALL THAT WAS FOR NOTHING?!
WELL?
SO WHAT *IS* YOUR WALL-PAPER?
HEH...
I TOLD YOU. I DON'T REVEAL MY PRIVATE LIFE.
IT'S A **SECRET**.
End

TIGER & BUNNY COMIC ANTHOLOGY 2

First, Catch Your Hare

WE RESPECT TIGER & BUNNY

TOMO, TEMARI MATSUMOTO, SUISU KANESHIKI, RIHITO TAKARAI,

JUN KUSUKI, NOKIYA, SAWAIKE, UKA NAGAO, MIN SAKUSAKA,

SUZU KOHNO, RENJI KURIYAMA, ARATA SHION, SOUJI ISHIDA,

HAZUKI MATSUO, WATARI, TAKUMI YOSHIMURA, MAMIKA MITSUSHIO,

AYA SAKURAI, KAZUKI SOMA, NAP, MAYU SHINJO

Special Guest Mayu Shinjo

Every week, Tiger & Bunny makes me writhe in pain due to cuteness overload! The story is great and never what I expect—in a bunny, jumpy sort of way. By the time this book comes out, the final episode will have already aired, so I don't know what I'll be doing then, but I hope I'll be dancing with joy because they've announced a sequel. These two completely changed my life! Someone's gotta take responsibility for that!

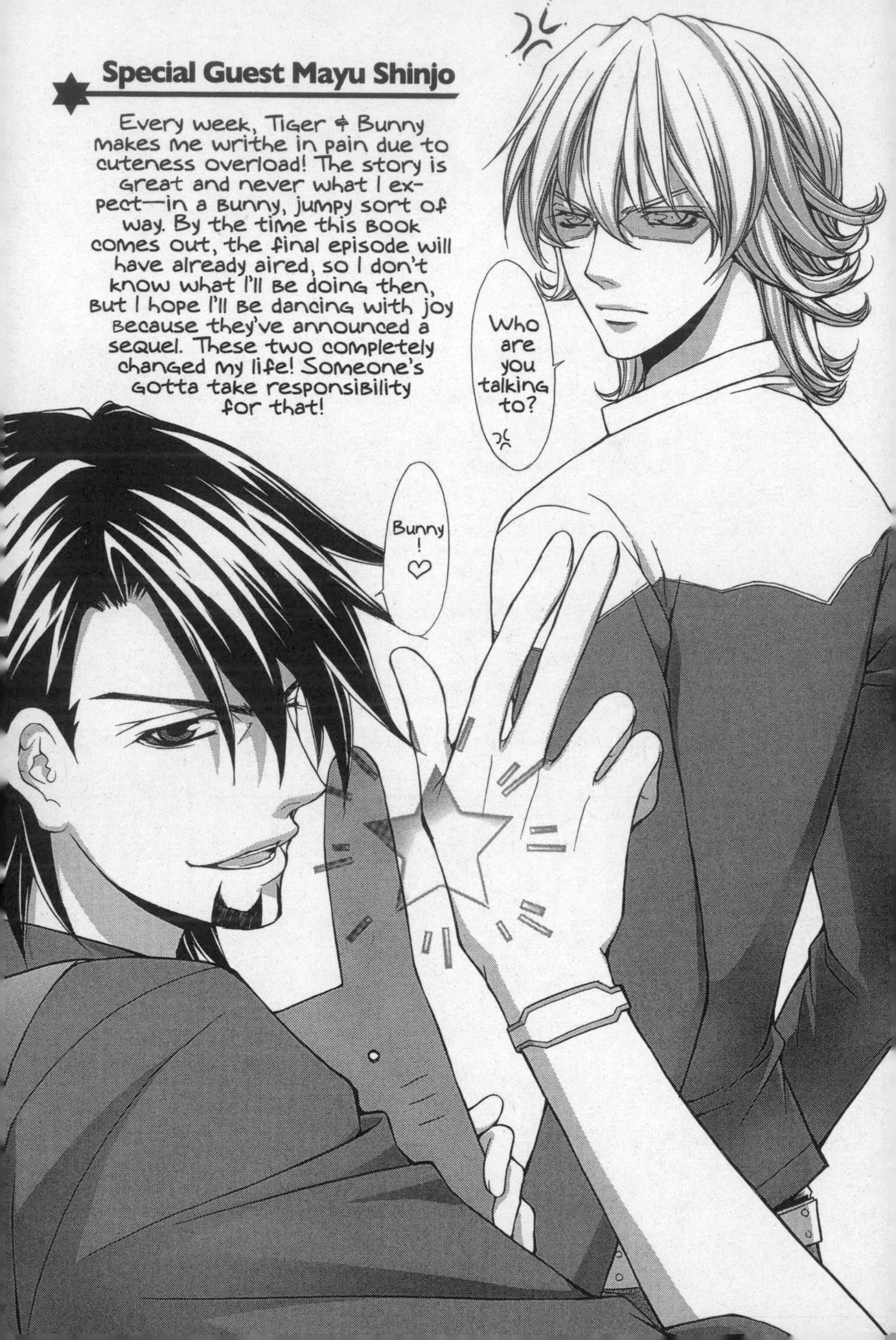
Who are you talking to?
Bunny! ♡

TIGER & BUNNY OFFICIAL COMIC ANTHOLOGY #2

First, Catch Your Hare

COMMENT

WE RESPECT TIGER & BUNNY

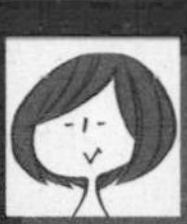

Tomo

I drew those two addressing crimes not just in front of the camera, but in their private lives too. I'm very happy to be able to draw for this anthology. Thank you!

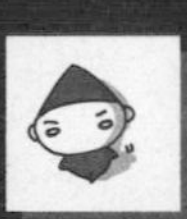

Temari Matsumoto

I'm honored to have been a part of the *Tiger & Bunny Anthology*! Every character is so cute and wonderful! I'll be looking forward to the book when it comes out filled with all these wonderful characters!

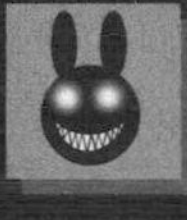

Suisu Kaneshiki

Hello, my name is Suisu Kaneshiki. I'm so glad to draw a chapter for this series that I love so much! I always fantasize about seeing a tiny Bunny.

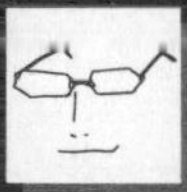

Rihito Takarai

I get both expectant and happy when I think about this book filled with so many wonderful *Tiger & Bunny* scenes. I can't wait!

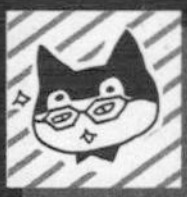

Jun Kusuki

My brain is always filled with Tiger & Bunny! Thank you so much for bringing this wonderful series into the world! I love *Tiger & Bunny*!

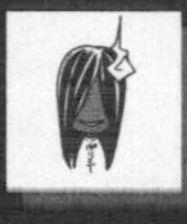

Nokiya

My stagnant life is much better now thanks to *Tiger & Bunny*. I love it! Receiving an invitation to be a part of this was an honor! I can't sleep at night just thinking about what the other artists' chapters will be like.

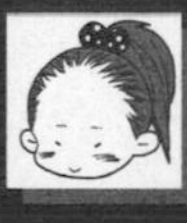

Sawaike

I'm Sawaike and I'm thrilled to be a part of this anthology. I looked forward to every episode of *Tiger & Bunny*. Barnaby is just too adorable! I love him!

WE RESPECT TIGER & BUNNY

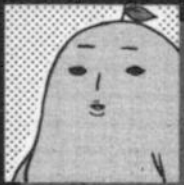

Uka Nagao

All the characters look cool in their hero suits, but they can be cute, too! I love them just the way they are! But I think everyone except Blue Rose and Dragon Kid must have a hard time in the summer!

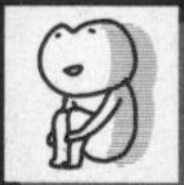

Min Sakusaka

I had trouble drawing the characters since I'm not used to them, but it was a blast nonetheless! Thank you very much for inviting me!

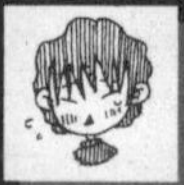

Suzu Kohno

I'm very happy to have been a part of the popular *Tiger & Bunny* franchise. I love mixing it up like this!

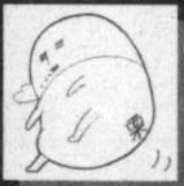

Renji Kuriyama

The more I draw Nathan, the more I love him! I just wanted to dress Tiger up in the wildest outfit I could think of! But as shown in the anime, Kotetsu has a great body, so he could wear any outfit and still look good. The more I draw Nathan, the more I love him! I just wanted to dress Tiger up in the wildest outfit I could think of! But as shown in the anime, Kotetsu has a great body, so he could wear any outfit and still look good.

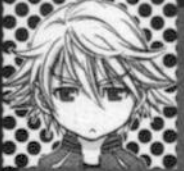

Arata Shion

Thank you very much for reading this! I look forward to *Tiger & Bunny* each week and I'm happy to have been able to draw a chapter for it! I love how the heroes are rivals but also good friends!

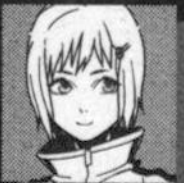

Souji Ishida

I enjoyed watching the show, so drawing this chapter was a huge honor! I love the three (?) girls, so it was fun drawing them! I'm so into *Tiger & Bunny* that I can't sleep at night!

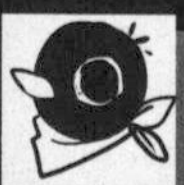

Hazuki Matsuo

I love Tiger and Bunny, but I also like Bison and Agnes. I love them all!

TIGER & BUNNY COMIC ANTHOLOGY 2

First, Catch Your Hare

COMMENT

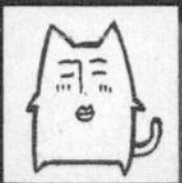

Watari

Thank you for putting together this anthology! I've been waiting forever for something like this! I love it so much that I was nervous the whole time I was drawing! I hope everyone enjoys it as much as I have!

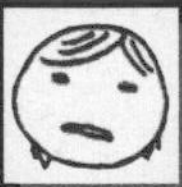

Takumi Yoshimura

I can't help but scream out "Sky High!" whenever I draw Sky High. Thank you for giving me the opportunity to draw this!

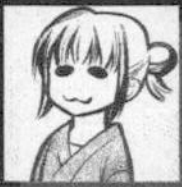

Mamika Mitsushio

I'm so glad to have participated in the Tiger & Bunny Anthology. If there's a next time, I want to do a chapter called "Kotetsu's Continent of Passion"!

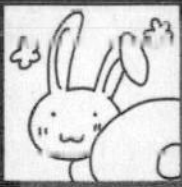

Aya Sakurai

I got fired up and had a fun time drawing Nathan and Blue Rose.

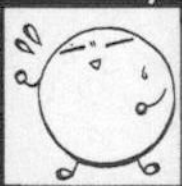

Kazuki Soma

Thank you for this opportunity to draw for *Tiger & Bunny*! I was overjoyed! I love it so much that it's taking over my life!

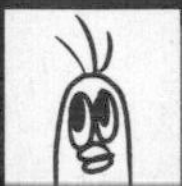

nap

I'm so glad to have been able to draw Bison! Thank you!

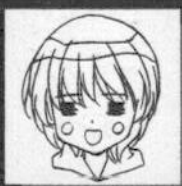

Mayu Shinjo

You guys gotta stop this. Bringing such a great series into the world is a crime. Now this single manga artist is being pushed to the edge of the cliff because of it. Do you want to be responsible for me never getting married?! Sunrise! SIGH... I wish I could marry Kotetsu...

TIGER & BUNNY
COMIC ANTHOLOGY

END | Volume 2

STOP!

YOU'RE READING IN THE WRONG DIRECTION!

This is the END of the graphic novel

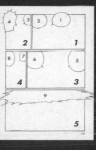

To properly enjoy this VIZ graphic novel, please turn it around and begin reading from **RIGHT** to **LEFT**. Unlike English, Japanese is read right to left, so Japanese comics are read in reverse order from the way English comics are typically read.

This book has been printed in the original Japanese format in order to preserve the orientation of the original artwork. Have fun with it!

←┘ Follow the action this way.

TIGER & BUNNY COMIC ANTHOLOGY

Volume 1
VIZ Media Edition

Edited by: **ASUKA HENSHUBU**
Production: **SUNRISE**

COVER:
Illustration **ASAKO NISHIDA**
Coloring **JUNKO HAKAMADA**
Finishing **RUMIKO NAGAI**

LAYOUT:
MASAMI SUZUKI

TIGER & BUNNY OFFICIAL COMIC ANTHOLOGY #01 It takes two to make a quarrel.
TIGER & BUNNY OFFICIAL COMIC ANTHOLOGY #02 First catch your hare.

First published in Japan in 2011 by KADOKAWA SHOTEN Co.,Ltd.,Tokyo.
English translation rights arranged with KADOKAWA SHOTEN Co.,Ltd.,Tokyo.

Translation & English Adaptation **LABAAMEN & JOHN WERRY, HC LANGUAGE SOLUTIONS**
Touch-up Art & Lettering **EVAN WALDINGER**
Design **FAWN LAU**
Editor **MIKE MONTESA**

The rights of the author(s) of the work(s) in this publication to be so identified have been asserted in accordance with the Copyright, Designs and Patents Act 1988. A CIP catalogue record for this book is available from the British Library.

Printed in the U.S.A

Published by VIZ Media, LLC
P.O. Box 77010
San Francisco, CA 94107

10 9 8 7 6 5 4 3 2 1
First printing, August 2013